Kiev, Jewish Metropolis

THE MODERN JEWISH EXPERIENCE

Paula Hyman and Deborah Dash Moore, editors

KIEV
JEWISH METROPOLIS

A HISTORY, 1859–1914

NATAN M. MEIR

INDIANA UNIVERSITY PRESS
Bloomington and Indianapolis

Preparation and publication of this book were generously supported by a Cahnman Publication Subvention Grant, awarded by the Association for Jewish Studies, and by the Institute for Israel and Jewish Studies, Columbia University.

Portions of chapter 4 were originally published as "From Pork to Kapores: Transformations in Religious Practice among the Jews of Late Imperial Kiev," in *Jewish Quarterly Review* 97.4 (Autumn 2007), and are reprinted by permission of the University of Pennsylvia Press. Portions of chapter 5 were originally published as "Jews, Ukrainians, and Russians in Kiev: Intergroup Relations in Late Imperial Associational Life," in *Slavic Review* 65, no. 3 (Autumn 2006), and are reprinted by permission of the publisher of *Slavic Review*, the American Association for the Advancement of Slavic Studies.

This book is a publication of

Indiana University Press
601 North Morton Street
Bloomington, Indiana 47404-3797 USA

www.iupress.indiana.edu

Telephone orders 800-842-6796
Fax orders 812-855-7931
Orders by e-mail iuporder@indiana.edu

♾ The paper used in this publication meets the minimum requirements of the American National Standard for Information Sciences—Permanence of Paper for Printed Library Materials, ANSI Z39.48-1992.

Manufactured in the United States of America

Library of Congress Cataloging-in-Publication Data

Meir, Natan M.
Kiev, Jewish metropolis : a history, 1859–1914 / Natan M. Meir.
p. cm. — (The modern Jewish experience)
Includes bibliographical references and index.
ISBN 978-0-253-35502-7 (cloth : alk. paper) — ISBN 978-0-253-22207-7 (pbk. : alk. paper)
1. Jews—Ukraine—Kiev—History—19th century. 2. Jews—Ukraine—Kiev—History—20th century. 3. Jews—Ukraine—Kiev—Social conditions—19th century. 4. Jews—Ukraine—Kiev—Social conditions—20th century. 5. Kiev (Ukraine)—Ethnic relations. I. Title.
DS135.U42K5453 2010
305.892'404777—dc22

2009049723

1 2 3 4 5 15 14 13 12 11 10

Dedicated to

the memory of my beloved grandparents:
Saba and Savta
Rabbi Judah Nadich, Ephraim Yehudah ben Yitzhak ve-Leah ve-Nessa *z"l*
Martha Hadassah Ribalow Nadich,
Marta Hadassah bat Menachem ve-Shoshana *z"l*
and
Bubby and Zayde
Jeanette Meyers, Sheindl bat Sarah *z"l*
and Abe Meyers, Avraham ben Natan ve-Sarah *z"l*

and to Ema and Aba
Leah Nadich and Aryeh Meir
she-yibadlu le-hayim tovim va-arukim

CONTENTS

ACKNOWLEDGMENTS

During the researching and writing of this book, which has been ten years in the making, I lived on three different continents, so I have the pleasure of thanking a great many people who assisted me in one way or another (and sometimes in many ways). First I would like to thank Michael Stanislawski, who guided this project and gave me the support and encouragement that were so crucial in my formative years. Among many other things, I have learned from him the value of committed skepticism and scholarly detachment combined with a deep love for Jewish history. It is also a delight to thank others who guided my training in Jewish history and Russian history: Yosef Hayim Yerushalmi, Mark von Hagen, Richard Wortman, and Aryeh Goren. Jane Burbank and Benjamin Nathans gave me invaluable feedback, which helped me shape the development of the book.

I have had the good fortune to work with a number of senior colleagues who have encouraged my scholarly work, supported my research, and served as true role models for what an academician should be. Among these are Marsha Rozenblit at the University of Maryland; Shulamit Magnus at Oberlin College; Tony Kushner, Anne Curry, and Mark Cornwall at the University of Southampton; and Michael Weingrad here at my new home of Portland State University. At Southampton, I enjoyed the support and advice of many colleagues, including Nils Roemer, Dan Levine, George Bernard, Jane McDermid, Julie Gammon, and Joan Tumblety. Special thanks to Lorna Young, Frances Clarke, and Marie-Pierre Gibert for their loving assistance at many junctures along the way. The late John Klier supported this project at every step, and I am deeply saddened that I will not be able to show him the final results.

I spent several years of research for this book in Washington, D.C., where Tom Pitt and Steve Rodes were always ready with a warm meal, a cold drink, and a loving cat. The support I received from Edna Friedberg and Stig Trommer was truly invaluable. Nancy Roth and Richard, Jacob, and Miriam Mazer became true friends who never fail to take a genuine interest in the results of my research. Others whose support made all the difference are Jordan Potash, Adam Tenner, Jeremy Rosenblatt, Dan Furmansky, and Alex Goldberg. Joel Alter's moral, spiritual, and material support sustained me for many years, and for this I am truly grateful.

I was lucky to have had assistance in my research from many individuals and institutions. In this country, I am indebted to Edward Kasinec, formerly chief librarian of the New York Public Library's Slavic and Baltic Division (now Curator Emeritus, NYPL Slavic and East European Collections) and the staffs of the library of the Jewish Theological Seminary, the libraries of Columbia University, and several departments at the Library of Congress, including the African and Middle Eastern Reading Room (with special thanks to Peggy Perlstein) and the European Reading Room. In Ukraine, I was assisted by the staffs of the Central State Historical Archive of Ukraine, Kyïv; the Scientific Research Library of the Central State Archives of Ukraine; the State Archive of Kyïv Oblast; and the State Archive of the City of Kyïv. The superb archivists and librarians at these institutions went out of their way to make sure I had access to the documents I needed. I am especially grateful for the support provided by Irina Sergeeva, director of the Judaica Division of the Vernadsky National Library of Ukraine, and her able staff. I also thank the staffs of the library's Newspaper and Dissertation reading rooms and especially Viktoriia Matusevich.

The staff of the Institute of Judaica in Kiev, and especially its director, Leonid Finberg, provided me with an academic home during my stay in their city. Their support and assistance were incalculable. Special thanks to Misha Kal'nitskii for sharing his encyclopedic knowledge of Kiev's history and to Arsenii Finberg for his computer assistance. I am also appreciative of the sponsorship of the Jewish University of St. Petersburg and its rector, Dmitrii Elyashevich, and of the European University in St. Petersburg and its Center for Archival Training. Victor Kelner of the Russian National Library helped to unlock some of the treasures of that institution's Judaica holdings. My research at the Russian State Library's Newspaper Division and the State Public Historical Library in Moscow was greatly facilitated by the helpful librarians at those institutions.

In Israel, I was privileged to do research at the Central Archives for the History of the Jewish People (CAHJP), the Central Zionist Archives, and the National and University Library. I am particularly grateful to Hadassah Assouline and Binyamin Lukin of the CAHJP for their assistance, and to Vera Solomon and Eliezer Niborski for their help with the Index to Yiddish Periodicals. Thanks too to the staffs of the Hartley Library's Special Collections Division at the University of Southampton, the Main Library and the School of Slavonic and East European Studies Library at University College London, and the Newspaper Reading Room of the British Library.

Those family members and friends in distant places who opened their homes to me made my time abroad incomparably easier, not to mention more fun: Shoshana Ribalow, Volodia Ribitskii and babushka Zinaida Grigorievna, Jeff Rosenberg and Glenn Tasky, and Ayelet Cohen.

My years as a graduate student were made more enjoyable by the companionship and support of my peers in Columbia's doctoral program in Jewish history, including Olga Litvak, Michael Miller, Annie Polland, Marina Rustow, Magda Teter, and Kalman Weiser. Victoria Khiterer generously shared her knowledge of Kiev's archives with me at a crucial stage of this project. Among other colleagues and friends to whom I extend my heartfelt appreciation for their comments and assistance are David Assaf, Eugene Avrutin, Paula Eisenstein Baker, Israel Bartal, Michael Berkowitz, Richard Cohen, Bernard Cooperman, Jonathan Dekel-Chen, Lisa Epstein, Chae-Ran Freeze, Abigail Green, Robin Judd, Gwynn Kessler, Rebecca Kobrin, Olga Litvak, Sam Norich, Avraham Nowersztern, Steven Rappaport, David Rechter, Shaul Stampfer, and Scott Ury. Special thanks to Phyllis Deutsch for her imaginative title suggestion.

The research for this book was enabled by support from a number of institutions, including Columbia University's Institute for Israel and Jewish Studies and Harriman Institute, the Fulbright-Hays Doctoral Dissertation Research Abroad program of the U.S. Department of Education, the National Foundation for Jewish Culture, the YIVO Institute for Jewish Research, the Hadassah-Brandeis Institute, and the British Academy. Preparation and production of this work were generously supported by a Cahnman Publication Subvention Grant, awarded by the Association for Jewish Studies, and by Columbia's Institute for Israel and Jewish Studies. I thank Jeremy Dauber for his kind facilitation in making the latter subvention possible.

I would like to thank my editor at Indiana University Press, Janet Rabinowitch, for her insight and assistance, as well as Katie Baber, and Jeffrey Veidlinger for his helpful comments. My thanks also to Paula Hyman and Deborah Dash Moore for including this book in their superb series. I am grateful to David Banis and especially Margaret Seiler for their hard work on the beautiful maps.

Throughout the researching and writing of this book I had the loving support of my family: my brother Adin and sister Vered, my aunts and uncles and cousins, and my parents-in-law Hans and Hennie van Herpen. My husband Elchanan van Herpen spent many Sundays on his own so that I could have the time I needed to "finish the book," and I am grateful to him for his patience and encouragement. Dank je, Chananchik. I was lucky enough to have all my grandparents until very recently, and I miss their presence greatly; they remain a constant source of inspiration to me in all that I do. Finally, I thank my parents, *be-ahavah rabah rabah,* for always being there for me, and always believing in me.

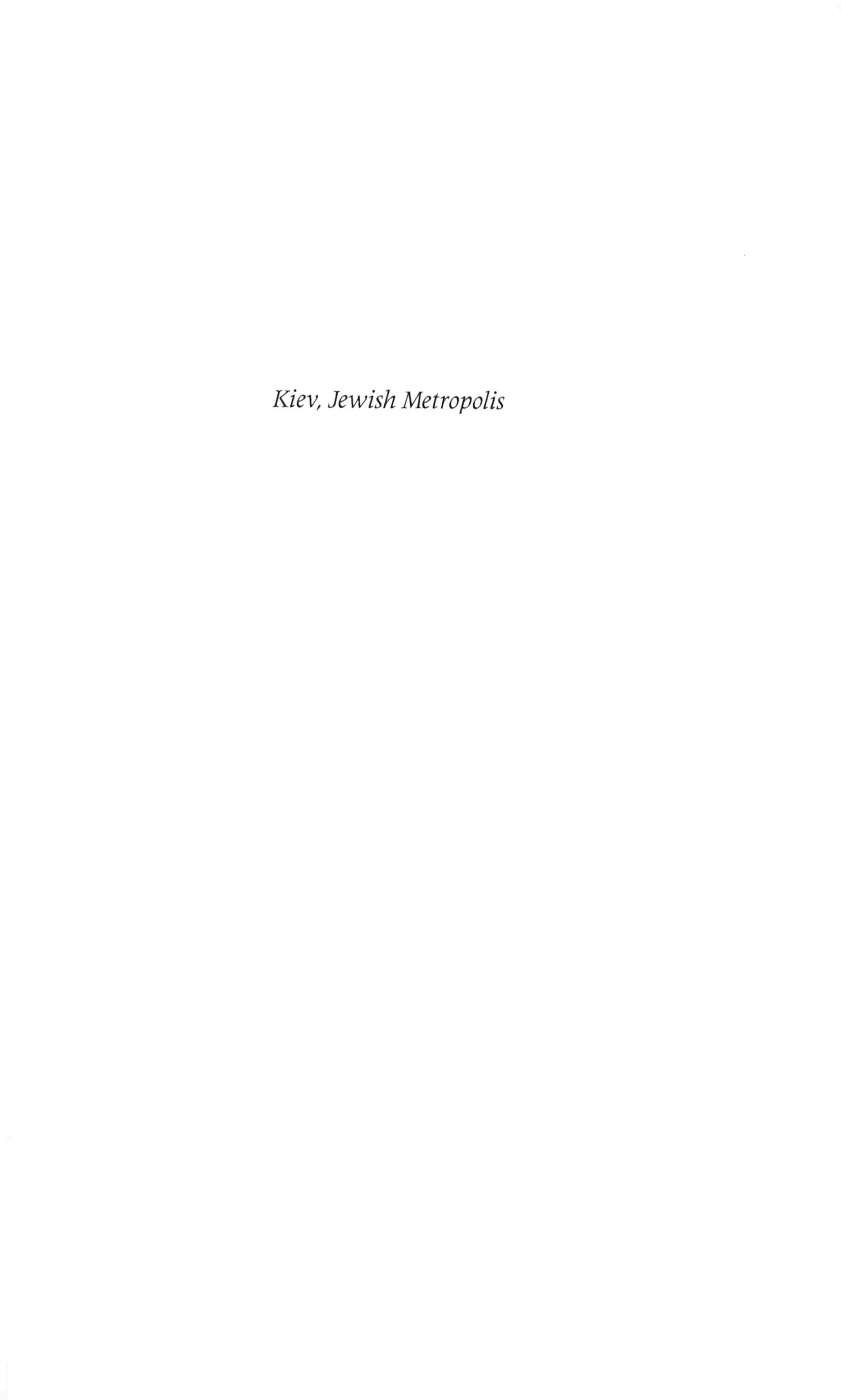

Kiev, Jewish Metropolis

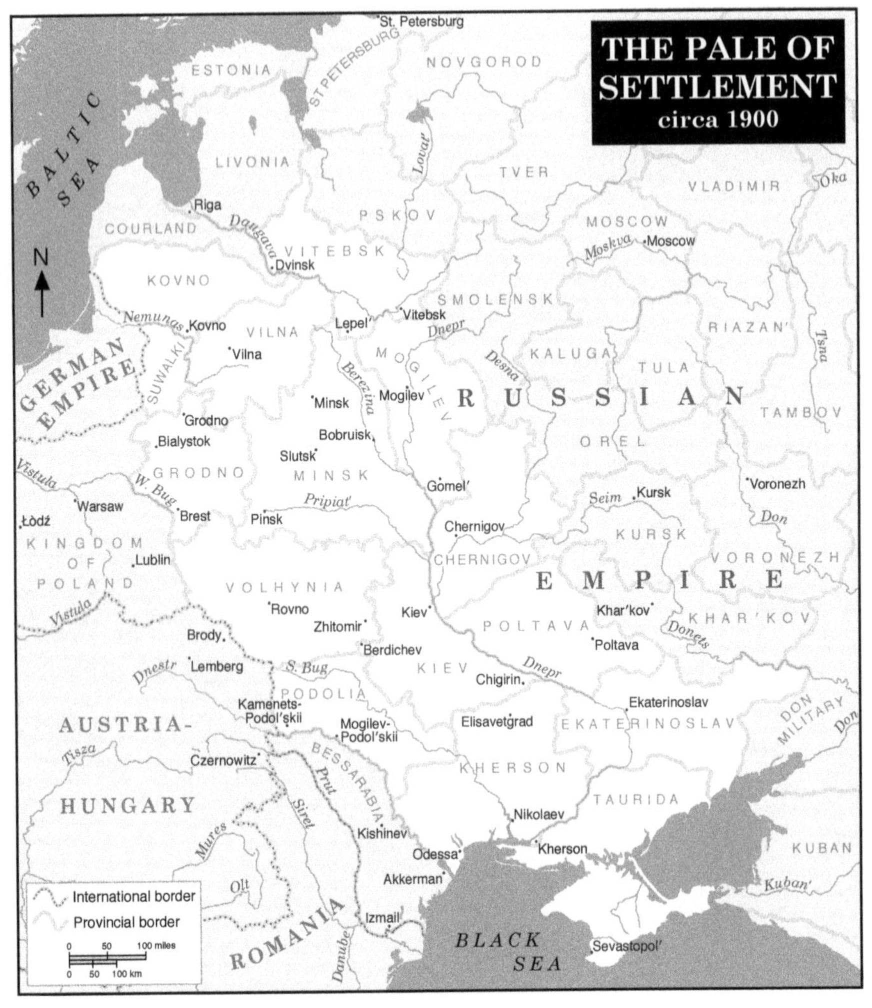

The Pale of Settlement, c. 1900. *Cartography by Margaret Seiler, based on map in* The YIVO Encyclopedia of Jews in Eastern Europe.

The southwest region of the Russian Empire, c. 1900. *Cartography by Margaret Seiler, based on map in* The YIVO Encyclopedia of Jews in Eastern Europe.

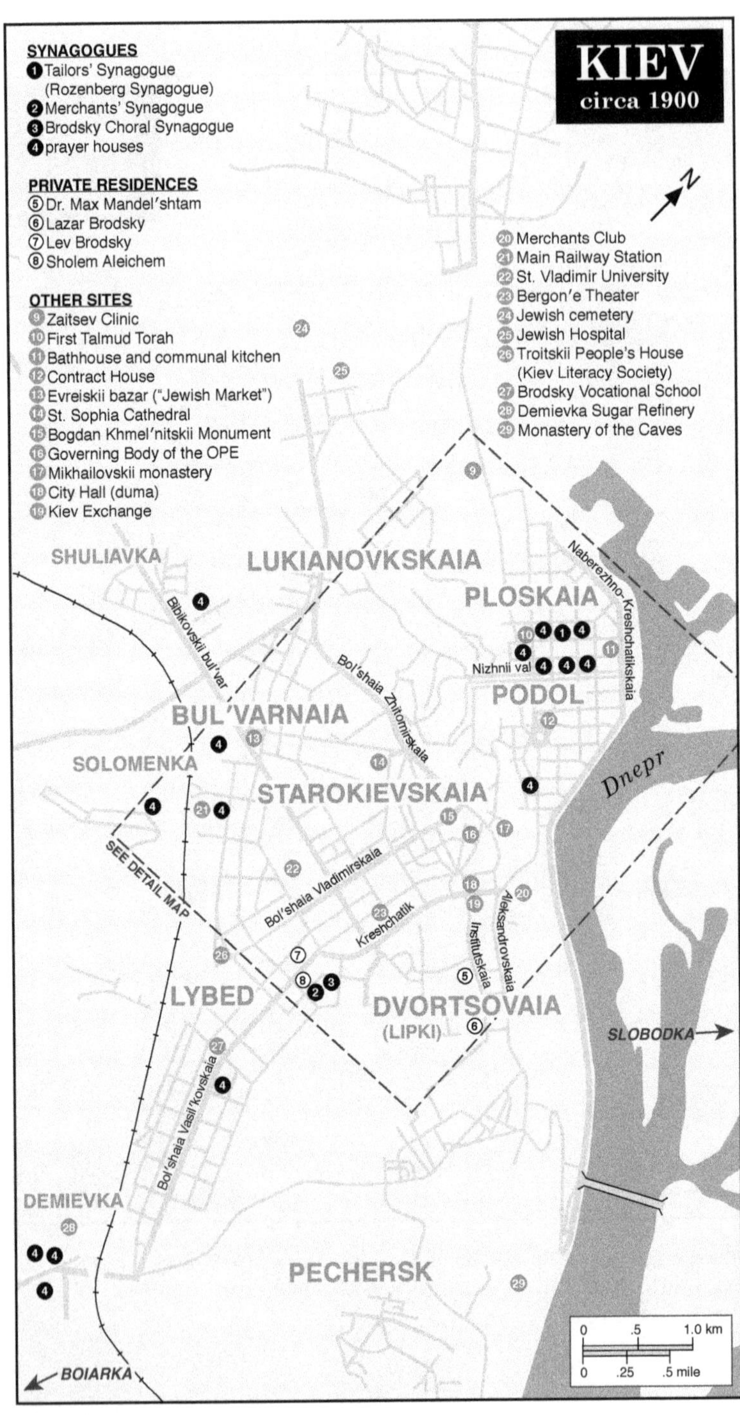
KIEV
circa 1900
SYNAGOGUES
1 Tailors' Synagogue (Rozenberg Synagogue)
2 Merchants' Synagogue
3 Brodsky Choral Synagogue
4 prayer houses
PRIVATE RESIDENCES
5 Dr. Max Mandel'shtam
6 Lazar Brodsky
7 Lev Brodsky
8 Sholem Aleichem
OTHER SITES
9 Zaitsev Clinic
10 First Talmud Torah
11 Bathhouse and communal kitchen
12 Contract House
13 Evreiskii bazar ("Jewish Market")
14 St. Sophia Cathedral
15 Bogdan Khmel'nitskii Monument
16 Governing Body of the OPE
17 Mikhailovskii monastery
18 City Hall (duma)
19 Kiev Exchange
20 Merchants Club
21 Main Railway Station
22 St. Vladimir University
23 Bergon'e Theater
24 Jewish cemetery
25 Jewish Hospital
26 Troitskii People's House (Kiev Literacy Society)
27 Brodsky Vocational School
28 Demievka Sugar Refinery
29 Monastery of the Caves
N
SHULIAVKA
LUKIANOVKSKAIA
PLOSKAIA
Naberezhno-Kreshchatikskaia
Bibikovskii bul'var
Bol'shaia Zhitomirskaia
Nizhnii val
PODOL
BUL'VARNAIA
SOLOMENKA
STAROKIEVSKAIA
Dnepr
SEE DETAIL MAP
Bol'shaia Vladimirskaia
Kreshchatik
Institutskaia
Aleksandrovskaia
LYBED
DVORTSOVAIA
(LIPKI)
SLOBODKA
Bol'shaia Vasil'kovskaia
DEMIEVKA
PECHERSK
BOIARKA
0 .5 1.0 km
0 .25 .5 mile

Kiev, c. 1900. *Cartography by Margaret Seiler, based on map in* The YIVO Encyclopedia of Jews in Eastern Europe.

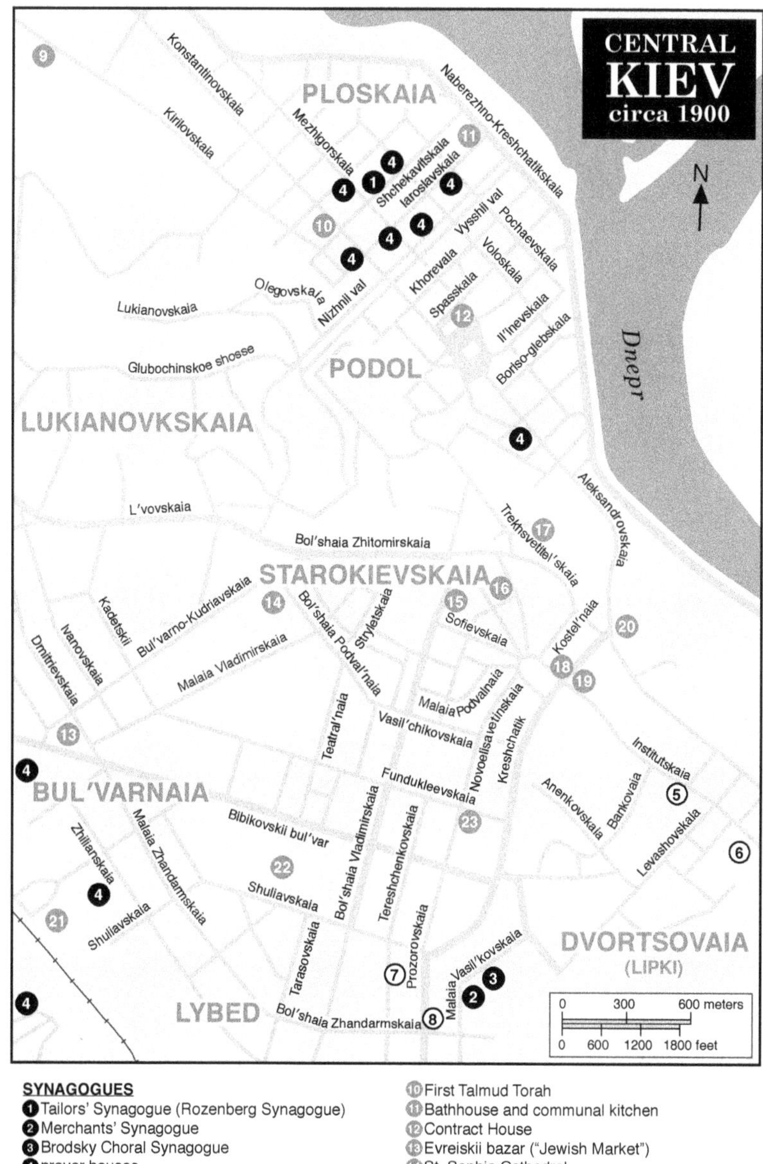

SYNAGOGUES
1 Tailors' Synagogue (Rozenberg Synagogue)
2 Merchants' Synagogue
3 Brodsky Choral Synagogue
4 prayer houses

PRIVATE RESIDENCES
5 Dr. Max Mandel'shtam
6 Lazar Brodsky
7 Lev Brodsky
8 Sholem Aleichem

OTHER SITES
9 Zaitsev Clinic
10 First Talmud Torah
11 Bathhouse and communal kitchen
12 Contract House
13 Evreiskii bazar ("Jewish Market")
14 St. Sophia Cathedral
15 Bogdan Khmel'nitskii Monument
16 Governing Body of the OPE
17 Mikhailovskii monastery
18 City Hall (duma)
19 Kiev Exchange
20 Merchants Club
21 Main Railway Station
22 St. Vladimir University
23 Bergon'e Theater

Central Kiev, c. 1900. *Cartography by Margaret Seiler, based on map in* The YIVO Encyclopedia of Jews in Eastern Europe.

Introduction

Kiev, Jewish Metropolis is a study of the Jews of late imperial Kiev, and of Jewish institutions and Jewish leadership in that city, from the official readmission of Jews to Kiev by Tsar Alexander II in 1859 to the outbreak of the First World War. The book examines the inner life of a dynamic and rapidly changing urban Jewry over the course of half a century, exploring its communal politics, leadership struggles, socioeconomic and demographic shifts, religious and cultural sensibilities, and relations with its Christian neighbors. The setting of Kiev, a city at the heart of both the dense Jewish population of the Pale of Settlement and the Russian imperial consciousness, lends itself to an analysis set in the dual context of both Russian Jewry and of imperial society, culture, and politics. Surrounded by the historic heartland of Ukrainian Jewish settlement, populated by a curious mixture of urbane Jewish merchants and professionals and "green" Jewish artisans and brokers newly arrived from the shtetl, famed for its opportunities for education, culture, employment, and stock market speculation, cursed for its often pitiless persecution of its Jews—Kiev embodied all the promises that the Russian Empire held for Jews, as well as all that many of them came to hate and fear about the disabilities, restrictions, and chauvinism of the tsar's realm.

After decades of official exclusion, Jews were permitted to settle in Kiev, now capital of independent Ukraine but then the chief city of the Russian Empire's southwest, beginning in 1859. This late date permits us to use Kiev as a laboratory to examine the development of Jewish communal institutions, both official and unofficial, in the late imperial period, as the city was something of a tabula rasa on which its new Jewish residents could inscribe their vision of corporate Jewish existence. The governing alliance between wealthy notables and *maskilim* (proponents of the Jewish Enlightenment), accepted without protest for the first few decades of communal existence, came under attack from several fronts in the last years of the nineteenth century, paving the way for the revolution in community affairs—and Jewish life as a whole—that was to come in the early twentieth century. Imperial authorities, troubled by the untrammeled power of the Jewish elite, moved to check the dominance of the notables by changing the legal basis of communal organization in Kiev, which had far-reaching consequences for the city's Jews. New elements from Kiev's educated Jewish classes began to make their voices heard by pushing for change within official structures and by creating their own organizations that would be responsive to their needs. And a new generation of community activists and philanthropists, many of them women, initiated new and independent institutions for the provision of welfare and education to the needy and the sick.

By the early twentieth century, the socioeconomic, religious, and political fissures that had begun to appear over the previous decades were now beyond bridging, and there was very little on which the would-be leaders of Kiev's Jews could agree. Nor is there much evidence that they consulted with the working Jewish masses whom they claimed to represent. The growing diversity of Kiev Jewry and increasing levels of acculturation, however, made possible new forms of association similar to those taking shape in the larger Russian imperial society. Indeed, just as civil society was developing and taking on a central role in the Russian Empire starting in the 1890s, it is possible to speak of a kind of "Jewish civil society" emerging in that same milieu to replace the traditional form of Jewish community that was no longer appropriate for the changing circumstances in which Russian Jews found themselves, and above all for the new definitions of Jewish identity that emerged in the last quarter-century of imperial rule. This "self-conscious public sphere" was characterized by some of the same features that were central elements of *obshchestvennost'* (Russian civil society): democratic institutions of self-government, voluntary associations, and forums for the expression of public opinion such as the press.[1] As in the larger Russian society, much of the energy of the new civil society was given over to solving the problems of modern life, of which poverty and its attendant ills loomed largest. Hence, charity and welfare were issues central to Jewish communal life, and are among the primary foci of this study.

While new forms of Jewish collective existence were a feature of Jewish life throughout the empire, they usually emerged first and most intensely in the large cities. Circumstances and conditions in Kiev make it a particularly favorable place to examine specific aspects of late imperial Jewish life, elements that have as yet not been adequately analyzed by scholars: Jewish communal development and associational life, the realm of welfare and philanthropy, contacts with non-Jews, and acculturation. Like Odessa, Kiev was the endpoint of migration for thousands of Jews and, placed in the heart of the region of densest Jewish settlement in the Pale, was even more favorably located than its southern counterpart in this regard. But, unlike Odessa, settlement in Kiev was restricted to certain categories of Jews; as we shall see, this did not necessarily prevent other Jews from trying and succeeding to gain residence in the city, but it did mean that those who ended up there had to want to be there. Settling in Kiev was not something one did lightly; that is not to belittle the efforts involved for a Jew traveling hundreds of miles in order to find a job in Odessa, but those who settled did not have to spend months or even years obtaining an official residence permit or expend time, money, and pride in bribing the right policemen and officials. The self-selecting aspect of migration was thus greatly intensified, and in this sense Kiev might be more favorably compared to St. Petersburg, which was also outside the Pale of Settlement, but with a Jewish population that constituted a much smaller proportion of the total urban population: 2 percent in 1897, compared with 13 percent in Kiev in the same year.[2]

Residence requirements and the particular attractions of Kiev contributed to the somewhat eclectic makeup of the city's Jewish community: wealthy merchants and industrialists concentrated in the sugar trade, the economic engine of the southwest region; upwardly mobile clerks, bookkeepers, and shop workers legally "attached" to their magnate employers in order to attain legal residence in the city; brokers, agents, and speculators (often without residence permits) trying to make a quick ruble in Kiev's fast-paced commodities and properties markets; and large numbers of impoverished artisans and students. Kiev's central geographical location also meant that diverse Jewish migrants came from many parts of the Pale of Settlement: *Litvaks* and Ukrainian Jews, Misnagdim and Hasidim, *yishuvnikes* (village Jews), and Jews from large market towns. Finally, its proximity to the heartland of compact Jewish settlement meant that Jews could easily travel back and forth between the bustling city and the sleepier shtetlekh, which could serve both to soften and to underscore the differences in Jewish communal, religious, and cultural life in the two settings. Thus, Kiev was uniquely both a central hub attracting thousands of Jews a year from the surrounding, densely Jewish provinces and a frontier city in which one had to make a conscious effort to settle.[3]

Many of the migrants who chose to come to Kiev were ready to leave the tightly regulated community of the shtetl and—though most were simply looking for a better living—perhaps even sought a place where they could experiment with different ways of being Jewish.[4] Certainly, in the last few decades of the *ancien régime,* Kiev was known as a city with a vibrant and diverse array of Jewish institutions and communities, and conformity of any kind was not necessarily a requirement for belonging. The city was the capital of the modern age, and modernity, "a world laced with possibilities," represented choice: of language, religious practice, communal affiliation, and new gender and familial roles.[5]

Restrictions on Jewish life, however, were not absent in Kiev. The tsarist regime imposed legal limitations on Jewish settlement in the city, making life quite onerous for contemporaries but, ironically, aiding the historian. Surveillance of Jewish activities—of which there is abundant evidence in the archives—was often more intense in Kiev than in the Pale, which made it quite difficult for many people to engage in nationalist Jewish politics in any constant or meaningful way, especially when illegal residents risked expulsion if discovered by the police. This heightened the importance of communal politics and local associations in Jewish life—hence the sustained treatment that those phenomena receive in this study.

Russian Jewish Historiography

Simon Dubnow and Iulii Gessen, who were themselves born and raised in the Russian Empire, laid the foundations for Russian Jewish historiography in their sweeping surveys, both attempting syntheses of "external" and "internal" history: Jewish relations with state and society, and Jewry's inner religious, cultural, economic, and political dynamics. Dubnow's *History of the Jews in Russia and Poland,* while dated in some respects (especially in its evaluation of the motivation behind tsarist legislation on the Jews), nonetheless remains the standard survey of East European Jewish history.[6] The work is particularly valuable for its thoroughgoing coverage of all aspects of the Jewish experience, embracing politics, society, religion, and culture. Though Gessen, in comparison, did not have the linguistic tools to plumb the inner workings of Jewish society, in his *History of the Jewish People in Russia* he nonetheless provides remarkable insight into the inner life and development of Russian Jewry, an analysis oftentimes just as sharp as that of government policies on the Jews (which, given his access to a broad range of archival sources, has in many ways not been surpassed since the publication of the book in 1927).[7] The one major flaw is Gessen's insistence, clearly suggested by his context and perhaps his own ideology, on the centrality of the class struggle within the Jewish community, with the alliance between the wealthy elite and the rabbinate taking the place of the bourgeoisie in the Marxist schema. The fact that the theme of class struggle appears only sporadically throughout the book, though, suggests that it was introduced more for the benefit of others than because of Gessen's own convictions.[8]

Other members of the first circle of Russian Jewish historians include Elias (Eliyohu) Tcherikower, Jacob (Yaakov) Lestschinsky, and Saul (Shoyl) Ginsburg, who began their careers in the tsarist empire and eventually emigrated to Western or Central Europe and then to the United States. Tcherikower, Lestschinsky, and other scholars in Berlin, Warsaw, and Vilna established a tradition of social science and quantitative research methods in their work under the institutional umbrella of YIVO, the Jewish Scientific Institute, and in such publications as *Bleter far idishe demografye, statistik un ekonomik*.[9] Russian Jewish academics who remained in the Soviet Union and continued to write on Jewish topics were often active in the state-sponsored academies of "Jewish proletarian culture" in Kiev and Minsk, and produced several studies on Jewish history and culture that, while marred by ideological bias, remain of value for contemporary scholars (for example, the work of Nokhem Shtif). Also eminently worthy of mention is Arcadius Kahan, one of Lestschinsky's few successors in the field of the economic history of Russian Jewry.[10]

Since the Holocaust, however, most scholars in North America and Israel have focused not on the social, communal, and economic history of Russian Jews but on other topics that can be divided into three primary foci.[11] The first is the relationship between the Russian state and the Jews, encompassing the dynamic between the imperial bureaucracy, which sought to shape, control, redefine, and limit the Jew, and the Jewish subjects of the tsar, who both responded to these attempts and actively sought to deploy for their own purposes the power of the state.[12] A second and related focus examines the interactions between Jews and Russian imperial society; many of these center on the issues of antisemitism and violence.[13] A third category of study examines the evolving internal culture of Jews in the Russian Empire, especially the changing self-definition of those Jews in political, intellectual, literary, and cultural terms but also religious traditions such as Hasidism and Musar.[14] These studies, along with a small number of excellent surveys, have provided us with a rich portrait of Russian Jewry.[15]

But there is another category of Russian Jewish history that relates to all of those mentioned above and yet deserves its own place: that of the lived experience of Jews in tsarist Russia. The history of Russian Jewry's *Lebenswelt* or

Alltagsgeschichte has begun to be explored in a number of recent monographs, but much ground remains to be covered.[16] This book seeks to bring to life the everyday struggles and triumphs of Kiev's Jews, from the market trader to the commodities broker to the sugar baron; at home, at work, at prayer, and in community (or, perhaps more accurately, *communities*). To do so, it draws on a wide variety of sources: statistics, annual reports, individual and collective petitions to the authorities, correspondence between government officials, reports and letters in the press, memoirs, and contemporary works of fiction. The resulting portrait is an attempt to capture the complex textures of Jewish existence and consciousness in a time of rapid change and modernization.

A City without a History

The absence of historiography on Kiev is striking and is not matched by any other large city in the Russian Empire. Michael Hamm's *Kiev: A Portrait* and a small number of scholarly articles are the only satisfactory works available in any language.[17] The Soviet *Istoriia Kieva,* published in two editions in the 1960s, is so sparsely referenced as to be almost useless to the scholar.[18] Moreover, the Marxist-Leninist framework within which its authors interpret all events and trends ensures that the issue of ethnicity is almost completely neglected, which is akin to trying to ignore the elephant in the middle of the room. Several recent collections of historical sketches (most notably those by Vitalii Kovalyns'kyi), as well as a series of guidebooks by Mikhail Kal'nitskii and a number of Soviet-style reference works (*spravochniki*) provide some solid information on various aspects of life in tsarist Kiev, but these are obviously no substitute for a comprehensive and overarching analysis of the themes that these works raise.[19]

Why the paucity of works on Kiev, and especially imperial Kiev? Ukrainian intellectuals were often more interested in the periods that predated tsarist control of the city and of historic Ukraine, and thus produced a number of works on medieval Kiev, capital of Kievan Rus', as well as on the Hetman period.[20] Under the tsars, Kiev enjoyed only a brief period as a flourishing center of Ukrainian nationalism after the 1905 Revolution, and this, along with the fact that until well into the 1920s the city was (officially, at least) minority Ukrainian, meant that it did not garner the attention of a truly "Ukrainian" city such as L'viv. In the early Soviet period, Kiev had its capital status stripped from it in favor of Kharkiv, and even after it regained that title in 1934, it continued to be seen as "a provincial backwater of Soviet Russian culture," with scholarship on Ukrainian history relegated to the second-class standing reserved for all "national minority" histories.[21] And perhaps most of all, the decimation of the Ukrainian intelligentsia by Stalin ensured the end of a vibrant academic culture devoted to the study of Ukrainian history and culture, which would of course include the history of Kiev.

Nor have Jews embraced Kiev as their own, remembering it most often as a place of persecution and medieval-style ghettos and preferring to write about cities that they considered to be, in the words of the Hebrew phrase, "mother cities in Israel," such as Vilna, Odessa, and Warsaw. Vilna and Warsaw, both included within the borders of interwar Poland, also survived for much longer as world centers of Jewish culture, while Kiev—despite its large Jewish population and Bureau of Jewish Proletarian Culture, liquidated by Stalin in the late 1930s—quickly lost whatever Jewish cachet it had once had. It did not even benefit from the mass emigration of Russian Jews to outposts of the Russian diaspora that made their metropoles of origin famous once again for their Jewishness (take the example of Odessa and Brighton Beach).

Capital of What?

The dearth of scholarship on a city that was a major center for both Ukrainians and Jews is striking . . . and suggestive. Certainly in collective memory, and perhaps even in the scholarly worlds of Ukrainian and Jewish Studies, it is the hinterland rather than the metropole that has been the preferred subject of study: for Jews, the mythical shtetl and its "traditional" Yiddish culture; for Ukrainians, the village and peasant folkways. And one of the intriguing aspects of Kiev as a multiethnic city is the different imagined hinterlands the city could claim as its own. In the imperial geography, Kiev was the capital of the "southwest region," a somewhat artificial construct made up of Kiev, Volhyn, and Podol provinces, corresponding roughly to Right-Bank Ukraine. Paradoxically, Ukrainophiles viewed it as the principal city of Little Russia, which corresponded to *Left-Bank* Ukraine—previously ruled by the Hetmanate; but of course those taking an expansive view of an entity called "Ukraina" would see Kiev as the natural capital of both banks of the River Dnepr/Dnipro. The situation became no less complicated when it came to Kiev and the Jews. Here, Kiev could be viewed as a natural metropolis for the great hinterland of the Pale of Settlement—starting with the three southwest provinces and neighboring Chernigov province and extending to Polesie and the southern provinces of the "northwest" (i.e., Belorussia) as well as to New Russia in the south. But it could just as well be seen as a gaping hole in the geographic fabric of the Pale, for legally it was off-limits to Jewish settlement and thus not an obvious "center" for the surrounding Jewish "periphery."

Although Kiev is not an obvious "border town"—officially, it held that status for less than a century after it fell under Muscovite rule in 1686, straddling the frontier between Muscovy and Poland—I would argue that it remained a metaphorical border town for many centuries after the "reunification" of Left- and Right-Bank Ukraine.[22] If one imagines the Russian southwest, the Left and Right Banks of Ukraine, and the Pale of Settlement (and even the former Polish–Lithuanian Commonwealth) placed one over the other on a map, Kiev is somewhere near the center of the resulting geographical amalgam—and its symbolic importance then becomes clear. The seat of the Metropolitan of Kiev, the city was claimed by the Orthodox faithful (both Russian and Ukrainian) as a historic center of Eastern Christianity, but through the centuries prelates in Kiev representing both the Uniate (Greek Catholic) and Orthodox churches battled over the leadership of the Ukrainian Church.[23]

Indeed, another problem we shall confront in the pages that follow is the definition of center versus periphery, for it is not always clear now, as it was not then, which was which.[24] For all intents and purposes the booming city seemed to be the hub toward which all things—people, intellect, capital—gravitated, but as the forces of acculturation became ever stronger some Jews, most notably the Jewish *intelligenty* of Kiev (and many other cities), began to wonder if perhaps the shtetl was not, after all, the true center of Jewish life. Thus Sholem Aleichem's many stories set in the shtetl, Sh. An-sky's expeditions to record Jewish folkways, and Simon Dubnow's quest to collect *pinkasim* (communal record books) and other invaluable documents.[25] Ukrainian intellectuals, too, have invariably sought "authentic" Ukrainian culture in the countryside, not in the city.

A Jewish Metropolis?

But why was Kiev different? Like Odessa and Warsaw, it had its Jewish writers: Sholem Aleichem and the Hebrew poet Yehudah Leib Levin both spent significant time there. Like St. Petersburg, it had its illustrious Jewish plutocrats: the Brodsky family was known throughout the empire and even had marriage connections with the "noble" Gintsburg family of the capital. Like Odessa, it had its famous Jewish Zionists: Max Mandel'shtam even served as the model for Dr. Eichenstam, president of the Hebrew Commonwealth in Herzl's *Der Judenstaat.* And like Vilna, Kiev had a (somewhat) illustrious Jewish pedigree, boasting the presence of Jewish scholars as early as the twelfth century. Was Kiev Jewish? Or was it the epitome of a Russian city, indeed a veritable "non-Jewish" city, if there could be such a thing? As we shall see, one of the central tensions that Kiev Jews and non-Jews expressed about their city throughout the tsarist period was the extent to which it was, if at all, a Jewish city. Starting from the first decades of Jewish settlement, residents and visitors found that Kiev was becoming an increasingly Jewish city, not only in sheer numbers but also in its very character; those hostile to Jews even claimed that the latter were intent on "conquering" Russia's holiest city. But as it became more and more "Jewish," Kiev became ever more inhospitable to Jews. Many if not most of the Jews in Kiev lived in constant fear of arrest and expulsion simply for not being in possession of the proper papers that would allow them residence in the city. As the influence of Russian nationalists in the city grew, so did the role of antisemitism: from hateful but empty threats to the violence of the 1905 pogrom to the almost constant specter of pogroms in subsequent years. Of one thing there could be no doubt: Kiev was an imperial city, a place where numerous ethnic and religious groups falling under the umbrella of the great *Rossiiskaia imperiia* met and mingled.

This book will not attempt to argue that the dominant culture of Kiev was actually a secularized Jewish culture, as has been argued for other cities.[26] It will, however, claim that the Jewish presence there was one that had a palpable impact on the character and profile of the city in a way that epitomized the tensions in the uneasy relationship between the Russian Empire's Jews and imperial society. Though Jews were but tolerated strangers in Kiev, they influenced—indeed shaped—the city to a remarkable extent. The fact that by the turn of the century urban Jews were such a visible and inextricable strand within the tapestry of that society makes an exploration of their experience in the city even more important. As was true for the empire as a whole, Jews played a central role in the economy of Kiev and most agreed that the city could not do without them and even owed to them much of its spectacular growth in the final decades of the nineteenth century and first decades of the twentieth. Yet as integrated as they were into the fabric of the city in some ways—and a good number were fully acculturated into Kiev's urban Russian milieu—in other respects they continued, nolens volens, to live apart—a problem that continued to vex the intelligentsia and the bureaucracy alike. As Harriet Murav has demonstrated, the very act of acculturation provoked anxiety among ethnic Russians because it destabilized the idea of *Russianness:* if a Jew could speak Russian well enough and become sufficiently acquainted with imperial Russian (*rossiiskii*) culture to pass for an ethnic Russian (*russkii*), then how could one continue to define *Russian*? It is no accident that Sholem Aleichem set half of his tragicomic farce *The Bloody Hoax* in Kiev: the city was the perfect setting for a tale of a Christian pretending to be a Jew. The total lack of familiarity with Yiddish and Jewish customs exhibited by the Christian student Popov masquerading as the Jewish student Rabinovich is—at least at first—put down by the Jewish family with which he boards to extreme assimilation. And perhaps Sholem Aleichem chose to set the second half of the novel, in which the Jewish student pretends to be an Orthodox Christian, in Moscow to heighten the dramatic tension of the plot—for a Jew pretending to be a Christian in Kiev was quite an ordinary occurrence.

The Meaning of Community

This book also looks closely at the development of a continued corporate identity among Russian Jews, which in its organized manifestation was called the "community," and at the various groupings that attempted to claim a leadership role within Russian Jewry. First, by mapping the contours of communal leadership and organization in one locale from their very beginnings, the following pages will contribute to our very murky understanding of how Jews ran their communities after the abolition of the official *kahal*—the governing body of the Jewish community—in 1844.[27] Following in the footsteps of Azriel Shohat and Eli Lederhendler, each of whom attempted in his own way to unravel the tangled skein of internal Jewish leadership (both actual and attempted), representation, and political networks, I explore not only how the Jewish community functioned after 1844 but also what it meant to those who were supposed to constitute its membership and to those who supposed themselves worthy of acting as its leadership.

Several works in European Jewish history have recently appeared that attempt to understand Jewish modernization and the formation of a modern hyphenated Jewish identity (French-Jewish, German-Jewish, Austrian-

Jewish, etc.) through the lens of the individual community, and many devote attention to the significance of associational life within the framework of community.[28] Indeed, any discussion of community development must, of course, relate to changing conceptualizations of Jewish self-understanding, for a corporate body can only be constituted if its members agree that they share a core element of their individual makeup. In the late Russian Empire, that agreement was absent among a Jewry divided by class, religious observance, political disposition and affiliation, and language. Commonalities that had previously been taken for granted were no longer necessarily so, especially in a metropolis. The pressure that one invariably felt in a small town to affiliate with the official Jewish community was not nearly as strong in the anonymous city. How would Jewish community, or any sort of collective existence, be defined now that even the word *community* itself was indeterminate? The "communal" tax was paid on kosher meat, but not by everyone—not even those who allocated the proceeds. The "communal" rabbi was elected by prayer house parishioners, but not everyone wanted to or could afford to belong to a prayer house. The community could not be defined by restrictions on Jews to which the elite was not subject (which, as we shall see, was indeed the case in Kiev). Perhaps only during pogroms were all Jews linked by the threat of injury or death common to all, but even this fleeting moment, if it can be considered "communal," was overshadowed by the bitter quarrels that ensued once victims demanded assistance and leaders were charged with deciding who would benefit and who would not. Like many Russian subjects, Jews could now choose to be members of one or more of the hundreds of voluntary societies sprouting up in Kiev and other cities, but in an era of growing interaction between Jews and non-Jews, there was no guarantee that that society would be a Jewish one. At times, the vagaries of Jewish observance, behavior, and affiliation in Kiev made identity almost impossible to pin down.[29] As Martha Bohachevsky-Chomiak notes, "Works on imperial Russian society outside the Russian center have rarely focused on community organizations. . . . They often overlook the organic process of local organization and concentrate on political developments."[30] This has been true of the historiography of Russian Jews, as well, and this study's microhistorical focus attempts to understand just that organic process that has been so elusive for scholars, if they have tried to find it.

This account's focus on Jewish leadership in Kiev means that it must spend considerable time investigating the lives and works of the Jewish haute bourgeoisie, the "notables" who were so prominent in both Jewish and general life in Kiev, thus contributing to a history of the Russian Jewish merchant elite—a desideratum noted by many historians.[31] Far from claiming the mantle of leadership because of their close ties to the existing Jewish community, these merchants were often quite far removed from the mechanisms of Jewish self-rule—both because they often saw themselves occupying a higher social plane than most of their fellow Jews and because at a relatively early stage in Russian rule over Polish Jews, imperial legislation had removed them from formal affiliation with the *obshchestvo* (Jewish community). So why were they interested in a leadership role at all? Cynics would not be wrong in ascribing the drive toward leadership exhibited by some of these men to the urge for power, but there were surely positive motivations as well, including feelings of responsibility toward their coreligionists; a desire to help their fellow Jews move toward enlightenment and acceptance by the Russian polity and society; and, no doubt, a sense of shared fate (*Schicksalgemeinde*) in an empire that classified both the richest Jewish merchant and the lowliest Jewish water bearer as *evrei* above all else. I have been unable to find memoir or epistolary material by these men that would enable me to ascertain such assumptions through their own words. I hope that material will yet be found.

The notables' detractors accused them of taking advantage of their leadership position within Jewry and even of betrayal, but many of them saw themselves as loyal Jews and dedicated leaders, a claim that the historian may interrogate but not contest. Indeed, the findings of this study seem to confirm one scholar's conjecture that "further research . . . is likely to reveal a higher degree of attachment to Jewish society than was implied by contemporary Jewish critics."[32] The matter is complicated by the possibility of multiple loyalties, a concept that any discussion of developing national identity must take into account and one that was not foreign to Russian Jews in the late imperial period. It was only with the advent of mobilized Jewish nationalism around the turn of the century that Jews started speaking of exclusive loyalty to the Jewish nation and its historical destiny, and even then significant strands of Jewish political thought continued to insist on the possibility of nationally conscious Jews living within the framework of a federative state (the Bund, to take one obvious example). Many members of the Jewish elite and bourgeoisie committed to liberal politics did not see themselves as "assimilationists" but as comfortably maintaining their loyalty to the Russian tsar and empire along with a commitment to some form of Jewish communal, cultural, and/or religious identity. For them, an exclusively Jewish self-definition was unthinkable, let alone totally impractical.[33]

Nor are they the only actors in this story who were concerned with authority and influence. Much of this story is about power—who wielded it and how, over whom, for what purposes—and about the struggle for power. Power was not always for base purposes: many of those engaged in the struggle sincerely wanted to improve the lot of the Jews in Russia. The Russian state insisted on its sovereignty over its Jews and its ability to do with them as it wished (integration or segregation, depending on the era); those in power at the regional, provincial, and especially the municipal levels also argued for their right to intervene in Jewish affairs. Among the Jews, various individuals and groupings vied for power and leadership based on a number of qualifications: religious authority (rabbis); wealth and influence (notables); insight and education, and connection to wealth and influence (maskilim, Crown rabbis); political awareness (nationalists, socialists, liberals); and, increasingly, "the will of the people" (any of the above).

Kiev, an Imperial City

At a 1993 workshop entitled *Revisioning Imperial Russia*, a number of leading historians of the Russian Empire discussed how a new history of the empire might appear. Among topics to be included in that history were "multiple searches for national identity, as well as the much-neglected subject of the prevalent and ordinary intermingling of ethnic cultures."[34] Among the suggestions was a reevaluation of imperial culture—in the context of the expanding empire—as an amalgam of the various ethnicities and other groups that made up that empire. And just as the identities of the other nationalities of the empire were developing in the late imperial period, so too was a Russian national self-definition—far from being an *idée fixe*—also taking shape, often in response to those others.[35] Quite distinct from that identity was "Russianness itself,'" as Michael Stanislawski put it, which dominated the empire in very subtle ways, and with which so many non-Russian groups wanted to be affiliated.[36] But ethnic identity—or any other externally imposed classification—must not be the only category used to understand imperial Russia; probing questions must also be asked about, as Nancy Kollman argued, the "self-definition of individuals and groups, and their interaction with the state"—and, we might add, with other individuals and groups as well. This leads to the next desideratum, voiced by Richard Stites: a more intimate history of individual experience, including "emotions, human expressiveness, personal relations."[37] Such a history can promote a new emphasis on agency, whether of the individual or the group, thus moving away from the traditional historiographical treatment of peasants and many other groups as "faceless, inert, acted-upon."[38] The sources themselves, of course, can either hamper or facilitate the new cultural history, and they must be mined carefully for personal narratives and interactions as well as for expressions of collective self-definition. Indeed, Reginald Zelnik suggested "that the investigation of social identity and the 'subjective parameters of experience' could provide the basis for a new imperial history."[39]

These ideas correspond felicitously to many of the aims of this book, which is very much part of the "new history" of the Russian Empire that has been emerging over the past several decades, focusing on culture and society from the bottom up as well as on the empire's non-Russian nationalities or peripheral regions.[40] In particular, the book joins the ranks of those recent works that attempt to balance analyses of the "internal" society and culture of a particular ethnic group with the "external" view that takes in imperial policies and contexts.[41] My analysis of the Jewish experience in imperial Russia is informed by an understanding of identity as fluid and dynamic, always interacting with other individual and corporate identities and changing in response to those interactions—for Jews, and all subjects of the tsar, defined themselves just as much as they were defined by his government. Nor is identity limited to ethnic or religious group, but it encompasses a wide range of descriptors and categories: occupation, socioeconomic class, familial status, linguistic abilities and choices, and political consciousness or affiliation. It is more accurate, then, to speak of Jewish communities made up of many elements and many different kinds of collective self-understanding, rather than an elusive singular community to which all belonged and which spoke with one voice. Indeed, some Jews rejected formal or informal membership in *any* kind of Jewish community, and we must consider them as well. Thus the account that follows pays close attention not only to institutions and organizations—representational bodies, communal welfare institutions, rabbinates, voluntary organizations, political groupings—but also to the non-institutional spheres of communal life: commerce and industry, the street, the world of leisure, popular religion, and family life. And at the center of all these are the individuals and families that constituted them, and their personal experiences as real people living in this specific place and time. The book also "asks questions about the meaning of institutions in daily life"—the significance of Russian and especially Jewish institutions for the daily life of Jews.[42]

Looking Back, One Hundred Years Later

Walking around Kiev today, and seeing how many of its Jewish buildings have survived, one might think that it would be relatively easy to reconstruct the history of the Jewish community here. But revolutions, wars, Stalinism, and genocide have taken their toll. The spaces are the same, but you might as well be in Vladivostok for your proximity to the Jewish community that once existed in the city. Just as the city itself is totally transformed, and none of its former spirit can truly be said to remain, so is it with the Jewish community. The decimation is total, and to a certain extent it even extends to the documents of that community. Of the many Jewish institutions in the city, the full records of only two survive. Everything else must be reconstructed using government documents such as petitions and interdepartmental memoranda, newspapers, memoirs, and so on. And even then the picture we get is hazy, only half-there, shimmering in the twilight like the ghost of a friend from the past. What does it mean for the historian, existentially, hermeneutically, to work in an archive with documents from a long-dead community, only several yards away from the killing fields of Babi Yar, where so many members of that community were murdered? What does it mean for the graduate student who is able, with the help of a generous government grant, to rent an apartment in Kiev in the neighborhood where the wealthiest Kiev Jews used to live, steps away from the synagogue attended by the cream of the Jewish elite? Sometimes it seems to mean nothing: the people are long gone, as is the context in which they lived. But the presence of the past is heavy, or perhaps its absence. The historian must acknowledge these burdens, these shadows, these gaps, as he or she sets about to describe this community that once was. How does one give honor to what once was, to the people who inhabited these spaces and created something meaningful that is worth reconstructing, to the extent possible, and understanding, without sentimentalizing, without claiming that this picture is a complete one, that we can ever truly know this time and place, its smells, tastes, joys, sorrows? Nonetheless we forge ahead, trusting the historian's tools, some scientific, some less so, not the least of which is instinct. And detachment, which does not mean a lack of honor for the subject. If we can try to understand the choices that people made and the contingencies and conditions that lay behind those choices, then we will have achieved something.

Structure of the Book

The following chapters trace the evolution of Jewish life in Kiev from its beginnings in a tiny community at a time of expansive optimism; through decades of continued Jewish settlement and communal activity—despite two pogroms and growing hostility toward Jews; to the emergence of a Jewish metropolis and civil society, with a form of elected self-government, a thriving associational culture, and outlets for independent public opinion. The book is divided into two parts that correspond roughly to the "early years" (the first two or three decades of renewed Jewish settlement in Kiev after 1859) and the age of the "Jewish metropolis" (the turn of the century to the outbreak of the First World War). Each part leads off with an economic, demographic, and cultural profile of Kiev Jewry, and then moves on to investigate specific issues of Jewish communal organization and self-understanding.

Chapter 1, "Settlement and Growth, 1859–1881," provides the reader with an overview of the history of Kiev and of Jewish settlement in the city from the medieval period. It then sketches in detail the first twenty years of Jewish life in late-imperial Kiev, including migration, residential, and occupational patterns, set within the context of the city's multiethnic population and dynamic urban life as well as the larger context of Russian Jewry as a whole. The chapter closes with the 1881 pogrom. Chapter 2, "The Foundations of Communal Life," traces the development of an organized Jewish community in Kiev during the first decades of Jewish settlement into the 1890s. This chapter ascertains how the established leadership of Russian Jewry at the time—wealthy merchants and maskilim, proponents of the Jewish Enlightenment—understood and reimagined the concept of "Jewish community" in the decades after the government's abolition of the official Jewish community, and the kinds of institutions they sought to establish to bring that community into being. These institutions, to be controlled by the Jewish economic and intellectual elite, would help to modernize Russian Jewry and facilitate its integration into Russian society. The analysis focuses specifically on the official communal governing board, the municipal Jewish hospital, the state rabbinate, and the Choral Synagogue. The chapter also examines the Russian state's attempt to engineer the kind of Jewish community that it viewed as most appropriate for a modern Russian Jewry, often (but not always) in conjunction with Kiev's Jewish establishment, and reveals the government's unrealized plan to reduce the Russian Jewish community to an entity of a purely religious character, stripped of all independence and autonomy.

Part 2 begins with a survey of the Jewish community of Kiev in the last decades of the tsarist regime as it grew rapidly into one of the largest urban Jewish conglomerations in the empire. Chapter 3, "The Consolidation of Jewish Kiev, 1881–1914," explores the emergence of a large Jewish working class and a smaller Jewish bourgeoisie, the diversification of the local Jewish economy, the gendered economic roles of Jewish men and women, changing residential patterns, and the pogrom of 1905, which—together with the revolution of that year—proved to be a caesura in the life of Kiev Jewry, after which things would never be quite the same. Chapters 4 and 5 take a closer look at specific aspects of Jewish life in Kiev around the fin-de-siècle. Chapter 4, titled "Modern Jewish Cultures and Practices," charts a complex transformation in cultural practices and religious observance among Kiev Jews. Challenging the received categorization of Russian Jews into "traditional" and "secular," the analysis here examines new religious trends that included an unexpected laxity of observance even among groups traditionally considered "pious" and the establishment of a modern-style Choral Synagogue by Kiev's Jewish oligarchs. Chapter 5, "Jew as Neighbor, Jew as Other: Interethnic Relations and Antisemitism," analyzes the dynamics of relations between Jews and other ethnic groups in the city, particularly Ukrainians, and reveals that there were a number of contexts—philanthropic societies, social clubs, political groups—in which a surprisingly large number of contacts between Jews and non-Jews could and did take place. The chapter reflects on the role that interethnic relations, both positive and negative, played in the development of a Russian Jewish identity.

Chapters 6 and 7 return to the theme of Jewish communal and institutional life. "Varieties of Jewish Philanthropy" explores a central component of modern Russian Jewish communal existence by examining the wealthy benefactors who were behind many of the city's Jewish charitable initiatives and the types of institutions they chose to establish. In accordance with their vision of the ideal community, health care was their first priority, followed by education; but whatever the field, they often made sure that the institutions they supported broadcast a political message to the authorities and to Russian society in addition to providing for the poor and the sick. The field of welfare also became an arena in which women could take on leadership roles that were denied to them in official communal structures, and where they introduced new forms of welfare provision that were often more efficient than those of the official governing body of the community. The chapter also shows that philanthropy, often overlooked by scholars, became a new vehicle for the maintenance of Jewish identity and the expression of political opinions—and not only for wealthy Jews—at a time when Russian Jewry was becoming more and more fragmented and there were ever more ways of being Jewish. This network of modern Jewish philanthropic institutions also formed the basis for a "Jewish public sphere" that became vital for Kiev's Jews who, because of official restrictions on Jewish activities, expression, and movement in the city, were compelled to channel their political energies into their many welfare, cultural, and self-help societies. Chapter 7, "Revolutions in Communal Life," continues the focus on communal developments by examining the upheaval in Jewish communal life that accompanied the first Russian Revolution of 1905. As Jews began, not in tiny pockets of maskilim and litterateurs, but en masse, to create new ways of expressing their Jewishness (with the emergence of an acculturated hybrid Russian–Jewish identity, the rise of Jewish nationalism and socialism, and the flowering of modern Jewish culture in Hebrew, Yiddish, and Russian), they also began to challenge the communal status quo by finding alternative ways of affiliating Jewishly through voluntary associations and philanthropic societies. This is Jewish politics in its most local—and perhaps rawest—form. The chapter demonstrates how the central tensions in Russian Jewish society, which usually related in some way to the question of self-definition (as in the ubiquitous problem of Jewish languages or the conflict between nationalism and socialism), played out in local politics, as activists demanded communal governance that would be elected, transparent, and accountable to constituents. In the analysis of the fortunes of the newly reorganized Jewish Communal Board of Kiev and the Kiev Branch of the Society for the Dissemination of the Enlightenment Among the Jews of Russia (OPE), we witness the porousness of Jewish politics in its formative years, as ideologies were still taking shape and communal leaders attempted to stake out ideological territory on ever-shifting ground. In this context, charismatic leaders and ideologues in the national and socialist movements had to compromise not only with each other, but also with one of the driving forces of community—men with money—if they wished to stay realistic about achieving their strategic goals. On the plane of ideas, politics could afford to be as idealistic as it wished, but in the realm of action and practice, it could not be anything other than pragmatic. In Kiev, where perhaps more than any other locality in the Russian Empire Jews felt the heavy weight of restrictive legislation and administrative practice, local politics and organizational life provided the sole outlet for the emerging Jewish public sphere, which, though oriented toward the Jewish masses, was heavily middle-class in its makeup and perhaps its goals as well.

A Note on Sources

I have used a wide range of sources in order to reconstruct a profile of Kiev Jewry. The 1874 census of the city, conducted by the South-West Branch of the Imperial Russian Geographical Society, and the 1897 imperial census provide some basic information about language and occupation, though the two censuses often used different measures and are thus difficult to compare.[43] While the 1874 census furnished fascinating data on the Jewish population in individual neighborhoods of the city, such information is much harder to find for later decades. Moreover, the official enumerations surely did not count Jews who resided in the city illegally and did not want to be noticed by authorities of any kind. (I have not used the 1917 census because the radical demographic changes that took place during the First World War make any comparison of the 1917 numbers with the prewar censuses meaningless.) In the late 1880s, economist A. P. Subbotin undertook an expedition to the Pale of Settlement, providing a mine of information about the economic and occupational patterns of Russian Jewry (Subbotin was also the author of a report on Russian Jewry for the government's Pahlen Commission, appointed after the pogroms of 1881–82 to review Jewish legislation). The survey of Jewish economic life in the Russian Empire carried out under the auspices of the Jewish Colonization Association in 1897–98 also contains a wealth of information; though the survey did not include data on Kiev, I draw on it for its general conclusions on Jews in the province and region of which Kiev was the capital, as well as for Russian Jewry as a whole. The local press (in Russian) and Jewish newspapers published for the entire empire (in Russian, Hebrew, and Yiddish) provide statistics and anecdotal information, as do archival documents of various kinds, especially governmental memoranda and petitions. I have tried to be particularly cautious when drawing on articles in *Kievlianin,* which was in certain periods the city's only newspaper, since its editorial perspective was one of russification and often Judeophobia.[44] Annual reports of philanthropic societies also yield quantitative and qualitative data, and memoir and belletristic literature help to provide details about everyday life. But the picture is far from complete: five wars, three revolutions, and decades of Soviet suppression of Jewish-related documents have done their part to draw a curtain around Jewry in imperial Kiev, since many of the sources that would shed light on all aspects of Jewish life in a West European or American city have been destroyed or are missing without a trace.

Note on Transliteration

Though the official name of the capital of modern-day independent Ukraine is Kyïv, throughout this book I use "Kiev," the designation familiar to most English-speakers and the city's official name during the imperial period. For Russian and Hebrew transliterations, I follow a simplified Library of Congress format (omitting diacritical marks). I have chosen not to distinguish between Hebrew aleph and ayin, as well as to omit initial apostrophes. Yiddish is romanized according to the system established by the YIVO Institute for Jewish Research. Personal names are generally given in their Russian versions, with Hebrew variants provided where appropriate (e.g., Ionna and Yona); exceptions are names for which an English spelling is widely known, such as Brodsky and Dubnow.

PART 1
THE EARLY YEARS

1

Settlement and Growth, 1859–1881

The first two decades of Jewish settlement in Kiev were years of rapid growth and adaptation, as ever larger numbers of Jews took up residence in the city and quickly became acclimated to their new home. Christian Kievans, too, had to become accustomed to the sight of Jews in a city that had been (officially, at least) off-limits to Jewish settlement for several decades. This chapter attempts to understand the people and groups that began to constitute "Kiev Jewry": which Jews migrated to Kiev, where they came from, how they made their livelihoods, and where they stood in relation to one another in terms of economic and social class. We begin with a brief survey of Jewish settlement in Kiev prior to the modern period.

Jews in Kiev prior to 1861

Jewish settlement in Kiev goes back to the first years of the city, when it was the capital of Kievan Rus' and an important stop on the trading route between Europe and Central Asia. Although the sources are few, from the ninth century there were probably both Rabbanite and Karaite Jews in Kiev, whose communities were branches of Byzantine Jewry, in addition to Khazars, members of a Turkic clan whose ruling class had converted to Judaism in the eighth century. Medieval Kiev was at the height of its power in the eleventh century, and about a century later there were references to a "Jewish gate" in the city walls as well as to a Talmudic scholar named Moses of Kiev. After the Principality of Lithuania conquered the region from the Mongols in the fifteenth century, a short-lived expulsion of local Jews was followed by the reestablishment of the Jewish community and a century of peaceful existence. In 1619, however, Christian merchants successfully petitioned for the status of *de non tolerandis judaeis,* putting an end to permanent Jewish settlement and allowing Jewish merchants to enter the city only for limited periods of time. After the Armistice of Andrusovo in 1667 and the cession to Muscovy of Left-Bank Ukraine, Kiev was relinquished to the tsar. New Jewish settlement began in 1781 after the first partition of Poland

and the annexation of Belorussia to the Russian Empire, and intensified after the city was reunited with its hinterland with the second partition in 1793, when Right-Bank Ukraine—with its hundreds of thousands of Jews—was annexed to the empire. The establishment of the Pale of Permanent Jewish Settlement, with the inclusion of Kiev province, legalized Jewish residence in Kiev, which picked up pace with the removal of the Contract Fair, the largest trading fair in the region, from Dubno to Kiev in 1797.[1] In 1795 there were about one hundred Jews in the city, a number that grew in just six years to almost seven hundred. As evidenced by surviving pinkasim, a Jewish community with a cemetery, burial society, and several other institutions was established in these years.[2]

Kiev's Christian merchants, however, were unhappy with the competition from Jewish traders, and petitioned the government several times in the early nineteenth century for the restoration of Kiev's hoary right to exclude Jews from its precincts.[3] In 1827, their request was granted by Nicholas I, but explanations for the expulsion vary.[4] Contemporaries accused the Jews of trying to dominate and exploit the local Christian population, and thus the official edict of expulsion wrote that the Jews' "presence in [Kiev] is injurious to the industry of the city and to the treasury itself, and is moreover in opposition to the rights and privileges granted at various times to the city of Kiev. . . ."[5] However, historian and ethnographer Mikhail Kulisher, writing in the early twentieth century, contended that it was the goal of Nicholas, ever the soldier-king, to transform Kiev into a "fortress city," as opposed to a trading center, that led to the expulsion of its Jews. Presumably, Jews were not seen as loyal enough to be tolerated in an important military center, which explains the simultaneous expulsion of Jews from the garrison towns of Nikolaev and Sevastopol'.[6] After a number of delays—during which local Jews requested in vain that a special Jewish settlement be created just inside or outside the city limits—the expulsion was finally carried out in 1835, at which time Kiev was officially excluded from the Pale of Settlement.[7] From then on, Jewish merchants were permitted into the city for stays of several days only, and were required to lodge in two Jewish inns leased out by the municipality. During the Contract Fair, however, Jews could enter the city freely, and did so: in 1845, some 40,000 of the fair's 60,000 attendees were Jews.[8]

Under the reforms of Alexander II, certain categories of Jews were permitted to settle outside the Pale, including in previously closed cities such as

Kiev.[9] While his decree of 1859 allowed only first-guild Jewish merchants to reside in the interior provinces of the Russian Empire and in Kiev, in 1861 the city was opened to both first- and second-guild merchants, who immediately began to move there.[10] Later decrees permitted settlement by artisans, soldiers who had finished their service, and graduates of institutions of higher education. Jews were permitted to settle in two neighborhoods, Ploskaia and Lybed, and those wishing to live elsewhere in the city had to apply for special authorization.[11]

The Growth of Kiev after 1861

The rapid growth of the Jewish population of Kiev in the 1860s and 1870s, as of the city as a whole, was due to migration. Many Jews were on the move in search of a living, for they had found that the environment around them was undergoing swift transformations. After the emancipation of the serfs in 1861, the long-standing economic structure within which Jews had played the roles of middleman, agent, petty trader, and tavern-keeper began to change rapidly; the beginning of the intensive growth of Russian industry and trade and the advent of the railroad in the 1860s and 1870s brought about yet further changes in the economy. Many Jews were adversely affected by these changes, finding that there was less demand for their services and that their unique niche in the economy of the western borderlands was disappearing.[12] On the other hand, a small but influential number of Jewish entrepreneurs played a central role in the industrial and commercial development of the western provinces, and their activities would open up new avenues of employment for many of their coreligionists.[13] Just as important a motivating factor in Jewish migration was the population explosion among Russian Jewry that began in the early nineteenth century; it increased the Jewish population 150 percent in the years 1820–1880, while the non-Jewish population grew by 87 percent.[14] Jewish migration within the Russian Empire was generally north to south, from regions that had been settled by Jews for centuries (Lithuania and Belorussia) to provinces of the southwest (Right-Bank Ukraine and Chernigov and Poltava provinces) and the south (the New Russian and Bessarabian provinces that had been appended to the Pale of Settlement in the late eighteenth and early nineteenth centuries).[15] From the mid-nineteenth century until the outbreak of the First World War, the Jewish population of these regions increased by 844 percent (seventeen-fold), in comparison to an increase in the general population of 265 percent (five-fold).[16] Aside from emigration, mostly to the United States, the other leading trend in Jewish migration was urbanization; but whether Jews were city-bound or south-bound, the motivation was almost always economic: they migrated in the hope of finding a better living. Jews looked to communities where a thriving economy could offer more opportunities and, since Jewish society was not diversified economically, where a smaller Jewish community would mean fewer of their coreligionists with whom to compete. Thus, the most popular destinations were the new communities of Odessa, Ekaterinoslav, and Kiev, located in the economically flourishing provinces of the south and southwest. Moreover, in the immediate aftermath of the Polish Uprising of 1863, the authorities broadly approved of intensified Jewish settlement in areas of former Polish influence so as to develop "a socioeconomic force that could stand in opposition" to the once powerful Poles.[17]

All of these factors contributed to the rapid growth of Kiev in the post-emancipation period, its population almost doubling in the decade between 1864 and 1874, when it reached 124,000.[18] The tremendous flow of migration to the city can be seen in the fact that in 1874, only 28 percent of its population were natives of Kiev. Indeed, just 45 percent were from the southwest region, testifying to the geographical diversity of Kiev's new arrivals.[19] The Jewish population grew much more swiftly in the first decade, multiplying five-fold from 3,000 in 1863 to 14,000 in 1874 (11 percent of the total population).[20] The Jewish population grew so quickly—and was so heavily migrant-based—that an independent Jewish postal office was established in Kiev in the 1880s, which a local newspaper used for sending subscriptions to nearby towns.[21] As Michael Hamm writes, "The rapid growth of the Jewish community constituted the single most dramatic change in the composition of the city's population during the ensuing decades [i.e., after the 1860s]."[22] The heavy stream of Jewish migration to Kiev was not difficult to understand: at 253,000, the Jewish population of Kiev province was far and away the most numerous of any province in the Pale in 1864, and the entire southwest region, of which Kiev was capital, had about 635,000 Jews (with another 35,000 across the Dnepr River in Chernigov province).[23]

The expanding railway network facilitated migration. Kiev was already a water transport hub due to its situation on the Dnepr River, and in the immediate post-emancipation years, the railroad began rapidly to tie Russia's cities together. The Kiev–Moscow line was completed in 1869, and lines to

Odessa and to Poland followed within a few years. Kiev's railway station was opened in 1870, making the city more accessible than ever for visitors, pilgrims, and of course migrants. One of the neighborhoods that sprang up around the station, Solomenka, soon became a heavily Jewish area. In the four years after the inauguration of the station, Kiev's population jumped by 80 percent, from 71,000 to 127,000. Indeed, throughout the 1870s Kiev's growth came exclusively from migration, since deaths outnumbered births among the city's population.[24]

The establishment of the Kiev Commodities Exchange in 1873 was yet another element drawing migrants, especially Jews, while the annual Contract Fair continued to be a mainstay of the Kiev economy and a contributing factor to its rapid growth, since it drew thousands of visitors every year, some of whom probably made the decision not to leave.[25] Of the 60,000 merchants and traders who visited Kiev annually on business in the 1840s, two-thirds were Jews, and they continued to play a significant role in Kiev's commercial fairs throughout the nineteenth century.[26] The city played an especially important role as a processing center for agricultural products grown in the rich earth of the surrounding provinces, including sugar beets, tobacco, wheat, fruit, and timber.[27] In the 1870s and 1880s, a number of industrial concerns built large, modern factories in the city, drawing large numbers of laborers from the hinterland.[28] Kiev's status as the political capital of Kiev, Podol, and Volhyn provinces and the principal city of the entire southwest region, comprising five provinces, also made it an attractive base for financial and commercial concerns, and its reputation as an educational and intellectual center attracted students and *intelligenty.* Though Kiev's significance as a military center was not as great as it had been earlier in the century, the soldiers stationed there and the city's arsenal contributed to its standing and import.

Settling in Kiev

In 1861, two years after Alexander II began to allow Jewish first-guild merchants to settle in the city, Jewish residence in Kiev was extended to graduates of institutions of higher education, artisans, and several other categories of Jews. Judging from reports that Lithuanian Jews chose to move the long distance to Kiev in that same year, we may assume that Kiev was a very attractive destination.[29] It was somewhat easier for Jewish members of the merchant estate to gain access to Kiev than to the inner provinces of the empire: the circle of eligible merchants was expanded to include second-guild merchants in addition to first-guild merchants, and the requirement that they have entered the merchantry at least five years prior to leaving the Pale was dropped.[30] Nonetheless, the vast majority of Jewish merchants in Kiev had first-guild status; merchants who would not normally have paid high sums to obtain first-guild status did so because the law then granted them permanent residence rights in Kiev.[31] By contrast, most other categories of Jews permitted to settle in Kiev received temporary residence permits.

Jewish residence in Kiev was officially subject to strict regulations and afforded only to members of certain professions or certain other categories, but because of the rapid multiplication of decrees and circulars regarding the exact meaning of the law, the meager wages of policemen and other municipal officials and their openness to bribery, and Kiev's geographical location in the heart of the Pale of Settlement, Jews began to take advantage of or evade the regulations almost as soon as they were announced in 1861.[32] By 1874, a Ministry of Interior report showed that "at least 458 Jews were not officially registered and 303 did not possess internal passports," and there were surely hundreds more whom bureaucrats did not manage to find.[33]

Kiev was perceived to offer many opportunities for Jewish businessmen or traders, and even many Jews who did not fall into one of the categories of eligibility for residence still moved to the city. Jewish merchants were permitted to bring a certain number of clerks to help run their business affairs, many of whom were employed in name only and immediately struck out on their own.[34] To preserve the ruse, however, they carried out their petty trade under the name of their official employer.[35] As early as 1864, the newspaper *Kievlianin* (The Kievan) was complaining that Jews were taking advantage of the openness of the city and the lack of resources of the police, and were ignoring the law and entering the city under the pretense of serving as clerks and assistants to first-guild merchants.[36]

Artisans were another category of Jews permitted to settle in Kiev, and though many truly practiced a craft, others did not. It was widely known that officials at the Artisan Board made it easy to obtain an artisan's license—as easy as handing over 3 rubles, as long as one displayed a bucket and brush (for men) or a bolt of cloth (for women). The law stated that Jewish parents with children studying in Kiev's educational institutions were to be granted temporary residence permits, but there were some stories of individuals bending the rules, such as the woman who received a permit based on her daughter's attendance at a music conservatory; she had failed to reveal that the girl was three years old. Moreover, many parents did not leave the city when their children graduated, as the law required.[37] Jews requiring medical treatment in the city could also receive permission to live there for a set period, but here, too, there were instances of abuse (such as the woman who needed to be under the constant supervision of a Kiev doctor for "inflammation of the nasal mucous membranes"—in other words, a common cold).

Lack of organization on the part of the police meant that temporary permits often became permanent simply because they were never checked after being issued; more often, though, police had to be bribed.[38] Bribery was a fact of life for most Kiev Jews if they wished to be left alone by the law—so much so that, as one Kievan's memoirs claim, the policemen with the best service records or with connections were actually assigned to the Jewish neighborhoods so they could reap the rewards of institutionalized corruption. Bribes were demanded of Jews whether they were in possession of residence permits or not, because the law regarding Jewish settlement was so confusing and labyrinthine that no one really understood it. Jews might lodge an official complaint if a particular policeman got too greedy, but it would never occur to them to request that policemen not be allowed to take bribes; even the chief of police was on the take![39] But bribes did not always work, and the police would sometimes conduct surprise raids on Jewish houses to find and arrest Jews staying there illegally. Even opponents of the growing Jewish presence in Kiev did not always approve of these raids; in 1864, the editor of *Kievlianin,* V. V. Shul'gin, criticized "the capriciousness and violence with which the 'hunts' were conducted."[40]

Information about the origins of Kiev's Jews is sparce and anecdotal, and tsarist-era restrictions on organized religious activities in Kiev have greatly impeded the contemporary scholar's efforts to unearth information on the city's synagogues and prayer houses, which were often organized by town of origin. According to a report from 1869, only two prayer quorums existed in Kiev, one a group of Talner (Tal'noe) Hasidim and the other a group of Misnagdim (non-Hasidic Jews).[41] But a slightly more accurate depiction is probably provided by Crown Rabbi Tsukkerman in a memorandum to Kiev's chief of police that same year, in which Tsukkerman referred to two prayer houses in Ploskaia and another in Podol. A later account (written in 1891) seems to confirm Tsukkerman's report, relating that in 1866 the authorities permitted the establishment of three prayer houses.[42] It is unclear whether one of these was what *Kievlianin* referred to in 1866 as the "communal synagogue" (*obshchestvennaia sinagoga*), possibly the prayer quorum of the Jewish elite and the forerunner of the Choral Synagogue.[43] However, all was not what it seemed. When, starting in 1869, groups of Jews began to request permission to open additional prayer houses (one each in Ploskaia, Podol, and Lybed), the authorities discovered the existence of another *five* prayer houses that had originally been opened for Jewish soldiers in the 1850s, in which other Kiev Jews were now praying as well.[44] This kind of underground Jewish life was common throughout the entire period: time and time again, officials found out about secret synagogues or Jewish educational institutions, attempted to get rid of them or regularize their existence, and then new ones would take their places. This also makes our task difficult if not impossible: secret institutions frequently left no trace behind for the historian to find. Thus, to say that there were already at least eight prayer houses in the first decade of official Jewish settlement in Kiev is an educated guess at best (an additional two in Ploskaia and Lybed were authorized for groups of artisans by Governor-General Drentel'n in 1876).[45]

Who prayed in these synagogues? Beyond the traditional divisions of Hasidim and Misnagdim, the former category was made up of a great many smaller groups. Ukrainian Hasidim included members of sects based throughout Kiev and Volhyn provinces and neighboring areas, including followers of the *tsaddikim* (charismatic rabbinic leaders) who lived near Kiev.[46] Most, if not all, were members of the Twersky Hasidic dynasty, the dominant strain in Ukraine; scions of the original rebbe, Menahem Nahum, lived in towns near Kiev such as Chernobyl, Makarov, Vasil'kov, and Rotmistrovka.[47] A pinkas from a *havura mishnayot* (Mishnah study brotherhood) at Beit ha-midrash Makariv (Makarov Prayer House) survives in the manuscript section of the Vernadsky National Library of Ukraine; the contents refer specifically to "the synagogue of the *Admor* [Hasidic term for "Our master, teacher, and rabbi"] of Makariv of this place, Kiev."[48] His analysis of the pinkas leads Yohanan Petrovsky-Stern to argue that the urbanization process "transformed the traditional societies of Hasidism into urban headquarters of this or that trend in Hasidism"; donations to the brotherhood supported not only the synagogue but also "the courts of the Makarov and Chernobyl dynasty."[49] The society was in existence—and thrived—until the end of the tsarist period, though we have no evidence about specific activities or trends within the brotherhood. Other sects included those based in Tal'noe, Skvir, Cherkassy, Korishchev, and Gornostopol'; there was also a prayer house of the Gornostopoler Hasidim on Iaroslavskaia street in Ploskaia.[50] A petition of Jewish clerks in 1880, requesting permission to establish a mutual aid society, was signed by thirty men, of whom nine were from Vasil'kov.[51] We know of the existence of a "Chernobyl" prayer house in Kiev in the 1880s, and in a cemetery consecration dispute between the Lithuanians and the Hasidim of Kiev in 1892, the latter requested assistance from the tsaddik of Rotmistrovka.[52] There were also Polish and Lithuanian Hasidim of various stripes, the latter including Chabad or Lubavich Hasidim.[53] Indeed, in 1866 *Kievlianin* reported that Kiev's Jewish leaders were attempting to install a grandson of the Hasidic leader Menahem Mendl of Lubavich as rabbi.[54] Other than this episode, we lack detailed information about Kiev's religious leaders in this early period, though we know that by 1879, there were "four or five rabbinic law judges" (*dayonim mo"ts*) in the city. Traveling preachers, or *maggidim,* would of course stop in Kiev for a few weeks, as in the case of the famous Horodner Maggid from Minsk, whose preaching—according to Yekhezkel Kotik, with whom the maggid boarded during his stay in the city—attracted many Kiev Jews of all stripes, even students.[55] (To the maggid's dismay, his words had no effect on Kotik's other boarder, a student, who challenged him to a debate and called him "an old fool.") Kotik, who lived in Kiev in the late 1870s, wrote in his memoir that of the Jewish groups in the city, the Lithuanians were the most stable and secure; they played an important role in Kiev, and had "the best businesses, the finest synagogues, the most aristocratic Jews, and the most respectable rabbi."[56]

In addition to the Hasidic and Lithuanian prayer houses, the tailors had their own synagogue, as was the case in many Jewish cities and towns. This institution was known variously as the Tailors' Synagogue, the Rozenberg Prayer House, the Large Prayer House (Beit ha-midrash ha-gadol), and Beit Midrash Poalei Tsedek. Its official name was the Artisans' Prayer House (Remeslennaia molel'nia) no. 10.[57]

A native of the town of Kamenets in the Polesie region, Kotik likely typified many Jews from market towns and villages who migrated to the big city. Upon arrival, he was thrown into despair by the scale of the place (and by the fact that his brother-in-law had lost many business undertakings): "How can I come, a village Jew, to find business in a big, noisy city? Who needs me here?"[58] He only returned to himself that evening, when his brother-in-law took him to the *shtibl* (prayer house) of the Karliner Hasidim. No doubt for many Jewish migrants to Kiev, the prayer house served as a kind of *landsmanshaft* (society of fellow townsmen), where the artisan or broker could take refuge from the anonymity and impersonality of the big city and mingle with like-minded people from the same town.

In his memoir *From the Fair,* Sholem Aleichem recalled a similar sense of loneliness and despair upon arrival in Kiev:

> Being a stranger in a large city is like being in a forest. Nowhere does a person feel more lonely. Sholom never felt as lonely as he did then in Kiev. The people in that big, beautiful city seemed to have conspired to show the young visitor no signs of hospitality or warmth. All faces were grim. All doors were closed to him.[59]

Although there was a prominent semi-russified Jewish elite in the city, most of the Jewish migrants in the first fifteen years had received little if any secular education; some, including most women, were probably totally uneducated. In 1874, Jewish women made up a larger proportion of the unlettered—60 percent—than did women in other religious groups (55 percent for Orthodox and Catholics, 47 percent for Protestants).[60] The overwhelming majority—about 97 percent—of Kiev's Jews declared Yiddish to be their native tongue, defined by the census as the language customarily used in the home. Only 483 out of the 13,800 Jews in Kiev identified a language other than Yiddish—in most cases Russian—as their primary language.

The growing Jewish student population was, of course, literate in Russian. Jews were allowed to reside in Kiev in order to enroll in educational institutions. Accordingly, while the total male gymnasium population increased by just 40 percent between 1874 and 1879, the number of Jews in that group grew by 140 percent to 257 (the sharp rise was probably due in large measure to the Universal Military Statute of 1874, which offered exemptions for higher education).[61] Almost 60 percent of Jewish male students in Kiev were enrolled at the Third Gymnasium in the heavily Jewish Podol district, where the student body was almost one-third Jewish.[62] At girls' schools, the percentage of Jews was often higher, and the rate of increase over time sharper: there were thirty-one Jewish girls at the Podol Girls' School in 1885, compared with fifteen the previous year; at the Ploskaia Girls' School, the number was twenty-two, up from twelve.[63] Kiev's St. Vladimir University counted seventy-six Jewish students in 1876 (the most of any of the empire's eight universities), who made up 9.8 percent of the student body, a proportion surpassed only by Warsaw University.[64] In 1878–80, sixty-seven of these students were enrolled in the medical faculty.[65] As Lisa Epstein writes, "The large number of Jewish medical students seeking to study in Kiev heightened the issue of residence and sojourn rights [there]."[66] According to an account from the 1850s, Jewish students came from two backgrounds: from wealthy and acculturated families, and from more traditional homes. In later decades, the former contingent probably grew as the younger generation of Jews became progressively more russified.[67] The student boarding in Yekhezkel Kotik's home who had called the maggid an "old fool" was a young man by the name of Lipski, a socialist and nonreligious Jew (*apikoyres*) from Vilna who had studied in the state-sponsored rabbinical seminary in Zhitomir until its closure.[68] Lipski then came to Kiev to prepare for his admission to the university there. At night he studied for his exams, but during the day he hauled sacks of flour at Brodsky's mill, to pay for his living expenses. He later found work as a tutor, as did many students, and was able to leave the mill.[69]

When the Higher Women's Courses opened in 1878, offering university-level education, they also attracted Jewish women interested in advancing themselves. The four-year study program was often taught by professors from Kiev's St. Vladimir's University, and graduates could obtain a teaching certificate upon graduation.[70] Between 1878 and 1882, Jewish women constituted 16 percent of students at the courses, the second-largest group after Russian Orthodox women.[71] Jewish women also made up a sizable proportion—more than one-fifth—of pupils at the city's Midwifery Institute.[72]

There were even small numbers of Jewish radicals in Kiev. The young revolutionaries Pavel Akselrod and Grigorii Gurevich established a Chaikovskyist circle—espousing a radicalism that was "a combination of maskilic idealism, nihilist scientism, and Lavrovist Populism"—in the city in 1872, which soon turned into a small commune with a predominantly Jewish membership.[73] All the Jews in the group had had traditional upbringings and some had even been dedicated adherents of Haskalah, but now their socialism demanded that they reject Judaism and any allegiance to the Jewish people. Ironically, several members of the commune continued to live with their parents in Podol even after joining the radicals and beginning to conduct propaganda among workers. Their activities were short-lived, however, for in 1874 the circle was uncovered by the police and its members left Kiev or went into hiding.

The Jewish Geography of Kiev

Kiev's history, as well as its hills and ravines, helped create a number of distinct neighborhoods that were fixed as official districts in the nineteenth century. The upper town, high on the bluffs above the Dnepr River, consisted of Old Kiev (Starokievskaia) with its ancient churches and monasteries, and Dvortsovaia, home of the Royal Palace and aristocratic mansions; Kiev's main avenue, Kreshchatik, cut through the ravine that formed the boundary between the two areas. Further south along the bluffs was the religious and military district of Pechersk, home to the Caves Monastery, one of the holiest in the Russian Empire. The lower town, a port area close to river commerce and transportation, was called Podol. Newer neighborhoods that took shape with Kiev's phenomenal growth in the second half of the nineteenth century were Ploskaia, a northern extension of Podol on the floodplains along the banks of the Dnepr, and Lybed, stretching from the upper town near Kreshchatik south to the railway stations at the edge of the city. In the upper part of the city, Lybed's Bol'shaia and Malo-Vasil'kovskaia streets became "the focal point of Jewish life in the city."[74]

The law required most Jews settling in Kiev to reside in outlying Ploskaia and Lybed, two of the poorest districts that lacked amenities such as running water and sewage systems. Kiev was the only place in the Russian Empire where Jews (or most Jews) were limited to specific neighborhoods, and it was for this reason that the city was often referred to as the only "ghetto" still extant in Russia.[75] The Ploskaia Jewish ghetto actually included several blocks in Podol, which seem to have been considered a bit more desirable than the rest of the neighborhood. Ploskaia was home to a number of factories of various sizes—several breweries, a brickworks, a tannery, a candle factory—while Lybed had less industry, with two brickworks and a distillery/brewery, all located at its outer limits. In 1874, Ploskaia, with almost 6,000 Jews out of the city's 13,800, was home to 43 percent of the city's Jews; with just under 2,400 Jews, Podol had 17 percent, and Lybed followed behind with 13 percent (1,900 Jews). Ploskaia also boasted the highest concentration of Jews: 29 percent of its residents, while the figure for Podol was 15 percent. Solomenka and Demievka, small neighborhoods adjacent to Kiev's two railway stations that were outside the bounds of Kiev proper but were actually extensions of Lybed, were also heavily (one-quarter) Jewish.[76] Demievka, in particular, as well as Slobodka, a suburb across the Dnepr from Kiev, became very popular destinations because Jews were not required to hold residence permits to settle there; in his memoirs, Jewish communal activist Genrikh Sliozberg claimed that "only the May Laws [of 1882] stopped them from becoming huge Jewish cities," because their village status meant that no new Jewish settlement could be established there.[77]

According to 1874 census data, Ploskaia and Lybed's Jewish populations were mostly poor and Yiddish-speaking. Only 1.4 percent identified a language other than Yiddish as the language customarily used in the home, and two-thirds were unable to read or write in Russian (versus 40 percent in the other neighborhoods). The overwhelming majority belonged to the *meshchanstvo,* the catch-all "townspeople" estate in which most Jews in the Pale of Settlement were inscribed. There were almost as many Jewish merchants in Ploskaia and Lybed as in the neighborhoods of the upper city; these were likely those who belonged to the second guild or had belonged to the first guild for less than five years, for these categories of merchants did not have the right to live outside of Ploskaia and Lybed. Presumably they moved to finer neighborhoods as soon as they were able to attain a higher estate status.[78]

In a city that was fairly sparsely populated, Jews lived three times more densely than Christians.[79] In the 1870s, Ploskaia and Lybed had the highest mortality rate for Russian Orthodox (30–35 per 1,000), but at 30.7 per 1,000, the Jewish mortality rate for the city as a whole was no better—indeed, it was poorer than for any other group.[80] Among the worst areas were the slums of Ploskaia, referred to as "beyond the canal," located north of the open ditch (Glubochitskaia Canal) that carried fetid runoff water from two nearby factories.[81] Apartments were cheaper there than almost anywhere else in the city; the average annual rent of 160 rubles was far less than Kiev's overall average, 411 rubles, not to mention the rents in the best neighborhoods, which ranged from 700 to 850 rubles a year. Ploskaia abounded in cheap, low-quality housing, and a working-class individual searching for an apartment or room for 15 rubles or less per year had practically no other choice of neighborhood (it is no surprise that Ploskaia had the highest illiteracy rate, 70 percent, of any central neighborhood).[82] Only one-quarter of the buildings in Ploskaia had gardens or kitchen plots, fewer than anywhere else in the city.[83] For those unable to afford an apartment or even a room, Ploskaia and Podol offered eleven flophouses where laborers could bunk down for the night.[84] With an average annual apartment rent of 325 rubles, Lybed was on a somewhat higher plane, but still below the city average. Like other outlying districts, it lacked most of the amenities enjoyed by the central neighborhoods, including access to running water.[85]

Astoundingly to those familiar with this period and accustomed to lower mortality rates among Jews, in the period 1866–70 Jewish children had a higher mortality rate than any other confessional group in Kiev: 37 percent of children died in their first year, and 56 percent in their first five years; the corresponding rates for Christian Orthodox children were 29 percent and 45 percent while the five-year rate for Catholics and Lutherans dropped to 36–37 percent.[86] These high rates may have been due to poor living conditions, hygiene, and sanitation in the crowded neighborhoods where Jews were compelled to live, but they may also have been associated with the particular cohort of Jews who chose to migrate to Kiev and the lives they found upon arrival: the more poorly educated individuals who had more children, working at jobs that paid little, were less likely to be able to create a healthy home for an infant and to be able to provide medical care in case of illness. That the mortality rate was so high in the early years of Jewish migration to Kiev, and the fact that it dropped in subsequent years, may suggest that the earliest arrivals were those most desperate to leave their current circumstances to start a new life elsewhere. The data also points to the undeveloped state of communal support and philanthropy in Kiev at that early stage. Both inferences are supported by anecdotal evidence.[87] Given these mortality rates, it is not surprising that *Kievlianin* should have hinted in 1873 that the ballooning Jewish population was to blame for the increased number and strength of cholera epidemics in Kiev: the two seemed to go hand in hand.[88]

At the opposite end of the spectrum were the refined neighborhoods of Dvortsovaia (known also as Lipki, after the lime trees along its boulevards), home to the Tsar's Palace (residence of the sovereign on his visits to Kiev) and spacious mansions on tree-lined boulevards, and Starokievskaia, with imposing brick buildings, the latest urban conveniences, and high-style shops and theaters. As might be expected, Jewish merchants, lawyers, and others with wealth and high aspirations settled there; in 1874, these two districts were home to only 5 percent of Kiev Jewry but to 40 percent of its non-Yiddish-speaking Jews. A language other than Yiddish was usually spoken in almost 30 percent of the Jewish homes of Dvortsovaia and Starokievskaia, with a Russian literacy figure of 66 percent. Slightly half of the Jewish population of these elite neighborhoods belonged to the merchant estate, compared to 15 percent in Kiev as a whole.[89]

Podol seems to have fallen somewhere in between the poverty and traditionalism of Ploskaia and Lybed, the districts where Jews without special privileges were required to live, and the wealth and acculturation of the genteel neighborhoods of the upper city. With the Contract House, site of Kiev's important trade fairs, at its heart, as well as the important mercantile thoroughfare Aleksandrovskaia Street, Podol was the commercial center of Kiev, rivaling Kreshchatik in the upper city in importance. Merchants made up one-quarter of Podol's Jewish population in 1874 (compared to 11 percent in the poor neighborhoods). At its northern end, however, Podol bordered on Ploskaia and in fact included several streets where Jews could live without special authorization, as in Ploskaia. Census data paint a picture of a Yiddish-speaking but educated Jewish population, as one would expect from those who might have been interested in settling in Podol: merchants and traders who wanted access to the lively commerce of the district as well as to the prayer houses within walking distance in the Ploskaia district. Almost all of Podol's Jews named Yiddish as the language spoken at home, but three-fifths of them could read and write Russian to some extent (a literacy rate similar to the upper town), pointing to a Jewish population that was at home in both languages, speaking Yiddish but able to read and write Russian. Thus, it makes sense that in 1867 a group of Jewish merchants wanted to establish a synagogue in Podol, "expressly for the Jewish merchantry"; the wording of the request suggests that they no longer wished to attend synagogues where they had to mingle with the impoverished masses of Ploskaia.[90] As in Dvortsovaia and Starokievskaia, Jews in Podol wanted to purchase real estate in the best parts of the neighborhood: in 1871, Moisei Vainshtein, a merchant, communal leader, and one of the overseers of the Jewish Hospital, petitioned for permission to buy a house next to the Church of the Nativity, on central Aleksandrovskaia Street.[91]

Economic Profile of Kiev's Jews

Unlike some of their Russian counterparts, who greeted the Jewish influx into Kiev with suspicion and even hostility, Jewish newspapers reflected, with wonder and pride, the perception that Jews were settling in great numbers throughout Kiev. As early as 1863, an observer in the Hebrew press exulted that no Jew had entered the city for so long, and now "many Jews can be found throughout its neighborhoods and on all its hills."[92] A historian of the Kiev Jewish community claimed that the authorities did not closely scrutinize the legality of all Jewish migrants in the early years because it was well-known that their economic activities were of benefit to the city.[93] Nonetheless, Jews—especially maskilim concerned with Jews' image within Russian society—were sensitive to the accusations being made against them, and Alexander Tsederbaum, the editor of the Hebrew weekly *Ha-melits* and its Yiddish supplement *Kol mevaser,* warned those settling in Kiev "that they should strive to be good citizens [*birger*] and to find useful occupations."[94]

The exaggerations on both sides were, as is often the case, rooted in reality. Jewish merchants had done well in the city over a short period of time, and soon threatened the once-dominant Great Russian merchantry.[95] As early as 1869, Jews made up three-quarters of all first-guild merchants, though less than 10 percent of the total of all merchants, both first and second guild. While it was clear that Jews were registering in the first guild in order to obtain greater privileges, in the eyes of many contemporaries the situation decreased the prestige of both the merchantry and the city as a whole. The proportion of Jewish first-guild merchants continued to rise, reaching 85 percent by the mid-1890s, when Jews made up over half of all Kiev merchants.[96]

It was sugar, refined from the sugar beets that grew in the soil around Kiev, that generated most of the city's wealth and created the wealthiest Jews in Kiev. Starting in the 1840s, a handful of enterprising Jews began moving from their traditional niche as middlemen for agricultural products; instead, they began to finance the growing sugar industry in the southwest region. Contracts between Jewish backers and the (usually Polish) nobles frequently gave the former a fixed percentage of the profits from the venture and granted them even some control over production. Jewish financiers could also acquire leases on sugar refineries, which in effect was but a short step from outright ownership.[97] Men such as Israel Brodsky and Ionna Zaitsev, two of the earliest Jewish entrepreneurs in the sugar industry, were pioneers in the burgeoning field, helping to develop markets for sugar and introducing new technologies into every step of the cultivation, refining, and marketing processes. By 1872, at least one-eighth of all sugar production in the Russian Empire was in Jewish hands. In order to get around the Temporary Laws of 1882, which placed heavy restrictions on Jewish ownership and leasing of land in the Pale of Settlement, the sugar industrialists simply converted their enterprises into joint-stock companies, which were not subject to the Temporary Laws. The Jewish sugar barons, chief among them Brodsky, played a central role in expanding the market for sugar in the empire; Brodsky pioneered the establishment of marketing agencies and storage warehouses throughout European Russia, the Caucasus, Siberia, and Central Asia, and made "Brodsky's Sugar" a household word from Tiflis to Bukhara to Vladivostok. Brodsky, Zaitsev, Moisei Gal'perin, and others also brought Russian sugar to Persia, Norway, and Western Europe. Christian sugar industrialists such as the Tereshchenkos and Bobrinskiis often operated on a much larger scale than their Jewish counterparts but were not as heavily involved in the marketing side of the business. This had important consequence for Kiev's economy—first in the annual Contract Fair, where both sugar and Jews played central roles, and after 1873 at the Kiev Exchange, which was dominated by the buying and selling of various sugar-related notes and securities, mostly by Jews. Genrikh Sliozberg claimed that Jewish entrepreneurs played a key role in forging a sense of solidarity and common purpose among the ethnically diverse provinces of the southwest; as members of a disinterested party, they were able to build bridges and create alliances (*sglazhivat'*) where others could not.[98]

Of all of Kiev's Jewish plutocrats, the Brodsky name was the most celebrated, known among Jews and non-Jews throughout the Russian Empire. The family, originally from Brody in Galicia, had settled in the small town of Zlatopol in Kiev province in the early nineteenth century. One of five sons, Israel Brodsky (1823–88) began to invest in the emerging sugar industry in the 1840s. He began by leasing and managing sugar refineries, and eventually owned an array of plants through the southwest, including a refinery in Demievka (near Lybed) that was one of the largest factories in Kiev. Brodsky himself moved to Kiev in 1876; at its height, his "sugar empire" would control a quarter of the sugar production in the Russian Empire.[99] His sons Lazar' and Lev (also known as Leon, he had started out in Odessa but, after experiencing business losses there, moved to his father's house in Kiev)[100] extended the family's holdings into other areas such as milling; Kiev's Brodsky wheat mill was the largest in the city. Their cousin Alexander was also a leading figure in the economy of Kiev and its region. There were other Jewish sugar barons as well—Gal'perin, Zaks, and Lieberman—while other Kiev Jewish entrepreneurs such as David Margolin made fortunes from other sectors such as shipping on the Dnepr and milling.[101]

Like the Gintsburgs of St. Petersburg, with whom they would eventually be linked through marriage, the Brodskys donated huge sums to Jewish philanthropic causes, "were well-informed sponsors of Hebrew culture in the spirit of the Haskalah, and became active spokesmen on behalf of the empire's Jews. Prominent maskilim . . . were employed as tutors, secretaries, and librarians in their household."[102] Lazar' Brodsky, whom Genrikh Sliozberg called "a man of enormous initiative," was known as the "king of Kiev Jewry," and maintained close personal relationships with all the governors-general of the southwest region.[103] "The Bible starts with the letter *beys* [B]—

for *'Breyshis'* [Genesis], and Yehupets, you should excuse the comparison, also starts with *beys*—for the *Brodskys,*" wrote Sholem Aleichem of the city's most celebrated Jewish family in one of Kiev's short-lived Yiddish newspapers (*Yehupets* was the Yiddish writer's name for Kiev, probably a play on the Russian word for Egypt, *Yegipet,* or, in its south-Russian or Ukrainian pronunciation, *Yehipet*).[104]

These wealthy Jews maintained a high profile in the city. After the Senate ruled that Jewish first-guild merchants were permitted to purchase real estate anywhere in the city, they immediately began to do so, especially in the most elegant neighborhoods, building opulent mansions on the plots.[105] Six members of the Brodsky family sat on the board of the Kiev Industrial Bank, leading *Kievlianin* to note dryly that the bank should be called the "Brodsky Family Bank."[106] A writer in a Jewish newspaper proudly noted that Jews were counted among the most honored citizens of Kiev, relating that two sons of Israel were among the invitees to a gala hosted by the Governor-General and were even provided with kosher food.[107]

While greater attention was often paid to the richest Jews, many more struggled to make a living in various small-scale commerce ventures. In 1874, almost as many Jews made their living from trade of some kind as did in industry and crafts, and one-third were petty traders. In that year, about one-fifth of Kiev's petty traders were Jews, and a good number of them were probably women, since three-quarters of all Kiev petty traders were female.[108] Some Jewish women probably came to Kiev on their own; Kiev province had one of the highest rates of divorce among Jews in the Pale of Settlement, and "many Jewish divorcees migrated to the city because they had often been associated with their husband's occupation in their hometown, and divorce deprived them of both income and employment."[109]

Apparently, many Jewish traders were officially registered as clerks to Jewish merchants, so as to avoid having to pay the expensive duties required for taking out a guild license and becoming a member of the merchantry.[110] But many others were unable or unwilling to take even this step; when the police wanted to inspect a large number of Jews who were likely to be lacking any permit authorizing them to do business in Kiev, they checked papers at the city's markets.[111] According to the 1874 census, even more Jews were engaged in retail trade than in petty trade: 42 percent of all Jews employed in some form of trade were owners or employees in Kiev stores; this group was equal to 25 percent of all Kievans in retail trade.[112] The journalist Starozhil remembered that, in the 1880s, many of Kiev's Jewish-owned stores were concentrated on Aleksandrovskaia Street in Podol, and they all sold ready-made clothing; competition was such that "they practiced a form of forcible recruiting" of customers that made it difficult to walk down the street.[113]

In 1864, one year before Jewish artisans were permitted to settle outside the Pale and in cities like Kiev, there were 7,200 artisans in Kiev. Ten years later, that number had grown by two-thirds, to 12,000, much of it probably due to Jewish migration.[114] Of Jews employed in crafts and industry in 1874, almost 70 percent were involved in some aspect of the garment trade; the 629 Jewish tailors and seamstresses made up one-fifth of all such artisans. Another 11 percent of Jews in handicrafts and manufacturing were in the tobacco and cigarettes industry, constituting 55 percent of laborers in that field; according to anecdotal reports, many were young women. Significant percentages of Jews also made livings from smithing and metalworking, tavern-keeping and distilling, and furniture-making and carpentering.[115] Women formed a substantial portion of artisans (17 percent in 1874), working mostly in the ladies' garment and food industries.[116] At times the police was apparently unsure how to handle cases in which a wife, working as an artisan, had the right to reside in Kiev while her husband, a lawyer or agent, did not.[117]

It seems that those Jews who entered the city on false premises most often did so to engage in petty commerce or the liquor trade—in retail sale of alcohol or tavern-keeping. Kiev had an inordinate number of liquor establishments (about 800, or one for every 112 adults, in 1874),[118] and many were run by Jews. This was a natural way for Jews to make a living, since distilling and the keeping of public houses had been traditional Jewish occupations in the formerly Polish lands that constituted Russia's western provinces.[119] Kiev's port area, also heavily Jewish, was especially overrun by pubs; *Kievlianin*'s claim that, on some streets, almost all the liquor traders were Jews must be taken with a grain of salt, but nonetheless suggests the extent of the Jewish share of the alcohol trade.[120] That taverns provided a steady source of income, for women as well as men, is demonstrated by a divorce case in 1865 in which the ex-husband declared that he had established a tavern in Kiev for his estranged wife to serve as a kind of alimony.[121] Jews were the majority of owners of alcohol-trading businesses of one kind or another: 112 of 195, or 57 percent.[122] The 1874 census probably did not count the *gandel'shchiki*, a Russian term that incorporated the Yiddish word for trade (*handel*) to refer, in all likelihood, to small-scale liquor dealers who, according to *Kievlianin*, were corrupting the simple people.[123] An 1874 law attempted to limit Jewish participation in the liquor trade throughout the Russian Empire by permitting Jews to sell alcohol only "in their own homes" (the meaning of the phrase was ambiguous); two years later, however, *Kievlianin* complained that the trade in Kiev was, in actuality, still in the hands of Jews, despite nominal changes in the ownerships of taverns and other such establishments.[124] Of those Jewish victims of the 1881 pogrom who declared an occupation on their applications for aid, 10 percent worked as tavern-keepers.[125]

Another visibly Jewish segment of the workforce were the cabmen and carters who transported passengers and cargo throughout the city; they served a particularly important role in Kiev, where the railway had never been extended to the port, necessitating a ground transportation link between the two depots.[126] The 1874 census actually listed a separate category of drayman called *balaguly,* from the Yiddish word *balagole,* wagon-driver or coachman; this term was used in the Russian south and southwest to refer to the wagons driven by Jews that carried passengers and light cargo inexpensively within and especially between cities and towns. Though the balaguly were, of course, all Jewish, there were Jews among the other categories of carters as well. Their visibility made them particularly vulnerable to expulsion, since most did not have Kiev residence permits; they were among the Jewish groups expelled in 1886, and in 1891 they were singled out to be the only group expelled.[127]

Jews, who had only recently begun to attend institutions of higher learning, were represented in small but growing numbers in the professions. Of sixteen attorneys authorized to practice before the Justices of the Peace of Kiev Region in 1874, four (and possibly five) were Jews; *Kievlianin,* of course, complained about the increasing number of Jewish attorneys and their dishonest practices.[128] The number of Jewish doctors was on the rise, and in 1874, a total of 28 of the city's 182 midwives, or 15 percent, were Jewish women.[129]

Kiev's most illustrious Jewish physician was the ophthalmologist Max Emmanuel Mandel'shtam (Mandelstamm) (1838–1912). Nephew of the maskilim Benjamin and Leon Mandel'shtam, Max attended Dorpat University and then received additional training in Germany. Settling in Kiev upon his return to Russia, Mandel'shtam served as docent at St. Vladimir University, which he left in 1880 when the university would not grant him a chair because of his Jewishness. He opened an ocular clinic in 1879, where he would often treat poor Jews at low cost or even for free; Yekhezkel Kotik remembered that "poor Jews streamed to him from all regions and corners."[130] In the 1870s, Mandel'shtam played a leading role in the Kiev Jewish Student Fund, forerunner of the Kiev branch of the Society for the Dissemination of the Enlightenment Among the Jews of Russia (known by its Russian initials as the OPE). This was a natural role for him, and he became a prominent activist in the Higher Education Division of the OPE.[131] Indeed, Mandel'shtam was known not only among Jews in the Russian Empire but also across Europe; the *Jewish Chronicle* described him in 1880 as "Dr. Mandelstamm, the eminent Jewish savant well known in London."[132] Jonathan Frankel writes, "In the crisis of 1881–2 Mandel'shtam was to emerge as a highly articulate spokesman and effective organizer."[133] In later years he would become a leading figure in the Zionist movement and then in the territorialist movement.

Work was available in Kiev, but life was not easy. In fact, between 1867 and 1886, prices went up by one-third to one-half, without a corresponding rise in wages.[134] The cost of living was actually 20–35 percent higher than in the imperial capital, so that even members of the middle class felt the pressure on their pocketbooks.[135] Jews might come to Kiev to earn a living or even to try to strike it rich, but they were more likely to remain poor. After only two decades of Jewish migration to Kiev, there was already a need for a free school for Jewish children, for which Israel Brodsky donated 40,000 rubles in 1880.[136]

"The Conquest of Kiev"

Jews, who had comprised an insignificant portion of Kiev's population prior to 1861, had by 1874 become the largest religious minority in the city: 13,800 individuals, or 11 percent of the total population (the second-largest, at 8 percent, were Catholics); this proportion did not change significantly until the outbreak of the First World War. Some observers began to complain about the increasingly Jewish character of Kiev, citing the influence and conspicuous consumption of Jewish merchants, the perception of Jewish traders "taking over" commerce in the city, and the visibility of Jewish brokers in front of the exchange on Kreshchatik. As early as 1864, *Kievlianin* was grumbling that all the newly opened groceries, stores, and public houses were owned by Jewish first-guild merchants.[137] The impression of a "Jewish Kiev" may have been due in part to the fact that there were undoubtedly large numbers of Jews living illegally in the city, bringing the true percentage of Jews closer to 15 percent (a *Kievlianin* journalist confirms this estimate, stating that the Jewish population exceeded 20,000 in 1873).[138] Traditional accusations against the Jews of Kiev were heard repeatedly over the decades: they were bent on corrupting the Christian Orthodox and working population of the city by selling them liquor; traded mostly in contraband and stolen goods; wanted to take control of the meat trade; engaged in unwholesome speculation, brokering, and usury; and drove up the prices of goods.[139] Some of these charges were cited by members of the commission established to examine the Jewish question in Kiev after the 1881 pogrom, as part of an attempt to lay the burden of blame for the pogrom at the feet of the city's Jews. These commission members were of the opinion that "a significant number of Jewish traders does not engage in honest trade, but rather speculation—in the negative sense of the word, and they stop at nothing [to achieve their goals]." They suggested that Jewish traders and all those involved in intermediary [*posrednicheskii*] activities be restricted and encouraged to move into more "productive" occupations and menial labor.[140]

The attack on growing Jewish economic roles was not limited to Kiev, but was actually a rather widespread phenomenon within the Russian intelligentsia beginning in the late 1860s, as various streams within Russian society began to identify the evils of capitalism and industrialization with the received notion of Jewish "exploitation" and the newly visible Jewish railroad magnates and other parvenus.[141] *Kievlianin* played a leading role in the national debate, passionately denouncing post-emancipation Jewish economic roles, especially leaseholding and trading in liquor, and claiming that most Jews were unproductive leeches on the Russian body economic.[142] The role of Jews in Kiev was particularly sensitive since, in addition to being a stronghold and symbol of the Russian imperial government, Kiev was also a bastion of Russian Orthodoxy, the "Jerusalem of Russia," second in religious importance only to Moscow. With seven monasteries, sixty churches, and 1,500 members of the clergy, it is no wonder a traveler in the 1880s dubbed the city "the Russian Rome."[143] Pious Russian Orthodox believers saw Kiev as the cradle of Holy Rus'. A guide to Kiev's Orthodox sights asked in 1861, "How can people who are totally alien to Kiev, unconnected to it by any patriotic memories, whose hearts have never beat fast at the sound of the Lavra's bell, ringing in the depths of the caves . . . hope to master Kiev? Its name and memory are alien to those who do not carry the name Russian."[144]

It was not uncommon to identify the fast-paced and bewildering changes that Kiev was experiencing as it entered the modern world of industry and commerce with the newly arrived Jews; as one writer put it, the "Jewish plague" that had infected the city was "growing . . . not by the day but by the hour."[145] Andrei Nikolaevich Murav'ev, a conservative nobleman and author of *Travels to the Russian Holy Places,* blamed holy Kiev's increasing secularization on its new role as a center of business and commerce, on the city fathers and new economic elite who cared little about the Church—and on the growing numbers and influence of Jews. Many poor people are in debt to Jews, he wrote in the early 1870s, and the greediness of Jewish and Polish lawyers has caused Kiev to become littered with signs advertising their services. Even worse, the naiveté of the local authorities has enabled the despotic Jewish kahal to subjugate Kiev as it has other cities and towns, and to "suck out the last juices from the Christians who have been given over to it."[146] Jews have taken over Kiev's industry, set about to corrupt the Russian Orthodox population with their numerous taverns, and acquired property in the very heart of the city. In short, Kiev is undergoing a transformation from the holy center of Christianity to "the capital of the zhids." To be sure, this charge was nothing new: in 1827, a petition urging the expulsion of the Jews had claimed that "Jews are transforming the ancient Russian capital into the capital of the Jews, who in their obstinate fanaticism are attempting to create temptations as regards religion (*v religioznom otnoshenii*) for the Orthodox nation."[147]

Echoing many of Murav'ev's charges, a correspondent in *Kievlianin* wrote in 1873 that Kiev was the Jews' "Promised Land," so dominant had they become.[148] Another writer claimed that the city had become so Jewish that most of the shops on Kreshchatik were closed on Saturday! A fear that seemed to lurk in the hearts of not a few Kievans was that their city might become "a second Berdichev"—all the more interesting when we consider that one of the reasons for lifting the ban on Jewish settlement in Kiev was the very real possibility that, due to its vigorous Jewish element, Berdichev would overtake Kiev in commercial importance.[149] It had seemed that Kiev could not live without Jews—but some now felt that it could not live long *with* them, at least not as the champions of "holy Kiev" knew it.

Not surprisingly, church officials were concerned about the influx of Jews into holy Kiev as well. When the merchant Vainshtein requested permission to purchase a house in Podol located next to the Church of the Nativity, the highest Orthodox prelate in the region, Metropolitan Arsenii petitioned against the sale, claiming that enabling Jews to settle only eight or nine yards from the very church altar "would be too burdensome for the Christian sensitivities of the parishioners and the entire Orthodox population of such an ancient holy place as Kiev." He even hinted darkly at the consequences of such a move, predicting that it "may lead to incidents unbecoming to the ruling Orthodox Church and that are impossible to foresee at the present time."[150] Vainshtein rescinded his request before any further complaints could be registered. A few years later, Arsenii's successor Filofei fulminated against the possibility of a Jewish school in Kiev, arguing that it would encourage "Talmudism" among Jews and thus hatred of Christian society.[151]

The authorities were aware of the complaints about Jews settling throughout Kiev, and agreed that Jews should be kept at a distance from the holy places of the city. In 1872, A. M. Dondukov-Korsakov, the governor-general of Kiev, Podol, and Volhyn provinces, wrote to the Minister of Internal Affairs, stating that several Jews had indeed been granted permission to settle outside of the Jewish districts of Ploskaia and Lybed, but that such a choice was limited to only those "Jews with whom the administration is acquainted to its satisfaction [*s khoroshei storony*], . . . quite educated and in general the kind of people whose presence in various districts of Kiev, judging from their lifestyle and occupation, leaves no expectations whatsoever of bad consequences." Because of Kiev's unique character as a religious pilgrimage center, however, Jews would not be granted blanket permission to settle throughout the city; after taking up residence near important Orthodox religious sites, their "fanaticism, religious intolerance, and arrogance" would inevitably lead them to ridicule Orthodox worshipers, and thus to confrontations with the tens of thousands of pilgrims arriving in Kiev annually.[152] It is clear that Dondukov-Korsakov also shared the opinion that, given the opportunity, Jews would pour into the city and virtually inundate it. In 1876, weighing in on the long-contested question of Jewish artisans' right to settle outside of the two Jewish districts, Dondukov-Korsakov again referred to the risk of confrontation with pilgrims, and added that if the issue were decided in the artisans' favor,

> all Jews, without exception, will reside throughout Kiev on the pretense of being artisans, and will flood the city to such a degree that the police will in no way be able to ensure order and tidiness. Jews have long been attempting to settle here under various pretenses. . . .[153]

Anxiety about the influx of Jews reached such a pitch that, in the early 1870s, the city council entertained the notion of establishing a quarter outside the city for undesirables: Jews, with or without residence permits, and pilgrims. Kiev, the project stated explicitly, would thus be protected from an influx of dirty and infectious pilgrims; implicit in the proposal was the defense that the suburb would provide against the deleterious influence of Jews.[154]

In 1880 and 1881, anti-Jewish sentiment was running especially high in Kiev, reflected in or perhaps encouraged by *Kievlianin*'s series of articles about the increasing menace of the local Jewish population. One of those articles was actually a reprint of a memorandum on the Jews in Kiev by the new governor-general of the southwest region, M. I. Chertkov, submitted to the imperial Commission for the Reorganization of Jewish Life in January 1880. Chertkov argued that current law, far from protecting Kiev from Jews, actually exposed it even further to their harmful influence. Kiev, as the last bastion of Russianness and Orthodoxy in a region that Jews had come to dominate, was in need of stricter protections against Jewish inroads so that Jews could not "conquer" Kiev the way they had the other cities of the western provinces. Not only had the official policy of russification and the attempt at the "merger" [*sliianie*] of the Jewish and Russian populations not succeeded, but just the opposite had come to pass: Kiev, once a pure Russian city, was becoming judaized (the Russian verb was *ob"evreivat'sia*).[155]

Using data from the 1874 census to back his argument, Chertkov argued that Kiev, once a "purely Russian city," was now well on its way to becomingjust like all the other cities of the western provinces in its subordination to Jewry. Only one-third of Kiev's Jews worked in industry, crafts, and trade, while more than 60 percent were engaged in "the customary Jewish exploitation of the passions, ignorance, and gullibility of the surrounding urban population."[156] The "native Russian" population, for historical reasons much more vulnerable to the advances of the Jews than their coreligionists in Russia's interior cities, had to be protected from abuse by the law. In a short period of time, Jews had managed to become owners and managers of private banks and joint-stock companies, and leading players in the sugar-beet trade. They had also taken over petty commerce and especially trade in alcohol,

> introducing a spirit of hot-tempered speculation and exerting a demoralizing influence everywhere. . . . In their attempt to seize the most profitable branches of trade and industry, Jews are spreading out through the entire city. The places of industry and the central districts of the city fill up with more and more Jews every year. From Podol and the outskirts they have penetrated into the very center of the city, everywhere occupying the best

> spots, purchasing houses there and settling with their large families, surrounded by an entire swarm of dependents under the name of relatives, clerks, agents, and servants; but they always remain closed off in their own world, alien to the population and the interests of the city, without any ties to the surrounding Christian milieu, from which they are separated by language, fanatic religious prejudices, differences in upbringing, and family life.[157]

Soon, as had already occurred in the other cities of the region, the Russian element in trade and industry would be "suppressed by the Jews," and the "'mother of Russian cities,' so dear to the Russian people by virtue of its religious and historical relics," would become a Jewish city like all the others in the western borderland region.[158] Like his predecessor, Chertkov also referred to the danger of conflict between Jews and Christians, especially pilgrims; reviewing his memorandum, however, several members of the all-imperial Commission on the Reorganization of Jewish Life commented somewhat cuttingly that he had failed to specify any actual incidents of such hostility.[159]

Other articles published in 1880 and 1881 stressed the recent influx of Jews into Kiev's schools. So-called "native" (*korennye*) Kiev children were in danger of being pushed out of their schools by Jewish children, who were receiving free education at the expense of the age-old inhabitants of the city.[160] A *Kievlianin* article entitled "More on the Subject of the 'Zhid Invasion'" warned that restrictions had to be placed on the number of Jews in Russian educational institutions, lest the Russian intelligentsia come to be constituted solely of "aliens" (*chuzherodtsy*).[161]

The articles seem to have had an effect on local attitudes. In May 1881, the city council appointed a commission to study the Jewish question and the influence of Jews on the city's economy. In June, after rumors started to circulate that Jews were poisoning flour and other foodstuffs, the provincial governor announced the establishment of a commission to study Jewish grocery stores.[162] Reports of police requests for a precise delineation of the categories of Jews permitted to reside in Kiev suggest that a crackdown on Jewish illegal residents was in the works.[163] The pogrom of 1881, one of a wave of violent attacks on Jews that swept the southern provinces of the Russian Empire following the assassination of Alexander II, showed even more poignantly the extent to which articles such as the ones in *Kievlianin* reflected—or perhaps influenced—the beliefs and opinions of the poor Christian population of the city. That they were mostly illiterate does not mean that they could not pick up the rumors spread by *Kievlianin* from those who were able to read. The report submitted by the Kiev Jewish community on the pogrom of 1881 testified that throughout the three-day ordeal, the mob could be heard crying that the Jews had illegally taken over all the commerce and trade in the city—whether the crowds were looting the wealthy shops on Aleksandrovskaia (the main thoroughfare of Podol) or the wretched shacks of Jews in the slums beyond the canal.[164] The belief that Jews had set out to "conquer" Kiev and make it their own was clearly not limited to aristocratic or literate circles. Moreover, the fact that the pogroms of 1881 and 1882 were mostly limited to the southern provinces of the Pale of Settlement suggests that the intensive Jewish in-migration of the kind experienced in Kiev contributed to the animosity felt by many Christians throughout the region.

Paradoxically, Kiev's Jews came under attack both for remaining isolated from the rest of the population and for insinuating themselves into the fabric of the city. Critics often bemoaned the fact that Kiev had separate Jewish neighborhoods, a sign of the size and permanence of its Jewish population. Critics also—and sometimes at the same time—wrote angrily about the fact that Jews also lived throughout the city, even in its finest districts.[165] On his travels through Ukraine (or Little Russia, as it was known) around 1880, a Frenchman was told by the hotelkeeper on his arrival in Kiev that the city consisted of three parts: the Old and New Town (the upper city), Pechersk (the center of religious life), and Podol—the Jewish quarter *and* the industrial and commercial center of the town.[166] There was no mystery to why certain areas of the city—the port area (Ploskaia and part of Podol) and Lybed, a southern neighborhood—became known as Jewish quarters: most Jews living in Kiev were restricted by law to residence in precisely those districts. As early as 1873, Podol was being called "a second Berdichev."[167]

The law forced the authorities into a contradictory position about the desirability of Jewish acculturation in Kiev: government decrees had created two heavily Jewish neighborhoods, ensuring that they would continue to be relatively isolated from the non-Jewish population. At the same time, city and provincial authorities forbade Jews from establishing formal associations of various kinds for fear that they would encourage Jewish isolation and self-segregation: it was feared that an 1880 proposal to establish a mutual-aid society for Jewish clerks in Podol would lead to "open segregation on the basis of nationality" (*obosoblenie otkrytoi natsional'nosti*), and the establishment of more prayer houses would "aid in the inordinate development of isolation, fanaticism, and superstition among the Jewish masses."[168] Reviewing the contradictions in the regulations on Jewish settlement in Kiev, several members of the Commission for the Reorganization of Jewish Life, established to eliminate Jewish "segregation," implicitly acknowledged that maintaining separate Jewish neighborhoods was inconsistent with the idea of progress and a modern Russian Empire. Forcing Jewish artisans and soldiers to move into Ploskaia and Lybed, they opined, "would be equivalent to establishing a special Jewish quarter (ghetto) in the city—a measure that has been abolished throughout Russia for its most injurious consequences, even from the hygienic point of view."[169]

According to publicist A. E. Kaufman, the restrictions that kept most of Kiev's Jews concentrated in the densely populated Ploskaia and Lybed ensured that the two neighborhoods would be "a miniature Pale of Settlement." Not only was the environment of the big city unfavorable for the acculturation of the Russian language and "Russian morals," wrote Kaufman, but Kiev Jews were actually among the least modernized of all the city's religious groups: fewer Jews than any other religious group spoke Russian or another European language, Jewish literacy rates were low, and few Jewish children were receiving a general education. The circumstances in which Kiev's Jews lived were serving to keep them chained by the fetters of ignorance and fanaticism, alienated and isolated from the Russian nation.[170]

Kaufman was not the only one who considered Kiev's Jews to be isolated from the rest of the population. In a spat between *Kievlianin* and the prominent Kiev Jewish merchant A. A. Kupernik in 1871, the latter apparently protested the newspaper's lack of reportage on the Jewish Hospital and its special cholera wing, claiming that the newspaper was actually reinforcing the Jewish isolation that it so abhorred. *Kievlianin* responded that it saw no need to pay special attention to the Jewish Hospital, since mortality rates there were no different from those elsewhere; indeed, Jews were only ignorant of this plain fact because of their very segregation from larger society.[171] In his memorandum in 1880, Governor-General Chertkov agreed that Jews were keeping to themselves, but offered a different solution: rather than lifting restrictions on residence to encourage russification, he recommended that the existing regulations be enforced more severely or even that Jewish settlement in Kiev be banned outright, because Jews had shown that they had not yet learned to intermingle with, and stop exploiting, the native population.[172]

The Pogrom of 1881

It is not surprising, then, that the pogrom wave that overran the southern provinces of the Russian Empire in 1881 and 1882 was seen by many as "retribution," not only for the alleged Jewish participation in the assassination of Tsar Alexander II, but more broadly for Jewish "exploitation" of their Christian neighbors, an accusation that dated back to the reign of Paul I (1796–1801).[173] The fact the pogroms were largely concentrated in areas of new Jewish settlement was hardly coincidental: as in Kiev, Jews throughout the Ukrainian and especially the New Russian provinces were often viewed as interlopers, competing for jobs with Christians and "exploiting" them by taking advantage of business opportunities to open up taverns and shops.

But the Jews of the empire *were* shocked by the scale and intensity of the violent riots. The investigation carried out after the pogrom by Count P. I. Kutaisov claimed that there were two opinions in Kiev on the causes of the pogroms. Some were convinced that they had emerged out of centuries of hatred for Jews. But local Jews were certain that the pogroms had been stirred up by revolutionaries, because however strong Christian hate, it could not have materialized in so powerful a fashion—and in so many places simultaneously—without an organization to coordinate it.[174] Whatever the validity of this assumption, it reveals that Jews in Kiev did not underestimate the extent of Christian animosity but rather doubted its ability to manifest itself in the form of physical violence. This, despite the fact that pogroms had occurred in recent memory (in Odessa in 1821, 1849, 1859, and 1871), while the horrific massacres that took place in the context of the seventeenth-century Chmielnicki and eighteenth-century Haidamak uprisings also continued to live in Jewish collective memory.[175] The fact remained, however, that most Russian Jews alive in 1881 had not themselves experienced mass violence on the scale of a pogrom. Indeed, neither Jews nor most anyone else could envision the wave of violence that would engulf the Pale, even given the considerable provocation that preceded it. After the pogrom, the Hebrew writer Yitshak Yaakov Vaysberg (Weisberg) wrote to the Hebrew newspaper *Ha-melits* that

> the rumors had been spreading in our city for quite some time that there were people planning ill for our people, but who believed that in our time

> and in a city as respected as ours, with thousands of soldiers as well as government officials, something like this would happen, something out of the Middle Ages?[176]

Hamm writes that "initially Kiev's Jews did not feel threatened by reports of pogroms elsewhere."[177] Jews in other parts of the empire were apparently just as unprepared. A report in another Hebrew newspaper written before the pogroms had started but published afterward told of rumors that had been spread throughout Poland stating that "the peasants were getting ready to attack the Jews during the coming holiday [Passover]," which, although they "cast fear into the hearts of Jews living in villages . . . [were] in and of themselves unworthy of attention. . . ."[178] As I. Michael Aronson has shown in his study of the 1881 pogroms, even those who wished ill to the Jews "did not expect rioting to occur as a result of the anti-Jewish newspaper campaign" or in the wake of the assassination of Alexander II; indeed, "the actual outbreak of rioting caught everyone off-guard."[179] The state of panic that Kiev Jews experienced seems to have begun only after the very first pogrom in Elizavetgrad on April 16, when a pogrom in Kiev became a very real possibility.[180]

In the week after the Elizavetgrad disorders, rumors surged through Kiev about the upcoming April 26th, which was not only a Sunday but a feast day, with large groups of workers and artisans milling about in the public squares and markets of Ploskaia and Podol from early in the morning, many of them drinking.[181] The police report on the pogroms from the Ploskaia district later claimed that "people were heard saying that the Jews should be beaten up and thrown out [*vygnat'*] of Kiev, since all the trade is concentrated in their hands, as a consequence of which bread and other products have become more expensive."[182] Though most studies have concluded that the *pogromshchiki*—or at least the most active ones—were mostly unemployed migrant peasants from the Great Russian provinces (*bosiaki* or the "barefoot brigade"), more recent work has posited that "most *pogromshchiki* were from the Pale, and the majority were probably local people"—townspeople resentful of Jewish competition along with peasants residing in the city who were eager for the excitement or plunder that would likely result from a pogrom.[183] The reality was probably some combination of the two: a heady mixture of local and imported animosity that combusted spontaneously in the context of rapid modernization and change, economic competition, social instability, religious antagonism, and the uneasy proximity of religious and ethnic groups as a result of migration. Gessen makes a suggestion that is not often considered but which makes a great deal of sense: at least some of the pent-up animosity that exploded during the pogroms was not directed at Jews but was a general feeling of anger and frustration caused by the rapid changes in society and the economic constraints experienced by many, especially in the lower-middle class. The Jews served as a scapegoat.[184] Vodka and rumors that the violence was sanctioned by the Emperor himself fueled the conflagration.[185] Certainly there were no "ringleaders," ideological leaders, or secret orders from St. Petersburg, as some accounts over the decades have attempted to demonstrate.[186] As to the ethnicity of the pogromshchiki, over which much ink has been spilled, it seems clear that there was a mixture of Ukrainians and Great Russians, though the former seem to have predominated (117 of the peasants arrested after the pogrom were from Kiev and the neighboring Chernigov provinces).[187]

In Ploskaia, the police tried to convince Jewish shopkeepers and traders at the Zhitnyi Bazaar and second-hand goods market to close up shop and go home to avoid confrontation with the mob, but according to the police report, "Jews at both markets responded distrustfully to the requests of the police to vacate the area." The violence in Ploskaia started at the Zhitnyi bazar when "the half-drunken mob started chasing after passing Jews and beating them, shouting 'Down with the bloodsucking zhids [*doloi zhidov-krovopiitsev*], we can't live among them any longer, they have taken everything into their hands.' . . ."[188] The police and troops were not able to protect all Jews because the huge crowd was in too many places at once, or at least so went the official police account. Shouts of "Beat the zhids" began to spread along the streets and, according to another source, although police and troops tried to disperse the crowds, they had not yet been given permission to use force. A few individuals started to throw rocks at Jewish homes, and then began to loot Jewish apartments and shops.[189] The pinkas of the Tailors' Synagogue noted that "they set fire to Tailors' Synagogue with [its] twelve Torah scrolls, and they tore up all the scrolls in the synagogue, after which they went into people's homes and stores."[190]

From the port neighborhoods with their dense Jewish populations, the mobs ascended Kiev's steep hills to the central districts, where they attached Jewish-owned shops and prominent landmarks like the house of Isaak Markovich Brodsky. But they did not get far: "at each of these places, the mob was either prevented from attacking or stopped in mid-attack by troops." In his report, Count Kutaisov found that the military served the city well in protecting "the best and central parts of the city, which remained untouched thanks only to the army." By contrast, violence raged in the suburb of Demievka, where the mob was totally unhindered by troops.[191] Some scholars have surmised that the authorities "dispersed the troops throughout the city rather than concentrating them in Jewish neighborhoods" and that "soldiers lacked the training to deal with urban disorders," but descriptions of the events in the center of Kiev seem to suggest that there were enough soldiers with sufficient training there to put down the mobs without much difficulty, while the same was not true for Podol, Ploskaia, and Demievka.[192] Archival records show that powerful local administrators such as Drentel'n apparently put a great deal of effort into quelling the violence, but they were unsuccessful in the face of inertia, ineptitude, and indifference.[193]

A striking pattern emerges from the police reports on the pogroms submitted by individual police precincts by district after the events of April 1881. Outside of the visibly Jewish neighborhoods, the mobs almost always headed for two targets first. These places were associated with the nexus—in the minds of the masses, at least—between Jews and commerce: the markets of Kiev, fulcrums of the city economy where Jewish traders played a prominent role; and homes or buildings owned by the city's wealthiest and most visible Jews. The latter, however, were often protected by troops or policemen, while the shops, stalls, and homes of Kiev's Jewish poor were rarely defended. In Starokievskii district (the Old Town), for example, a mob of about four hundred people ascending from Podol went directly to the Haymarket (Sennoi, also known as L'vov, Market), where they smashed and plundered Jewish stalls, and then moved on to a building owned by one Grebin', probably Meir Grebin', a businessman and wealthy patron of the Jewish Hospital and other Jewish causes.[194] When the police prevented them from attacking the building, they headed for the Evreiskii (Jewish) Market (also known as Galitskii), where they began to destroy Jewish stalls. A mob of similar size hurtled through shortly afterward, following the same route, and attacked the houses of two wealthy Jews (both with the surname Brodsky)—but they were soon stopped by police and troops.[195] Of course the markets in Podol and Ploskaia had been the original epicenters of the violence.[196] In neighborhoods with considerable Jewish populations, such as the port districts of Demievka and Solomenka, the mob then moved on (and presumably dispersed) to attack and plunder individual Jewish homes and apartments. Naturally, it was easier for the authorities to defend individual homes than to protect entire neighborhoods, but the contrast is nonetheless striking, and it must have seemed a coincidence to very few contemporaries that the homes and property of wealthy and connected Jews survived the violence mostly unscathed. Of the 896 victims recorded by official statistics, less than a third (254) were homeowners (28 percent), but this percentage would have been even lower had Demievka been taken into account.[197]

It is also interesting to note that the rioting mobs in Kiev were heard to cry not only the familiar "beat the zhids" (*bei zhidov*) but also to utter calls to expel the Jews from the city where they had taken over all the trade and pushed prices up (the reality was just the opposite: the admission of Jews into the city had brought prices down).[198] Expulsion was very much part of anti-Jewish discourse in Kiev, whether in the mouths of officials, disgruntled peasants and townspeople, or even Jews considering the hazards faced by illegals in Kiev. Pogromshchiki must have been aware of the terrible consequences that expulsion meant for Jews, and this threat may have been meant to terrorize in addition to being a genuine expression of animosity.[199]

The scale of the destruction is attested to by some of the statistics from the official report of the Kiev Jewish Society for Assistance to Victims of the Disorders in the South of Russia in 1881, which provided emergency shelter to 2,000 Jews and emergency food aid to at least 5,000. The aid distributed to Jewish victims in Kiev and its suburbs totaled 95,000 rubles, about 60 percent of the aid that the society provided to victims throughout the southwest region.[200] By some accounts, the Kiev pogrom was the most serious in scope of all those that occurred in 1881–82.[201] The misery of Kiev Jewry was compounded by a large-scale expulsion of illegal residents in the autumn of 1881.[202] This, in a cruelly ironic sense, brought to fruition the cries of the pogromshchiki to expel the "zhids" from Kiev.

As in other cities throughout the Pale of Settlement in January and February 1882, Jews in Kiev observed a fast day and held special penitential services (on February 1st). John Klier claims that these events "were extensively planned," and that the main service, led by Rabbi Tsukkerman at the Tailors' Synagogue in Podol, included a sermon by Tsukkerman, speeches delivered by university students, and musical pieces performed by the "celebrated Jewish opera singer, Medvedev."[203] In addition to many of the city's Jews, the audience included over one hundred Jewish students (including also, possibly, *gimnaziia* students), "virtually the entire enrolment of the university."

In addition to giving money and providing practical guidance for the aid effort, some Jewish leaders also attempted to provide explanations for the unprecedented violence. As we have seen, some were inclined to agree with the government's initial assessment that revolutionaries were to blame for stirring up the riots, because that "served to pre-empt the accusation of Judeophobes that the pogroms were a popular defense against Jewish exploitation."[204] Or at least this was the official Jewish line given in the Russian language. Quite another explanation appeared in the Hebrew press, one that highlighted Jewish–Christian tensions and the socioeconomic aspect of the pogrom's destructive dynamic. An open letter from the unnamed "Jewish nobles of Kiev" (*atsilei b'nei Kiyov*)—the city's Jewish aristocracy—in December 1882 reproved the prosperous Jews of the city for flaunting their wealth in the eyes of Kiev's Christian population. While the authors of the letter acknowledged that the Jews were not to blame for the pogrom, they nonetheless urged them to maintain a lower profile so as not to provoke their neighbors' envy. The letter spoke disapprovingly of Jewish mansions bedecked with costly furniture and of lavish Jewish weddings, but devoted most of its censure to Jewish women, who—regardless of their family's means and social status—insisted on dressing in luxurious garments and expensive jewelry. The "nobles" urged all Jews to lead their lives modestly, and even discouraged Jews of more humble means not to keep their children in school if they could not afford it, but rather to teach them a trade and thus ensure an honest living for them. Finally, in a passage replete with citations from the Talmud and other traditional texts, the writers discouraged all forms of cheating and fraud in business dealings, lest Christians be able to point to even one Jew's actions as an excuse for their poor impression of Jews as a group.[205]

Clearly, the pogrom had provoked soul-searching among Kiev's Jews. But unlike the standard narrative of the Jewish reaction to 1881–82, these Jews were not despairing of an eventual Jewish integration into Russian society, nor engaging in traditionalist self-flagellation over sins against God. In some ways it was a classic maskilic argument, advocating that Jews "fit in" as much as possible into the surrounding society: too much visible embourgeoisement without enough real integration and rapprochement between Jew and Christian could lead to disaster, as the pogrom showed. But at least one maskil found this warning nothing but an insult to the intelligence of Kiev's Jewish masses: in a response to the letter from the "aristocrats," Moshe Leib Lilienblum retorted that the pogrom mobs had spent most of their energy attacking not the wealthy or even the middling Jews, but the Jewish poor and working class of the city.[206]

For many Christians in Kiev, and particularly for Russian bureaucrats, there was little question as to who bore the lion's share of responsibility for the pogrom. A memorandum on Jewish residence privileges in Kiev written after the pogrom concluded that Jews had managed to settle throughout Kiev (contrary to regulations) thanks only to bribery, and Kiev residents did not generally believe that Jews had ever had the right to do so. This line of reasoning could lead only to the inference that Jews had stepped beyond all legal and societal bounds in their dealings in Kiev, and in doing so had provoked the animus of the local "native" population. Moreover, went the memorandum, Jews were the instigators of the quarrels that sparked the violence, and thus the pogrom was caused mostly [*bolee vsego*] by the Jews.[207] This conclusion was similar to those reached by most of the provincial boards of inquiry established by St. Petersburg in the wake of the pogroms, and led eventually to the restrictive May Laws instituted by Interior Minister N. P. Ignat'ev.[208]

Not everyone agreed about the precise portion of blame to be apportioned to the Jews, however. A curious article in the Moscow-based *Russkii kur'er,* which the correspondent from Kiev claimed to have written after the first day of pogrom violence, argued that although economic exploitation by Jews was an unmistakable fact, it was hardly their fault alone—indeed, the municipal administration had actually invited Jews in certain occupations to come to Kiev in order to lower the prices![209] The writer went on to maintain that Kiev had become "zhidified" [*ozhidovlen*], and the process of "zhidification" was continuing; but that it was Christians as well as Jews who were responsible for that state of affairs. Apparently the writer was condemning the exploitation of the common people by anyone, regardless of religion; however, he then returned to the subject of Jews, noting that "Jews are strong where we are weak: the Jews have real community spirit (*obshchestvennost'*) . . . [and] solidarity." In other words, Christians made the mistake of turning on one another while Jews continued their inexorable rise, thanks to their cohesion and unity of aims.

Conclusion

The opening of Kiev, in the very heart of the Pale of Settlement, to limited Jewish residence put tsarist officials in an impossible bind. Some Jews met the requirements for a residence permit and were able to take up legal residence in the city, but even more did not meet those requirements and decided to take their chances. Thus, from the very beginning an entire caste of Jews lived an existence in the shadows, hoping that bribing the right policemen and hiding in the attic during police raids would be enough to keep themselves in Kiev for another few months. Even Jews who entered the city legally could find their situation transformed overnight; if their child graduated from school, for example (parents of children attending school in Kiev were granted residence permits), or if their occupation was declared no longer in the category of "craft." Official figures can only tell us so much about a Jewish life—religious, economic, and otherwise—which tried so hard to stay out of view. On the other end of the spectrum, we witness the growing visibility of the "most favored" Jewish denizens of the city: the first-guild merchants living in sumptuous houses in Lipki and riding through the city in their carriages. No wonder some Christians felt uneasy about a city they felt was rightfully "Russian" and "Christian": the Jewish contribution to the city's economy and everyday hustle and bustle grew by the day, and even official statistics—which described an explosion in Kiev's Jewish population in the 1860s and 1870s, climbing to about 13,000 in 1874, or 12 percent of the total population—clearly did not correspond to the true number of Jews in the city. This was especially true in the neighborhoods where Jews had already achieved the heroic proportions similar to those of heavily Jewish Odessa and Warsaw. But imperial Russia was not a police state, and sometimes there seemed to be more cracks than actual bricks and mortar in the legislative and administrative walls it attempted to put up. If this was ever the case, it was certainly so with the regulations governing Jewish entry into and settlement in Kiev.

As we will see in the next chapter, the visibility of Kiev's Jewish elite, and their quest for a sense of rootedness and permanence in their adopted city, meant that their religious and communal institutions would almost always have to be above board and subject to official review and approval. Working-class Jews, by contrast, would often find that their petitions to establish Jewish institutions—such as the Vasil'kover mutual-aid society that we saw above—were summarily rejected. Not surprisingly, therefore, most of those institutions were organized and run secretly, which, while a useful state of affairs for the members of those institutions, makes knowing anything about them extraordinarily difficult, if not impossible, for historians. It is with that caveat in mind that we proceed to take a close look at some of Kiev's central—and legal—Jewish institutions in the first two decades of Jewish settlement in the city.

2

The Foundations of Communal Life

As is often the case with the establishment of new communities, patterns set in the first years frequently remain paradigms for years to come. So it was in Kiev. A number of blueprints for communal governance and philanthropic activity were laid down in the first years of Jewish settlement; these became "tradition" in more ways than one. As we will see in this chapter, the establishment of the Jewish Hospital, the communal governing board, and the first educational institutions were all ad hoc developments that were nonetheless to have a tremendous impact on Jewish life in Kiev until the turn of the century and, in some ways, to the very end of the tsarist regime. Although the Jewish Hospital was, as its name made clear, a distinctly separate institution that was meant for the welfare of the Jewish community, it was in no way cut off from the wider life of the city and indeed maintained close ties with non-Jewish institutions and society. At the same time, it was made clear from the outset that Jewish welfare was to be funded *solely* from Jewish money. Christian Kiev demanded that Jews pay for their own institutions but insisted at the same time on municipal and local philanthropic oversight of those institutions. The same, it eventually emerged, would be true for the very mechanisms by which the Jews of Kiev governed themselves; an early forbearance for a form of semi-independent Jewish self-governance in Kiev, one based on the government's vision of an acceptable form of Jewish leadership, gave way in the 1880s and 1890s to intolerance for any autonomy and a wholesale takeover of the Jewish communal governing body by the government. This takeover must be understood in light of the tsarist government's deep suspicion of all independent Jewish associations—indeed, of all civil society activity by any Russian subjects—and its long-term, though vague, strategy to place checks upon the activities and influence of Jewish organizations.

Little is known about this attempt by the Russian state to transform the leadership and structure of the Jewish community, which was actually part of a larger bid to reform Russian Jewry as a whole and "merge" Jews with the surrounding society. The story that is better known and more often told is Russia's attempt to make over its Jews through education by establishing, beginning in the 1840s, a network of state Jewish schools and seminaries that eventually produced a cadre of Russian-speaking Jewish intellectuals and professionals seeking to integrate into Russian society.[1] This chapter will examine the emergence of Jewish communal governance in Kiev and explore the fraught relationship between the heads of the Jewish community and the Russian authorities. Examining the history of the official governing body of Kiev Jewry and two other central Jewish institutions in the city, the Crown rabbinate and the Choral Synagogue, we will see that the Jewish community was indeed transformed, though not quite in the fashion that the authorities had envisioned. The government's bid to concentrate communal authority in the Jewish elite and to vest it with official government authority failed because the widening gap between that elite and the masses it claimed to represent led to a crisis in authority. A similar, previously extant rift between the Jewish masses and the government also expanded, echoing the larger crisis in Russian society leading up to the 1905 Revolution. Democracy and public accountability—whether for the sake of the ideal of representation or in order to gain power for one's own faction—became the watchwords of the day in the Jewish community, as in the Russian society of which it was an integral part.

The Communal Governance of Russian Jewry

In his pioneering work on Jewish political structures in the Polish–Lithuanian Commonwealth and the Russian Empire, Eli Lederhendler showed that among those who benefited from the breakdown of traditional structures and institutions—brought about mostly by state intervention into Jewish affairs during the reign of Nicholas I—were precisely the Jewish "notables" who stepped in to fill the power vacuum, both as internal leaders and as representatives of the Jewish community.[2] While ostensibly similar to the elders of the kahal, the often oligarchic governing board of the autonomous Jewish community, the new Russian Jewish aristocracy—consisting primarily of liquor-tax farmers who then branched out into trade and industry—was actually a different phenomenon altogether.[3] Where the kahal elders had been elected, at least on a pro forma basis, and often governed with the active support of rabbinical authorities, the notables had no formal ties to the organized Jewish community, and in a certain sense were not even members of it.[4] Their authority emanated from their wealth—which provided them with "economic independence from Jewish communal authorities"—and their contacts with and (often exaggerated) influence in high circles of the Russian governmental bureaucracy.[5] Fairly soon after the Russian conquest of the western borderlands, Jewish merchants were differentiated from Jewish members of other estates, not least in their freedom from payment of community taxes, the taxes that the Jewish/meshchanstvo community was required to pay the government, as distinct from taxes that Jews paid to support their own communal and welfare institutions. Instead, they were required to pay a portion of their capital to the treasury.[6] Thus, as early as the early nineteenth century, a divide emerged and sharpened between the economic elite of the Jewish community and those below them on the rungs of the financial ladder. Of course this kind of rift had existed in the oligarchic community structure under the Rzeczpospolita, but now the state sanctioned a formal distinction between the two classes. In 1831, new legislation required the merchants to contribute toward the taxes of the Jewish meshchane in certain cases, but their unwillingness to comply with this law only brought into sharper focus their sense of disconnectedness from the townspeople estate, to which the vast majority of Russian Jews belonged.[7]

The abolition of the kahal in 1844 was part of the government's attempt to encourage rapprochement (*sblizhenie*) between the Jews of Russia and the surrounding population. As the government saw it, the elimination of Jewish self-government, as well as the newly introduced Jewish state schools and official rabbinate, would ultimately lead to the transformation of the Jews, as they abandoned their medieval isolation from society and "merged into the Russian social order."[8] This merging was to be particularly encouraged by the transfer of the kahal's functions to the organs of municipal government. However, the crucial matter of taxation was not wholly given over to the local authorities; rather, Jews would elect "collectors" (*sborshchiki*) to be directly subordinate to the local governing bodies, who would collect and administer the *korobka,* the kosher meat excise also introduced in 1844 that served as "the basic internal tax of the Jewish community."[9] Writing on the abolition of the kahal, Isaac Levitats maintained that "its administrative functions were turned over to the police, while its fiscal responsibilities were allocated to the municipalities."[10] This formulation, however, is probably too strong, and Simon Dubnow's slightly more nuanced description is more accurate. Dubnow argued that the process of "municipalization," which had begun as early as the reign of Catherine II, "managed to destroy the self-government of the Kahal and yet preserve its rudimentary function as an autonomous fiscal agency which was to be continued under the auspices of the municipality."[11]

Gessen agreed: "The Jewish commune [*evreiskoe obshchestvo*], as a financial-administrative unit, continued to exist, and . . . sborshchiki and *starosty* [elders responsible for finding recruits] replaced the earlier kahal elders."[12] According to this version, Russian Jews did hold onto some shred of autonomy under the new system, a supposition substantiated by Russian legislation's use of the term *evreiskoe obshchestvo* (Jewish community or commune). But who was in charge now that the governing board of the community was, at least in theory, no longer in existence?

Clearly, someone had to be in charge because legislation on the korobka compelled the Jewish obshchestvo to provide for the enlightenment of the masses, welfare or "communal care" (*obshchestvennoe prizrenie*), and charity (*blagotvoritel'nost'*), and these matters required organization and oversight.[13] In many communities, the sborshchik and his assistants were in fact simply kahal officers by another name, and in his encyclopedic investigation of the post-abolition kahal, Azriel Shohat demonstrates that the Jewish obshchestvo retained—at least for a time—some of its earlier authority, such as the right to grant passports.[14] Another new figure of authority was the *deputat,* also called the *upolnomochennyi* (representative), an elected position probably connected to conscription and the allocation of tax revenues for the needs of the poor, but this post was apparently not obligatory upon the community and thus did not appear in all localities. In a few places, the local burial society took over the functions of the kahal, while in many others, "prosperous and settled" (*zazhitochnye i osedlye*) members of the community whom the law allowed the local authorities to invite (or coopt) to assist in administering the korobka—in other words, the wealthiest members of the community—came to be de facto communal officers.[15] (This phenomenon was fairly standard practice for the Russian Empire, as the administrators of the already overstretched imperial bureaucracy well understood that the western borderlands could only be efficiently governed by allowing the elites of their relatively "advanced" cultures to retain a certain amount of power).[16] We also hear of the governing body of the main synagogue in a particular locality acting as a communal board.[17] The reality is that we simply do not know—and may never know—exactly how the organized Jewish community carried on its functions.[18]

By the 1860s and early 1870s, the sborshchiki and deputaty began to lose their relevance. This was due to the easing of the harsh conscription regime for Jews in 1856, the abolition of the poll tax in 1863, and the new conscription law of 1874.[19] (This shift was part of the larger transformation of the meshchanstvo as a result of these legislative changes.)[20] Within the Jewish community, the changes may have opened the way for "prosperous and settled" Jews, or, as they were often called in Hebrew and Yiddish, the notables (*gvirim*), to take on an even more prominent role in Jewish communal life.

The reforms of the Jewish community undertaken by the Russian state must be understood not only in the context of similar measures taken to diminish Jewish separatism by Austria-Hungary and various German states, but also in light of the Russian government's policies in the western borderlands after the Polish Uprising of 1830. These policies first restricted and then abolished remnants of local autonomy that had survived from the era of the Polish–Lithuanian Commonwealth. As Michael Stanislawski has shown, one of the most important lasting effects of the 1844 abolition of the kahal was not in the functioning of the community, but rather in the *perception* on the part of Russian Jews that the kahal's authority had been substantially diminished.[21] Indeed, the goal of the government's plan—if haphazard legislation over the course of decades can be considered a plan—was to reduce the Jewish community to an entity of a purely religious character, consisting of the synagogues and prayer houses in a given locality and the Crown rabbi that they elected. In terms of the day-to-day functioning of Jewish communal institutions, it was the notables coopted by individual municipalities—and the municipalities themselves—who truly held power.[22] Of course, bound up in this question was the issue of competing spheres of influence within the urban body politic: municipalities, especially with the new powers granted them by the Municipal Statute of 1870; *soslovie* (estate) institutions, such as the townspeople's and artisan boards (*upravy*); and religious communities, such as the Jews, with historic privileges confirmed by the government in various acts of legislation.[23]

This was especially true of cities outside of the Pale of Settlement, as Benjamin Nathans has demonstrated in the case of St. Petersburg, where the authorities sharply restricted the areas in which the governing board could function, barring it from operating a burial society or philanthropic institutions.[24] However, the policy later came to be applied to cities within the Pale, such as Odessa. In 1883, minister of internal affairs Tol'stoi wrote that because the Jewish community had previously been defined as relating only to religious ritual, there could be no separate Jewish communal governing board in Odessa, other than a body to administer the korobka.[25] Since Jews were members of the municipal body politic and Jewish autonomy was no longer tolerated, Jewish communal affairs had to be governed by the municipality. Ultimately, the government's goal was to atomize the Jewish community, transforming it from a self-contained, independent entity with a variety of functions into a mere collection of synagogues.[26] Authority over fiscal matters was to be transferred to local government; formerly autonomous and unregimented charitable societies were to be carefully supervised by the authorities; and synagogues would be restricted to electing their own boards to govern financial, not communal, matters.[27] As had been the case for decades, the only communal leader recognized by the state was its own: the state, or Crown, rabbi.[28]

While the state's policies did have an impact on the functioning of the Jewish community, the evolution of Russian Jewish leadership from the 1840s through the 1870s did not conform to the government's blueprint. Crown rabbis were mostly rejected by the communities to which they were sent, while traditional rabbis began to take on both local and national political roles, as did the new maskilim (proponents of Enlightenment) and the notables. These last two groups became linked to the state in various ways, whether through official sponsorship of the enlightenment project, as proponents and beneficiaries of a plan for "selective integration" of the Jews, or as local communal leaders, elected or self-appointed with the approval of the authorities.[29]

As in many cities of the Russian Empire, an informal alliance developed in Kiev between the maskilim and the acculturated elite. Both groups saw the good of Russian Jewry linked closely with the state. As Lederhendler makes clear in *The Road to Modern Jewish Politics,* maskilim solidified their connection to the state in the governmental positions that were bestowed upon Jews who had received some secular education: Crown rabbis, "expert Jews" (*uchenye evrei;* i.e., government advisers on Jewish affairs), and official censors.[30] For their part, Jewish merchants and industrialists—who had first proposed the selective integration scheme to the government—were awarded official titles such as commercial counselor. Members of both groups were permitted to settle outside the Pale of Settlement. While the maskilim strove to act as intercessors on behalf of Russian Jewry, in reality it was often Jewish millionaires such as Lazar' Brodsky and Baron Gintsburg, men with influence and connections with officials high in the tsarist bureaucracy, who were the true *shtadlonim* (the traditional Hebrew/Yiddish term for intercessors).

The Jewish case was highly typical of a broader pattern within the Russian Empire in which the central government coopted the elites of the empire's national and religious minorities in order to gain access to the peoples who acknowledged these elites as their leaders.[31] Significantly, though, in many cases these elites were not long-established leadership groups with traditional claims to leadership but new factions or familiar factions with new claims. In the Muslim case, as Robert Crews writes,

> State backing confirmed some customary prerogatives, but many of the "traditional" rights for which clerics sought support were, in fact, novel. . . . The authority of these new elites rested less on clerical or lay consensus than on police power.[32]

In the case of the Jews, such new groups as the maskilim and the "notables" were only too happy to take on the mantle of leadership that the state offered them in exchange for loyalty to the regime and a pledge to help carry out the state's intentions with regard to the reform and enlightenment of the Jews.

The Jewish Hospital

In its first decades, much of Kiev Jewry was transient. There were as yet few Jews residing permanently in the city, and apparently many of the Jews who could be seen in Kiev on a daily basis were passing through: itinerant traders carrying their goods, artisans in search of temporary employment, sick Jews seeking medical care, and all manner of other people whom fate had carried to the city on the Dnepr, some of whom arrived without a penny to their names.[33] Such Jews had been coming to Kiev as visitors well before 1861; indeed, a monthly distribution of charity to poor and sick Jews was started as early as 1860—not by their fellow Jews, but by Princess Ekaterina Vasil'chikova, wife of the Governor-General and chair of the Kiev Philanthropic Society for Aid to the Poor.[34] This piece of evidence helps to corroborate contemporary impressions that in the first ten years after Jews were readmitted, it was every man for himself, and most Jews with means were likely to have been too busy establishing themselves to worry about the growing numbers of needy Jews passing through, and sometimes staying on in, Kiev. In addition, wrote the Hebrew poet Yehalel (Yehudah Leib Levin) in 1871, Jewish traders in Podol were divided among themselves, their only common denominator being "the spirit of commerce," and no one was interested in education or doing good (*ve-ein poneh le-haskil u-le-heitiv*).[35]

Another contemporary account, however, maintained that although Jewish charity was administered through a Christian organization, Jewish initiative was, in fact, responsible for this first Jewish charitable undertaking in Kiev. According to the pseudonymous Tmol bar Yente's 1872 account in the Odessa Yiddish weekly *Kol mevaser*, immediately after Jews were permitted to settle in Kiev, the first *otkupshchik* (holder of the franchise for Jewish taxes in Kiev), whom Tmol named only as "B.," donated 10,000 rubles to the Kiev Philanthropic Society, which was headed by Princess Ekaterina Vasil'chikova. "This donation was on such a grand scale," marveled Tmol, "that it was possible to provide for the Jewish poor and sick in the same numbers as for the Christians."[36] Vasil'chikova and Avraam (Avraham) Kupernik, one of the trustees (*popechiteli*) of Jewish charity in Kiev, apparently decided that B.'s donation would be used solely to provide aid to poor Jews.[37] A precedent was thus set that would serve as a model for decades: even if Jews were to be served by Christian or nonsectarian philanthropic institutions, they would almost always be served separately from the Christian population, with discrete funding streams. A description of Jewish philanthropy in Kiev from 1880 confirms that the established community paid for the medical costs of poor Jewish patients in the city's hospitals.[38]

It was not only poor Jews coming to Kiev who needed caring for, but the sick as well, for Kiev was known as a center for medical expertise. Thus, Tmol's account continues, Kupernik suggested to the princess that a Jewish clinic or sick care society [*biker khoylim*] be established, and her subsequent petition to the tsar requesting permission for such a clinic was granted in 1862. This was the genesis of the Jewish Hospital, an institution that would dominate charitable and, to some extent, communal affairs in Jewish Kiev for the next fifty years. The hospital remained part of the Kiev Philanthropic Society until the adoption of its new charter in 1891. According to the hospital's first charter, 2,500 rubles were added to the total amount of the tax to be collected from kosher meat sales, one-fifth of which was to go to the Philanthropic Society (presumably for administrative costs) and the remainder for hospital expenses.[39] In Tmol bar Yente's account, the annual operating budget consisted of 2,500 rubles from the korobka, supplemented by donations from householders and the whole city (meaning, presumably, the entire Jewish community), which brought the total to 3,000 rubles. Thus, from its inception the Jewish Hospital was closely linked both with non-Jewish institutions and society in Kiev and with Jewish taxation in the city, and both connections remained significant in the decades to come.

The dedication ceremony for the new hospital in 1862 was an opportunity for the merchants who made up Kiev's small Jewish community to introduce the city to Jews and Jewish ways. A report in the local paper *Kievskii telegraf* (Kiev Telegraph) explained to readers that the small group of Jews present included "a rabbi, holding in his arms a scroll (Toira [*sic*]) and a cantor, who are necessary for the performance of certain rituals." Also in attendance were Governor-General Vasil'chikov and his wife, the governor of Kiev Province, the marshal of the nobility, trustees of the Philanthropic Society, and many local officials. This audience witnessed, many of them probably for the first time, the recitation of a Hebrew prayer; naturally, it was *Ha-noten teshu'a,* the traditional supplication on behalf of the monarch. While both speakers made clear that the hospital was for indigent Jews coming to Kiev for medical care, they diverged in their vision of the Jewish future in the city; the Governor-General stressed the fact that only Jewish merchants were permitted to live in Kiev, whereas hospital trustee Kupernik chose to emphasize that the hospital's small size (twenty beds) was due only to insufficient resources and that the institution would be expanded as soon as it was possible.[40] Thus, the Russian official indicated that the establishment of the hospital should not be taken as evidence that any expansion of Jewish settlement in Kiev would be viewed favorably, while the Jewish notable painted a picture of continued growth—if not of the Jewish population itself, then at least of its charitable institutions. The location of the hospital—at the city limits in the far reaches of the Ploskaia district, as specified in the hospital's charter—was in itself symbolic of the position of the small and new Jewish community in Kiev. Ostensibly, this area was deemed advantageous because it was near the Kirillov Institution, a mental hospital, almshouse, and school for physicians' assistants, where Jewish Hospital staff would be able to obtain advice for difficult medical cases.[41] Clearly, though, the Jewish institution was placed in the same category as the mental hospital—somewhat undesirable and thus relegated to the outskirts of the city.

The boundaries between Jewish and Christian welfare systems, such as they were, were not yet clearly drawn in these early decades. Not only was the Jewish Hospital formally a branch of the city's Philanthropic Society, but in 1870 the society was also distributing monetary aid to Kiev's poor Jews in advance of the upcoming Passover holiday.[42] As with the hospital, though, both the initiative and the funds for these offerings almost certainly came from Kiev's Jews, a supposition supported by the fact that the list of honorary members in the society's report grouped all the Jews together, after the Christian members, signaling that their participation in this Russian institution was somehow conditioned by their difference.[43] Still, the very fact that a non-Jewish institution was involved in the distribution of aid for a Jewish holiday, and that it was acceptable for Jews to be assisted through the city's general charitable organization, is significant. This phenomenon also points to the fact that Jewish welfare in Kiev was as yet fairly unorganized.

For their part, Jews were eager to show that they, too, were prepared to aid the needy, regardless of confession. In 1866, local Jewish merchants proposed taking up a collection in honor of the miraculous saving of the tsar's life (the reference was to the failed assassination attempt of Dmitrii Karakozov), but they did not immediately determine how to allocate the funds. Eventually, the merchants agreed to establish a fund to assist needy Jewish and Christian students attending local gymnasia.[44] This gesture echoed an earlier charitable donation made by A. M. Brodsky, who added a scholarship endowment for Christian students at St. Vladimir University to a fund for Jewish students already established by Brodsky and other Jewish merchants—in order to emphasize his "sincere rapprochement with his fellow Russian citizens."[45] (Interestingly, the annual benefit events for the cause of Jewish students were well-known in Kiev and attended by Christian as well as Jewish Kievans; an 1865 editorial in *Kievskii telegraf* noted that among the many kinds of entertainment one could enjoy in Kiev, in addition to theater, opera, masquerades, balls, concerts, and restaurants, were spectacles to raise money for poor Jewish students.)[46] These moves were significant, setting a long-term precedent for Jewish charity in Kiev: Jewish philanthropy was to have a political as well as a humane goal, and would exemplify the best of Russian Jewry by illustrating their willingness to live in peace alongside their fellow citizens. More prosaically, providing for Christians helped avoid the appearance of insularity, an important goal for a new Jewish community that was small but growing and whose members interacted on a daily basis with non-Jewish businessmen, merchants, and bureaucrats. Brodsky's move also points up the impact that Kiev's restrictions on Jewish settlement may have had on would-be philanthropists, since they would have wanted to avoid the appearance of attracting illegal Jews to the city.

The Jewish Welfare Committee of Kiev

Examining two cases of Jewish communities founded at the beginning of our period affords us the opportunity to follow the evolution of communal structures and governance from their very inception. In both St. Petersburg and Kiev, Jewish notables came to lead the community. This was not surprising given that under the policy of selective integration, first-guild merchants were the earliest to be allowed to settle in localities of restricted Jewish settlement. In the capital, the Jewish communal governing board was elected, if only by a limited group of merchants and graduates of institutions of higher education.[47] Because of the complex history and status of Jewish rights and restrictions in Kiev, however, the governing board there was not elected or appointed but rather was self-selected, and came to govern the community by fiat. As far as the law on Jewish settlement in Kiev could be clearly interpreted (and much effort was put into such interpretation over the years), the only Jews who enjoyed full residence privileges there—and were not restricted to the neighborhoods of Ploskaia and Lybed—were first-guild merchants. Thus, they were the natural candidates for members of a communal governing board.

Moreover, it was only logical that a welfare board be selected from the Jewish elite, since the law stipulated that local authorities consult with "prosperous and settled" Jews in managing the korobka. As the governor of Kiev province wrote in 1890, "these individuals, by virtue of their social and property status, represent a sufficient guarantee of reliability."[48] The fact that some of these prosperous Jews were members of Kiev's city council made that move all the more natural.[49] (It did not, however, seem natural to all observers of Russian Jewry; some antisemites decried the "tyrannical and despotic" Jewish leadership that, in their eyes, kept control over the Jewish masses with an iron fist, inculcating in them hatred toward Russia.)[50]

Yet it is likely that the authorities had other motives for sanctioning communal governance by the elite in leading communities such as Kiev, St. Petersburg, and Odessa. As we have seen, the Russian government—or at least certain bureaucrats who thought along similar lines—was interested in shaping an acculturated Jewry that would be integrated into Russian society. In their eyes, members of the Jewish elite, who spoke Russian at home, interacted with non-Jews in business and social circles, and practiced a modernized, German style of Judaism, were just the right individuals to be governing communal affairs and deciding priorities. These, then, were the men who eventually constituted the Representation for Jewish Welfare, as the governing board came to be known.

It is not an easy task to reconstruct the history of the Representation for Jewish Welfare, but archival documents, press reports, and several publications of Kiev's Jewish Hospital allow us to trace a sketchy outline of its origins and development. The predecessor of the Representation, the Jewish Welfare

Committee, was originally established to deal exclusively with the affairs of Kiev's Jewish Hospital (in contrast to St. Petersburg, where everything began with a synagogue governing board).[51] The hospital was the city's first and most prominent Jewish institution, and was tended to with great care by the Jewish elite. The revenues from the kosher meat tax in Kiev—which was not formally a korobka but a form of reimbursement to the city for the income lost after the abolition of the Jewish hostels where Jews had been required to stay when visiting the city before 1861—originally went entirely toward hospital expenses, and were thus administered by the Hospital Committee. Several later documents referred to a decision of the city council of August 4, 1875, assigning the responsibility for allocating the kosher excise revenues for the entire Jewish community to the Hospital Committee. For example, "The representatives of the Jewish community [assigned] to deal with the korobka should be the members of the Jewish Committee, which was originally confirmed by the City Council on 4 August 1875 for Jewish Hospital affairs"; ". . . General management of all matters of Jewish welfare falls on the local 'Jewish Committee,' confirmed by the Kiev City Council on 4 August, 1875. . . ."[52]

However, the minutes of the city council show that the committee established was only to deal with hospital affairs; it was not for general communal governance. The fourth point discussed by the council on that day stipulated only "that the administration of the hospital and the management of all hospital affairs be under the authority of the local Jewish merchants, elected by a majority of the city council, and that the revenues assigned from the korobka for the maintenance of the Jewish Hospital be transferred to its control."[53] Apparently, because most of the kosher excise went toward the hospital, it was understood that the Hospital Committee, in allocating revenues for the hospital, would also take care of distributing the balance of funds to Kiev's other Jewish institutions.[54] Thus, the Hospital Committee came to be known as the "Jewish Welfare Committee" or simply the "Jewish Committee."[55]

According to Tmol bar Yente's somewhat obsequious account in *Kol mevaser,* when *balebotim* (householders) and gvirim began to settle in Kiev (i.e., in the early 1860s), a committee on communal affairs was formed of the finest well-to-do Jews (*di sheynste balebotim*).[56] This committee, realizing that government recognition would be vital for its work, submitted petitions to the city duma requesting official approval for their committee so that—in Tmol's words—"there should be named in Kiev a Jewish community [*es zol heysen in Kiev a yidishe obshchestvo*]." The wording here is crucial, as the author employed a Russian word that was usually used to describe a formal association; according to Vladimir Dal''s comprehensive dictionary of the Russian language, compiled in the early 1860s, this was the same word used in the contemporary phrases *dvorianskoe obshchestvo* (noble corporation), *krest'ianske obshchestvo* (peasant association; i.e., the commune), or even *obshchestvo sapozhnikov* (a cobblers' association; i.e., a guild or union).[57] A contemporary archival document on the formation of an official Jewish community in Kiev consistently used the same word.[58] This account seems to imply a somewhat more self-conscious act of organizing a community than that suggested by the documents related to the Jewish Hospital, but we are not in a position to reach a definitive conclusion about how communal governance emerged in this early period—especially since the very term *obshchestvo* was used so loosely in the imperial period and to describe so many different concepts.[59]

In the first few decades of Jewish settlement in Kiev, the Jewish Committee did not attract much attention. We know that in 1876 kosher tax revenues funded the Jewish Hospital as well as prayer houses, the Talmud Torah (school for children of poor families), the bathhouse, and the Crown rabbi's salary; an account from 1880 mentions relatively small sums (up to 2,000 rubles annually) given for the maintenance of Jewish orphans, aid to poor artisans, tuition support for Jewish gymnasium students, and the burial of the dead.[60] Press reports, however, focused instead on the munificent endowments of individual members, above all sugar magnate Israel Brodsky and his son Lazar', to various local institutions, especially the Jewish Hospital: a maternity clinic at the hospital in 1871, a donation of 15,000 rubles in 1875 toward a new building for the hospital, 40,000 rubles for a Jewish trade school in 1880, and in 1884, 50,000 rubles for St. Vladimir's University and 40,000 rubles each for the hospital and a building to house a bathhouse and communal kitchen in 1884.[61] Apparently, Israel Brodsky assisted needy Jews on an individual basis, giving 1,000 rubles a month to alleviate their plight and even more for the more desperate cases.[62]

Starting around 1880, complaints began to appear in the Hebrew press (notably *Ha-melits*, published in St. Petersburg) about the organization—or lack thereof—of charity and welfare in Kiev. Critics charged that benefactors, while generous, gave unsystematically to whichever causes appealed to them or when they were asked to give, while important needs went untended because no one took initiative. Prominent institutions such as the hospital received huge sums of money that could, it was suggested, be better spent on assisting the Jewish poor of Kiev; this particular critique would be heard many times over the decades. One detractor asserted that some wealthy Jews became involved in charitable causes for the sole purpose of making a name for themselves.[63]

Non-Jewish sources were even more critical, seeing in the dominance of the Kiev Jewish plutocracy remnants of the hated kahal; the local newspaper *Kievlianin,* in particular, was (in John Klier's words) "the vigilant watchdog of the reputation of [Brafman's] *Book of the Kahal.*"[64] Its tendentious articles must be examined with great suspicion, yet certain observations are corroborated by other sources: the Jewish Committee was unelected; the funds it managed were not subject to any oversight; and the entire operation lacked accountability—though *Kievlianin,* of course, attributed that defect to the "kahal structure of the local Jewish community." Interestingly, the newspaper claimed that complaints could be heard from the local Jewish population about their so-called "plenipotentiaries" and the disorderly state of their communal institutions.[65] An 1880 account from within the Jewish community seems to confirm this state of affairs: the correspondent wrote that some Kiev Jews grumbled that the Hospital Committee, which ran all Jewish communal affairs in the city, was "usurping various rights and duties."[66] (The hostility was mutual: members of the committee complained that the Jewish community did not appreciate the heavy burden the committee had to carry.) An "exposé" of the internal workings of the Kiev Jewish community in the Judeophobic *Novoe vremia* a decade later also referred to widespread corruption—including charges of nepotism related to the allocation of kosher tax revenues—though the grotesque exaggerations made throughout the article diminish the reliability of this source.[67] The article also claimed that once a week, the Jewish destitute—"a crowd of Jewish ragamuffins"—waited on line in the cold outside of Lazar' Brodsky's mansion as he personally gave out alms by the kopeck to each petitioner.

A more trustworthy measure of the Jewish community's resentment of the committee's policies are two petitions, dated 1890, from a group of Jewish artisans led by two men by the names of Gershtein and Khodes complaining about the lack of accountability on the part of the committee and its unfair allocation of the kosher excise. The tax was paid "almost exclusively" by Jewish artisans, they wrote in their first petition, implying that the men who managed the tax did not pay it themselves (which, it is to be presumed, also meant that they did not personally follow the laws of kashruth). When the petitioners had applied to the municipality and other official bodies for information on who, exactly, constituted the Jewish Committee, the authorities refused even to identify them. In an apparent reference to the uncertain legal status of the committee, the writers of the petition remarked that the committee "does not officially exist"; thus, they argued, its members were private individuals—"whether elected by anyone, whether confirmed by the municipality or not, we do not know." Since they could not obtain any information about the committee, the petition continued, they were unable to submit declarations to it about the needs of Kiev's poor artisans. Their request from the Governor-General was to take the committee "under his guardianship," presumably to eliminate its independence and institute official oversight over its activities.[68]

One of the most revealing and even surprising aspects of this document is its assertion that most ordinary Kiev Jews did not even know who sat on the Jewish Committee that served as the de facto governing board for their community. Apparently, they had so little access to the committee and the wealthy circles from which its members were drawn that they felt they had no choice but to appeal for outside assistance to rectify the situation. Moreover, by noting that the committee members were neither elected nor appointed, the petition's authors skillfully made apparent the committee's quasi-legal and near autonomous status, which could never be tolerated by the all-encompassing bureaucracy of the Russian Empire. The accusation that Jews of the upper ranks were using the korobka tax, which they themselves did not pay, to fund their own priorities within the Jewish community was by no means unique to Kiev; the same phenomenon occurred in St. Petersburg and was likely common in most cities and towns large enough to support an acculturated Jewish elite.[69]

In the second petition, submitted six months later, the artisans went even further, requesting that one-quarter of the funds from the kosher excise be allocated directly to be used to care for the needs of poor and disabled Jewish artisans of the city.[70] Although the petitioners did not say so explicitly, it seems clear that they meant for the funds to be granted without the mediation of the Jewish Welfare Committee. In other words, not only were these artisans opposed to the independence of a committee of unelected plutocrats, but they also wanted to remove themselves from the authority of those plutocrats altogether, setting up an alternate institutional structure through which a different class of Jews would enjoy more equitable welfare assistance. These two petitions are evidence of dissatisfaction with the leadership of the elite and of the wide rift between that elite and at least some of the poorer

Jews of Kiev—so wide, indeed, that the institutional links tying them together no longer seemed relevant to the latter group. These documents also constitute a rare window into the structure and functioning of the community, providing insight lacking in other contemporary records because communal organization in Kiev was so opaque and complex.

In his response, the governor took exception to the artisans' desire to manage their own welfare outside of the already established framework. He saw their request as one for special benefits, and argued in response that artisans had no more right to funds than any other poor Jews in Kiev, nor were Jewish artisans to have any undue advantages over Christian artisans that aid from the kosher tax might render. He also made clear the threat he saw in Kiev's Jewish artisans receiving "special" assistance, a practice that might attract even more Jewish artisans to the city in their hopes of receiving a share; as we have seen, most government bureaucrats worried that Kiev would become flooded with Jews from surrounding provinces. Finally, wrote the governor, the artisans had no organization of their own to manage the distribution of benefits.[71] Clearly, the governor did not view with favor the petitioners' proposal of alternate Jewish welfare structures to parallel the existing one.

He may, however, have taken their recommendation to abolish the independence of the Jewish Welfare Committee more seriously than might have been apparent from his initial response, for that step was taken only a few years later. We cannot know, of course, whether the artisans' petition planted a seed in the minds of the responsible officials, articulated an already popular notion, or simply happened to correspond to the very solution eventually devised by the government for the committee. What is clear is that the plutocrats' unquestioned authority was beginning to be questioned both by other Jews and by the government itself, and the doubts regarding that authority on both sides may well have reinforced each other.

As fate would have it, Avraham Kupernik published his *History of the Israelites in Kiev* just as the debate over the Jewish Welfare Committee was roiling the community. Ostensibly, the book had nothing to do with contemporary events, for its *terminus ad quem* was 1865 and it dealt primarily with the pre-expulsion Jewish community of Kiev at the turn of the eighteenth century and arguments made for the readmission of Jews to the city. More specifically, Kupernik reprinted the pinkas of the *hevra kadisha* (burial society), founded in 1794, and mounted a defense of the organization against attacks that were apparently being leveled at it from elements in Kiev society.

Kupernik argued that the pinkas proved that the founders of the society were not alcohol dealers, as was alleged, nor were they corrupt. He stated, more generally, that Jews did not fit the Judeophobe stereotype but were rather charitable and beneficent in their actions. (It is interesting that Kupernik himself started his career in Kiev in 1858 as tax-farmer on alcohol for Kiev province.)[72] Jew-haters, Kupernik took pains to point out, were not the worst enemies of the Jews; those could be found within the Jewish community in the form of Jewish slanderers and backbiters.[73]

Why did Kupernik compose this apologia for the organized Jewish community at this precise moment? As a veteran leader of the Kiev Jewish community, philanthropist, and maskil, he may have chosen this means to respond to what he perceived as an attack on the contemporary communal leadership. Although he was clearly concerned about antisemitic aspersions cast on the community, this Hebrew book was meant for internal Jewish consumption—a rebuke to those who would libel altruistic communal leaders with claims of corruption and malfeasance. His reference to the expulsion that followed the attacks made on the hevra kadisha a century earlier may have been a disguised warning to unruly elements in the community: by assailing the leadership, you are endangering your own position in Kiev, and that of the entire community.

The Municipalization of Jewish Welfare

A number of factors entered into the government's decision to eliminate the autonomy of the Jewish Welfare Committee. As we have seen, the committee had always had ties to the Kiev city authorities, since the kosher meat tax in Kiev was officially municipal revenue and was included in the municipal budget.[74] At the same time, the committee remained basically independent, often functioning and perceived as the de facto Jewish communal governing board. But in 1895 the government moved to sever the last links between the Jewish Welfare Committee and the Jewish community by abolishing the committee and replacing it with a new body within the city administration; the new group was called the Representation for Jewish Welfare (Predstavitel'stvo dlia evreiskoi blagotvoritel'nosti).[75]

It seems that the government's primary concern was the autonomous, unsupervised nature of the committee's workings. The press reported that local authorities were dissatisfied with the way funds had been handled by the committee; for example, sums that were supposed to be allocated to the

Jewish Cemetery Supervisory Administration (the cemetery had been placed under the supervision of committee members several years earlier) had never been recorded in the books of the latter body but "were returned to the general fund of the Jewish Welfare Committee."[76] Kiev newspapers reported that various communal expenses were exceeding income and that the shortfall was being covered by an unknown source; in general, "Jewish institutions are notable for their great secretiveness [*zamknutnost'*], and information about their activities is notable for its exceedingly general nature."[77] These comments point to a familiar trope in the Russian official language regarding Jewish institutions: suspicion of their closed nature was considered to indicate Jewish separatism. Indeed, the Russian government was not comfortable with, and usually deeply suspicious of, private associations of any kind.[78] In Kiev, this meant that even the partial autonomy of the committee could no longer be tolerated. The fact that the Jewish Cemetery Supervisory Administration, another semi-independent body that was abolished and then reconstituted within the city administration, called itself the Kiev Burial Society was also proof that the official Jewish institutions in Kiev were all too characteristically "Jewish" for the authorities' taste. As the governor-general wrote in his memorandum to the minister of the interior, it was a mystery to the local authorities why that body had chosen to call itself the Kiev Burial Society; the unspoken implication was that "burial society," the Russian equivalent of the Hebrew term *hevra kadisha,* was inappropriate for an organization that was not supposed to have retained anything of the traditional association or hevra.[79]

Archival documents show that the municipalization of Jewish communal governance in Kiev took place in the context of the Russian government's wider plan to restrict the activities and influence of Jewish charitable associations that many officials saw as reinforcing Jewish particularism and isolation. As early as the 1860s, the imperial authorities had begun to collect data and opinions on Jewish welfare institutions in order to determine if they should be given government oversight or, perhaps, be banned altogether.[80] The matter was later taken up by the High Commission for the Review of Laws Regarding the Jews (Vysshaia komissiia dlia peresmotra deistvuiushchikh o evreiakh zakonov), which operated from 1883 to 1888.[81] In the early 1890s, A. R. Drentel'n, governor-general of the southwest region, wrote that "Jewish charitable institutions . . . are a formidable tool for the maintenance of national differences and often serve other purposes from those for which they were established. . . . It is essential that this charity . . . not serve as the bearer [conduit, transmitter] of Jewish isolation."[82] The proposed solution was to abolish most such institutions, or at the very least to introduce regulations so strict and narrow that most would be forced to close.

In the early 1890s, departments of the Ministries of Interior and Justice provided opinions on the matter of Jewish charitable societies throughout the empire to the Department of Spiritual Affairs of Foreign Confessions, which was conducting an inquiry into the subject. The economic department of the Ministry of Interior commented in 1891 that the societies needed to be reorganized so that they did not exist in a legal vacuum, unsupervised, especially since they tended to "further Jewish national interests and especially Jewish isolation." The societies were often plagued by corruption and the misappropriation of communal taxes. In short, it might be a good idea to abolish them in most cases, unless the need for the existence of a particular society was clearly demonstrated.[83] The jurisconsultation section of the Ministry of Justice, for its part, noted that the government's goal had to be to restrict the deleterious influence on the Jewish masses of Jewish charitable societies and the powerful individuals who controlled them, and that one method to be employed was abolition, especially of burial societies. However, those individuals would likely retain their power even if the societies were banned.[84] A memoir written by chairman of the Committee of Ministers, N. Kh. Bunge, sometime during the last years of the reign of Alexander III expressed similar sentiments, as it recommended the abolition of particularist Jewish institutions and the subjection of Jews to "the authority of local governments at every level."[85] It is thus no surprise that two years later, in 1893, the department of spiritual affairs corresponded with officials in Kiev about the possibility of abolishing that city's Jewish Welfare Committee and the Jewish Cemetery Supervisory Administration.[86]

At about the same time, the new governor-general, Lieutenant-General Count A. P. Ignat'ev, argued that Jewish charitable associations filled an important need in the Jewish community and that existing official welfare institutions could never take on the extra burden should their Jewish counterparts be abolished. Ignat'ev nonetheless admitted that most of the Jewish societies remained "inaccessible to government supervision and frequently governed by individuals pursuing narrowly nationalist and sometimes illegal goals. . . ."[87] His ambivalence about the need for separate Jewish institutions points to the continuing inconsistency in official policy about Jewish integration into Russian society: Jewish isolation needed to be eliminated so as to do away with the deleterious influence of Jewish separatism on Russian society, yet the abolition of restrictions and independent Jewish institutions would inevitably mean an influx of Jews into Russian institutions of all kinds—a proposition that made most officials very uncomfortable, given the widely accepted understanding that the "native" population needed protection from the Jews. Moreover, as an exchange in 1903 between interior minister V. K. Plehve and finance minister S. I. Witte about a proposed Vilna Jewish workhouse illustrates, the government regarded Jewish poverty as a threat to the very well-being of the empire, and Jewish welfare institutions as crucial in keeping the dissatisfaction and hostility caused by that poverty to a minimum. At the same time, the government could not be seen to be granting "special privileges" to Jews by allowing them to establish large numbers of Jewish institutions.[88] A compromise the government could live with was the coopting of Jewish communal welfare into the mechanism of the state itself, which would ensure official oversight of Jewish activities while keeping the state from having to take over the day-to-day administration of Jewish welfare institutions. This arrangement was, in the government's eyes, particularly suited for a city like Kiev, whose administrators were uneasy about its rapidly growing Jewish population and did not feel it proper for large numbers of independent Jewish institutions to take root there. (Their ambivalence and inconsistency on these matters is pointed up by the official removal of the Jewish Hospital from the administrative structure of the Kiev Philanthropic Society in 1891. In this case, a major Jewish philanthropic institution was actually excluded from the purview of a body with quasi-official status and granted independence—presumably because it was no longer deemed appropriate or feasible for such a large and visibly Jewish institution to be officially associated with a nominally Christian establishment.)[89]

In another memorandum of 1893, the governor-general warned that it would be counterproductive to ban all Jewish participation in the allocation of excise revenues, since alienating Jews from welfare affairs would lead to their ceasing charity work altogether or organizing charity independently, without any government oversight at all.[90] His prediction was not fulfilled. As we shall see, the city's takeover of the Jewish Welfare Committee did little to improve the delivery of services or assistance to the city's Jews, and thus actually added to the existing resentment of governance by the plutocrats. In this way, it may have served—along with the 1897 model charters law, facilitating the creation of voluntary societies throughout the empire—to encourage the establishment of myriad new Jewish associations in Kiev.

At exactly the same time that the Representation for Jewish Welfare was being established, new regulations were decreed for the elections of synagogue boards. As in the case of the communal governing board, Kiev was to join St. Petersburg as both a test case and a model for Russian Jewry. The positions of elder and treasurer, corresponding to responsibilities in traditional synagogue governance, were abolished and replaced by "members" and "alternates," terms more familiar to the world of voluntary associations than traditional religious bodies. Moreover, a voting requirement was introduced, limiting the franchise to those paying at least 10 rubles a year in dues, a high sum that for the most part restricted voting to merchants.[91] Most importantly, in locations outside the Pale of Settlement boards governing communal matters (*dukhovnye pravleniia*) were no longer permitted; only boards regulating the financial affairs of a synagogue (*khoziaistvennye pravleniia*) were allowed.[92] In effect, all communal self-governance was expropriated by the government, leaving the Jewish community to govern itself solely on the level of the synagogue—and even here its responsibilities were limited to those of a financial nature.

But restricting participation in the synagogue was also cause for ambivalence among some officials, this time about the power of the Jewish elite over its poorer coreligionists. As we have seen, bureaucrats at the Ministry of Justice were concerned that powerful Jews not be allowed to continue to hold power and exert their harmful influence on the Jewish masses. This attitude probably stemmed from the widely held conception among bureaucrats and Russian nationalists that Jewish figures of authority used their control of Jewish institutions to inculcate hostility toward the Russian state and society in the Jewish masses.[93] The newspaper *Kievlianin* had long expressed concern about the oppression of the Jewish poor at the hands of wealthy Jews who controlled the Jewish community.[94] A memorandum from the governor-general's office to the Ministry of Interior brought this question to bear on the issue of synagogue board elections: while the authorities in St. Petersburg might be interested in regularizing Jewish religious bodies and bringing them into line with similar Russian institutions, the author was concerned about the growing influence of the wealthy in the Jewish community, which the proposed regulations only abetted. Even if the minimum dues were lowered to 10 rubles per year, he argued, there were still two prayer houses in Ploskaia, a poor Jewish neighborhood, that would have to shut down for lack of dues-paying members to elect a board. Those Jews would then have to attend other prayer houses, where they would be nonvoting worshipers and thus subject to the authority of the wealthy. Such dependence, he continued, would only exacerbate the already unhealthy situation of Jewish communal governance in Kiev: "If the Jewish masses are put in such a situation, it will significantly strengthen the influence of the Jewish capitalists, who are even now almost all-powerful masters of the Kiev Jewish community, answerable to no one." He recommended setting the minimum annual dues necessary for voting eligibility at 5 rubles.[95]

Criticism of the Representation for Jewish Welfare

The annexation of the Jewish Welfare Committee by the municipality, which deprived it of its independence but lent it the authority and imprimatur of the Russian government itself, only served to widen the gap between the members of the committee and their wards. This should not be surprising, given that the new body, the Representation for Jewish Welfare, was staffed by the same plutocrats as the old committee, and moreover was now part and parcel of the city administration that so many Kiev Jews regarded with suspicion and hostility, given its generally antagonistic approach toward the city's Jewish community, of which the frequent nighttime roundups and arrests of illegal Jews were only the most obvious example. Indeed, complaints about the Representation's unresponsiveness to the needs of Kiev Jewry began to multiply right around the time that the body was established. This held true despite the representatives' initial attempt to establish a certain measure of independence vis-à-vis local authorities, as seen in their successful appeal of the city's initial order that only Jews holding Kiev residence permits would be eligible to receive assistance from the Representation (as opposed to the thousands of temporary Jewish residents).[96] A clear illustration of the wariness of Kiev Jews about the welfare administration is the warning given by one frequent correspondent from Kiev in the pages of the Jewish newspaper *Ha-melits,* who, even as he was praising the actions of the new Representation, wrote, "I am writing this in *Ha-melits* so that the benefactors of our city will know that their actions are being watched, and they should continue to do acts of charity for all days, and so that all those engaged in communal affairs should do the same."[97]

At first, the founding of the Representation for Jewish Welfare seemed to bode well. Under the new system, charity was systematized; for example, before Passover the city was divided up into districts and the would-be recipients of holiday assistance had to apply to their district board, which then decided on eligibility.[98] The needy had previously received cash, but were now given packages of matzah, wine, meat, and potatoes; according to the report of a correspondent who was thrilled with the new dispensation, this change eliminated improprieties such as using the Passover charity to bid on synagogue honors or to purchase valuables or household goods. In years past, funds had even gone missing.[99] Russian Kiev agreed: after the Passover of 1895 ended, one Jewish newspaper reported that Kiev's Russian press had praised Jews for their holiday charity and the orderly manner in which it had been distributed.[100]

The new order did not, however, please everyone. Some Jews were apparently unhappy about having to "grovel" to those who distributed the food, likely a reference to the required application to the local district board; it is probable that Passover aid had previously been given to anyone who declared that he or she was in need.[101] More important, however, is the fact that the new arrangement brought into relief the lack of accountability of the Representation. The Municipal Statute of 1892 denied Jews in cities outside the Pale of Settlement any representation in their municipal government; hence, if Jews had had little say in the decisions of the Jewish Welfare Committee, they were now even more disenfranchised, given that the Representation for Jewish Welfare was officially part of the municipal government.[102] Despite the fact Jewish "representatives" still sat on the committee, most Kiev Jews had no voice in how the money they paid in taxes was spent, just as they had no voice in how their city was run. Indeed, the electoral restrictions of the municipal statute and the abolition of the independent Jewish Welfare Committee were part of a broader trend of widening limitations on Jewish participation in communal and public affairs, which also included a decision in 1891 by the Committee of Ministers allowing the Kiev municipality to appropriate additional funds for itself from the kosher tax revenues.[103]

Evidence of general rancor against the Representation for Jewish Welfare was now found not only in sealed petitions such as those submitted by the artisans in 1890, but also openly, in the press. In 1899, the korobka system in Kiev received national attention after a correspondent from Kiev wrote a letter to the editor of the Russian-language Jewish weekly *Khronika Voskhoda,* complaining that those who distributed revenues did not consult with taxpayers, thus leading to a situation in which the municipality spent the money on whatever it chose. The author claimed that a recent gala dedication of Kiev's new port had been paid for out of the korobka proceeds, and thus out of the pockets of the Jewish destitute.[104] In a subsequent letter to the editor,

Kiev's Crown rabbi P. A. Iampol'skii—a member of the Representation for Jewish Welfare—defended the Kiev korobka, writing that the city administration had "always energetically defended the interests of the Jewish population." Iampol'skii claimed that it was only after the provincial government had usurped the tax from the city and made drastic cuts in allocations that circumstances for Kiev's Jews had declined.[105] The editor of *Khronika Voskhoda* then weighed in with his own commentary: the Kiev kosher excise, as the only municipal tax in the empire to be levied from subjects of a particular faith, was illegal; the Jewish masses should not have to shoulder the burden; and Jewish representatives, rather than defending the tax, should be defending the interests of the Jewish poor. This, he claimed, they were not doing.

Perhaps it was no coincidence that the very same issue of *Khronika Voskhoda* printed a report from Kiev about a new Jewish day shelter for children, established jointly by the Kiev Society of Day Shelters for Children of the Working Class and the wife of a local Jewish doctor. The paper's correspondent condemned the "indifference" of the Jewish aristocracy. According to him, it was imperative that the Kiev Jewish community (i.e., the Representation for Jewish Welfare) make this institution a priority; indeed, the center, established without initiative or assistance from the Representation, was proof of the apathy of the Jewish elite.

> It's shameful to say: despite the influence and wealth of the representatives of the community, there is still much to do here. The huge numbers of poor artisans and employees do not even have the opportunity to give their children elementary education; we do not have even one Jewish school, and other basic needs also go unmet.[106]

Clearly, the communal board was out of touch with its constituents, and was ignorant or neglectful of their most elementary needs. What was required of the representatives, continued the correspondent, was an entirely new approach to communal affairs to replace the current inertia: energetic activity in order to encourage public initiative, reorganize and ameliorate existing institutions, and establish new ones.

Another Kiev Jew writing to *Voskhod* seconded the charge that the plutocrats were out of touch with the reality of most of Kiev's indigent Jews. If the organizers of Jewish welfare in Kiev were simply to become acquainted with the living conditions in the Jewish slums, they would know how better to assist their denizens. "Unfortunately, the contributors are too far away from the poor folk and their circumstances." What was really needed was proper housing, instead of the current hovels, and employment opportunities so that the poor could make an honest living. In essence, the author was calling for a modern welfare system that went far beyond what traditional Jewish charity had attempted to provide. Moreover, the attempts the Representation had made to systematize welfare were apparently unsuccessful, at least in the eyes of some critics; the letter charged that "a central organization to coordinate the aid" was still lacking.[107]

The day shelter was only one of a number of independent voluntary associations and institutions established after the government's introduction of model charters for charitable associations in 1897 (another leading example were sanatoria for Jewish tuberculosis patients, of which Kiev had several).[108] This measure regularized and facilitated the establishment of such associations by providing them with a standard set of by-laws that, in most cases, had to be approved of only by the provincial governor and not the minister of the interior in St. Petersburg.[109] Indeed, in late 1899 the editor of *Khronika Voskhoda* noted that "there are more and more 'Societies to Aid the Needy' cropping up all over the place, in every community," and that they were now transparent and accountable, thanks to the new model charters law. However, the new organizations were having to do battle with the old societies, run by the "notables" and often infamous for embezzling or other financial improprieties, since the trend was now moving toward uniting all Jewish welfare institutions under one roof. The notables did not want to give up their independent fiefdoms.[110] The editor's observation on the ubiquity of Jewish charitable associations was in line with reality, for they made up almost half of all those founded in the Russian Empire in 1898.[111]

The notables of Kiev were no exception: they too did not want to give up control over the Representation for Jewish Welfare and the power it embodied, nor would they allocate funding for the new societies. Calls for an elected governing board began to multiply. In a series of articles entitled *Letters from Kiev*, an anonymous author defended the Representation for Jewish Welfare from charges of abuse, but at the same time suggested diplomatically that the Kiev Jewish community would benefit greatly from an elected communal governing board. The current members of the Representation, he insisted, approached their responsibilities conscientiously, but since they were chosen by the city administration, they tended to be financiers and industrialists who had little extra time to devote to communal affairs and in general were indifferent to "the new needs of Jewish life."[112] Elections with the participation of all Kiev Jews would bring "new, fresh, and energetic forces" to the Representation and to Jewish welfare in Kiev.[113] Such forces were now essential, he argued: with the huge influx of Jews, mostly poor, into Kiev in recent years, "a vital need has arisen for the expansion of the existing philanthropic institutions and the organization of new forms of communal assistance."[114] Against claims, perhaps heard from the representatives, that Kiev's peculiar status did not allow for an official (i.e., elected) Jewish governing board, the author noted that the city already had an elected Crown rabbi.[115]

Interestingly, the suggestions found in *Letters from Kiev* are quite similar to those that had been made by St. Petersburg rabbi Avram Neiman almost thirty-five years earlier in a report to the governor of St. Petersburg province, in which he described the "disorders and stagnation" that troubled the community. In St. Petersburg as in Kiev, communal leaders were too busy with their own business affairs to attend to their voluntary commitments. Neiman suggested that elections were necessary in order to provide the community with the stability and firm foundation that it needed. Also common to both cities' Jewish communities was the charge of corruption in communal elections.[116]

To a certain extent, the figures for the korobka budget in the 1898–1902 period, cited in *Letters from Kiev*, spoke for themselves. More than one-quarter of the 116,000 rubles in income were handed over to the municipality and the police department. Of the balance, fully 45 percent went to the Jewish Hospital—the favored institution of the Jewish elite—18 percent were designated for burial and cemetery expenses, and 17 percent to pay the salaries of the Crown rabbi and the kosher inspectors. Only 12 percent of the funds were left for the Representation's own programs for the needy: aid to the indigent and unemployed, care for orphans, and Passover assistance. The only outside organizations to receive allocations were prayer houses and the city's subsidized cafeterias—a total of 1,800 rubles, or 2 percent of the total.

Accounts from Kiev testified to the fact that the city's Jews were not miserly in their charity: private individuals gave donations in addition to the kosher excise revenues, but because the Representation for Jewish Welfare was either incompetent at distributing to those in need or did not take responsibility for doing so at all, the funds were delivered late or to the wrong recipients.[117] The veteran Jewish welfare organizations in Kiev were also accused of lacking supervision over funds, secrecy in accounting, and nepotism; the Jewish organizations were contrasted to charitable societies of Kiev's Catholic and Lutheran communities, which were governed according to the 1897 model charter, publishing annual reports and avoiding a great deal of red tape.[118]

One piece of evidence hints that not all the blame should have been placed on the shoulders of the Representation for Jewish Welfare, but rather that the policies of the government were at least partially responsible for the absence of well-organized Jewish welfare in Kiev. In 1897, three prosperous Jewish merchants, including Lazar' Brodsky, petitioned the authorities to allow the establishment of a Society for Aid to Poor Jewish Artisans and Workers, arguing that the money that was currently being spent on assistance to needy artisans was not having its desired effect because of the unsystematic nature of the aid and the lack of official government sanction. The provincial governor recommended that the application be rejected, remarking that the establishment of such a society would attract even more Jewish artisans to Kiev and prove harmful for Christian craftsmen. The governor-general acted on his subordinate's advice, noting that "rich Jews can provide material assistance to their coreligionists without establishing a special society."[119] Not surprisingly, such government bureaucrats felt that it was safer to leave welfare activities in the hands of the wealthy, who were, it was felt, generally more reliable than poor Jews who had a reputation for revolutionary tendencies. Thus, it may well be the case that at least some Jewish "notables" in Kiev *wanted* to establish other, independent welfare institutions, but were not permitted to do so.

The author of *Letters from Kiev* who had suggested that the representatives be elected, noting that the Kiev Jewish community already had an elected official—the Crown rabbi—turned out to be quite prescient. And it was no coincidence that he was writing in 1901, the year the government made regulations governing rabbinical elections uniform throughout the entire empire and enfranchising all members of synagogues and prayer houses, regardless of how much they paid in dues.[120] While extending the vote to many more than had had it previously, the government was also following the policy it had set down decades before: the Jewish community was to be defined as a religious entity only—hence, the official rabbi was to be elected by dues-paying "parishioners" only, and not simply by any Jew. The elected status of the rabbi quickly became a flashpoint for many of the issues of governance and power in the community. It is thus important to review the history and nature of the Crown rabbinate in Kiev before proceeding further.

The Crown Rabbinate of Kiev

A Crown rabbi [*kazennyi ravvin*] was at first appointed for Kiev immediately after the city was opened to Jewish residence in 1861, but the Jewish merchants who had settled there protested that they wanted an elected rabbi, an educated man who would command respect. In the election that ensued, Evsei Tsukkerman, a new graduate of the state rabbinical seminary in Zhitomir, defeated one Avraham Binshtok to become Kiev's Crown rabbi.[121] Tsukkerman was indeed fortunate to obtain the position in Kiev. A young graduate of a state seminary—so different from most Jews in his European dress and secular customs—often spent years struggling to be more than a functionary recording vital records in the metrical books and writing reports, the responsibilities to which many communities attempted to limit the official rabbi.[122] Many also received meager salaries apportioned to them by communities that preferred to save their funds to pay the salary of the "real" rabbi (the so-called spiritual rabbi [*dukhovnyi ravvin*]).[123]

Unlike many state rabbis at the time, Tsukkerman had received a traditional Jewish education and was reasonably well-versed in Jewish law and lore. Though many official rabbis were treated by their Jewish communities as little more than lower-level bureaucrats, those in the newer communities of the southern Pale often had some success in making a place for themselves as organizers of communal affairs, welfare, and charity, thus earning the trust of their communities—as Tsukkerman was to do quite effectively.[124] Indeed, Kiev, a new community without the established traditions of most Jewish towns, was the ideal post for a new Crown rabbi.

Because Kiev's Jewish community governing board, at least in its first years, was a self-selected group of merchants and businessmen, men on the path of embourgeoisement and acculturation, it is no surprise that they requested the right to choose their own rabbi. Unlike most Russian Jews of the period, they saw in the Crown rabbi a religious official and, as such, someone who would be in the public eye and, perhaps more importantly, representing the community to the government. Judging from his three decades-plus term of service, Tsukkerman did his job well. He was reelected time and again, always by the same small circle of first-guild merchants, the only Jews with full privileges in Kiev. He served them well, delivering homilies and sermons at community events and dedications (in Russian, as correspondents to Jewish newspapers noted proudly).[125] In the 1880s and 1890s, he was among the leaders of the drive to obtain permission for a Western European–style choral synagogue, which was clearly to be a house of worship for the more acculturated elite and bourgeoisie.[126]

Eventually, Tsukkerman himself was able to join the ranks of the elite he served: he was granted personal Honored Citizen status, which bestowed a number of valuable privileges on its bearer. In 1886, he even petitioned for this status to be made hereditary in recognition of his twenty-five years of service to the Kiev Jewish community. In a revealing evaluation of the worth of his own work as a Crown rabbi, he argued in his petition that had he been a merchant, he would have received hereditary Honored Citizen status after only twenty years—and were not his achievements at least as valuable as trade?[127] His salary toward the end of his career, approximately 6,000 rubles per annum, was a great deal of money by any measure of the time.[128] While slyly poking fun at the rabbi, in his memoir Sholem Aleichem also conveyed his impression of Tsukkerman's striking stature and mien, which may also have served him well in securing and maintaining his position: "Compared to [all the crown rabbis of the smaller towns he had known], the Kiev crown rabbi was a magnate. Compared to him, they were monkeys, midgets. He was a giant. A good-looking man. His one flaw was that he had a sallow complexion and was phlegmatic. He spoke slowly, moved slowly, thought slowly. A man without fire."[129]

In the eyes of some, the money used to pay Tsukkerman's wages was well spent, for he was an advocate for the Jewish poor as well as the wealthy and middle class, and he was praised in the empire's Jewish newspapers for his dedication to the less fortunate. In the early 1870s, he intervened in the running of the city's Talmud Torah to insist that its pupils be properly fed during the school day; a correspondent to *Kol mevaser* from Kiev wrote, "Luckily, the Rabiner Tsukerman endeavored to ensure that some of the children would receive food from the communal soup kitchen [*gorkekh*]."[130] As one report from Kiev related in the 1880s, "since his election, Rabbi Tsukkerman has initiated a number of important projects, and he is always looking out for the welfare of the poor."[131] Another writer described him as "the spirit of all charitable enterprises here."[132] Among the philanthropic projects he reportedly helped initiate were a society to provide artisan training for poor Jewish youths and a fund to provide financial aid to poor Jews attending Kiev's gymnasia.[133] His influence with non-Jews was another boon to the community; for example, in an article he wrote for *Kievlianin,* he defended the legitimacy of oaths taken by Jews, putting to rest the doubts of many local judges who had read an earlier article about the supposed simple annulment of oaths offered by the Talmud.[134] Tsukkerman was also active in local Hebrew culture and Palestinophile organizations such as the Judaica library, the Society of Lovers of Jewish Science and Literature, and the local branch of the Palestinophile Hibbat Zion (see chapter 4 for more on these organizations).[135]

Tsukkerman not only worked behind the scenes to initiate projects, but also held important leadership roles in the community's institutions. Thus, for example, Israel Darewski, a frequent correspondent from Kiev and an expert on local history, wrote that Tsukkerman was serving as the chairman of a select committee appointed to supervise the excise tax contract and its orderly execution and accounts, since the law gave responsibility over the korobka to the Crown rabbi.[136] At various times he was also a member of the Jewish Hospital Committee (1875), the Pogrom Aid Committee (1881), and boards of other institutions. Tsukkerman was also one of the overseers of the Talmud Torah in Kiev's heavily Jewish suburb Demievka.[137]

In 1892 Tsukkerman engineered a takeover of Kiev's burial society that was widely viewed as a triumph for the benefit of the community. According to Darewski, the society had been run by Jewish soldiers, dating back to the previous period of Jewish settlement in Kiev in the early nineteenth century. Burials were carried out crudely and without dignity, and the finances were totally hidden, but no one had dared to wrest control of the society from their hands until Tsukkerman stepped in, using his connections in high places to successfully request that a new burial society be authorized. The takeover clearly benefited the reigning Jewish plutocracy, for the new burial society was to be led by "the heads of the Jewish community of Kiev," twelve trustees to be chosen by the municipal administration, "great men of Torah and of wealth."[138]

The burial society episode was characteristic for its time. In the same period when new, independent relief societies began to crop up throughout the empire, a parallel trend toward centralization was also occurring. In some places, the new modern welfare association naturally coopted existing aid organizations (the traditional *hevrot*) by virtue of the education and resources—and therefore better access to funds and government assistance—of its more acculturated and often younger leaders. In cities and large towns, it was almost universally true that the new associations were led by the most influential members of the Jewish community, often those with secular education, wealth, and connections, or some combination of the three. Knowledge of the law and connections in high places also often meant easier access to korobka funds, no small asset in the cash-starved Jewish communities of the Russian Empire.[139] And the modern associations, with their promise to alleviate the poverty of Russian Jews through the most up-to-date methods of relief, attracted the energies of young, acculturated Jews; such Jews had had no interest in participating in the old hevrot, which, in addition to their reputation for shady financial dealings and lack of transparency, lacked the social incentives offered by the modern obshchestvo.[140]

Kiev's situation, however, was somewhat different. Its main welfare institution was not organized along the lines of the new associations, but was a closed, unaccountable group without a membership. It did not seem interested in adopting the methods of "scientific charity" espoused by the new voluntary sector. Moreover, in the case of the takeover of the burial society, the abolition of the hevra and the transfer of its responsibilities to the new association were coerced. Such phenomena were not unique; in Khotin (in Bessarabia), for example, the municipal administration ordered that all the property of the old Jewish welfare organization be transferred to the new Jewish Relief Society.[141] However, in Kiev, the "expert Jew" Aaron Tseitlin had, only a few months before the burial society takeover, been asked by the governor-general to compile a report on the history, necessity, and utility (or lack thereof) of the Jewish hevra kadisha and specifically Kiev's Jewish burial society; this may have signaled, as right-wing newspapers were warning, that the authorities were unhappy with the state of affairs in this sector of the Jewish community.[142] In that case, Tsukkerman's actions, perhaps motivated by information he had obtained through his many well-placed contacts, may well have saved an important institution of Jewish Kiev from restriction (abolition was unlikely) by the authorities. From this perspective, the "coercion" appears rather different.

Some outspoken members of the community were probably not surprised at Tsukkerman's actions against an independent communal institution—and potential rival for leadership—on behalf of the powerful elite. Such critics saw a different side of him, and paid less attention to his activities in the charitable sphere than to his connections to the Jewish oligarchs and possible explanations of his incredibly lengthy tenure in the post—thirty-three years, one of the longest of any Crown rabbi. In the mid-1890s, allegations began to emerge that Tsukkerman was in the pocket of Kiev's Jewish elite, with Lazar' Brodsky at its head, and that kosher excise funds paid by Kiev's poor Jews were being used to pay the salary of a rabbi who fought *against* the interests of those very Jews. It was argued that the Crown rabbi's long dependence upon certain wealthy members of the community had stripped him of his ideals.[143]

In 1896, a Kiev Jew by the name of Lev Shtammer wrote a letter to the local newspaper *Kievskoe slovo,* claiming that Tsukkerman, the Jewish plutocrats, and the authorities had colluded to limit the electorate and the candidate pool to make the rabbi practically "irremovable." Those who truly cared about the rabbinate did not have the right to vote in the Crown rabbinical elections.[144] Shtammer may even have gone as far as to submit a petition to the local authorities on the matter. An internal memorandum of the Kiev municipal administration from 1896 maintained—apparently in response to a claim (from Shtammer?) that the most recent rabbinical elections had been illegitimate—that, *despite the lack of participation by local artisans,* the rabbinical elections of 1894 had "in no way been compromised."[145] Archival records show that the circle of those eligible to participate in rabbinical elections was indeed small; in 1884, for example, invitations were sent to only 134 individuals out of a total Jewish population of at least 11,000.[146] The very fact that the elections were announced by invitation or, at best, by the placement of a tiny notice in the local papers was, according to Shtammer, proof that a deliberate attempt was being made to ensure a specific outcome—that Tsukkerman would remain in the position of Crown rabbi. The wealthy Jews cared so little about the rabbinate—presumably because, since they had little need for religion, their only use for the rabbi was as a metrical records clerk—that only those who intended to vote for Tsukkerman actually showed up at the polling place. Further, argued Shtammer, the election was announced in such a way as to guarantee that no other applicants would have time to present their candidacies.

A pamphlet that Shtammer wrote a decade later was even harsher in its indictment of Tsukkerman and his patron Lazar' Brodsky. Shtammer accused Brodsky of using his unlimited power in the community before each rabbinical election to ensure Tsukkerman's election—but only after the latter fawned upon him, "our Jewish protector [or champion, *zashchitnik*]," to guarantee his own success. Why was it that only the Jewish elite could vote in Kiev, when rabbinical elections were open to the entire Jewish community in all other locales? It was, claimed Shtammer, because Tsukkerman had craftily taken advantage of a previous case in a far-off provincial town, in which the circumstances were completely different, in order to argue that Kiev's Jewish artisans and clerks were actually "nonresidents." He had thus managed to disenfranchise all of Kiev's Jewish poor in one stroke.[147]

The plot thickened, continued Shtammer. Because of Tsukkerman's growing self-assurance in his position, he had neglected to pay proper obeisance to provincial authorities, who then initiated an inquiry into the legal status of Kiev's rabbinical elections. When the Ministry of Internal Affairs declared that all of Kiev's Jews, including artisans and clerks, were eligible to vote for Crown rabbi, Brodsky and Tsukkerman hastily pressed for legislation to avert a universal franchise: the Crown rabbi would now be chosen by electors, who would in turn be elected by members of Kiev's prayer houses. And, according to Shtammer, a subsequent petition that was granted by the authorities defined members as those paying over 10 rubles a year.[148] That sum was high enough to exclude most of Kiev's Jews, working-class artisans and clerks, from eligibility, as a 1907 petition from poor parishioners of a Kiev prayer house demonstrates. As with rabbinical elections, elections for synagogue boards were limited to those paying at least 10 rubles a year, which the petitioners protested gave control over their prayer house to the wealthy.[149]

This was probably not the only case in which a Crown rabbi used questionable means to ensure his reelection, since all Crown rabbis had to face election every three years, meaning that if they wanted stable employment they had either to win the trust of the community or limit the electorate to those who trusted them. The general rule for election of a Crown rabbi was that he, along with the spiritual rabbi, had to be elected by all "synagogue pewholders."[150] This eventually also became the rule for Kiev, and probably meant all those who paid above a certain amount in dues. But Tsukkerman was likely in a very different position from most, since his job was virtually guaranteed and he had only to please the wealthy. He was thus in a position to do some unpopular things, such as introducing reforms in worship—as in the case of the Choral Synagogue.

Kiev's Choral Synagogue

The burial society was not the only Jewish institution that the plutocrats took over and made their own. In order to make possible the German-style choral synagogue that they sought to establish, a group of notables apparently engineered the takeover of an existing traditional prayer house. The complicated history of the Kiev Choral Synagogue illustrates the growing rift between wealthy, russified Jewish merchants and industrialists and their maskilic hangers-on and the unacculturated Jewish majority of the city.

The image projected by the traditional prayer houses, and those who prayed in them, was clearly a source of anxiety for some Jews in Kiev—and not only there. In 1869 (perhaps after a trip to Kiev?), Alexander Tsederbaum, editor of the Odessa-based Hebrew *Ha-melits* and the Yiddish *Kol mevaser,* berated Kiev's Jews (particularly Hasidim) for attracting attention by insisting on wearing heavy prayer shawls and traditional Sabbath garments in the street even in the summer. Kiev had no *eruv* (ritual boundary to mark off a symbolic private space to enable one to bypass the prohibition of carrying on the Sabbath) and carrying on Sabbath was thus forbidden. Tsederbaum wrote,

> We don't even want to talk about what a Christian says when he sees such get-ups; the Jew doesn't even care what the Christian thinks, even though he's living in a really Christian city (*ekht kristlikhe shtodt*) and our wise men have said that in a majority-Christian city, Jews should not dress to attract attention.[151]

Tsederbaum's real gripe was with traditionalist rabbis, who insisted that Jews continue to wear the clothing that Jews in Eastern Europe had been wearing for centuries instead of allowing them to dress as their Christian neighbors did. But the trope resurfaced again in the Jewish press, as publicists tried to impress upon Kiev's Jews that they represented Jewry and Judaism to one of the most important audiences in the empire, and should act accordingly. A year later, a local Jew complained in a letter to *Kol mevaser* that "the places where Jews gather to pray in Kiev are shameful"—temporary rented quarters next to pubs that were often littered with garbage.[152] "How do we look to the other residents of the city, to the Christians, who consider the church to be such a holy place?" he asked. "How can people have a better opinion of us if we ourselves do not protect our own honor?" The only respectable place of worship were the rooms rented by a few householders (balebotim) in Podol for the High Holy Days, but that was simply not enough for a city with so many Jews, both residents and passers-through. By 1880, there were four authorized prayer houses in Kiev, only one of which was in Ploskaia, a fact that makes it beyond certain that there were many more existing underground.[153]

There is evidence that the Jewish elite of Kiev began a quest to establish their own prayer house as early as 1867, only a few years after Jews were officially readmitted to the city. In 1866, *Kievlianin* made mention of a "communal synagogue" where the merchants worshiped, and the next year, Rabbi Tsukkerman petitioned for permission to rent a facility "expressly for the Jewish merchantry" in which the latter could hold services—seemingly so they would not have to mix with the poorer artisan folk.[154] (In a letter to the chief of police two years later, Tsukkerman criticized the modes of worship he had observed in three prayer houses in Podol and Ploskaia: "There is noise and disorder, [and] behavior is permitted that is inappropriate for a holy place, such as the smoking of tobacco and the like. There are often arguments between parishioners.")[155] The proposed prayer house was to be located in Podol, where we may assume most Jewish merchants were living at that time.[156] Just a few years later, Tsederbaum called the erection of a synagogue in Kiev "one of the greatest needs" of the local Jewish community.[157]

By 1880, thirty petitioners calling themselves the "educated constituency" of Kiev Jewry requested permission to open their own synagogue, not in Podol but in the center of the city, where there were already more than one hundred Jewish homes.[158] The petition was rejected, but they tried again six years later. In addition to the problem of location—most of the petitioners lived in the central Dvortsovaia and Starokievskaia districts, too far to walk to the existing prayer houses in the outlying neighborhoods—the request explained that

> the internal configuration of the aforementioned prayer houses does not conform to the contemporary religious requirements of educated Jews because of the absence of choral singing and, in general, that order in divine worship which has already been introduced into Jewish prayer houses in several important Russian cities such as Petersburg, Moscow, Odessa, and others.[159]

Choral singing and orderly worship, the two elements missing from services in the prayer houses, were construed not only as desiderata of the petitioners, but as *requirements*. From their perspective, worshiping in a traditional prayer house was no longer a possibility; they had to have their own synagogue. Thus, they clearly differentiated themselves from the masses of Jews in Kiev: they were "educated" Jews who desired "order" in worship. The desire for an orderly and regularized service is remarkably similar to Osip Rabinovich's depiction (written over thirty years earlier) of the reaction of the young maskil to services in the local prayer house: "The very format of the prayers, with violent cries, hand clapping, convulsive movements, *without any system,* as if in the forest, evoked in us not reverence but horror."[160] Seemingly, little had changed in the traditional Jewish prayer house, prompting the same horrified response in generation after generation of educated Russian Jews. Rather than attend such an institution, the wealthiest of Kiev's Jews requested and received permission to establish chapels or prayer quorums in their own homes; others apparently preferred to worship at home on an individual basis rather than attend a prayer house, a practice reminiscent of Moses Montefiore's private synagogue on the grounds of his Ramsgate estate.[161]

The petition went on to aver that without a modern synagogue, the younger generation—which was not attending services at all—"is thus deprived of the moral support that all find in religion and can more easily fall prey to pernicious influences."[162] We learn, then, that even if the heads of families were attending services at a private home, their children and other younger Jews (students, for example, who were explicitly named in a later petition) were not, and evidently had no other consistent or reliable link to Judaism at all. Indeed, an 1893 report in the Hebrew press on the progress in the matter of the choral synagogue voiced the hope that the new institution would attract the Jewish students of the city, who usually spent their Sabbath mornings in Kiev's cafes.[163] Another observer went so far as to claim that the students did not know anything about Judaism—indeed, the very spirit of Judaism was foreign to them—and that a modern-style synagogue was the only hope for attracting them to services, for they would never attend the traditional prayer houses with their antiquated customs, so distasteful to modern sensibilities. Moreover, the new synagogue promised not only to draw them to worship but also back to Judaism and the Jewish world in general, for "if they come to a modern synagogue, they will learn from the rabbi about the principles of the faith, topics in Jewish history, Sabbath and holidays, and they will honor God and love their people.[164]

For many, then, the choral synagogue promised to be the key to a Jewish future for the acculturated Jews of Kiev: by establishing a respectable Jewish presence in the very heart of the city, it held a promise to stop the flow of assimilation. As maskil Yitshak Yaakov Vaysberg wrote, the new synagogue would be a spiritual center for all the maskilim of the city, not just a theater where diploma-holders would pray once a year. Moreover, the synagogue would be a symbol and model of enlightened Judaism for Kiev's unenlightened Jews, a "holy setting" without such "shameful and disgusting" customs as "chattering and gossiping" during services as were to be found in the Hasidic synagogues.[165] In addition, some Kiev Jews felt that a decorous synagogue housed in a beautiful building in the center of the city was only appropriate for one of the leading Jewish communities of the empire.[166] It would serve a political purpose, wrote Israel Darewski, to improve the image of Jews in the eyes of other Russian subjects, so that in Kiev, "a city that is majority Christian . . . our Christian neighbors will see that we are called by the name of God." He envisioned high-level bureaucrats being invited to the synagogue on the emperor's birthday to behold the loyalty of Jews as they prayed for the ruler and his kingdom.[167]

After having received permission to hold their own high holiday services for several years in succession, the group—including Tsukkerman, L. I. Brodsky, and four others—submitted yet another request for permission to establish their own synagogue in 1893, this time apparently citing the crowded conditions at their current prayer house, the Chizik Synagogue, as justification for a new one.[168] According to Eliezer Friedmann, Chizik had good connections with the chief of police, and the merchants and householders who prayed in his synagogue probably did so because of its central location, close to the city center, but also, perhaps, because of Chizik's connections; Friedmann observed that all the synagogue's parishioners kowtowed to Chizik.[169] In his denial of the petition, the governor remarked that outside of the high holidays, the "Jewish intelligentsia and students" would simply have to worship at one of Kiev's twelve licit prayer houses. They could not establish their own because the law set the number of Jewish prayer houses in Kiev at that number. An appeal to the governor-general was also rejected, the response calling into the question the petitioners' stated motivation for desiring a new prayer house: if the current space was "truly" crowded, they should simply request to move it to a new location.[170] Given the group's many previous entreaties and justifications on the matter, the governor-general had good reason to suspect that its members were concerned not so much with the spaciousness of their surroundings as they were with separating from other Kiev Jews and creating their own place of worship.

The group took the governor-general's advice—but gave it their own particular spin. Two years later, in 1895, they applied not to establish a new prayer house but to move an existing one to a new location. Having left the Chizik Synagogue and become parishioners of an artisans' prayer house in the delapidated Shmidt Building, they requested authorization to relocate to a new plot of land purchased only several months before by Lazar' Brodsky. Since the only existing building on that plot was also too old to be used for their purposes, they suggested tearing it down and erecting a new one. Although the local authorities denied the request, noting that the government had already ruled that no choral synagogue could be built in any part of Kiev, an appeal to the Senate was successful, that body agreeing that the proposed plan was no more than a relocation of an existing prayer house. Thus, permission was finally obtained for the long-awaited choral synagogue—which was officially not a synagogue at all but only a prayer house, albeit to be housed in a grand Romanesque edifice.[171]

Examining the protocols for board elections at the two prayer houses from 1890, we discover that the first, the Chizik Synagogue, was for both merchants and artisans, while the second, in the Shmidt Building, was solely for artisans, the majority of whom were illiterate.[172] By 1895, however, the notables involved in the choral synagogue petition had not only joined the Shmidt artisans' prayer house but even formed a majority on its governing board.[173] There seems little doubt that these men engineered their takeover of the prayer house precisely in order to move it or, more accurately, to *recreate* it, at a new location—the grand edifice that they planned to build on the plot that Brodsky had purchased. The takeover was facilitated by new regulations for the elections of prayer house boards in Kiev introduced by the government in 1895, on the model of those for St. Petersburg: parishioners wishing to vote had to contribute a minimum of 10 rubles a year to gain eligibility, a sum that few artisans could afford.[174] Perhaps some or even most of the original members of the prayer house were pleased that so many notable Kiev Jews had joined their shul, but if they were at all traditionally oriented in their approach to prayer and Jewish custom, they could not have been happy with the style of worship in the new Choral Synagogue (see chapter 4 for more on the details of the innovations introduced there).

Comprehending the government's role in the choral synagogue episode, whether as active participant or passive observer, enhances our understanding of its ambivalent attitude toward Jewish society and its constituent groups. In the 1890s, the government was clearly bent on restricting authority within the Jewish community to the wealthy elite, as demonstrated by the creation of the Representation for Jewish Welfare and the introduction of eligibility requirements for synagogue board elections. Similarly, in 1894 the provincial administration (*gubernskoe pravlenie*) reaffirmed that only Jews with permanent residence rights were allowed to vote in Kiev rabbinical elections.[175] This was natural for a state that was ever more fearful of its impoverished Jewish masses and the revolutionary tendencies they were assumed to harbor. At the same time, however, in other ways it seemed to support broader participation of all Jews in Jewish institutions. Thus, it maintained the regulations allowing all prayer house parishioners in a given community, regardless of their income level, to vote in elections for Crown rabbis and even required that those regulations be applied to Kiev when it discovered in 1901 that the city's prayer houses were not abiding by them.[176] In a similar vein, we have seen that at least one bureaucrat voiced fears that the existing law on prayer house boards would enable "Jewish capitalists" to maintain control in the Jewish community and influence their poorer coreligionists for the worse. In formulating his response to the elite's request to build its choral synagogue, the governor-general wrote that the establishment of such an institution would lead to an undesirable increase in Jewish migration to the city, given "the influence of the local Jewish merchants on their fellow tribesmen (*edinoplemenniki*)." At the same time, because the government maintained that a certain amount of autonomous activity on the part of the masses could be—indeed, *had* to be—tolerated as long it was regulated, a certain number of prayer houses had to be allowed to prevent the multiplication of secret prayer quorums, which would encourage "the development of isolation, fanaticism, and superstition among the Jewish masses.[177] In sum, the tsarist government trusted wealthy Jews only marginally more than their poor coreligionists; the former had to be entrusted with communal leadership, but would probably exploit their wards, while the latter were still unfit to be integrated into Russian society, and their communal and religious activities had to be closely supervised.

Conclusion

As the examples of the Representation for Jewish Welfare, the Kiev Burial Society, and the Choral Synagogue make clear, the plutocracy's authority in Jewish communal governance in Kiev and general prominence in the Jewish community were growing, and so was dissatisfaction with that authority on the part of the city's other Jews. The accusation that the leadership of plutocrats and educated intellectuals was out of touch with its constituents and insensitive to the reality of their lives was bolstered by the thoroughgoing dissimilarity of the world they lived in: they worshiped in a different synagogue, spoke Russian in their homes, maintained a radically different attitude toward Jewish observance, and presumably did not have the constant financial worries of most Kiev Jews. The situation was exacerbated by inconsistent government policies that at times strengthened the hand of the elite while at other times encouraged the expansion of popular authority.

The 1905 Revolution and its aftermath helped abstract ideals of democracy and self-determination become real goals for many Jews in their prayer houses and in their Crown rabbinates. How would communal institutions, so long controlled by Kiev's Jewish elite, fare in the revolutionary era? This story unfolds in part 2, which will explore Jewish socioeconomic, residential, cultural, and religious patterns, as well as relations with Christians, before returning to the subjects of philanthropy and communal governance in chapters 6 and 7.

PART 2
JEWISH METROPOLIS

3

The Consolidation of Jewish Kiev, 1881–1914

In the last thirty-five years or so of Romanov rule, the Jewish population of Kiev continued to grow, and Jews continued to take root in the city despite increasingly strict enforcement of the regulations on Jewish residence there. In this chapter, we will survey the nuts and bolts of Jewish existence in Kiev—numbers, occupations, residential patterns—and then examine the bloody pogrom of 1905, the Beilis Affair of 1911–13, and their impact on the city's Jews. Subsequent chapters will investigate other aspects of Jewish life in this period: Jewish literary and political culture, patterns of acculturation, interethnic relations and antisemitism, charity and philanthropy, and the democratization of communal and cultural politics after 1905. Constantly hampered by official restrictions on Jewish residence and institutional life in Kiev, the city's Jews nonetheless managed to fashion an array of institutions—some legal, others underground—to serve their religious, cultural, educational, and political needs. The revolution of 1905 brought about a flurry of activity in the city's communal and welfare organizations, which rapidly became heavily politicized, but after the first enthusiastic months, the meetings presided over by the Jewish notables and middle-class professionals—well-meaning as they may have been—could have but little relevance for most working-class Jews, struggling to recover from the 1905 pogrom, piece together a living, and survive from day to day without being expelled from Kiev.

Insecurity amid Continued Growth

The 1881 pogrom dealt a heavy blow to Kiev's Jews, especially in the years immediately following the "disorders": according to one source, the Jewish population had dropped to 11,000 by 1885 (the official count had been 14,000 in 1874 and was certainly higher just prior to the pogrom).[1] If true, this would have meant that Jews now formed only 7 percent of Kiev's populace, the lowest level for decades.[2] However, another, more reliable source gives a figure of 18,000 Jews in 1887, so the decrease in population—if there was one at all—was probably slight and fleeting (as is the case throughout the entire period under study in this book, the population statistics available to us are, at best, educated guesses).[3] The city's Jewish population soon returned to its upward trajectory, and Jewish visibility—despite the pleas of the "nobles"—did not diminish but, if anything, only increased, especially in the realm of philanthropy (Jewish philanthropy will be discussed in greater detail in chapter 6). Nor did the pogrom seem to have a decisive impact on Jewish–Christian interaction in the ensuing years; as chapter 5 will show, in the everyday life of Kiev's workplaces, social clubs, and voluntary organizations, a mixture of segregation and integration between Christians and Jews meant that toleration and even camaraderie was practiced in some circles, while interethnic tension and hostility remained a fact of life. Government policies mandating or encouraging segregation, which multiplied in the 1880s and 1890s, bolstered the latter trend. On the other hand, the Kiev Literacy Society counted both Christians and Jews among its board members and operated programs open to individuals of both religions, in addition to courses geared specifically to the needs of Jewish students.[4] The percentage of Jews in some public school districts was as high as 29 percent, but universities and gymnasia imposed quotas on Jewish students, while some private schools barred them altogether.[5] What all this meant for the security of Kiev's Jews is difficult to determine. Residential patterns are similarly ambiguous in meaning for the historian: does the fact that there was a decrease in Jewish residential concentration in a few neighborhoods mean that Jews felt more comfortable living among Christians, or did they fear that the continued existence of Jewish "ghettos" could serve as provocation for animosity and even violence?

One piece of evidence that seems to demonstrate that interethnic tensions were—at least to some extent—always brewing beneath the surface is a report from Kiev in 1884 to a St. Petersburg newspaper, recounting the tale of a dispute between two market-women, one Jewish, the other Russian Orthodox, at the Zhitnyi bazar, which escalated to a brawl that threatened to explode into a full-scale pogrom. According to the report, the Jewish trader's husband, "a hefty Jew," gave his wife's antagonist a whack, whereupon a crowd of artisans and laborers moved in to defend the Russian woman and began to rain blows upon the Jewish man, who managed to escape from their grasp. Part of the throng scattered the Jewish woman's dried fish all over the market, while others went after the woman's husband, crying "Beat the Jews!" A passing trader managed to calm the crowd, averting large-scale violence.[6] Was this a common occurrence? It is difficult to say: on the one hand, opportunities for tensions to erupt were myriad; on the other, the fact that this fracas was worthy of being printed in one of the capital's newspapers suggests that incidents of this kind were rather more rare. The incident may well have started as a simple dispute, without religious or ethnic differences playing a role, and then turned into a brouhaha when someone with an axe to grind began to yell that this was an opportunity to beat the Jews. The many details, sometimes rather peculiar, included in the report seem to vouch for its authenticity, though certain aspects—"the Jew started it by provoking a Christian"; "the mob shouts, 'Beat the Jews!'"—are reminiscent of common tropes from pogrom (or near-pogrom) narratives. (The 1883 pogrom in Ekaterinoslav was touched off by "the cries of a peasant woman at the market" after her unruly son was cuffed by a Jewish salesman.)[7] Perhaps the figure of "the passing trader" is somehow representative of the pacifying effect of the small but growing sphere of civil society in urban Russia; individuals who had meaningful interactions (i.e., outside the realm of commerce) with members of other religious or ethnic groups were less likely to engage in violence against others from the same group. There is no doubt, however, that some Kievans were resentful of the so-called Jewish "takeover" of their city, which was apparently worthy of a long article in one of the capital's newspapers; in 1885, *Sankt-Peterburgskie vedemosti* found that Kiev was "although not yet a zhid city, will undoubtedly be that [soon]."[8] The author deplored the recent "flood" of Jews into Kiev and insinuated that local officials had lost control over who was permitted to settle in the city legally.

There is no doubt that many of Kiev's Jews experienced insecurity on a daily basis, but not because of the threat of physical violence per se. Rather, they lived in "constant anxiety and fear" of the round-up (*oblava*), a phenomenon unique to Kiev and its labyrinth of legislation on Jewish settlement in the city. In a pattern that became increasingly frequent over the last two decades of the nineteenth century and into the twentieth, Kiev police would raid Jewish homes in the middle of the night to uncover individuals or families staying in the city without the requisite permission; they were then detained, fined, and expelled (sometimes in chains along with common criminals).[9] One local observer described it this way:

> The ones who suffer are mostly the migrants who have come from small towns for meager earnings, but the local Jews with rights also suffer. Someone's servant is expelled, another one's clerk from the store, and sometimes, even an old mother who has come from the Pale to visit her son. In addition to ongoing surveillance, there are also frequent general "cleansings" in the

> form of nighttime visits to Jewish homes during which those without rights are taken away from their beds. And the ghetto has become so used to this that all the persecutions are considered to be the necessary conditions for existence here.[10]

Almost without exception, every description of Jewish life in Kiev from the 1880s on includes a reference to the oblavy, the disgraceful treatment of the arrestees, and the bribes required to remain in the city.[11] Sholem Aleichem's works contain several fictionalized descriptions of raids that are apparently based, at least in part, on his own experiences, as told in his memoir:

> But [the threat of police raids and expulsion] didn't prevent anyone from going to Kiev. The Russian proverb says, "If you're afraid of the wolf, don't set foot in the forest." But despite everyone's fears of the midnight inspections, they traveled to Kiev anyway. The innkeeper saw to it that the inspections proceeded smoothly and that, God forbid, no unkosher merchandise [i.e., illegal Jews] was discovered. How? Simple. The innkeeper greased those palms that had to be greased. He got advance word of a raid and knew what to do. The forbidden goods were hidden, one in an attic, another in a cellar, someone else in a clothes closet, a fourth in a chest and a fifth in a place where no one ever dreamed that a human being could be hidden. Best of all, when they crawled back into God's world from their hiding places, everyone laughed at the whole thing, like children at hide-and-seek. If worse came to worse, they consoled themselves with a sigh: "So what! We've lived through worse times and bigger Hamans!"[12]

Despite the light tone of the memoirist's tale, oblavy were not usually laughing matters. In one of his fictional works, Sholem Aleichem has his protagonist Menachem-Mendl recall "that terrible time . . . when I trembled like a thief, lay freezing in misery in an attic all night or curled up like a dog in a cellar."[13] In periods of stricter oversight, raids were carried out not only at night but in the daylight hours: Jews might be stopped to have their papers inspected while waiting to board the tram, or even in synagogue during services, which created a climate of "constant anxiety and fear."[14] Over the course of three nights in May 1895, for example, a total of 78 Jews were arrested in the Jewish neighborhoods of the city, and all were slated for deportation.[15] Both advocates and opponents of the tactic of expulsion acknowledged that many of the deportees soon returned to Kiev, so plentiful were the economic opportunities there. However, in some cases entire groups, such as porters and cabmen, were expelled en masse, usually because the authorities decided that the particular occupation in which these men made their living would no longer be classified among those giving Jews residence rights in the city; this happened in 1881, 1886, and again in 1891 (Simon Dubnow cites a figure of 2,000 expelled Jewish families in 1886, a huge number).[16] Jewish artisans who did not meet the exact criteria required for a residence permit were summarily expelled. Another, more mundane but no less menacing, danger was economic downturn leading to a dearth in employment opportunities. In the early 1890s, it seems to have been a combination of these two factors that led to the departure of high numbers of Jews from Kiev.[17]

Specific examples from the archives allow us to understand how the lives of Jewish artisans could be embittered by the regulations on expulsion. In 1892, Simkha Osadchii's deaf-mute son received an expulsion order after he reached his eighteenth birthday. The local authorities ruled that the son, once of the age of majority and despite his disability, could no longer remain with his father in Kiev, but Osadchii appealed the ruling all the way to the Senate in St. Petersburg, which overturned the order in 1894 and allowed the two to stay together in Kiev.[18] A more mundane case—but one that nonetheless generated sheaves of memoranda and petitions, as did many of these cases (that folder alone contains sixty-six folio pages)—was that of one artisan Efshtein, who was given an expulsion order in 1894 for living in Kiev without a residence permit, and then appealed to be accepted back into the Kiev Artisan Board (*remeslennaia uprava*) in order to avoid the expulsion.[19] The archives stacks are full of such cases, each one of which cost the government untold resources in time and money. The cost to the artisans cannot be measured by the historian. Nor was it only artisans who lived under the threat of expulsion: when the owner of a cast-iron works died in 1911, his sons were charged by a factory supervisor of trading in fabric without the necessary permit. Because Jews trading illegally outside the Pale could have their wares confiscated, the authorities ruled that the factory could be impounded. Thus, according to a correspondent for the Warsaw daily *Unzer leben*, a family that had lived in Kiev for several decades was expelled from the city and, most likely, ruined economically.[20]

While the situation of Kiev's Jews was in some ways unique, the insecurities that they faced—particularly the threats of expulsion and economic failure—were not very different from those faced by Russian Jewry as a whole. The May Laws of 1882 included a clause forbidding "new settlement" by Jews in a rural area or village; the clause was often interpreted broadly and used to expel families from areas they had inhabited for generations, forcing them into the ever more crowded towns and cities of the Pale (here we must also note the brutal expulsion in 1891 of thousands of Jews from Moscow).[21] And, of course, millions of the empire's Jews, hemmed in by residential, occupational, and educational restrictions, lived in poverty, many seemingly surviving on the very air. These, indeed, were the chief threats to Russian Jewry and the primary incentive for emigration. Whether it is wise to refer to government restrictions as a "legislative pogrom," a "cold pogrom," or a "silent pogrom" is open to debate, but perhaps these terms obscure unnecessarily the very important distinction between physical violence and administrative measures, however cruel.[22] More significantly, they elide the largely socioeconomic factors that contributed to the 1881–82 pogroms (which were *not* organized by the government) and the political and ideational characteristics of the official restrictions that followed.

That the real threat to Kiev's Jews lay not in the mob but in the authorities seemed to be bolstered by a suggestion made by right-wing city councilor F. N. Iasnogurskii in 1902, that the city petition the government for permission to expel all of its Jews. The mayor moved that as the proposal did not fall under the purview of the municipal administration, that it not even be accepted for consideration. While this was clearly not an idea that most people considered desirable or even realistic, the fact that such a suggestion could be made in the city council at all must have been unsettling, to say the least.[23]

Numbers and Origins

A. P. Subbotin, an economist and writer who surveyed the economic condition of the Jews in the region in 1887, gives a figure of "up to" 18,000 Jews out of a total city population of 170,000 in 1887, or about 10.5 percent, which is almost identical to the percentage in the 1874 census.[24] By 1897, the year of the All-Imperial Russian Census, Kiev's population had risen to just under a quarter of a million, of whom about 13 percent were Jews (32,000).[25] This figure was commensurate with their proportion of the population of the entire province (12.2 percent), and an increase of only a few points from the share of Jews in the total population in 1874: Jewish movement into Kiev had slowed from its early breakneck speed and was now keeping pace with total migration to the city.[26] However, Jews now formed the city's largest religious minority, with Catholics coming in second with 19,000. The share of Jews who spoke Russian as their mother tongue was not much greater than that in the Jewish population of the empire as a whole: 6 percent, or about

2,000. For comparison, 37 percent of St. Petersburg's Jews and 10.5 percent of Odessa's claimed Russian as their mother tongue, while less than 1 percent (0.83 percent) of the Jews of Kiev province did so.[27] In the imperial census of 1897, "mother tongue" probably meant something more like *Umgangsprache*—the language of everyday use—as even those Jews who spoke Russian at home had probably not been raised with it as children. Thus, while Kiev had a higher concentration of acculturated Jews than the average shtetl, it had fewer such Jews than most of the empire's large cities with significant Jewish populations. Of Yiddish-speakers, half were literate in Russian (a statistic somewhat higher than the 42 percent literacy rate among the total population of the city), and only 5 percent had had any education higher than the primary grades. As was the case among Russian Jewry as a whole, women were less likely than men to be literate in Russian (41 percent versus 61 percent).[28]

The 1897 census also shows that Kiev was largely a city of relatively young and unattached people: of Yiddish-speakers, fully 60 percent had never been married, the same proportion as for Russian-speakers in the city and indeed for all Jews in the Russian Empire.[29] Two-thirds of Kievans had been born outside the city, and almost half of them outside Kiev province.[30] Jews certainly had reasons to want to move to Kiev: Subbotin noted that Jewish poverty in Kiev province and the southwest region as a whole was at a higher level than in the northwest: living conditions were worse, it was more difficult to find work, and competition with non-Jews was more intense.[31] These circumstances were likely another factor that attracted Jews to Kiev, the one locality in the region one could hope would be an exception to the continually worsening conditions in the surrounding provinces.

The heavily migrant character of the community may also explain the imbalance in the representation of the sexes: for every one hundred Jewish men, there were eighty-nine Jewish women. Lestschinsky points to the legal restrictions on Jewish settlement, theorizing that many of the merchants and artisans who were permitted to live in Kiev were not yet married.[32] Married Jews attempting to live in Kiev illegally might have been more likely to leave their families behind; however, some—like Yekhezkel Kotik—may have succeeded in bringing their wives and children with them, despite the difficulties.

After 1881, some Jewish migrants to Kiev were undoubtedly victims of the many expulsions from rural areas brought about by the Temporary Laws of 1882, or had arrived from other towns overburdened with expellees. But where did they come from? Eliezer Friedmann, who arrived in Kiev in 1893, concluded that the city's Jewish community was so diverse—since Jews from different regions differed so greatly in character and outlook—that it was practically unique in the Pale of Settlement. Even prayer houses, which were usually organized around place of origin or occupation, could muster true communal feeling only during prayers, and the prayers themselves were often recited in disparate melodies or musical modes (*nushaot*) characteristic of different regions within the Pale.[33] In attempting to determine the place of origin of Kiev's Jews, we may note that the provinces surrounding Kiev were among those with the densest Jewish population; in Kiev province in the mid-1880s, 20 percent of the Jewish population of 300,000 was crammed into the town of Berdichev, and Kiev—which had had practically no Jews twenty years earlier—was already home to more than 5 percent of the province's Jews. Still, the Jews of the southwest were less urban than those in the Lithuanian, Belorussian, and Polish provinces, where fully 85 percent of the Jewish population was urban (versus about 70 percent in the southwest).[34]

We do not know if Jews from the same town or region tended to stick together, as did peasant *zemliaki* (countrymen) in many Russian cities.[35] If Jewish immigrants to the U.S. and Europe prayed together with their fellow townspeople from the old country and formed *landsmanshaft* mutual-aid societies, why would the same not be true for internal migrants within the Russian Empire?[36] We have some references relating to synagogues that mention particular places of origin (for example, there were "Lithuanian" and "Polish" shuls), but in general the evidence is too patchy to confirm or deny a zemliak-based Jewish community.[37] Thus we have no way of knowing if this was one way that a sense of continuity with shtetl life was preserved after migration to the city, or whether "familiar social bonds" were present that could "foster a sense of security. . . ."[38] On the other hand, we do know that Jews might move back and forth between shtetl and city, whether because of family ties, work obligations, or simply because they were registered in their hometown and had to return there to obtain important documents. Many Kiev Jews probably experienced a double identity as both natives of their hometown and residents of Kiev.

By 1910, the Jewish population of Kiev had risen considerably from its proportions at the 1897 census—but to what, exactly, we cannot say. Lestschinsky, without citing specific sources, names a figure of 51,000, or 11 percent of the total population.[39] The approximate figure cited by the editors of *Die Judenpogrome in Russland* is 70,000, or 15.5 percent of a total

450,000, but no year is given. Perhaps this is an estimate of the pre-1905 pogrom population.[40] A very high estimate given by rabbi and Hebraist Moshe Rozenblat, who lived in Kiev for years, is 150,000; Rozenblat may have been the correspondent from Kiev who wrote in a 1912 issue of the Russian Jewish newspaper *Novyi voskhod* that there might be 150,000 Jews in the city, maybe even more.[41] If not, we have two Kievans speculating that the Jewish proportion of the population might actually be about one-third; but this is much more akin to the number in 1926, after the influx of tens of thousands of Jews during the years of war and revolution, and can safely be disregarded.[42] Still, with thousands of Jews living in Kiev illegally and thousands more in its suburbs, something on the order of 75,000 or even slightly higher would not be impossible.

An ever-present segment of the Jewish population were students. In 1886, there were 237 Jewish students at St. Vladimir's University, making up 12.9 percent of the student body. This was the third-largest Jewish student body in the empire after Moscow and St. Petersburg universities (with 298 and 268 Jewish students, respectively), not surprising given that Kiev's university was the largest after those in the two capitals. It was also the third-largest in terms of proportional representation, after Novorossiiskii University in Odessa (29.8 percent) and Khar'kov University (28.3 percent).[43] By 1909, there were more than 900 Jewish students at the university and another 400-odd at the Polytechnical Institute, in each case constituting a significant proportion (about 17 percent) of the total student body.[44] Many other young people came to Kiev to study in its many gymnasia and institutes; the archives preserve hundreds of petitions from Jewish teenagers and young adults who asked the authorities for permission to reside in Kiev during the school year or even just for the exam period, if the student was an extern studying independently. This situation continued right up to the end of the imperial period. A late example is that of Iankel' (Yankel) Kharmats of Rzhishchev, a heavily Jewish town south of Kiev, whose father Shloma (Shlomo) applied in March 1908 for permission for his son to live in Kiev temporarily in order to sit his exams for a gymnasium that required all students to reside in Kiev during the examination period. The mark "OTK" (short for *otkazat'*), written in blue pencil on the bottom of the petition, tells us that Shlomo's request was denied; whether Iankel' ever managed to take the exams, we do not know.[45] Some students lived in the suburbs rather than apply for residence rights, but it was a difficult commute by coach or horse-drawn cab, and later by streetcar.[46] Relatively large numbers of students were probably involved in the revolutionary movement in the 1880s.[47] Students were also key in the founding of Kiev's first Bundist cell, Frayhayt (Freedom) around 1900, after a split between Zionists and socialists in the Jewish student organization at St. Vladimir University; the Frayhayt group officially joined the Bund in 1903 as the Kiev Bund Group.[48] This may be the "leftist radical group" to which Nokhem Shtif refers in his autobiography, whose members he describes as "not clearly knowing what we wanted."[49]

Making a Living

As noted in chapter 1, the proportion of Jewish first-guild merchants had reached the 85 percent mark by the mid-1890s, when Jews made up more than half of all Kiev merchants.[50] Subbotin remarked that Jewish firms represented a relatively small portion of the total enterprises in the city while accounting for a great deal more of its business: in 1887, the 113 Jewish merchants made up 13 percent of the total, but accounted for 45 percent of annual returns. Moreover, the average turnover [*oborot*] of each Jewish merchant was 3½ times that of his non-Jewish counterpart.[51] Although Jews did not play a significant role in the development of large-scale industry in Kiev, Jewish-owned concerns, apparently mostly small-scale, were responsible for about a quarter of industrial production: ten of the eleven tobacco factories were owned by Jews, as were the largest and most important tannery and wheat mill.[52] Jews were active in the region's grain trade, both as middlemen between producer and exporter, and as exporters themselves. They dominated the alcohol trade, as well as commerce in tobacco: all eighteen of the city's wholesale storehouses were Jewish-owned, as were 80 percent of the tobacco stores.[53]

Around 1897, three-fifths of the total value of sugar produced in Kiev province (13.6 million rubles out of 21.8 million rubles) was the output of Jewish-owned factories.[54] By the last years of the tsarist regime, 76 of the 234 sugar refineries in the Ukrainian provinces—almost a third—were owned by Jews. Over 40 percent of board members of sugar-related joint-stock companies were Jewish, as was almost as high a percentage of board directors. Among the largest undertakings were the Alexander Company (owned by the Brodskys), which comprised a number of refineries throughout the region and generated one-fourth of all the refined sugar produced in the Russian Empire in the early 1890s, Gal'perin's Kursk Company, and Zaitsev's Grigorii Company. These corporations employed large numbers of Jews as clerks and other white-collar workers as well as in higher echelons of management, though their ethnic Russian names were clearly an attempt to project an image of "wholesome" or "native" Russianness. The proportion of wealthy Jews in Kiev may have been higher than in any other place in the Pale of Settlement—in the 1880s, as many as fifteen Jews possessed fortunes of at least 100,000 rubles.[55] The elite Jewish families made it possible for dozens if not hundreds more Jews to live and work in Kiev by employing managers, clerks, accountants, salesmen, and servants; members of the Jewish intelligentsia were also able to settle in Kiev by serving the Brodskys and their ilk as "teachers, secretaries, accountants, and cashiers."[56] The overwhelming influence that Jews had on trade in the city was striking: by some measures, they controlled two-thirds of the city's trade at the turn of the century. The 1897 census showed that (depending on how one understands the categories imposed by the bureaucrats who devised the census) anywhere from 20–30 percent of all Yiddish-speaking Jews in Kiev were employed in trade (versus about 12 percent of Russians), and if one were to take the Russophone Jews into account that number would surely be higher.[57] Antisemites, of course, pointed to these statistics as evidence that Jews were intent on "taking over" the local economy for their own benefit.[58]

On the other hand, Subbotin downplayed the importance and visibility of Jews in his analysis of their role in Kiev's economy. It is possible that he did so because he was aware that local Jews were facing charges of dominating the city's commercial and financial sectors, but his analysis cannot easily be dismissed, given his serious approach to his subject and his reputation. Subbotin wrote that though Jews had indeed made advances in the fields of trade and credit, they were in no way as prominent in Kiev as they were in other cities (the example he gave was Berdichev, with a population that was 80 percent Jewish, not a particularly convincing contrast). Jews were not only fewer in numbers, but they also conducted themselves so unobtrusively that there seemed to be even fewer of them than in actuality. There were, Subbotin acknowledged, many large Jewish firms, but they could not compare to the competition offered by the large Russian and foreign concerns. He did not hide the important fact that each Jewish merchant's revenues were, on average, 175 percent greater than those of non-Jewish merchants, but he offset that figure with another: the profit margins of Jews, taken as a group, were less than those of their non-Jewish counterparts (3.5 percent versus 4.6 percent).[59] (He even claimed that due to legal restrictions "there is no typical Jewish bazaar" in Kiev as in the other cities of the Pale of Settlement, despite the fact that Galitskii market was also known as Evreiskii bazar at least as early as 1881 and kept that name into the Soviet period.)[60] In the end, it seems, whether Kiev's Jews were conspicuous or not depended in large measure on the observer. This was certainly true of the press: while *Kievlianin* often accused Jews of usurping all economic activity in Kiev, *Ha-melits* boasted that the large numbers of first-guild Jewish merchants were proof that Jews were the number-one cause of the fantastic growth of trade in the city.[61]

The archives enable us to become acquainted with the lives and livelihoods of individual merchant families who did not receive the same attention from contemporaries as did the most prominent families in the city. Gerts (Herts) Iakovlevich Timen, for example, was a successful first-guild merchant who owned two grocery businesses, one wholesale and the other retail, at the Zhitnii bazar in Podol (the largest market in the city), the net receipts of which came to about 70,000 rubles annually. He was also a contracted supplier for government agencies to the tune of 80,000 rubles a year. Timen and his wife Tuba (probably a Russian version of the Yiddish Toybe) Izrailovna resided in their own home—a sign of their prosperity—in Podol, not the Upper Town. Their choice of location was probably predicated on a desire to be close to their businesses, but may also have reflected the lower real estate costs in Podol as well as the proximity to prayer houses. When Gerts died in 1904 after working for more than twenty years as a merchant in Kiev, his wife requested permission from the authorities to maintain the five clerks who managed the enterprises. Since Tuba was illiterate, her son David signed for her. Her lack of formal education, however, had no bearing on her ability to manage the businesses left to her by her husband, which she clearly intended to do. (An interdepartmental memorandum refers to Timen as *kupchikha,* which can be translated as "merchant's wife" but also as "female merchant.") The document also illustrates how five Jewish clerks—and if they had families, as many as twenty souls or more—depended on one Jewish merchant for their livelihood and very authorization to live in Kiev.[62]

In much the same way, Sonia Zlobinskaia of Demievka, who worked as a cashier in "Petersburg," a linens store owned by merchant Ruvin Gershman, could only obtain residence rights in Kiev if Gershman agreed to count her as one of his "clerks" (*prikazchiki*).[63] In her petition to the authorities, Zlobinskaia wrote that she wished to move into Kiev proper because she was losing a great deal of money on transportation costs between Demievka and the city center. Another example of a migrant attached to a merchant family was

Ita-Khaia Zuseeva Tsypman of Mstislavl (Mogilev guberniia), a cook named in a petition submitted by Ester Moiseevna Gol'dshtein, wife of first-guild merchant Movsha-Leib (Moyshe-Leyb) Itskovich Gol'dshtein, which stated Ester's need—because of the demands of "Jewish ritual"—for a Jewish cook to live with her in Kiev.[64]

According to Subbotin, artisans did better for themselves in busy, bustling Kiev than elsewhere in the Pale, where there was usually an overabundance of craftspersons. In the mid-1880s, Jews made up 45 percent of all tailors in Kiev (up from 20 percent in 1874), 40 percent of silversmiths, one-quarter of all blacksmiths (6 percent in 1874), and almost one-fifth of cobblers (6 percent in 1874). More than a third of Kiev's 8,500 artisans were Jewish, a significant proportion but one basically in consonance with the region (Kiev and Chernigov guberniias), where the Jewish share of artisans varied between 25 and 40 percent; that paled in comparison with nearby cities such as Berdichev, where Jews constituted more than four-fifths of the artisan population.[65] This was the one group in Kiev that did not engender the usual complaint from critics that they were supplanting their Christian counterparts; indeed, Subbotin relates that Christian artisans competed successfully with similar Jewish workers.[66] By 1897, at least 40 percent of all Yiddish-speaking Jews in Kiev were artisans; the corresponding statistic for Russians, by comparison, was about one-quarter.[67]

Again, the case of a specific family helps to humanize the statistics. Rukhlia (Rokhel) Aronovna Roitman moved to Kiev with her husband Aron and child in 1901 from Odessa; the couple was originally from Zhitomir. According to a petition that Roitman submitted to the Kiev provincial governor in 1904, Aron, a typesetter by trade, found work at a printing shop and applied for a residence permit, but soon fell ill and traveled to stay with relatives so that he could convalesce. Since the relatives could not be expected to support their entire family—they now had three children—Roitman decided to stay in Kiev to work as a seamstress; she had received a certificate attesting to her mastery of the craft from the Zhitomir Artisan Board in 1894. Since details are sketchy, we do not know if Roitman practiced her craft while her husband was working or why the couple decided to move to Kiev. However, it seems likely that they had left Odessa for Kiev in the hopes that Aron would find employment there; perhaps the downturn in the Odessa economy had put him out of work. As for Roitman, it may be that she had obtained her artisan certificate while an unmarried adolescent or young woman and had worked as a seamstress until she married Aron or perhaps until they had their first child; the wording of her petition suggests that she had not been working while Aron was employed.[68] Around the turn of the century, the marriage age was rising for both Jewish women and men, and many women were taking the time to learn a trade or craft before getting married. This enabled "the emergence of a sizable artisan class composed of Jewish women."[69]

The case of another family, the Manilovs, gives additional anecdotal evidence that many Jewish women were well-equipped to provide for their families when necessary. Fania Kadysheva Manilova, originally from Gostomel' (a town just outside Kiev), but registered in the *meshchanstvo* (townspersons') estate in Nezhin, seventy-five miles away, lived in Kiev with her two small children, and worked as a milliner and seamstress, bringing in 25 to 35 rubles a month. Her husband Mendel Kopelevich had stayed in Nezhin, where he worked as a clerk and was able to send Fania 5 or 10 rubles to supplement her monthly income.[70] Why Fania came to Kiev is unclear—perhaps the family was hoping to make a new start in the big city and they decided that she would be the first to go, since she, as an artisan, could more easily obtain a residence permit than could he (we know about Fania from her 1904 petition for permission to have her father join her in Kiev). Perhaps, too, they had their children's education in mind, hoping to get them into good schools and get them started on a promising career path. Or they may have had marital problems and chose not to divorce at that time. Whatever the reason, Fania Manilova—like Rukhlia Roitman and many other young women—had joined the ranks of working women in Kiev, who now made up a growing proportion of all Jewish artisans. In 1897, 15 percent of Jewish artisans in the southwest region were women, and about 6 percent of all Jewish women over the age of ten earned a living in crafts. At 20 percent, the female share of Jewish craft positions in Kiev was somewhat higher than the average for the surrounding region.[71]

For the women who needed to work to support themselves or their families, the needlework and retail trades were the most prevalent occupations—perhaps because they corresponded closely with traditional female skills in the Jewish small-town economy. These vocations also met the growing demand in urban centers for haute couture driven by the fashions displayed in store windows and on the pages of catalogs and magazines.[72] In the southwest, three-quarters of all female artisans worked in the garment trade as seamstresses, dressmakers, milliners, and stocking-makers.[73] The situation of women like Fania Manilova and Rukhlia Roitman—alone in the city with several children to care for—makes apparent the need for outside assistance with child care and other aspects of what was for all intents and purposes single motherhood, a need that new Jewish charitable societies began to fill at this very time. (These societies are discussed in detail in chapter 6.)

The 1914 annual report of the Kiev Chapter for Care of Jewish Girls and Women, a branch of the Russian Society for the Defense of Women, is a rich source of data on young Jewish women who arrived in Kiev hoping to find employment.[74] The chapter's labor exchange was unable to locate positions for many of the women, in part because of the war but also because of the low demand for female employees and laborers and the low wages paid to those who did manage to find a job. The greatest demand was for nannies, while educated women looking for professional positions were least likely to be successful in their search. Of the 262 women registered by the labor exchange in the second half of 1914, almost three-quarters of whom were under the age of thirty, more than 20 percent were graduates or students of an institution of higher education (including the Higher Women's Courses, the equivalent of university education for women, as well as medical, dentistry, law, and commercial schools), while another 43 percent had received some gymnasium or professional school education. This sample, while not representative, does give some sense of the generally high educational levels of young Jewish women who lived in large cities like Kiev or undertook to travel there for employment.[75]

A comparison between this group and the women who wrote to the labor exchange from throughout the Pale of Settlement requesting assistance in locating employment is instructive: while 45 percent of the women in Kiev declared their desire to work as white-collar professionals—teachers, clerks, saleswomen, or cashiers—less than 10 percent of the women from outside of Kiev were interested in (and presumably qualified for) such positions. Comparable proportions wanted to work as caretakers for children as governesses or nannies or for the sick as midwives or sick-nurses (30 percent of the Kiev group and 40 percent of the non-Kiev group), and as artisans in the garment trade (15 percent and 20 percent, respectively). There was a marked difference, however, in the inclination toward domestic service: only 10 percent of the Kiev women were interested in working as housekeepers or domestic servants, while the proportion for the non-Kiev women was 30 percent. These numbers suggest that Jewish women in urban centers were much more likely than their counterparts in smaller cities and towns to have a higher education, as well as the converse: women outside of the metropolis were more likely to be educated at home or to have only a few years of elementary schooling, if at all, and thus to fall back on domestic service when looking for a job.[76] Apparently, however, Jewish women with professional training or experience of some kind in fields such as midwifery and dressmaking could be found in similar proportions throughout the Pale.[77] Whatever their education and training, one symbol of the restrictions that women had to cope with was the difficulty in obtaining a residence permit for the many who were registered under their fathers' names and were thus willy-nilly inscribed in a locale where they had no intention of living.

At the turn of the century and into the early twentieth century, Jews, and especially women, continued to play a prominent role at Kiev's markets, as they had in earlier decades. A survey of Jewish market traders undertaken by the police in 1890 found many women selling bread, fruit, dairy products, and notions. Eleven of the fifteen Jewish traders at the Galitskii (Evreiskii) bazar, for example, were women. Among Kiev's women traders: Liba Abramovna Kolis, a joiner's wife, selling fruit; El'ka Ioseleva Rudak, widow of a soldier, selling pottery wares; and Khaia Shmuleva Tsypirukha, a cobbler's wife, selling fruit. One example of a man making a living in the market was Gershko (Hirsh) Faivelev Berman, a retired soldier, who sold candles and blacking (polish).[78]

Of 146 mothers of poor children assisted by a Jewish philanthropic society in 1910, ninety were listed without an occupation. Of the remainder, almost half worked as market-women while 30 percent were seamstresses or other garment trade-related artisans.[79] Two years later, the corresponding proportions were 42 percent and 46 percent, though it is difficult to say if the change represented a larger trend. The 1913 report of the Representation for Jewish Welfare, the official charitable body, gives us further details about Jewish women working as traders in Kiev (for the most part, needy artisans applied for assistance to the local Jewish Artisan Aid societies, not the Representation). In 1913, a total of 78 percent of all applicants for aid were women, 62 percent of whom were widows and 13 percent abandoned wives. Of the female applicants, 37 percent listed their occupation as "traders in food products," while 16 percent were clothing traders and 13 percent were secondhand dealers; one-fifth were categorized as "lacking a specific occupation."[80] Thus, we learn that the vast majority—80 percent—of needy women worked outside the home, and two-thirds of nonartisan working women were traders or market-women of some kind.

As in most cities of the Pale of Settlement, Jewish poverty in Kiev in the last years of the empire had taken on striking proportions. According to a 1911 report in *Unzer leben,* Jewish begging in Kiev had reached monumental proportions: "one finds Jewish poor folk in almost every part of the city," wrote the correspondent. The 1912 annual report of the Society of Summer Colonies for Sick Children of the Poor Jewish Population of Kiev related that more than 80 percent of its 235 wards, whose average age was eleven, lived in one room or less (either a one-room flat, a kitchen, or part of a room), and that there was an average of eight people per room in their homes. Only twenty of the children had their own bed, and fifty-five of them slept on the floor. About 10 percent, according to the report, did not receive the main meal of the day (*obed*) at all, while another 30 percent ate only a poor, unfilling meal. Over a quarter of the children did not attend school at all.[81]

Although one lady's dressmaker at one time ran a brothel in the center of town, we have no evidence that there were Jewish prostitutes in Kiev, and the 1897 census listed no Jews out of the 155 female and male prostitutes in the city.[82] It is conceivable that there were Jewish prostitutes who went unregistered by the census, or who appeared in the city in later years; one of the residents of the brothel in Aleksandr Kuprin's *Yama,* a fictional treatment of Kiev's seamy underworld in the last years of the tsarist regime, is "Sonka the Rudder, a Jewess."[83] Kuprin even has the prostitutes speaking to each other in a secret language combining elements of Yiddish, Gypsy (Romany), and Romanian, but this may be more a reflection of contemporary bias toward the speakers of these languages as "criminally inclined" than a representation of reality.[84]

The Lure of the Stock Exchange

Many of the Jewish artisans who arrived in the city under false premises, wrote the memoirist Starozhil, went immediately into brokerage at the Kiev Exchange or other shady pursuits such as money lending. Before 1886, Kiev's commodities exchange, a national center for the sugar trade, did not have a building of its own, and business took place in the open air on the sidewalks of Kreshchatik, where "from morning till night hundreds of wheeler-dealers [*gesheftmakhery*], mostly Jews, darted to and fro."[85] *Kievlianin* complained that many of them did not even bother to put up a pretense of working as craftsmen, and that regular folk could not even walk on Kreshchatik because of the "masses of Jews jamming the sidewalk and wangling their affairs in the open air."[86] It is possible that some artisans, as well as clerks, servants, and others with residence rights, worked as brokers, agents, and realtors on the side.[87] The exchange certainly was enticing for anyone who thought he could persuade 10 rubles to become 20 or even 50, as Sholem Aleichem described so well in his fictional letters between Menakhem-Mendl and his wife Sheyne-Sheyndl: after the former failed to make his fortune in Odessa, he went on to Yehupets (a.k.a. Kiev) to buy and sell "little pieces of paper"—that is, stocks—on the exchange.[88]

But the construction in 1886 of a building to house the exchange, which was by then the third-largest in the empire, did not solve the problem of brokers gathering on the street.[89] By 1900, the chief of police was giving orders that crowds of Jewish brokers from the exchange not be allowed to gather on the sidewalks of Kreshchatik, and after the 1905 pogrom a group of brokers even banded together to form a mutual-aid association.[90] On the eve of the First World War, a Jewish school listing parents' occupations revealed that 46 (12 percent) gave their profession as "brokers and '*voyageurs*'" and an anecdotal report in the Yiddish newspaper *Haynt* gave a figure of three thousand brokers living in Kiev.[91] Although women apparently did not take part in the business of the exchange, some did play a role in the financial sector: for example, one recipient of aid from a Jewish philanthropic society was listed in its 1910 annual report as a "female moneylender" (*faktorsha*).[92]

An 1895 feuilleton in *Kievskoe slovo* entitled "Pictures of Stock Exchange Manners" painted an unflattering portrait of two of the city's many Jewish speculators and brokers, who filled the bank offices on Kreshchatik to such capacity that that "you might think that you had arrived in a provincial town near Vilna or Minsk on market day."[93] The author made his subjects out to be boorish Jews who had made their money by cheating innocent people, and then posed as educated and cultured members of the middle class who moved comfortably in the Jewish and non-Jewish worlds. Eliezer Friedmann, also writing of 1890s Kiev, noted in his memoirs that the speculators, brokers, and traders who did business at the Kiev commodities exchange were among those Jews most likely to cease traditional religious observance; no doubt some observers associated this behavior with the immorality that was said to reign among them.[94] A report in *Haynt* in 1910 remarked that most of the brokers did not live too badly—"some even perhaps a little too well, too liberally, and too boisterously." No one in Kiev thought particularly highly of the brokers, but they were such a unique and picaresque phenomenon that Sholem Aleichem even wrote a satirical drama on their social-climbing ways entitled *Yakneh"oz* (the Russian title was *An Exchange Epic*), portraying them as philistines who attempted, with little success, to take on the manners and mores of the Russian bourgeoisie (for more on the play, see Chapter 4).[95] Not everyone appreciated his humor: apparently, some brokers denounced the piece to the authorities (ostensibly because it used biblical quotes in a derogatory manner), and it was censored.

Residential Patterns

In the last decades of the nineteenth and into the twentieth century, Podol/Ploskaia and Lybed continued to be the primary Jewish neighborhoods in Kiev. One Aizenberg, an engineer living in Kiev, wrote to the St. Petersburg–based Russian-language Jewish newspaper *Nedel'naia khronika Voskhoda* in 1901 that life in these neighborhoods was inexpensive, and that there were many cheap apartments. Jews were motivated to live there by the significant degree to which commerce was developed and, perhaps more meaningfully, by "a general gravitation towards one's one people" [*obshchee tiagotenie k svoim*]:

> The result of such a concentration of Jews is that Kiev has streets and even whole parts of the city where not one Jew lives and it's difficult to even meet one on the street, and on the other hand there are entire quarters where the entire population is Jewish, without exception. In other words, a real ghetto. Everywhere Jewish faces, Jewish speech. We can find here the heightened competition, poverty, density of population, and unsanitary conditions that are characteristic of all kinds of other centers that are densely populated by Jews.[96]

But Aizenberg also noted that conditions were improving, and that even the poor now had access to some amenities—both physical and cultural—that had previously been the province of the wealthy. Indeed, Jews in Kiev were materially better off than their coreligionists in other cities of the Pale. Where they could not be envied, however, was in their constant persecution by the police.

We lack data for residential patterns at the turn of the century, as the 1897 census did not break down population by neighborhood. By 1908, however, almost 10 percent of Kiev's Jews now lived in the Starokievskaia district, suggesting that a new professional class of Jewish doctors, lawyers, and engineers was taking up residence in this desirable area (municipal almanacs confirm this supposition).[97] Also of interest was the shift in the center of Jewish population from Ploskaia, in the north of the city, to Lybed in the south; Ploskaia held 43 percent of Kiev's Jews in 1874, while in 1908 Lybed claimed almost exactly the same proportion, 42 percent (up from 13 percent in 1874). In that year, more than 20,000 Jews lived in this one neighborhood alone, a number that would have constituted a small city almost anywhere else in the Pale of Settlement. Yet Jews still made up only a fifth of the total population of Lybed. Indeed, in this respect little had changed since 1874: in no neighborhood did Jews constitute more than a third of the population. There were clear concentrations of Jews in particular parts of the city, but no district could be called exclusively Jewish. This does not mean, however, that particular *streets* were not heavily or even almost entirely Jewish, which may well have been the case. Moreover, percentages of 20–35 percent Jews in a given area were similar to the substantial proportion of Jews in many of the shtetlekh, market towns, of the Pale. Indeed, one guidebook to Kiev noted that "nowadays, Podol is a heavily populated and commercial district of Kiev, making up, as it were, a separate city (*sostavliaiushchaia kak by otdel'nyi gorod*)."[98]

Living conditions in some of the neighborhoods were just as bad as, or even worse than, they had been several decades earlier. Descriptions of Ploskaia from 1900, for example, speak of the unhealthy living caused by the swampy ground and frequent flooding, with many poor families living in damp, airless basement apartments, sometimes two or three families to a one-room apartment.[99] Of 158 children assisted by a Jewish philanthropic society in 1910, 65 percent lived in one room or even less—a kitchen or part of a room.[100]

Although most detractors of the Jewish population in Kiev were resigned to Ploskaia and Lybed being Jewish neighborhoods, there was active opposition to the "judaization" of the more genteel areas of the city, especially the central avenue of the upper city, Kreshchatik, and its financial and commercial institutions. There was an ongoing legal question about whether Jews were even allowed to conduct business outside of the two Jewish neighborhoods.[101] A report from the southwest region in the St. Petersburg newspaper *Novoe vremia* in 1890 warned readers in the capital about the transformation that the main avenue of Russia's ancient mother of cities had undergone; a stroll down Kreshchatik, wrote the author, will have one saying about Kiev, formally off-limits to Jews, that "this is a Jewish city." The article continued: "Look in the shops—190 Jewish first-guild merchants and only 20 Russians; stop into the banks—Jewish faces there; get to know the artisan folk—their leaders are Jewish and there's a special Jewish guild."[102] According to the article, tens of thousands of Jewish residents held trade and industry in their hands, and each one was an "exception" to the rules regulating Jewish activity in Kiev.

That there was a good deal more Jewish communal and religious activity in Kiev than met the eye of officials is made clear by a list of prayer houses compiled by bureaucrats in the early 1890s.[103] Most of these had had their permits issued in the 1880s or in 1890, testifying to the surge in Jewish population in that decade and official recognition of the religious and communal needs of Kiev's Jews. The list includes seventeen authorized—and one unauthorized—prayer houses: nine in Ploskaia, two in Podol, four in Lybed, and three in Bul'varnaia (which included the Solomenka and Shuliavka neighborhoods). Assuming there was an absolute minimum of 25,000 Jews in Kiev in 1890—and there were likely many more—then each prayer house would have had to accommodate an average of anywhere between 200 and 250 adult males, which seems unlikely given that most of these were probably housed in small converted apartments. If the authorities knew of the existence of one unauthorized prayer house, then surely there were many more underground synagogues.

Any discussion of the residential patterns of Kiev's Jews must also include the dacha suburbs such as Boiarka and Pushcha-Voditsa that were so popular among the Jewish bourgeoisie. These were village-like settlements on the outskirts of Kiev, easily accessible (sometimes even by streetcar), yet distant from the dirt and noise of the city.[104] In a letter to Y. H. Ravnitsky in 1895 from his dacha in Boiarka, Sholem Aleichem waxed poetic about the garden with sour cherries, raspberries, apples, and pears; the free plays and concerts on offer; and the delicious roast chicken and duckling that one could eat. "Believe me, it's really a slice of paradise here."[105] Even the poor Jews of Kiev could experience the wonders of the dacha suburbs if they were lucky enough to be granted a stay at one of the sanatoria operated by Jewish institutions such as the Society of Summer Colonies for Sick Children of the Poor Jewish Population of Kiev. By the last years of Romanov rule, however, permission to rent a dacha for the summer was not a foregone conclusion: Jews had to apply individually for such permission, and many did not receive it.[106] Even this simple pleasure was now subject to administrative restriction, one in a seemingly endless list applicable to Kiev's Jews.

The Pogrom of 1905

The bloody pogrom of 1905 was adumbrated by the threat of a pogrom two years earlier, in the wake of the Kishinev pogrom of 1903. In mid-April, several days after the events in Kishinev, rumors spread that there would be a pogrom in Kiev. A telegram from local authorities to the Ministry of Justice in St. Petersburg on 14 April read, in part, "Panic among Jews, packing up belongings, leaving Kiev. The city is still quiet."[107] The local Social Democrats, who had originally planned a large demonstration for 20 April, soon cancelled that event because—as they wrote in a proclamation that was distributed throughout the city—they feared that it might, "thanks to the police and the enormous unorganized army of idle populace [*prazdnogo naseleniia*], turn into a pogrom."[108] According to a report of the procurator of the Kiev high court tribunal (*sudebnaia palata*), the Kiev Committee of the RSDRP called a meeting at the Polytechnical Institute on 18 April, which was attended by both students and local Jews. According to the report, the Jews demanded that the students present a request to the director of the institute that in the event of a pogrom, the building be made available as a refuge to Jews. Confirming the telegram of four days earlier, the procurator wrote that the Jewish population of Kiev was in panic, many of them leaving the city after depositing their valuables at banks and pawnshops, and that others had moved from their apartments into hotels.[109] (Clearly, these were among the most affluent of the city's Jews; the poor could not leave at a moment's notice, let alone move into a hotel.) A report in *Nedel'naia khronika Voskhoda* in early May described a "commercial stagnation"—a noticeable downturn in economic activity—in the wake of the panic engendered by the Kishinev pogrom.[110] Kishinev also helped to radicalize Kiev's Jewish students and to push some of them toward the Jewish nationalist camp.[111] The archives reveal that the Kiev branch of the *okhrana* (secret police) was aware that representatives of revolutionary groups were planning self-defense activities in case of a pogrom; a certain Dr. Lev (or Leiba) Ovseev Mandel'berg, a member of the Poalei-Tsion, hosted such a planning meeting in his clinic in March of 1904.[112] In his autobiography, Nokhem Shtif recalled that he and other radical leftist Jewish student responded to Kishinev "with a self-defense group and with revolutionary proclamations," and in autumn 1903 they and Jewish students from other cities convened the first conference of the Vozrozhdenie (Rebirth) group, later to become the non-Marxist, socialist-autonomist Sejmists (Sotsialisticheskaia evreiskaia rabochaia partiia, or SERP).[113]

Despite the events of April–May 1903, the 1905 pogrom, a by-product of the revolution, apparently took most of Kiev's Jews by surprise, as it followed a time of optimistic chaos.[114] As with the 1881 pogrom, the pretext was an attack on the tsar: in 1881, Jews had been linked to the assassination of Alexander II; in 1905, Jews were said to be playing a disproportionate role in the revolutionary movement. In Kiev, the sparks that set the pogrom off on 18 October were rumors spread by ultraconservative forces that Jews were desecrating portraits of the emperor at a demonstration celebrating the handing down of the October Manifesto.

In Kiev as throughout much of the empire, the strikes and disorders of the 1905 Revolution surged several times: early in the year, following Bloody Sunday; in the heat of summer, when many of the confrontations between strikers and revolutionary youth and the police "appear to have involved Jews" (a July strike by dressmakers and shoemakers and an August demonstration in Lybed likely included many Jews); and in October.[115] By September, crowds were forming "more or less continuously" in Kiev's Jewish neighborhoods."[116] Conservatives saw in the city's Jews a potential threat, as was the case in many other localities with large Jewish populations. This was especially true because it seemed to them that, as Senator E. F. Turau would later state in his report on the pogrom, "some of the most zealous attendees and organizers of the local antigovernment organizations and meetings are young Jews and Jewesses."[117] There was certainly a kernel of truth to this perception, but the numerous citations of Jews as leaders and ringleaders of the revolutionary movement in Turau's report seem calculated to inspire in the reader some kind of understanding of the subsequent anti-Jewish violence as a "measure-for-measure" reaction to the "impudence" of the Jews. As tensions continued to mount through September and into October, the stage was being set for a confrontation between progressive forces and Jews, on the one hand, and the authorities and the conservative masses, on the other.[118] The large antigovernment "people's demonstrations" (*narodnye mitingy*) held at St. Vladimir's University and the Polytechnical Institute, attendance at several of which numbered in the thousands, were attended by students, workers, nationalist- and revolutionary-minded professionals, and Jews.[119] Again, Turau's report, based on the eyewitnesses that he interviewed, maintained that, other than the workers present, the attendees at some of the meetings were largely Jewish, a claim that is impossible to verify.[120] Claims of bias and distortions in these reports go back to the days immediately following their publication; *Nedel'naia khronika Voskhoda,* for example, commented that the Russian Telegraphic Agency's "Judeophobic tendencies" led it to describe the crowd attending the people's meetings and demonstrations in Kiev as "mostly Jewish" and "riffraff."[121] It is abundantly clear that the reporting of RTA and other right-leaning organs, as well as the reports and memoranda written by local officials—to which Turau had access—influenced the senator's report as well as subsequent histories and impressions of the days and weeks leading up to the pogrom.[122] *Kievlianin,* for example, characterized one of the demonstrations at St. Vladimir's University as a "Jewish meeting," with speeches on Zionism and the Jewish question. Patently aiming to pass the revolution off as an attempt by Jews to inject their parochial issues into the life of the nation, the newspaper wondered aloud why the attendees could not have held the meeting in a synagogue or prayer house instead of bothering the professors and students.[123]

On 2 October, a funeral procession for a member of the Kiev Committee of the Socialist-Revolutionary party turned into a confrontation with police that left one protester dead—a young Jewish woman, who was subsequently memorialized in Yiddish at another revolutionary meeting held at the university.[124] According to reports in *Nedel'naia khronika Voskhoda,* some of the meetings in early October included or focused on issues relating specifically to Jewish students, such the demand for the elimination of separate admissions standards for Christians and Jews and the abolition of Jewish quotas.[125] The empire-wide railroad strike began in Kiev on 11 October, and was followed by the largest people's meeting yet, with a reported attendance of 10,000, where speeches were made by local leaders of the Social Democrats and the Bund, including assistant attorney Mark Ratner, who would soon play a leading role in the revolution within the Kiev Jewish community (discussed in chapter 7).[126] One of the main topics of the meeting was the organization of a general strike in Kiev, for which the revolutionary activists began to plan.[127] As a result, martial law was declared on 14 October. A joint revolutionary committee was established that crossed ethnic and religious lines, with "equal representation for Bolsheviks, Mensheviks, SRs, Bundists, Polish Social Democrats, and the leaders of [the Ukrainian] Spilka."[128]

On 18 October, celebrations of the tsar's manifesto granting limited civil and political rights apparently became muddled with revolutionary rallies.

Turau claimed that unsuspecting Kievans who gathered to show support and reverence for their tsar were shocked as they witnessed workers and students desecrating portraits of Nicholas II and statues of Nicholas I and Alexander II. He describes the revolutionary crowds marching toward Kreshchatik, shouting, "Down with autocracy! Down with the bloodsuckers!" (*doloi krovopiits*), as well as individual Jewish "agitators" insulting a priest (snatching his hat off his head to force him to pay respect to their red flags) and a group of soldiers—actions which aroused the indignation of passers-by.[129] Whether or how these incidents actually occurred is less important than the *perception* that Jews were playing a prominent role in the anti-tsarist demonstrations, which was apparently fairly widespread.

Later in the day, a large crowd "gathered in front of City Hall to listen to political speeches and celebrate the news of the October Manifesto," but things began to get ugly when the patriotic flags on the building were replaced by red banners and the flags of socialist parties.[130] In Turau's account, revolutionary activists flooded into city hall, and a young Jewish man even tore out the tsar's head from a portrait, stuck his own head through, and declared, "Now I'm the Sovereign." Again, what is most significant here is the perception that the revolutionaries, with Jews prominent among them, were bent on taking over the city and, indeed, the entire empire.

The crowd was dispersed by troops, and mobs with violent intent quickly formed, perhaps sparked by rumors that Jews had damaged or mutilated portraits of the tsar.[131] (There is some evidence that there were also rumors circulating to the effect that the tsar had given permission to attack the Jews.)[132] The mob was heard to shout, "Blood!"—was this a signal, agreed upon beforehand, that the pogrom was to begin, as some later surmised?[133] The local civilian and military authorities did little or nothing to stop the pogrom until 20 October—by which time entire neighborhoods had been sacked. One military man in charge of troops in Kiev, Major-General Bezsonov, was reported to be very clear in his support of the *pogromshchiki*, maintaining that the Jews had played too large a role in the revolutionary movement and deserved the attack; Senator Turau noted that Bezsonov and Police Chief Tsikhotskii went so far as to "actively encourage the mob."[134] There are numerous reports of soldiers and policemen taking part in the looting and violence, and even those who did not take active part did not, for the most part, attempt to put down the riot or defend Jews.

As in 1881, the mobs set upon Jewish stalls in the markets (starting with the Troitskii Market in Lybed), and then Jewish stores and homes, smashing and stealing; however, they did not confine themselves to the Jewish neighborhoods, as before, but included Jewish-owned shops in the very heart of the city, on Kreshchatik, where they carted away loads of booty in wheelbarrows as the police stood by and watched.[135] In another departure from 1881, the violence went further than incidental injuries sustained in the course of confrontation over property: when they came upon Jews, pogromshchiki set upon them with often deadly force (and sometimes upon the Christians who defended or hid them). Zionist and Hebraist activist Moshe Rozenblat claimed that the mobs shouted not only "Beat the zhids" but also "Death to the Jews!"—a new escalation in the rhetoric of pogrom violence. As the pogrom was occurring, Rozenblat wrote, "Just now a Jew dared to set foot on the street, and the hooligans set upon him like wolves and killed him."[136] Jews feared for their lives; in the words of Sholem Aleichem, who witnessed the pogrom, there was "a general panic which does not lend itself to description. The lives of forty or fifty thousand Israelites hang by a hair."[137] By the third day, wrote A. Brusilovski from Kiev, "all the Jews of the city are hiding in holes and cracks and waiting. . . ."[138]

Dozens were killed and hundreds hurt, with millions of rubles worth of property either stolen or destroyed. Nor were Kiev's wealthy Jews spared, as they had been in 1881. Indeed, Rozenblat reported that when a large group of Jews holed up in a Kiev hotel tried to telephone the Brodskys, Zaitsev, and other grandees to implore them to speak to the governor-general about putting a stop to the pogrom, they discovered that they, too, were hiding in cellars and that their houses had been looted.[139] Sholem Aleichem wrote in a letter to his daughter,

> They have beaten our millionaires—the Brodskys, the Zaitsevs, the Baron [Gintsburg], Rozenberg, and the others. . . . The Brodskys tried to hide with good Christians, and many others did the same, but the good Christians . . . refused them hospitality. . . . Jewish converts, men and women, spent the night in Jewish cellars.

He described affluent Jewish women hiding in stables and attics; Lev Brodsky and his daughter climbed over a fence to the Institute for Noble Girls, but were refused entry. Other members of the Brodsky family tried to take refuge with the director of the state bank, but to no avail.[140] Sholem Aleichem's own apartment, however, was saved by his Christian cook, who placed icons and crosses in the windows.[141] In addition to attacking the Brodsky home, the mob also looted and destroyed the Brodsky Trade School, a lavishly outfitted institution that had been in operation for only a few years.[142]

Despite Tsikhotskii's account that as the mobs fell upon Jews, they shouted, "This is your freedom! Take that for your Constitution and revolution . . . ," Hamm argues convincingly that "Kiev's October pogrom was not a mass upheaval. . . . There was nothing popular or patriotic about it."[143] Rather, right-wing agitators and sympathetic police and military men stirred up drunken mobs to plunder, destroy, beat, rape, and kill. With little time or wherewithal to organize self-defense of any kind, Kiev's Jews were at the mercy of "small bands of thugs incited by agitators"; large groups of people took advantage of the chaos to steal and loot.[144] The Hebrew newspaper *Ha-zeman* reported that the cruelty and hatred of the pogrom mobs could be clearly seen in their actions: when they entered a Jewish house, they smashed and destroyed every last item.[145] Whereas the masses in 1881 had been mostly leaderless, disorganized, and intent on stealing and looting what the Jews had "stolen" from them, in 1905 members of the antisemitic Black Hundreds clearly had a hand in organizing and directing the violence, and perhaps even in whipping up its lethal side. The investigators who compiled the two-volume *Die Judenpogromen in Russland* found that the gangs consisted mostly of doormen, porters, servants, elementary school pupils, traders and market-women, tram workers, and sometimes also Russian workers. People also came in from outlying villages (such as Boiarka) to take part, some apparently egged on by implausible rumors: a Jew had killed a Christian woman; Jews were attacking monks; Jews were desecrating a Christian holy place; thousands of armed Jews were marching on Kiev.[146]

At the height of the violence, on 19 October, right-wing organizations coordinated "patriotic" demonstrations with the active participation of local priests, which appear to have given some kind of encouragement to the pogrom mobs, though one account has Bishop Platon of Chigirin attempting to fight the tide and exhorting the crowds to stop attacking Jews.[147] (There is evidence that the Caves Monastery, Kiev's hoariest and most celebrated holy place, may have played a role in the printing of a leaflet urging Russians to "defend the fatherland" against revolutionaries—and, by implication, Jews.)[148] The next day, the pogrom continued in the city's main markets, whence the mobs continued on to Jewish homes and apartments.

A telegram of protest sent to chairman of the Council of Ministers S. Iu. Witte by a collection of leaders of civil society on 19 October suggests that at least some Kievans were horrified by the breakdown of order in their city and the authorities' refusal to step in to stop the atrocities—and in some cases even demonstrating complicity with the violence.[149] Many others, however, were clearly content to watch on the sidelines without taking sides. The majority conservative city council also displayed indifference during the pogrom, showing little remorse or attempts at making amends afterwards, and rejecting a proposal to provide 5,000 rubles in aid to pogrom victims.[150]

The violence came to an end on 20 October, when the military finally took decisive action and used force to disperse the mobs, arresting more than one hundred people. In addition to the human casualties, the Kiev Central Committee for Assistance to Pogrom Victims estimated that damages were sustained by over two thousand shops, warehouses, workshops, and private apartments, and by more than seven thousand households. The sum total of damages to Jewish property was estimated at 7 million rubles, and to all property in the city at anywhere between 10 and 40 million rubles.[151] There was hardly a Jewish home, store, or workshop that had not been attacked during the pogrom.

In the Wake of Pogrom and Revolution

The shock and grief of the pogrom were intermingled with continued, though now much dulled, excitement about the ongoing revolution, the ramifications of Nicholas's October Manifesto, and the upcoming elections for the new Duma. While Jewish traders and artisans, many of them now impoverished by the pogrom, attempted to reconstruct their lives, Kiev's Jewish liberal activists were particularly engaged in mobilizing the city's Jews for the elections, and there was hope in the air that Jewish disabilities might soon be eased, if not even removed altogether (see chapter 7 for an in-depth discussion of the revolution and the elections). The new premier P. A. Stolypin gave added heft to these aspirations when he ordered governors of the interior provinces of Russia to cease expulsions of Jews who had settled there before August 1906; this circular seemed to apply to Kiev as well, over which fact the city's Jewish residents were jubilant.[152]

But the threat of violence still hung in the air. March 1906 brought rumors of an impending pogrom, and trains bound for Austria-Hungary were reported to be full of Jews fleeing the city.[153] In April, despite promises from the authorities to put a stop to antisemitic propaganda, a leaflet aimed at soldiers and distributed in large numbers claimed that Jews were dressing up as troops in order to sabotage the army from within and achieve their ultimate goal of destroying Russia. "Let us stand up against the Jews, the seditionists," called the leaflet, according to Yiddish newspaper *Dos lebn*.[154] The fact that laborers at one of Kiev's shipbuilding yards passed a resolution in May voicing their opposition to the possibility of another pogrom and calling on all workers to defend citizens from attacks on their freedom, life, and property was not necessarily reassuring to Jews; the incident seemed to reveal that the menace of pogrom still hung in the air.[155] A month later, there were reports that a leaflet was being distributed around the city, calling on Russians to beat their enemies, in the name of the Central Russian Patriotic Committee.[156] New rumors of an imminent pogrom sprung up every day, and a "depression has fallen on the local Jews," wrote the Yiddish newspaper *Der telegraf*.[157]

Life was affected in more ordinary ways as well. The records of the library of the Kiev Literacy Society record a precipitous drop in Jewish attendance in the year after the pogrom, from 55 percent to 32 percent; this, after the proportion of Jewish readers had climbed from one-fifth in 1897, to one-third in 1899, to 55 percent just before the violence broke out. Clearly, the pogrom severely damaged Jewish willingness to mingle with their Christian neighbors, even in such a benign environment as a lending library. Several years later, after a terrible flood of the Dnepr River, only seven of the thousands of Jewish families in the low-lying neighborhood of Podol took refuge at the district's solidly built Contract House; an observer claimed that most Jewish flood victims, remembering their experience of the pogrom, were too afraid to come to the Contract House and chose instead to take shelter in damp garrets where, presumably, they would not have to mingle closely with Christians or be an easy target for anti-Jewish violence.[158] Their fears do not seem out of place when we read that in that same year, bands of *soiuzniki* (members of the right-wing Union of Russian People) wandered the streets of Kiev, asking, "Jew or Russian?" and beating up those Jews foolhardy enough to tell the truth.[159] The increasing violence was accompanied by round-ups more vicious than those experienced before 1905—including humiliating daytime razzias and mass expulsions, not surprising given the threat that all Jews were now said to pose to the very existence of the Russian Empire itself.[160] Kiev's illegal Jews were said to live "like hunted animals," especially now that Stolypin's circular of 1906 about Jews living outside the Pale had been "clarified" to cover only Jews who had *not* had residence permits for those areas; those who had carried such permits but had then allowed them to lapse after the issuing of the circular were now living illegally in places such as Kiev—and thus were candidates for expulsion.[161] In 1910, more than one thousand Jewish families were expelled.[162] A report from 1911 describes policemen going into Jewish stores and businesses, tearing people away from their work, gathering them in a courtyard, and marching them off to the police station where their papers would be examined.[163]

The Beilis Affair

The last few years of the tsarist regime can without doubt be called the most insecure of all those preceding them. An especially dark year for Kiev Jewry was 1911, which saw the beginning of the Beilis Affair and the assassination of Prime Minister Petr Stolypin—both events of national significance occurring in Kiev with direct implications for the city's Jews. After the murder of twelve-year-old Andrei Iushchinskii in March 1911 (probably at the hands of members of a criminal gang who knew that the boy had overheard information relating to crimes they had committed), members of the Union of Russian People (URP), a right-wing and antisemitic organization also known as the Black Hundreds, circulated leaflets claiming that Iushchinskii had been the victim of a Jewish ritual murder. They called for revenge—in the form of a pogrom.[164] Extremists rampaged through the Jewish suburb of Slobodka (across the Dnepr River in Chernigov guberniia), attacking Jews at random. The threat of pogrom was very real, especially at large-scale assemblies such as the memorial service for Iushchinskii, where police reinforcements were provided in order to avoid violence.[165] The assassination of Stolypin by Dmitrii Bogrov in September led to another frenzy of right-wing antisemitic rhetoric, and a pogrom was only averted when the governor-general issued a decree specifically banning such an occurrence.[166] Even Max Mandel'shtam, who had been a cornerstone of the city's Jewish community for four decades, now wrote to a friend in Vienna that he was considered leaving Kiev.[167]

Information about the case was quickly picked up by the right-wing press, and the empire's attention was focused on Kiev as the investigation picked up pace. Although the initial inquiry concluded that Iushchinskii had been murdered by criminal elements, Minister of Justice I. G. Shcheglovitov and other right-wing bureaucrats (though not the imperial government as a whole) worked behind the scenes to ensure that the case would proceed to trial as a ritual murder.[168] Thus it was that Beilis—whose only connection to the murder was the fact that he had worked at the Zaitsev brick factory, situated near the site where Iushchinskii's body had been found—was arrested for the murder in July 1911 and subsequently languished in jail for the next two years awaiting trial.

As the affair dragged on, with more than two years separating Beilis's arrest in July 1911 and the start of the trial in September 1913, Kiev's Jewish community continued to be the target of chauvinist and antisemitic hatred. Right-wing organizations published publications such as a leaflet blaming the "zhids" for Iushchinskii's murder and warning Christian parents to protect their children from Jews, and soiuzniki distributed them at places like the Podol markets—no coincidence, as these markets, in the heart of a heavily Jewish neighborhood, were weekend gathering places for Christian workers and peasants.[169] The authorities seemed to be doing little or nothing to suppress these provocations—in some case even attending local gatherings of right-wing forces—and Jewish newspapers reported that Kiev's Jews feared the outbreak of a fresh pogrom.[170] Before Easter 1912, a delegation of Kiev's rabbis called upon the governor and asked him to prevent a pogrom during the upcoming holiday.[171] The Beilis Defense Committee—which included such local leaders and notables as Lev Brodsky; Rabbi Shlomo Ha-Cohen Aronson, the best-known "spiritual" rabbi in Kiev; Beilis's defense attorney Arnol'd Margolin; Mark Zaitsev, son of Ionna Zaitsev; and Dr. G. B. Bykhovskii, chief physician of the Zaitsev Surgical Hospital—discussed taking steps to defend the community, including offering a reward for information on the true murderer of Iushchinskii and bringing in experts to investigate the case, but they were apparently not sure whether, in Kiev's tense atmosphere, these would redound to the benefit of the community.[172] The battle they were fighting was uphill indeed.

Sholem Aleichem attempted to capture the mood of Kiev's Jews in these difficult days in his *Further Adventures of Menachem-Mendl:* when his protagonist Menachem-Mendl arrives in Kiev around 1912 and asks his friend about Jewish cultural issues, the friend replies, "'Eh, who can think of that? Now there is nothing else for us but Beiliss [*sic*], only Beiliss!'"[173] Later, Menachem-Mendl writes,

> You hear nothing these days but [hopes for Beilis's release]. I went past the stock exchange on the Kreshtshatik [*sic*], stepped in to Semadeni['s cafe], where I once spent my days, better to forget them. I had some coffee, looked around and didn't recognize the place! What stock exchange?

> What Semadeni? A ruin! I saw a few familiar faces, sad-looking, miserable brokers. . . . You didn't hear them laughing. Apparently there was nothing to laugh about.[174]

If this fictional depiction is anything like the reality, the Beilis Affair weighed heavily indeed on Kiev's Jews. Even the brokers at the exchange, normally preoccupied with only one thing—money—now could think of nothing but the affair.

The Kievan context for the trial was an ambiguous one. On the one hand, there could be no better site for a ritual murder trial than Christian Kiev, stronghold of the Black Hundreds and a Slavic island in the middle of the Pale of Settlement, at least in theory. On the other hand, as any student of Kiev's recent history could have told the trial's organizers, the situation was much more complicated. Far from being the fundamentalist Jew that prosecutors claimed had carried out the religiously motivated murder, Beilis was not particularly observant and in fact had worked the Saturday shift at the brick factory. Moreover, he lived in a non-Jewish neighborhood of the city and was apparently well-liked by all, Jews and Christians.[175] The fact that he was employed by Zaitsev, who was also active in the annual organization of the baking of Passover matzahs, was brought up at the trial as circumstantial evidence pointing to Beilis's guilt.[176] Even more bizarrely, some URP members were known to be friendly with individual Jews despite the virulent antisemitism espoused by their organization.[177] Indeed, there is evidence that the timing of the trial was motivated by national politics, as the extreme right wing was looking for something—perhaps a cause célèbre—to help it win the upcoming elections.[178] Nonetheless, local antisemites were enthusiastic about the trial, as is evidenced by the rhetoric in a retrospective published in 1914 by the ultranationalist Kiev Russian Gathering (Kievskoe russkoe sobranie), once a branch of the national organization by the same name but now independent. The report testified that the organization had sent congratulatory telegrams to various judicial and governmental figures, thanking them for following through on the case; blamed the "all-powerful Jewish kahal, [and] its willing and unwilling agents, the Jewish press" and others for covering up what was clearly a case of ritual murder; and protested the "indignation endured by those Russian Kievans who will not yield to Judaic reprimands and temptations [*iudeiskim vnusheniiam i iskusheniiam*]."[179] On the other hand, several local conservatives not known for their great love of Jews—monarchist politician V. V. Shul'gin and nationalist publicist D. I. Pikhno, writing in *Kievlianin,* of all papers—came out publicly against the trial in 1912 and 1913, which shocked the Russian nationalist movement.[180] As Kievans involved in the Beilis Affair, Shul'gin and Pikhno, along with defense attorney Margolin, were actually exceptions to the rule: most of Russia's prominent Judeophobic activists as well as its eminent Jewish advocates who devoted their energies to the trial were not from Kiev. (As Michael Hamm writes, "in fairness to Kiev, the Beilis Affair was more a national than a local crusade.")[181]

Historians now know that the jury was rigged and that some witnesses were bribed. Nonetheless, the jury found Beilis innocent—though it still asserted that the killing had indeed been a ritual murder. Thus, this was a Phyrric victory for progressive forces and particularly for Russian Jews; the acquittal was clearly a terrible blow for the tsarist government, but the affair "could not but contribute to the general feeling of despondency among Russian Jews in the last years before war and revolution."[182]

Conclusion

A twenty-first-century observer might guess that the pogrom of 1881 would have put a stop to continue Jewish migration to Kiev, or that the official restrictions on Jewish residence, which under some bureaucrats were enforced very harshly indeed, would have been a deterrent for many. But Jews continued to settle in Kiev. Of the hundreds of interactions between Jews and Christians that took place every day in the city, very few seem to have been openly hostile. Surely some fraction of such incidents would have made their way into the press and memoirs, but those sources contain very few descriptions of everyday animosity. It seems unlikely that they were so common as not to be considered worthy of mention.

The 1905 pogrom was not only an outburst of antisemitic violence; it was a symbolic reconquest of Kiev from the "seditionist Jews" whose influence, in the minds of many Christians, had grown far too great in the city. The "patriotic" demonstrations on the main thoroughfares of Kiev that took place throughout the pogrom were a show of force and strength; they were meant to broadcast a message: we control the city. The violence and looting were yet another way of saying, albeit in a less civilized manner, that the "true Russians" and the "native population" were the only people who had the right to be in Kiev, and Jews, their property, and even their lives were all "rightless"—what in Yiddish might be called *hefker.* The inaction of the authorities, and the lack of self-defense among Jews, only strengthened this argument.

After the 1905 pogrom, however, Jewish insecurity grew to unprecedented heights. Now Jews not only feared being caught without a residence permit and being expelled from the city, but they also dreaded the next deadly riot. An observer remarked in 1912 that Kiev's Jews, always haunted by the specter of pogrom, "lived with a sword hanging over their heads."[183] What would spark the next pogrom? Whether it was Passover, the anniversary of Stolypin's assassination, or even Election Day, their enemies were sure to find a propitious time to attack. The numerous near-pogroms that occurred during these years were fictionalized poignantly by Sholem Aleichem in his novel *The Bloody Hoax* (*Der blutiger shpas*), which described wealthy Jews taking out foreign passports to ensure a quick escape, prosperous middle-class Jews hocking furs and jewels at the city's pawnshops, and poor Jews rushing to the train station only to sit waiting with thousands of others like them until, finally, the governor issued a declaration banning a pogrom.[184] For all their talk of defending Jewish national pride, self-defense groups such as those organized by the Bund had little chance of success in the face of official repression and internal division.

Nonetheless, Kiev continued to be a magnet for Jews. Perhaps Kiev's Jews so needed (or wanted) to remain in the city, despite all the problems, that they learned to downplay the gravity of their situation, as in their reported reaction to the expulsion of 1910: "The affair was not as terrible as the newspapers make it out to be."[185] The article, one of a series in *Haynt* entitled "The Truth about Kiev," added that this opinion was expressed by "all kinds of Jews in Kiev, from the communal leaders to the people in the street." In another article in the series, the correspondent wrote that to understand the importance of Kiev for Jews, one had to understand its geographical and economic role in the region. When Jews were restricted from going to a city outside the Pale like Moscow, they figured out a way to do it through agents. But, he explained, it was different with Kiev: it was full of Jews, and right in the middle of the Pale—indeed, it was the heart and nerve center of the entire region: "Kiev is where merchandise is bought and sold; the seat of the district court and all of the administrative and governmental bureaus that almost everyone has need of; . . . Kiev is where you find a good lawyer, and where you go when you are sick. . . ." Kiev was a hub for the sugar industry, for import–export, for trade in real estate and forested properties, and was a port handling tens of millions of rubles of merchandise. In short, "without Kiev, a Jew is lost."[186]

FIGURE 1.1. Lazar' Brodsky. *Photograph courtesy Leonid Finberg and the Kiev Institute of Jewish Studies.*

FIGURE 1.2. D. S. Margolin. *Photograph courtesy Leonid Finberg and the Kiev Institute of Jewish Studies.*

FIGURE 1.3. Max Mandel'shtam. *Photograph courtesy Leonid Finberg and the Kiev Institute of Jewish Studies.*

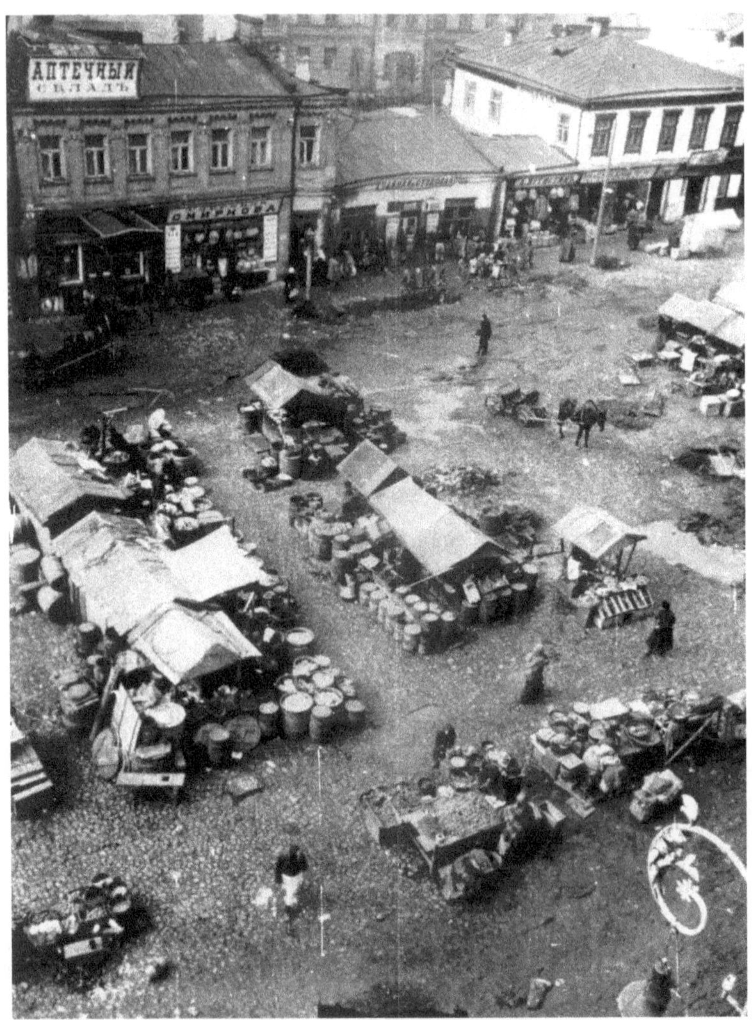

FIGURE 1.4. Evreiskii bazar ("The Jewish Bazaar"), also known as Galitskii Market, undated photograph. *Courtesy Leonid Finberg and the Kiev Institute of Jewish Studies.*

FIGURE 3.1. Studio portrait of the Rutov family, 1911: Mordkhe, who ran a hardware store, his wife Eta Bella, and their sons Iosif (r.) and Aleksandr. *From family collection of Viktor Khamishon. From the Archive of the YIVO Institute for Jewish Research, New York (RG 120, Russia II, folder 145.13).*

FIGURE 3.2. Evreiskii bazar ("The Jewish Bazaar"), also known as Galitskii Market, 1905. *Courtesy Central Archives for the History of the Jewish People (Ru 441, no 49). Original in Tsentral'nyi derzhavnyi arkhiv kino-foto-fonodokumentiv, Kiev.*

FIGURE 3.3. View of Podol, ca. 1890–1900. *Courtesy Library of Congress Prints and Photographs Division.*

FIGURE 3.4. View of Podol, ca. 1902. *Courtesy Library of Congress Prints and Photographs Division.*

FIGURE 3.5. View of Kreshchatik, ca. 1890–1900. *Courtesy Library of Congress Prints and Photographs Division.*

FIGURE 3.6. Crowd in front of City Hall (Duma), 1905 or 1906. Photograph taken as part of relief mission of the Russo-Jewish Committee in the wake of the pogroms of 1905. *Courtesy University of Southampton Special Collections (MS 128, Papers of Carl Stettauer, AJ 22/A/7).*

FIGURE 3.7. House on Zhilianskaia street with windows smashed and debris in front of building as a result of the 1905 pogrom. *Courtesy University of Southampton Special Collections (MS 128, Papers of Carl Stettauer, AJ 22/A/7).*

FIGURE 3.8. Entrance hall in house of M. B. Gal'perin showing destruction after 1905 pogrom. *Courtesy University of Southampton Special Collections (MS 128, Papers of Carl Stettauer, AJ 22/A/7).*

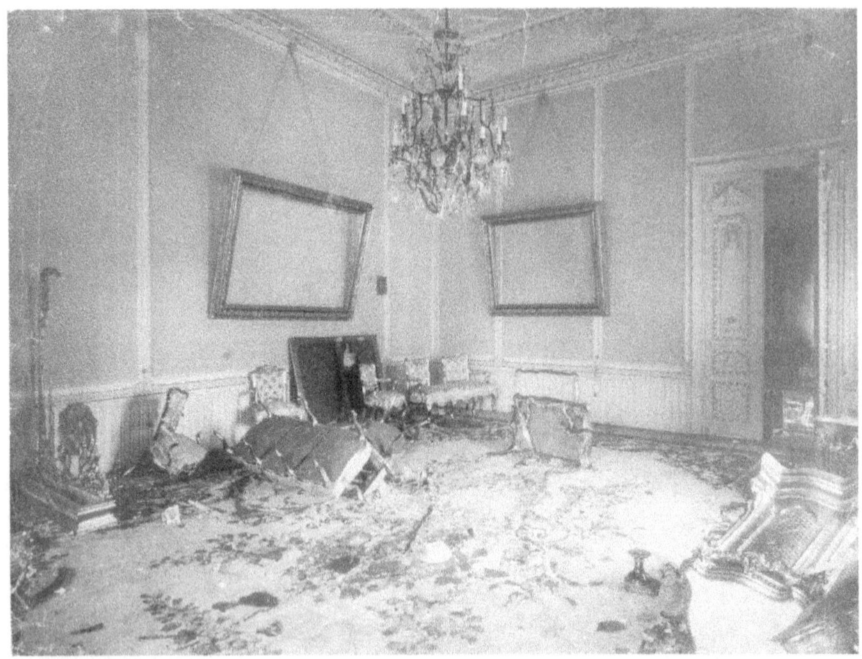

FIGURE 3.9. Salon in house of M. B. Gal'perin showing destruction after 1905 pogrom. *Courtesy University of Southampton Special Collections (MS 128, Papers of Carl Stettauer, AJ 22/A/7).*

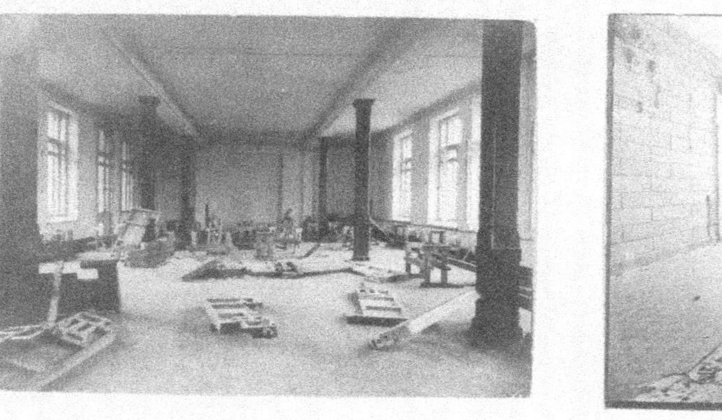

FIGURE 3.10. Destruction inside Brodsky School, 1905. *Courtesy University of Southampton Special Collections (MS 128, Papers of Carl Stettauer, AJ 22/A/7).*

FIGURE 3.11. Crowd of peasants marching with flags and portraits of the tsar, 1905. *Courtesy University of Southampton Special Collections (MS 128, Papers of Carl Stettauer, AJ 22/A/7).*

FIGURE 3.12. Two bodies (pogrom victims) on stretcher with crowd staring at photographer, 1905. *Courtesy University of Southampton Special Collections (MS 128, Papers of Carl Stettauer, AJ 22/A/7).*

FIGURE 3.13. Mendel Beilis with his family, ca. 1913. *Courtesy of YIVO Institute for Jewish Research (collection MG).*

FIGURE 3.14. Bodies of pogrom victims with onlookers. *Courtesy University of Southampton Special Collections (MS 128, Papers of Carl Stettauer, AJ 22/A/7).*

4

Modern Jewish Cultures and Practices

Jewish historiography has often regarded the Jews of Eastern Europe as an exception in the European Jewish encounter with modernity. Along with Romania, the Russian Empire was the only European country that had not emancipated its Jews by the time of the First World War. External assimilatory pressures and internal forces for change had also apparently made fewer inroads on the masses. Preserving Yiddish and traditional piety for much longer than did other Jewries, they were seen as more authentically Jewish.[1] As Eli Lederhendler has written, however, the experience of East European Jews in the nineteenth century—even lacking emancipation and assimilation—was not a special case that must be viewed separately from that of Jews in Western and Central Europe.[2] Benjamin Nathans has shown that Russian Jews did indeed encounter emancipation, albeit in a different form from the classical model offered by the French Revolution or Joseph II's Toleranzpatent.[3] The "selective integration" of the tsarist regime was in some ways not very much different from the gradual, quid-pro-quo schemes found in the German states. As for "assimilation," the Russian Empire offered Jews as individuals the possibility of wholesale absorption into Russian society through conversion, as was true elsewhere in Europe. In a fashion less radical than apostasy, Jews became "Russian" in much the same way that other national minorities in the empire did, through gradual acculturation and russification. However, as assimilated or traditionalist individual Jews might have been, all Jewries across Europe maintained some level of corporate identity and consciousness and all experienced some degree of acculturation and Europeanization.[4]

Recent trends in assimilation theory—which is most often used to understand the social psychology of immigrants and immigrant culture but can be applied more widely to multinational and multiethnic contexts—are useful in understanding Russian Jews and their relationship to the larger society in which they lived. Milton Gordon's straight-line theory of assimilation posits seven dimensions of assimilation, the first of which is behavioral assimilation or acculturation: the adoption of cultural patterns of the host by the minority without social contact and interaction between the two groups.[5] Gordon's second dimension is "structural assimilation," which includes social contacts of the minority with the dominant group on two levels: primary relations and secondary relations. To some extent, the category of primary relations—contacts within the realms of family and friendship networks and clubs and neighborhoods—is applicable to Jews in fin-de-siècle Kiev, especially when we consider that other social traits such as class and individual characteristics can, in this instance, become more important than ethnicity. However, "secondary relations"—equal access to power and privilege within society's main institutions and elimination of minority status—are unequivocally inapplicable to the case of Kiev's Jews. More recent formulations have attempted to add nuance to this model by stressing the complexity of the acculturation process: for example, the "two-culture matrix" and "multidimensionality" models posit slightly different variations on what is basically a multifaceted process of adaptation in which members of the minority group adopt some aspects and practices of the majority culture but retain characteristics of their native culture "in a flexible and situationally dictated manner."[6] Whichever theory we attempt to apply, we must conclude that there was a wide range of acculturation among Kiev's Jews depending on class, educational background, linguistic abilities, and a number of other factors.

It must be remembered that Kiev's Jews were not the only minority in the city, nor was the city unequivocally Russian in language or in culture, despite a veneer of imperial culture that was shallower or deeper depending on the context and circumstances. At times there must surely have been more Ukrainian, Yiddish, and the local combination of Russian and Ukrainian known as *surzhik* spoken at Kiev's markets than any form of literary Russian. When it came to the city's governmental institutions, official bureaucracy, high commerce, and education, it was not only Kiev's Yiddish-speaking Jews, but also its Ukrainians—as well as Poles and Germans—who had to negotiate a Russian-speaking city.

The case of the Jews of Kiev reinforces the reevaluation of the place of Russian Jewry in the larger historiography of European Jewry. To a surprising degree, Jews became Russian, participated in municipal life, and interacted with their non-Jewish neighbors. At the same time, as occurred in Western and Central Europe, bourgeois Jews became acutely conscious of their distance from an "authentic" Jewish existence and strove to strengthen their Jewish identity by creating new forms of Jewish culture that were seen as genuine because rooted in the quasi-mystical people or *Volk* (Russian *narod,* Yiddish *folk,* Hebrew *le'om*). This phenomenon came about in part because of growing hostility to Jews within Russian society, but paradoxically it was also a measure of how comfortable Jews felt in that society, or at least as carriers of its culture.[7] So "Russian" were Jews becoming that one of the central tasks facing the leadership of Russian Jewry was to bring Jews back to their heritage. And in multiethnic cities such as Kiev, it was increasingly acceptable and even stylish to be an adherent of a particular national culture while retaining one's primary allegiance to the Russian state. This was, by its nature, a concern of the middle class alone; the toiling masses were for the most part too busy eking out their daily bread to be overly concerned about the character, quality, and future of Jewish culture.

The sources make it frustratingly difficult to get a firm grasp on the extent of Russian acculturation among Kiev's Jewish masses. It was probably not as clear-cut a process as is portrayed in the classic historiographical literature (and especially in works with a socialist slant), such as the description of the transformation of the family of Grigorii Gol'denberg in a Soviet historian's account. After the Gol'denbergs' move from Berdichev, where "they had been an observant merchant family," to Kiev, where David Gol'denberg "opened up a flourishing hardware store,"

> currents of modern life poured into the Kiev home of the Goldenbergs. And together with these currents there penetrated the progressive ideas of the epoch. . . . Even the parents succumbed to the influence of this new atmosphere. This was shown in the first place by their willingness to give their children a secular education.[8]

Some families and individuals may indeed have experienced a radical transformation after arriving in the big city, but for most, changes occurred more slowly. The acculturation process is incredibly complex; choices and practices cannot be assigned to any category or class of Jews with any certainty. One university student might not even know Yiddish, yet identify as a Jewish nationalist and observe important aspects of Jewish practice. Another might have Yiddish as a native language and think in both Russian and Yiddish, yet live a completely secular life and endorse the possibility of conversion for those Jews who chose it. Jewish migrants to the city were likely to adhere to traditional religious practices, but might also pick and choose from individual rituals and observances. Economic, occupational, political, and even leisure activities brought Jews and non-Jews together, requiring from Jews a knowledge of spoken Russian, at the very least. Jewish professionals who had attended Russian gymnasia and universities usually spoke Russian in the home, and many had tenuous links, at best, with organized Judaism. Then too, wealthy merchants and industrialists created their own mode of Jewish affiliation, frequently worshiping separately from other Jews and staking out a claim to leadership of the community. Members of the middling and haute bourgeoisie, especially women, came together in "associational Judaism" to create a network of Jewish social service organizations that in some ways built on traditional models of charity while standing in the mainstream of Russian philanthropic culture. As Steven Zipperstein has remarked for Odessa, Jewish acculturation was not an intellectual or ideological stance but simply made economic and practical sense; thus, it was not planned, but developed ad hoc as circumstances dictated.[9]

Jews settling in Kiev entered a city that was known as the mother of Russian cities, and it was indeed a bastion of Russianness in a sea of Ukrainian villages, Jewish shtetlekh, and even Polish estates. But as their numbers and influence grew, Kiev grew ever more Jewish, as we saw in detail in chapters 1 and 3. Despite the exclusion of Jews from the city's political life after 1890, they played a significant role in local life—its economy, philanthropies, and associations, from the Jewish-dominated commodities exchange to the "Jewish Bazaar" and the neighborhoods of Podol and Lybed, to the dozens of institutions and welfare organizations throughout the city endowed by Kiev's Jewish millionaires. These establishments served as models for other communities. At the same time, the community shaped a new Jewish culture rooted in the traditions and conventions of premodern Jewish society and adopting the urban culture of the Russian Empire and the sensibilities and aesthetics of fin-de-siècle Europe.[10]

Jewish Culture to 1907

The small Jewish intelligentsia of pre-1905 Kiev felt isolated and beleaguered—not so much because the city's Jews were so russified, but simply because they seemed indifferent to Jewish culture (or culture of any kind, for that matter). Scholars have pointed out the ironies of the turn of events wherein the maskilim, proponents of secular education and European culture, were victims of their own success when new generations of Jews became so thoroughly Russian that they could not even read the literature that the maskilim worked so hard to produce. A handful of Hebrew and Yiddish writers lived in the city, most of them making their living as secretaries, clerks, or teachers for the Jewish magnates. They gathered every Thursday at the Iudaika, the small library containing scholarly books on Jewish topics in Hebrew and European languages that had been established by "expert Jew" (*uchenyi evrei*) Aaron Tseitlin in 1885, to discuss the affairs of the day and the Jewish question. These maskilim, we are told, were joined by national-minded professionals such as Dr. Max Mandel'shtam, lawyer German Barats, and Crown Rabbi Tsukkerman.[11] Such intellectual engagement could scarcely compete with the excitement and quick fortunes to be made at the Kiev Exchange, where young Hebrew poets "wasted their talents" (Rozenblat complained) by playing the market, or the entertainment offered by the city's theaters and billiard halls. Unlike Vilna, Eliezer Friedmann complained, few young Jews were involved in Jewish affairs of any kind.[12]

The most popular leisure activity among Kievans, whether Jewish or not, was not cultural discussion, but card-playing.[13] On Friedmann's first evening in Kiev in 1893, people started gathering at his brother-in-law's house for what he assumed was a meeting—especially since one of the arrivals was Sholem Aleichem. Instead, they set up cardboard-covered tables and threw themselves into cards, the Yiddish writer as enthusiastically as everyone else, one hand holding his cards and the other a drink or a leg of goose. In the morning, Friedmann found Sholem Aleichem in the same place, asleep on some chairs.[14]

Luckily, Sholem Aleichem took time out from his card games to write, and revealed his familiarity with Kievans' love of cards when he had his fictional Menakhem-Mendl explain to Sheyne-Sheyndl:

> [Yehupetz is] a lovely town, there's no comparing it to Odessa. You couldn't wish for nicer, more considerate people, men and women alike. Their only weakness is cards; they stay up calling "Deal!" until the wee hours. The older folk favor a game called Preference while the young ones play whist, rummy, and klabberjass.[15]

It should come as no surprise, then, that the chief source of income for the Kiev Literature and Art Society in 1903 was cards, apparently derived from the fee that members paid for each game they played.[16]

According to most accounts, Sholem Aleichem himself had first come to Kiev in 1887 because of its business and investment opportunities, not because of literary prospects. Nonetheless, in his third-person memoir *From the Fair* he tells a different story:

> He was drawn to the big city, like a child attracted to the light of the moon. For a great town contained great people—the bright stars that shone down on us here on earth with the clear light of vast and endless skies. I refer to the great writers and divinely graced poets of the Haskala whose names made such a great impression upon—what shall I call them?—well, the young maskilim, the naive, innocent youth.[17]

His first dablings in business did not have a happy ending, and he left Kiev in 1890 after going bankrupt, returning three years later to support himself and his family with trading and brokering.[18] He eventually secured a job at the Kiev Exchange and, according to anecdotal reports, lived a comfortable life in the city, summering in a dacha in the suburb of Boiarka (which he fictionalized as Boyberik in the "Tevye the Milkman" cycle).[19] His presence in the city contributed greatly to the eclectic Jewish cultural scene; the Yiddish writer and critic Nakhmen Mayzel even claimed that Kiev only became a "Jewish city" thanks to Sholem Aleichem's activity.[20] Yiddishist and political activist Nokhem Shtif, a student at the Polytechnical Institute at the time, later remembered, "I first heard about Yiddish in a serious vein when Sholem Aleichem read his stories at Zionist gatherings in Kiev in 1900–1902."[21] In a letter to his brother in 1889, Sholem Aleichem himself wrote, "Any educated person will find it of use to visit me, as my house is a gathering place for the wise and enlightened (*hakhamim u-maskilim*) of Kiev, as all who enter the gates of my city know."[22] In the late 1880s, for example, he produced the first Yiddish literary almanac, *Di yudishe folks-bibliothek*, which had a significant impact on the subsequent development of Yiddish letters (I. L. Peretz made his Yiddish-language debut in the 1888 volume). In 1894, he wrote "Yakneho"z (or the Great Exchange Comedy)," a send-up of the Jewish speculators at the Kiev Exchange, which was so offensive to some that it was denounced to the authorities (apparently by some of the brokers who were mocked in the piece) and confiscated.[23]

The "Yakneho"z" incident makes clear that to the extent that Jewish culture was alive in Kiev, its existence was bound up with the money around which life in the city revolved, dependent on the sugar industry on which so many Jews relied. There was no state Jewish school in Kiev to provide maskilim with a measure of independence and a base for influence in the community, as was the case in Odessa.[24] Jacob Sheftel, a researcher of Talmudic and medieval literature and owner of a Jewish bookstore in Kiev, made his living by managing the affairs of the wealthy widow Rozenberg. The Hebrew poet Yehalel (Yehudah Leib Levin) worked as a tutor and secretary for the Brodsky family. Eliezer Schulman, one of the first historians of Yiddish language and literature, was the treasurer of one of the Brodsky enterprises.[25] Throwing in one's lot with the Brodskys was potentially quite lucrative, but it also had its risks. According to Friedmann, Schulman married the daughter of a Brodsky underling in exchange for a position with the sugar magnate, thereby not only securing a job for himself but also enabling himself to leave the provincial town of Zlatopol for Kiev.[26] Yehalel's precarious and dependent relationship with the Brodskys is made clear by an 1872 letter in which he pleaded for a raise, showering praise upon his employer while describing his own insolvency and miserable existence in pitiful terms. "Am I such a heavy burden that you cannot have mercy upon me? Do you consider my salary to be a great fortune?"[27] The poet's final fate was a dramatic one: after he published a poem describing the inner workings of the family business, Brodsky banished him from bustling Kiev to the provincial hamlet of Tomashpol.[28]

Their proximity to plutocrats like Brodsky could at times help to secure support for causes dear to maskilim. For example, a collection was taken up for the family of the late Hebrew nationalist writer Peretz Smolenskin, whose greatest advocate in Kiev was Eliezer Schulman; contributions were secured from Lazar' Brodsky and other Jewish notables in Kiev.[29] The apparent commonality of interests between the literary intelligentsia and the merchantry was also revealed by memorial services for deceased writers and scholars dedicated to the national cause; these included Samuel Joseph Fuenn (Rashi Fin), Heinrich Graetz, and Y. L. Gordon and were held at the merchants' synagogue, also referred to as the "reformed" service (*ha-minyan ha-metukan*) and the "quorum of the enlightened" (*minyan ha-ne'orim*).[30]

Clearly, not all those of the new generation were lacking in Jewish spirit and knowledge, as some claimed.[31] *Ha-melits* reported that a group of young Jewish men from families of means had founded a society for the study of Hebrew language and literature in 1894, but its members evidently lost interest quickly, for the society had to be revived only two years later.[32] Some observers alleged that Kiev's older maskilim cared little about the youthful Hebraists, and failed to offer assistance to the new society in its formative period. The established Hebrew writers, it was intimated, preferred organizations and events on a grand scale and could not be bothered with a piddling new society.[33] At the same time, a call went out to revive the Iudaika library, which had also dwindled in active membership and activities. Aharon Ha-Levi Iznor echoed earlier criticism of Kiev's maskilim, writing in *Ha-melits* that the institution should not be the exclusive province of the enlightened but must belong to all Jews. For that reason, he repeated his call of earlier in the year that it should be moved to Podol, where most Jews lived.[34] Podol was, indeed, the site of meetings of the newly reactivated Hebrew society, which met at the new Rozenberg Synagogue; youths "from all walks of life" came to hear lectures in Bible, Jewish history, grammar, literature, and the like. Iznor exhorted Kiev's maskilim to support the fledgling organization and not to keep their distance.[35] Hebraist and Zionist Moshe Rozenblat corroborates the existence of the society in his recollections of the Hebrew movement in Kiev: according to him, it was first called Sefat Tsiyon (The Language of Zion), and was later changed to Ivriya (the name is something akin to "Hebraica") as a branch of the organization by the same name that already existed in Odessa.[36] Exhibiting the social conscience characteristic of Russian youth, the young people active in the society resolved at one of their meetings to establish a Hebrew and Russian literacy school for young artisans' apprentices that would be held on Saturdays and Sundays.[37]

Yitshak Ya'akov Vaysberg, one of the older generation of maskilim, suggested that a Jewish library be established not in Podol but in the new Choral Synagogue.[38] But others disagreed: wealthy Jews, busy with their own affairs, could not be expected to help support Jewish culture in Kiev; it was up to the middle class to act, one Elhanan Kalmansohn opined in *Ha-melits*.[39] A description of a literary event to mark the jubilee of the Hebrew writer L. L. Shulman in 1901 is notable for its omission of the categories of "students" and "youth" from the long list of groups attending: the list mentioned "literati, authors, correspondents, poets, doctors, lawyers, Zionists, millionaires, maskilim, merchants, teachers." Such a large-scale event in support of Hebrew culture—with illustrious guests such as Zionist thinker Ahad Ha-am and teacher David Yellin, a leader of the *yishuv* in Palestine—was clearly rare in those years: "this Jewish celebration was a novelty, the likes of which has almost never been seen before here."[40] Even then, when Kiev's Jewish population numbered in the tens of thousands, the author of this article betrayed a continuing insecurity, referring to his home as "our non-Jewish Kiev, where Jews hang [suspended] as in the air."

Indeed, Friedmann complained that "the new generation does not have a Jewish spirit" and knew nothing about Judaism or Jewish culture, a critique that others echoed. Some blamed the poor state of Jewish education in the city, since most Jewish schools were forced underground because of restrictions.[41] In 1902, Sholem Aleichem wrote to S. Y. Abramovitsh (Mendele Mokher Sforim), "You have forgotten that Yehupets [Kiev] is not Odessa. In

Yehupets, even if someone bursts,[42] he will die a cruel death trying to find a copy of *'Fishke'* or *'Susati'* (My Horse)—they are not to be found! This hole which is Yehupets, may it go up in flames!"[43] Several correspondents in *Ha-melits*, openly envious of Lithuania with its many yeshivas and teachers, lamented the sad state of Jewish education throughout Ukraine: boys were trained to make a living, while girls went to school to learn Russian well, and only sometimes learned Hebrew.[44] Friedmann also referred to southern Jews as *"am ha-arets"* (boors).[45] These critiques must, however, be taken with a grain of salt, since their authors were usually maskilim with open hostility toward Hasidism, the dominant religious mode in the Ukrainian provinces.

Palestinophiles in Kiev

There was a brief burst of successful Palestinophile activity in the mid-1880s following the pogroms of 1881–82 and the establishment of the Hibbat Zion movement. Max Mandel'shtam and the Hebrew poet Yehalel were the driving force behind the branch and were indeed leaders of the movement on the national level; Mandel'shtam, together with Pinsker, Lilienblum, and others, worked to forge a confederation out of individual Hibbat Zion groups.[46] As with almost every aspect of organized Jewish life in Kiev, successful activity depended on the support of the notables, and the Kiev Palestinophiles consistently tried to win over the city's Jewish elite. Some Jewish plutocrats donated money to support emigration in the immediate wake of the pogroms, but ceased contributing when they regained confidence in the Russian government and its actions to stop anti-Jewish violence. A celebration in 1884 of the one hundredth birthday of Moses Montefiore, patron of Jewish settlement in Palestine and advocate for Jewry the world over, was made simultaneously into an occasion to honor Israel Brodsky. Funds raised at the festivities were to be earmarked for Jewish settlers in Palestine. Israel Darewski, describing the event, added that although Brodsky and his son Lazar had not yet actually donated to the cause, it was hoped that they would contribute a large sum (!).[47] Hebrew writer Y. Y. Vaysberg also voiced the hope that Kiev's notables would hearken to the call to assist in settling the Land of Israel, just as many middle-class Kiev Jews were doing.[48] Some apparently did: internal memoranda within the Kiev provincial administration reveal knowledge of an 1885 meeting of both rich and poor Jews at the home of merchant Moisei Vainshtein, a leader of the city's Jewish community, where 8,000 rubles were raised for the Love of Zion movement.[49] Vainshtein's home was in Ploskaia, which indicates that he was a businessman of a somewhat lesser order than Brodsky, Margolin, and the other grandees; this, however, did not hinder him from raising over double the sum raised at the meeting in 1884.

An apocryphal story was told about an encounter between the plutocrat Lazar' Brodsky and the Zionist leader Mandel'shtam, in Brodsky's office. When Mandel'shtam returned from the First Zionist Congress in 1897, he presented a report on the proceedings in a private meeting with some of the plutocrats. Brodsky asked him, "If you like this plan so much, why don't you go to Palestine yourself?" Mandel'shtam responded, "You are now building all these hospitals in Kiev—why don't you be one of the first patients in them?"[50] Whether or not the story is actually true, it does provide insight into the perspectives of Kiev's two most prominent Jewish leaders, each of whom took a very different approach to Jewish communal affairs. While both men lived comfortable lives in Kiev and devoted considerable energy to bettering the lot of the Jewish masses, Mandel'shtam saw no future for Jews in Russia—in an 1887 letter to a colleague in Berlin, he described himself as "without homeland; a mixture of Jew, Russian, and German"—and thus poured all his energy into Zionism (and later Territorialism), while Brodsky was a classic liberal who believed that the tsarist government would eventually grant equal rights to Russian Jews.[51]

In 1894, Eliezer Friedmann, lamenting in *Ha-melits* that Jews no longer seemed to care about Hibbat Zion, took up the cudgel: the notables and great Jewish patrons of the city were especially to blame for the decline, apparently because they had withheld essential financial support.[52] He would later recall that during his first years in Kiev, from 1893 to 1899, there had been almost no substantive Palestinophile activity in the city.[53] This may have been an exaggeration, because other sources tell of meetings at the progressive prayer quorum (the forerunner of the Choral Synagogue), a two-hundred-strong volunteer or member corps, and collections of hundreds of rubles.[54] Moshe Rozenblat also recalled semi-clandestine Zionist meetings at Brodsky's synagogue as well as at the Rozenberg (Tailors') Synagogue in Podol and, for the intelligenty-professionals (doctors, lawyers, engineers, and the like), in private homes.[55] Sholem Aleichem was also very active as a Palestinophile propagandist in the late 1890s; among his works was "Der yudisher kongres in Bazel," a Yiddish version of a speech about the 1897 Zionist Congress that Mandel'shtam had given in a number of Kiev prayer houses.[56] Friedmann wrote that both Brodsky and Zaitsev were opposed to Hibbat Zion, and an anonymous article in *Ha-melits* in 1896 confirms that the movement had only had limited success in winning over the notables, in Kiev as elsewhere in the empire. Exulting that Baron Gintsburg and Jacob Poliakov, leading figures in Russian Jewry, were now members, the writer continued on a more somber note: "we can hope that the rest of the Jewish notables [*atsilei yisra'el*], in Kiev and in the other cities, will not stand against the society forever."[57] However, a published list of investors in the Jewish Colonial Bank in 1899 reveals that Zaitsev had bought five hundred shares, more than anyone else in Kiev, so perhaps his initial hostility turned into acceptance.[58] Overall, it seems clear that general interest in the cause was declining in the 1890s, as another Kiev observer wrote and as was the case throughout the empire.[59] Police harassment may have been another factor; archival documents reveal that Mandel'shtam, chair of the Kiev branch, denied any knowledge of a Hibbat Zion organization in Kiev when questioned by the chief of police in 1885.[60] Mandel'shtam himself wrote to a colleague in Vienna that official restrictions were hampering the growth of the movement, but added that the character of the Jews in southern Russia was also a problem, especially those of better means, who demanded immediate, concrete results. He also intimated that the Jews of the south were somewhat less energetic than those of Lithuania, where "countless societies" had already been organized.[61]

In a speech on the Zionist Congress in London in 1900, Mandel'shtam upbraided his fellow Zionists in Kiev, just as he had criticized the Zionist movement in general at the congress: "[As elsewhere,] we in Kiev have not done one-tenth of that which we could have done. Other than ten or twelve energetic individuals . . . everyone else slept, awakening only we shook them forcefully. Let every Zionist fulfil his duty . . . !"[62] At home in Kiev, from the turn of the century on, Mandel'shtam, together with Hillel Zlatopol'skii, a successful businessman who was also a donor to Jewish causes and a Hebraist, were kept busy as the heads of Russian Zionism's "financial center" (*merkaz ha-kesafim*), based in Kiev.[63] Students were also active in the Zionist movement; as he later recalled in his memoirs, Nokhem Shtif, a student at the Polytechnical Institute, belonged to "the general Zionist organization" before seceding with other students and founding "a leftist radical group."[64]

Linguistic Patterns

The threads of Jewish integration and segregation in Kiev were closely interwoven and are difficult to pull apart; hard and fast conclusions are difficult to draw. Nonetheless, the underlying trend seems to be that residential, cultural, and social isolation in the earlier decades began to give way around the turn of the century to a greater degree of acculturation and integration, which in turn prompted hostility on the part of non-Jews and a turn toward Jewish nationalism by Jews. (Interactions between Jews and the other nationalities in Kiev, Ukrainians and Russians, are discussed in more detail in chapter 5.) The years 1874–81 and 1905 provide good representative poles by which to contrast the two periods. In 1874, most Jews lived in Podol and Lybed, with scattered settlements in other parts of the city. The vast majority of the Jewish population cited Yiddish as its language of household use. According to journalist A. E. Kaufman, whose evaluation may have been influenced by his pro-integration convictions, Jews were almost totally isolated linguistically and culturally from those around them.[65] His ideology dictated that this isolation stemmed from the restrictions placed on Jews, but there is no reason not to think that some Jews were content to continue living in a Jewish context in which they were not required to adapt wholesale to the surrounding, foreign culture. That Jewish life in Kiev was centered in Podol is evident from the fact that the 1881 pogrom started in that neighborhood and only later moved to other areas of the city, according to the official investigation by Count Kutaisov.[66]

By contrast, in 1905 the pogrom started not in Podol but in central Kiev. To be sure, it was a demonstration in front of the city council building on Kreshchatik that sparked the violence, but this was also a symbol of the fact that the Jewish presence was now spread throughout the city, including its central neighborhoods. There were now sizable Jewish populations in such areas as Bul'varnaia and Lukianovskaia with 5,000 Jews in the former and almost 1,200 in the latter in 1908; these were official figures, with true numbers probably a good deal higher.[67] In the traditionally Jewish neighborhoods of Podol and Lybed, Jewish concentration was dense but by no means exclusively or even majority Jewish. Many of Kiev's physicians and lawyers, especially its most visible ones, were Jews; a reader of *Kievskie otkliki* (Kiev Echoes) would have found that ten of the sixteen doctors' advertisements on the front page had been placed by Jews.[68] In the 1897 census, 6 percent of Kiev's Jews claimed Russian as their mother tongue, but far more must have been functionally bilingual, speaking it as their language of everyday use in a city where over half of the population was Russian-speaking.[69] Even for Jewish market women, tailors, and brokers who had never had any formal Russian education, some knowledge of the language—or perhaps surzhik—

must have been essential for everyday interactions. Perhaps these were the types of students at the Saturday adult literacy school of the OPE to whom the 1907 annual report referred as "unacquainted with Russian speech" and to whom Jewish history should be taught in Yiddish.[70] Among the student population, which was more prone to acculturation than older or less educated Jews, linguistic acculturation had made much further inroads: by 1910 almost 70 percent of Kiev students either never spoke Yiddish or spoke it rarely, while more than 80 percent reported that they thought in Russian.[71] The extent of Russian's influence on even the most traditional Jews is betrayed by the use of the Russian word *chlen* ("member") in the Yiddish regulations found in the pinkas (record book) of Kiev's Hevra magidei tehilim, a traditional association with religious, social, and mutual-aid functions.[72]

Among Kiev's Jewish youth, Russian, not Yiddish, was the lingua franca.[73] In Sholem Aleichem's fictional account of a blood libel in Kiev, *The Bloody Hoax* (*Der blutiger shpas*), gymnasium student Syomke, excited about the upcoming holiday of Passover, exclaims to his mother in Yiddish, "Passover? Matzos? Matzo balls?" Then, switching to Russian, he adds, "I can ask the Four Questions, I can get a grade of five-plus [A+] in that!"[74] The irony here is thick: the four questions of the Passover seder are traditionally asked by the youngest child in a singsong Hebrew, but Syomke is announcing in *Russian* that he will ask them, and placing them in the context not of the religious ritual of the seder but of the Russian gymnasium with its one-through-five grading system. His mother Sara answers, "All right, all right. Tomorrow tell me stories in Russian, not today. The child can only speak to me in Russian, may a curse fall on my enemies!" The fact that Syomke speaks to her in Russian is a source of both pride and disappointment: while she is proud of his academic achievements, she is ambivalent about the russification that accompanies his gymnasium education. The complexity of these cultural transmutations is pointed up by Sara's appellations for her son, which are Yiddish diminutive versions of his everyday name, Syomke, which is in turn a Russian rendition of his official (Yiddish) name, Shlyomke: "Syomke! Syomkenyu! Syomketchke!"

Personal names were indeed a good gauge of acculturation. Many of the wealthy and middle-class Jews used European—though not necessarily ethnic Russian—names. Examples of such names were Ernestina (Zaks), Klara (Gintsburg), Sofiia (Gal'perin), Pavla (Gal'perin), Vera (Levin), Avgustina (Brodskaia), and Luiza (Ettinger). Men's names tended to be either Russian calques of Hebrew/Yiddish names or generic European names: Moisei, Solomon, Lazar', Mark, David.[75] A list of patients at the Free Jewish Sanatorium from 1908 suggests that the Jewish working class continued to use traditional names such as Kalman, Pinkhus, Gersh [Hirsh], Izrail' [Israel], Mordko [a version of Mordkhe or Mordecai], Shulim. Among women's names we find Rukhlia, Ester, Sarra, Tsipa, Masha, Feiga, Khaia, Malka, Mania, and Berta.[76]

While most Kiev Jews may have spoken Yiddish, it was a Yiddish increasingly inflected by Russian, of which we find examples in one of Kiev's Yiddish newspapers, *Yudishe naye leben*. One article exclaims, "*Shteh oyf du goles-yid! Du eyved, du rab, shteh oyf!*" (Stand up, you diaspora Jew! You slave, stand up!) Here, the author used two words for *slave*, the first of Hebrew origin and the second a Russian import not usually utilized in Yiddish. Another example is the use of the Russianism *priznayen* to mean classify or categorize in an official manner (as by the state), or the adjective *strashne* (frightening, from the Russian *strashnyi*).[77] While Yiddish as a language is known for its openness to foreign vocabulary, the extent to which Russian influenced the tongue as it was spoken in Kiev is noteworthy.[78] On the other hand, Jews also felt free to "translate" their city, as in for example the appellation "Groys-Vasilkover gas," a literal translation of Bol'shaia Vasil'kovskaia ulitsa, one of Kiev's main thoroughfares. The influence was mutual.

According to the 1897 census, more than 6 percent of Kiev Jews claimed Russian as their mother tongue, fewer than the 11 percent in Kiev but far more than the proportions in the provinces—for example, 0.83 percent for Kiev province and as low as 0.35 percent for Volhyn.[79] An article in the Russian-language *Evreiskaia zhizn'* (Jewish Life) in 1905 claimed that Kiev, thanks to its many educational institutions, was "an even bigger center of russification for the southwest region than Vilna is for the northwest."[80] Russian was the language of the new generation of Jews, and was heard more and more frequently at communal events; for example, at an 1891 memorial service for the Hebrew writer and Palestinophile Samuel Joseph Fuenn, Crown Rabbi Tsukkerman and Aaron Tseitlin, the latter of whom held the official government position of "expert Jew," spoke in Russian, while the rabbi of the Lithuanian community in Kiev, Aaron Zeev Weil, addressed the assembled in Yiddish. The service was held at the merchant's prayer house, the predecessor to the Choral Synagogue, where some parishioners may already have felt more at home in Russian than in Yiddish; notices for the events were placed in Kiev's *Russian* newspapers.[81] At a comparable community event ten years later, Yiddish was apparently no longer being used, and many more speakers chose Russian (or even German) over Hebrew for their addresses—and this at an event celebrating the life and work of a Hebrew writer.[82] The choice of language may, however, have been compelled by administrative regulations operative in Kiev banning the use of most languages other than Russian at public events.

According to Eliezer Friedmann, Jews in government service such as the Crown rabbis and learned Jews even wore their facial hair in the same style as the tsar—a shaved chin with a strip of beard on either side.[83] In *The Bloody Hoax*, Sholem Aleichem portrays his fictional Kiev rabbi as a mixture of traditional and acculturated: he sported sidecurls, but they were "short and straight"; he wore a long black kaftan and spoke with his bewigged wife in Yiddish, yet he could speak Russian perfectly.[84]

The Jewish Press

Sholem Aleichem provided an incisive analysis of the role of Yiddish among Kiev's Jews in a 1910 feuilleton in the short-lived *Kiever vort* (this piece was sent from abroad, as the Yiddish writer had left Kiev after the 1905 pogrom).[85] Asking, "Who needs a Yiddish newspaper?" he enumerated the city's Jewish groups and their attitude toward the language. The wealthy elite looked down on Yiddish as something shameful and uncultured; it might be good for a joke or a song, but nothing more. The brokers at the exchange had no use for Yiddish, since during the day they spoke in the rarified dialect particular to the exchange, a Russian of economic and commercial terms (*vyvoz* [export], *obmen* [exchange], *perechislennyi* [transferred]) while at night they spoke "French"—at the card tables, playing *Macao, Diabolique, Bézique,* and *Ecarté.* The "simple Jews" in Podol and Demievka loved the Yiddish word, continued Sholem Aleichem (perhaps playing on the name of the newspaper for which he was writing), "but we ask ourselves: how have they gotten along without a Yiddish word till now?" The upshot was that even the masses, who still used and loved Yiddish, were unwilling to actively support it and its expression. Even among those who spoke it, much less among those who did not, Yiddish was an orphan language in Kiev.

To survive, a Yiddish newspaper needed a willing audience, but it also needed cooperative authorities, who were increasingly rare in the last decade of the empire. Only a few would-be publishers were granted permission to print newspapers, and none of the publications that saw the light of day lasted for more than a few months. *Dos folk* (The People), a radical, anti-establishment daily, emerged out of the ferment of 1905 and lasted through 1906, but folded early the next year. In 1910, *Kiever vort*, also a daily, lasted all of eleven issues over thirteen days.[86] Were these short-lived newspapers closed down by the authorities? Were their publishers expelled from Kiev, or did they simply run out of money? The answers are unclear, though the fact that *Kiever vort* was fined 150 rubles for some offense—a detail found in the records of the Kiev Committee for Publications, a government body—suggests that all of these could have been the case.[87] An idiosyncratic publication with a territorialist slant, *Yudishe naye leben* (New Jewish Life), lasted somewhat longer (1912 to 1914, irregularly), perhaps because it was a monthly.[88] Applications for proposed newspapers called *Folks-shtime* (People's Voice; 1907) and *Kiever tagblat* (Kiev Daily Paper; 1909) were never approved.[89] An unsolved mystery is a Hebrew organ with the title *Ha-tsofe u-mabit* (The Observer and Watcher), whose publisher, D. A. Fridman, submitted an apparently unsuccessful petition for permission to publish in 1906 and had better luck on his second try in 1912, when he shortened the title to *Ha-tsofe*. It was still being published in 1913, but almost no information on the newspaper has survived—nor, seemingly, have any copies of the paper itself.[90] The fact that it was so difficult to publish a Jewish newspaper in Kiev must have been a serious hindrance to the development of Jewish civil society in the city; other than learning through word of mouth and rumors, the only ways for Jews to learn about the goings-on in their own Jewish community was from national Jewish newspapers published in St. Petersburg such as *Ha-melits* or *Nedel'naia khronika Voskhoda*, or from local newspapers—which often took their irregular reports on Jewish Kiev from Russian Jewish organs like *Nedel'naia khronika Voskhoda*![91] If one of the fundaments of civil society is a free and thriving press, then Kiev Jewry did not pass the test; building a separate Jewish public sphere would be nigh on impossible without a Jewish press.[92] As a Jewish political activist wrote in a letter intercepted by the secret police, "Without a newspaper, without a language (*iazyk*) as it were, we can do too little."[93] Perhaps Kiev was also an inhospitable place for the written word: in 1890, it had only 38 bookstores compared to Moscow's 205, Warsaw's 137, and Odessa's 68. Even Saratov had more bookshops (42) than Kiev![94]

Religious Observance

Evidence about religious observance from the first two decades of Jewish settlement in Kiev is spotty, and much of the reporting tendentious. However, the overall impression is that the small community, made up of newly arrived migrants from the towns of the Pale of Settlement, was fairly traditionally pious. An 1873 report in the newspaper *Kievlianin* claimed that most of the shops on Kreshchatik, Kiev's main commercial avenue, were closed on Saturday, but it must be kept in mind that the author's intent was to reveal the extent of Jewish domination of Kiev.[95] Around the same time, the Judeophobic A. N. Murav'ev—also set on showing that Kiev was becoming "the capital of the *zhids*"—wrote that the Jewish magnates living in the wealthiest parts of the city had still not given up their "*pesiki*" (a derogatory term for *peyes*, sidecurls) and "zhid rituals."[96]

Because of government restrictions on organized Jewish life in Kiev, access to Jewish education was difficult. Apparently, a Talmud Torah lasted in the city until 1878, when it was shut down; thereafter, it operated in a semilegal limbo, which did not bode well for the quality of pedagogy at the school. Until 1895, men with Kiev residence rights were forbidden from working as *melamdim* (teachers of Jewish religious subjects); according to one cynic, this state of affairs led to an unregulated situation in which anyone who could not find work in his hometown could try to pass himself off as a melamed, spelling doom for the quality of the city's *hadarim* (traditional Jewish schools).[97] Thus, other than the wealthiest families who could afford to hire private tutors for their children, parents moving to Kiev found a city with an abundance of opportunities for secular education for their children but little in the way of Jewish schooling.[98] Indeed, a correspondent from Kiev in the early 1880s wrote that many Jewish children in the city were educated in non-Jewish institutions, and did not receive religious instruction.[99] The city could certainly never hope to have its own yeshiva. This circumstance undoubtedly had an impact on the Jewish knowledge and perhaps even observance of the next generation of Kiev Jews.

It is difficult to mark a turning point in Jewish observance in Kiev, but 1880 may serve as an approximate fulcrum, after which we begin to see large-scale changes in religious practice. There are reports of widespread abandonment of ritual starting in the 1880s: "most of this city's Jewish inhabitants have abandoned the Torah." This correspondent to the Hebrew newspaper *Ha-yom* claimed that many Jewish shopkeepers kept their businesses open on the Sabbath and Jewish holidays.[100] It was in 1880 that the self-proclaimed "educated constituency" of Kiev Jewry petitioned the authorities for permission to open their own synagogue in the center of the city (the synagogue is discussed in greater detail below).[101] The mid-1890s saw accusations that the wealthy elite hired tutors in Jewish subjects for their children for only half the year; another observer remarked cynically that the tutors were hired by the month and fired when the lady of the house realized that she needed the money to pay for the extra costs associated with renting a dacha for the summer.[102] In a feuilleton about the poor state of Jewish education in the Russian Empire, Hebrew writer Yitshak Yaakov Vaysberg, a resident of Kiev, placed part of the blame on the lack of Jewish education for girls, who when they became mothers had nothing to pass on to their sons. He referred particularly to wealthy ladies who adored novels and the theater, and even worse, the social-climbing women who aspired to nobility, for whom one word of French was preferable "to all of Judaism, of which they know nothing."[103] (Vaysberg himself was a Hebrew teacher and his firsthand experience surely influenced his opinions. Several years later, he would write an article on "Learned Jewish Women from the Biblical and Talmudic Periods until Today" for *Di yudishe folks-bibliotek,* and then a book titled *The Women's Question according to the Talmud*!)[104] As in Western Europe, Jewish women—ostensibly responsible for the religious and moral upbringing of their children—were often blamed for the corruption of Jewish youth.[105]

In his remembrances of Kiev in the late 1870s, Yekhezkel Kotik remarked that he was surprised from his very arrival in the city at the licentiousness (*oyslasnkeyt*) that cohabited so easily with superstition among Kiev Jews. Amazingly, Kotik paints a picture of Hasidim smoking cigars on the Sabbath while having a Gypsy woman read their palms![106] Kotik, himself a product of a pious Hasidic home in the town of Kamenets in the Polesie region, criticized Kiev's Hasidim for not truly understanding Hasidism; they believed in its miracles and wonder-working but not in the faith, love, and ecstasy that underlay the Hasidic way.[107] Strangely, Kotik claims that although there were many Hasidim in Kiev, there were few *shtiblekh* (prayer houses). Assuming he was correct, it is impossible to know whether this was because of the legal restrictions on private prayer quorums or the widespread "licentiousness" he observed. Archival records from the late nineteenth century, however, document the existence of fourteen official prayer houses (there must have been many more underground), six "spiritual" (communal) rabbis, and eleven religious teachers.[108]

The laxity described by Kotik could be found elsewhere in the empire. Writing of his childhood in Bialystok in the 1870s and 1880s, Yeshaya Heshl Perelstein wrote of Jewish homes where many basic strictures (such as those relating to eating and Sabbath observance) had been dropped.[109] In Odessa of the 1870s, "the most sacred rituals were casually ignored and the most stringent prohibitions publicly transgressed," while Warsaw Jewish charities hosted galas where mixed-sex dancing was an unremarkable occurrence.[110] And Chae-Ran Freeze has charted the decline in the late nineteenth century of the observance of Jewish legal requirements associated with marriage and divorce, such as that of *halitsa* (levirate divorce) and the payment of child support.[111]

E. E. Friedmann's memoirs of 1890s Kiev also portray a city where Jewish observance may have been honored more in the breach, at least in some circles. According to his account, Jewish observance in Kiev could not be neatly categorized; he reported that many Jews picked and chose from traditional rituals, usually observing those that related to major holidays. A Jews might desecrate the Sabbath and eat nonkosher food—even on the Day of Atonement—yet would be careful about *kapores,* the custom of casting one's sins onto a chicken on the eve of that solemn holiday, or about eating only unleavened food products on Passover. A Jew who ate pork would nonetheless organize a prayer quorum in his house for the High Holy Days.[112] Friedmann observed much of this kind of behavior among the speculators, brokers, and traders who did business at the Kiev commodities exchange; he remarked that their behavior was not motivated by any conscious choice but simply by the fact that they were "free from the yoke of Torah."[113] Friedmann makes clear his impression that, due to the extremely heterogeneous makeup of Kiev's Jewish population, communal life and controls in the city were very weak.[114] This impression is bolstered by the fact that the *takanot* (regulations) found in the pinkas of the Kiev Psalms Recitation Society (Hevrat magidei tehilim shel Kiev) were apparently not officially endorsed by a rabbi or scholar, as was customary.[115] As in Odessa, the ardor for making money was overwhelming for many, who could not be bothered to be fastidious about religious observance when more important things demanded their valuable time.[116] Oftentimes a compromise worked out with the help of a halakhic loophole—a Christian hired to work in a shop on a Saturday—

simply seemed unnecessary after a certain period of time.[117] Perhaps their libertinism was linked to the fact that many of them were alone without family in the city, like Sholem Aleichem's fictional Menakhem-Mendl, who also tries his hand at trading and brokering; many were also young, for who else but a young man without a family to support could take the risk of speculating in Kiev, where a "fortune" could be made one day and lost the next? Menakhem-Mendl writes to his wife that the sugar traders are "rich as the devil, ride around in carriages, live in dachas in Boiberik, play cards all day long, and have courtasins and conquerbines [*sic*]."[118] In fictional Yehupets, as perhaps in the real Kiev, Jewish mores were somewhat loose: "It's not unusual for a man to throw over his wife for another woman he's fallen in love with, or for a woman to throw over her husband."[119]

The kosher dietary laws were not strictly observed by all Kiev Jews. In 1895, a concerned Kiev Jew warned that non-Jews had begun to hire unscrupulous Jews to place a stamp of kashruth on wines that were not in fact kosher for Passover. And, whether out of carelessness or ignorance, Jews were falling for the ruse and buying the wine! The author cautioned the bogus supervisors that they were being watched, but their actions suggest that there were few people in Kiev willing or able to guard against such scams.[120] Furthermore, though Kiev Jews were still largely Passover-observant, at least some of them were relaxed enough that they found it unnecessary to verify the supervision on the products they purchased for the holiday. More disturbing for some, a significant number of Kiev's Jewish communal leaders no longer bought kosher meat for their tables, a fact stressed by a local dissident who made public the fact that those very leaders continued to be responsible for allocating the revenues from the kosher meat tax even though they did not pay it themselves.[121] Though Crown Rabbi Joshua Tsukkerman received ample remuneration from the communal purse, the city's six "spiritual" rabbis, complained one observer in 1892, had had their salaries cut completely by the communal leadership. "'Rabbi' is a dirty word in Kiev," remonstrated the dissident. Thus, yet another challenge was added to the maintenance of proper religious leadership in Kiev—in addition to that posed by residence limitations.[122]

There are reports of students and young people transgressing Jewish law, though this is not particularly surprising, as students were known for their rebellion against tradition and were not usually representative of the Jewish community as a whole. In 1894, a Mrs. M. Gol'dberg organized a subsidized kosher cafeteria for Kiev's Jewish students who, according to *Ha-melits,* had been eating at nonkosher dining halls because of their miserable financial circumstances.[123] About the same time, a report in the Hebrew press remarked that the Jewish "enlightened youth" (*tse'irim mitna'orim*) of the city usually spent their Sabbath mornings not in synagogues, but in cafes.[124] The fact that this was worthy of acknowledgment in the press is in itself telling, for it means that this type of behavior was still unusual. As we will see, by 1909 lack of observance was so common among Jewish students that it would probably have been unusual to see a Jewish student in the synagogue on Sabbath!

Other press condemnations of aberrations in religious practice are also reliable evidence that this behavior was still relatively rare. These charges included mixed-sex dancing at weddings and the improper observance of some fasts.[125] But the decade also witnessed several cases that were far more serious. In 1896, apprentice lawyer Iakov Gol'denveizer lodged an official complaint against Crown Rabbi Joshua Tsukkerman for refusing to register Gol'denveizer's newborn son in the official metrical books. The reason for Tsukkerman's resistance? Gol'denveizer had not had his son circumcised. The official records do not reveal the motivation for Gol'denveizer's highly unusual action, but it is clear that it was not on medical grounds. And this was not the first such case that Tsukkerman had been faced with: documents refer to the case of Benedikt Mandel'shtam, who had declined to circumcise his son in 1891.[126] (A similar case, perhaps the first of its kind in the Russian Empire, is recorded in 1873 in Odessa.)[127] Far from minor variations in ritual, these cases, while extreme, reveal the extent to which some Jews were willing to jettison traditional practice while at the same time declining to convert to Christianity. Unfortunately, the extant records do not allow us to probe the motivations of the historical actors in these cases, as has been done with excellent effect in the case of German Jews.[128] We may speculate, however, that these parents hoped to make it easier for their sons to move freely in imperial Russian society without the physical marking—or perhaps any other indicator—that might set them apart as Jews.

The Choral Synagogue

The Choral Synagogue in Kiev, or the Brodsky Synagogue as it was known, was not built until 1898, but those interested in gathering in a European-style house of worship met in rented premises until they were able to secure permission to erect their own building. Like the choral or great synagogues in Warsaw, St. Petersburg, and Odessa, the Brodsky Synagogue in Kiev did not deviate from Jewish religious law, but the changes it made in custom (*minhag*) were significant, especially for Eastern Europe where minhag played a central role in Jewish religious culture. A hired cantor led the services, often with the help of a choir; the rabbi delivered sermons in Russian; the layout of the pews was changed (all seats now faced the eastern wall); and extraneous conversations were banned.[129] Unlike in most Jewish prayer houses, great attention was paid to ensuring that the architecture and decor of the synagogue were both lavish and aesthetically pleasing. One newspaper account gives a hint that, as in Warsaw's Great Synagogue, men called up for honors to the Torah were required to wear black hats.[130] We do not know whether, as in Odessa's Brodsky Synagogue, medieval *piyyutim* were eliminated from the service; this would have been a step further in the process of change.[131] What is clear is that the synagogue did not go as far in its innovations as some of the more radical synagogues in the Odessa area, such as that of the Society of Jewish Shop Attendants, which featured an organ and a mixed-sex choir on the High Holy Days.[132]

Details are sketchy, but there is evidence that there was a certain amount of struggle among the synagogue's members over the tone of the services. Friedmann wrote that Lazar' Brodsky, like his father Israel, was a pious Jew whose philanthropy and public-mindedness were motivated by his wholly traditional desire to do good deeds.[133] According to this account, Brodsky, who donated the lion's share of the funds for building the new synagogue, attempted to instill in it a traditionalist spirit, in apparent opposition to the other members of the board who were proponents of a more formal, decorous German-style Judaism. In Friedmann's heavily Zionist-influenced analysis, the latter eventually won out over the "living national spirit," and the synagogue became a "factory" for the recitation by so-called assimilators of the mourner's kaddish and dry ceremonies on Sabbath and festivals. It may be, then, that the physical trappings of a choral synagogue did not necessarily mean that the services themselves would be "modernized."

Apparently Lazar''s less-prominent brother Lev was also traditionally minded. Several years after the opening of the Choral Synagogue, he endowed another synagogue immediately adjacent to the one his brother had founded. This new institution, which came to be called the Merchants' Synagogue, was evidently much closer in aura to a traditional prayer house, and may have been intended to be a very prominent answer to the Choral Synagogue. The worshiper would likely find things more disorderly here than next door.[134] That the Merchants' Synagogue was apparently built as a traditionalist answer to the Choral Synagogue is at least one piece of evidence that the choral synagogues were a significant and momentous innovation in Jewish life that could be viewed both positively and negatively—as is also implied by the fact that in Odessa several synagogues (even an "Orthodox" prayer house) copied innovative elements of that city's Brodsky Synagogue, such as its choir and seating arrangement.[135]

It is difficult to know what most Kiev Jews thought of the Choral Synagogue and its proponents. Commenting on local religious life in 1885, Israel Darewski noted that most of the city's Jews were opposed to a choral or "reformed" synagogue in the city, since they were hasidim, followers of the tsaddikim who resided in the area surrounding Kiev.[136] The next year, Darewski commented acidly that the "enlightened" Jews of Kiev only attended synagogue three days a year, on the high holidays, and many were not even present for the New Year because they had not yet returned from their summer homes. A few more came back for the *yizkor* memorial services conducted on the Shemini Atseret holiday because, according to Darewski, "they have decided that *yizkor* is more important than prayer."[137] A few years later, another correspondent remarked that he had heard many people speaking ill of the choral High Holiday services organized by the notables.[138] At the same time, the grandiose building clearly piqued the curiosity of both Jews and non-Jews; after the gala dedication in 1898 (held on Lazar' Brodsky's fiftieth birthday!), the doors were opened to the masses gathered outside so they could enter and marvel at the architecture and craftsmanship.[139] The handsome exterior concealed a soaring sanctuary with fittings of the finest materials as well as a chapel, library, bridal chamber, meeting room, and a room for choir practice. The building was also centrally heated and ventilated using state-of-the-art technology.[140]

Many proponents of choral synagogues did not view them as the "deviations" that others saw, but as just the opposite: as tools to bring progressive, acculturated Jews back in touch with Judaism and the Jewish people. Writing in the Hebrew press in 1896, a defender of the soon-to-be-built choral synagogue in Kiev remarked that the early choral synagogues had been built by modernizing Russian Jews eager to distance themselves from the "backward" ways of traditional synagogues. The new Kiev synagogue, however, was a reversal of that trend as maskilim returned to their roots, building a synagogue "in order to come closer to the Jews."[141]

Clearly, though, to many Jews the innovations of the choral synagogues were departures from the norm, as were the new burial paraphernalia introduced by the Kiev hevra kadisha (burial society) soon after its 1892 "takeover" from traditionalists by members of the acculturated elite, a move that had the sanction of Crown Rabbi Tsukkerman.[142] Here Kiev was following a trend begun two decades earlier in Odessa, which had subsequently spread to many cities in the south.[143] The new options were meant to satisfy the modern tastes of the acculturated elite as well as the requirements of tradition: coffins with black writing on a white background, instead of plain wooden boxes; a hearse drawn by black horses; and special mourning garb for the undertakers. (Apparently not everyone would be entitled to such lavish treatment; some or all of these burial extras were dependent on "the honor of the deceased.") While one observer emphasized that the new caskets were not Christian catafalques, another claimed that the new coffins did, indeed, look like catafalques, and that they had been introduced for the precise purpose of preventing the enlightened and wealthy from buying coffins from non-Jews (such an incident had already occurred once).[144] What remains unclear is whether this change was for the elite's own convenience, as it transformed the burial society in its own image, or if it was rather an attempt to incorporate certain modernizations into the society so that it would remain relevant to all Kiev Jews. The Jewish elite plainly had an interest in transforming in its own image the communal institutions it controlled, but one wonders if all Kiev Jews—the majority of whom were far from acculturated—approved of such changes. While the Choral Synagogue incorporated newfangled elements such as Russian preaching and a choir on days other than Sabbaths and festivals, it was meant for the exclusive use of the acculturated Jews. The burial society, by contrast, was a communal institution to which almost every Jew in Kiev would sooner or later have to turn.

On the occasion of the marriage of scions of the empire's most illustrious Jewish families, Lazar' Brodsky's daughter Klara and Vladimir Gintsburg (son of Baron Horace, the St. Petersburg financier), Yitshak Ya'akov Vaysberg wrote that "Jews and non-Jews streamed in their masses to the synagogue" and waited for hours, presumably for a chance to glimpse the rich and famous dressed in their finest.[145] The very fact that the choral synagogue could be a kind of tourist attraction for most poor and/or uneducated Kiev Jews, conspicuous in its difference from most other prayer houses in the city, underscored the disparity between the groups.

Despite his role in the establishment of the Merchants' Synagogue, Lev Brodsky's own religious inclinations were somewhat idiosyncratic, as with other Kiev Jews we have already discussed. Indeed, it may have been just those inconsistencies in his own religiosity that convinced him of the importance of a new traditionalist synagogue in Kiev and, in general, of "old-time religion" as the foundation of Jewish life. Although Brodsky himself lived a life of libertinism, wrote Friedmann, he was concerned that the Jewish masses maintain their traditional religiosity and that their children be educated in hadarim, learning Bible, Talmud, the prayer book, and psalms. (Apparently, Brodsky's "libertinism" was part of family lore, as Alexandra Fanny Brodsky describes her ancestor as a "womanizer" in her memoir *Smoke Signals*.)[146] When it came to communal funding for Jewish matters, he was interested only in Talmud Torahs, ritual baths, and kashruth.[147] The secular, acculturated life that bourgeois Jews wanted for themselves, then, was deemed inappropriate for the masses. Clearly, they were anxious about the future of the "Jewishness" that they viewed as genuine, and saw it as their duty to preserve traditional Judaism. It is interesting that philanthropy here played a central role in the maintenance of Jewish identity: by sponsoring traditional schools for the poor, well-to-do Jews could ensure that the authentic piety that they themselves had abandoned would be sustained. The role of the poor, then, was just as important in this transaction as that of the benefactors, for they—or their children—were charged with "being Jewish" as proxies for all Jews.

Brodsky was not the only member of the Jewish elite—especially those prominent in the communal leadership—who was anxious about the growing secularization among the Jewish masses in the early years of the twentieth century. According to a writer in the short-lived Yiddish newspaper *Kiever vort*, the members of the schools commission of the official communal body, the Representation for Jewish Welfare, demanded that an archaic, old-fashioned heder-style curriculum of prayers and psalms be preserved in communal schools. Although these men were themselves irreligious and did not teach their own children Yiddish, complained "Pedagogue," they demanded piety from the Jewish poor and refused to be guided by the expertise of trained teachers. But the new generation of maskilim, activists in the Kiev branch of the OPE, the primary educational and cultural organization of the Russian Empire, were not much better, wrote "Pedagogue," despite their reputation for progressive thinking. Here, too, the bourgeoisie attempted to impose its vision of "authentic" *yidishkayt* (Jewishness) on the poor who attended the schools it controlled. For example, when contemporary pedagogy dictated that children learn the Bible in abridged form, these "bourgeois maskilim" cried heresy and demanded that traditional methods of Jewish education be adhered to. While educational theory called for children to be educated in their mother tongue, the OPE activists threatened to cut school subsidies if teachers did not rid the curriculum of Yiddish and teach the prayer book and psalms instead.[148]

As the example of the Brodsky brothers demonstrates, we cannot simply classify all wealthy merchants as acculturated and modernizing in their approach to religion; patterns of religious observance did not always break down according to the socioeconomic lines we might expect. According to Friedmann, most of the wealthy sugar merchants—including the wealthiest men, Lazar' Brodsky and the Hasid Ionna Zaitsev—were "Orthodox" Jews who were knowledgeable of Torah, attended synagogue, and participated in traditional Talmudic and midrashic study circles.[149] (To confuse matters, this would not necessarily obviate taking on, to some extent, the trappings of imperial Russian society in dress and mannerisms: trimmed beards, European dress, and Russian speech.) Sholem Aleichem gives a fictional example of this kind of Kiev Jew in *The Bloody Hoax* in the form of Shlomo Familiant, a wealthy, "worldly merchant" who is at the same time a pious Hasid who disapproves of going without a hat, "a terrible sin."[150] Some of these men were relatively unacculturated, wearing the traditional "long kaftan and large prayer shawl," like Familiant, who is reminiscent of Ionna (Yona) Zaitsev, one of Kiev's richest industrialists.[151] Zaitsev was a Hasid who remained strictly observant his whole life and apparently refused to attend the Choral Synagogue, as evidenced by his 1904 request for permission for a private chapel in his mansion.[152] Zaitsev's claim that he was too old to walk to prayer houses in the two heavily Jewish neighborhoods of Kiev reveals that he preferred to walk several miles to Sabbath worship over taking a much shorter stroll to the nearer Choral Synagogue, which had been open since 1898. Conversely, those whom we might view as the most opposed to acculturation were not necessarily so: the Hebrew press reported that members of the household of the Hasidic Rebbe Yohanan of Rotmistrovka were all literate in Russian. This lax attitude came back to haunt the rebbe, however, as—according to one report, at least—when his son came to Kiev, he began to read the newspapers every day and eventually "ran off to study secular wisdom."[153]

Even ordinary Jews were criticized for their lax ways. One observer lamented the immodest behavior that could be seen at some Jewish weddings, where men and women mingled and even danced together.[154] Jews were also dressed down for improperly observing various religious fasts.[155] One critic alleged that, while it used to be said that "from K[iev] comes forth Torah," these days it had left for good; though he hastened to add that it was difficult to generalize about Kiev, since the Jewish population there was so diverse, one learned and another ignorant.[156] That the city's Jewish masses remained traditionally pious, at least in moments of crisis, is indicated by Sholem Aleichem's account of the reaction to the 1905 pogrom, when a fast day was decreed a month after the massacre. The Yiddish writer, visiting Kiev's prayer houses, witnessed large candles burning, Jews reciting the penitential prayers and the confession, beating their breasts, and singing *Ha-noten teshu'a*—the prayer for the monarch.[157] A similar response had followed the pogrom of 1881, a quarter-century earlier. However, the fact that even nonobservant students often chose to join in such fasts as an act of solidarity is proof that many Jews who were lax in their ritual observance may have returned to traditional forms of piety at moments of despondency.

Apparently, criticism of Jewish observance or piety stopped at the doors of the commodities exchange; in Voltaire's words, "When it's a question of money, everybody is of the same religion." Truly, what mattered was not how one lived, but how much money one made. The brokers, speculators, and runners who gathered on the sidewalk in front of the Kiev Exchange were Jews of all types—young and old, rich and poor, some dressed in finery and others in rags, "skinny Lithuanians who knew Torah and . . . boorish, rude, strapping, ungainly Volhynians and Podolians." According to Friedmann, most were clean-shaven, irreligious types—not conscious heretics but simply "free from the yoke of the Torah"—but there were also observant Jews with *peyes* among them.[158] In the hubbub of the exchange, these differences were insignificant; the pursuit of profit united them all. Sholem Aleichem's fictional Menakhem-Mendl wrote to his wife Sheyne-Sheyndl:

> You should see Kreshchatik Square. It's mobbed with Jews. . . . The word from Petersburg is, buy Transports [stocks] for all you're worth! The whole world is holding them: Jews, housewives, doctors, teachers, servants, tradesmen—who doesn't have Transports? When two Jews meet, the first question is: "How are Transports today?"[159]

Friedmann's entertaining anecdotes reveal that the all-pervasive culture of money made its mark among the "pious" as well, and some nouveaux riches apparently believed that their wealth had given them Jewish erudition too. One sugar trader came to Kiev from a Hasidic court in Volhyn, where he had been a *gabai* (treasurer), selling entrance tickets to see the rebbe. After making his fortune in speculation and money-lending, he became a bigwig in one of the Kiev synagogues and, considering himself a great scholar, even wrote a work of Talmudic casuistry; another time he demanded to lead the prayer for rain in place of the cantor, though his voice was far from melodious.[160]

The Twentieth Century

By the early twentieth century, it is clear that many Kiev Jews did not or could not maintain some of the most basic practices such as Sabbath and kashruth. Worsening economic conditions probably made it impossible for many to refuse to work on the Sabbath for fear of being fired, while for others the rapidly spreading ideologies of Jewish nationalism and socialism provided an alternative sense of Jewish identity and belonging.[161] The 1907 annual report of the Kiev branch of the OPE remarked that shop clerks made up a very small proportion of the students in the organization's Saturday school for adults because many Jewish businesses were open on Saturday.[162] "A significant portion of the more prosperous classes do not use kosher meat," noted the annual report of the Representation for Jewish Welfare in 1913.[163] On the other hand, kashruth and Passover continued to be observed by the majority of Kiev's Jews, many of them poor; by the first decade of the twentieth century, there were three subsidized kosher cafeterias in the city serving thousands of reduced-price or free meals every year, while Passover aid was still one of the community's major annual expenses. An advertisement in *Kiever vort,* a Yiddish newspaper unlikely to be read by acculturated Jews, screamed: "Kosher Food! Pure! Fresh! Inexpensive! A Jewish restaurant M. Likhter has opened at the newly improved hotel 'Louvre'! Groys-Vasilkover Gas, No. 6."[164] It must also be noted that Kiev, while in the heart of the Pale of Settlement, lacked even a moderate traditionalist influence such as could be found in other large cities; even Odessa had a yeshiva, while the most prominent (and often only) face of Jewish Orthodoxy in Kiev was the "spiritual" rabbi Shlomo Ha-Cohen Aronson (Aharonson), who was something of a maskil and had actually worked in trade before turning to the rabbinate.[165] A Rabbi Aharon Sudarski is mentioned in one press report, but there are few if any other references to him in other sources.[166]

For many, abandoning certain religious practices or making changes in religious life was not a choice. Government restrictions on the number of prayer houses in Kiev, for example, meant that Jews in some neighborhoods of the city did not have a synagogue to pray in and were unable to bring up their children in an environment of traditional Jewish worship. In various petitions to the authorities for permission to hold services in private homes, groups of Jews bemoaned the deleterious effects that nonattendance of synagogue had on their children; several memorials noted that there had been a drop in religiosity among the younger generation, which was falling into a life of immorality.[167] Frequent expulsions of Jews who lacked the legal status to be in the city also meant that synagogues had to make do without religious professionals; High Holy Day services, for example, might have to be led by a tailor instead of a proper cantor.[168]

Comparisons of the Jewish population of Kiev and the number of legally permitted prayer houses make clear that only a small percentage of Kiev's Jews could squeeze into the usually small makeshift synagogues. What did everyone else do? Some Jews gathered illegally in their homes to worship on the Sabbath and festivals, and were sometimes caught.[169] Israel Darewski confirms this practice in his 1885 letter to *Ha-melits* about the synagogues of Kiev. Undoubtedly, some Jews did not attend such clandestine meetings for fear of arrest, while others were not there because they were a priori inclined to less consistent religious behavior and did not mind not attending communal worship. These individuals prayed at home or not at all.

Also of note is the wording of the petitions requesting permission to meet not only during the autumn holidays, but also during the year on Sabbaths and festivals. None of the petitions that I viewed in the archives asked to be allowed to meet every day or even on Mondays and Thursdays, arguably more important than other weekdays because of the Torah readings inserted into the service on those days. This may be because the petitioners, aware of the many restrictions on Jewish life in Kiev, did not want to ask for too much for fear of receiving nothing. But it is a telling contrast to life in the small-town Jewish community, where the prayer house (often known as the house of study or *beys medresh*) was used not only on Sabbath and holidays but every day of the week.[170]

Not surprisingly, students were among the most irreligious of Jews. A 1910 survey of male and female students at a number of institutions of higher education in Kiev reveals that about half the Jewish students were totally unobservant. Anywhere from one-quarter to half reported observing Passover and/or the fast of Yom Kippur, but no more than about one-fifth of respondents said that they kept kosher, while less than 10 percent observed the Sabbath.[171] Here there was a gender gap: men were about as likely to pray as observe the Sabbath, but between 5 and 10 percent of women kept the Sabbath while 2 percent or less reported that they prayed.[172] This phenomenon is striking, for while traditional Jewish practice required only men to attend public worship, women often came to synagogue on Sabbath and festivals and frequently had rich prayer lives of their own based on the women's prayer book (including *tkhines,* or personal supplications) and the *Tsene-rene,* the women's Bible (actually a compilation of rabbinic commentaries and legends).[173] Among this new generation, that tradition of prayer had all but disappeared. Unfortunately, we do not know whether the prayer that the male students referred to was public or private, so we cannot reconstruct the kind of piety this would have entailed.

Also of interest is the lack of correlation between religiosity and observance. Seventy percent of those students who identified themselves as "religious" were observant, which meant that the other 30 percent were not; clearly, religion for them meant a more spiritual or universalistic faith. On the other hand, 30 percent who described themselves as indifferent to religion, and 12 percent of self-classified irreligious students, were observant! As some of the students' remarks show, ritual observance was not necessarily performed out of commitment to God or the Jewish way of life. Many students wrote that habit played an important role in observance; in other words, they were so used to fasting on Yom Kippur, for example, that they did it out of rote instead of dedication to the meaning of the day. Others used ritual to strengthen their connection to the Jewish people when feeling isolated.

Surprisingly, the younger the student, the more religious and the more observant he or she was likely to be.[174] About 40 percent of the youngest cohort (17–19 years old) was observant, compared to 20 percent of the oldest men and only 6 percent of the oldest women (26–28 years old). It may be, then, that young Jews in their twenties and thirties, like the students and the clerks in Kiev's shops, were representative of a passing trend of secularization among urban Jews in the Russian Empire, while a younger generation was increasingly likely to observe some customs. This phenomenon may well have been related to the growing isolation and inward-looking "retreat from politics" felt by Jewish students and from the confusion of the outside world described by Nathans.[175]

Also noteworthy is the finding that students from families where the breadwinner worked in the Jewish community were more likely than students from families in any other occupational category to be irreligious.[176] Perhaps this is not surprising, given patterns of rebellion within families and, specific to the Jewish case, students' rejection of Jewish communal affairs in favor of nationalist or socialist-oriented politics or even universalistic ideals. The survey also showed that embourgeoisement did not necessarily mean secularization: students from families in economic brackets categorized as large or middling capitalist and higher-income white-collar/professional were more likely to be religious than students from lower-income brackets. Again, this may be evidence of rebellion, as children of well-to-do, acculturated families began to "return to their roots" while the offspring of working-class families turned their backs on traditional piety in favor of a more cosmopolitan lifestyle.

Russian Jews were not the only subjects in the empire to be influenced by secularizing forces. In just the period we have been examining, the Orthodox Church identified a need to "rechristianize society" as a response to creeping secularization and the loss of the loyalty of many educated (nominally Orthodox) citizens.[177] Urban dwellers, especially those of the more comfortable socioeconomic classes, were known to be somewhat relaxed in their religious practices, and even peasants who migrated from the countryside in search of work "tended to be extremely lax in their religious observances when living in the city. Uprooted from village life, where the parish church . . . was an important centre of activity, many workers also lost touch with their faith."[178] This did not mean, of course, that such individuals lost their abiding reverence for the Orthodox Church, its saints, and symbols, but that their lives were no longer governed by the rhythm of the church and its rituals (*bytovoe pravoslavoe*).[179] But, like some Jews, once removed from the village or town setting where religious authority infused all aspects of life, they were not knowledgeable or zealous enough to maintain an observant lifestyle. And for members of the educated and professional classes, the church, sullied by its use as a tool of the state, was not a viable option for the expression of spirituality, as witnessed by the growth in popularity of spiritualism, mysticism, and evangelicalism in the last years of the empire.[180]

Jewish Culture after 1907

Once Stolypin had achieved his goal of a right-wing, conservative State Duma with a change in the electoral law in June 1907, many of those who had been politically active in Jewish parties and movements turned to cultural, communal, and economic organization-building, the so-called "organic work."[181] As in many localities, Jewish life in Kiev in this period took on added dimensions with the establishment or revival of a number of nationally and culturally oriented organizations. Over the previous decade, there had been talk of the need for a new Jewish library and plans to create one, but it never materialized.[182] Now, the Kiev branch of the OPE opened the long-awaited Jewish library.[183] A branch of the Jewish Literary Society was founded.

The first Zionist ball in Kiev, held in 1908, was an opportunity for Kiev's Jewish nationalists to demonstrate their strong Jewish spirit and opposition to assimilation. Though the event was the last of the series of Jewish charity balls traditionally held in Kiev in March and thus seemed to be just another event of Jewish Kiev, its content was intended to distance "national Jews" from those lacking national consciousness. A local Zionist noted with scorn that the Concordia Club, while Jewish, refused to host a dinner for a number of prominent visiting Hebrew poets because, not being sugar brokers, card sharks, or stock exchange bigwigs, they did not correspond to the measures of "greatness" of Kiev's acculturated Jews. The ball was intended to reinvigorate the discouraged Zionists with national spirit: the hall was decorated with Zionist flags, pictures of scenes of life in Palestine, and portraits of Zionist leaders. An "oriental" fountain was installed to enhance the illusion of a Jewish–Palestinian enclave in the heart of the Russian Empire. Because of restrictions on the use of Hebrew in public events, the performances were in Russian, but were national in content nonetheless: Bruch's *Kol Nidre* (op. 47), and readings by poets Leib Jaffe and Simon Frug, the latter greeted with tremendous enthusiasm. Reinforcing the national feeling of Kiev's Jews was particularly important, wrote the Zionist, because of the overwhelming Christian character of Kiev and its assimilating influence on Jews. Assimilation was not an ideology for Kiev's Jews, he explained, but it took its toll nonetheless. "The influence of Russian culture devours the inner Jewish 'I' to such an extent that he unconsciously begins to look at everything through the eyes of a cultured Russian man."[184]

As this quotation reveals, Kiev's Jewish intelligentsia was concerned with its distance from "authentic" Jewish life and creativity, what Steven Zipperstein has called "cultural slippage."[185] As early as the 1890s, educational activists in the OPE had become concerned with the marked lack of Jewish identity or sense of belonging among the new generation of secularly educated students. The pendulum had swung too far: the first maskilim had pressed the importance of a Russian education upon Jews, but now Jewish children were in danger of losing Jewishness altogether. For the OPE, the question of "national education" now became how to make Jews Russian and European "while preserving the essence of an authentic Jewish culture."[186] Just as some pedagogues looked for succor to what they saw as the locus of authentic Jewish education, the heder, Jewish *kulturträger* became convinced that modern Jewish culture had to draw from the wells of "living" culture, presumably as it existed in the shtetlekh of the Pale, uncorrupted—as it were—by modernity.

Inevitably, this vision of culture led to accusations of "inauthenticity" as one organization after another was founded and then declared to be lacking in true Jewishness. The Kiev branch of the Society of Lovers of the Hebrew Language (Hovevei sefat ever) was reestablished in 1908 (it is unclear when the first incarnation of the society became defunct) under the leadership of Zionist activist Hillel Zlatopol'skii.[187] At the first meeting, Zlatopol'skii criticized the educational commissions of the Representation for Jewish Welfare and the OPE, respectively, for neglecting the cause of Hebrew: the language was not flourishing at any of Kiev's Jewish schools, nor was there a clear plan for its instruction at the high schools or institutes. The teaching of Hebrew at the Commercial Institute, it was charged, was limited to the Mourner's Kaddish. He urged that Hebrew be introduced at Kiev's sixty-odd municipal schools, and evening courses, lectures, and informal conversation groups were needed as well. The unkind disposition of the tsarist authorities in the southwest region toward Zionism and Jewish cultural activities, however, cast a dark shadow over these plans; even the society's aspiration to hold its meetings in Hebrew was unlikely to meet with approval by the authorities (similar requests by groups in Kiev province had previously been rejected).[188]

Soon—almost immediately, in fact—the Society of Lovers was, in turn, censured for its amateurish approach to the cause of Hebrew (in a pun on the society's use of the word "amateur" in its name), and a new organization dedicated to Hebrew language and literature was founded.[189] Members of the new organization would pledge to use Hebrew in daily and communal life and devote themselves to disseminating Hebrew literature. Despite its rapid growth and large membership—it reached almost a thousand members less than two years after its founding—the Jewish Literary Society (Evreiskoe literaturnoe obshchestvo) was also criticized for a superficial approach to Jewish culture.[190] (Here, too, there was a struggle for power, this time between Zionists and Yiddishists, with the former winning out in what some called a "usurpation" of power.)[191] At the same time, a Jewish National Student Group was established at Kiev's Polytechnical Institute.[192] According to its charter, the group's aim was "the unification of all nationally minded Jewish students in order to awaken Jewish life at the Institute and satisfy their national-cultural needs."[193]

Students were a good gauge of trends in cultural affinities. Like other big cities, Kiev was a place where young people were known to shake off traditional ways quickly—if they had not come there to be rid of them in the first place. Once a Hasidic child had run off to become a student, as did the son of the Rotmistrovker rebbe, chances were that he or she would not return to observance. Students were the archetypal *apikorsim,* heretics and freethinkers: they were reported to sit in cafes on Sabbath rather than attend synagogue, and ate nonkosher food at cheap dining halls before the founding of the Jewish student cafeteria.[194] Crown Rabbi Iampol'skii's lecture series in 1899 was meant to draw Jewish students back to their heritage, while even the activist Jewish youth who established a Hebrew language society in Kiev did not, apparently, know the language particularly well.[195] Now, a number of observers noted the "return" of Jewish students to Jewish culture with satisfaction; OPE board member L. Dynin, for example, wrote in *Raszvet* that even nationalist students—let alone assimilated ones—were far removed from their heritage and knew little about Jewish culture or history. Things were changing.[196]

Kiev was now a major hub in the Russian and European Zionist and Hebraist movements. The Association for Hebrew Culture and Language, founded in Berlin in 1909, held a major (though secret) conference in Kiev in 1911, attended by dozens of leading figures from Moscow, Odessa, Vilna,

Warsaw, and provincial cities and towns; only the last session of the conference was open and, according to Moshe Rozenblat, was attended by so many thousands of Kiev Jews that people had to be turned away at the door.[197] The gathering bore witness to a debate about the impact of the organization. Hillel Zlatopol'skii, the chair, argued that much progress had already been made and that one could hear Hebrew being spoken on the streets of Kiev and throughout the province; but an interlocutor contended that everything that was truly new, exciting, and spiritually sustaining in the Jewish world was being created by the Zionist movement and especially by the yishuv in Palestine. What impact, he seemed to be asking, could an organization in Kiev really have?[198]

Perhaps another manifestation of the desire to create a Jewish cultural existence that would be closer to its roots was the call to increase the number of Yiddish books in the OPE's library while moving it to Podol. In the society's report of 1907, the audit commission suggested dryly that the library commission purchase books with the reading public in mind: the acquisition of a 50-ruble Hebrew dictionary and several volumes of past years of the Hebrew newspaper *Ha-magid* was inappropriate considering that less than 3 rubles had been spent on literature in Yiddish.[199] L. Dynin noted in 1909 that there were only 250 Yiddish volumes in the library versus 1,400 Russian books and 3,400 in Hebrew. If the library commission wanted workers and clerks to use the library in addition to "so-called *intelligenty*," there needed to be more Yiddish works in an accessible location.[200] The library's location and collection are also poignant testimony to the distance of Kiev's Jewish educated classes and communal leaders from the Jewish masses.

Among the obstacles to "authentic" Jewish cultural life in Kiev were the restrictions placed on the use of languages other than Russian. In an example of the heights of absurdity that were sometimes reached, when the Yiddish writer I. L. Peretz was the guest of honor at the Jewish Literary Society, his works were read in Russian translation.[201] Similarly, a jubilee celebration of Sholem Aleichem had to be postponed because the authorities would not let it take place with the planned Yiddish readings; Russian translations had to be substituted.[202]

A communal critic writing under the pseudonym Wladeldo charged that Kiev Jewry, despite its concentration of talented intelligenty, was unable to produce "authentic" or "living" Jewish culture.[203] Many of these intellectuals, wrote Wladeldo, were totally russified and active in the city's Russian cultural and public life; they were unaware of the new Jewish national life, and continued to be ashamed of their ancestry. But even Jewish organizations were far from authentic. The Kiev OPE was still a maskilic institution, as yet ignorant of Jewish nationalism and its new culture. Its annual gala was Jewish, yes—but only because its organizers and audience were; featuring Italian aria and Russian folk songs, the concert itself contained nothing Jewish at all. The Jewish Literary Society, while officially Zionist in orientation, was unable to achieve anything of substance; for example, nothing had been done for the jubilee of Yiddish writer Mendele Mokher Sforim. As for the student organization, Wladeldo remarked that its members were simply not Jewishly knowledgeable enough to keep it alive.

The only bright spot for Wladeldo was Demievka, a Kiev suburb officially outside the city limits that served as a kind of "model shtetl" (not his term) cheek-by-jowl next to the bright lights of the big city. There, one could hear "living Jewish speech" and genuine expressions of Jewish culture—signs of "healthy . . . national life." But here too there were problems: the primitivity associated with small-town life, a lack of cultural aesthetics and talented individuals. Back in Kiev, hundreds of Jews packed the local Merchants' Club for a concert of Jewish folk music that included renditions of Hasidic melodies. "The diverse audience was united in its desire to hear a native [Jewish] song, and was in rapture, demanding more and more." Some Jews who were hearing their national music for the first time were converted to the national cause. The result, concluded the writer, was gratitude to those in St. Petersburg engaged in the creation of Jewish national culture, and shame that such activity was not taking place in Kiev. Actually, this was inaccurate: Dovid Bergelson, Der Nister (Pinhas Kahanovitch), Nakhmen Mayzel, and other Yiddish writers were active in a small circle that came to be called the Kiev Group; these writers strove to create a new style of secular Yiddish literature and "sought from Russian and European literatures the techniques of impressionism and symbolism for their prose."[204] Members of the group produced the journal *Der yidisher almanakh;* another literary journal out of Kiev was the miscellany *Fun tsayt tsu tsayt* (which featured the work of Bergelson and Mayzel, among others), which appeared in 1911 and 1912. Although the other center of Yiddish modernism at the time was hoary Vilna, it may be that the Kiev modernists found their city, which could not boast a specific Jewish literary tradition or a Jewish "literary marketplace," particularly suited for their needs; after all, they wished to create something quite new in the field of Yiddish letters: "a new literary tradition, a new literary school," as Der Nister remembered it three decades later.[205] Other Hebrew and Yiddish writers, such as Uri Nissan Gnessin, had also spent time in the city but, like Gnessin, were often isolated and unnoticed, and in any case would certainly have not caught the attention of Jews who only read Russian.

For Wladeldo, national culture could only be created by modern Jews, educated in contemporary methodologies of music, art, and literature, who were also in direct contact with the authentic life of the nation as it existed in the Pale of Settlement. If "indifference" and "a lack of ideals" could be overcome, Kiev—a modern metropolis in the heart of the Pale of Settlement—could be an ideal center for the creation of Jewish national culture. With the benefit of hindsight, we can see that a modern Jewish culture and way of life was indeed being created in Kiev, but mostly not in the self-conscious manner envisioned by Wladeldo. Like other cities on the cutting edge of modernity in the Russian Empire such as Odessa, Kiev's very contradictions, its freedoms and restrictions, communal structures in the midst of the anonymity of the metropolis, physical proximity yet psychological distance from shtetlekh such as Demievka—all of these created an environment ripe for experimentation in Jewish modernity, as each individual Jew developed his or her own brand of Jewishness, collectively creating a Jewish future unlike any that could be envisioned by a single individual.[206]

Conclusion

In his letter to Sholem Aleichem that served as the introduction to the literary almanac *Di yudishe folksbibliotek,* Dr. Isaac Kaminer, a Hebrew writer and poet, compared Kiev to the Jewish communities established by the Nikolaevan soldiers in the Russian interior—a collection of individuals from many places who found themselves thrown together and thus started a community:

> We came here one by one, from Lithuania, from Reisen, Vohlyn, Poland; each was a stranger to his fellow, everyone was his own individual (*adam bifenei atsmo*): poor, rich, hungry, caught up in worries about the future. [But before you knew it, we had] a *minyan* [prayer quorum], *beys medresh* [study hall], *biker khoylim* [visiting the sick society], *khevras mishnayos* [Mishna study brotherhood], *hakhnasas orkhim* [society to support the community hostel], and so on. The strong and lively spirit of Judaism was growing.[207]

Kaminer's was an outlook colored by the optimism of his time, the 1880s. Then, Jews could move to a new city and, at least in his eyes, not be substantially changed by their new environment. True, Jews differed in their regional customs and accents, but their fundamental religious and communal needs and aims were the same. By the second decade of the twentieth century, Jews streamed en masse to events like the folk music concert at the Concordia Club and the Conference on Hebrew Culture and Language, hungry for Jewish culture that was both "old" and "new" at the same time. Students and middle-class professionals, who had grown up and been educated in the bosom of Russian culture and were now increasingly shut out of many (though not all) areas of imperial life, turned back to Jewish culture for a sense of meaning and belonging. Many "ordinary" working-class Jews felt a natural connection to Jewish nationalist culture because of its mobilization of symbols from the world of Jewish religious observance, most notably the Hebrew language and the Land of Israel.

Indeed, as we have seen, Kiev not only became a city with a large Jewish population but was seen by some as a Jewish city in the same way that the very character of Warsaw and Odessa was permeated with Jewishness. It may well be that the very impression that Russian Kiev had become "too Jewish" helped to stimulate or intensify the pogroms when they did occur; a nationalist publication explicitly linked the 1905 pogrom with the purported Jewish attempt to "take possession of Kiev and its ancient sacred places," which was the key to conquering all of Russia.[208] Gennady Estraikh writes that Jews were "more marginal" in Kiev than they would have been in the shtetlekh of the Pale where they often constituted the majority of residents, but marginality is a difficult concept to pin down.[209] It is likely that a Jew, especially a young one, would feel much more a part of the mainstream of Russian and European—and even Jewish—life in a big city, the center of culture, politics, and finance.

As Jews became more Russian and more integrated into the city's institutions, the counter-reaction on the part of the government was to restrict Jews from those very institutions. The first and best example of this phenomenon was the numerus clausus instituted by the Ministry of Public Enlightenment under Alexander III, but in later years it extended to many other areas of society. And the popularity of Jewish nationalism was fueled not only by rising hostility to Jews but also by widespread acculturation among Jews and the sense that Jews were losing their uniqueness and an authentic culture.

By the time the tsarist regime had reversed its stated goal of merging the Jewish population into Russian society in favor of a segregation that would "protect" the narod from the dangers of Jewry, a significant proportion of Russian Jews, especially those educated in Russian gymnasia and universities, were now fully Russian in their cultural affinities and sensibilities: Russian, that is, in the all-imperial sense, *rossiiskii*, not the ethnic *russkii*.[210] If they were to "return" to Jewish cultural production, as some of them did, it would be in an unmistakably imperial, Russian mode.

In a complex dance with Russian state and society, as Jews became more and more Russian and at home in Russian culture, they yearned for an authentic way of being Jewish that they felt was disappearing. Thus, antisemitism and pogroms were not the only cause for the turn to Jewish nationalism. Even nationalism and modern Jewish culture—in Yiddish and Hebrew as well as Russian—were expressed in particularly "Russian" ways. Wealthy, acculturated Jews wanted poor Jews to study traditional heder curricula, while the middle class wanted to recreate some kind of "authentic," "living" Judaism they felt they had lost.

A history of Kiev Jewry published in 1902 by communal activist Israel Darewski provides insight into local Jewish identity. Darewski argued that the Khazars (a Turkic people who had converted to Judaism) had settled Kiev in the eighth century, before the city was settled by Russians (or the Rus') in the ninth century.[211] Darewski also argued that the Khazars had called the place *Zion*, perhaps because of the connection between the hills of Kiev and the mountain called Zion. Later, the Russians corrupted "Zion" into "Kiev" in a complex linguistic transition that Darewski described in detail.

Darewski audaciously turned received history on its head: Kiev was not the "Jerusalem of Russia" and the mother of Russian cities, but rather a second Jewish Jerusalem, having been originally named after the holy city itself. Indeed, Jews had been there even before Russians and, as Darewski went on to show, had maintained a presence for much of subsequent history. Darewski's stance is even more daring when we call to mind the continuing charges on the part of Judeophobes that Jews were bent on taking over Kiev and using it as a base from which to enslave all of Russia. Keeping in mind that the book was written in Hebrew, we may interpret his project in a number of ways. Perhaps it was his way of expressing that Kiev's Jews felt at home in the city, and rightfully so, since they had been there for a millennium. The message to his home community was one of reassurance, providing them with a local Jewish myth that would help to bind them to the place despite charges (written into law) that Jews did not belong there. It may also have been an attempt to create a shared sense of community among Jews who were divided among themselves, sometimes seemingly irrevocably. The book might also be seen as a historical foundation for a confident Jewish existence on Russian soil; that even the city reputed to be most hostile to Jews was in reality a Jewish city. While some Kiev Jews who were secure in their place in the city and in imperial society as a whole would probably have chosen to read Darewski's interpretation as confirming their own self-confidence, most would likely have seen it as a call for Jews to fight for their right to call Russia their rightful home, and for equal rights as equal citizens. A decade after the book's publication, the chances that Jews would be optimistic enough to subscribe to either position were remote indeed.

5

Jew as Neighbor, Jew as Other: Interethnic Relations and Antisemitism

The two pogroms surveyed in earlier chapters, along with local anti-Jewish restrictions, day-to-day hostility, and rising nationalist sentiment, would seem to have made impossible the prospect of Jewish integration of any kind into the larger society. However, there were small but significant islands of neighborly interaction, cooperation, and even conviviality; and thus the reality of meaningful interaction between Jews and non-Jews in Kiev cannot be discounted, nor can the extent to which some Jews felt at home in the society and culture of imperial Russia. As this chapter demonstrates, such interaction was not limited to commercial contacts, which had existed for centuries and, as Todd Endelman has written of England, "were generally of an instrumental and formal character" and at times could even hinder contact of a warmer nature when individuals evaluated each other purely on the basis of how they conducted business.[1] People coming together in the context of voluntary societies, charities, and educational institutions had something in common other than personal gain, and that sense of common purpose surely made it easier to overcome prejudices and forge working partnerships, acquaintanceships, and even friendships with members of other ethnic and religious groups.

Scholars have recently pointed out the importance of the voluntary sector within late imperial Russia's small but growing civil society. Kiev and other large cities were home to a rapidly growing number of associations, societies, clubs, and charities that provided a middle ground between the state and the individual, offered an outlet for political energies that until 1905 could not be expressed outside the limited municipal sphere, challenged the established social order based on soslovie (estate) and rank, promised the amelioration of many aspects of municipal life (especially in the realms of education and health) as well as individual self-improvement, and encouraged professionalization.[2] For Jews, whose opportunities to enter public life were becoming ever fewer as government restrictions blocked or severely narrowed the way to participation in municipal government, higher education, and the bar, the voluntary sector offered an alternative—and a chance to be active in a nonsectarian quarter of society that was truly "all-imperial."[3] But as Joseph Bradley points out, even as associational life fostered a new spirit of *obshchestvennost'* in the empire's cities, the associations "also promoted new identities and groupings based on craft, profession, culture, and choice"—and, we may add, nationality.[4] Nowhere could this contradiction be seen more clearly than in Kiev, a city of a quarter-million in 1897 where three prominent ethnic groups—Russian, Ukrainian, and Jewish—lived side by side with smaller populations of Poles, Germans, Czechs, and others.[5] Even as individuals came together to improve city life for specific socioeconomic, religious, or occupational groups, the pull of national identification remained strong and grew only stronger as the empire, and especially its western borderlands, grew more polarized in the last decades of tsarist rule.[6] Kiev's voluntary sector provided common ground where Jews and non-Jews could come together, but ethnic tensions present everywhere in society could not be erased or forgotten even here. Without discounting the significance of the national question, however, the evidence also points to class as a secondary but still important factor in the formation of civil society in Kiev; as Michael F. Hamm writes, "toward the end of the nineteenth century . . . occupation, education, and income came increasingly to determine status and recreational choices."[7]

This chapter highlights the ambiguities inherent in the partial integration that some Jews, especially educated middle-class Jews, experienced in Kiev. As we shall see, the few decades before 1905—not quite a "golden age" but still relatively peaceful—yield a number of fascinating examples of interethnic contact. However, even after the 1905 pogrom, which shattered the hopes of most Jews for peaceful coexistence with their Christian neighbors in Kiev, we can find Jews and non-Jews coming together in professional and even social contexts. Moreover, these encounters did not necessitate Jews "becoming" Russian or even abandoning their Jewishness, though many of the individuals whom we will have cause to mention were acculturated to some degree. This point is crucial because the field continues to suffer from the impressionistic duality of isolated shtetl Jew versus assimilated, russified, or even deracinated Jewish *intelligent*.[8] Kiev—a city seen by many Russian officials and subjects as quintessentially Russian and Orthodox yet home to thousands of Jews, a city legally "beyond the Pale" yet sitting right in the heart of a territory of historic Jewish settlement—is an ideal place to view the encounter between the average urban Jew and the Christian townsperson. In a city where ethnic segregation was the norm, the extent of interaction and cooperation—even when imperfect or restricted in some way—was truly remarkable, and allows us to point to a very limited but no less real Jewish integration even in Kiev.

The nature of relations between Jews and Christians in the Ukrainian lands varied depending on ethnic group and socioeconomic class. Most Russian bureaucrats and merchants moving to Kiev from the inner provinces of the empire had probably met few if any Jews before, and their knowledge of Jews and Judaism was likely limited to the stereotypes that surfaced in official imperial policy, the press, and in the relatively few works of Russian literature that discussed Jews; that is, as exploiters of the peasantry, enemies of Christianity, and individuals detrimental to the economic well-being of the state.[9] Poles and Ukrainians, on the other hand, had a long history of interaction with the Jews of the former Polish–Lithuanian Commonwealth, characterized by both economic interdependence and mutual antagonism. Starting in the late sixteenth century, Polish (and polonized Ukrainian) magnates had begun to invite Jews to settle on their estates and in private towns in the Ukrainian lands in order to provide essential economic services; the Christian burghers in this region, however, often resented Jewish competition.[10] Some citizens' groups attempted to attain the *de non tolerandis judaeis* right for their town, and at times—such as in Kiev in 1619—they succeeded. The relationship between Jews and peasants was also problematic, melding peaceable (or at least uneventful) day-to-day interaction with religious antagonism (including anti-Judaism on the part of Christians and a negative valuation of Christianity on the part of Jews) and peasant resentment of Jews for the supporting role they played in Polish economic hegemony in the region and especially the *arenda* leaseholding system.[11] The two groups often inhabited different sociogeographical terrains, Jews predominating in the market town (or shtetl) and Ukrainian peasants residing in agricultural village settlements. The modern period brought rapid change and upheaval for all these groups, however, and, though individual migrants to the city surely brought with them traditional images of how a typical Jew, Ukrainian, or Russian was supposed to behave, in the context of the late imperial city, economic and social roles could not remain as rigid as in past times or in rural areas.

Kiev (or Kyïv, as it has always been known by Ukrainians) held a special place in the symbolic world of Ukrainians, which began to achieve expression with the emergence of the Hromada (society) movement of Ukrainian national and cultural consciousness in the mid-nineteenth century.[12] The attitudes of Ukrainian *intelligenty* toward Jews ranged from friendly to hostile and, understandably, the question of relations between the two groups often hinged on the perception of the Jewish role in the complex triangulation of national interests in the region. Were Jews shills for the imperial government and its program of russification, or were they another oppressed nation that might be interested in allying with the Ukrainians to throw off the tsarist yoke? Many Ukrainian intellectuals and political leaders were resentful of what they saw as a Jewish alliance with the repressive Russian state.[13] (For obvious reasons, acculturating Jews in the late empire chose to learn Russian, not Ukrainian.) A concrete illustration of resentment of Jews by Ukrainians—or perhaps of Russian perceptions of that resentment—is the original design for the statue of Bohdan Khmel'nyts'kyi (Bogdan Khmel'nitskii, in Russian) in Kiev, showing the Cossack leader's steed crushing a Polish noble and a Jewish *arendator.*[14] Nationalist Ukrainians hoped, of course, that the Jews would see themselves as an oppressed nation that might ally with the Ukrainians to throw off the tsarist yoke, as evidenced quite concretely by advertisements—in Ukrainian—placed in Jewish publications for Ukrainian-language newspapers and journals such as *Ukraïna* and *Khata.*[15] The Revolutionary Ukrainian Party (RUP), founded in 1900, condemned the persecution and official repression of Russian Jewry in strong terms.[16] And in response, not only did Jewish socialist parties often ally themselves with Ukrainian and Russian groups, but individual Jews also joined the Kiev Hromada and later the Ukrainian socialist party Spilka (Ukrainian Social Democratic Union).[17] Liberal Jewish organizations in Kiev (the Non-Party Jewish Organization [Vnepartiinaia evreiskaia organizatsiia] and the Kiev branch of the Union for the Attainment of Equal Rights for the Jewish People in Russia [Soiuz dlia dostizheniia polnopraviia evreiskogo naroda v rossii]) collaborated with the Kadet party and Polish and Ukrainian organizations to mobilize the electorate in preparation for the first Duma elections in 1906.[18] According to some reports, many peasants voted for M. R. Chervonenkis, one of the Jewish candidates for Duma deputy in Kiev province. For their part, after the elections two of the non-Jewish deputies—one Ukrainian, the other Polish—pledged to fight for Jewish rights as well for those of their own nationality.[19]

Interactions between the ethnic groups took place in the realm of ideas—in books, newspapers, and political programs—but also in the sphere of everyday life: in voluntary societies, schools, libraries, mutual-aid societies, and social clubs. While most Jewish participation in associational life was in the context of specifically Jewish societies, many Jews were also active in—or at least took advantage of the benefits offered by—non-Jewish institutions. It is to these more mundane but not less significant arenas for intergroup contact that we now turn.

Public Education and Literacy

The Russian Empire's small but growing civil society, most visible in large cities like Kiev, was one area where people of goodwill from different nationalities could come together to improve society. Within this arena, the public (i.e., informal) education movement has been called "the central locus of philanthropic efforts."[20] In this regard, the Kiev Literacy Society (Kievskoe obshchestvo gramotnosti) is an interesting example of Jewish–Christian and Jewish–Ukrainian interaction.[21] The society, established in 1882 with an all-Christian board and a church-oriented program including the creation of parish-based village libraries, was by 1898—at the behest of two Jewish members—petitioning the authorities for permission to open a Jewish Saturday adult literacy school in addition to its existing Sunday literacy schools in Kiev. From the moment it opened its doors in 1897, the society's library and reading hall attracted a large proportion of Jews; these numbers ballooned over the next decade, from one-fifth in 1897 to one-third in 1899, to 56 percent in 1904 (this figure represents the over 1,500 Jews who were library subscribers). In 1902, almost 18,000 visits were made by Jews out of a total of 54,000; the overwhelming majority of library users were under the age of twenty.[22] The increase in Jewish numbers was due in part to the library's move to the Literacy Society's new Troitskii People's House (Narodnyi dom) in the heavily Jewish Lybed neighborhood, a change about which the 1902 annual report commented positively.[23] Construction of the new building was funded wholly by the Jewish sugar baron Lazar' Brodsky (by means of a gift of 14,000 rubles in memory of his daughter Vera), while his daughter Baroness Klara Gintsburg donated significant sums each year for book acquisition. By 1906, many of Kiev's most recognizable Jewish names were on the membership list.

The extent of Jewish involvement in the Literacy Society is even more interesting when we take into account that the organization's leadership was strongly Ukrainophile, not surprising given the fact that the literacy movement in Ukraine had close ties to the Hromadas and nascent Ukrainian nationalism, especially through the Prosvita Ukrainian enlightenment movement.[24] The society's publications commission put out works in "Little Russian" (the official tsarist moniker for Ukrainian) as well as Russian, and the board urged the presentation of Ukrainian dramas alongside plays in Russian at the society's "people's theater" (*narodnyi teatr*).[25] The theater also offered pieces with Jewish themes, such as *Jews* by E. Chirikov and *Uriel Acosta*, a play about the Sephardic philosopher, as well as plays by Max Nordau.[26] In 1906, the publications commission was reestablished in two separate Ukrainian and Jewish sections devoted to clarifying and disseminating "correct views on the questions of Ukrainian life and on the Jewish question," an initiative likely prompted in part by the previous year's pogrom.[27] The overall picture is one of an institution in which Ukrainian interests were the first priority but—whether out of a true concern for other minority groups and the healthy development of their national consciousness, or out of baser financial interests—in which other constituencies found an institutional infrastructure open to their interests as well (at a price, perhaps?). More prosaically but no less significantly, the society's institutions served as "neutral territory" where Kievans of all faiths and nationalities could and did mingle in the pursuit of knowledge and leisure.

It is interesting to note that several other libraries and reading halls throughout Kiev carried Russian Jewish literature—such as the works of Grigorii Bogrov, Lev Levanda, and Simon Frug—in addition to more "mainstream" Russian fare. The fact that one could find the likes of Frug at a reading hall suggests that administrators or librarians were aware of the high proportion of Jews among their readers and did not mind catering to their perceived needs, or perhaps even that Russian Jewish literature was considered important for any "good" library or reading hall.

Another Ukrainophile institution hospitable to Jewish interests was the Russian-language *Kievskaia starina* (Kievan Antiquities), a journal of Ukrainian historical and cultural studies established by members of the Ukrainian intelligentsia in 1882. From that year until 1907, when it ceased publication, the journal published dozens of articles devoted to Jewish history in Ukraine, such as "Jewish Cossacks in the Early Seventeenth Century" and "Notes on the History of the 1768 Uman' Slaughter," the latter by I. V. Galant, a noted historian of Ukrainian Jewry and a resident of Kiev. Galant's article presented a newly discovered Hebrew document, translated into Russian, in order to shed light on the Haidamak rebellion of the eighteenth century.[28]

Here we may note that one of the few Christian families to support Jewish charitable causes in Kiev was the Ukrainian Tereshchenko family.[29] Perhaps this was a consequence of the close working relationship between the Tereshchenkos and the Brodskys in the sugar cartel that the two families helped establish. Or there may have been an unspoken rule that each family donated to the favorite causes of the other. A third possibility, though more remote because of the solidly establishment nature of these wealthy dynasties, is that out of principle they supported the "national" institutions of any oppressed minority within the empire, whether their own or that of another.

The Ambiguities of Civic Life

Other areas, such as formal education, could also accommodate shared spaces where ethnic and religious interaction was possible, though those spaces were frequently accompanied by significant tension and unease.[30] Government policies mandating or encouraging segregation, along with outright antisemitism—while simultaneously condemning the "isolation" engendered by the existence of separate Jewish charitable societies—contributed to the ambivalence.[31] For example, Jewish and non-Jewish children mixed in Kiev's public schools: Jews made up 11 percent of pupils in the municipal system in 1906, up from 5 percent in 1899 and, with more than 15 percent of all applications submitted by Jews, even more wanted to attend.[32] In some schools in neighborhoods with dense Jewish populations, the percentage of Jewish students in public schools was as high as 29 percent. Even the municipal school commission counted two Jews among its twenty-two members.[33] Yet quotas led to a concentration of Jewish students in those schools offering unrestricted admission—Jewish schools, of course, but also commercial academies under the auspices of the Ministry of Trade, where Jewish pupils constituted half and even three-quarters of the student body.[34] In addition to the official quotas established in official educational institutions with the introduction of the numerus clausus for Jewish males in universities and gymnasia in the mid-1880s, Jews began to be barred from other kinds of facilities on an ad hoc and individual basis.[35] Even private schools and academies, which did not fall under the numerus clausus law, began to institute Jewish quotas—especially schools for women, where Jews could often be found in large numbers. For example, the regulations of the Volodkevich Women's Commercial School, established in 1900, maintained that Jews were to constitute no more than 40 percent of the student body.[36] That very number reveals the overwhelming presence of Jews in Kiev's educational sector; clearly the school's founders feared that if no limit were set, Jewish applications and admissions would be at least if not more than half of the total. In 1906, one Jewish newspaper announced that the wife of a priest was opening a private girls' gymnasium that would educate pupils in the "true Russian spirit"; Jews would not be admitted.[37] Those Jews lucky enough to obtain admission to Kiev's St. Vladimir University were refused support from the local Student Aid Society (Kievskoe obshchestvo posobiia studentam) beginning in 1899.[38] And at least one gymnasium forbade its Christian students from being tutored by Jews, thus eliminating another important source of income for Jewish students.[39]

A passing reference in Sholem Aleichem's epistolary work *The Further Adventures of Menachem-Mendl and Sheyne-Sheyndl* illustrates the "challenge" that acculturation posed to Christians (and especially to antisemites) who, in earlier times, had been used to being able easily to identify Jews. Arriving in Kiev in 1912 or 1913 to cover the Beilis Affair as a journalist, Menachem-Mendl hails a cab and asks to be taken to Podol. "Hearing the words, 'Podol,' and 'Nizhne Rampart' [one of the neighborhood's main streets], the driver, a goy, turned his head to look me over and decided I must be a Jew, not otherwise, because all the Jews live on the Podol."[40] Even Jews whose mother tongue was Yiddish, like the fictional Menachem-Mendl, could be indistinguishable from their fellow Russian subjects in dress, speech, and manner—in the first moments of an encounter, and perhaps even for longer.[41]

The exclusion practiced by such institutions as the Student Aid Society was by no means a uniform trend, and in many cases a peculiar mixture of interaction and segregation seemed the norm. A relief committee set up after the Dnepr flood of 1895 was composed of both wealthy Jews and Christians and provided for victims of both religions, albeit in separate facilities.[42] (As in many cases, the primary motivation for the separation of the groups was likely the need for a separate kitchen to provide kosher food for observant Jews.) The charter of the charitable society established by the Blagoveshchenskii parish in 1908 stated specifically that the society would assist all the needy of the parish, "not excluding nonbelievers"—even though membership in the society itself was restricted to Christians.[43] Another variation on Christian–Jewish interaction within the sphere of civil society was the semi-segregation of Jewish interests within a larger, nonsectarian organization, as had been the case in the first decades of Kiev's Jewish Hospital and was now true for the city's largest and most distinguished charitable societies, the Society of Day Shelters for Working-Class Children (Obshchestvo dnevnykh priiutov dlia detei rabochego klassa) and the aforementioned Kiev Literacy

Society. At the behest of Jewish activists, the two institutions set about to establish facilities for Jews in the late 1890s; the former succeeded in founding a Jewish shelter while the latter, despite several years of effort, was unable to obtain permission for its proposed Saturday literacy classes for Jewish adults.[44] Despite the integrated presence of Jews in schools and programs established by a number of philanthropic organizations in Kiev, including the Literacy Society—one of the society's Sunday schools had a Jewish enrollment of over 10 percent, while Jewish students made up approximately 6 percent of students at its Kiev Women's Prison School[45]—both the Literacy Society and Society of Day Shelters were clearly determined to create institutions specifically for Jews. The pertinent documents show that this need was taken for granted by all those involved, perhaps because it was self-evident that most Jewish children would need a day shelter where Yiddish was spoken and kosher food was provided, while the majority of Jewish adults in need of literacy lessons would have a better chance of success if taught in their native tongue (Yiddish). And as far as funding was concerned, segregation seemed to persist even in the integrated schools, with all or most of the expenses for teaching Jewish students shouldered by Jews.[46] Although the question of whether Jews were expected to contribute to the general fund was left unasked, major Jewish donors often gave for general support as well as for specifically Jewish causes. Despite the fact that some of the most generous donors to the Literacy Society were Jewish (in 1901, at least one-fifth of the largest contributions originated from Jewish homes),[47] few or no Jews sat on the society's board. Apparently, this was an organization willing to cater to Jewish interests but reluctant or uninterested in having Jews participate in the running of its (non-Jewish) activities, other than by giving money.

The evening classes for adults sponsored by the local Committee for Public Sobriety (Popechitel'stvo o narodnoi trezvosti) provide another angle on Jewish participation in informal education. Ten of the sixteen classes had only one Jewish student or none at all, while an additional three—all in heavily Jewish neighborhoods—were between 80 and 90 percent Jewish. Only the three remaining classes had Jewish student bodies roughly commensurate to the Jewish share in the overall city population.[48] While these last three cannot be discounted, there is certainly a marked trend toward segregation, perhaps owing to residence patterns—or perhaps to the undesirability in the eyes of Christians of attending a school perceived as "Jewish."

Separate Jewish welfare institutions, while meant to facilitate integration by firmly establishing Jews in the local institutional setting, often reinforced Jewish apartness. Jewish welfare institutions such as the Kiev Jewish Hospital welcomed the Jewish poor as well as non-Jews, but there is evidence that some Jews chose to frequent the city's non-Jewish hospitals and clinics as well, which by and large did not exclude Jews in the early years.[49] But eventually at least one and possibly a number of institutions began to bar Jews, citing the existence of Jewish facilities.[50] By contrast, one of the reasons cited for the founding of the new Jewish maternity clinic in 1901 was that some Kiev clinics did not admit Jews, while the Brodsky Vocational School (Kievskoe evreiskoe uchilishche imeni S. I. Brodskago) was established to educate Jewish boys, who were barred from Kiev's main trade school.[51] Thus, separate Jewish welfare institutions could be both the impetus for anti-Jewish restrictions and a consequence of such restrictions.

Not surprisingly, Jews with a more nationalist bent often argued that shared institutions would never fully satisfy the needs of the Jewish public. Thus, despite the presence of Russian-language Jewish literature in Kiev's general libraries and reading halls, Jews called for an independent Jewish reading hall that would stock literature of all kinds in Hebrew and Yiddish in addition to Russian.[52]

Increasing Ethnic Cleavage

In the last decade before the First World War, ethnic segregation in the realm of charitable work seemed increasingly to be the rule in Kiev. This is not a surprising development given the growth of nationalism and antisemitism in the Russian Empire in these years, and specifically in Kiev—where Russian nationalists were particularly strong—expressed in the 1905 pogrom and the Beilis Affair (1911–13). A fascinating case is the Kiev Branch of the Russian Society for the Protection of Women (Rossiiskoe obshchestvo zashchity zhenshchin), under whose auspices a special division for the care of Jewish women and girls was established in 1914.[53] The scant documents relating to this organization seem to indicate that the Jewish chapter was initiated by outside activists in conjunction with the Kiev branch of the OPE. The 1912 annual report revealed that only 5 women of the 562 housed at the organization's shelter were Jewish, while for most of the year there were no Jews at all among the students at its evening and Sunday classes—a circumstance that the report declared troubling. The report called the phenomenon "inexplicable" in view of the "attitude of the teachers (among whom there have always been Jews), which is wholly benevolent and impartial toward all nationalities." The report's authors speculated that Jewish women had only begun to sign up for the society's classes later in the year owing to the very recent closure by the authorities of educational organizations in Kiev.[54] One possibility that was not considered was that many working Jewish women, having taken Saturday as a day of rest, could not afford to lose precious working hours on Sunday, when classes were held from 11 AM to 2 PM. Similarly, only 3 percent of women seeking legal assistance at the society were Jewish, as were less than 1 percent of those being housed in the society's shelter for migrants.[55]

The history of the society's Division for Care of Jewish Girls and Women (Otdel popecheniia ob evreiskikh devushkakh i zhenshchinakh g. Kieva), as related in its first annual report, reveals a few more interesting details about the assumptions shared by Jews and Christians with regard to their integration (or lack thereof) in charitable organizations. The history recounts that a Mrs. K. L. Geller initiated the founding of the branch, mooting the proposal to the board members of the Kiev branch of the OPE; it was only after she had gotten their enthusiastic promise to assist in the matter that Geller approached the board of the Kiev branch of the Society for the Protection of Women and began to negotiate with them about the establishment of a Jewish branch. The history noted specifically Geller's justification of the new institution in pointing to "the great cultural significance" that such a branch would possess, perhaps suggesting that by caring for Jewish women and girls in need, the branch would help to raise the cultural level of the Jewish community and of society in general (*cultural* here being used in the sense of *Bildung,* denoting a certain level of civilization, propriety, and education).[56] In response to the initiators' petition, the national board of the Society for the Protection of Women wrote from St. Petersburg that it did not find necessary an autonomous Jewish division in Kiev, but that a shelter and other institutions "especially for Jewish women" could be set up under the auspices of the existing Kiev branch of the society. Why the Petersburg board decided that a Jewish division was unsuitable for the Kiev branch of the society when such a division already existed in the capital was unclear.[57] The board stipulated that funding for these institutions "could be provided by Jewish donors" on the condition that the board of the society's Kiev branch would have the final say on their internal structure and governance. Neither the initiators nor the board of the Kiev branch were happy with this suggestion, and wavered over whether it was even worth going ahead under such circumstances. The resolution of the impasse came through the intervention of the society's copresident Princess Elena Al'tenburgskaia (probably at the prompting of Baron Gintsburg, another of the society's patrons, or perhaps by Baroness Anna Gintsburg, who moved in the highest circles in Petersburg and had close ties with the Al'tenburgskii family), at whose recommendation an autonomous Jewish division was swiftly agreed to.

Parsing this episode carefully, we can learn a good deal about the assumptions of the individuals involved, likely shared by many members of society. First, Jewish women were apparently unwilling to take advantage of the services offered by a non-Jewish organization, even when it declared itself "impartial" to the ethnic origins of its clients and was clearly, at least in theory, dedicated to serving all segments of society.[58] The low numbers of Jewish clients described by the 1912 report may well have been a product not only of worsening conditions for Jews within the Russian Empire but specifically of the Beilis Affair; with tensions mounting between Jews and Christians, it is not surprising that Jews tended to steer clear even of those Christians who professed a desire to help them.[59] Second, the group of Jewish women who initiated the Jewish division originally intended it to operate autonomously: within the general framework of the Society for the Protection of Women, but not as a constituent part of the Kiev branch. The activists of the Kiev branch shared this vision. Perhaps here they had in mind that only an organization with a specifically Jewish character would attract the very women it aimed to serve—the question of the language of instruction may have been an issue here, as well—but whatever the reason, all the individuals involved in the founding of the Jewish division apparently *assumed the necessity* of separate services for Jews. Moreover, even when the division was established as an integral part of the society, the society's governors were clearly not interested in providing the necessary funding for it. Thus, it seems that even when the need was demonstrated for similar services to Jewish women as were being provided to Christian women, the assumption was that the Jewish community needed to step forward to make them available; Christians could not be expected to support a Jewish institution.

Professional and Social Associations

Jews and Christians could also meet in the framework of trade-based organizations, often mutual-aid societies.[60] Government registries reveal that there were at least a few such societies with mixed memberships (though some of them may have come into existence to circumvent the law banning mutual-aid societies with majority-Jewish memberships).[61] Significantly, these were organizations of proprietors who evidently hoped to strengthen their position vis-à-vis their employees by allying with one another. Charters of professional societies registered with the provincial authorities include a Society of Proprietors of Ladies' Apparel, founded in 1906 by Shmuilo Iomtefovich Gutmanovich, Avrum Ruvinov Veiner, Gersh Itskovich Katsenelenbogen, Khaim Mikhelevich Polevik (all Jewish names), Tikhon Mikhailovich Bondarenko, and Semen Lavrenteevich Martinenko (Ukrainian or possibly Russian names). The primary goal of the society was "the raising of the material well-being and amelioration of the living and working conditions of Society Members," while objectives included "the elucidation and coordination of economic interests of members" as well as the seeking out of peaceful means of settling labor disputes between the proprietors and the artisans in their workshops (either by mediation or third-party arbitration). The society would also provide support to members whose workshops were shut down by strikes, as well as access to production materials at reduced costs. A Society of Hairdresser-Proprietors, established in 1906 or 1907 by four Jews and a peasant living in the same neighborhood, aimed to unite all businessmen in their métier to defend their professional interests as well as to provide assistance to members.[62] Evidently, ties of class and economic interest were strong enough to cross the divide of religion and ethnicity, especially in an era of frequent strikes and worker protests. It is striking that these associations were founded in the year or two after 1905—perhaps serving as evidence that not all opportunities for interethnic contact were wiped out by the pogrom.

Whether workers of different nationalities—such as the dressmakers and hairdressers who might have labored in the shops owned by the members of these two organizations—came together in similarly formal societies is unclear. Certainly some and perhaps most artels (traditional workmen's cooperative associations), such as the First Kiev Laborers' Artel of Floor-Polishers, required members to be Christians.[63]

Even if they did not work together, Jewish and Christian workers may have socialized with each other in the context of Kiev's many social clubs. In 1909, a workers' club was established to enable laborers of all nationalities and religions to come together for educational activities and classes in Russian and other subjects, and by early 1910 membership had reached 350. Judging by the names—Berman, Metushchenko, Smirnov, Gal'perin,

Svirskii—the governing board included both Jews and Christians.[64] An announcement for an upcoming masquerade ball for members of the Kiev Podol Society Club (Kievskii podol'skii obshchestvennyi klub) could be found in the "Workers' Chronicle" column of the Yiddish newspaper *Kiever vort,* suggesting that, like the Workers' Club, the membership was largely proletarian. Archival documents reveal that the club's founders were non-Jews, while the membership was mostly Jewish with a smattering of non-Jews; that a Yiddish paper advertised the club's events further complicates the picture, suggesting that even unacculturated Jews whose primary language was Yiddish might mingle socially with non-Jews of the same socioeconomic status.[65]

In addition to the workers' clubs, the more bourgeois Kiev Social Assembly (Kievskoe obschestvennoe sobranie), dedicated "to the development of community spirit" (*obshchestvennost'*), was open to members of all religions.[66] The club provided meeting space for community organizations such as the Society for Literature and the Press (Obshchestvo deiatelei literatury i pechati), the Religio-Philosophical Society (Religiozno-filosofskoe obshchestvo), the Jewish Literary Society (Evreiskoe literaturnoe obshchestvo), the Society of Lovers of the Hebrew Language (Obshchestvo liubitelei drevno-evreiskago iazyka), and the Society for the Protection of Women. The Kiev Community Library (Kievskaia obshchestvennaia biblioteka), purchased by the club after its closure by the authorities in 1910, included books in Russian as well as Ukrainian, Yiddish, and Hebrew, while periodicals subscribed to included the Ukrainian *Rada,* Yiddish *Der fraynd,* and Russian Jewish *Razsvet* and *Evreiskii mir* in addition to a variety of mainstream Russian dailies and weeklies.[67] An unscientific survey of the names of members listed in the 1915 annual report suggests that a majority were Jews with a significant number of non-Jews as well.[68] Thus, even if this ostensibly nondenominational organization was known to most middle-class Kievans as a "Jewish" institution, it nonetheless counted non-Jews among its members and interacted regularly with the non-Jewish public sphere of the city.

In his memoirs of fin-de-siècle Kiev, E. E. Friedmann remembered that Jews attended Russian clubs, and that "equality reigned at the green table" on which card games were played; since everyone played cards in Kiev, they served as an equalizing force that brought together people of all walks of life.[69] We have evidence that an organization calling itself the "Russian Society Club" (Kievskii russkii obshchestvennyi klub), which existed in 1912 but may have been founded earlier, was open, at least in theory, to members of all faiths and nationalities.[70] Such a club would surely have consciously juxtaposed itself over and against nationalist organizations such as the "Club of Russian Nationalists" (Klub russkikh natsionalistov) which explicitly excluded Jews; indeed, with the rise in antisemitism, recalled Friedmann, Jews eventually founded their own club which they called, perhaps not without some irony, the "Concordia Club" (Obshchestvennoe sobranie "Konkordiia"). As this case and that of the Society for the Protection of Women demonstrates, in the last years of tsarist rule Jews responded to rising hostility by turning inward and, in many cases, creating Jewish institutions that were replicas of those in which they no longer felt comfortable or were unwelcome.

Whether hated or grudgingly tolerated, however, Jews were too important an element in the city to be ignored. That Jews were an integral part of the fabric of municipal life as early as 1865 is demonstrated by the casual inclusion by a local newspaper surveying Kiev's entertainment scene of a "benefit performance in aid of poor Jewish students" among other leisure opportunities available to the public.[71] The trading house of the Brothers Lepeiko (a Ukrainian name) advertised its ready-mades in the Yiddish newspaper *Kiever vort;* the advertisement itself was in Yiddish, though the paper did also carry Russian-language notices.[72] Jewish shop-owners such as Isaak (Yitshak) Shvartsman and the Rozental Brothers placed prominent advertisements, worded in Ukrainian, in the daily Ukrainian-language *Rada.*[73] The semi-weekly *Kievskoe slovo* often carried articles of Jewish interest, including a feuilleton piece by Sholem Aleichem entitled "Confusion" featuring a character by the name of Tevel', better known to his Yiddish- and English-language readers as Tevye.[74] Footnotes explained the meaning of unfamiliar Yiddish words such as *shadkhen* (matchmaker). Yiddish words that had entered Russian were used widely in Kiev; the city's *balaguly* were Jewish carters known in Yiddish as *balagoles*, while a Russian slang word for pickpocket, *marvikher*, was clearly derived from a related Yiddish word meaning profit or gain.[75] On the other end of the socioeconomic spectrum, Kiev's Jewish millionaires were recruited for the boards of all the city's major institutions; Lazar' Brodsky sat together with N. Pikhno, the conservative and nationalist owner of the Judeophobic newspaper *Kievlianin,* on the boards of the Kiev Literacy Society and the Bacteriological Institute.[76] As Thomas Owen points out, sugar magnates of all ethnic backgrounds worked together to promote their product: individuals of Russian, Ukrainian, Polish, and Jewish extractions were members of both the Society of Russian Sugar Producers and the

Kiev Exchange Committee.[77] These men, and their wives, may even have mingled socially. And in the eyes of ordinary Kievans, Jewish plutocrats were just as much a part of the city's firmament of wealthy constellations as their Christian counterparts, as evidenced by the composition of the multiethnic crowd that came to the Brodsky Synagogue in 1898 to gawk at the wedding of Klara Brodskaia and Baron Vladimir Gintsburg. Although of a particularly Jewish nature, the event clearly had overtones of civic pride as well.[78]

Antagonism and Animosity

Kiev also had its share of groups that explicitly excluded Jews from membership or advocated anti-Jewish policies. Anti-Jewish groups such as the Union of Russian People were quite active in Kiev, viewing themselves as defenders of Russianness in a part of the empire "threatened" by the existence of significant minorities such as Jews and Ukrainians, especially with the rise of openly nationalist movements among these groups after 1905.[79] As Eugene Avrutin notes, the Revolution of 1905 also "popularized racist stereotypes and images as violence and disorganization erupted, as censorship laws and public opinion were liberalized, and as commercial culture proliferated."[80] Also very influential—in addition to the hoary myth of Jewish exploitation and parasitism—was the growing belief among many non-Jews that Jews represented a serious threat to the very existence of the empire. Indeed, one of the most prominent groupings within the Russian nationalist movement as a whole in the post-1905 empire was the Kiev Club of Russian Nationalists.[81] The Kiev Russian Assembly (Kievskoe russkoe sobranie; originally a branch of a national movement but later independent) was founded to promote "Orthodoxy and Autocracy, the rights of the state, and the distinctive features of the Russian people."[82] Non-Christians could not be members. Lectures held in the years leading up to the First World War included a talk on the evils of Ukrainian separatism, but much more energy was devoted to what club members viewed as the Jewish threat to Russia. In the eyes of the organization's leaders, the most important of whom was Father G. Ia. Prozorov, organized Jewry was planning to destroy the Russian state and enslave the Russian people. The "all-powerful Jewish kahal" was also blamed for the Beilis affair, which was an opportunity to do away once and for all with the "indignation that Russian Kievans must suffer who do not submit to Hebrew suggestions and temptations."[83] The Kiev Russian Sports Society (Kievskoe russkoe sportivnoe obshchestvo) restricted its membership to individuals of Russian descent and Christian faith: even Jews who had converted to Christianity were banned.[84]

Two of the organizations mentioned above—the Union of Russian People and the Russian Assembly—joined forces with four other nationalist groups or local party branches (the Party of Legal Order, the Russian Monarchist Party, the Union of Russian Workers, and the Russian Brotherhood) after the elections to the First Duma to establish "a powerful rightist coalition" that campaigned in the next election as the United Rightist Parties of Kiev. This coalition, adopting a stridently conservative and at times antisemitic platform, and drawing on support from wide swathes of ethnic Russians from across the socioeconomic spectrum, "gained an absolute majority of the vote, making Kiev the only city in the empire, except for Kishinev, to go rightist in the second elections."[85] With 51 percent of the vote against the Kadets' 48 percent in the elections of late 1906, the rightists were empowered to decide who would be chosen as Kiev's representative to the Second Duma.[86] In the 1907 elections to the Third Duma, Kiev was the only city of the six in the empire with separate representation to elect a rightist, who was one of two deputies from Kiev (the other was a Kadet).[87]

As we have seen, the leader of a constituent organization of the rightist coalition, the Kiev Russian Assembly, was a priest. This was hardly a coincidence, since some segments of the Russian Orthodox Church—usually on the lower levels of the ecclesiastical hierarchy—took an active role in promoting Judeophobic sentiment. After the 1905 pogrom, the authorities investigated claims that proclamations calling for the beating of Jews and Poles had been printed at Kiev's Caves Monastery.[88] In 1912, the anniversary of the slaying of Andrei Iushchinskii, the boy who had supposedly been the victim of a Jewish ritual murder at the hands of Mendel Beilis, was marked with a commemoration at the Cathedral of St. Sofia.[89] And the upper ranks of the clergy of Kiev province were reported to be in attendance at a provincial conference of the Union of Russian People, along with the governor and the regional military commander.[90] Notably, however, no Orthodox priests could be found who were willing to testify to the truth of the blood accusation in the Beilis case.[91]

It is worth noting that even after the 1881 pogrom, which dealt a considerable blow to the Jewish community, the threat of pogrom seems to have played strikingly little role in the lives of Kiev Jewry in the quarter-century that followed (i.e., until 1905). In this period, at least, interethnic violence was seen as a rare phenomenon; Kiev Jews lived in far greater fear of the oblava, the police roundup of Jews living illegally in Kiev, who were subject to arrest and immediate expulsion from the city.[92] As we have seen, the opportunities for Jewish–Christian interaction in the civil sphere that existed in some numbers before 1905 shrank considerably after that year and the pogrom it brought for Kiev's Jews. One clear illustration of this trend is the drop in Jewish attendance at the library of the Kiev Literacy Society in the year after the 1905 pogrom: Jews as a proportion of all subscribers fell from 55 to 32 percent.[93] This suggests that the outbreak of anti-Jewish violence, while generally outside the norm, made Jews much less likely to mingle with Christians even in public spaces like libraries. Although it is possible that the pogrom was, at least in part, a backlash against increasing Jewish participation in civic life and civil society, it seems more likely that, as Hans Rogger suggests, it was the image of the Jew as revolutionary and seditionist that drove the xenophobic nationalists who whipped up the riotous mob and—when it was not vodka and plunder that was motivating them—the members of the mob themselves.[94]

Some non-Jewish Kievans made deliberate attempts to show their Jewish fellow subjects that not everyone supported the violence: many donated to the fund established after the pogrom to aid needy victims.[95] Moreover, in the wake of the pogrom, workers at some factories held meetings, vowing to expel from their collectives anyone who had participated in the pogrom; some pledged to defend Jews against future attacks.[96] And in May 1906, about 150 workers at one of Kiev's shipbuilding yards passed a resolution decrying the possibility of another pogrom, calling for an end to attacks on defenseless citizens, and asking all workers "to defend citizens from attacks on their freedom, life, and property."[97]

In the years that followed, Kiev's civil society continued to show a certain resistance to anti-Jewish policies and attitudes. At various times after 1905, Kiev merchants petitioned the government to call off planned expulsions of Jews from Kiev, since these would cause economic harm to the city, and even to include Kiev within the Pale of Settlement, presumably to eliminate the burdensome restrictions on Jewish economic activity.[98] The administrations of institutions of higher education were apparently also interested in alleviating the onerous conditions under which their students lived: in 1906 the rector of St. Vladimir's University and the director of the Women's Higher Courses requested liberalized residence permits for their students.[99] For their part, middle-class Russian and Jewish professionals established a Society for the Promotion of the Dissemination of Accurate Information on Jews and Judaism (Obshchestvo sodeistvuiushchego rasprostraneniiu vernykh svedenii o evreiakh i evreistve) on the model of the first such society in Moscow. The Kiev society took the opportunity to address Jewish stereotypes prevalent in Ukraine with the publication of its first brochure, "Did Jews Lease Christian Churches in Ukraine?"[100]

Despite these efforts, the trend among Jews after 1905 was to turn inward. Discouraged by growing persecution and political reaction, many sought succor in the Jewish nationalist movement. Those who did not give up hope in a multiethnic and harmonious Russian Empire faced an uphill battle in a society growing more fragmented by the day.

Conclusion

Against a backdrop of centuries of interethnic tension, government-sponsored segregation, rising nationalism, and sporadic violence, Kiev's ethnic and religious groups got along better than might have been expected, in the period before 1905 and even to some extent in the years after. Russian Jews could not hope for full acceptance into the fabric of urban society, but the extent of their integration ranged widely from outright segregation or rejection to grudging toleration to acceptance—the latter especially to be found in the world of voluntary associations. In many ways the same was true for other European societies, notwithstanding the broader rights that Jews formally enjoyed; in German, Austrian, and Hungarian cultural contexts, for example, modernity and emancipation ushered in Jewish acculturation but not necessarily full integration or assimilation—if these were indeed possible (or even desirable).[101] The examples of interethnic contact and collaboration that we have seen in Kiev were probably fairly unusual, but they are nonetheless strikingly similar—both in quality and in relative rarity—to what we might observe in the cities of Central Europe.

In Central as in Eastern Europe, integration in all its varieties was often accompanied by a measure of adaptation to the culture and norms of the hegemonic society, but as Jonathan Frankel writes, "The loss of linguistic and cultural distinctiveness [does not] necessarily bring . . . with it a loss of ethnic identity."[102] To be sure, many and even most Jews had no desire entirely to lose their Jewish identity even if they could, and even the term *identity* itself is made more complex by the reality of *situational ethnicity*, the individual's ability to consciously emphasize or deemphasize his or her identification depending on the context.[103] Identity is almost never a zero-sum game.[104] As Harriet Murav has shown in her study of Avraam Uri Kovner, when Jews took on aspects of Russian identity, they often made themselves more, not less, suspect in the eyes of ethnic Russians, because they were seen as attempting to disguise their true nature.[105] This may help to explain why Jewish acculturation from Berlin to Odessa usually took place within a specifically Jewish sphere; Jews identified as German, Hungarian, or even "Russian" (*rossiiskii*) even as they maintained a particularly "Jewish" social and professional profile and even as their primary associational circles continued to consist almost exclusively of other Jews.[106] Another pan-European phenomenon were the separate Jewish welfare institutions that were meant to anchor Jews in their milieus but instead all too frequently underlined Jewish difference.[107] Growing secularization among European Jews (including those in the Russian Empire) meant that more and more of them were finding the voluntary association, and not the traditional Jewish *hevra*, an ideal instrument for the expression of their most cherished values and ideals, as well as an alternative to the conflict-ridden official Jewish community [*obshchina, Gemeinde*].[108]

Moreover, the Russian Empire was not unique in the choices that it forced Jews to make. Across multiethnic Central and Eastern Europe, as hegemonic imperial cultures slowly gave way to regional and usually nationalist cultures, Jews had to choose to which society or culture it was most prudent to acculturate. We must also remember that the choice on the part of Jews to join non-Jewish organizations cannot always be ascribed to a conscious attempt to integrate into the larger surrounding society.[109] The many opportunities available outside the Jewish community for making social change, defending one's rights, or participating in leisure activities proved a powerfully attractive force for some Jews. As in Kiev, it was Jews of the middle class and haute bourgeoisie who were the most likely to participate in general civic culture, but working-class Jews crossed ethnic and religious lines as well.

But when evaluating the implications of mixed-membership associations in the Russian imperial context, it is impossible to divorce them from the generally hostile environment in which Russian Jews found themselves in the last years of tsarist rule—the terrible post-1905 decade, when Kiev's Jews were said to live "with a sword hanging over their heads."[110] In those years, events and policies on the national stage created an atmosphere of intolerance and fostered clannishness and self-segregation. For all the similarities we have seen among European Jews across the continent, the fact that Russian Jews were without civil rights and faced a constant threat of violence made their circumstances decidedly different. They were challenged not only by the ingrained hostility and prejudice of imperial society but also by the antagonism of the Russian state, a state that, at least in its dying years, was determined to saddle its Jews with ever more legal disabilities and to stir up national and even world opinion against them. Thus, imperial Russia's growing civil society could serve both as a neutral territory where Jews, Ukrainians, and Russians could come together as well as a space in which old habits of ethnic particularism—as well as new forms of xenophobia—could thrive even in an atmosphere of ostensible egalitarianism. In this environment, voluntary societies could bring people together but could also be used to keep them apart, as is clear in the case of the Jewish school or branch—with specifically Jewish funding—within the larger voluntary association.[111] Clubs that espoused ethnic chauvinism as their primary raison d'être are an even more extreme example of this trend.

The possibility must be entertained, then, that some Jewish members of mixed-membership associations saw them as prophylactics against the threat of pogrom, while others viewed their continued engagement with non-Jewish Kievans as a philosophical statement in the face of anti-Jewish violence and continuing state persecution. Both possibilities have far-reaching implications for scholars: the former is a strong statement about the reach and efficacy of the voluntary association and its impact on society, while the latter is a conviction that historians must take as seriously as those expressed in political brochures and at party conferences.

As Joseph Bradley has shown, civil society and its voluntary associations provide a key with which to unlock many of the riddles of imperial Russian society, and one that helps the scholar "to understand the civil society that [Russia] did achieve" rather than "explain[ing] the liberal-democratic civil society that Russia clearly did not become."[112] In other words, we must strive to see what was, rather than what was not. Voluntary associations can indeed be used as a microscope of sorts through which to examine Russian Jews and their Christian neighbors on the levels of their most mundane interactions. In the context of the late empire, however, even the least of these interactions was far from ordinary, and that they occurred at all is significant in and of itself.

6

Varieties of Jewish Philanthropy

As Derek Penslar has suggested, modern Jewish philanthropy must be examined not only in the context of traditions of Jewish charity but also "within the framework of the modernization of philanthropy on the Continent as a whole."[1] The philanthropic and welfare institutions that Russian Jews developed in the nineteenth and early twentieth centuries cannot be fully understood if they are seen simply as extensions of the ramified system of communal welfare that was at the core of the autonomous Jewish community in premodern Eastern Europe. The new Russian Jewish leadership that we examined in chapter 2 looked to new models for the provision of medical care, poor relief, and education not only because Russian law required them to care for their sick and indigent, but also as a tool in their effort to reform and modernize Russian Jewry; they hoped to shape a new, healthy, productive, and "cultivated" generation of Russian Jews. A rational and "scientific" system of philanthropy could bring order to the very chaotic world of Jewish charity. Heinz-Dietrich Löwe writes,

> Jewish charity became transformed from an activity which dealt with ameliorating symptoms to one which aimed at changing the structural constraints which affected Jewish economic activity and would enable the impoverished elements of Jewish society to attain economic self-sufficiency.[2]

Charitable giving and communal welfare could also serve as political strategies to lobby for greater acceptance of Jews in Russian society. And finally, philanthropy was an ideal vehicle for the expression of a modern Jewish identity; Jews who felt uncomfortable relating to their Jewishness as religion or nationality were often much more at ease with the universalist and humanitarian conceptions of Judaism. In all of these, Russian Jews were perhaps a bit later chronologically but fundamentally no different from Jews in Western and Central Europe in their search for a modern ethos of Jewish charity. "The centrality of philanthropy as a source of collective Jewish identity is indeed a hallmark of modernity."[3]

A number of groups were involved in developing new forms of charitable work with the Jewish community: the wealthy notables; maskilim and their successors, the nationalist (and sometimes radical) intelligentsia; *polu-intelligenty* who rose from the proletariat to provide initiative and leadership for artisans' and workers' self-help organizations in the twentieth century; and women—who could be members of any of these groups and played an increasingly significant role in charity, especially private philanthropic organizations. Indeed, by creating a realm of independent, progressive philanthropic institutions, women played an important role in extending the boundaries of Jewish community and creating a Jewish public sphere that mirrored new developments in the larger Russian milieu.

Unlike the many other European states that developed welfare systems in the nineteenth century, the Russian Empire had neither an official welfare policy nor any organized system of public relief.[4] As was the case in all of the cities of the Russian Empire, Kiev's poor were cared for by a patchwork of public and private institutions supported by the state, municipal government, and, above all, individual donors. Like all of Russian society, welfare was usually organized according to the social status, profession, nationality, and religion of the recipient, and it was thus natural for Jews to establish charitable societies to provide for their less fortunate coreligionists. Moreover, as we have seen, Russian legislation mandated that the proceeds of the kosher meat tax be used to care for the poor and the sick. At the beginning of our period, there were only a handful of welfare institutions in Kiev; by its conclusion, the city counted over 150 welfare institutions, including 30 children's shelters and orphanages, 23 societies to aid needy pupils, and 22 hospitals.[5]

As was the case in Western Europe, Jews in Kiev understood their philanthropic organizations as a means toward the end of integration into the surrounding society; it was hoped that institutions such as the Jewish Hospital would show Russians the true face of Judaism and Jews: caring for all, regardless of faith; forward-looking and progressive; helping to advance the country of which they were an integral part.[6] Charity was also one of the few realms in which Jews could exert leadership in the public sphere, since Jewish political participation was restricted by the state (especially on the municipal level, where Jews lacked representation even after they had received the right to vote for the State Duma in 1906). And the "model institutions" they founded were indeed intended to be shining examples for the city, the region, and the entire empire: the Jewish Hospital was declared one of Kiev's finest; the Brodsky Trade School was patterned after the best educational institutions in Europe; the OPE's kindergarten adopted the latest pedagogical methods of Friedrich Fröbel, its German educational reformer and founder of the kindergarten. Not coincidentally, this new Jewish welfare network bore a good deal of resemblance to similar networks emerging across Europe in London, Berlin, Vienna, and other great cities with established Jewish communities and large influxes of Jewish migrants or immigrants. In all these places,

> the philanthropists' motives combined humanitarianism and self-interest, [as] trepidation about antisemitic reactions to the presence of vast pools of impoverished and unmistakably foreign Jews combined with a sincere concern for the welfare of Jews struggling to make ends meet and crowded into filthy and unsanitary slums.[7]

On a wider level, the institutions that Kiev's Jews created were nearly identical in their organization, goals, and methods to analogous hospitals, schools, shelters, and relief agencies then being established throughout the empire and elsewhere in Europe; more Russian (or European) than Jewish, the only thing they had in common with traditional Jewish brotherhoods or *hevrot* were some nomenclature choices, such as calling poor relief "*Tmikhe.*"[8] The only differences, it seemed, were the kosher food and, in schools, the teaching of "Divine Law" (religion classes) in Judaism and not Christianity. Thus, the civil society that was developing throughout imperial Russia, and especially in its urban centers, was being replicated within Russian Jewish society as well.

A good example is the introduction of district committees for Passover relief by the Representation for Jewish Welfare in 1895, clearly modeled after Moscow's district guardianships (*popechitel'stva*), introduced in the 1880s. (As we shall see, a form of the popechitel'stvo model was put into use as early as 1881 by Kiev's Pogrom Aid Committee.) The evaluation of applicants on a case-by-case basis to determine their need and merit—a practice unknown in premodern Jewish charity—was a pillar of modern scientific philanthropy. It is no surprise, then, that some Kiev Jews protested this new development in the administration of welfare. Later, other Jewish welfare agencies also adopted the guardianship model.[9]

Paradoxically, however, the Jewish welfare system that many hoped would facilitate acceptance and integration helped to maintain the separateness of Jews from non-Jews.[10] While it is true that some non-Jewish institutions did not serve Jews, by the early years of the twentieth century Jews could and did turn to general charities for various types of assistance.

For their part, Jewish benefactors could also participate in charitable giving outside the Jewish community. Nonetheless, the Jewish philanthropic sector expanded steadily, serving the material needs of growing numbers of Jewish poor as well as the social needs of the Jewish haute bourgeoisie. As Benjamin Nathans has noted in the case of St. Petersburg, philanthropy, in "new and large-scale forms," became "a defining communal activity."[11] It also provided employment to increasing numbers of Jewish professionals, especially medical professionals (doctors, physicians' assistants, and midwives) and educators but also economists and statisticians. In this way, with every Jew playing a role, charity united the socioeconomically differentiated Jewish community as perhaps no other cause or activity could.

At the same time, however, it pointed up the differences between haves and have-nots, serving as a framework within which the wealthy and educated could attain prestige while wielding power over the less fortunate. Some tried to use this power to transform the poor in their own image into healthy, civilized, cultured Russian subjects, similar to the *Bildungsbürgertum* that German Jews strove to become (perhaps in the Russian case it is more appropriate to speak of a "*Bildungsproletariat*"); as we saw in chapter 4, others seemed to want to petrify poor, uneducated Jews in their "traditional" roles, withholding progressive, secular education for the sake of the preservation of Judaism.[12] A third way was to narrow the charitable focus to those with promise, since it was simply impossible to give any more than the most cursory assistance to all those in need; here, donors promised "productive assistance" to artisans who proved themselves industrious and capable of independence. In all cases, the indigent now had to apply for support and prove that they deserved it; indiscriminate distribution of charity to all comers was a thing of the past. As community secretary G. E. Gurevich put it, "incoherent giving creates parasites and beggars." Gurevich warned anyone thinking of entering communal service that it was "not easy to refuse many, assist most only partially, and satisfy very few."[13]

Jewish philanthropy in Kiev was characterized by projects on a grand scale: the Jewish Hospital was endowed with building after elaborate building; the Brodsky School was "more like a palace" than a school; the Jewish cemetery was lavished with expensive stone edifices; and the list of structures costing tens and even hundreds of thousands of rubles went on. This emphasis on large-scale capital projects could be found among the city's Christian patrons as well, but sources suggest that it had special significance for prosperous Russian Jews. The buildings they erected were a visible testament to the presence, success, and beneficence of Jews in Kiev toward their coreligionists as well as toward Russian subjects of other religions and nationalities. They broadcast a message of solidity and permanence to the surrounding society. They were also ways for the very wealthy to gain prestige and eternal fame, insinuating their names into the very fabric of the urban environment, as in the cases of the Zaitsev Clinic, the Brodsky School, and the Brodsky Synagogue (known by the name of its founder to this day). Names of benefactors or the memorialized deceased were also attached to hospital wings or, for those of more modest means, beds in a sanatorium. Even in the latter case the name of the donor and, if desired, of the individual being honored or memorialized, were literally inscribed on a plaque displayed above the bed for all to see.[14]

As the importance of the Jewish Hospital testified, health was another concern of Kiev's Jewish philanthropists—perhaps, like the capital projects, by dint of its visibility. In this case, however, it was not something to show off but to conceal or transform; Russian Jews were often noted in popular literature and the press for their poor health, and the growing poverty among Jews often made that reputation well-deserved. The crowded and unsanitary conditions of the city only made things worse. For acculturated Jews seeking to put a positive face on Jewry for the benefit of Russian society, sickly Jewish masses who were liable to put other populations in danger (through cholera epidemics, for example) were to be avoided. By the Great War, Kiev had literally dozens of Jewish medical facilities, from hospitals and clinics to sanatoria and hospices to home health agencies and free dispensaries. But the crowning jewel of them all was the Jewish Hospital, whose founding we examined in chapter 2. Now we return to the hospital and follow its development in the last two decades of the nineteenth century and into the twentieth.

The Jewish Hospital: Expansion and Growth

When Kiev's Jewish merchants petitioned in 1875 to expand the hospital from forty beds to eighty, they proposed that the plot they intended to acquire and the buildings upon it would remain "the property of the Kiev Jewish Hospital in perpetuity," while the hospital itself would be governed by Kiev Jewish merchants, elected by the city council.[15] The city council agreed to the expansion on the condition that the land and structures, while given over for the permanent use of the hospital, would constitute *municipal* property.[16] For some reason, then, the council was interested that the hospital be owned and subject to city authority. The chair of the Kiev Philanthropic Society, Princess Nadezhda Andreevna Dondukova-Korsakova, intervened on behalf of the trustees, requesting that the hospital remain under the auspices of her organization, and the council acquiesced. After years of an unsuccessful search for a suitable plot, the council offered several acres of municipally owned land for the new hospital building; it had only to decide whether to sell the land to the hospital's trustees or grant it outright. To this the hospital's representatives, who were also city councilors themselves, replied that the Jewish community wished to purchase the land.

Even though the details surrounding them are unavailable to us, these negotiations bear some analysis. It seems that the Jewish Hospital was an institution of some significance, whether materially or symbolically, for the Philanthropic Society, the city of Kiev, and the Jewish community (or at least the hospital's board) all wanted control of it. In some ways, this is not surprising. In reform-era Russia, municipalities were often reluctant to spend their scant resources on welfare, so a hospital funded entirely by the Jewish community would have been an unmitigated good on the city's balance sheet. From this perspective, it was also advantageous for the Philanthropic Society to have control over an institution for which it needed to pay nothing.

There may, however, have been ulterior motives involved. As we have seen, the original charter of the hospital contained a provision advocating that it be located in an area distant from the city center, near the Kirillov Institution. The plot later offered by the council for the hospital was also not far from the Kirillov, on the outskirts of the Lukianov district. Though by that time the hospital was housed in a rented complex at a more central site (Starozhitomirskaia Street), an attempt on the part of the hospital trustees to purchase the site was unsuccessful.[17] Was it a coincidence that both of the locations suggested by the city council were as far as one could get from the center of Kiev without actually leaving the city? To be sure, no one wanted a hospital in the city center for fear of spreading disease, but it is also likely that the city councilors, while not opposed to the existence of the hospital, were interested in reducing its visibility as much as possible. This was to be expected in a city where Jewish settlement was restricted and, as we saw in chapter 1, the profile of Jewish residents was highly contested.

The hospital trustees had their own goals in mind. Their proposal that the new structure and the land upon which it was situated belong to the Jewish Hospital, and their insistence on purchasing the plot offered by the city council when they could have obtained it at no cost, suggests that they, too, were interested in having as much control as possible over the institution (a later account that they proposed that the hospital building and grounds be the property of the Kiev Jewish community is conceivable, though less likely).[18] Their specification that Jewish merchants govern the institution was also an attempt to reserve power for the wealthy elite of the Jewish community, consistent with the history of the Representation for Jewish Welfare surveyed in chapter 2. At the same time, their offer for the hospital administration to be selected by the city council implies that they saw an advantage in an institutional linkage to the municipality. The vesting of power in them by city authorities would put the final seal, as it were, on their dominance in Jewish affairs in Kiev.

The acquisition of the hospital complex, though hailed by many at the time, was in subsequent years subject to regular criticism because of the site's distance from the city and its Jewish neighborhoods. One critic, for example, wrote that the distance from the center of town put off both Jews and non-Jews from visiting the hospital; only "the most destitute [of Jewish women] go there, those engaged in heavy physical labor and those without their own kin."[19]

The dedication of the new Jewish Hospital in October 1885 was a grand affair, reported in the Hebrew press and in Kiev's Russian papers. The ceremony, attended by the governor-general, the governor, and other local dignitaries, was an opportunity for the leaders of Kiev Jewry to broadcast a political message about their hopes for acceptance by Russian society, and revealed some of the genuine motivations behind the building of the new hospital.[20] The proceedings emphasized that Kiev's Jews, while remaining true to their faith and heritage, felt quite at home in the Russian context. Crown Rabbi Tsukkerman preached in Russian, the choir sang songs in both Hebrew and Russian (a Russian folk song, according to one attendee), and the plaque dedicating the institution in memory of Israel Brodsky's wife was inscribed in both Hebrew and Russian. That Jews could and did make important contributions to their city and country was suggested by one witness's testimony that the "Great Jewish Hospital," as he called it, was "the best hospital in the city, both in terms of outward beauty and inward level of medicine and care, and some say one of the three or four best in the country."[21]

The same correspondent reported that the Russian dignitaries, impressed by the fact that the governor-general had chosen to honor the Jewish community with his presence, showered praise upon Jews; they noted that Jews, always a charitable nation, did not neglect those outside their faith, assisting others "for the love of mankind" without differentiating between Jew and non-Jew. This nonsectarianism, they indicated, must surely extend to the Jewish Hospital, which would accept any non-Jew who needed its services. The Jewish notables present, continued the correspondent, confirmed that this was indeed the case and that the institution was only called a "Jewish" hospital because it provided kosher food. This politically fraught exchange enabled both sides to express their assumptions about the hospital: Russian officials, clearly uncomfortable with the notion of a specifically Jewish institution in Kiev, asked for confirmation that the hospital would also serve non-Jews, making it a more universalist undertaking. Not only did their Jewish interlocutors affirm that this was the case, but they went even further in watering down the Jewish character of the hospital by explaining that it was only the adherence to one ritual practice—kashruth—that made the institution "Jewish" at all.[22] (Not incidentally, this was a practice to which bureaucrats could hardly object, seeing as the tax on kosher meat provided thousands of rubles in income to the municipal coffers.)

The comments of the correspondent for *Ha-melits,* one Y. N. Goldberg, and of Alexander Tsederbaum, who edited the newspaper from St. Petersburg, reveal the hopes that Jews in Kiev and throughout the empire placed in the new hospital and similar institutions. Goldberg repeatedly described his hope that the impressive event would convince the authorities of the integrity and probity of the Jews and lead them to change their minds about Jews and Judaism.[23] Echoing Goldberg, Tsederbaum wrote that he hoped that the event had made a lasting impression on the officials present and—now that they had seen cultured Jews familiar with European ways, decorous Jewish worship, and Jewish preaching in Russian—that they would change their minds about Jews. "Now they know that even in a city that barely tolerates Jews, the Jewish community gathers together to heal its sick, and even welcomes non-Jews into its hospital."[24] Accurate information about Jews and especially the acculturated and Europeanized among them would serve to combat the slander and misrepresentation that the officials had always heard. The Kiev Jewish Hospital, a concrete representation of the new, genuine face of Russian Jewry, would thus serve as a tool in the quest for acceptance and emancipation. That this tool was in the arena of health care was no coincidence; as Lisa Epstein argues, it was precisely in the 1860s, when the hospital was founded, that maskilim, and the acculturating, usually prosperous Jews whom they influenced, began to point to health care as a field in which reforms were necessary in order to eliminate "backwardness" among Russian Jewry and to bring them up to the level of Western society:

> The desire to remold the attitudes and practices of the Jews regarding hygiene was motivated by both altruistic and self-serving goals, to improve the health of the Jews but also to improve their image and status within modern society, in order to render them worthy of acceptance as equals in the eyes of other peoples.[25]

The expectations some Kiev Jews had of the hospital were no different from those regarding the proposed choral synagogue, which Darewski advised should be "full of sanctity and beautiful to the eye, more so than other synagogues in the Pale, so that our Christian neighbors will see that we are called by the name of God." Such a synagogue would prove to Christians not only that Jewish worship was just as decorous and thus worthy of respect as theirs, but that Jews were just as loyal as well—if not more so. As Darewski wrote, "On [the tsar's] birthdays, we can invite one of the government ministers to the synagogue when we pray for the peace of the kingdom so that they will see that we are more loyal to our king than his loyal servants."[26]

The hospital dedication was also significant from the point of view of Kiev's Jewish communal politics, serving as a kind of coronation of Israel Brodsky and his son Lazar' as indisputable leaders of the hospital and the community as a whole. (Interestingly—given the fact that the Brodskys would later be dubbed the Jewish "kings" of Kiev—Israel Brodsky's initial pledge of 15,000 rubles for the hospital was made in 1875, one year after a donation of 12,000 rubles for a children's ward at the city hospital was made by Princess San-Donato, wife of Kiev Mayor Petr Demidov.)[27] Much of the ceremony was devoted to praise of Israel for providing the lion's share of the funds for the new building (165,000 rubles); not only was the sugar magnate made honorary trustee of the hospital, but the position was made hereditary, to be inherited by the eldest Brodsky son in each generation. A portrait of Israel Brodsky to be hung in its halls, as well as the dedication inscription, would always remind patients, employees, and visitors alike of the moving force behind the institution. Israel was compared to the biblical forefather Jacob (who was renamed Israel)—both had "struggled with God and with man, and emerged victorious."

In a sign of the passing of the mantle of leadership from father to son, Lazar' Brodsky—who had served as chair of the building committee—was presented with a calligraphed epistle composed by the local Hebrew poet Yehalel in the form of an acrostic spelling out his name. In a gesture of homage, the epistle had been signed by all the men of note in the community and was proffered to Brodsky *fils* by Crown Rabbi Tsukkerman. A witness noted that the honoree accepted the gift with modesty, acknowledging his youth (he was then thirty-seven years old). Remarking that Lazar''s first accomplishments showed great promise, the writer intimated that he would soon be serving as leader of the Jewish community in Kiev and that under his guidance, communal affairs would be conducted in an orderly and successful manner.[28] Institutions such as the Jewish Hospital thus served a dual function: sending a political message to Russian officialdom and society, and creating a new sphere within which acculturated Jews could maintain a Jewish identity and a connection to the larger Jewish community.

Moshe Reikhesberg, a frequent contributor to *Ha-melits* from Kiev, praised Israel Brodsky for his many charitable works but nonetheless maintained that the huge outlays on the hospital could better have been spent on aid to Kiev's many poor Jews (other causes included the Talmud-Torah, Bikur Holim [biker khoylim, sick care society], the maternity clinic, care for orphans and apprentices, and aid for poor gymnasium and university students). Indeed, he accused some of Kiev's Jewish philanthropists of giving to the hospital project solely to enhance their prestige. (The previous year, Lazar' Brodsky had been similarly criticized for making large donations to non-Jewish institutions to enhance his reputation, despite their disrespectful treatment of him; for example, his name was not mentioned at a university ceremony despite his large gift to that institution.)[29] This rare instance of criticism among coverage that was usually nothing less than glowing, if not sycophantic, adumbrated a more widespread critique of Jewish philanthropic practices that would follow within only a few years. Despite his reservations, however, Reikhesberg recommended that the Jewish Hospital be named after Brodsky so that the gratitude of Kiev Jewry could be expressed not just in words but in concrete action.[30]

Tolerance and Segregation

Kiev's Jewish Hospital illustrated the paradox to which Reinhardt Liedtke points in his discussion of Jewish philanthropy in Hamburg and Manchester: Jewish welfare institutions, illustrating the universal value of charity, promoted acceptance of Jews by the larger society; at the same time, the institutions remained separate and thus reinforced Jewish distinctiveness.[31] Indeed, in the very year of the dedication of the new building of the Jewish Hospital, the Kiev newspaper *Zaria* reported on a decree that no more Jews were to be accepted at the Kirillov Hospital because Jews now had their own hospital.[32] Thus, the attempt to encourage integration apparently backfired: the hospital that was supposed to be the equal of its non-Jewish counterparts, showing that Jews could operate model institutions, as well as serving both Jews and Christians, actually led to the barring of Jews from non-Jewish hospitals.

The continuing segregation between Christians and Jews would be reinforced several years later by the "categorical refusal" of S. S. Ignat'eva, chairwoman of the Kiev Philanthropic Society, to serve as head of the Jewish Hospital, a position she automatically inherited when she took on the mantle of leadership at the society. The new (1891) charter of the hospital removed it from the administrative structure of the Kiev Philanthropic Society at least partly as a result of Ignat'eva's demurral.[33]

However, Kiev's Jewish magnates could continue to attempt to influence the current state of affairs with their philanthropy. In 1895, Kiev's Jews celebrated the opening of the new children's ward of the Jewish Hospital, funded by Lazar' Brodsky, and in that very same year Brodsky announced at a board meeting of the Kiev Society for Aid to Sick Children his intention to finance the construction of a free pediatric outpatient clinic in honor of the birth of Princess Ol'ga Nikolaevna.[34] Did Brodsky, perhaps concerned about being criticized for being clannish or miserly toward Russian society, feel an obligation to provide the same institutions for Christians in Kiev that he was bestowing upon his fellow Jews? Perhaps. But an analysis of his patterns of giving suggests another likelihood: he was rewarding the Society for Aid to Sick Children for its acceptance of Jews. Almost without exception, the institutions to which Brodsky contributed all served Jews and were sometimes intended specifically to replace similar institutions where Jewish admission was restricted (institutions of higher learning, for example). Brodsky refused restrictions on the number of Jews to be permitted to sit on the board of his planned artisans' loan fund. Around 1895, he offered a large sum to establish a trade school for children of all faiths, but some members of the city council mandated that the number of Jews on the school's board would have to be limited, while others demanded that the number of Jewish students be proportional to their Christian peers. Brodsky rejected these conditions, and the school project did not go forward.[35]

The chain of events is remarkable: turned down by the authorities in his initial request to open a Jewish trade school to train the poor boys of Kiev, Brodsky then attempted to gain approval for a school that would school both Jews and Christians. Stung yet again when this proposal, too, was rejected, Brodsky, together with his brother Lev, finally returned to the original plan for an exclusively Jewish school, for which they finally received permission. If the government's segregationist policies could not be defeated, they would have to be adopted. Brodsky was also a major force in the establishment of Kiev's Polytechnical Institute in 1898, which became known as a welcome alternative for Jewish men to other institutions of higher learning where the numerus clausus was strictly enforced.[36]

It is no coincidence that these episodes took place in the 1890s, and they are even more striking when compared with this Brodsky brother's earlier giving patterns. In 1884, for example, after he had presented Kiev's St. Vladimir University with a princely gift of 50,000 rubles, his name was not mentioned at the festivities celebrating the university's fiftieth anniversary. In *Ha-melits*, Alexander Tsederbaum moralized that the money would have been better spent on the poor of Brodsky's own people—the Jews. Tsederbaum went on to argue that Brodsky was even more deserving of reproach because the university was known for its anti-Jewish policies.[37] Given the growing burden of anti-Jewish legislation and administrative practice that became especially notable in the 1890s, it is not unlikely that Brodsky began to heed such advice and appropriate his funds with a more discerning eye. Institutions that did not discriminate against Jews would be rewarded, while Jewish institutions serving Jews exclusively—which Brodsky would previously have rejected—were now acceptable and even desirable. If Brodsky's giving, including his gift of a new clinic to the Kiev Society for Aid to Sick Children, was indeed motivated by such quasi-political aims, it is not without irony that his endowment of the clinic should have moved no less a personage than the emperor himself to offer Brodsky his personal thanks (tied, of course, to the naming of the institution after his new daughter).[38]

Lev Brodsky seems to have followed his brother's example. In 1894, he endowed scholarships at a Kiev gymnasium and at the medical faculty of St. Vladimir University that were to be restricted to Jewish students.[39] That same year, he offered to defray tuition for a large number of students at two of the city's women's gymnasia, most of which had high percentages of Jewish students.[40]

But we must not hasten to assume that the earlier motivation attached to philanthropic generosity—to "bring peace," as it were, between Christians and Jews, had disappeared. Certainly others continued to see the Brodskys' large gifts in this light. The founding of Kiev's Bacteriological Institute in 1896 was an opportunity for one Barukhovitsh of Kiev to write an article entitled "Works of Charity [Lead to] Peace." The author noted that Lazar' Brodsky gave charity to Jews and non-Jews alike, and that all Jews could exult in the honor that had been showered upon the great humanitarian by Russian officials and scientists. Barukhovitsh also described Brodsky's proposal that all sugar processors in the southwest region donate a fixed percentage of their income to the Kiev branch of the Imperial Russian Technical Society, another act that brought honor not only to Brodsky himself but to all Jews. Barukhovitsh encouraged other Jewish industrialists to follow Brodsky's example.[41] Another observer wrote that "we are doubly happy [about the Bacteriological Institute] because the founder is a Jew," and commented that all those present at its dedication had heaped accolades upon Brodsky.[42] The project unquestionably underlined Brodsky's loyalty to the empire and its ruling family, as the institute was named after the assassinated Tsar Alexander II and the dedication itself was held on the anniversary of the coronation of Nicholas II.

Model Institutions: Jewish "Civilization," Civilizing Jews

In Kiev, Jewish philanthropic institutions were often planned as "model" hospitals, clinics, and schools. In many cases, participants in the undertaking or observers drew an overt comparison between the new institution and existing ones based on traditional models of Jewish welfare. There were several goals at work here. Activists were eager to show the surrounding society that Jews were not, as prevailing stereotypes portrayed them, backward and primitive, but rather were in the forefront of progress and scientific achievements. Moreover, their model institutions contributed not only to the well-being of Jews, but to that of the city as a whole, and even of the empire. Integral to this project was an attempt to transform Jewish institutions and, through them, Jews themselves. Clearly inherent in this new Jewish image was the hope for acceptance by Russian society, though many of those involved genuinely desired to create a new, healthy, educated Russian Jewry and were less concerned about the approval of the Christian world. Kiev was the ideal place to set such a project in motion: unlike St. Petersburg and Moscow, both city and hinterland had significant numbers of poor and sick Jews in need of relief; unlike Odessa, it was a particular object of national scrutiny because of its historical and religious significance.

In an overview of the hospital's history written in 1913—far removed from the actual events but possibly still reflective of the motivations of the original actors—chief doctor Petr Timofeevich Neishtube wrote that after slow growth in the first years, the institution began to develop more rapidly as it strove to maintain a position for itself among the city's other hospitals and clinics. The number of staff physicians rose, and professors from St. Vladimir University were invited as consultants, "but nonetheless the hospital had still not attained the physiognomy and character of a clinic: it could not yet free itself from the disposition [*poriadki*] and character which were reminiscent of the pre-reform 'gekdysh' hospitals."[43] The reference is to the *hekdesh*, a combination of poorhouse, old-age home, and primitive hospital that often served as a stand-in for a medical clinic in traditional Jewish communities. As Neishtube describes it, the trustees were not simply engaged in building up a hospital, but were also exorcising demons, as it were: though no hekdesh existed in the post-1861 period of Jewish settlement in Kiev, somehow the specter of the hekdesh continued to haunt the city's Jews. We can safely state that the hospital officers harbored no nostalgia about traditional Jewish welfare and viewed their institution as an opportunity for a new, thoroughly modern start.

Their anxiety to avoid replicating familiar Jewish models was exacerbated by the desire to have the Jewish Hospital measure up to the non-Jewish medical institutions in Kiev, which it could never do, they felt, as long as it was housed in rented premises. Reflecting the arduous and lengthy negotiations that led to the purchase of land for the hospital in 1885, Neishtube wrote,

> Over the course of twenty-three years, from 1862 to 1885, the hospital leaders continued their difficult work, doggedly pursuing one goal, one secret dream: to have their own building for the hospital. . . . a building constructed to the requirements of medical science, satisfying hygienic and sanitary precepts. . . . in their own building it would be possible to achieve everything.[44]

The goal of "their own building" symbolized the independence of the hospital from the Jewish past, personified by the unsanitary hekdesh, and the creation of a modern, scientific institution. The new building signified a break with the old Jewish past—including its legacy of rightlessness—for in this new context, Jewish accomplishments would not be limited: "everything" could be achieved.

The dedications of the hospital's new wings and wards, of which there was one every few years after the opening of the new building in 1885, were opportunities to show off the hospital, with the latest scientific and technological advances, to Russian society; to educate the Jewish public about modern medicine; and even to model an exemplary way of life for Russian Jews. That Neishtube described the hospital as "a small town" was no coincidence: far from the crowds and bustle of the city, the forty-acre hospital compound with its numerous wards and auxiliary structures (a chapel was added in 1902) could indeed be considered a kind of model community.[45] In 1891, on the occasion of the dedication of the new convalescent ward, an article in *Ha-melits* explained the ward's purpose and functioning to readers who had never before heard of a special establishment for recuperating patients. The account gave a detailed description of the many amenities of the ward, and depicted its ideal setting, looking out onto the beauty of nature with fresh breezes blowing in from all sides.[46] This was a far cry from the typical hekdesh with its mean, unsanitary conditions (the Yiddish adjective *hekdeshdik* actually means soiled or dingy).

Not only were Jews to feel pride in their model institution, but Kiev's Christians were also welcomed to the hospital, following the model of Israel Brodsky's pioneering endowment for Jewish *and* Christian students. The treatment of Christian patients at a Jewish hospital was a novelty in the Russian Empire, as attested to by the fact that contemporaries frequently stressed the "trust" or "faith" that the Christians had in the institution. In the first half of 1894, more than 40 percent of outpatient division patients were Orthodox Christians.[47] Indeed, during the cholera epidemic of the early 1890s, the city council requested the hospital's assistance in countering the outbreak and, according to one witness, "many non-Jews streamed to it in full faith."[48] Not only had the hospital officers succeeded in elevating their institution to the level of the other hospitals in Kiev, but the Sanitary Commission pronounced the hospital's cholera wing the best in the city and noted that many Christians stricken with cholera only consented to be hospitalized on the condition that they be admitted to the Jewish Hospital.[49] In 1895,

Kiev's chief medical inspector called the hospital a model establishment serving both Jews and Christians, "who have complete trust in the institution."[50] The hospital was gaining a reputation for excellence not only within Kiev, but even throughout the empire; for example, the hospital was the first in the country outside of the two capitals to attempt a pioneering operation to correct a hunchback.[51] The hospital's admirable physical plant and extensive resources likely induced envy among some; an article in the Judeophobic *Novoe vremia* called the "beautiful" Jewish Hospital "the envy of the wretched neighboring Christian hospital."[52] According to the 1891 charter, all patients were to receive room, board, linens, hospital garments, and even shoes at no cost during their stay.[53]

Israel Brodsky's decision to build (or purchase and renovate—the sources are unclear) a bathhouse and ritual bath (*mikvah*) in Podol at the same time as the hospital may also have reflected the attempt by acculturated Jews to cultivate and "civilize" their coreligionists—raising their quality of life and thus bringing them closer to a European-Russian lifestyle—while at the same time assisting them in maintaining Jewish observance. The bathhouse was supposed to serve as a source of supplemental income for the hospital, but the new facility was, according to one contemporary, also intended to encourage women who had stopped visiting the old, dirty mikvah to resume the observance of the menstrual purity laws. Surely the new institution, located in a heavily Jewish neighborhood, was also designed to raise the general level of cleanliness of Kiev Jewry.[54]

A second model Jewish public health institution was the free surgical clinic established by Yonah (Ionna) Zaitsev in honor of the wedding of Tsar Nicholas II and Alexandra in 1894. In addition to the 30,000 rubles that he donated to build the clinic, Zaitsev granted the plot of land on which it would be constructed. The institution was specifically intended to serve the needy of all religions and estates, and would be open year round to help fill the gap in service created when most of Kiev's hospitals closed for the summer, when the city filled with pilgrims and migrant workers. Moreover, the clinic's central location in Podol made it much more convenient for most Kiev residents than the distant Jewish Hospital.[55] Like the Jewish Hospital, it was equipped with the most up-to-date equipment, including sterilization apparatus for surgical instruments. Tellingly, the establishment was to be governed by a committee consisting of Zaitsev (and his descendants after him), the chief doctor, and a representative of donors to the clinic to be chosen by the city council.[56] Thus, at both the Jewish Hospital and the Zaitsev Clinic the most prominent patrons (Brodsky and Zaitsev) were granted a role in the governance of the institution in perpetuity. Zaitsev also created a 36,000-ruble trust, the income of which was to maintain the clinic, thus ensuring that his name would continue to be linked with the institution for decades to come.

Model Institutions: Creating Model Jews

Hospitals, clinics, and sanatoria could treat the poor once they were sick, but the new scientific philanthropy was also concerned with preventing poverty. There were several initiatives in the pre-1905 years that aimed to assist in the "productivization" of Jews: assisting poor artisans and training needy Jewish children in useful crafts.[57] Some Jewish artisans had the privilege of settling outside the Pale of Settlement, and it was felt that encouraging the next generation to enter a field other than trade could only serve its interests and those of Russian Jewry as a whole, as more Jews moved to the interior provinces and integrated into Russian society. There was particular concern with providing an education for orphans so that they would not become a burden to the community. In 1879, around the same time that he was involved with the planning of the expansion of the Jewish Hospital, Israel Brodsky donated 40,000 rubles for a Jewish trade school to be built in Kiev.[58] It is no surprise, however, that the project did not receive official permission for over thirty years; the authorities were perpetually concerned with the possibility that Kiev would become a magnet for poor Jews, whether artisans or not, and sought to prevent an "influx" of Jews into the city. The reality that they could not seem to come to terms with was that that influx had started almost from the very moment of Kiev's opening to Jews, despite the restrictions on settlement.

Interestingly, there is some evidence that Jewish poverty in Kiev was not as dire as it might have been. In 1887, A. P. Subbotin claimed that on the whole, Jewish indigence in the southwest was worse than in the northwest, but noted that, thanks to residence restrictions, "Jewish poverty in Kiev is not striking." He expanded on this phenomenon by remarking that "the small number of poor Jews is not so noticeable compared with the relatively comfortable non-Jewish population and especially with the masses of poor Christians"—including the 100,000 pilgrims who arrived each year, many of whom stayed in Kiev and ended up begging. His conclusion was that Jews made up a smaller percentage of poor than in other cities, and were being effectively assisted by the large number of wealthy Jews.[59] A decade later, the situation was now just the reverse: a U.S. government report compiled on the basis of statistics gathered in 1897 and 1898 maintained that "the economic condition of the Jews in the south of Russia is so much better than that of those in the northwest that only since the recent disturbances has the emigration fever touched the Jews of that region."[60] The upshot was the same, however: though there were many poor Jews in Kiev, overall the city remained a desirable destination for Jews (and non-Jews as well).

Despite their inability to establish the trade school, it seems that Kiev's communal leaders did organize a training program in crafts for Jewish boys from indigent families (most were probably orphans). The project, according to one account initiated by Crown Rabbi Tsukkerman, was declared pioneering in its supervision of the youths after their assignation to master artisans, and in its instruction in Hebrew, Russian, and other academic subjects. As a model program, it would help eliminate the prevailing circumstances wherein boys were "sold off" to long, cruel apprenticeships.[61] Thus, like the Jewish Hospital, the training program was planned as a model project that would help teach Russian Jews the proper way to care for the poor. It was also reported that the chair of the training commission, M. Rozenberg, took an active interest in the program, even visiting workshops to check on the progress of the apprentices.[62] A decade after its founding, the initiative was still in existence, with nine orphans in apprenticeships.[63]

Nonetheless, by the 1890s the absence of any Jewish schools in Kiev had become a serious problem in light of the ever-increasing quotas in many state and private schools. A group of Kiev Jews requested permission for a Jewish school in 1891 and then again two years later; archival documents reveal that the schools were apparently intended for the children of artisans and soldiers. It is unclear if this school was intended to replace the Talmud Torah or was meant for children of Kiev's lower-middle-class Jews who were not willing to send their children to an institution meant for "the poor."[64] In any case, the governor-general turned down the request on the grounds that these Jews did not have permanent residence rights in Kiev and that allowing the establishment of a school would only encourage more such Jews to come to the city. A lower-level bureaucrat writing a memorandum on the same question argued that once one such school was allowed, there would be no way to stop the inevitable establishment of many more Jewish schools. He noted that there were already enough schools in Kiev which Jews could attend.[65] Indeed, many Kiev children studied in the city's numerous gymnasia (this was a means to obtain a residence permit for Kiev), and another educational cause that was taken up by Kiev's Jews was support of needy Jewish gymnasia students, a fund originally created through donations from maskilim who were graduates of institutions of higher education.[66]

But the centerpiece of Jewish educational efforts in Kiev was the Brodsky trade school. Around the turn of the century, Lazar' and Lev Brodsky decided to establish a Jewish boys' primary school with a vocational division. The brothers, who wished their school to be the best of its kind in the Russian Empire, traveled throughout Europe to visit vocational schools before sparing no expense in planning and erecting the academy in Kiev. After they purchased a plot, they constructed a building with state-of-the-art appurtenances; its total cost was more than 300,000 rubles, a truly princely sum. "They imported the grand scale" of those schools, wrote G. E. Gurevich about a decade later, creating a facility that looked "more like a palace than a school . . . a gymnasium for wealthy children or an institute for noble girls."[67]

Izrail' Kel'berin, close associate of Lazar' Brodsky and author of a booklet celebrating the school, expressed explicitly the Brodskys' aspiration that the school—like the Jewish Hospital—be the leading institution of its kind in the Russian Empire, not only among Jews but among all the realm's peoples: "The Kiev Jewish School possesses unique characteristics that cannot be found in any other educational institution in Russia." Moreover, the school would serve as a pedagogical center for the entire Russian southwest, making its "museum of educational media" (collection of visual aids for teaching) available free of charge to all educators in the Kiev Educational District, a five-province region. As with many other welfare and educational institutions in the Russian Empire at that time, the school was consciously modeled on similar institutions in the West; in his brochure, Kel'berin quoted John Locke and made reference to schools in Germany and the United States after which the Brodsky School had been patterned.[68]

The Brodsky School was not only to be a model educational institution, but was to produce graduates who would themselves be model Jewish citizens of the Russian Empire. According to Kel'berin, the moral aspect of the school's mission was as important as the educational: pupils were to be instilled with "a love of activity and labor, a sense of duty, the instincts of civic spirit, national consciousness, and the like." The Brodsky School would provide not only education (*obrazovanie*), but also *vospitanie*, moral edification and upbringing, similar to the German *Bildung*, with its overtones of transforming the pupil into a cultured and civilized individual. Kel'berin made it clear that both were crucial because of the background of the pupils, "mostly children of artisans, petty traders, and clerks of modest means, and sometimes of utterly penurious parents who have neither the resources nor the opportunity to give their children even the least tolerable *vospitanie*."[69] The founders of the school plainly considered a working-class background to be deficient in culture, civility, and the civic virtues, as well as adequate discipline, as witnessed by Kel'berin's unequivocal statement that "the first and principal rule for the pupils in the new school is strict discipline." Also to be emphasized were cleanliness and tidiness, which would lead in turn to "moral tidiness" and a love for elegance—all of which, it was assumed, were not to be found in Jewish homes of modest or scant means. Music and physical education were additional curricular elements that would not normally be found in Jewish schools. Not only would the pupils imbibe these qualities during their lessons, but they would then, through their own examples of good behavior, exert a beneficial influence on their brothers and sisters at home.

The school, then, was not only a model institution that would provide Jewish boys with excellent training for a craft to enable them to make a living, but would also create a core of new working-class Russian Jews worthy of emulation by all their peers. Industrious, dutiful, patriotic, and nationally conscious, their cultured character and bearing would set a shining example. Its benefit for Russian Jewry as a whole could be seen in its aspirations for its graduates, who as certified artisans would not only be able to make a living but also to obtain residence rights outside the Pale of Settlement.[70] This vision, constituting the final words in Kel'berin's brochure, was clearly at the center of the school project, and encapsulated the Brodskys' continuing belief in progress and gradual emancipation for Russia's Jews. This was the same notion that had been expressed four decades earlier, when residence rights for the Russian interior had been granted to some artisans (as well as merchants like the Brodskys)—that the opportunity for an "honest" livelihood (i.e., one unrelated to trade) and domicile among Russians would lead to acceptance of Russian Jews and their eventual integration into the Russian body politic. Lazar' Brodsky's gift of a few thousand rubles to endow a scholarship at the traditionalist Volozhin Yeshiva, compared with the hundreds of thousands spent on the vocational school at about the same time, reveals how great the difference was between his enthusiasm for a "new" model of Jewish education and his continued but by no means generous support for old-style institutions.[71]

It is significant that the Brodskys, who had contributed many thousands of rubles for the construction of the school, then provided only half of the school's annual expenses; the other half was to come out of the kosher meat tax proceeds, specifically from the funds allocated for the education of orphans and the poor. This arrangement may well have been designed to ensure ongoing communal investment in the institution, but also had a symbolic impact: the school, with its particular goals and priorities, was not the Brodskys' alone but belonged to the entire Jewish community, and the political statements that it made were by implication agreed to by all of Kiev's Jews.[72]

Other Jewish philanthropic institutions also stressed the importance of moral education for the working classes. The Society of Summer Sanatorium Colonies for Children of the Indigent Jewish Population of Kiev, for example, stressed that its program focused on building up the health and strength of sickly youngsters as well as their education and "elevating their spiritual level."[73]

Higher Education

Jewish philanthropists were also quite active in the field of higher education, and played a central role in the establishment of Kiev's Polytechnical and Commercial Institutes. The former was established in 1898 on the initiative of the Brodsky brothers, who, together with other magnates such as N. A. Tereshchenko, helped to raise much of the capital. (Lazar' Brodsky himself donated 100,000 rubles.)[74]

Because neither institution was under direct control of the Ministry of Education but rather supervised by the Ministry of Trade, each had a bit more flexibility when it came to the regulations governing the numerus clausus for Jewish men, and as a result both institutes enabled many more Jews to obtain a professional education than would have been possible otherwise. There is little doubt that the significant role of Jews in the founding of the institutes and presence on their governing boards had something to do with this policy.[75] In 1905, official statistics showed the Jewish proportion in the Polytechnical Institute's student body to be 16 percent, just over the quota, but by 1909, the institute's administration had become embroiled in a dispute with the government over its apparent admission of Jews at a rate of 40 percent of the total (the additional 25 percent were to be considered externs [*vne otdelenii*]!).[76] Even after the authorities had intervened and ordered the institute's administrators and governors to adhere to the strict construction of the law, they refused to back down, and the board even passed a resolution that it would not comply with the government's order.[77]

As for the Commercial Institute, its first trustees included David Margolin and Lev Brodsky, who also served as chair of the board of overseers, and among its many Jewish students were such future Soviet Jewish cultural luminaries as Solomon Mikhoels and Isaak Babel.[78] This strong Jewish presence may help to explain the anonymous denunciation submitted to the authorities in 1914 about antigovernment tendencies within the institute. The writer complained that entire board of overseers were "zhids and zhid sympathizers" (*zhidy i zhidovstsvuiushchie*)—an exaggeration of the Jewish presence on the board, no doubt, but nonetheless an interesting insight into how some outsiders perceived the institute and its sponsors.[79]

The Rich and the Poor; Power and Politics

Family sponsorship of one or more medical institutions was to become a familiar pattern in Kiev Jewish philanthropy. In this, Kiev's well-to-do Jews relied on the precedent set by Jewish tradition where, for example, a prosperous man might pledge a large sum for a certain communal institution—often in memory of a loved one—on the occasion of the honor of an aliyah to the Torah in the synagogue. But they were also following the example of their non-Jewish neighbors, as in the case of sugar magnate N. A. Tereshchenko's founding of the hospital of the Kiev Philanthropic Society and the noblewoman A. V. Vasil'kova's bequest of her estate to the city of Kiev for use as a school for indigent children.[80]

The convalescent ward of the Jewish Hospital was financed by Yoel Natan and Gitel Beile Tulchinskii, who also offered to donate 500 rubles annually for continuing expenses.[81] In 1895, the Pediatric Wing, donated by Lazar' Brodsky, was dedicated in honor of Sara Semenovna Brodskaia (neé Lur'e) (40,000 rubles).[82] Only a year later, the new obstetric-gynecological ward (80,000 rubles) was dedicated by Lev Brodsky in memory of his late second wife Flora Ignat'eva; at the same event, Chief Doctor Neishtube announced that Sara Brodsky had told him of her plans to establish a disinfection ward at the hospital.[83] From 1898 to 1912, Lazar' Brodsky (and after his death in 1904, his heirs) made five significant grants to the hospital for, among other facilities, an infectious diseases ward, a new children's ward, and a generating station to provide electrical power to the entire hospital complex. Close behind the Brodskys was Maks Rafailovich Zaks, who financed an ophthalmology ward, a chapel, a bakery, and a carbonated water production facility. The Gal'perin family, for their part, facilitated the construction and outfitting of a ward sanatorium for first-stage tuberculosis patients and a urological ward.[84] A nervous diseases ward donated by the Frenkel' family brought the total number of hospital divisions to fourteen. In this fifteen-year flurry of expansion, a new facility was added approximately every two years.

The hospital was not the only arena for large-scale building. G. E. Gurevich maintained that the burial commission's expenses for capital improvements had gone beyond all bounds; in 1913, new structures included an undertaker's house, a new stable, and a stone fence, giving visitors "the impression of a fortress." It was wonderful that this important communal institution was in good physical condition, wrote Gurevich, but "splendor and luxury" were inappropriate.[85] Given the constant interest in construction we have seen in other areas of philanthropy and welfare, the "addiction" to new buildings on the part of the burial commission's members is not surprising.

Can we interpret the continued building as an expression of faith that Kiev's Jewish elite had in the future stability of Jewish life in the city and the empire? In a certain sense, the hospital buildings may have been political statements expressed in stone, not words, by individuals who did not usually engage in oppositional politics: they proclaimed to the tsarist regime that Jews were here to stay. If so, this would be a remarkable, perhaps courageous, and possibly even foolhardy behavior given the pogrom of 1905, the Beilis Affair of 1911–13, and the intensifying official oppression of Jews throughout the Russian Empire and especially in Kiev. On the other hand, the buildings may also be seen as increasingly desperate (and expensive) pleas for acceptance by a society that seemed to be moving from a position of, at best, ambivalence toward its Jews, to one of outright hostility.

The Jewish Hospital's 1912 Jubilee Volume, celebrating the fiftieth anniversary of its founding, gives a sense of how the millionaires who endowed the many structures on the hospital campus, as well as others involved with the institution, saw themselves. The book, published in a limited edition, was itself a small monument—as wide around as a small table (18 inches, to be exact)—and contained many full-page, lavish photographs of those who had contributed to the growth of the hospital: three tsars, governors-general, governors of Kiev province, mayors of Kiev, and so on. The text started with an interesting historical error: the author claimed that "until 1858, the right of residence in Kiev for Jews was granted only to merchants of the first guild."[86] In actuality, no Jews of any estate had been permitted to live in Kiev before 1859.[87] This rewriting put first-guild merchants—to which group belonged almost all the past and present benefactors of the hospital—in a category of their own; not only were they not now subject to the same restrictions as were most Jews in Kiev, but they had *never* been subject to them at all! Another telling linguistic slip was made in the use of the phrase "the Kiev Jewish Community [*Obshchina*]"; the author, Chief Doctor Neishtube, remarked that Israel Brodsky's munificent donation of 1885 "enabled the Kiev Jewish Community to finalize this weighty and crucial matter: the erection of its own [*sobstvennoe*] building."[88] As we have seen, there was never a formal Jewish community in Kiev, though in the early decades the hospital committee at times served as the de facto communal governing board, and was referred to as "the Kiev Jewish Corporation" or "Society [*obshchestvo*]" (most often by the city council, which either did not recognize a difference between the hospital and the community, or did not want to acknowledge the existence of a community for political reasons). It is revealing that as late as 1913, when the Jewish Hospital and the Representation for Jewish Welfare were clearly separate bodies, the chief doctor of the hospital was equating the hospital with the Jewish community.

In some ways, the hospital was very similar to the community, for both received their funding from the richest and the poorest Jews of Kiev, who were also the two groups most visibly associated with both institutions—the benefactors and administrators, and the patients and other recipients of social services. According to the original charter of 1861, the hospital was to be financed by voluntary contributions.[89] It was also to be exempt from paying the tax on kosher meat, but no subsidies were provided for. But Kiev Governor L. Tamara wrote in 1886 that donations were so insignificant in the first few years that they did not even allow for the hospital to hire a chief doctor as director of the institution. It was concluded, wrote Tamara, that the hospital would not be able to survive on contributions alone, and it was thus allocated a subvention from the kosher meat tax revenues.[90] By 1890, the institution had three sources of income: the interest from capital in the amount of 50,000 rubles donated by Israel Brodsky (3,000 rubles a year); income from the bathhouse that Brodsky had purchased (2,500 rubles a year); and the korobka subsidy of 2,500 rubles a year.[91] It is indeed striking that the hospital's funds came from the most affluent—Brodsky was one of the wealthiest men in the empire—and the most deprived, for it was mainly poor Jews who paid the korobka tax.

The division of labor between rich and poor was evident elsewhere, too. The 1861 charter had called the institution the "hospital for indigent Jews," and the 1891 charter reiterated that services were meant for the poor only: "Sick individuals of means [*sostoiatel'nye*] will be admitted into the hospital only in exceptional cases." By contrast, only "distinguished" Jews with residence rights in Kiev could be selected as trustees.[92]

It is thus no wonder that a medical clinic was founded expressly for the middle class, who had sufficient means for medical care and did not "want to stand with the thoroughly poor or be treated by a ha'penny doctor," but who also could not afford the private doctors who treated the wealthy. Charging 30 kopecks for medical advice and 3–6 rubles a day for inpatient stays, the fifteen-bed clinic was established in 1898 by three Jewish doctors and provided patients with kosher food.[93] In a city known for its medical care, a facility founded by and for middle-class Jews seemed to be something of a novelty. Either the Jewish middle-class was very small or they simply went to non-Jewish clinics (and either ate nonkosher food or made other arrangements). As with their private prayer quorums, Kiev's wealthy Jews also had their own doctors.

There is evidence of some dissatisfaction with the running of the Jewish Hospital: one writer complained that not only was the hospital far from the city, but outpatient visits were made even more burdensome by the regulation requiring that medicine be dispensed a day after the prescription was submitted, requiring patients to make the long trek to the hospital *again*. Moreover, the wards were always full. A suggestion to open a free pharmacy in the center of Kiev had for some reason been rejected by the hospital's trustees.[94] It is no surprise that criticism of the Jewish Hospital emerged at the same time as criticism of the Representation for Jewish Welfare: both were creations of the Jewish elite that had traditionally been praised for their good works, but with the changing character of Jewish society were now vulnerable to critique. Also, the two hospitals prided themselves on being open to both Jews and Christians, a feature that may or may not have enhanced acceptance or respect for Jews on the part of other Russians, but seems to have meant that fewer Jewish patients could be served. In 1897, almost half of all Jewish Hospital patients were Orthodox Christians.[95]

By the post-1905 period, some Kiev Jews were no longer willing to tolerate what they saw as major flaws in the governance of the hospital, especially when the flaws stemmed from the board's continuing use of the institution as a showcase for Russian–Jewish relations. Moreover, as in other community institutions, the lack of transparency and democracy would no longer be tolerated. In 1910, there was an exposé in the local Russian-language press uncovering neglect and negligence in patient care. To charges of overcrowded wards and unsanitary conditions the Yiddish newspaper *Kiever vort* added its own accusation of a doctor's malpractice that had almost led to a child's death. According to the paper, the commission of inquest set up by the hospital board was more interested in discovering which employee had ratted on the institution than on introducing needed reforms.[96] Communal activist G. E. Gurevich also deplored the "disorder" at the hospital, which included—according to the many complaints he had heard—serious problems with hospital management, conducted with no oversight or accountability, and patient food. The fact that the hospital, funded from exclusively Jewish sources, served a large number of Christian patients was also not acceptable to Gurevich: "If it made any sense twenty-five, or even fifteen years ago, in recent years it has lost any rationale."[97] Clearly, Gurevich and probably many other Jews considered the attempt to use the hospital as a political tool for the acceptance of Jews to be obsolete. The noises of approval registered in earlier years about the fact that the hospital was open to people of all faiths, and the hopes that this policy would lead to toleration, were no longer heard. In fact they had died out years before, and many new Jewish institutions served only Jews. The year 1905 and subsequent events had changed Jewish expectations.

Worst of all, according to Gurevich, was the fact that the hospital board—more concerned with protecting its own interests than those of patients or the community that financed the institution—did nothing about the problems. Hospital trustees were elected by the city council and thus were theoretically accountable, but apparently the accepted procedure was for the community bigwigs to vote privately on their preferred slate of trustees, who were then simply confirmed by the council. Thus, claimed Gurevich, the same "obedient" trustees were elected each time, having neither the courage nor the experience in communal affairs to denounce the abuses they knew to be taking place. In 1913, however, "circles independent of the influence of the community bosses and the hospital board became interested in the elections"—Gurevich is probably referring to nationally minded Jewish activists—and managed to convince the city council to replace two of the trustees on the slate with two independent individuals (one of them being

Gurevich himself).[98] We may well wonder whether this "revolution" in the administration of the Jewish Hospital was any more effective at changing the standard modus operandi than the upheaval that brought about the elected Representation for Jewish Welfare, which will be examined in the following chapter. In any case, the hospital existed for only a few more years before its nationalization by the Bolsheviks.

Female Philanthropists and Private Charity

In the 1890s and 1900s, the Jewish Hospital was joined by a number of additional charitable medical institutions intended to serve Kiev's poor Jews. In this period, the number of voluntary, self-help, and philanthropic organizations rose dramatically throughout the empire and especially among Jews. Poverty was growing among Jews, living conditions in poor neighborhoods remained appalling, and some Kiev clinics for the poor did not accept Jews. More simply, Kiev's Jewish population continued to grow rapidly, with many of the new arrivals quite poor and thus more susceptible to disease and illness. The criticism of the workings of the Jewish Hospital also helped to stimulate the founding of new, independent institutions.

In addition to the Zaitsev Surgical Hospital, founded in 1896, a free sanatorium for consumptives was established in 1899 by A. P. Tul'chinskaia in Boiarka, a dacha suburb of Kiev (and model for Sholem Aleikhem's fictional Boyberik, home of Tevye the milkman). Two years later, a group of wealthy Jewish women founded a maternity clinic for poor Jewish women. The benefactors were especially concerned about the lack of a medical facility for poor Jews near the center of the city; the Jewish Hospital was far from the Jewish neighborhoods and the roads leading to it unsafe at night. The clinic would also send midwives on home visits.[99] A home health organization providing the sick with free medicine and food—a branch of the Representation for Jewish Welfare—was also in operation by the late 1890s. In Hebrew sources it was called by the name of the traditional hevrah for visiting the sick, Bikur Holim (or biker khoylim), which was apparently also the name by which it was known in the Jewish community; for example, the 1907 Russian-language report of the Society for Care of Poor Artisans referred to it as "the Kiev 'Bikur-Khoilim' Society."[100]

Many of the new institutions were initiated by women. Women were prominent in the new scientific philanthropy throughout Europe, and the Russian Empire was no exception. Contemporaries viewed the "female character" as naturally warm and tender and thus perfectly suited to care for those on the margins of society. It was common, even expected, for the wives of Russian nobles, high officials, and wealthy merchants to participate in local philanthropic causes or even to found their own societies.[101] While women played a significant role in private charity, men continued to dominate at public, state-run institutions.[102] This pattern was duplicated in the Jewish community, where throughout the late imperial period communal institutions were a male domain while many private, independent relief institutions were founded and run by women. The restriction of women's roles in Jewish communal welfare agencies was also a legacy of the male dominance of the kahal and traditional hevrot, which were often religious in nature. There were cases of women becoming members of these associations—such membership was usually financial and did not extend to active participation in the group—but it was much more common for women to form their own charitable groups—to clothe needy students, for example.[103] One example of the former is provided by the pinkas of the Kiev Mishnah Fellowship of the Makarov Prayer House, which stipulated that if a woman wanted the society "to fulfill these regulations on her behalf" ("le-kayem negda . . . et ha-takanot ha-n"l")—presumably to study Mishnah in her merit—she was to donate a sum that she and the society's wardens would agree upon, and then her name and donation would be noted on a special page in the pinkas.[104] (The pinkas of the Kiev Psalms Recitation Society, however, lists seven women members on a separate page; Gershon Bacon surmises that, in addition to gathering in the women's section to recite Psalms, they also visited sick women and recited Psalms on their behalf. But the fact that the hevra's regulations make no mention of women seems to show that they "formed a kind of abstract group . . . whose presence was recognized only unofficially.")[105] Just as charity was "the only significant activity that allowed women to participate meaningfully in public life" in Russian society, so did it enable Jewish women to contribute to the otherwise male-dominated Jewish community.[106] There was, then, a division of labor in the world of Jewish voluntarism: men dominated the realm of communal governance and welfare, while women—usually from prosperous households—created a constellation of independent charitable societies to serve particular groups such as women, children, and the chronically ill. However, women, like men, could and did engage in philanthropy as individuals, making names for themselves as benefactors to one or more of their favorite causes.[107]

Soon after the Jewish Hospital was founded in 1862, we hear of a female trustee, Tsirlia Fimilevna Zevin. One of the major contributors to the hospital's cholera division in the mid-sixties was the wife of hospital trustee Moisei Vainshtein—probably Gitele Vainshtein, who together with Hayya Brodskaia endowed (or facilitated the establishment of) a small maternity ward at the hospital in 1871.[108] This model of Jewish women founding institutions for causes that were considered of typical female concern became the regnant pattern. Thus, in 1886, a number of prominent Jewish women petitioned for permission to establish a Society of Shelters for Girls of the Jewish Faith. The shelters, explained the petitioners, would give orphans and girls of poor parents a safe place to spend the day while their parents and guardians were busy working.[109] By contrast, no women sat on the board of the official pogrom aid society after the Kiev pogrom of 1881, though well-to-do Jewish women collected and distributed donations of clothing and other items for victims.[110]

Many of the most important Jewish philanthropic institutions in Kiev to be founded around the turn of the century were initiated or led by women. Around 1894, a Mrs. M. Gol'dberg organized a subsidized kosher cafeteria for Kiev's Jewish students who, according to *Ha-melits,* had been eating at nonkosher dining halls because of their miserable financial circumstances.[111] The same article, noting that "Jewish women are among the most generous here [in Kiev]," praised Gol'dberg for her involvement in an array of charitable works. The Free Boiarka Sanatorium for Poor Consumptive Jews of Kiev was founded in 1899 by Anna Tul'chinskaia (perhaps daughter or wife of Honored Citizen Natan Klement'evich Tul'chinskii, one of the leaders of Kiev Jewry in the 1860s).[112] Sofiia Mandel'shtam, wife of the Zionist leader, established the Day Shelter for Children of the Jewish Working Class and in 1900 petitioned the authorities for permission to organize evening classes in Russian literacy for Jews.[113] Another children's shelter, the Fifth Day Shelter for Children of the Working Class of the Jewish Faith, was also established and run by women, and the major donors were the women of Kiev's most illustrious Jewish families: Brodsky, Gintsburg, Rozenberg, Zaks, and others.[114] Some of the same women also gave money to help Dr. Bykhovskii establish a Jewish maternity clinic in 1901; the chair of the clinic's board was Mrs. Gal'perin.[115] In 1903, E. V. Brodskaia founded a subsidized kosher cafeteria in the heavily Jewish Lybed neighborhood.

That it was normal and even taken for granted that women would serve in positions of leadership in relief efforts was illustrated by the fact that Countess S. S. Ignat'eva served as chair of the 1895 flood aid committee on which Sara Brodskaia, wife of Lazar' Brodsky, also sat as a member. *Ha-melits* took pains to point out that Ignat'eva was accompanied on her visits to the flood victims by Brodskaia. It was no doubt considered a great honor for the Jewish community for its most prominent gentlewoman—indeed, the wife of the man known as Kiev's Jewish "king"—to be seen in the company of a countess (who was also the wife of the governor-general, the tsar's representative to the southwest region) as they together tended to the less fortunate.[116] It was also likely seen as natural for two of the most eminent women of Kiev—one Christian, the other Jewish—to engage in charitable work together. The extent of Brodskaia's charitable endeavors can be grasped from the fact that she gave almost 10,000 rubles to Jewish philanthropic societies in her home city of Minsk on a visit there in 1895, a deed found worthy of mention in at least one Jewish newspaper.[117]

Another Brodskaia, Sara's sister-in-law Flora Ignat'eva (wife of Lev), was eulogized in 1894 as one of Kiev's "most active charitable women," who devoted a great deal of her time to philanthropy.[118] The construction in the mid-1890s of the splendid new building of the Tailors' Synagogue in Podol was financed in large measure by the wealthy Rozenberg family, and there is an intriguing reference to "the synagogue of the wealthy lady Rozenberg," suggesting that Etil Rozenberg herself, sister of wealthy entrepreneur Evzel Gintsburg of St. Petersburg, had been the primary benefactor.[119] Yekhzekel Kotik recalled that Rozenberg used to travel in her carriage every day from the Kreshchatik to the subsidized cafeteria founded by her husband in Podol, and would go through the written requests for charity submitted by "beggars, poor *intelligenty,* fallen merchants, hungry brokers, and the like."[120] The picture is something akin to a female version of Israel Brodsky, who, as we saw in chapter 2, was also known for his charitable gifts to individual Jews who requested his assistance in person or in writing. Brodskaia and Rozenberg were also involved to some extent in Jewish communal affairs, as illustrated by the request of the members of the Representation for Jewish Welfare that the two women, along with E. V. Brodskaia, be permitted to participate in the activities of the Representation as associates [*sotrudnitsy*].[121] Women were also singled out for thanks in their role as donors to the Passover aid fund in 1892.[122] However, it is clear that women played a subordinate role in Jewish affairs: after all, they could not actually be members of the Representation for Jewish Welfare or the Passover aid committee. The 1905 pogrom aid committee, though established a quarter-century after its predecessor, followed the same model with regard to the roles of the sexes: women participated through separate Ladies' Circles in charge of distributing food and clothing to pogrom victims, especially children.[123]

The 1913 report of the Representation for Jewish Welfare makes it clear why women felt compelled to establish their own organizations for charitable work: members of the subcommissions of the official Jewish communal organization were all men—not only those that might have been associated with religious duties, such as the Schools Commission (in charge of the Talmud Torahs) and the Passover Aid Commission, but even those charged with providing more typically "feminine" types of relief, such as the Commission for Home Health Aid. The Relief Commission was also all male. Clearly, Jewish communal affairs in Kiev were still a man's world. By contrast, there was an Evangelical [Lutheran] Women's Society in addition to the Evangelical Philanthropic Society, and two of the institutions run by the Roman Catholic Philanthropic Society—the shelter for elderly women and the children's soup kitchen—were governed entirely by women.[124] This is why (as we shall see in the following chapter) the call for the OPE to enlist the participation of Jewish women in 1905 was considered so revolutionary; heretofore, Jewish education, like other aspects of communal life, had been restricted to men.[125] And the new elections to the Representation for Jewish Welfare instituted in 1906, while hailed as a radical change in the nature of communal governance because of the diverse socioeconomic background of the new members, did not allow women to stand as candidates. Indeed, such a change was hardly conceivable, given that the body was elected in large measure by the city's prayer houses, which were governed exclusively by men. Even more telling, however, is the fact that the very possibility of women representatives was never even suggested in the press. It is not surprising then, that wealthy Jewish women were not significant contributors to the Representation for Jewish Welfare, judging from the list of donors in 1913; of 131 individuals giving 50 rubles or over, only ten were women.[126]

Even after the revolutionary upheaval of 1905, however, the established order of the Jewish community remained the same in this regard: the board of the OPE in 1907 was still all male, while its three commissions included only one woman. Continuing the tradition of women as auxiliaries assigned to take care of traditionally female concerns, the board organized a Ladies' Circle to take on the establishment of the society's new kindergarten.[127] Women might also be drafted to help raise funds, as in the case of the "Gmilus Khesed" Relief Society for Poor Jews, which decided in 1913 to organize ladies' committees that would bring in additional resources.[128] In a marked change from traditional relief agencies, and perhaps reflecting the society's two-sided nature as the descendant of the free-loan hevrah while at the same time an adherent of scientific philanthropic methods, the executive board of "Gmilus Khesed" included a woman as treasurer, while another woman sat on the general board of eight members.

As in the surrounding society, in the Jewish community many of the most innovative institutions were founded and headed by women.[129] In his survey of the Jewish community of Kiev, G. E. Gurevich criticized the management of the Representation for Jewish Welfare and its constituent institutions on many points, while reserving his praise for the city's independent welfare societies. He termed the day shelter for Jewish children "very sympathetic" and the Jewish sanatorium "one of the most popular and worthy institutions in Kiev."[130]

The shelter was a good example of the division of philanthropic labor between the sexes. Full membership in its parent organization, the Society of Day Shelters for Children of the Working Class, was limited to women, which seems also to have been the case for the Jewish society. Even the major donors were mostly women: prominent contributors included Etil Rozenberg, Sara Brodskaia and her daughters Margarita and Baroness Klara Gintsburg (daughter-in-law of the celebrated Baron Gintsburg of St. Petersburg), and other distinguished Jewish women of Kiev—mostly wives of men active in Jewish communal affairs and welfare. Clearly, Jewish charity was a family affair. A decade after its founding, the institution moved into its own building, erected by Margarita Brodskaia (now known by her married name of Gol'dsmidt-Brodskaia). Women were also prominent among the major donors to the OPE's Jewish kindergarten, which began functioning in 1907. The governance of the Jewish consumptives' sanatorium was also heavily female; in addition to chair Avgustina Brodskaia and treasurer Luiza Ettinger, the driving forces behind the institution after the death of founder Tul'chinskaia, three other women sat on the board out of a total of seventeen members.[131] In that year, three of the four new buildings constructed as part of the sanatorium complex were endowed by women (all wives of prominent Kiev Jewish men). There is a tantalizing reference in one of the sanatorium's annual reports to a large donation from "the ladies' philanthropic society," but nowhere else is such a society mentioned.[132] Whether this was a Jewish organization or a nonsectarian group of both Jewish and Christian benefactors, it seems to have been unofficial in nature, since it is not listed in any municipal directories or almanacs. Were such organizations a kind of political strategy by which Jewish women in Russia, as Marion Kaplan argues for their sisters in Germany, managed to "create their own power structures alongside the political and business spheres dominated by men"?[133] Whether or not their moves were consciously political or in pursuit of "power," women were certainly staking out a territory of their own within the world of good works and community welfare.

Though many of the women prominent in Kiev's Jewish charitable works were of the haute bourgeoisie, sources suggest that middle-class women became more involved in philanthropy over the course of our period, especially after the turn of the century. Such a phenomenon stands to reason, given the large numbers of female members of the intelligentsiia in Kiev with its many educational and vocational training institutes for women. Jewish students had a reputation for membership in illegal political groups, but there must have been an equal number of educated women who chose to become involved in organized Jewish life in Kiev. We know that some of the leading male intelligenty found their way into the leadership of the OPE; at first, women interested in the cause of Jewish education had to be content with participating in the society's Ladies' Circle and taking part in general meetings (as did one Mlle Tsetner at a meeting in 1906).[134] However, Jewish women seem to have gained leadership positions a bit later on: for example, a Mrs. Rozenshtein was one of the Kiev branch's four delegates to the national OPE conference in St. Petersburg in 1911.[135] Women also seem to have played a significant role in the Kiev branch of the OZE (Society for the Protection of the Health of the Jewish Population), which started operations in 1912 or 1913.[136] Drawing from these examples, a plausible conjecture is that, while the visible female leaders of Jewish philanthropy and self-help were wealthy, many of the lower-level activists and organizers were middle-class women. This makes sense when one considers that rich women did not work outside the home; indeed, some of them may have considered philanthropy "real work," since it often required a serious investment of time and resources. These women had time to serve as chairs and treasurers; women of more modest means, however, often worked in health care or education and would only have had time for limited involvement in charitable work. On a more elementary level, the regulations governing Jewish residence in Kiev did not allow for the development of a substantial middle class, at least not one of any means; as Hamm points out, "a lower-middle class of Jewish property owners apparently did not exist" in Kiev.[137]

We must also consider the accusation of apathy leveled at the intelligentsia. In an article on Jewish education in Kiev, *Kiever vort* alleged that "the intelligentsia is indifferent to communal affairs," while G. E. Gurevich concluded that the intelligenty and middling merchants were too busy with their own affairs to spend the time required to truly make a difference in the Jewish community.[138] In an article entitled "Kiev Jews and Philanthropy" published in the Russian-language newspaper *Kievskoe utro* (Kiev Morning), the anonymous author, commenting on the recent annual report of the Kiev OPE, noted the inaccuracy of the widely held notion that the Jewish classes of means did not skimp on charity. The society's donors were mostly wealthy magnates and the poor, while the petty and middling bourgeoisie were glaring in their absence.[139] Intelligenty, who made up most of the board of the Society for Care of Poor Jewish Artisans, did not bother to attend the general meeting of that organization, remarked communal observer L. Dynin.[140] A report from the Kiev branch of the Russian Society for the Defense of Women complained that although many women had volunteered enthusiastically to teach in the branch's literacy classes, in the end only a few had actually shown up.[141] Even when the middle class was involved in philanthropy, it was—according to some—in name only. A scathing feuilleton in *Dos folk* (The People, a short-lived Yiddish newspaper published in Kiev) accused the bourgeois doctors constituting the OPE's Medical Commission of utter neglect of the poor schoolchildren about whom they purported to care; their one accomplishment, the issuing of a set of "hygienic regulations," only reflected their ignorance of the plight of the masses. The regulations warned the children, many of whom lived in filthy surroundings and never got enough to eat, to protect themselves from disease and not to study on an empty stomach (!).[142] Apparently, the phenomenon of middle-class indifference was not limited to Jewish society; an article in *Kievlianin* alleged that the city's philanthropic organizations were supported only by the most prominent individuals by virtue of wealth or position.[143]

This apathy marks a striking difference from the Jewish communities of England and especially Germany, where the middle class funded and managed the communal welfare bodies, and probably reflects the fact that Russian Jewish communities did not experience the democratization or the embourgeoisement that Germany's communities did in the late nineteenth century.[144] There was also the larger problem of the relative size and strength of the bourgeoisie in those societies: civil society in the Russian Empire had developed measurably since the Great Reforms, but the middle class was still small and weak compared to that of Western European countries. The structure of philanthropy could not but reflect this deficit.

The Pogrom Aid Committees

There was one kind of charity that could never be proactive in its approach, and this was the aid organized by the Jewish community after each of Kiev's pogroms in 1881 and 1905. What these committees needed more than anything was resourcefulness and efficiency, and for the most part they were very successful in providing both immediate relief in the days and weeks after the pogroms as well as longer-term assistance to those whose homes and businesses had suffered damage. In the half-year after the 1881 pogrom, the Kiev Jewish Society for Assistance to the Victims of the 1881 Disorders in the South of Russia had raised almost 220,000 rubles, of which 38 percent was a donation from Baron Gintsburg of St. Petersburg, 33 percent came from abroad, and 29 percent from throughout the Russian Empire. By October 1, 1881, the committee had already distributed more than 150,000 rubles worth of assistance—about two-thirds of it to Kiev Jews and the balance to other cities and towns throughout the southwest. This heroic sum was nonetheless a drop in the bucket compared with the 2.5 million rubles in losses that the society estimated Jews had suffered in the pogroms.[145] The estimate given by Count P. I. Kutaisov in his official investigation came up with a lower figure: 1,474,168 rubles in damages, of which the largest two categories were individuals with losses of under 100 rubles and between 100 and 500 rubles (561 individuals out of a total of 889). (That there were also a substantial number of wealthy Jews in Kiev was confirmed by the seventy individuals who claimed losses of between 5,000 and 40,000 rubles.)[146]

In the days immediately following the pogrom, the society organized emergency tents and hot food for thousands of Jewish refugees. After two weeks, as the refugees began to return to their homes or find interim housing, the tents were taken down and distribution points for food and money (5 kopecks per person) set up at several points around the city. The society then divided the city up into districts for the purposes of applications for aid, which were reviewed by "commissions of trustworthy local residents" and assigned an amount to be awarded based on losses. This plan was clearly based on the "district guardianship" model, based on new theories of welfare and philanthropy, which would be adopted in many cities throughout the empire in the 1880s and 1890s. In addition to small one-time grants to families, the committee also made substantial loans (of 500–1,500 rubles) available to merchants to enable them to rebuild their businesses.[147]

The Kiev Society had originally been intended to provide aid exclusively to Kiev Jews, but soon found itself assisting Jews from throughout the southwest region. This was testament not only to the extent of the destruction wreaked by the pogromshchiki and the shock it left in its wake—many Jewish communities were simply unable to organize themselves to provide effective aid—but also to the effectiveness of the existing organizational structures within Kiev Jewry and the competence of its leadership. Certainly the local authorities could not be relied upon to assist the pogrom victims, just as they had failed in protecting them from the pogromshchiki; the city council refused to release 15,000 rubles from the korobka funds for pogrom aid, and then—only after being asked by the Jewish community—did councilors vote to make a 3,000-ruble grant from the municipal coffers, not a particularly large sum.

Several years later, Mordecai ben Hillel Ha-Cohen published a review of the Kiev Society's activities in *Ha-melits*, praising it for its efficiency, honesty, impartiality, and lack of bureaucracy. Whereas the notables in St. Petersburg had not lived up to expectations in raising funds for aid to pogrom victims or coordinating an effective policy vis-à-vis the government, wrote Ha-Cohen, the Kiev Society had triumphed on both counts, sending its own representatives to the capital to meet with Minister of Interior Ignat'ev and working with the press to put a stop to harmful rumors.[148] The Society's success can be attributed at least in part to its chair, Max Mandel'shtam, who, as Jonathan Frankel notes, emerged in the crisis of 1881–82 "as a highly articulate spokesman and effective organizer."[149]

By contrast, the activities of the "Kiev Committee for Provision of Aid to the Victims of the Pogroms of 18–21 October 1905" were received somewhat less favorably, at least by some. Of course, the scale of destruction here was much greater than that of the 1881 pogrom—two months after the pogrom, total losses were estimated at 7,000,000 rubles—and thus the task much more difficult.[150] But there was another important difference: as the committee's report testifies, Kiev Jewry was now divided up into many more groupings and constituencies, each of which had its own demands. This was a factor of the community's size, of course, but also of the many associations and societies that had sprung up in the previous decade or so, as well as of the politicization and factionalization of Russian Jewry overall. Thus, for example, representatives from the Subsidized Kosher Cafeterias, the Jewish Day Shelter for Children, the Sanitorium in Boiarki, the Artisans' Association, and the Committee for Aid to the Working Class all requested funds from the committee, and a newly organized but as yet officially unregistered association of brokers (*maklery*).[151] At one meeting, a man by the name of I. L. Raikhlin appealed for aid to the spiritual rabbis of Kiev (the committee rejected the request, but then granted it when it was brought again at the next meeting); at another meeting, I. B. Esman asked for assistance to "four anonymous tsaddikim."[152] Amazingly, even non-Jewish institutions applied for assistance on the grounds that some of their constituents were Jewish; this was the case with the Women's Trade School, the Kiev Trade Guild, and even the Russian Orthodox Boris and Gleb Brotherhood, which requested aid for warm clothing and shoes, as Jewish children were being educated at their facility.[153] Was this a testament to the extent of integration of Jews into Kiev society, or simply greed on the part of these institutions? If we take these requests at face value, perhaps the administrators of the school, the guild, and the brotherhood felt duty-bound to care for pogrom victims who were associated with their institutions, or possibly felt even a religious or moral obligation to make up for what other Christians had done. If, however, the Pogrom Aid Committee was the only source to which they turned for funding (and this is unclear), then the gesture of assistance—to be provided with Jewish money alone!—was somewhat less altruistic.

The report also betrays a certain lack of trust among Kiev's Jews; committee members frequently requested verification of the aid applications of a number of individuals and groups—often, apparently, with reason; an association calling itself the Society for the Provision of Bread to Poor Jews was told that it could not receive aid so long as it was under the oversight of just one individual and not the official community organization. Twenty percent of the aid applications from petty and middling traders were rejected, as were 12 percent of those from artisans.[154] The committee had nowhere near enough money to provide for all those who were in need, and thus had to husband its resources carefully. Despite the apparent attention it paid to a fair distribution of aid, the committee still came in for criticism; an article in the St. Petersburg–based Jewish weekly *Khronika Voskhoda* complained that its activities were marred by favoritism, funds were not being distributed by need, and no criteria for fair distribution had been established.[155] The comparison with the reception of the activities of the 1881 Pogrom Aid Society is instructive. The Kiev Jewish community was smaller in 1881, as was the scale of the destruction; nor were recipients of philanthropic aid or indeed the wider public accustomed to criticizing the leadership who came to their aid. The large and diverse audience that was Kiev's Jews in 1905 had also become a critical one, and demands for transparency and probity would now become the norm, as we shall see in the next chapter.

A total of 676,000 rubles was raised by the committee, almost 400,000 of it in Kiev and another 270,000 sent by the International Aid Committee in Berlin. In January 1906, the committee reported that many of those who had received aid had already used it up (artisans, for example, had received an average of only 37 rubles each) and, not having been able to rehabilitate their businesses, were living "in dire need, in hunger and cold." Local sources of private charity had been exhausted.[156]

Conclusion

In 1910, Baron V. G. Gintsburg informed the mayor of Kiev that he wished to donate to the city a statue of Tsar Alexander II by the renowned Jewish sculptor Mark Antokol'skii. The statue was to be poured in Paris and brought thence to Kiev, where Gintsburg requested that it be placed in the main hall of the public library.[157] Carefully parsed, this seemingly ordinary civic-minded gift shows just how loaded with symbolism philanthropy could be. If they wished to show their patriotism, for Jews there was really no other choice among the tsars of the previous century than Alexander II, who was still remembered fondly by most Jews for his role in expanding Jewish rights in the 1860s. Liberals who still insisted on viewing Russian history through Whiggish lenses (as did most Jewish "notables" such as Gintsburg) hearkened back to those happy days of optimism and progress, and an effigy of the "Tsar Liberator" in Kiev was almost a talisman—a statement of hope that perhaps some day Russia would return to his path. Of course, the choice of artist was no coincidence: a sculpture created by a Russian Jew was a fine example of the contributions that Jews made not only to the world of commerce and industry (as with Gintsburg) but to the arts as well. The placement of the sculpture in Kiev's public library was a reminder of the important role that Jewish contributions played in advancing literacy in the city. And finally, the artwork's provenance in Paris showed that just as Jewish philanthropists had brought the best medical and technological expertise from throughout Europe to the Russian Empire for the good of its Jewish and Christian subjects alike, so would they continue ever to brighten the urban landscape of the empire in other ways as well—with delightful monuments such as this one, for example.

In a sense, all Jewish charitable initiatives in Kiev were destined to be laden with symbolic meaning in addition to their more practical, rational aims. Even those engaged in more traditional forms of charity not discussed in this chapter—hevrot for dowering the bride or visiting the sick, for example—would not have been ignorant of the significance of a positive Jewish profile in holy, Russian Kiev. But for acculturating Jews in particular, modern philanthropy was a way of expressing their own sense of what being Jewish was about no less than it was a means to the transformation of the Jewish masses and the creation of a new Russian Jewry in the image of the Jewish bourgeoisie. Jewish philanthropists and community activists used social services to mold the (as yet) unacculturated Jewish migrants who settled in Kiev as well as to shape public and official opinion of Jews and Judaism. The institutions they built were a crucial—and as yet largely unrecognized—pillar of modern Jewish self-expression in the Russian Empire. As donors both large and small, administrators, employees, and clients, most Russian Jews were implicated in the project of Jewish welfare in one role or another. In an era of Jewish ideological division, communal fragmentation, and socio-economic differentiation, this was a remarkable achievement indeed. No less an attainment was the mobilization of philanthropy for political or quasi-political aims and to project Jewish leadership from the realm of the parochial to the wider imperial stage.

Some measure of integration into Russian society was surely one of the goals of the leaders of philanthropic projects—but the results of their efforts were mixed. The communal welfare system they created, though identical in many ways to that which lay at the heart of the emerging Russian civil society, was often a world apart: a separate, Jewish institutional world that (often unconsciously) hindered integration and interaction with non-Jewish society. With the increasing exclusion of Jews from Russian society in the early years of the twentieth century, however, this world took on a very significant role and significance of its own. However unwittingly, the grandees had fashioned a network of institutions that would form the kernel of a separate Jewish public sphere—albeit one that was heavily bound about with restrictions. While increasing governmental oppression and growing antisemitism in the last years of Romanov rule had a chilling effect on the faith of Russian Jews in philanthropy's ability to effect political or anti-defamatory change within Russian society, they did not lose their conviction that organized networks of individuals—after 1907 largely in the form of cultural, educational, welfare, and self-help organizations—could have a decisive impact on both everyday life and the long-term prospects of Russian Jewry. It is to these organizations that we now turn.

FIGURE 4.1. Sasha Rutov with unidentified girl (possibly his sister). *From family collection of Viktor Khamishon. From the Archive of the YIVO Institute for Jewish Research, New York (RG 120, folder 145.02).*

FIGURE 4.2. The Choral Synagogue. *Photograph courtesy Leonid Finberg and the Kiev Institute of Jewish Studies.*

FIGURE 4.3. The Choral Synagogue (interior). *Photograph courtesy Leonid Finberg and the Kiev Institute of Jewish Studies.*

FIGURE 4.4. Unidentified woman, possibly a student. On the back of the photo: "Remember 'Strange' Chava." *From the Archive of the YIVO Institute for Jewish Research, New York (RG 120, folder 015).*

FIGURE 5.1. Khmel'nitskii Monument, Kiev, ca. 1890–1900. *Courtesy Library of Congress Prints and Photographs Division.*

FIGURE 6.1. The Bacteriological Institute (ca. 1900). *Photograph courtesy Leonid Finberg and the Kiev Institute of Jewish Studies.*

FIGURE 6.2. The Brodsky School. Note the inscription at the top of the façade with the name "BRODSKII." *Photograph courtesy Leonid Finberg and the Kiev Institute of Jewish Studies.*

FIGURE 6.3. Interior view of grand staircase inside the Brodsky School, 1905. *Courtesy University of Southampton Special Collections (MS 128, Papers of Carl Stettauer, AJ 22/A/7).*

FIGURE 6.4. The Commercial Institute (undated). *Photograph courtesy Leonid Finberg and the Kiev Institute of Jewish Studies.*

FIGURE 6.5. The infectious diseases ward of the Jewish Hospital (undated).
Photograph courtesy Leonid Finberg and the Kiev Institute of Jewish Studies.

FIGURE 6.6. The Ophthalmology Ward of the Jewish Hospital (undated).
Photograph courtesy Leonid Finberg and the Kiev Institute of Jewish Studies.

FIGURE 7.1. "Board of the Podolia-Kiev Zionist Socialists," 1905. *Standing (l–r):* Shmuel, Berta the Nurse, Khayem the Hatmaker, Noyme, Isak the Orator. *Seated:* Khayem the Tailor, Yankl Holtsman, Arn the Purveyor, Dovid Miller, Nokhum. *Courtesy of YIVO Institute for Jewish Research (Collection R1).*

FIGURE 7.2. Studio portrait of participants at the General Meeting of the Jewish Emigration Society, Kiev, Feb. 23–25, 1911. *From the Archive of the YIVO Institute for Jewish Research, New York (Collection R1).*

FIGURE 7.3. Ginzburg House (headquarters of the business operations of industrialist L. B. Ginzburg), on Nikolaevskaia street. *Photograph courtesy Leonid Finberg and the Kiev Institute of Jewish Studies.*

7

Revolutions in Communal Life

The tumultuous period from the Kishinev pogrom in April 1903 through the years of the First Russian Revolution of 1905–1907 witnessed the beginning of the mass politicization and mobilization of Russian Jewish society, as of the entire empire, and the legitimization of the leadership of new political forces in Russian Jewry, the socialists and the nationalists.[1] Revolutionary groups—among them the Bund (the General Union of Jewish Workers, the most prominent Jewish socialist party in the Russian Empire)—seized the initiative, especially during the heady days of the industrial strikes leading into the crippling general strike of October and November. The Bund's activities during the months of upheaval, and especially its leadership role in Jewish defense operations, worked to its political advantage, especially among the radical youth. Its self-defense initiatives made it particularly popular among Jews in many cities and towns whose lasting impression of 1905 was not one of liberation but of a series of vicious pogroms initiated by chauvinist groups like the Black Hundreds against Jews as ostensible "revolutionary agitators" and "enemies of the tsar." Russian Zionists, who had previously focused their energies on settlement in Palestine, found themselves without clear direction when revolution came, but managed to win back some political capital in the months immediately following the revolution. Zionism needed to change rapidly in order to maintain its relevance; it was due in large measure to Vladimir Jabotinsky—journalist, brilliant orator, and new leader on the Russian Zionist stage—and his call for Zionist participation in Russian political life that the movement once again regained a central position in the Russian Jewish arena.[2] For their part, Jewish liberals weighed their options in the face of a radically new political climate. After October 1905 and the Bund's crisis of confidence leading to its reunification with the Russian Social Democratic Party, other political camps attempted to take advantage of the opportune moment in order to gain momentum. Zionists advocated a Jewish National Assembly to offer leadership for all of Russian Jewry; liberals, along with some Zionists and other parties, created the Union for Equal Rights to lobby for emancipation; and socialist Zionists, who had broken off from the labor Zionist Poalei-Tsion to establish independent parties such as the revolutionary territorialist SERP just before the revolution, now tried to push their agendas forward. As Elise Kimerling Wirtschafter writes, "the revolution of 1905–1907 was a time of massive societal organizing and broad-based 'unionization' among economic, educated, and administrative elites, as well as among peasants, artisans, workers, and common laborers."[3] Jews were only one of many ethnic groups in the empire for whom the revolution became a vehicle for rising nationalist feelings.[4]

The impact of the revolution on the Jewish community was far-reaching. Russian Jewish society was transformed by widespread hopes for the democracy that the October Manifesto would bring about, political mobilization on a mass scale, and the legalization of political parties, trade unions, the press, and other institutions. The parties themselves experienced an unprecedented "drive for democratization and openness."[5] But as the case of Kiev reveals, Jews reacted differently according to their socioeconomic position and relationship to imperial society. Particularly after the bloody pogrom of October 1905, the masses, for the most part, withdrew into themselves, distrustful of the city that had betrayed them so cruelly and violently and intent on pouring their remaining strength into assisting the victims of the pogrom. The intelligentsia, on the other hand, continued to look hopefully outward for allies during the heady days of campaigns and elections for the new Duma, and saw the salvation of Russia's Jews in political affiliation and participation.[6] For them, and for those members of the Jewish proletariat whom they managed to convince, the widespread sense of possibility and excitement lasted through 1906 and into 1907, until the dispersal of the Second Duma in June of that year. Jewish participation in the elections for the State Dumas, and the Jewish National Assembly proposed by the Zionists, made electoral politics and the issue of representation even more central than before.

Thus, the new labor Zionist and territorialist parties founded in the wake of 1905 steadily gained strength, and their energized members were often at the forefront of a new "democratic" movement within the newly politicized local Jewish communities, including Kiev. Even Max Mandel'shtam and his Territorialists, who saw no long-term future for Jews in Russia and poured much of their energy into making mass emigration a real possibility for Russian Jewry, also devoted themselves to the democratization of the institutions of Russian Jewish life.[7] By contrast, the Bund went into a steep decline, with the government cracking down on its activities and publications and many party activists and members emigrating to the United States. As

Joshua Zimmerman writes, "One symptom of declining membership and moral was the sharp reduction in funds after 1907. The party lost over two-thirds of its income between 1908 and 1910."[8] Nonetheless, many of those Bundists who remained in the Russian Empire continued to play an active role in the liberationist movement, as well as in communal politics. That this decline played out on the local level is evidenced by the intracommunal struggles in Kiev in the immediate post-revolutionary years.

Indeed, it is not hard to see why many Jews wanted change at the local level: how could there be a revolution in national politics without any change in communal governance? Progressive Jews were no longer willing to allow "their" institutions to be led by individuals whom they considered to be governing unjustly and without democratic sanction. With local partisans fighting bitterly for control of institutions and funds and for the claim to the mantle of local leadership, the loci of the struggles in Kiev were the Kiev branch of the Union for the Attainment of Full Equality for the Jewish People in Russia (Soiuz dlia Dostizheniia Polnopraviia Evreiskogo Naroda v Rossii), the Crown rabbinate, the Representation for Jewish Welfare acting as the communal governing board, and the Kiev Branch of the OPE. The new politics forced public figures to demonstrate the legitimacy of their claim to power: the established, plutocratic leadership tried to maintain its authority with claims of experience and influence, while nationalists insisted that only they spoke for the masses. Some scholars have argued that the shift in Russian Jewish political orientation toward self-liberation in the late nineteenth and early twentieth century obviated further leadership by the "notables."[9] However, events in Kiev suggest that this was not the case, but rather that the wealthy continued to lead the community. Especially in the earliest years of Jewish "self-emancipation," but later on as well, new organizations such as Hovevei Zion did not at first constitute an alternate base of power but rather were supported by both maskilim and notables.

As Jewish liberationist politics matured and spawned movements and ideologies, it often found itself in confrontation with the notables and their vision for Russian Jewry; in this, Kiev was no exception, as we shall see.[10] Indeed, those who continued to believe in the liberal vision of emancipation ascribed to a politics of their own.[11] In the battle between the two camps, however, neither side could maintain its uncompromising position for long; local circumstances and contingencies called for pragmatism, not stubborn idealism. Rabbi Solomon Lur'e, Crown rabbi of Kiev from 1903 to 1906 and a self-proclaimed representative of the Jewish masses, began to display some of the same despotic tendencies of which he accused the elite; then, after engineering Lur'e's ouster, the notables actually proceeded to appropriate some of his political objectives (or at least his rhetoric). The OPE opposed the Kiev Jewish establishment, but was unable to make headway without the financial support it had lost by doing so, while the plutocrats were compelled to hold elections for the Representation for Jewish Welfare and adopt the populist language of their opponents. While ideological resoluteness might play well in party platforms and the partisan press, activists on the ground were finding that communal politics of necessity required compromises of all.

Amid the sea of words, arguments, opinions, and denunciations that we will wade into, however, we will find precious few emanating from the mouths of the very masses whom the wealthy elite and the educated professional claimed to represent. Other than the glimpses we catch in the words of a few petitions submitted to the authorities, they were silent. So where was this "community," these "masses," whose leadership our protagonists wanted to capture? Undoubtedly, they were hard at work trying to make a living, recovering and recouping their losses after the 1905 pogrom, and perhaps evading the police to avoid expulsion from the city. Some lived just outside the city limits and thus had to spend additional time commuting every morning—many even by ferry, across the Dnepr from the suburb of Slobodka. For these Jews, communal politics, despite its importance in some respects (the funding of Jewish institutions was clearly a significant matter), could not be a full-time pursuit.

Jewish Revolutionary Activity

As we saw previously, the first Bundist cell in Kiev was founded by students in 1900 eager to mobilize the city's Jewish workers. This was relatively late, but it was difficult to organize in Kiev because of legal restrictions on Jewish settlement; moreover, the Bund was less popular in the south of Russia than in the Lithuanian and Belorussian provinces because Ukraine was less industrialized and working conditions were generally better. According to 1897 statistics, Jews made up 38.1 percent of the urban population in the southwest as opposed to 57.9 percent in the northwest.[12] Still, laboring Jews were much more likely to have a "class consciousness" than the peasants who worked in the factories and mills of the capitals and the Donbass region, "most of whom retained ties to the countryside" and did not form a clearly delimited, self-conscious working class.[13] Before the founding of the Bundist Frayhayt in Kiev, Gomel, in the Belorussian province of Mogilev, was the southernmost city to have a Bund committee. As Henry Tobias notes, for the students in Kiev "the Bund was at once an answer to their Zionist opponents and the perfect wedding of their ideology and their feelings of Jewishness."[14] By 1903 the group was already in rivalry with other activist groups, as revealed by a letter from Chaim Khazatskii of Kiev to Fania Gotkina of Bobruisk, written in August 1903 and intercepted by the secret police, which referred to a dispute between Zionists and Bundists in Kiev.[15] Another rival was the Jewish Comradely Union (*Evreiskii tovarishcheskii soiuz*), which Nathans describes as "a mutual aid society as well as a forum for discussion and debate"; at a meeting that year, Bund activists apparently held a meeting to deliberate about whether the Union should exist—not surprisingly, the answer was no.[16] After the pogrom in Smela in 1904, Bundists distributed a leaflet explaining that the government's antisemitic policies were a tool of oppression of the bourgeoisie over the entire working class, in an attempt to divide and weaken the working class. Interior Minister Plehve, argued the leaflet, had orchestrated the pogroms in order to fight with the working class.[17] The Bundists continued their activities in the revolutionary months of 1905. For example, they organized demonstrations in Podol in mid-June together with local Social Democrats and distributed a leaflet in October arguing that the oppression of the Jews was part of tsarism's counterrevolution, which actually oppressed all people.[18] However, as Michael Hamm writes, "the Kiev Bund seemed more effective in organizing Jewish workers in the smaller towns outside of Kiev than it did in Kiev itself."[19] As we have noted, this may well have been because of the logistical challenges involved in organizing in a city where restrictions on Jewish activities were much harsher and more severely applied than in localities in the Pale.

Autonomists and Socialist Zionists such as the Poalei-Tsion had begun to be active in Kiev just after the Bund cell was established. In the first years (1901–1902), there was no united organization but only individual cells in cities, including Kiev, which hosted the Vozrozhdenie (Renaissance) conference in 1903.[20] The SERP/Seimist party—"the smallest of the three new [labor Zionist] parties"—was established in Kiev in April 1906.[21]

Like Zionists throughout the Pale of Settlement, Kiev's Zionists began to "reactivate" in the wake of the revolution, hoping to seize their share of Jewish political energies, now made easier with the Zionist turn toward *Gegen-*

wartsarbeit (cultural and political work among Russian Jewry), which enabled Zionists to demonstrate to the Jewish street that they were relevant to the current situation and pressing political tasks in the here and now. The Russian-language Zionist newspaper *Evreiskii narod* reported in November 1906 that, after a long period of inactivity, a new board had been elected to lead the growing numbers of local members and head up activities that would "fulfill the demands of the Central Bureau."[22] The newly independent Territorialists, led by Mandel'shtam, a global figure in the movement, also showed new vigor by holding a conference in Kiev in February 1906, at which a new organization was established.[23] From January 1907, Kiev was also the headquarters of the Territorialists' new Jewish Emigration Society (Evreiskoe emigratsionnoe obshchestvo), which worked together with the ITO (Jewish Territorialist Organization), the German-Jewish Hilfsverein, the U.S. Industrial Removal Office, and a group of wealthy New York Jews led by banker Jacob Schiff to send emigrating Jews to the port of Galveston, Texas, whence they could be settled in the American West.[24] After Mandel'shtam's death in 1912, Lev Brodsky replaced him as president of the society, evidence of the latter's loss of faith in a future granting of full rights to Russian Jews.[25]

Who were the new activists? They might best be described as radical members of the intelligentsia—or, as they are often referred to in contemporary sources, the "radically inclined" (*radikal'no nastroennye*). Otto Müller argues that there is no single definition of the intelligentsia, and that it is more a "self-image" than an actual group or a "moral code." In the Russian context, intelligenty have been defined as "various groups of writers and politically active men in Russian society," which bears some resemblance to the Jewish situation, though it is too narrow a definition.[26] Not only were there women among the new generation of activists, but also many *polu-intelligenty,* such as schoolteachers, *fel'dshers* (something like a physician's assistant or nurse-practitioner), and professionals (perhaps what we might call "activist professionals").[27] This helps to explain why, as we shall see, the new Organization of Jewish Teachers was so heavily involved in the struggle over the OPE—as Wirtschafter explains, "the impulse to organize [professionally] often assume[d] an oppositionist character"; only here it was in opposition to the Jewish establishment and not to the government. There is also a question of socioeconomic class, and Haimson's definition is thus particularly helpful:

> [The intelligenty's class] identities were fluid and fluctuating, depending on the particular representation of their group identity that they felt most appropriate at any given point. The intelligenty could be middle-class *meshchane,* or they could be the thinking head of the Jewish [working-class] masses, a title that they often appropriated for themselves. Moreover, these intelligenty offered to their putative "followers" (i.e., the masses) one of a number of possible representations of identity. Would they be the Jewish masses? the toiling Jewish workers? the national masses? etc.[28]

The Union for the Attainment of Full Equality for the Jewish People

Most middle-class Jews in Kiev were strongly drawn to the liberal movement, and many Jewish professionals joined the liberal activist groups established in the autumn of 1904 such as the Union of Lawyers and the Union of Physicians. Another new organizations that formed a constituent member of the Union of Unions was the Union for the Attainment of Full Equality for the Jewish People in Russia, a number of whose leaders resided in Kiev.[29] As even the leftist liberals became more radicalized over the course of 1905, moderates within the Jewish community had to decide whether they could in good conscience call for the overthrow of the autocracy. Surely a constitutional democracy would give Jews full rights, but on the other hand the anarchy that could conceivably follow a coup might be a greater evil than the current regime, however oppressive. The dark days of the October pogrom seemed to prove these fears well founded indeed. The Union for Full Equality decided to call on Jews to take part in the elections for the new Duma, joining forces with Kiev's Kadet (Constitutional Democratic) Party and progressive Polish and Ukrainian Groups.[30]

The split between liberals and nationalists that was to characterize so much of communal politics in the immediate post-revolutionary years was already evident in the politicking involved in the establishment of the Kiev branch of the Union for Full Equality. In July 1905, leaders of the Union in St. Petersburg wrote to G. B. Bykhovskii, asking for the help of Kievans in expanding the organization.[31] By September, there was already an elected provisional committee which, crucially, included both members of the plutocratic establishment such as Lev Brodsky and his associates and of the (mostly) younger generation of nationalists: Max Mandel'shtam, Mark

L'vovich Tsitron (a territorialist), Mark B. Ratner (a leader of the Jewish nationalist socialist SERP party as well as a member of the Union for Equal Rights of the Jewish People and the Russian Social Revolutionary Party), G. E. Gurevich, and others.[32] In a letter to Iulii Gessen, Gurevich revealed the nationalists' state of mind when he wrote that "we do not want to submit or to come to an agreement with the plutocracy."[33] The primary point of contention was apparently who would put himself forward as candidate for the Duma in the forthcoming elections. The split was aggravated by personal resentments and attempts at self-aggrandizement. The situation deteriorated to the point that leaders of the Union in St. Petersburg sent several telegrams in October, pleading the Kiev activists to unite their efforts in advance of the provincial conference to be held later in the month.[34] Some of the rifts were patched over, but others were too serious to be healed: Mandel'shtam and Ratner telegraphed that they could not unite with Brodsky, and a telegram from Brodsky sounded similar: "[I] find unification unsuitable. Doubt success of conference."[35]

The local branch of the Union for Equality poured most of its energy in the following months into mobilizing the Jewish vote in Kiev province.[36] But the feuding did not go away, and—as best as can be judged from the collection of letters and telegrams surviving in the archives—several radicals eventually resigned from the board of the local branch in protest against its heavily establishment character.[37] Things went from bad to worse when it became clear that the plutocrats were putting forward their own candidate for Duma representative (apparently the son of prominent industrialist David Margolin) and when a public split appeared between the Union for Equality branch and the new Nonparty Jewish Organization (*Vnepartinnaia evreiskaia organizatsiia*), with each body competing to mobilize and register Jewish voters in Kiev province.[38]

The focus on national politics did not preclude discussions of local communal matters; indeed, the strains revealed in the fabric of local Jewish affairs may actually have encouraged a rethinking of communal governance. In May 1906, Gurevich wrote to St. Petersburg that there was now talk of establishing a nonparty organization to manage Jewish political and communal affairs in Kiev. Perhaps mindful of Kiev's past experience with communal governance, while acknowledging that this was an important goal, Gurevich nonetheless stressed that any new organization must not "include any guardians of routine or any abuses that would demoralize the population and lead to the misappropriation of and attempts on communal funds or property."[39]

As the situation developed, it became clear that both the supporters of the Union for Equality branch and of the Nonparty Jewish Organization wanted their respective organization to form the core of a new communal body for Kiev's Jews. Activists within the Union for Equality seemed to see the other organization as a nothing more than a vehicle created to fulfill the aspirations for power of several individuals within the Jewish community who, according to one observer, enjoyed "the patronage of the local authorities" and thus a good deal of clout.[40] One of those they were referring to may have been Crown Rabbi Lur'e, a charismatic upstart on the Jewish communal scene in Kiev and a leader of the Nonparty Jewish Organization. We shall have cause to speak again of him soon.

Whatever the biases of the Nonparty Jewish Organization, it was apparently successful in mobilizing Jews to vote and in combating the apathy prevalent among the Jewish masses, a condition that was hardly surprising given that a large number of working-class Jewish men were ineligible to vote in the first stage of the elections because they were not employed in factories or workshops with "fifty or more eligible male workers (the number required for voting at the place of work)."[41] The workers' curia in Kiev sent only two electors to participate in the election of the city's Duma representative, while only about 12 percent of Kiev's total population, 29,500 people, were eligible to vote.[42] In addition to the fundamental challenge of a wary conservatism based in a traditional religious worldview or in lack of political experience, there were other problems.[43] In November 1906 a correspondent reported that many Jews were indifferent to the upcoming elections to the Second Duma because they saw no point in voting. How could elections help them with the most pressing problems: unemployment, sick family members, the threat of pogrom? But the writer acknowledged that—thanks to the Nonparty Jewish Organization—the intelligentsia had managed to transform apathy into enthusiasm in many places, and to increase voter registration throughout the province.[44] The result was that two of the Duma representatives elected from Kiev province were Jews (out of a total of twelve Jewish representatives elected empire-wide): M. R. Chervonenkis and S. Frenkel'.

New Leadership against the Old, I: The Kiev Crown Rabbinate

Our story now takes us back several years to just before the dawning of the new century. As demonstrated by the cases of the new burial society and Choral Synagogue discussed in chapter 2, a gulf had opened up between the Russian Jewish elite and those it was supposed to represent. The tenor of awe and respect that had generally accompanied articles and letters to the editor about the Jewish notables and their vast enterprises, works of charity, and contacts with the empire's rich and powerful in the 1870s and 1880s had given way to mistrust and skepticism about the plutocrats' motives in the 1890s; now they were accused not only of indifference to the needs of the Jewish masses, but also of active attempts to disenfranchise them so that they, the plutocrats and their lackeys, could remain in power.

Many of the plutocrats could not see the benefit of broadening participation in communal affairs to the masses. M. I. Polinkovskii, a merchant, Palestinophile, and a spokesman for the elite who responded to Lev Shtammer's 1896 letter on the Crown rabbinate in the local newspaper *Kievskoe slovo*, argued that in communities where everyone voted for the rabbi, the winner was invariably someone incompetent of holding the position. In other words, universal suffrage led to poor leadership.[45] Moreover, the agitation that elections might cause meant that they were not worth the scant benefits they might provide. It would be better to have Crown Rabbi Evsei Tsukkerman serve in his position for life, wrote Polinkovskii, than "to carry out elections that might take the artisans away from their work for many months and stir up ferment, which is undesirable everywhere but especially in Kiev."[46]

But popular opinion seemed to indicate otherwise. We have seen that the authority held by the Representation for Jewish Welfare, an unelected and unaccountable body, was increasingly coming under assault from the community at large, accompanied by accusations that its "representatives" were out of touch with the reality of most of Kiev's Jews. It was no longer taken for granted that communal leadership would be chosen by those with wealth or influence, which had always determined primacy. Now, under the influence of liberal and revolutionary ideologies, new ideas were gaining currency, chief among them the "electoral principle": communal leaders should be elected; the wider the franchise and the electorate, the more legitimacy the elected leader gained; and those who were chosen through elections—the Crown rabbis—were now to be considered popular leaders by virtue of their election.[47] The people were now to decide who was best fit to serve them. As Shtammer wrote, "As far as the intellectual and moral qualities of the elected, that's the business of the voters: let them elect for themselves the man who, in their view, will be most beneficial for them and will . . . fulfill the duties that they place upon him."[48]

After Tsukkerman was forced to resign in 1898 due to a sermon he gave of which the governor-general disapproved, Kiev's next two Crown rabbis were both maskilim and Zionists who attempted to transform the rabbinate, using it to advance the Jewish national cause in order to come to the aid of Russian Jewry. Their approaches, however, were quite different.

Petr Abramovich Iampol'skii, born in 1850, graduated as a medic from the Imperial Academy of Army Medicine and served on the front during the Russo-Turkish War. After his retirement from army life in 1888, he served as Crown rabbi in Rostov-on-Don for nine years and was active in the local Zionist circle there; Azriel Shohat, historian of the Russian Empire's Crown rabbinate, speculates that Iampol'skii may have been the first Palestinophile (member of Hovevei Zion) to be elected Crown rabbi.[49] Characteristically for the older generation of Hovevei Zion (he was forty-seven at the time of his election in Kiev in 1899), he envisioned a synthesis between nationalism and religion that would attract Russian Jewish youth back to their roots *and* to their faith. And like other activist Crown rabbis, he was intent on using the title of rabbi in order to effect a reform of sorts in the Russian Jewish rabbinate and even in Judaism itself, revitalizing them and making them relevant by infusing them with the new national spirit. In the inaugural lecture of a series that he delivered for Kiev's Jewish youth at the Brodsky Choral Synagogue, entitled *Spiritual Conversations*, he told those assembled that if they wished to come to the aid of their nation, they had to learn about its history, religion, and culture—and there could be no better teacher than the synagogue. Iampol'skii would serve as guide through their "spiritual process."[50] In this vision, with rabbi and synagogue serving as teachers of Jewish nationalism—a worthy goal in and of itself—deracinated Russian Jews would be drawn nolens volens back to Judaism, as well. That Iampol'skii intended not only to insinuate religion into the teaching of Jewish nationalism, but also systematically to introduce Zionism into his rabbinate, is evident from a postcard that he sent to Zionist leader Menahem Ussishkin in Ekaterinoslav in 1899, one day after he was confirmed in his new position: "On Saturday I gave a *programmatic* speech at the main (Brodsky) synagogue."[51]

However, Iampol'skii had no intention of putting an end to Tsukkerman's good relations with the ruling plutocracy, as is evident from the letters he wrote to *Khronika Voskhoda* defending Kiev's kosher tax and its management by the municipal authorities.[52] Any criticism of the administration of the tax would likely have provoked a serious conflict with Kiev's ruling elite.

Iampol'skii certainly had the support of that elite, whether or not we believe communal dissident Lev Shtammer's claim that the Crown rabbi had only gained his position with the backing and corrupt electioneering of Lazar' Brodsky; Shtammer alleged that Brodsky had stood next to Iampol'skii's ballot box during the election, signaling to voters that they had better cast their ballot "correctly" if they knew what was good for them.[53] At the same time, Iampol'skii announced his intentions to bridge the gaps between rich and poor in the Jewish community, an oblique reference to the tensions that Tsukkerman's long tenure had left behind.[54]

But Iampol'skii served only one term before being replaced by Solomon Arkad'evich Lur'e in 1903, in Kiev's first rabbinical election to be carried out in accordance with the government regulation allowing all parishioners of prayer houses in a given locality to vote for the Crown rabbi.[55] Born in 1858, Lur'e was of the second-generation maskilim who had come of age in the post-reform era; having received a traditional education, he then fell under the influence of Haskalah literature, taught himself Russian, earned a gymnasium diploma as an extern in 1879, and graduated from a communications institute in 1885. While studying to be an engineer, he published Hebrew poems and Russian-language articles on the scientific study of Judaism in various Jewish journals, and continued to publish original monographs and translations over the next decades, at least one on the topic of Palestinophilism.[56] In the 1880s, he studied in Berlin with the Jewish academic Moritz Steinschneider for a short time and, upon returning to St. Petersburg, began to study law and to work at one of the factories of the wealthy industrialist Baron Goratsii [Horace] Gintsburg. In 1894, his marriage apparently brought him to the provincial town of Pereiaslav, where he earned a living in the grain trade. As he wrote in a short autobiographical sketch in 1898, the first year in which he stood as a candidate for election to the Crown rabbinate in Kiev, his current situation did not allow him to devote any time to literary and academic pursuits, but he still hoped to be able to "labor in the name of the eternal truths and ideals of Jewry and for the sake of my people."[57] Presumably, he hoped and expected that the rabbinate would furnish him the opportunity for such pursuits.

The plutocrats refused to allow Lur'e to participate in communal governance as had his predecessors Tsukkerman and Iampol'skii. Only two years before, a correspondent from Kiev had written that "the participation of the municipal rabbi in the meetings of the twelve representatives is considered essential, as he is best able to encourage the city government to enact plans regarding Jewish philanthropy."[58] An 1899 almanac for the southwest region also noted that the Crown rabbi participated and voted at meetings of the Representation for Jewish Welfare, the de facto communal governing board.[59] Now, however, as Lur'e requested and then demanded to be included in the deliberations of the Representation regarding the allocations of the kosher excise revenues, he was shut out of the corridors of power.

Though his curriculum vitae made reference to his acquaintance with Baron Gintsburg, the most important Jewish communal leader in St. Petersburg and an in-law of Lazar' Brodsky, Lur'e was received with animosity by the Kiev Jewish establishment. Tantalizing clues to this hostility can be found in Lur'e's earlier, unsuccessful attempt to gain the rabbinate, in 1898. In that election, Lur'e had been one of three challengers to the long-serving Tsukkerman, and after his defeat he submitted a complaint that the elections had been carried out unfairly. The authorities then received a letter countering that notion, insisting that the balloting had been completely equitable and that Lur'e "is an individual completely foreign to the Kiev Jewish community, and his complaint is simply an expression of the dissatisfaction of the losing candidate, who has no concern for the interests of the local community."[60] It seems likely that the authors of the letter were those powerful Jews who had always supported Tsukkerman and who maintained that they (and their rabbi) had the best interests of the Jewish masses in mind in their governance of the community. Their reference to Lur'e's allegedly egotistical motives seems to be a direct rebuttal of his claim that he aspired to the Crown rabbinate in order to serve his people, and their accusation that he had no ties to Kiev Jewry an endorsement of their own long-established leadership. We can only imagine their chagrin when Lur'e finally achieved his goal and was elected Crown rabbi five years later—with a much broader franchise than ever before attained in a Kiev rabbinical election.

One of his first actions as Crown rabbi was to submit a proposal to the municipal administration about using some of the kosher excise monies to fund Jewish religious instruction in Kiev's public schools and improve Kiev's hadarim. The proposal was not reviewed by the Representation, but whether it was deliberately ignored or only neglected because of "red tape," as one correspondent from Kiev opined, is unclear; although Lur'e wrote that he had submitted his proposal to the city administration, he must have known that it would be passed immediately to the Representation, which dealt with all matters concerning the funding of Jewish institutions. Lur'e immediately began to appeal to public opinion for a redress of this wrong, writing a letter to *Kievskaia gazeta*, a left-leaning, Russian-language, general-interest newspaper, calling on the members of the board to join him in assisting their poor and uneducated brethren. Lur'e detailed the plight of the poor Jewish artisans of Kiev, who (he claimed) were too indigent to afford to pay melamdim to teach their sons, and thus sent them to municipal and parish schools without any Jewish education whatsoever, "not even teaching them Jewish literacy or even the daily prayers." Lur'e continued:

> What will the consequences be of such a situation, when poor Jewish children are not assimilating at home the moral principles that a judicious religious education inculcates in the impressionable infantile soul, and on the other hand are deprived of any religious instruction in the municipal and parish schools?[61]

Lur'e indirectly criticized the members of the Representation for Jewish Welfare for neglecting this crucial matter, and called on them to ensure that the surplus in the korobka budget be set aside for Jewish education so that the "heavy burden" of the kosher meat tax would serve Kiev's poor Jews in at least this way. The representatives answered in a subsequent issue of the same newspaper by stating flatly that the budget for the coming financial period was already decided and closed. Lur'e shot back that it was impossible for the budget to have been finalized—because he had not participated in the deliberations! Not only was he to be considered a member of the Representation, but he was "the closest individual to the [municipal] administration" in matters of Jewish philanthropy. Lur'e reminded the members of the Representation that this debate was taking place in the public sphere, that he was appealing to public opinion (*obshchestvennoe mnenie*), and that "thousands of eyes" were now focused on the Representation with hope.[62]

Indeed, the increasingly bitter exchange was not going unnoticed by other Kievans. A few days later, a feuilleton appeared in *Kievskaia gazeta*, accusing the members of the Representation for Jewish Welfare of hypocrisy, "shameless favoritism," and nepotism. The author, one M. Voloshin, argued that the Jewish grandees called the huge sums of money they disbursed "philanthropy," but none of it went to fund education for the sons of poor Jewish artisans ("education, which is the Jew's only defense against hunger and only access to a life without round-ups"). Some of the money, Voloshin continued, even went into the pockets of friends and acquaintances of the "bosses" (*zapravili*) who sat on the so-called "Oversight [Supervisory]

Committee." Only "zeal for the people" could change the current lamentable situation.[63]

Continuing this public epistolary saga, Lur'e wrote that he was moved by Voloshin's piece, but that it had had no effect, as the meeting of the Representation for Jewish Welfare on October 16 had not discussed his proposal, which, he made clear, had the support of at least some local Jews. "Those expectations were shared with many members of the local Jewish community [*obshchestvo*], some of whom sent me written declarations of support for my petition with the signatures of many highly educated [*diplomirovannye*] and other individuals." Lur'e appealed to the Jewish community for support: "I am appealing through the press to encourage sympathetic people to add their forces to this effort, for I cannot accomplish it alone."[64]

Within a month, Lur'e proceeded to submit a memorandum to the city council, appealing the refusal of the city administration to allow him to participate in the meetings of the Representation for Jewish Welfare. In the document, he specifically referred to himself as "the *only elected* representative of the tens of thousands of payers of the [kosher] excise," that is, the poor Jews of Kiev; while he had been elected by the entire Jewish community, "the so-called 'representatives' for Jewish welfare are in actuality not invested with any authority by the Jewish population, but are rather appointed by the administration. . . ."[65] While the plutocrats were "distant from the life of the poor populace," the rabbi was the only individual to come in contact with the Jewish masses on a daily basis, thus gaining intimate knowledge of their spiritual and material needs. (Lur'e's claim that Jews turned to the Crown rabbi "in times of joy and sorrow" was somewhat undermined by the obvious point—which he did not mention—that Jews had no choice but to come to the Crown rabbi, the only official empowered to issue Jewish birth, death, marriage, and divorce certificates.) Moreover, he claimed that Jewish voters had taken advantage of the new law on rabbinical elections in order to elect him for the precise purpose of participating in the allocation of the kosher excise revenues and making sure that their needs were provided for—since those needs had been neglected for years by the Jewish elite. The members of the Representation for Jewish Welfare, he hinted, had worked actively to prevent the election of a popular rabbi such as himself.

Lur'e played shrewdly on the general distrust of the plutocratic leadership, portraying it as removed from the genuine concerns of its constituency and suggesting that it no longer lived by the same norms and values (he made it clear that the "representatives" did not even pay the kosher tax, presumably because they had no need for kosher meat).[66] At the same time, he positioned himself as a more legitimate and natural leader, one with a direct connection to the masses. This was something of a revolutionary reworking of the role of Crown rabbi: from government apparatchik and, in the case of Kiev, establishment toady, to elected representative. As Lur'e surely knew, in establishing the Crown rabbinate—which had been an elective office from the very beginning—the Russian government had never meant to create a popular spokesman and advocate for the needs of the Jewish masses. Nevertheless, Lur'e had determinedly taken on precisely those roles, or at least claimed that he had.

In the course of the following two years, 1904 and 1905, Lur'e continued his direct and at times confrontational approach to local Jewish politics, demanding greater accountability to the needs of Kiev's poor Jews, especially in the realm of taxation. The dismay of the notables, used to achieving their goals through quiet negotiations and behind-the-scenes deputations to figures of authority, was surely great—especially given his numerous demands of the city council, not known for its friendliness toward the local Jewish community. In early 1904, Lur'e petitioned the mayor to exempt Jews from a proposed hospital tax since, he argued, they already supported an important local hospital—Kiev's Jewish Hospital, serving both Jews and Christians—through their payment of the tax on kosher meat.[67] According to the correspondent from Kiev who described the affair, Lur'e's petition was announced at a meeting of the city council but was not presented or explained; the position then, not surprisingly, languished in committee. In spring 1905, he submitted a complaint to the city council protesting the lack of representation on the council for the Jewish masses, despite the large sums that they contributed to the city's coffers through the various taxes and duties that they paid.[68] The author of this report to the Jewish newspaper *Voskhod* noted that, because of Kiev's status outside the Pale of Settlement, no Jews could sit on the city council, a situation aggravated by the Judeophobic tendencies of the mayor and most of the veteran councilmen. Several months later, Lur'e went so far as to threaten to bring a suit against the city if it continued to apportion 15,000 rubles for itself from the tax on kosher meat as had been its practice for years.[69] As the empire plunged headlong into revolution through the course of 1905, Lur'e's direct and no-nonsense approach to dealing with the authorities clearly embodied the heady spirit of the times, and probably appealed to a great many Kiev Jews who had grown accustomed to abuse and persecution on the part of the various levels of bureaucracy in the city. In a city with as many poor Jews as Kiev, his down-to-earth focus on the inordinate tax burden shouldered by the Jewish masses could only enhance that appeal.

With the outbreak of revolution in 1905, Lur'e stepped up his activism that, thanks to the new freedoms granted by the October Manifesto, could now be openly political. He was one of the founders and most active leaders of the Nonparty Jewish Organization, which, as we saw above, aimed to mobilize the city's Jewish population for the elections to the first State Duma in 1906. At the founding meeting of the organization, he expressed his continuing belief in the importance of active participation in representative politics and in the life of the empire: Jews must be inspired with the awareness that they are Russian citizens and have a duty to vote.[70] At the same time, there is some evidence that Lur'e was not open to a fully democratic process in his own organization: *Der telegraf*, a Warsaw newspaper established by Zionist leader Nahum Sokolow, reported that at one of the meetings, Lur'e refused to allow any discussion about a possible boycott of the Duma elections, nor would he give the floor to a worker who wanted to criticize the candidates that Lur'e had presented to the floor. This would not be the last criticism of his leadership style.[71]

Lur'e's other projects also reveal his dedication to the education of the Jewish masses and his belief in the importance of the rights and responsibilities of citizenship. He attempted to establish a Jewish library in Kiev and, after the Ministry of Internal Affairs denied him permission, appealed to the Senate, referring in his memorial to the right of every Russian citizen to open an institution for the use of the public.[72] Archival records show that sometime in 1905 he submitted a petition to start publication of a Russian-language Jewish newspaper in Kiev, to be called *Kievskii evreiskii vestnik* (The Kiev Jewish Herald), the editor of which was to be none other than Lur'e himself. The lead articles were to be about state and public life as they concerned the needs of the Jewish population.[73] (For reasons unknown, not one issue of the paper was ever published.) A year later, Lur'e succeeded in establishing Kiev's first Jewish savings and loan society, which would play an important role in the Kiev Jewish community over the next decade.[74] (Lur'e's combative nature seems to be on display here too: for some reason he was one of three individuals to petition that the first meeting of the society, at which board elections took place, be declared illegal.)[75] He also requested, but did not receive, permission from the authorities to establish a Jewish *Realschule* (vocational school) in Kiev.[76]

Lur'e also tried to play a role on the national stage. In 1904 he attempted to carry out his own statistical survey of two hundred Jewish communities throughout the Pale of Settlement by sending letters and forms to their Crown rabbis; in early 1906 he was one of five representatives from localities affected by pogroms who traveled to St. Petersburg to meet with chairman of the council of ministers S. I. Witte; and several months later he sent invitations to rabbis throughout the Russian Empire to the first Constituent Congress that would found an All-Russian Rabbinical Union.[77]

While some undoubtedly saw Lur'e as the incarnation of a new style of leadership for the Jewish masses, others claimed that his newfound power was going to his head. Even more important, observers from the left of the political spectrum were dissatisfied with leadership on the part of Crown rabbis, despite their elected status. While some felt that a national religious leadership was right for the Jewish community, others wanted leaders without ties to either religion or the state. One Kiev Jew, writing to a Russian Jewish newspaper under the pseudonym "Tsvi," challenged Lur'e's claim to leadership on the basis of his election as Crown rabbi. His participation in the deputation to Witte without any kind of authority from the Jewish community demonstrated that his power had gone to his head, inspiring visions of messianic grandeur. (Though he did not say so, Tsvi may also have considered Lur'e's behavior reminiscent of the intercessionary activity of the notables to whom he was so opposed, most notably Lazar' Brodsky's delegation to St. Petersburg after the 1881 pogroms.)[78] His attempt to convoke a contemporary "Great Sanhedrin"—a congress of Crown rabbis—was further proof of Lur'e's delusions of grandeur, and of the wrongheadedness of his priorities. Nationalism, not religion, was the inspiration of the Jewish masses. In this vein, Tsvi attacked the very foundations of Lur'e's leadership: Crown rabbis could never be the true representatives of the Jewish people. Indeed, he predicted that when Jews attained autonomy, they would get rid of the Crown rabbis and elect their own officials.[79]

There is some evidence that Lur'e had allowed his position of authority and crusade for the Jewish masses to get the better of his judgment in his role as Crown rabbi. In a petition submitted in 1906 in the name of "the Jewish working and artisan class of the Jewish population of Kiev," he was accused of demanding money for conducting rituals and of not handling the metrical books correctly. An investigation by the provincial government found that many poor families had indeed been forced to forgo rituals or to borrow money in order to pay the sums that Lur'e had been demanding, and he was officially reprimanded. In his own defense, Lur'e insisted that he had only taken money from those Jews whom he had judged capable of paying, revealing that he considered himself a sort of Robin Hood for the poor Jewish masses.[80] That same year, a petition submitted by parishioners of three prayer houses in Ploskaia complained that Lur'e was trying to postpone the rabbinical elections scheduled for 1906, allegedly because he knew that the community was dissatisfied with him. The petitioners characterized Lur'e's rule as "arbitrary" and "burdensome" for the community, and requested that he be dismissed.[81] A month later, a similar petition pleaded with the authorities to "deliver [the Jewish community] from the oppression of Mr. Lur'e," who was continuing to rob the population with "ever greater energy."[82] That the charges of interference with elections were at least partially true is supported by the fact that when elections were finally called, they had to be cancelled because Lur'e failed to appear to administer the oath to the electors.[83] Lur'e's actions were thus in flagrant contradiction to the values he had been so vigorously championing since his election: accountability of leadership and the centrality of free and fair elections to a just and equitable society. After a case was brought against him in Kiev District Court in 1904, charging that he had failed to record some entries in the metrical books in Hebrew as well as Russian, parishioners of one of Kiev's prayer houses petitioned in November 1906 that Lur'e be sacked for his abuse of rabbinical duties.[84]

Lur'e, however, had enemies far more important and dangerous to worry about than petitioners calling for his dismissal. The established leadership of the Kiev Jewish community, so clearly opposed to his participation in the mechanisms of communal leadership in the years after his election as Crown rabbi, were taking steps to bring about his fall from power and to ensure that the Crown rabbinate in Kiev would never again serve as a rival locus of power.

The drama started in early 1906 when Lur'e appealed to the city council to intervene in the matter of his salary for the month of January which, he claimed, had been left out of the municipal budget because of a plot against him. Since the salary of the Crown rabbi was paid by the Representation for Jewish Welfare, it is clear that Lur'e suspected the members of that body were deliberately trying to undermine his office.[85]

The "plot," as Lur'e saw it, eventually led to the end of his career as Crown rabbi. As he wrote in an open letter to the parishioners of Kiev's Jewish prayer houses dated October 8, 1906, he was resigning from his post in protest over the unlawful division of Kiev into two rabbinical districts, a move that he claimed had been instigated by "an insignificant group of individuals." The fracturing of an integral Jewish community into two fragments, Lur'e wrote, was unprecedented in Russian history and would serve only the interests of "a small group of pretenders who have arbitrarily seized Jewish communal funds and manage them without accountability!" (Of course the idea that there existed an "integral Jewish community" in Kiev was absurd, but it served Lur'e's purposes.) Over the past years, his denunciations of that clique had succeeded in drawing public attention to it, and his influence had held its power in check; even now, continued Lur'e, preparations were being made to take back communal funds from those grasping hands. The division would detract from the authority of the rabbinate, which had in many cases worked "for the good of Jewish spiritual, cultural, and civic interests," and make it impossible to attract individuals to the rabbinate of the caliber appropriate for such an important center as Kiev. Even more importantly, the elimination of a strong central rabbinate would mean that the unaccountable communal leaders could continue their arbitrary rule without protest of any kind. Lur'e noted that the request for the division of the city had been approved despite petitions of protest from nine prayer houses in Kiev.[86]

Ostensibly, the division of Kiev into two rabbinical districts was nothing more than a solution to the problem of the city's rapidly growing population, which could not be adequately served by one Crown rabbi. A copy of the Kiev governor's decree from April 19, 1906, reveals that the boards of prayer houses nos. 10, 11, 12, and 13 had requested the division in view of the fact that the 32,000 Jews of greater Kiev, with 22 prayer houses, needed more than one Crown rabbi to attend to the registration of their life events.[87]

A petition to the provincial administration from January 1907, after the division of the city into two districts was formalized, sheds additional light on the intrigue. Residents of Kiev's first rabbinical district (which included the wealthier neighborhoods of the upper city) pleaded that, in the temporary absence of a Crown rabbi for their district, the rabbi of the second district (consisting primarily of the poor areas of Podol and Ploskaia) not be given temporary jurisdiction over both districts for fear that such an action would endanger the existence of the two separate districts. With the preservation of the division, "which we worked so long to attain, the inconveniences of one rabbi will be eliminated and *our interests will be protected.*"[88] The vagueness of the preceding sentence and the reference to "interests" leaves ample room to conclude that the "inconveniences" to which the petitioners referred were about more than simply having to travel across the city to reach the Crown rabbi's office. As Lur'e correctly noted in his open letter, never before had a city in the Russian Empire been divided into two rabbinical districts; when Jewish communities grew too large for one Crown rabbi alone, the standing solution was simply to appoint assistants to the rabbi. Also, the petitioners' reference to their long travails to bring about the division contradicts the official decree, according to which the division was requested by prayer houses in Podol, located in the *second* district, not the first.

Lev Shtammer's pamphlet "In the Court of Public Opinion," published a year later in 1908, helps explain the matter. Bringing a stinging indictment against Kiev's wealthy Jewish leadership in the matter of the rabbinical districts, Shtammer accused the plutocrats, whom he sarcastically called "our Jewish protectors," of arranging for Kiev to be split into two rabbinical districts as a result of their hostility toward Lur'e—who was greatly respected by the entire Kiev Jewish community for being a true defender of its interests. Lur'e's opponents, claimed Shtammer, were careful not to be implicated in the affair, submitting their petitions "by means of several tractable members of synagogue boards"—which may explain why the January 1907 petition cited above was not signed by anyone associated with the Kiev ruling elite. Shtammer further imputed them with bringing a lawsuit against Lur'e (apparently the action regarding the metrical books). According to Shtammer, the stress caused by these incidents led to Lur'e's premature death, about which no further details were given.[89]

But why did Lur'e not simply accept the division and then submit his candidacy in one of the newly created districts—could he not have thus continued to serve at least some of the Jews of Kiev? The evidence shows that, far from accepting the division or even trying to broker a compromise, Lur'e and his supporters attempted to fight power with power: over the months of May, June, July, and August, they submitted no less than five petitions to the Senate requesting that it overturn the original decree. Then, on October 1, they sent a telegram to the Oberprokuror; and on November 6, one day before the decree was to go into effect and elections were to be held for the second rabbinical district, Lur'e cabled the minister of internal affairs, requesting that he intervene in the matter.[90] Given the evidence that Lur'e had taken advantage of his position for personal gain and that he saw himself as the leader and even the savior of Kiev's Jewish masses, his actions here only underscore the fact that he was loath to give up the prestige and power of one of the empire's largest and most important rabbinates.

Though Lur'e may have been gotten rid of, the populist goals and tactics he had introduced into Kiev Jewish communal affairs left a lasting impression. Indeed, even before Lur'e's disappearance from the scene, the established communal leaders began to co-opt some of his goals and tactics in their own leadership. Though the plutocrats had never protested against the Jewish taxation system before, in September 1905 two of the leading members of Kiev's Jewish elite, Lev Brodsky and David Margolin, submitted a petition to Governor-General N. V. Kleigels to abolish the tax on kosher meat in Kiev. They argued that the burden of the tax fell disproportionately on the Jewish poor of the city, and that it should be replaced by a "just and uniform" communal assessment to be determined by income, as was done in Warsaw (where only 13 percent of the Jewish population paid communal taxes, totaling almost 200,000 rubles, providing for the whole community). The petitioners assured the governor-general that the funds would continue to be collected by the municipality and allocated by the Representation for Jewish Welfare, and that the absence of an official Jewish community in Kiev did not pose an obstacle to the plan, since other interest groups had been permitted self-assessment for various purposes. The petitioners concluded by noting that by allowing the abolition of the kosher meat tax, Kiev could serve as an example for the future, when the korobka would be abolished throughout the Pale of Settlement—a suggestion of a more political nature than was usual for the plutocrats.[91]

Only a few months later, another petition was submitted in the name of the Representation for Jewish Welfare itself, requesting that the governor-general put an end to the city's practice of allocating 14,550 rubles from the meat tax proceeds for the Kiev police. In unusually strong language, the petition called the city council's actions "illegal and manifestly unjust with regard to the entire Jewish population of Kiev, violating the principle of equality of this population with the other citizens of the city," and asked "for what fault" Kiev's Jews were again having their tax monies expropriated for foreign purposes. The petitioners noted that Jews paid the same municipal taxes as their non-Jewish neighbors, and did not receive any special benefits from the city; indeed, the city council had refused to provide any assistance to the victims of the 1905 pogrom. That the authors of the petition touched upon both the principle of equality and the pogrom suggests that the events of October 1905 had had a significant impact on the established communal leaders, shattering any illusions they had held about the attitudes of the municipal authorities toward Jews. Unlike Brodsky and Margolin in their petition (and Lur'e before them), however, the board members did not refer to the Jewish poor of Kiev and their interests. Rather, they spoke of the entire Jewish population of the city, the poor residents of *all* religions and nationalities served by the Jewish Hospital (the primary beneficiary of meat tax funds), and "the interests of the Jewish charitable institutions"—which had no defenders other than the board members themselves.[92] The elite communal leadership was still uncomfortable taking on the role of defender of the interests of the Jewish masses, at least in its correspondence with the authorities.

Moreover, there is evidence that Iakov Meerovich Aleshkovskii, Lur'e's successor in the post of Crown rabbi for Kiev's second rabbinical district, which included the poor neighborhoods of Podol and Ploskaia, followed in the path of his predecessor in his engagement in communal politics—though not to the same extent as Lur'e. From his first days in the city, Aleshkovskii was an active participant in the Kiev Branch of the OPE, a member of the branch's Library Commission (the OPE's Podol library was housed in his apartment), and a leader of anti-establishment politics in the city's Jewish community.[93] At a provincial rabbinical conference in 1908, Aleshkovskii spoke on the reorganization of the Jewish community, arguing that since the community was a "national-religious institution," its members should be those individuals who paid communal taxes.[94] This asseveration put him in the camp of Lur'e and other nationalists who based their definition of Jewish community on the kosher tax that financed that community and those who paid them, a definition that would exclude many of the prosperous, acculturated leaders of the Kiev Jewish community.

The dangers inherent in the politicization of the Crown rabbinate are made clear by a denunciation of Aleshkovskii submitted to the governor of Kiev province by one Aron Khaimovich, witnessed by a group of Podol Jews, around the time of Aleshkovskii's election in November 1906. The indictment charged him with belonging to the Zionist Socialist Party (SS), and of delivering a speech in which he told his listeners that Jews could expect nothing from the current government and must act for themselves. Just as soon as Aleshkovskii was confirmed in his new position, the complainants warned, he would begin to organize antigovernment parties. "What kind of rabbi will he be, if he is a socialist?" they asked in language that was sometimes crude and ungrammatical (these men's mother tongue was clearly not Russian).[95] This is a clear example of how partisan Jewish politics—most notably the ongoing struggle between Zionist and socialist parties—was manifested on the local, communal level as well as on the national plane. Of course, denunciations of Crown rabbis were fairly common and might just as often be motivated by personal or business concerns as by political considerations.[96] Indeed, the secret police in Kiev reported that they had no information on any criminal activity on the part of Aleshkovskii.[97] But the heavily politicized struggle over leadership in the Kiev Jewish community and the thoroughgoing politicization of Russian Jewry at all levels leave no reason to doubt that the accusation was sincere. It is quite possible that Khaimovich had been a supporter of the general Zionist Lur'e, and resented the authority now being wielded by a Zionist of the socialist stripe.

An article in *Dos folk* (The People), the short-lived Yiddish newspaper, illustrates the thorough disenchantment with the Crown rabbinate felt by some Jews in 1906 and probably earlier. On the occasion of rabbinical elections, the anonymous author took the opportunity to deliver a caustic critique of the "evil worm"—the Crown rabbi. The candidates would do whatever it took to win, and would promise or assure anything to any constituency: European respectability for the haute bourgeoisie, Zionism and decades of experience in communal affairs for the middle class, and even bribes for the poor. The upshot: "No respectable person would dirty his hands in this business, where consciences are bought and sold for a penny!"[98] For this author as for other Jews, men such as Lur'e, far from being legitimate leaders, were actually a dead weight around the community's neck; no good could ever come of them.

New Leadership against the Old, II: The Kiev Branch of the OPE

During the very months when Lur'e was battling the plutocracy to retain his position and his authority, another clash was taking place in a different arena of Jewish communal politics in Kiev, this time within the Kiev Branch of the OPE. Here, too, wealthy men with a long history of involvement with a Jewish institution found themselves fighting upstart nationalist-minded intellectuals and professionals for control of that organization over issues of mass participation and democratization. Indeed, though the plutocrats emerged victorious from the battle with Lur'e, they lost the struggle for control of the Kiev OPE.[99]

The Kiev branch was established in 1903 on the foundations of an already existing organization, one of the first Jewish charitable organizations to be founded in Kiev—the Jewish Student Fund, an endowment that assisted needy students attending St. Vladimir's University.[100] As a result, the first members of the board of the branch were those who had contributed most generously to the student fund and had served as its leaders, most notably Baron Vladimir Goratsievich Gintsburg (son of Goratsii) who, according to communal activist E. E. Friedmann, founded the branch after his marriage to the daughter of Lazar' Brodsky and relocation to Kiev from St. Petersburg.[101] As one of their number wrote to *Voskhod,* they saw themselves, contributors to the cause of needy students, as the most natural pretenders to the leadership of the OPE.[102]

For several decades after the establishment of the OPE in St. Petersburg in 1863, student aid had been the society's primary undertaking, despite an initial commitment to elementary school reform.[103] This was consistent with the organization's stated goal of encouraging the education of Russian Jewry and its integration into Russian society. But in the 1890s, thanks to growing concerns over the alienation of the new generation of Russian Jews from their cultural heritage as well as an influx of nationally minded members into the OPE, the focus of the Society's Central Committee in St. Petersburg shifted to the schooling of Jewish children. The change in the makeup of the OPE membership had also forced the democratization of the organization, resulting in the lowering of dues so a broader constituency could join and the institution of annual conferences at which members could actively take part in determining organizational priorities.[104] Before the founding of the Kiev Branch of the OPE, several Kiev Jewish intellectuals were active members of the society, but the focus of the local haute bourgeoisie remained the Jewish Student Fund; the educational priorities of the conservative Kiev Jewish elite had, not surprisingly, remained those of the 1860s and 1870s. Moreover, the plutocrats continued to reserve decision-making power within the fund for themselves, an approach they carried over to the new OPE branch. All these factors, combined with the fact that the OPE's Kiev branch was established in 1903, on the eve of revolution, meant that the organization would, willy-nilly, be plunged into a political maelstrom immediately after its very birth. Indeed, during those months of revolution and turmoil, when educational activists were much more heavily involved in political action than in educational work per se, the OPE as a whole was engaged in a furious debate over the direction of the society.[105] The changing focus of the Zionist movement—as exemplified by the decision taken at the 1906 Helsingfors Conference to commit to Gegenwartsarbeit—also contributed to rapidly shifting dynamics in communal activity.[106] The stage was set for a struggle for the very soul of the organization, in Kiev as elsewhere. Indeed, an almost identical battle took place within the national executive board of the OPE in St. Petersburg, with representatives of the "old regime" defending their control of the organization against the attacks of "the aspiring new elite"—nationalists and democrats.[107] (One of the latter, Mark Ratner, even played a leading a role in the stormy meetings in both St. Petersburg and Kiev.) Before the subject of education could even be broached, however, Kiev Jews committed to the existence of the OPE in their city would have to work out more basic issues of communal and institutional authority and governance.

At one of the new branch's first general meetings, in January 1905, Mark Tsitron voiced his opposition to the management of the society's board, charging that its "inertia and sluggishness" were the reasons why nothing had been accomplished in 1904, the branch's first full year of existence. Tsitron blamed the problems on the centralized and undemocratic nature of the board, which consisted only of the original contributors to the student fund, not of members of the organization. The secretary, a pivotal board position, and members of the branch's various commissions had not been elected but were simply designated by the chairman—a charge that Izrail' Kel'berin, former secretary of the branch and close associate of the Brodsky family, denied in a rejoinder published several months later.[108] Tsitron left no doubt as to where his political sympathies lay, exulting in the fact that "the demands of the masses" were finally making themselves known. He called for the board to consider itself temporary until it had recruited a sizable number of new members and elected a secretary.[109] In other words, Tsitron considered the governance of the OPE as it was presently constituted to be illegitimate.

The battle over the meaning of legitimacy and the desire of the old guard leadership of the Kiev OPE to maintain control over the organization against the designs of current activists and new members who might take it in a different direction were well illustrated by the general meeting of June 1905. Baron Gintsburg, chairing the meeting, declared immediately that only contributors to the Jewish Student Fund would have the right to vote at the meeting, while board member G. B. Bykhovskii added that the primary school teachers who were in attendance—who were apparently representing a new teachers' organization—could not vote either. The teachers, he claimed, had been elected as members and invited to the meeting illegally, while their very organization itself was useless, since the OPE already had a commission on primary education. The upshot of their pronouncements was that despite the appearance of new forces interested in participating in and contributing to the organization, there would be no change in its governance.

Not all board members were in Gintsburg and Bykhovskii's camp: the new secretary, Mark B. Ratner (the SERPist who had been a leading figure in the mass demonstrations of September and October 1905), objected that the definitions of participation and membership could not be changed arbitrarily according to the whim of board members; if they were, the current board would have to be considered illegitimate. (Ratner and board members Mandel'shtam and Gendel'man later resigned from their positions to protest the uncompromising position of the board.)[110] Tsitron, now a member of the commission on primary education, added that the wealthy old guard was attempting to alienate the organization's most active members: anyone who was not one of the elite had been denied the right to vote. Not only the OPE, but also the entire Kiev Jewish community, was dominated by the "antisocial . . . representatives of legality, order, and material power"—but soon, warned Tsitron ominously, Jewish communal institutions would be led by other people. The board was furthering its own decay.

Tsitron's revolutionary rhetoric was characteristic of the mood in many Jewish circles. The order (the word was repeated over and again in these debates) of old was slipping away, they felt, and those who continued to identify with its reactionary, top-down politics would be consigned to oblivion along with it. No institution or segment of society was exempt, and soon the OPE, the Kiev Jewish community and its institutions, and indeed all of society, would yield to the democratic impulse and to progress.

But the conservatives refused to agree that a democratic vote in and of itself signified legitimacy. After the assembly had voted to recognize the teachers as members with full rights, Bykhovskii and Gintsburg protested that the meeting, disturbed by outside elements for personal gain, was proceeding illegally; accordingly, they declared it unsanctioned (or unauthorized; *nesostoiavshimsia*). As stalwarts of the organization and defenders of the existing order, it seemed clear to them that proceedings taking place against the established rules were illegitimate and not to be tolerated. But Ratner retorted that it was the plutocrats who had come to settle personal accounts, a charge endorsed with cries of "We don't need guardians of order!" and "Obscurantists!"[111]

That personal conflicts were entering into the political debate was pointed out by a former member of the schools commission, who opined that the bitterness of the confrontation at the meeting was due not to an overall communal split between "old" and "new" camps, but rather to the personalities involved: Bykhovskii's dry formalism versus Tsitron's lack of collegiality and tyrannical leadership style. The goals of the teachers' organization were laudable, he wrote, but Tsitron should not have attempted to impose them forcibly upon the commission.[112]

Nonetheless, the support demonstrated for Tsitron in the general meetings suggests that there was, indeed, general dissatisfaction with the established leadership. And at the next meeting, on September 20, Tsitron led a successful coup by pushing through a proposal—opposed by the board—according to which new members would be approved by acclamation and not by ballot. Having lost this struggle, the board consequently resigned.[113] Newspaper reports on the meeting make it clear that the central issue continued to be the legitimacy of authority: who was sovereign in the Jewish community; in whose hands did the basis for power lie? As Tsitron and his supporters made clear, the Jewish masses were sovereign, and only the "electoral principle" would guarantee that they maintained hegemony in their communal organizations. In practice, this meant the election of all OPE commission chairmen and members, not their designation by the board, as well as autonomy for all OPE commissions, meaning freedom from subjection to board directives. The "democrats" maintained that the unwillingness of the board to allow change, which was tied up with its lack of initiative and "sluggishness," was undermining public faith in the OPE as a whole.[114] This, too, marked a significant break with the past. Organizations had previously set their agendas without concern for public support, at times even determining to reshape or reform the Jewish masses against their will. But the Jewish community (and Russian society as a whole) now demanded a broad base of support and faith in a public institution and, indeed, in the very government itself.

Various groups of OPE members acknowledged the impact of the 1905 Revolution in different ways. (As David Fishman writes of the struggle within the St. Petersburg OPE, "the very divisions and radical impulses that underlay the Russian revolution of 1905 were now being reenacted in microcosm within the confines of the organization.")[115] A memorandum submitted by a group of moderate members pointed out that the branch had been founded before 1905, in the era of Plehve and the reign of tyranny—and its governance had thus presumably been characteristic of that period—but now times had changed and the electoral principle had to be introduced throughout the society.[116] The organization would be best served by eliminating parochial class-minded thinking and giving everyone the opportunity to participate in communal affairs, continued the document. It recommended initiating programs such as reading rooms and lectures to serve the wider public, and attracting more women to active membership.[117] Other, more radical activists, such as SERPist Ratner, demanded that the OPE take on an active role in the revolutionary struggle, standing at the forefront of the movement of Jewish national liberation.[118] The Kiev OPE could be the leader of "education and culture as liberation" throughout the Russian southwest, joining forces with other constituents of the liberation movement. One way of achieving this goal would be to lower dues and thereby to attract the proletariat as members, for "education must become an affair of the people"; more generally, the OPE's activities must be designed to "meet the needs of the Jewish masses." As a means toward the end of national liberation, the OPE had to embody the ideals of the democratic future.[119]

The radical opposition insisted not only that the old guard, creatures and guardians of the old order, would never be able to introduce the reforms needed to transform Kiev's institutions, but also that they were completely unfit to lead the Jewish people in this era of the revival of the Jewish nation and Jewish self-respect. They had always shown themselves too willing to abandon Jewish pride by negotiating and compromising with the "enemy," while real leaders helped Jews "stand erect" and did not engage in "deputations to the executioner."[120] The OPE was yet another communal institution that they wished to control through the force of their wealth. Since they lacked any real authority from the people, however, their monopoly over the leadership of Kiev's communal institutions had to be brought to an end. For those who were doubtful that such a "revolution" was in the best interests of the community, the opposition leaders reassured those present that not only would the current conflict bring about a change in leadership, but that it would also attract new energy to the society and revive its activities.[121]

The issue of membership was a major point of friction. The established leadership was clearly anxious about the impact on the organization of an influx of poorly acculturated teachers and artisans. One member warned that eighty melamdim joining the OPE would not further the cause of enlightenment but possibly hinder it. At the same meeting, the approval of new members by acclamation was proclaimed illegal by certain old-timers who insisted that the board had to authorize the members first. From their perspective, a reluctance to share power was justified: as they saw it, their experience in communal affairs, influence with important officials, and wealth made them the natural leaders of the community. They viewed themselves as guarantors of the stability and well-being of the community, due to their long experience in communal affairs; "by contrast, complete novices" at communal leadership would inevitably fail their constituents.[122] The old guard also had a radically different approach to accomplishing organizational priorities from that of the revolution-inspired democrats; they were accustomed and resigned to the fact that, in the undergoverned and bureaucracy-heavy Russian Empire, one could not be impatient with the slow course of any project, no matter how important. As Lev Brodsky counseled at an OPE general meeting, "Time will take care of everything." For these veterans of communal affairs, the coming of a "new era" was greatly in doubt. Nonetheless, change had indeed come to the Kiev Jewish community, and its influence was being felt in all corners, even at the Representation for Jewish Welfare.

The Democratization of the Representation for Jewish Welfare

At the same time that the Kiev OPE was being taken over by democrats, important changes were taking place in Kiev's Jewish communal governing body, leading to the first-ever elections for the members of the Representation for Jewish Welfare, in November 1906. As no original records of the body have survived, what exactly prompted the introduction of an elected board is unknown, but it is clear that the revolution and its accompanying upheaval had brought the years of criticism of the board to a head and made the further existence of an appointed body an impossibility. As the new board's secretary wrote in 1910, "the current board took shape immediately after 1905 and was permeated with the spirit of that year."[123] (Of course the final decision was up to the municipal authorities, and probably the governor-general and the minister of internal affairs as well.)

Until 1906, the board had had nine members; now, twenty-four members were elected by about one hundred electors from Kiev's synagogues and Jewish communal institutions.[124] According to secretary G. E. Gurevich, the elections, organization, and transparency (*otchetnost'*) of the Representation were to a certain degree considered models among Russian Jewry, and were even the subject of discussion at the 1909 Kovno conference on Jewish communal affairs.[125] The elections, as with those for the State Duma, were characterized by open campaigns among various parties and groups, many of them calling for fundamental changes in the culture of Jewish welfare in Kiev: allocation of communal resources not by "the whim of large contributors or their stooges" but according to communal needs; attentive oversight of finances; and the democratization of communal affairs, including greater civility, openness, and equity.[126]

While the representatives had previously been drawn from the merchant estate alone, professionals and artisans were now included as well.[127] According to guild and professional listings in the municipal almanac of 1907, five of the twenty-four were merchants, and another six were members of the free professions (doctors, lawyers, and an engineer); thus, it does seem that a majority of the newly elected representatives hailed from a socioeconomically diverse background.[128] (Only two of them, Zaks and Gol'denberg, had sat on the Representation in 1895.)[129] The influence of 1905 is clear from Gurevich's statement that "attracting artisans to participate in the Representation became logical and right from the moment representatives of the urban workers and peasants began to participate in the governing of the Russian Empire." Many probably shared his opinion that what was good for the Russian Empire was good for its Jewish communities as well. (Note, however, that he made no claim that the Jewish community either was or should have been more democratic or inclusive before 1905 than the surrounding society had been.) However, there were apparently only two artisans on the Representation, making up 8 percent of all members in a city where artisans formed a sizable proportion of the Jewish population.[130] This phenomenon can only be explained if two (and only two) seats were reserved for artisans; that is, representation was not proportional.

That a new era had arrived seemed evident from the new Representation's first achievement, one that had long been desired: a reduction in, and eventual elimination of, the subsidy for the Kiev police force that had been appropriated from the kosher meat tax.[131] According to Gurevich, important reforms were implemented in the institution's procedures to do away with all corruption: previously, relatives and friends of representatives had been shown favoritism in the awarding of contracts, but now the bids process was conducted according to strict standards. These changes actually brought down costs associated with providing for the poor.[132] The Representation members instituted regulations for all procedures throughout the organization—including, most importantly, in its accounting—and began to issue reports and hired a director for the main office.

The representatives used their first two years in office to study and expand the Representation's various branches of activity. Results were noticeable immediately; Gurevich noted that the Representation responded "more or less sensitively" to the needs of the Jewish community, and to emergencies that arose such as floods, epidemics, and mass expulsions. Not only was assistance provided, but commissions were created and legal aid made available—signs of a more scientific approach to philanthropy. The result, wrote Gurevich, was an upswing in public trust in the Representation and a consequent increase in income, both from general collections and individual contributors.[133] This point is crucial: before 1905, the representatives had simply relied on the kosher tax revenues in additional to the contributions of individual plutocrats, as they saw fit. Now, the body had to earn and keep the public trust—not least because contributions, and thus the Representation's financial health, now depended on it. The new Representation also augmented communal assets when one of the members volunteered to take on the lease for the kosher meat excise at a substantially higher price than before, increasing the proceeds by almost one-third (from 144,000 to 187,000 rubles a year).[134] Funds available for support of Kiev's communal institutions grew by over one-quarter in only two years, so that by 1908 that sum had reached 260,000 rubles.[135]

Observers from the outside, however, were not as enthusiastic about the results of the reforms and complained that, in effect, little had changed since the old days of the appointed Representation. In 1908, L. Dynin (a member of the OPE's Adult Education Commission) wrote to the Russian Jewish newspaper *Razsvet* that the Representation's response to a recent flood in Podol had left much to be desired: the hundreds of Jewish victims who had taken refuge in the Contract House, a large municipal building, were not being provided with enough food. According to Dynin, the Representation had not initiated the systematic response that was required: registering the number of victims, estimating their losses, and finding appropriate shelter for them.[136]

L. Efimov, another correspondent to *Razsvet,* was stronger in his critique, censuring the new Representation not only for "inconsistency and carelessness" but also "indifference and negligence," terms reminiscent of pre-1905 criticisms. Promises to study important issues went unfulfilled, educational institutions continued to be underfunded, and large portions of the budget were still spent on salaries of corrupt functionaries—prompted by the fancy of one or another wealthy bigwig.[137] A Jewish communal leader from Warsaw visited Kiev in 1908 or 1909 and commented that while the generosity of Kiev's Jews was admirable, the funds were not being put to the best use; Warsaw's Jewish institutions were run much more cheaply.[138]

Both internal and external critics agreed that certain areas were in need of improvement, most notably organization–client relations. The Representation's main offices remained understaffed even after the reorganization, and applicants for aid traveled long distances only to be turned away or told that they would have to come again several days in a row. Dynin claimed that the office staff treated applicants coldly and that the aid commission met so infrequently that the demoralized recipients often had to wait months to receive their 5 or 10 rubles; Gurevich maintained that a more educated and accountable staff was what was needed. Both agreed that the attempt that had been made to assign Representation members to office duty for several hours per week had been a failure, since only a few members had shown up at all, and even then they came late or stayed for only a short while.[139] At the 1908 general meeting, some complained that applicants often found the office totally empty! Gurevich claimed that the primary problem was that the Representation members expected too much of the office staff and did not fully carry out their own responsibilities—exhibiting the same lack of energy as before. Apparently, district guardians from among the Representation members had been assigned to evaluate applications in individual neighborhoods, but had never actually made themselves available for the task.[140] Representation and individual commission reports—nonexistent before 1905—were now being issued late because members refused take responsibility for preparing them, and dumped them on the office staff.[141] Critic Efimov charged that, as ever, thousands of rubles were being wasted on the salaries of rabbis and kashruth supervisors, some of whom were collecting wages for doing absolutely nothing or even selling their positions to the highest bidder.[142]

A primary complaint against the Representation, as in the pre-1905 period, was the favored treatment that certain institutions continued to receive. In 1907, subsidies for most institutions were cut while grants to the Jewish Hospital and the Brodsky State Jewish School were untouched or even increased; the Jewish Hospital continued to receive about one-third of all allocations.[143] Fourteen community schools received 4,260 rubles, 10 percent of their annual budget, while the Brodsky School alone was allocated 6,000 rubles—almost a third of its budget.[144] Critics complained that the community schools were poorly run and in terrible condition.[145] Gurevich agreed that the plutocrats continued to insist on special benefits for their favored institutions, such as the Jewish Hospital and the Zaitsev Clinic, and to shield them from the oversight of the Representation, which provided the lion's share of their funding (or at least for the Hospital—60 percent), though in their capacity as Representation members, they hypocritically agreed to the importance of Representation supervision of *all* subsidized institutions.[146] The hospital continued to ask for ever more money from the Representation while spending more than double per patient what other hospitals spent.[147]

Gurevich came out forcefully against the self-serving attitude of these wealthy Representation members, claiming that the new system of accountability was not something to which they could easily adapt: "They do not like either collegial discussions and decisions of issues, or being subject publicly and openly to public opinion." In sum, Gurevich maintained, the wealthy Representation members treated communal affairs as "a kind of game" that they never considered serious enough to warrant investing a great deal of their time in a thorough manner. Representation members from the middle class and the intelligentsia, who could be relied upon for greater equanimity and even-handedness, were too busy with their own affairs to give adequate time to the problems of the Representation.[148] At the same time, they raised no objections to the city's long-established practice of taking thousands of rubles from the kosher tax revenues for itself; even as poor Jews were forced to give their hard-earned rubles to the city, which gave them nothing in return, the wealthy Jews spent huge sums on non-Jewish philanthropic causes to aid Kiev's Christian population. "Where is your energy, where is your dedication to the interests of the Jewish population?" asked Gurevich of the Jewish elite, echoing the critic of the Representation in *Khronika Voskhoda* almost a decade earlier.[149] The middle class had no time for communal affairs, it seemed, while the haute bourgeoisie lacked both competence and patience.

Another example of a wealthy leader objecting to encroachment upon his territory as part of the reforms was that of M. R. Zaks, a prominent industrialist and one of the longest-serving Jewish communal leaders in Kiev. Zaks had headed the burial commission until the Representation voted to liquidate the commission's independent finances and merge them with the general finances of the Representation. According to Gurevich, Zaks considered this move "a personal insult," resigning his chairmanship and all further participation in Representation affairs.[150] As this particular incident demonstrated, reforms could be implemented institutionally, but it was another matter altogether to change the venerable practices and ingrained habits of communal leadership. Moreover, the election of middle- and working-class members could not bring significant change to the Representation if the only members who had sufficient time to devote to communal responsibilities remained the wealthy.

Electoral Politics in Kiev's Prayer Houses

The "electoral principle" was now so central a principle in Jewish life that it even extended to the religious sphere. In 1907, a group of poor parishioners of a Kiev prayer house submitted a petition to the authorities requesting that the usual minimum annual dues of 10 rubles required to participate in synagogue board elections be lowered, since most working-class Jews could not afford such a sum:

> All of us parishioners would like those elected as members of the board to be worthy individuals from the ranks of the poor parishioners, who form the majority of the worshipers. Among the parishioners, who are made up mostly of artisans, there are very few paying dues of 10 rubles. Three-quarters of the parishioners pay 3 rubles and higher, but do not have the right to participate in the elections. . . . We are pained that we cannot participate in the elections and thus concede the fate of the prayer house to a small group of prosperous individuals, who have only their personal interests in mind and do not care about us.[151]

The revolution had come to the synagogue. These petitioners were no longer working on the assumption that those with more money should automatically be granted the privilege of governing an institution, for, in a break from the past, it was no longer taken for granted that the wealthy understood the needs of the poor and worked in their best interest. The only truly deciding factor was that poor Jews formed the majority of parishioners, and should thus control the "fate" of their prayer house. And it was no mistake that they insisted that "worthy" men could not only be drawn from the ranks of the wealthy—poor men could be worthy too.

Several petitions relating to the rabbinical elections of 1906 further demonstrate the growing importance attached to elections and universal suffrage. The provincial authorities received memorials from parishioners of two Podol prayer houses, charging that elections for rabbinical electors (who would then elect the Crown rabbi) had been based on corrupted parishioner lists and should be invalidated.[152] In both cases, the complainants alleged that a small group of parishioners had seized control of the governance of their prayer house against the will of the majority. One petition asserted that at Prayer House No. 10, "it is convenient and profitable [or advantageous, *vygodno*] for a small handful of bosses that all elections at the prayer house and its entire governance depend exclusively on those bosses and their stooges, and not on the masses of parishioners."[153] As in the previous example, the assumption here was that the governance of the prayer house should, by rights, be vested firmly in the majority. The issue of class also seems to have been at play, at least at Prayer House No. 10, judging from the petitioners' claim that only those parishioners who had contributed to the prayer house had been invited to participate in the elections when, as the document stressed as its very first point, the law of 1901 allowed all parishioners to vote for rabbinical electors—"without any relation to how much one or another parishioner contributes to the prayer house or even contributes anything at all."[154]

The complainants asserted that the ruling clique had been voted off of the prayer house governing board in 1904, but had refused to yield power to the new board. The fact that a complaint was only being registered now, in 1906, points again to the influence of the events of 1905 and the much-heightened sensitivity within the Jewish community to issues of representation, suffrage, and equity in communal governance. The vocabulary chosen to express the outrage of those who felt they had been wronged was similar or identical to that used in other communal battles that we have seen: those who were accused of holding power illegitimately were called "cliques" (*kuchki*) of "pretenders," their actions "arbitrary," the elections they had corrupted "illegal" and "unlawful," and those they had harmed "the general masses of parishioners."[155]

Politics was even inserting itself into the life of the elite Merchants' Synagogue, founded and patronized by Lev Brodsky. A 1906 report related that a worshiper had intended to make an announcement about an upcoming boycott of a local Black Hundreds member, but was prevented from speaking by the synagogue wardens, just as on other occasions they had stopped Zionists and Territorialists from giving political speeches—even when they had received permission from Brodsky. In one instance, the speaker was dragged off the pulpit and the police called.[156] No aspect or arena of Jewish life was immune from politicization.

The OPE: Power, but No Money

That the Representation for Jewish Welfare, despite its newly elected status, was still a stronghold of the plutocratic establishment is made clear by its relationship with the Kiev branch of the OPE. In 1907, the year after the coup that replaced the old guard leadership of the organization with nationalists, the OPE requested 11,000 rubles from the kosher tax revenues—but received only 4,000 toward its library and adult education activities (a sum that was later further reduced). The Representation explained that it could not grant funds to the OPE for support of Jewish schools in Kiev since all Jewish education in the city was under the exclusive purview of the Representation itself.[157] Clearly, the Representation was not about to allow the parvenu OPE to encroach upon its territory, and that hostility was probably aggravated in the minds of some of the wealthier Representation members by the memory of the previous year's coup.

But the OPE, in turn, resolved that if it could not give financial assistance to Kiev's schools, it would at least provide them with "moral" support—in other words, organizational assistance. To this end, its schools commission began consulting with individual school boards about how they might petition the government for legalization and thus do away with the semi-legal limbo in which they had existed for years. This was to be the first step toward the eventual unification of the schools into some sort of integral educational system that would be managed by the OPE. But the OPE went even further, entering into discussions with the school boards about an institutional linkage between the boards and the OPE itself, whereby members of the school boards would sit on the OPE's schools commission and the commission, in turn, would send one of its members to each of the boards. The agreement also stipulated that, although responsibility for the financial well-being of each school still rested with the individual school boards, the OPE would have oversight over the schools' budgets. Presumably, this arrangement would correct what the OPE called the schools' "abnormal existence" due to lack of regulation or communal supervision. In effect, then, the OPE was planning a virtual takeover of Jewish education in Kiev—in direct violation of the Representation for Jewish Welfare's directive that the city's Jewish schools remain under its direction alone. The OPE was also demonstrating that leadership in communal affairs was not dependent on money alone, but also on the initiative and innovation that it felt the Representation lacked—for clearly the schools were cooperating with the OPE despite the fact that they had received no funding from it at all (surely this had at least something to do with the leftist leanings of many Jewish teachers, who had been an active force at many of the crucial OPE meetings in 1906). Moreover, in 1907 the OPE also submitted a petition to the authorities for permission to establish four of its own Jewish schools in Kiev, plainly another attempt to stake out a place for itself in an arena that officially belonged to the Representation for Jewish Welfare.[158]

In 1908, the Representation for Jewish Welfare answered the OPE's actions by slashing its subsidy for the coming year in half, to 2,000 rubles. OPE activist Tsitron charged that the cut was "an act of revenge,"[159] while the society's board appealed to the Representation to restore its funding and even to transfer sums designated for the boards of Kiev's Jewish schools to the OPE, for the purpose of creating a "unified schools commission" with a uniform curriculum for all schools.[160] As before, the issue of public accountability was central, the OPE calling itself "the only legal Jewish educational institution in Russia working under the permanent oversight of the Jewish population." Significantly, the OPE seemed to propose a quid pro quo, offering the Representation the opportunity for oversight over the educational society's activities in return, as it were, for supplemental funding and the right to govern Jewish education in Kiev through the unified schools commission.[161] At the same time, despite the OPE board's repeated insistence that it was not interested in subsidizing schools in Kiev because of the Representation's policy of exclusive control, it announced plans to grant a subsidy to one of those schools, which would then come under the jurisdiction of the OPE schools commission.[162]

At the general meeting of the OPE membership of October 21, 1908, M. L. Tsitron introduced a resolution to appeal to the municipal authorities to overturn the Representation's cuts in the OPE allocation; others, however, urged peaceful means to resolve this intra-Jewish quarrel, and the resolution did not pass.[163] This turn of events points to a subtle shift in the course of Jewish communal politics and leadership: activists with a tendency to be outspoken, idiosyncratic, and even choleric such as Lur'e and Tsitron had no qualms about appealing to the Russian authorities for redress. Lur'e's semiofficial position in the government bureaucracy only made that path more appealing to him, for his authority as Crown rabbi came from the state itself. However, the OPE, an organization with a clear nationalist orientation, not only had no links to the state but was also constantly engaged in struggles to extract more rights and funding from the government for Jewish education; moreover, many of its officers had been active in the revolutionary movement and continued to be hostile to the tsarist regime. The majority's choice to keep the battle with the Representation within the fold, then, may well be characteristic of the new brand of Russian Jewish welfare, educational, and cultural organizations that became prevalent throughout the empire in this period.

If the OPE saw itself as pitted against the state, why—we might ask—did it continue to seek funding from the Representation for Jewish Welfare, which was, after all, an organ of the Kiev municipal government? It might have seemed more logical to break away from any dependence on the Representation. There was a different logic at work here, however. As board member L. E. Mandel'berg reported to the Central Committee of the OPE in St. Petersburg in 1908, relying solely on charitable donations or philanthropic institutions for support would not enable the OPE to achieve its goals and, indeed, was contrary to the very principles on which the society was based.[164] Receiving a subsidy from the kosher tax revenues that the Representation for Jewish Welfare distributed represented the support of the Jewish people itself for the OPE's activities. In an ideal society, Mandel'berg explained, universal education would be financed through universal and equitable taxes, but since the current state of affairs instead imposed a very inequitable tax, namely the kosher tax, the most that could be done was to use it correctly: to ensure that the money taken from the poor masses was used for their spiritual and material needs. One of the most pressing needs, in the eyes of the OPE leaders, was education, a vision that Representation members clearly did not share; Mandel'berg noted that they had given less than 10 percent of the kosher tax revenues to education-related causes. He also commented on the hypocrisy of the Representation members in denying the OPE funding because some of its activities took place outside of Kiev, when free Jewish medical institutions in Kiev, funded heavily with kosher tax money, served primarily non-Kievans.

A more cynical interpretation might be that the OPE was simply lacking the money it needed to carry out its activities, and had to have recourse to the kosher excise funds to survive; Mandel'berg's explanation was as good as any. In any case, there was clearly ambivalence about receiving kosher excise funds: while they were a symbol of popular support for an organization or cause, they also meant having to dirty one's hands in Jewish communal politics, tussle with the conservative leadership of the community, and fight government bureaucrats for a greater share of the wealth.[165]

The 1908 General Meeting of the Representation for Jewish Welfare

In December 1908, the general meeting of members and electors of the Representation for Jewish Welfare threw into sharp relief both the animosity between the Representation, little changed since the pre-1905 era, and the OPE, as well as Gurevich's charge that the Representation's plutocrats were hostile to the new openness of communal affairs. Here, as at the OPE meetings two years before, the "old guard" faced an "opposition" of democrats led by Mark Tsitron, though now that opposition was part of the OPE leadership, and the mutual hostility of the two institutions and their leaderships was clear and open. The meeting helps explain why the elections and reforms did little to change the organizational culture and politics of the Representation: the established leadership and its basic assumptions, especially as personified by Lev Brodsky and his somewhat domineering personality (hardly surprising for the surviving "king" of Kiev's Jews), remained the same, though masked by populist rhetoric. The record of the meeting also reveals the assumptions and tactics of the plutocrats and especially Brodsky, who clearly viewed himself as the natural leader of the community and, though the elected chairman of an elected Representation, saw no need for democratic procedures in the operations of the Representation itself. Also quite clear is the extent to which the authority of the Representation, supposedly a collective of twenty-four elected members, resided in the person of Brodsky.

As the local paper *Kievskaia mysl'* (Kiev Thought) reported, it was only after many requests and entreaties from the electors from Kiev's synagogues and philanthropic institutions that Brodsky agreed to call the meeting at all.[166] He opened it by announcing that he would preside and set the agenda (though the rules called for the election of a special meeting chairman), and would not tolerate any criticism. "I have called you here not so that you might criticize our activities, but only to read you my plan to replace the korobka with communal self-taxation"; the electors were also to be familiarized with the Representation's activities over the year. When several individuals protested against the meeting being conducted in this fashion, Brodsky replied, "The administration permitted me to call this meeting with the provision that I would personally preside over it." In other words, the Jews of

Kiev were not to take the democratic functioning of their communal institutions for granted; it was still the influence of plutocrats such as Brodsky—which influence had always vested him with claims to Jewish leadership—that made such meetings as this possible. Without him, the meeting would not have been permitted at all, so no one could rightfully oppose his presiding over it.

If we try to see this meeting through Brodsky's eyes, we might understand that his perspective was quite different. The fact that he had a plan to introduce a system of communal self-taxation as already existed in Warsaw and other cities was "progressive" in a certain sense; rather than maintaining the status quo, he was now actively working to overturn it in favor of a more equitable system. Nor was this a new initiative for him, as he and David Margolin had submitted a proposal of this kind to the governor-general in 1905. And, given the bitter intracommunal rifts that had riven Jewish Kiev over the previous years, Brodsky may have felt that maintaining strict control over the meeting, rather than allowing it to deteriorate into petty squabbling, would be in the best interests of all present.

Throughout the meeting, Brodsky frequently spoke in the first person when referring to the Representation as a whole, and kept the debate focused on himself: when Tsitron began to speak at length about the proposed budget for the Representation, Brodsky insisted that Tsitron respond to each individual budget entry after it had been introduced and described by Brodsky himself. As neither Brodsky nor Tsitron wanted to cede the spotlight to the other, the meeting threatened to become a face-off between two imperious and domineering personalities. At the end of the meeting, Brodsky responded to a move to put the most important issues to a vote by expressing his sympathy for them but refusing to hold a vote, as he was certain that all those assembled were also in favor of the proposals. This may have been the most logical decision from his perspective; his natural claim to leadership and accurate perception of the community's wishes and needs meant that the formalities of democracy were unnecessary. Another possibility is that, in the interests of communal unity and peace, he wished to avoid a vote that would inevitably bring with it additional strife and recriminations.

It is no accident, however, that the proposals to be voted on were initiated by OPE activists and related to OPE institutions. In the first instance, those activists protested the disproportionately large cut in the Representation subsidy to the OPE, and demanded that the subsidy be increased. They also proposed eliminating the rent that the OPE was paying to house its Saturday school for adults at the Brodsky School, one of Brodsky's pet institutions. Moreover, they demanded action on the establishment of a school for midwives and physicians' assistants at the Jewish Hospital, the darling of the plutocrats, because—the OPE members claimed—students of existing schools had been imploring them to create just such a school. The OPE members also proposed establishing a unified schools commission under the auspices of their organization, to which several Representation members objected; one of the bodies that would be subject to the unification was the Representation's own schools commission. Perhaps attempting to play the peacemaker, Brodsky was not opposed to this plan, saying, "I never objected and never will object to such a united commission." There is no doubt, however, that a struggle for power and resources was under way between the Representation, with Brodsky at its head, and the OPE, led by Tsitron. The battle to gain power, as well as the possibility of losing it, were motivating factors for action in communal politics.

Another important issue that resurfaced here was the legitimacy of power: as in the struggle between Lur'e and the plutocracy, the question was who had the right to lead and speak for the Jewish population. On this, the Representation and the OPE leadership (mostly in the person of Tsitron) clashed throughout the course of the meeting, each group claiming to care for and understand the needs of the Jewish masses and obliquely charging that the other group was not as sensitive to those needs. OPE activists claimed that young Jewish girls, students at Kiev's midwifery schools, were asking the OPE for help because they were forced to go hungry in order to pay exorbitant tuitions; the need for a Jewish midwifery school at the Kiev Jewish Hospital (funded in large measure by the Representation) was evident, but the Representation was preventing it. Brodsky answered that he was waiting to study the response of the Jewish population of Warsaw and Odessa to similar schools recently founded there, as such schools performed autopsies—not permitted by Jewish law. Brodsky thus responded to the OPE's indirect assertion that it was the address of choice for Kiev Jews in need by showing that he, too, was sensitive to the needs—material as well as religious—of the Jewish masses. Several other Representation members responded to criticism of their performance with the assertion that they were trying to ease the plight of the Jewish poor as much as circumstances allowed—and that the same shortcomings could be found in any society, including the OPE. In other words, as they saw things, the OPE was in reality no better than the Representation in being sensitive to the needs of the Jewish street.

The OPE's Great Compromise

In point of fact, the OPE board was in a bind: the nationalist coup had achieved the ideal of a totally new board, free of the conservative plutocrats, but had also led to a severe shortage of funds due to cuts in the kosher tax allocation. Neither could the organization expect to receive donations from the wealthy individuals who usually supported Jewish organizations in Kiev, for most of them had disapproved of the coup. The 1907 annual report noted plaintively, "the city's wealthy men are keeping completely aloof from the society, for obvious reasons."[167] One wag had commented only half-jokingly at an OPE meeting in 1905, "That's why we voted for Brodsky as chairman, so we would always have money!"[168] And indeed, there was serious discussion at one of the first general meetings after the coup about inviting Lev Brodsky to serve as chairman of the new board. On one hand, Brodsky's role as the "king" of Kiev Jews was so entrenched that he was seen by some as above the fray, and a vital figurehead for any Jewish organization; on the other, his contributions were essential for the health of any society. Apparently, though, having him as chairman was too risky and had too many associations with the old order; Dr. Max Mandel'shtam was elected instead.[169]

Not surprisingly, the lack of funding proved to be a serious problem: the 1907 annual report repeated over and again that many important activities had to be put on hold "in view of limited resources."[170] The OPE was already facing criticism from the community for its lack of accomplishments.[171] Even a member of the society's own Adult Education Commission, L. E. Dynin, wrote in the newspaper *Khronika evreiskoi zhizhi* (Chronicle of Jewish Life) that the society was good at promising things but not delivering on them.[172] What was the use of the revolution in leadership if nothing had changed—except for a radical loss of funding?

Moreover, members and supporters of the old board now accused the new one of abrogating the very democratic principles it had advocated so strenuously; for example, of arbitrarily eliminating organizational committees. Tsitron was personally accused of "despotic leadership and usurpation of power"—the same allegations he had originally made against the plutocratic establishment! The new board was also imputed with arranging for its new pedagogical commission to be elected not by all of Kiev's Jewish teachers, but rather only those teachers who supported the "abandonment" of Hebrew.[173] A charge of manipulation of democratic procedures was quite serious, especially in the days of revolution and incipient democracy.

As we have seen, despite the OPE board's appeals to the Representation for Jewish Welfare, the society's subsidy from the kosher tax was not restored, and in 1909 the board took the fateful step of recommending that Lev Brodsky and Baron V. G. Gintsburg be elected to the board. The invitation to the two men was scorned by some OPE members as a slap in the face of the democratization process, but the apparent consensus was that the society had to make the compromise for its own good, and both men were voted onto the board (though Gintsburg declined the position).[174] It is interesting to note that while Brodsky served as chairman of the Representation for Jewish Welfare, so hostile to the OPE, and had not made any financial contributions to the society since the 1906 coup, he *had* made several significant in-kind donations, paying for the electrical and maintenance expenses of the OPE's Saturday adult education classes, which were housed at the Jewish school that he had founded, and making available one of his country houses for an excursion of the society's kindergarten.[175] Clearly, he had been unwilling to abandon the educational organization altogether, and perhaps this history provided the board with the face it need to save when inviting the king of Kiev Jewry to join them. Compromise could no longer be avoided.

The OPE's decision may also have been affected by a government crackdown on similar educational organizations with a nationalist bent: in 1908, the Kiev Literacy Society, with a pronounced Ukrainophile bias in its activities, and the Polish society Oświata (Education) had been shut down by the authorities.[176] Members of the literacy society had also played a role in the revolutionary activities of 1905.[177] Bringing in men with contacts in high places like Lev Brodsky would no doubt help to defend the society from administrative attack.

The changes that Brodsky ushered in were striking. Though the character of the society's programs was apparently not affected, its fiscal standing improved dramatically, as did—perhaps more significantly—its standing among Kiev's Jewish haute bourgeoisie. Brodsky chaired a new finances commission (listed ahead of all the other commissions in the 1909 annual report, signaling its crucial role in the organization's operations), and three of the seven members were new faces in OPE governance; two of them (L. B. Ginzburg and D. S. Margolin) were wealthy industrialists, while a third,

I. P. Kel'berin, was Brodsky's right-hand man and a powerful force in Kiev Jewry. Brodsky was also listed as honorary chairman—a new title, apparently created for him—of the library commission and the board of guardians of the society's Model Heder.[178] And he proved his worth by immediately calling a special fund-raising meeting at which he personally pledged 3,000 rubles, attracting almost 1,000 rubles in additional donations from attendees. (By contrast, the largest single donation in the previous year had been 400 rubles.)[179]

A new gala concert and ball, organized by Brodsky and to which invitations were sent in his name, netted more than 5,000 rubles for the OPE, well over three times the receipts from the concert of Jewish folk music held the year before.[180] The new event was also a significant shift for the public profile of the organization: folk music, while clearly in keeping with the character of a nationalist society devoted to the education of the masses, did not have the appeal of a society soiree to which, moreover, one had to be invited by none other than Lev Brodsky himself! Indeed, one Jewish nationalist complained that but for the Jews in attendance, there was nothing Jewish about the evening at all; one might hear an Italian aria or a Russian folk song, but "not the slightest hint of a Jewish word, motif, sound. . . ."[181] Despite such complaints, however, no one could deny that the Kiev Branch of the OPE was no longer a pariah but was now an integral part of the Kiev Jewish establishment. In subsequent years, similar and even more successful fund-raisers netted well over 6,000 rubles.[182]

Another tactic using Brodsky's name, influence, and contacts was to send out letters to specific individuals asking for their support of the OPE.[183] Brodsky's first year on the board also saw a tremendous increase in special income, consisting mostly of interest-bearing securities; these, too, were likely linked to the "king."[184] Perhaps most important of all for the nationalist leaders of the OPE, the society's subsidy from kosher tax revenues was restored to its previous level before the split between the two institutions had taken place.[185] Indeed, by 1911 five of the seven members of the executive board of the Representation for Jewish Welfare also sat on the board or on various commissions of the OPE, and by 1913 almost one-third of the members of the Representation's schools commission were also active in the OPE.[186] The days of exile and ostracism were over.

The 1909 annual report noted in an understated fashion that "the activity of the board . . . differed slightly from [that] of the previous five years"; thanks to the significant influx of resources in 1909, "the board succeeded in realizing its goals."[187] Indeed, the new infusion of funds enabled the society to carry through with many more activities than ever before. However, Brodsky's presence did not enable the society to achieve its long-standing goal of dramatically increasing its membership rolls; the new contributions were mostly in the form of one-time donations, perhaps pointing to a dependence on Brodsky's influence rather than any new commitment to the OPE and its goals.[188] The society might be "serving the people," but it did not achieve the popular mandate it had so ardently wished for in the form of a broad membership base.

We have noted that the arrival of Brodsky did not influence the OPE's direction. Remarkably, the organization was actually exporting the communal revolution that it had achieved in Kiev to the smaller cities and towns of Kiev province, where it actively encouraged the development of modern community schools. (Moshe Rozenblat claims that, thanks to the Zionist tendencies of OPE board members, all the schools in Ukraine supported by the Kiev OPE adopted a Hebrew-language curriculum.)[189] For legal reasons, Jewish communities lacked the rights to establish girls' schools, and thus the OPE's policy was to advocate the founding of official Societies for the Care of Poor Children, which were permitted to open schools of their own. As the OPE clearly acknowledged, these new societies served as a welcome counterweight to the influence of both individual benefactors and conservative communal elders, and created schools that were publicly accountable: "The opening of girls' schools on the basis of society charters freed the schools from the most undesirable tutelage of private individuals and transformed them from semi-official into entirely legal institutions, under broad communal oversight."[190] The new schools, then, led to the development of an array of societies in the image of the Kiev OPE itself—declaring their independence from the communal establishment in favor of a nationalist agenda.

Other Institutions

Other communal institutions in Kiev also experienced various forms of democratization after 1905, lasting for longer or shorter periods. The Society for the Care of Poor Jewish Artisans and Workers of Kiev, for example, was founded in the last decades of the nineteenth century as a branch of the Representation for Jewish Welfare. In 1906, it gained its independence and, as its annual report explained, participated with other "progressive social groups" in demanding reform of the Representation; namely, sound representation and just distribution of the meat tax proceeds.[191] The goals enumerated in its charter included the intellectual improvement of Kiev's Jewish artisans, as well as their moral and material betterment, and the charter provided for the establishment of a number of institutions oriented toward self-help and education, such as vocational bureaus, schools, and savings and pension funds. These were in addition to the traditional establishments providing assistance of a more temporary nature, such as almshouses (*bogadel'ni*).[192] (The following year, recognizing that one-time monetary assistance was not sufficient in and of itself, the board created a special commission for reorganization to figure out which additional types of aid the society should provide.)[193] At the same time, the society's board tried to attract a large number of artisans as members in an attempt to achieve "democratization," while acknowledging that it also needed to attract well-to-do members in order to grow. The society's membership did indeed expand dramatically, from 134 to 273, half of whom were "supporting members," a category created in 1905 so that artisans and workers could join as full members (notwithstanding the appellation) for only 1 ruble a year.[194] Five artisans had also been recruited to sit on the board alongside wealthy and middle-class members.

The annual report for 1906 was composed in the revolutionary spirit of the day, voicing disapproval of the current "conditions of State life" (i.e., the social and political order); the establishment of a loan fund, it declared, was especially significant "for those who view private philanthropy as a necessary evil under the present social order, which does away with human dignity." The report took jabs at both the Russian government's policies and the indifference of the Kiev Jewish elite, intimating that the bitter circumstances in Kiev would not improve until Russian Jews received equal rights, for those Jews living in the city with full rights would remain unsympathetic to the rightless Jews. It concluded by looking forward to the day when the Kiev Jewish community would "display responsiveness to its blood-brothers-laborers [*svoim rodnym po krovi brat'iam-truzhennikam*]."[195]

Despite these promising changes, the next year supporting members had dropped to just 20 percent of the total, suggesting that once the original enthusiasm had worn off, many artisans saw little reason to maintain their membership, or perhaps economic circumstances were so dire that they felt they could not even afford the 1 ruble. However, the number of artisans on the board had doubled to ten.[196] As OPE board member L. Dynin wrote in 1908, most of the members present at the general meeting were artisans, while those of the intelligentsia were mostly absent; at the same time, most board members were nonartisans (twenty-six out of thirty-six).[197] The annual report appealed to the membership at large for its participation, or perhaps its financial assistance, noting that "only with the concerted [or amicable] cooperation [*druzhnaia rabota*] of the members of the society will its high and humane ideals be realized."[198] Overall, this story suggests that after the exhilaration of the revolution had passed, it was difficult to maintain working-class participation in philanthropic organizations, even those that were intended to support and provide a voice for laborers. The active support of middle-class intelligenty continued to be crucial in the day-to-day workings of bodies like the Society for the Care of Poor Jewish Artisans and Workers.

The next year, the board announced that it was preparing to establish a girls' vocational school and a tailoring school for both sexes, and would prepare plans to found a technical school for artisans (*remeslennyi muzei*). The fact that vocational training would be made available to girls was important, since the only Jewish trade school in Kiev, the Brodsky School, was for boys only.[199] Perhaps it is not by chance that this working-class organization proposed to fill a crucial gap left by an institution established by Kiev's Jewish plutocrats.

We do not have a great deal of evidence about traditional hevrot in Kiev, but the pinkas of Hevrat magidei tehilim shel Kiev (Kiev Hevra for the Recitation of Psalms)—formed by worshipers at the Rozenberg (Shchekavitskaia Street) prayer house in Kiev—provides a tantalizing glimpse of the lives of pious working-class Jews. The record book, which covers the years 5655–5676 (1895–1916), shows that this hevra, and probably others like it, was not focused exclusively on its religious mission but also served as a primitive mutual aid society, the dues providing members with access to loans, medicines, and burial services.[200] A study of the pinkas shows that the members had at least basic literacy in Hebrew, since the regulations required each new member to read the *takanot* (regulations) in full, but on the other hand the many mistakes in the Hebrew reveal that they were not "particularly learned."[201] The pinkas also reveals not only that the leadership of the hevra "was not entirely open," but that there was actually a leadership clique, members of which were elected repeatedly to various posts. This was standard practice for hevrot in traditional Jewish society. Moreover the hevra did not hold elections every year as stipulated in the takanot.[202] Given what we have seen about how Jewish organizations tended to function before the revolutionary years, perhaps such hevrot were mostly unaffected by the transformations in acculturated Jewish society, and their members were happy to carry on with the oligarchic leadership that had existed since the society's founding. On the other hand, the pinkas does not reveal if there were internal disputes or even resignations from the hevra because of differences over leadership and power sparked by upheavals in other Jewish institutions. If the examples of Kiev's prayer houses are any guide, then such disputes were more than likely.

Conclusion

The Revolution of 1905 was not only a revolution for Russian society but for its Jews and Jewish society as well. Activists had brought the slogans and ideas of the revolution to the Jewish community, compelling the institutions that lay at the heart of Jewish self-governance to change the way they functioned and ruled. And while the course of Jewish communal affairs in Kiev reveals the politicization of Russian Jewry, at the same time it demonstrates there was not always a straight line leading from political and party ideologies to communal politics, which—as activists slowly learned—demanded compromise and consensus. Like civil society in the empire as a whole, the Jewish civil society that had begun to form in the 1890s now entered a period of maturation. The most fundamental and in some ways most significant aspect of this civil society was at the local level, where individuals came together to make change and take a gamble on staking a claim in society. At that plane, there was little room for strict and unbending party ideology; radicals, moderates, and conservatives would in many cases have to learn how to work together to effect change.

Just as Russian civil society formed in opposition to but also sometimes, out of necessity, in collaboration with the state, so did Jewish civil society also develop in opposition to the Jewish establishment—but found that in the end it had to cooperate with that establishment to make things work in the community and to satisfy a newly demanding constituency that had begun to know its own power. (This last was made explicit in Gurevich's comparison of the participation of Jewish artisans in the governance of the Kiev Jewish community to the participation of workers and peasants in the governing of the empire.) Jewish intellectuals of various political stripes could claim that they alone truly represented the masses of Russian Jewry, and had great plans for the future of those masses, but without the money that only the Jewish elite could provide from its own pockets and the communal coffers, their visions amounted to castles in the air. Even the introduction of elections for the communal governing board had little effect on the hegemony of the haute bourgeoisie. And new leaders who used confrontational methods in order to try to wrest the plutocrats' power away from them might in the end, like Lur'e, find themselves thrown out of the communal arena altogether.

At the same time, the new politics of the revolution and of Jewish nationalism and socialism introduced a populist rhetoric into community affairs that by 1908 was being used, whether sincerely or not, by all players. The notables could no longer point to their experience and influence as automatic qualifications for leadership; even if they had little respect for the democracy that had been instituted in communal institutions and treated communal affairs as "a game," they too now had to be representatives of the masses.[203] If in previous eras Jewish progressive institutions had tried to reform and reshape the masses, now people were demanding that the masses shape the institutions. But who was really doing the shaping? In much the same way that post-June 1907 Russia paid lip service to democracy but still functioned as an autocracy, the actions of the self-appointed leaders too often belied their words. We have heard many words from the mouths of the notables and the educated professionals, but little from the masses themselves. Critics of Jewish politics mocked the endless meetings held by activists and communal leaders, at which the only decision taken was often to call yet another meeting.[204] Against all odds, a tremendous amount was accomplished in these years to advance the cause of Jewry; whether more could have been done is a question not for the historian, but the philosopher.

Conclusion

This book has attempted to be two things: a history of late-imperial Kiev Jewry, and an evaluation of the development of Jewish collective existence in a Russian city under the last three tsars. First, some thoughts on the latter of these two. The drive to create new forms and conceptualizations of Jewish life in the Russian Empire was, as many historians have found, motivated both from without and from within. The Russian government's initial impulse, for the bulk of the nineteenth century, was to break down Jewish solidarity and communal self-governance, and it had some success in doing so. By the turn of the twentieth century, the old, premodern Jewish communal structures were gone, and new institutions had emerged to take their place, many of which were bound up inextricably with the rapidly expanding system of Jewish welfare, poor relief, and care for the sick. The new institutions of welfare and communal governance were mostly creations of the commercial and industrial elite, who, in the early decades, had a great deal of influence in the city, serving as city councilors, intervening with high-level bureaucrats on behalf of Jewish individuals or institutions, and even mixing socially with the Russian elite. However, even at the height of the Jewish elite's dominance, tsarist officials had great doubts about the wisdom of giving such men such vast power over their poorer coreligionists. And as anti-Jewish hostility grew, their power ebbed.

The government's attitude toward this system, then, was one of profound ambivalence: it abhorred Jewish "isolation," but in a certain sense the government *needed* to preserve separate Jewish welfare institutions because it saw Jewish poverty as a threat to the empire and feared an influx of Jews into Russian institutions if the former were abolished. In fact, continued Jewish institutional separation from Russian society became more and more expedient for the tsarist regime as its policy toward Jews turned into one of segregation and even outright Judeophobia. The converse was also true. Starting in the 1890s, Kiev Jews, like Jews across the Pale, had less and less say in how their city was run because they could no longer vote in municipal elections; and in Kiev particularly, the city council became more and more hostile to Jews. With absolutely no involvement in the running of the city, with little control over their own collective fate save through their communal and philanthropic institutions, Kiev's Jews were all but helpless in the face of the ever-growing persecution, both official and popular.

And this in a city whose population, including its professional element, was generally more conservative than other Russian cities, "a trait probably related to Kiev's non-industrial and religious nature."[1] The fact that it was home to a powerful coalition of rightist groups that was almost unique in the empire strengthened Jews' feeling of alienation.[2] That the third monarchist congress was held in Kiev in late 1906 is no coincidence—rightists saw the city as their natural political home, and an ideal base from which to fight against the "alien threats" to Russian autocracy, chief among them the Jews.[3] By the time of elections to the Third Duma in 1907, Kiev was the only large city in the empire with a rightist among its deputies. It was natural, then, for Jews to attempt (as in the case of Lazar' Brodsky) to exert control over their fate through philanthropy, and to control—as far as possible—whatever institutions of governance they could. The historical dynamic of the latter case helps us to understand the strong pressure around 1905 and beyond for Kiev's Jewish institutions to be fully representative.

In order to understand the threat that the Jews of Kiev—and the empire as a whole—were facing in the early twentieth century, we must understand the increasingly racial nature of Russian antisemitism. As Eugene Avrutin astutely observes,

> the tsarist regime may not have established a racial order based explicitly on biological theories of human development, but it did promote racial consciousness (the awareness of ethnocultural differences based on religions, customs, and ancestry) and racist attitudes (institutional and popular discriminations based on essential and ultimately unbridgeable differences).[4]

Indeed, by the turn of the century the mixture of curiosity, paternalism, religious animosity, and hope for Europeanization and integration (*sliianie*) with which Russians had viewed the Jews in the mid-nineteenth century had turned to a racialized hostility based on the perceived "otherness" of Jews—a "fixed, impermeable, and rigid" conception.[5] John Klier notes that "the expulsion of Jews from the countryside, residence restrictions, and quota systems in institutions of public education and free professions were among some of the most notable laws that attempted to preserve traditional social hierarchies and police the boundaries between Jews and their 'Christian' neighbors."[6] These restrictions, put into place starting in the early 1880s, were, of course, in part a reaction to the success of Jewish integration into imperial society and the "threat" posed by an influx of "disguised" or "invisible" Jews.[7] As we have seen, the fact that some right-wing societies and organizations banned even Jewish converts from membership points to a larger trend of classifying Jewishness as a racial trait as opposed to a religious heritage that one could shed. If in earlier years complaints had focused on Jewish "fanaticism" and "clannishness," which could—it was thought—be eradicated by government policies such as compulsory enlightenment and the abolition of institutions such as the kahal and separate Jewish dress, now the accusations were of sedition and perhaps even opposition to Russia itself. These charges were in many cases attached to the very nature of Jewishness itself, and thus made indelible.[8]

It is not enough, however, to say that by the dawning of the twentieth century, ever more virulent forms of antisemitism were convincing growing numbers of Jews that, despite all the advances of the previous decades, they had little hope of integrating into imperial society. Indeed, the greater degree of acculturation and integration visible in this period prompted a backlash from non-Jewish society and, in turn, a move toward Jewish nationalism on the part of many Jews. We must also acknowledge that, given the persistence of a strong ethnoreligious identity among the majority of the tsar's Jewish subjects, many doubted that full integration—whatever that might mean—was possible or even desirable for large numbers of Jews. In any case, the pogroms of 1905 and the government's continuing crackdown on the empire's Jews made the liberal option—emancipation on the model of Western Europe—an impossibility. Indeed, the absurdity of that choice within Russia's borders had been made even clearer by the granting of political rights to the tsar's subjects in 1905, among them Russian Jews—who now, as Shmarya Levin famously pointed out, could sit in the Duma in St. Petersburg as duly elected representatives but yet, as Jews, were forbidden to reside in that city without special permission to do so. The paradox of an increasingly rightless yet highly politicized Jewry was an apt one for the Jews of Kiev and many other cities of the empire; starting in 1905, the political and communal activity that had once been the province of intellectuals, radicals, and local elites burst out into a flurry of organizing, mobilizing, and planning among many groups and classes within Russian Jewry.

But even when they turned inward, Kiev's Jews faced restrictions that stymied the development of the quasi-autonomous institutions making up the "Jewish public sphere" that they sought to create.[9] Without a viable Jewish newspaper, unable to hold gatherings in the language of their choice, restricted in the number of prayer services they could organize, and at times even forbidden to gather at cemeteries for folk rituals or on the sidewalks to do business or talk[10]—the opportunities for Jews to build the kind of Jewish *obshchestvennost'* (in Habermas's term, *Öffentlichkeit*) that was emerging in Warsaw, Odessa, and other large cities were severely limited. (There was also a great deal of anxiety about whether "genuine" Jewish culture could even be found in Kiev, a big city that was too sophisticated—and too Russian—for the continued existence and flourishing of "the inner Jewish 'I'," as the local Zionist had noted in *Razsvet* in 1908. This made the project of building a Jewish public sphere even more complex and challenging.) This state of affairs helps to explain the tremendous significance of the transparency and wide participation in Kiev's Jewish communal affairs that had been such a desideratum for so many years and that was achieved by 1908 or so. Institutions in the fields of welfare, education, and culture constituted, in essence, the only specifically Jewish space that existed in Kiev, a space that was created in a variety of ways, both concrete and symbolic. While they could never take the place of a true Jewish press, annual reports did provide printed evidence of the existence of a separate and ramified Jewish community in Kiev, in all of its socioeconomic diversity. The reports, written by the same middle-class professionals who usually ran Jewish institutions, described the advancements of the nation, most often its working class masses who had received assistance in education, or health, or some other field. The Jewish elite also made an appearance in the report as the most generous contributors, but they were joined in the lists of contributing members found at the end of every report by their bourgeois and working-class coreligionists, no matter how small their donation. Yiddish theater was banned in Kiev, but almost every philanthropic organization had its fund-raising concerts and annual galas, which provided a "Jewish space" that helped give shape to the imagined community. No less important were the buildings themselves—the hospitals, clinics, schools, sanatoria, and many other edifices scattered throughout Kiev and its suburbs (many of them still standing today) that were very concrete expressions of a distinctly Jewish civil society, silent testaments to a community that, while laboring under untold checks and constraints, was nonetheless vigorous, multivocal, and wonderfully rich.

Indeed, the integration of these very buildings into the fabric of the city highlighted the paradoxical *Russianness* of the Jewish public sphere: Kiev's

Jewish welfare and philanthropic institutions, political groupings, and social-cultural clubs were all organized on Russian imperial paradigms (and served, in turn, as models for other such institutions, whether Jewish, Christian, or "imperial"). If at the beginning of our period it was still possible to refer to Jews in the southwestern provinces as "Polish Jews," thanks to the perseverance of structures and networks originating in early modern Poland–Lithuania, by the last years of Romanov rule there was no doubt that—in terms of sensibility and self-understanding—they were "Russian Jews." (This slow transition would, in due course, make the process of Sovietization that much more rapid.) To be clear: a Jew in Kiev might be a religious Jew in the synagogue, a member of the working class at the workers' club, a Jewish nationalist at a concert of folk music, or simply a Kievan while strolling in the park on the bluffs above the Dnepr on a sunny Saturday afternoon. All of these identities, however, were performed in a Russian imperial context and were colored to a greater or lesser extent by that context; as we have seen, Jews were an integral part of the fabric of Kiev's municipal life from as early as the mid-1860s. Thus, rather than helping us define and pin down Jewish identity in any clear or simplistic manner, studying the history of Russian Jewry only complicates things and muddies the waters. That is, of course, how it should be. Kiev's manifold contradictions created a fertile environment for experimentation in modern Jewish identities, both individual and collective.

Despite the fact that the institutions of Kiev's Jewish public sphere appeared to bring together *all* of the city's Jews, the roles for the different players were very clear. Those institutions were almost always about the elite and the bourgeoisie providing for the masses what they understood them to need and want—whether material, health, cultural, or even political needs (take, for example, Lur'e's demand that Jewish voters make the choices that he felt they *should* make). These organizations were established for the "good" and the "benefit" of the masses, but the masses rarely got to influence the direction of these institutions, other than perhaps by casting a vote at an annual meeting—if they could even afford the type of membership that granted one such a vote.

One of the major tensions within early twentieth-century Kiev Jewry, then, was the struggle over the leadership of the Jewish public sphere and, indeed, the legitimacy of that leadership. Who would decide? Who was most *fit* to decide: the leaders or the masses? The revolutionaries and democrats claimed to know the mind of the masses, but did they?[11]

And here is where we return to the goals of this work as stated in the opening sentence of this conclusion. A history of the Jews of late-imperial Kiev must be a history of *all* the city's Jews, and yet this book has said much more about the most articulate, the most politically and communally active, the most visible and prominent Jews in Kiev. The existing sources point to such an imbalance, a situation not easily rectified. The detailed minutes and descriptions of meetings are mostly those of the institutions founded by the professional middle class and the merchant notables. While I have attempted to portray working-class Jewish life by drawing upon archival material relating to their everyday existence and challenges, those are no more than samples drawn at random, rather than a representative survey. In terms of institutions, almost no evidence survives from the prayer houses (*batei midrash*), licit or illicit, or the hevrot; nor, for the most part, does the press discuss these kinds of institutions. And thus the historian must conclude that writing this history—as any history—is a challenging and deeply humbling experience. The more you learn, the more you realize you do not know. One conclusion we may draw—perhaps more from instinct than a scientific sampling of sources—is that Kiev's Jewish masses did not always agree to be led by those who claimed the mantle of leadership, nor did they necessarily heed the criticism of those who passed judgment on their ways—whether the subject was stubborn adherence to traditional ways or an insistence on doing whatever was necessary to earn one's daily bread, even if it brought shame upon the larger Jewish community. Individually and collectively, they chose their own path just as those with more education and broader horizons chose theirs. I look forward, then, to future studies not only of Kiev's Jews, but of the "broad masses" (as they were called in the literature of the day) of Russia's Jews—their lives, their struggles, their hopes, the religious institutions, cultural establishments, and political groups they were attracted to and that effected transformations in their lives.

* * *

The partial integration that Kiev Jews attained within Russian civil society continued, in some ways, beyond 1905. But the government's growing antisemitism—through its own restrictions and the tacit encouragement that it gave to the Russian right wing—gave the upper hand to groups that espoused an increasingly racialized antisemitism and chauvinism as their raison d'être, and made clear to more moderate Russians that ongoing and meaningful contacts with Jews would never be seen in a positive light by official Russia. Lev Brodsky's ascendance in 1912 to the presidency of Kiev's territorialist Jewish Emigration Society symbolized the end of the dream of Jewish liberalism in Russia; if even the Brodsky family supported large-scale Jewish emigration from the empire, what future could there be for Jews in Russia? It may well be that ordinary Russians and Ukrainians who would otherwise have been indifferent to Jewish matters were actually swayed by the "evidence" that Judeophobic officials and activists were so eager to make known to the Russian public. The growing conviction within the highest echelons of the Russian Empire that Jews—all Jews—were a fundamental threat to the very existence of the realm was translated into its most horrifying corollary during the First World War, when thousands of Jews were expelled from the front under suspicion of espionage. Indeed, the central role that the tsarist government played in fomenting anti-Jewish sentiment is made clear when we witness what happened under a government that not only did not encourage antisemitism but actively combated it: the Soviet regime in the 1920s and 1930s. In this period, Kiev became one of the largest Jewish centers in the world, and its 140,000 Jews formed one-third of the city's total population. To be sure, as throughout the Soviet Union most Jewish religious and cultural expression was repressed, and this played a significant role in pushing Jews, willy-nilly, into the new Soviet society; but it was also the full political and civil rights that Jews now enjoyed (or at least as full as the Bolshevik system would allow) that enabled them to achieve the kind of integration that had been unimaginable before the 1917 Revolution. Despite the new state-supported "Jewish proletarian culture," Jewish religious, cultural, and philanthropic culture was now undoubtedly poorer than in the difficult but creative period of tsarist repression, and the dynamic Jewish public sphere that had emerged under such constraints before 1917 was now all but eradicated. Individual Jewish lives, however, were unquestionably easier and opportunities for professional advancement and upward mobility greater. In the end, however, it was neither the Russian nor the Soviet government which struck the deadliest blow to Kiev's Jews, but occupying military forces: ultranationalist Ukrainian and Russian military bands who massacred thousands of Jews in the period of the Russian Civil War and, during the Second World War, German forces that (albeit with the help of some of the local Ukrainian population) turned a Jewish cemetery at the edge of the city into a killing field known as Babi Yar.

ABBREVIATIONS

Archives

CAHJP	Central Archives for the History of the Jewish People
CZA	Central Zionist Archives
DAKO	State Archive of Kyiv Region
DAmK	State Archive of the City of Kyiv
IR TsNB	Manuscript Division of the Vernadsky National Library of Ukraine
RGIA	Russian State Historical Archive
TsDIAU	Central State Historical Archive of Ukraine, Kyiv
YIVO	Archives of the YIVO Institute for Jewish Research

Archival Notations (R=Russian, U=Ukrainian)

f.	fond (collection) (R, U)
op.	opis' (inventory) (R, U)
d.	delo (file) (R)
spr.	sprava (file) (U)
l., ll.	list, listy (folio, folios) (R)
ark.	arkush, arkushi (folio, folios) (U)
ob.	oborot (verso) (R)
zv.	zvorotnyi bik (verso) (U)
EE	*Evreiskaia entsiklopediia: svod znanii o evreistve i ego kulture v proshlom i nastoiashchem.* Sankt Peterburg: Obshchestva dlia nauchnykh evreiskikh izdanii i izd-vo Brokgauz-Efron, 1906–13. 16 vols.

NOTES

Introduction

1. Lindenmeyr, *Poverty Is Not a Vice: Charity, Society, and the State in Imperial Russia,* 197.

2. Benjamin Nathans examines the communal politics of St. Petersburg in *Beyond the Pale: The Jewish Encounter with Late Imperial Russia,* chaps. 3–4 (pp. 83–164).

3. Steven Zipperstein notes that "traditional values tended to weaken" in frontier settings; the "traditional institutions, powerful sanctions, and respected authorities" that were absent in Odessa were also to a certain extent missing in Kiev, though—given Kiev's geographical location—physically closer. Zipperstein, *The Jews of Odessa: A Cultural History, 1794–1881,* 36.

4. The pioneering sociologist Arthur Ruppin reached a similar conclusion in his *Jewish Fate and Future,* 72–73.

5. Stein, *Making Jews Modern: the Yiddish and Ladino Press in the Russian and Ottoman Empires.*

6. Dubnow, *History of the Jews in Russia and Poland, From the Earliest Times Until the Present Day.*

7. Gessen, *Istoriia evreiskogo naroda v Rossii.*

8. See Nathans, "On Russian-Jewish Historiography," 410–417.

9. *YIVO Encyclopedia of Jews in Eastern Europe,* s.v. "YIVO." See also Dobroszycki, "YIVO in Interwar Poland: Work in the Historical Sciences," in *The Jews of Poland between Two World Wars,* ed. Israel Gutman, 495–518.

10. Kahan, "The Impact of Industrialization in Tsarist Russia on the Socioeconomic Conditions of the Jewish Population." See also Weinryb, *Neueste Wirtschaftsgeschichte der Juden in Russland und Polen.*

11. For a good introduction, see Nathans's introduction to Genrikh M. Deich, *Arkhivnye dokumenty po istorii evreev v Rossii v XIX–nachale XX vv.: putevoditel',* i–xi.

12. Stanislawski, *Tsar Nicholas I and the Jews: the Transformation of Jewish Society in Russia, 1825–1855;* Klier, *Russia Gathers Her Jews: The Origins of the "Jewish Question" in Russia, 1772–1825;* Nathans, *Beyond the Pale;* Freeze, *Jewish Marriage and Divorce in Imperial Russia;* Avrutin, "A Legible People: Identification Politics and Jewish Accommodation in Tsarist Russia."

13. Rogger, *Jewish Policies and Right-Wing Politics in Imperial Russia;* Aronson, *Troubled Waters;* Judge, *Easter in Kishinev: Anatomy of a Pogrom; Pogroms: Anti-Jewish Violence in Modern Russian History,* ed. Klier and Lambroza; Löwe, *The Tsars and the Jews: Reform, Reaction, and Anti-Semitism in Imperial Russia, 1772–1917;* Klier, *Imperial Russia's Jewish Question, 1855–1881.*

14. Mendelsohn, *Class Struggle in the Pale;* Frankel, *Prophecy and Politics: Socialism, Nationalism, and the Russian Jews, 1862–1917;* Zipperstein, *The Jews of Odessa;* Michael Stanislawski, *For Whom Do I Toil? Judah Leib Gordon and the Crisis of Russian Jewry* (Oxford, 1988); Lederhendler, *The Road to Modern Jewish Politics: Political Tradition and Political Reconstruction in the Jewish Community of Tsarist Russia;* Steven J. Zipperstein, *Elusive Prophet: Ahad Ha'am and the Origins of Zionism* (Berkeley: University of California Press, 1993); Gassenschmidt, *Jewish Liberal Politics in Tsarist Russia, 1900–1914: The Modernization of Russian Jewry;* Shaul Stampfer, *Ha-yeshivah ha-lita'it be-hithavutah* (Jerusalem: Merkaz Zalman Shazar le-toldot Yisra'el, 1995); Carole B. Balin, *To Reveal Our Hearts: Jewish Women Writers in Tsarist Russia* (Cincinnati: Hebrew Union College Press, 2000); Safran, *Rewriting the Jew: Assimilation Narratives in the Russian Empire;*

David Assaf, *The Regal Way: The Life and Times of Rabbi Israel of Ruzhin* (Stanford, Calif.: Stanford University Press, 2002); Shmuel Feiner, *Haskalah and History: The Emergence of a Modern Jewish Historical Consciousness* (Portland, Ore.: Littman Library of Jewish Civilization, 2002); Polishchuk, *Evrei Odessy i Novorossii: Sotsial'no-politicheskaia istoriia evreev Odessy i drugikh gorodov Novorossii, 1881–1904*; Murav, *Identity Theft: The Jew in Imperial Russia and the Case of Avraam Uri Kovner*; Parush, *Reading Jewish Women: Marginality and Modernization in Nineteenth-Century Eastern European Jewish Society*; Litvak, *Conscription and the Search for Modern Russian Jewry*.

15. Baron, *The Russian Jew under Tsars and Soviets*; Dawidowicz, *The Golden Tradition: Jewish Life and Thought in Eastern Europe*, introduction; Gitelman, *A Century of Ambivalence: The Jews of Russia and the Soviet Union, 1881 to the Present*.

16. Nathans, *Beyond the Pale*; Freeze, *Jewish Marriage and Divorce*; Assaf, *The Regal Way*; Stein, *Making Jews Modern*; *Luftmenschen und rebellische Töchter: zum Wandel ostjüdischer Lebenswelten im 19. Jahrhundert*, ed. Heiko Haumann (Cologne, 2003); Epstein, "Caring for the Soul's House: the Jews of Russia and Health Care 1860–1914."

17. Hamm, *Kiev: A Portrait, 1800–1917*.

18. *Istoriia Kieva*, ed. V. E. Dement'eva.

19. Kovalinskii, *Metsenaty Kieva*; Kal'nyts'kyi, *Kyïv: turystychnyi putivnyk*; A. M. Makarov, *Malaia entsiklopediia kievskoi stariny* (Kiev: Izdatel'stvo "Dovira," 2002).

20. The classic example is Mykhailo Hrushevs'kyi's *History of Ukraine-Rus'*. Notable exceptions are several essays in a volume under Hrushevs'kyi's editorship: *Kyïv ta ioho okolytsia v istoriï i pam"iatkakh* (Kiev: Derzhavne vyd-vo Ukraïny, 1926).

21. von Hagen, "Does Ukraine Have a History?" 663.

22. See Mark von Hagen's intriguing suggestion regarding the possibility of, instead of *a* Ukrainian history, a multiplicity of histories within Ukraine's history owing to "the fluidity of frontiers, the permeability of cultures, the historic multi-ethnic society" that are all characteristics of Ukrainian history. Von Hagen, "Does Ukraine Have a History?" 670.

23. Polonska-Vasylenko, "The Ukrainian Church in the Lithuanian-Polish Realm and the Kozak Hetman State," 154–155.

24. Stein remarks that Odessa was "at once both on the fringe and in the very center of secular Russian Jewish culture." Stein, *Making Jews Modern*, 25.

25. See the essays in *The Worlds of S. An-sky: A Russian Jewish Intellectual at the Turn of the Century*, ed. Gabriella Safran and Steven J. Zipperstein (Stanford, Calif.: Stanford University Press, 2006); Simon Rabinovitch, "Positivism, Populism and Politics: The Intellectual Foundations of Jewish Ethnography in Late Imperial Russia," *Ab Imperio* 3 (2005): 227–256.

26. Most notably Odessa; cf. Roshanna P. Sylvester, *Tales of Old Odessa: Crime and Civility in a City of Thieves*.

27. See Shohat, "Ha-hanhagah be-kehilot Rusyah im bitul ha-kahal," 3–4; Stanislawski, *Tsar Nicholas*, 123–154; Lederhendler, *Road to Modern Politics*, 74ff.; Freeze, *Jewish Marriage and Divorce*, 79–130. Isaac Levitats's study of the Jewish community is useful as a source of information about legislation and the workings of individual communities, but provides little overarching analysis of larger patterns in communal development. Isaac Levitats, *The Jewish Community in Russia, 1844–1917*, 201.

28. Bill Williams, *The Making of Manchester Jewry, 1740–1875* (Manchester: University Press, 1976); Rozenblit, *The Jews of Vienna, 1867–1914: Assimilation and Identity*; Paula E. Hyman, *The Emancipation of the Jews of Alsace: Acculturation and Tradition in the Nineteenth Century* (New Haven: Yale University Press, 1991); Steven M. Lowenstein, *The Berlin Jewish Community: Enlightenment, Family, and Crisis, 1770–1830* (New York: Oxford University Press,

1994); Shulamit Magnus, *Jewish Emancipation in a German City: Cologne, 1798–1871* (Stanford, Calif.: Stanford University Press, 1997); Stefanie Schüler-Springorum, *Die jüdische Minderheit in Königsberg/Preussen, 1871–1945* (Göttingen: Vandenhoeck & Ruprecht Gm, 1997); Rainer Liedtke, *Jewish Welfare in Hamburg and Manchester, c. 1850–1914* (Oxford: Clarendon Press, 1998); David Rechter, *The Jews of Vienna and the First World War* (London: Littman Library of Jewish Civilisation, 2001). Although not a study of a particular locality, François Guesnet's recent work on Polish Jewry pays close attention to the development of Jewish communal structures in his *Polnische Jüden im 19. Jahrhundert: Lebensbedingungen, Rechtsnormen und Organisation im Wandel* (Cologne, 1998). Michael Graetz's study of the transformation of Jewish identity among French Jews includes an investigation of a bourgeois elite that was similar in some ways (and especially in their use of philanthropy as a means of identifying with Judaism) to the Jewish elite of the Russian Empire. Michael Graetz, *The Jews in Nineteenth-Century France: From the French Revolution to the Alliance Israelite Universelle* (Stanford, Calif.: Stanford University Press, 1996). I am grateful to Nils Roemer for this reference.

29. By examining corporate identity among Russian Jews, the study also contributes to our developing understanding of how Jews fit into the empire's soslovie system. Most Jews were officially classified as "townspeople" (*meshchane*), yet, as Elise Kimerling Wirtschafter notes, "townspeople (*posadskie, meshchane*) represent the least studied and most poorly understood of all imperial social categories." She remarks further that as "a fluid mosaic of legal-administrative categories and socioeconomic groupings, urban society defied the juridical parameters and conceptual structures of the tsarist state." Wirtschafter, *Social Identity in Imperial Russia*), 130, 134.

30. Bohachevsky-Chomiak, "Women in Kiev and Kharkiv: Community Organizations in the Russian Empire," 160.

31. See, for example, Nathans, *Beyond the Pale*, 39.

32. Nathans, *Beyond the Pale*, 44.

33. For a similar debate among Ukrainians, see Kappeler, "The Ukrainians of the Russian Empire, 1860–1914," 122.

34. Burbank, "Revisioning Imperial Russia," 558. See also the edited volume that emerged from the initiative of which the workshop was a part: *Imperial Russia: New Histories for the Empire*, ed. David Ransel and Jane Burbank (Bloomington: Indiana University Press, 1998).

35. Burbank, 557, 566.

36. Ibid., 558.

37. Ibid., 560.

38. Ibid., 565.

39. Ibid., 560–562.

40. On ethnicity and nationalities, see Thaden and Thaden, *Russia's Western Borderlands, 1710–1870*; Theodore R. Weeks, *Nation and State in Late Imperial Russia: Nationalism and Russification on the Western Frontier, 1863–1914*; Daniel R. Brower and Edward J. Lazzerini, eds., *Russia's Orient: Imperial Borderlands and Peoples, 1700–1917* (Bloomington: Indiana University Press, 1997); Geraci, *Window on the East: National and Imperial Identities in Late Tsarist Russia*; Slezkine, *The Jewish Century*; Robert D. Crews, *For Prophet and Tsar: Islam and Empire in Russia and Central Asia* (Cambridge, Mass.: Harvard University Press, 2006). On ethnicity and ethnic relations in the Russian Empire generally, see Andreas Kappeler, *Rußland als Vielvölkerreich. Enstehung, Geschichte, Zerfall* (Munich, 1992) and D. A. Shevkulenko, *Mezhnatsional'nye otnosheniia v Rossii: vtoraia polovina XVI–nachalo XX vv.* (Samara, 1999). For a perceptive exploration of the development of ethnicity as a significant category for the organization of society, see Steinwedel, "To Make a Difference: The Category of Ethnicity in Late Imperial Russian Politics, 1861–

1917," 67–86. For a highly suggestive examination of the relationship between the state and religious community and identity, see Crews, "Empire and the Confessional State: Islam and Religious Politics in Nineteenth-Century Russia," 50–83. New social and cultural histories include Wirtschafter, *Social Identity;* Lindenmeyr, *Poverty Is Not a Vice: Charity, Society, and the State in Imperial Russia,* 197; Wynn, *Workers, Strikes, and Pogroms: The Donbass-Dnepr Bend in Late Imperial Russia, 1870–1905*; McReynolds and Popkin, "The Objective Eye and the Common Good"; Clowes, Kassow, and West, *Between Tsar and People: Educated Society and the Quest for Public Identity in Late Imperial Russia*; Patricia Herlihy, *Odessa: A History, 1794–1914* (Cambridge, Mass: Distributed by Harvard University Press for the Harvard Ukrainian Research Institute, 1986).

41. Geraci, *Window on the East* and Crews, *For Prophet and Tsar* are particularly good examples of this approach.

42. Burbank, "Revisioning Imperial Russia," 560.

43. Khodos, *Materialy po statistike naseleniia g. Kieva* provides a comprehensive comparison of all the censuses of Kiev from 1874 to 1923, while Shamrai, "Kyïvs'kyi odnodennyi perepys 2-go berezolia 1874 roku (Storinka z istoriï marksyzmu na Ukraïni)," 351–392 analyzes some of the defects of the 1874 census. Two of the many works on the 1897 census are Robert A. Lewis, Richard H. Rowland, and Ralph S. Clem, *Nationality and Population Change in Russia and the USSR: An Evaluation of Census Data, 1897–1970* (New York: Praeger, 1976) and *Research Guide to the Russian and Soviet Censuses,* ed. Ralph S. Clem (Ithaca, N.Y.: Cornell University Press, 1986).

44. See Klier, "*Kievlianin* and the Jews: a Decade of Disillusionment, 1864–1873," 1; and Klier, *Imperial Russia's Jewish Question,* 182–203.

1. Settlement and Growth, 1859–1881

1. *Evreiskaia entsiklopediia,* s.v. "Kiev"; *Jewish Encyclopedia,* s.v. "Kiev"; *Encyclopedia Judaica,* s.v. "Kiev"; Hamm, *Kiev,* 3–17, 117–121; M. I. Kulisher, "Evrei v Kieve: Istoricheskii ocherk," 351–66, 417–38; Iulii Gessen, "Getto v Rossii," *Evreiskii mir* no. 13, 1 April 1910; idem, "Mnogostradal'naia obshchina," *Evreiskii mir* 22, 25 Sept. 1910.

2. Darewski, *Le-korot ha-yehudim be-Kiyov.*

3. See Levanda, *Pol'nyi khronologicheskii sbornik zakonov i polozhenii, kasaiushchikhsia evreev,* 79–80, for the official rejection of the petition for expulsion.

4. For the expulsion order itself, see TsDIAU f. 442 (Kantseliaria Kievskogo, Podol'skogo i Volynskogo general-gubernatora), op. 1, spr. 504 ("Ukaz Nikolaia I ot 2 dekabria 1827 g. o vospreshchenii evreiam postoiannogo prebyvaniia v Kieve, vysylke ikh iz Kieva i pravakh kuptsov-evreev"), and Levanda, *Pol'nyi khronologicheskii sbornik,* 217–218.

5. Levanda, *Pol'nyi khronologicheskii sbornik,* 217.

6. Kulisher, "Evrei v Kieve," 424–427.

7. Gessen, *Istoriia,* II: 41–42. The expulsion came to pass despite the argument of Kiev Military Governor Levashev that Jews were useful to the city's economy and that their expulsion would lead to a rise in prices of certain goods. Ibid., 41; for the original legislation, see Levanda, *Pol'nyi khronologicheskii sbornik,* 332–335.

8. Kulisher, "Evrei v Kieve," 427–429; Ginzburg, "Ghetos in amoliken rusland," 335–340; Rybyn's'kyy, "Z istoriï getta v Kyïvi," 938–955; Hamm, *Kiev,* 119–120. For an overview and analysis of this policy, see Nathans, *Beyond the Pale,* chap. 4 (123–164).

9. Dubnow, *History of the Jews in Russia and Poland,* II: 161–172.

10. See the extensive explanation of Kiev's Jewish residence laws in Khiterer, "The Social and Economic History of Jews in Kiev before Feb. 1917," chap. 3.

11. Gessen, *Istoriia,* II: 154; Kulisher, "Evrei v Kieve," 430–433.

12. Gessen, *Istoriia,* II: 161; Klier, *Imperial Russia's Jewish Question,* chap. 13.

13. Kahan, "The Impact of Industrialization in Tsarist Russia on the Socioeconomic Conditions of the Jewish Population," 82–100.

14. Lestschinsky, *Dos idishe folk in tsifern,* 29–38; Baron, *Russian Jew,* 77.

15. Stampfer, "Patterns of Internal Jewish Migration in the Russian Empire," 29.

16. Baron, *Russian Jew,* 77.

17. Gessen, *Istoriia,* II: 157; Weeks, *Nation and State,* 117.

18. Lestschinsky, "Di idishe bafelkerung," 50.

19. *Istoriia Kieva,* I: 339.

20. Lestschinsky, "Di idishe bafelkerung fun 1897 biz 1923," 50.

21. Hamm, *Kiev,* 128 and Starozhil [Sergei Iaron], *Kiev v vosmidesiatykh godakh: vospominaniia starozhila,* 36.

22. Hamm, *Kiev,* 133.

23. Gessen, *Istoriia,* II: 159.

24. Hamm, *Kiev,* 33–34, 46.

25. *Istoriia Kieva,* 349.

26. Lestschinsky, "Di idishe bafelkerung," 50.

27. Subbotin, *V cherte evreiskoi osedlosti. Otryvki iz ekonomicheskago izsledovaniia v zapadnoi i iugo-zapadnoi Rossii za leto 1887 g.,* II: 159.

28. Hamm, *Kiev,* 33.

29. *Ha-melits* no. 251, 13 Nov. 1892: 4–5.

30. Kulisher, "Evrei v Kieve," 430–433. Inscribed in the so-called "merchant" estate [*kupechestvo*] were not only merchants and traders but also industrialists, entrepreneurs, and financiers.

31. *Khronika Voskhoda* no. 8, 21 Feb. 1899: 219.

32. Starozhil [Sergei Iaron], *Kiev,* 35.

33. Avrutin, "A Legible People: Identification Politics and Jewish Accommodation in Tsarist Russia," 122. See this entire chapter of the dissertation, "Who's a Jew? Where's a Jew?" (pp. 116–159), for an insightful analysis of Russian imperial practices in the documenting and "making visible" of Jews.

34. See, for example, *Kievlianin* no. 135, 19 June 1882: 2, where merchants are accused of not knowing the names of the clerks whom they had hired.

35. After the 1881 pogrom, the mayor accused prominent Jewish merchants of trying to collect compensation for losses incurred by the "clerks" who traded under their names, when in actuality the merchants had lost nothing of their own. TsDIAU f. 442, op. 534, spr. 87 ("Vedemost' o kolichstve remeslennikov-evreev v g. Kieve i gorodakh, mestechkakh i seleniiakh Kievskoi gubernii"), ark. 14–16zv.

36. *Kievlianin* no. 45, 3 October 1864.

37. Starozhil [Sergei Iaron], *Kiev,* 38; *Kievlianin* no. 158, 22 July 1883: 2.

38. Starozhil [Sergei Iaron], *Kiev,* 36–39.

39. Ibid., 35–36. The widespread bribery in Kiev is also described in Sliozberg, *Dela minuvshikh dnei,* 477.

40. *Kievlianin* no. 45, 13 Oct. 1864, cited in Klier, *Imperial Russia's Jewish Question,* 199.

41. *Kol mevaser* no. 31, 31 July 1869: 317–319.

42. TsDIAU f. 442, op. 528, spr. 450, ark. 12–12zv.

43. *Kievlianin* no. 42, 9 April 1866: 161.

44. TsDIAU f. 442, op. 528, spr. 450, ark. 13–13zv. On Jewish soldiers' being permitted

to establish prayer houses in Kiev under Nicholas I, see Petrovskii-Shtern, *Evrei v russkoi armii, 1827–1914*, 87.

45. A list compiled in the early 1890s provides seemingly contradictory information about how many prayer houses existed before 1881 and the dates of their establishment, but the confusion may be caused by the reissuance of permits years after the synagogues were first established; bureaucrats might then have noted that year instead of the original date of authorization. DAKO f. 1 (Kievskoe gubernskoe pravlenie), op. 336, d. 6197 ("Spisok sinagog i evreiskikh molitvennykh domov v g. Kieve i uezde"), ark. 1a–4zv.

46. *Kol mevaser* no. 17, 4 May 1872: 125–126; *Ha-melits* no. 6, 21 Feb. 1885: 88–93. On the tsaddikim of Chernobyl, see Klapholz, *Admorei Tshernobil* (s.l., [1971]) and, in a more critical vein, Assaf, *Ne'ehaz ba-sevakh: pirkei mashber u-mevucha be-toldot ha-hasidut*, chap. 3 (179–219), on the violent persecution of Bratslaver Hasidim of the mid-nineteenth century, perpetrated mainly by rabbis David Twersky of Talne and Yitzhak Twersky of Skver.

47. See Hamm, *Kiev*, 121.

48. IR TsNB f. 321 (Kollektsiia evreiskikh rukopisei), op. 1, spr. OR 71, n. 39.

49. See also Petrovsky-Shtern, "Hasidism, Havurot, and the Jewish Street," 42–43.

50. Petrovskii-Shtern, *Evrei v russkoi armii*, 87. On the development of Ploskaia as a Jewish neighborhood, see the next section in this chapter.

51. TsDIAU f. 442, op. 533, spr. 17 ("Delo o zapreshchenii evreiam-prikazchikam, prozhivaiushchim v g. Kieve, sozdat' obshchestvo vzaimnogo vspomoshchestvovaniia"), ark. 1–5.

52. Mykhaylo Kal'nyts'ky, comp., "Ievreis'ki adresy Kyieva"; *Ha-melits* no. 247, 9 Nov. 1892: 2.

53. The existence of a Polish community is corroborated by *Kievlianin;* see no. 78, 3 July 1879.

54. *Kievlianin* no. 40, 5 April 1866: 154.

55. Kotik, *Mayne zikhroynes*, II: 265–271.

56. Kotik, *Mayne zikhroynes*, II: 237.

57. Mikhail Kal'nitskii, *Sinagoga Kievskoi iudeiskoi obshchiny, 5656–5756: Istoricheskii ocherk*, 16; IR TsNB f. 321 (Kollektsiia evreiskikh rukopisei), op. 1, spr. OR 64, n. 38.

58. Kotik, *Mayne zikhroynes*, 226.

59. Sholem Aleichem, *From the Fair*, 259.

60. Iugo-Zapadnoe otdelenie Imperatorskago Russkago Geograficheskago Obshchestva, *Kiev i ego predmestiia*. This figure assumes, as is clearly the case, that the tabulators of the 1874 census considered a Jew who could read and write in Yiddish but not in Russian to be illiterate. Moreover, the census did not define exactly what "literacy" meant. See Stampfer, "Yedi'at kero u-khetov etsel yehudei mizrah eiropa ba-tekufa ha-hadasha: heksher, mekorot va-hashlakhot," 459–483, and Perlmann, "Literacy among the Jews of Russia in 1897: A Reanalysis of Census Data." For an analysis of the complexity of gauging Jewish women's literacy, see Parush, *Reading Jewish Women*, 93–96. For a general discussion of literacy in the Russian Empire, see Brooks, *When Russia Learned to Read: Literacy and Popular Literature, 1861–1917*, 3–34.

61. This brought the proportion up to 12 percent of all students (which was about the same as the proportion of Jews in the city as a whole).

62. *Kievlianin* no. 93, 25 April 1880: 1. The corresponding proportion for the Kiev educational district as a whole, which covered Kiev, Podol, Volhyn, Chernigov, and Poltava provinces, was 10.4 percent in 1876. Gessen, *Istoriia*, II: 230.

63. *Kievlianin* no. 91, 24 April 1885: 3. The growing trend of Jewish girls attending Russian gymnasia was visible throughout the Pale; see Parush, *Reading Jewish Women*, 83–89. On Jewish girls' education more generally, see Stampfer, "Gender Differentiation and Education of the Jewish Woman in Nineteenth Century Eastern Europe"; Eliyana R. Adler, "Private Schools for Jewish girls in Tsarist Russia" (Ph.D. dissertation, Brandeis University, 2003), and idem, "Rediscovering Schools for Jewish Girls in Tsarist Russia," *East European Jewish Affairs* 34, 2 (2004): 139–150.

64. Gessen, *Istoriia*, II: 230.

65. Dr. G. M. Gertsenshtein, "Universitetskie studenty-evrei," *Razsvet* no. 36 (1880): 1427–1428, cited in Epstein, "Caring for the Soul's House," 63.

66. Epstein, "Caring for the Soul's House," 64.

67. Ibid., 69. For an analysis of the development of a Russian-Jewish student culture, see Nathans, *Beyond the Pale*, chap. 6 (201–256).

68. On these rabbinical seminaries, see Verena Dohrn, "The Rabbinical Schools as Institutions of Socialization in Tsarist Russia, 1847–1873," *Polin* 14 (2001): 83–104.

69. Kotik, *Mayne zikhroynes*, 262–265.

70. *Istoriia Kieva*, 415.

71. Freeze, "Making and Unmaking the Jewish Family: Marriage and Divorce in Imperial Russia," 267; Nathans, *Beyond the Pale*, 224–225. For more on the courses, see Ivanovych Shcherbyna, "Do istoriï zhinochoï osvity u Kyïvi," 159–164. On the history of the Higher Women's Courses, see Johanson, *Women's Struggle for Higher Education in Russia, 1855–1900.*

72. Iugo-Zapadnoe otdelenie Imperatorskago Russkago Geograficheskago Obshchestva, *Kiev i ego predmestiia*, 222–223. On female Jewish medical students in this period, see Epstein, "Caring for the Soul's House," 53–57.

73. Haberer, *Jews and Revolution in Nineteenth-Century Russia*, 69–71.

74. Hamm, "Kiev: Dubnov's Inferno of Russian Israel," 58.

75. For details of the complicated laws on Jewish settlement in Kiev, see Mysh, *Rukovodstvo k russkim zakonam o evreiakh*, 284–294.

76. Iugo-Zapadnoe otdelenie Imperatorskago Russkago Geograficheskago Obshchestva, *Kiev i ego predmestiia*, 25.

77. Sliozberg, *Dela minuvshikh dnei*, 477.

78. Iugo-Zapadnoe otdelenie Imperatorskago Russkago Geograficheskago Obshchestva, *Kiev i ego predmestiia*, 67.

79. Subbotin, *V cherte*, 161.

80. Pantiukhov, *Opyt sanitarnoi topografii i statistiki Kieva*, 262–63, 285. Although the rate was calculated for the entire city, most Jews lived in Ploskaia and Lybed.

81. *Istoriia Kieva*, 356.

82. Iugo-Zapadnoe otdelenie Imperatorskago Russkago Geograficheskago Obshchestva, *Kiev i ego predmestiia*, 42–43.

83. Pantiukhov, *Opyt*, 290–292.

84. *Istoriia Kieva*, 398.

85. Pantiukhov, *Opyt*, 294.

86. Ibid., 246.

87. See, for example, the feuilleton "Kievskie nishchie" (*Kievlianin* no. 138, 18 Nov. 1872: 1–2), where the author complains that so many Jews streamed to Kiev after its gates were opened to them that many of them were, in the end, unable to make a living; for its part, the Jewish community was unprepared to provide aid to such a large indigent population.

We have evidence that there were Jewish beggars in Kiev by the early 1870s, mostly in the neighborhoods close to the train station. *Kievlianin* no. 138, 18 Nov. 1872: 1–2; *Ha-melits* no. 110, 20 May 1896: 2.

88. *Kievlianin* no. 40, 3 April 1873: 1.

89. Iugo-Zapadnoe otdelenie Imperatorskago Russkago Geograficheskago Obshchestva, *Kiev i ego predmestiia.*

90. TsDIAU f. 442, op. 46, spr. 35 ("Delo o razreshenii ravvinu Tsukkermanu postroit' v g. Kieve molitvennyi dom"), ark. 1–5.

91. TsDIAU f. 442, op. 50, spr. 302 ("Delo o zapreshchenii meshchanam evreiskogo veroispovedaniia priobresti uchastok zemli okolo tserkvi Rozhdestvo Khristova na Podole").

92. *Ha-melits* no. 31, 15 Aug. 1863.

93. Darewski, *Le-korot ha-yehudim,* 86.

94. *Kol mevaser* no. 31, 31 July 1869: 317–319.

95. Hamm, *Kiev,* 137.

96. Subbotin, *V cherte,* 168.

97. Landau, "Der ontayl fun yidn in der rusish-ukraynisher tsuker-industriye," 98–103. See also K. Voblyi, *Narysy z istoriï rosiis'ko-ukraïns'koï tsukro-buriakovoï promyslovosti,* 3 vols. (Kyïv, 1928–1930) and O. Plevako, "Do materialiv z istoriï tsukro-buriakovoï promyslovosti na Ukraïni," *Ukraïna* (Kyïv, 1925), vol. V.

98. Sliozberg, *Dela minuvshikh dnei,* 478.

99. Hamm, *Kiev,* 129–130; *Encyclopedia Judaica,* s.v. "Brodski"; *YIVO Encyclopedia of Jews in Eastern Europe,* s.v. "Brodskii Family."

100. Brodsky, *Smoke Signals: From Eminence to Exile,* 4.

101. Kalnizkij, "Juden in Kiew—Ein Gang Durch die Jahrhunderte," 21.

102. Nathans, *Beyond the Pale,* 43.

103. Sliozberg, *Dela minuvshikh dnei,* 478–479.

104. Sholem Aleichem, "Nito ver s'zol lakhen!," *Kiever vort* no. 11 (Jan.) 1910, emphasis in original. I am grateful to Victoria Khiterer for this explanation; Khiterer, "Social and Economic History of Jews in Kiev," 145.

105. Starozhil [Sergei Iaron], *Kiev,* 41.

106. *Kievlianin* no. 51, 30 April 1877: 2.

107. *Ha-melits* no. 47, 9 Dec. 1865.

108. Pantiukhov, *Opyt,* 305; Iugo-Zapadnoe otdelenie Imperatorskago Russkago Geograficheskago Obshchestva, *Kiev i ego predmestiia,* 186–187.

109. Freeze, "Making and Unmaking the Jewish Family," 288.

110. Subbotin, *V cherte,* 169.

111. *Kievlianin* no. 146, 10 Dec. 1866: 582–583.

112. Iugo-Zapadnoe otdelenie Imperatorskago Russkago Geograficheskago Obshchestva, *Kiev i ego predmestiia,* 186–187.

113. Starozhil [Sergei Iaron], *Kiev,* 12–13.

114. *Istoriia Kieva,* 391.

115. Iugo-Zapadnoe otdelenie Imperatorskago Russkago Geograficheskago Obshchestva, *Kiev i ego predmestiia,* 138–153.

116. Pantiukhov, *Opyt,* 305.

117. *Kievlianin* no. 163, 25 July 1881.

118. Hamm, *Kiev,* 163.

119. See *YIVO Encyclopedia of Jews in Eastern Europe,* s.v. "Tavernkeeping."

120. *Kievlianin* no. 130, 31 Oct. 1868: 51.

121. RGIA f. 821, op. 9, d. 289, l. 37, cited in Freeze, "Making and Unmaking the Jewish Family," 201.

122. Iugo-Zapadnoe otdelenie Imperatorskago Russkago Geograficheskago Obshchestva, *Kiev i ego predmestiia,* 140–141, 186–187.

123. *Kievlianin* no. 76, 27 June 1874: 1–2.

124. *Kievlianin* no. 150, 16 Dec. 1876: 1.

125. Kievskoe evreiskoe obshchestvo dlia vspomoshchestvovaniia postradavshim ot bezporiadkov na iuge Rossii 1881 g., *Otchet . . . po 1-e oktiabria 1881 goda* (Kiev: Ern. Perlis, 1882).

126. Hamm, *Kiev,* 35.

127. Subbotin, *V cherte,* 157–158; *Ha-melits* no. 82, 8 April 1891: 2.

128. *Kievskiia gubernskiia vedemosti* no. 105, 7 Sept. 1874: 474; *Kievlianin* no. 145, 28 June 1880: 2.

129. Iugo-Zapadnoe otdelenie Imperatorskago Russkago Geograficheskago Obshchestva, *Kiev i ego predmestiia,* 244–245.

130. Kovalinskii, *Metsenaty Kieva,* 356; Kotik, *Mayne zikhroynes,* 310; *Encyclopedia Judaica,* s.v. "Max Mandelstamm"; CZA, A3 (Mandelshtam, Max), 32.

131. Gol'denveizer, "Mandel'shtamm i studenchestvo," 40.

132. *Jewish Chronicle* 31 Dec. 1880: 13.

133. Frankel, *Prophecy and Politics,* 61.

134. *Istoriia Kieva,* 395.

135. Subbotin, *V cherte,* 173. The cheapest rent was 150 rubles. Fish cost, on average, 3.30 rubles/pud, i.e. 9 kop./lb. in 1874. *Kievskiia gubernskiia vedemosti* no. 82, 16 July 1874: 374.

136. *Jewish Chronicle* 25 June 1880.

137. *Kievlianin* no. 45, 3 Oct. 1864.

138. *Kievlianin* no. 40, 3 April 1873: 1.

139. *Kievlianin* no. 146, 10 Dec. 1866: 582–583; no. 138, 18 Nov. 1872: 1–2; Hamm, "Kiev: Dubnov's Inferno of Russian Israel," 62.

140. Cited in I. S. Bliokh, *Sravnenie material'nago byta i nravstvennago sostoianiia naseleniia v cherte osedlosti evreev i vne ee. Tsifrovye dannye i issledovaniia po otnosheniiu k evreiskomu voprosu,* III: 128. The two Jewish members of the commission, Mandel'shtam and Barats, replied that these accusations were made simply in order to maintain a monopoly of a small circle of local merchants, to the detriment of local consumers.

141. Zipperstein, *The Jews of Odessa,* 115–116, 124–125; Klier, *Imperial Russia's Jewish Question,* 320–328.

142. Klier, *Imperial Russia's Jewish Question,* 300–320.

143. Subbotin, *V cherte,* 161.

144. *Kiev i ego sviatynia,* 235 ("Kak zhe dumaiut usvoit' sebe Kiev, v svoikh nesbytochnykh mechtakh, liudi sovershenno emu chuzhdye, ne sviazannye s nim nikakimi vospominaniiami otechestvennymi . . ."). The term *chuzhdie* may have been a reference to both Poles and Jews, but a later reference to unbelievers (*inovertsy*)—as well as the early date—suggest that the author was primarily concerned with the Poles of Kiev. The reference to the Lavra is to the holiest monastery in Kiev, the Caves Monastery in Pechersk, founded in 1015.

145. Murav'ev, "Zapiska o sokhranenii samobytnosti Kieva," 264.

146. Ibid.

147. Kaufman, "Cherta osedlosti v miniatiure," 613.

148. *Kievlianin* no. 26, 1 March 1873: 1–2; this phrase was repeated in subsequent years.

149. *Kievlianin* no. 40, 3 April 1873: 1; no. 126, 9 June 1885: 2.

150. TsDIAU f. 442, op. 50, spr. 302, ark. 1–6.

151. TsDIAU f. 707 (Upravlenie Kievskogo uchebnogo okruga), op. 203, spr. 58 ("O zakritii sushchestvuiushchego bez razresheniia v g. Kieve, v Plosskoi chasti v dome Bazilevskoi evreiskogo uchilishcha"), ark. 24–24zv. Filofei's choice of words reveals the likely influence of Iakov Brafman's *Kniga kagala* (Book of the Kahal), an antisemitic work that had been partially reprinted in *Kievlianin* in 1868. On *Kniga kagala,* see Dubnow, *History of the Jews in Russia and Poland,* II: 187–190, Gessen, *Istoriia,* II: 200–202, and Klier, *Imperial Russia's Jewish Question,* chap. 7.

152. RGIA f. 821 (Departament dukhovnykh del inostrannykh ispovedanii MVD), op. 9, d. 97 ("Po voprosu o razreshenii evreiam zhit' vo vsekh chastiakh g. Kieva"), ll. 8–9.

153. RGIA f. 821, op. 9, d. 97, l. 88ob.

154. Merder, "Melochi iz arkhivov iugo-zapadnago kraia," 10: 23–24; also cited in Hamm, *Kiev,* 53. Curiously, it was Jews who had first proposed the idea of a special Jewish hamlet, after their expulsion from Kiev in 1827, in order to carry on economic activities in the city without residing in it. RGIA f. 821, op. 9, d. 121 ("Po voprosu o prave zhitel'stva evreev v g. Kieve"), l. 61.

155. *Kievlianin* no. 106, 11 May 1880: 1.

156. RGIA f. 821, op. 9, d. 121, ll. 59–60.; see also "Evrei v Kieve," *Kievlianin* no. 206, 14 Sept. 1880: 1.

157. RGIA f. 821, op. 9, d. 121, l. 68.

158. Chertkov also referred to the "powerful global Jewish association," revealing that he, like Filofei before him, had been influenced by Brafman's *Kniga kagala.* RGIA f. 821, op. 9, d. 121, l. 70.

159. RGIA f. 821, op. 9, d. 121, l. 79ob. On the Commission, see *EE,* s.v. "Komissiia dlia ustroistva byta evreev"; Klier, *Imperial Russia's Jewish Question,* 181, 296–297.

160. *Kievlianin* no. 93, 25 April 1880: 1.

161. *Kievlianin* no. 106, 11 May 1880: 1.

162. *Russkii evrei* no. 24, 10 June 1881: 942.

163. *Kievlianin* no. 163, 25 July 1881.

164. *Materialy dlia istorii antievreiskikh pogromov v Rossii,* ed. G. Ia. Krasnyi-Admoni, II: 428.

165. *Kievlianin* no. 126, 9 June 1885: 2.

166. *Kievlianin* no. 246, 6 Nov. 1882: 1, emphasis added.

167. *Kievlianin* no. 40, 3 April 1873: 1.

168. TsDIAU f. 442, op. 533, spr. 17 ("Delo o zapreshchenii evreiam-prikazchikam, prozhivaiushchim v g. Kieve, sozdat' obshchestvo vzaimnogo vspomoshchestvovaniia"); RGIA f. 821, op. 8, d. 153 ("Evrei v g. Kieve"), ll. 26–33.

169. RGIA f. 821, op. 9, d. 121, l. 79ob.

170. Kaufman, "Cherta osedlosti v miniatiure," no. 17: 649–652; no. 19: 725–729.

171. *Kievlianin* no. 107, 9 Sept. 1871: 2.

172. *Kievlianin* no. 206, 14 Sept. 1880: 1.

173. Klier, *Russia Gathers Her Jews,* 87.

174. Kutaisov, "Pogromy v Kieve i Kievskoi gubernii," 428.

175. See Shmeruk, "Yiddish Literature and Collective Memory: The Case of the Chmielnicki Massacres," 173–183.

176. *Ha-melits* 5 May 1881: 346.

177. Hamm, *Kiev,* 124.

178. *Ha-magid* 4 May 1881 (22 April 1881 o.s.).

179. Aronson, *Troubled Waters*, 75–93; Aronson, "The Anti-Jewish Pogroms in Russia in 1881," 45.

180. *Materialy dlia istorii antievreiskikh pogromov*, 413.

181. The police report on the pogrom in Bul'varnyi district claimed that "there were rumors in Kiev that what happened in Elizavetgrad would happen in Kiev too." DAmK f. 237 (Kievskaia gorodskaia politsiia), op. 3, spr. 46-B ("O pogromakh 1881–83 gg."), ark. 12.

182. DAmK f. 237, op. 3, spr. 46-B, ark. 16–19, 24–25zv.

183. Klier, "Ethnicizing the Anti-Jewish Pogroms in Ukraine," paper presented at *"Prelude to the Holocaust? The Mass Dynamics of Anti-Jewish Violence in Eastern and East-Central Europe"* (conference held at University of Southampton, 18–20 March 2007). For the "Great Russian" theory, see Aronson, "Geographical and Socioeconomic Factors in the 1881 Anti-Jewish Pogroms in Russia," 18–31, and "The Anti-Jewish Pogroms in Russia in 1881," 47 and note 9 there. As Klier shows, the standard explanation of the "barefoot brigade" was frequently based on Governor-General Drentel'n's original report on the Kiev pogrom, which was duplicated in the classic 1923 volume by Krasnyi-Admoni (*Materialy dlia istorii antievreiskikh pogromov v Rossii*). Drentel'n would naturally have wanted to distance the people in his own provinces from culpability for the pogroms.

184. Gessen, *Istoriia*, II: 218.

185. See, for example, the police report for Pechersk district, whose author wrote that "the arousal of [the animosity and violence] was facilitated by the intoxicated state [of the pogromshchiki] and the lack of awareness that these actions had a criminal character, emerging as a result of the dissemination of those disgraceful rumors that the attacks against Jews and their property were sanctioned by the Emperor." DAmK f. 237, op. 3, spr. 46-B, ark. 8–8zv.

186. See Klier, "S. M. Dubnov and the Kiev Pogrom of 1882," 71.

187. *Materialy dlia istorii antievreiskikh pogromov*, 80; Klier, "Ethnicizing the Anti-Jewish Pogroms"; Hamm, *Kiev*, 125. For a controversial and largely discredited work that attempts to remove blame from Ukrainians, see Pritsak, "The Pogroms of 1881," 8–43.

188. DAmK f. 237, op. 3, spr. 46–B, ark. 16.

189. *Materialy dlia istorii antievreiskikh pogromov*, 397.

190. IR TsNB f. 321 (Kollektsiia evreiskikh rukopisei), op. 1, spr. OR 64, n. 38 ("Pinkas me-ha-havura mishnayot mi-beit ha-midrash Rozenberg poalei tsedek Kiev"), ark. 6–7.

191. *Materialy dlia istorii antievreiskikh pogromov*, 397–400.

192. Hamm, "Kiev: Dubnov's Inferno of Russian Israel," 59. Hamm is referring to I. Michael Aronson's analysis of the Kiev pogrom. See also Hamm, *Kiev*, 126.

193. Klier, "S. M. Dubnov and the Kiev Pogrom of 1882," 69–71.

194. See *Ha-melits* no. 111, 20 May 1891: 1–2; no. 48, 24 Feb. 1892: 2. In the 1890s, Grebin' was known for his access to high officials and representations on behalf of the Jewish community, most notably for permission from the chief of police to allow a group of nonresident Jews to enter Kiev each year to help bake the Passover matzot. Perhaps the fact that his house was protected by the troops had something to do with his connections. *Ha-melits* no. 75, 30 March 1894: 2–3; no. 63, 16 March 1895: 2.

195. DAmK f. 237, op. 3, spr. 46–B, ark. 9–11.

196. In addition to the police reports cited above, see also the letter of Professor N. I. Petrov to his brother describing the pogrom, TsDIAU f. 1423, op. 1, spr. 28 ("Pis'mo professora i akademika N.I. Petrova k bratu Ivanu o evreiskom pogrome v Kieve v 1881 g., ot 29 aprelia 1881 g."), cited in Khiterer, *Dokumenty sobrannye Evreiskoi istoriko-arkheograficheskoi komissiei Vseukrainskoi akademii nauk*, 190–192.

197. *Materialy dlia istorii antievreiskikh pogromov,* 533 and Hamm, *Kiev,* 255 n. 32. It is unclear what portion of the 769 Jewish victims were householders, but the percentage was probably about the same.

198. *Materialy dlia istorii antievreiskikh pogromov,* 396.

199. Aronson, *Troubled Waters,* 87.

200. Kievskoe evreiskoe obshchestvo dlia vspomoshchestvovaniia postradavshim ot bezporiadkov na iuge Rossii 1881 g., *Otchet,* 2, 8. For more on the Pogrom Aid Society, see Chapter 6.

201. *EE,* s.v. "Kiev."

202. Frankel, *Prophecy and Politics,* 68. Jews were also expelled from Orel, Tambov, and Dubno. See RGIA f. 821, op. 9, d. 121, ll. 81–86ob for official memoranda and discussions of the Kiev expulsion.

203. Klier, "Jewish Responses to the Pogroms," unpaginated draft of chapter for Klier's forthcoming book, now being edited for posthumous publication by François Guesnet.

204. Klier, "S. M. Dubnov and the Kiev Pogrom of 1882," 65.

205. *Ha-melits* no. 50, 9 Jan. 1883.

206. *Ha-melits* no. 11, 7 Feb. 1883, and cf. Heinz-Dietrich Löwe, "Pogroms in Russia: Explanations, Comparisons, Suggestions," 21.

207. RGIA f. 821, op. 9, d. 121, ll. 87–91.

208. See Baron, *Russian Jew,* 56–57; Rogger, *Jewish Policies and Right-Wing Politics,* 144–156.

209. *Russkii kur'er* no. 116, 26 April 1881: 3.

2. The Foundations of Communal Life

1. See, for example, Stanislawski, *Tsar Nicholas,* 97–109; Levitats, *Jewish Community,* 45–55; Freeze, *Jewish Marriage and Divorce,* 79–130; Shohat, *Mosad ha-rabanut mi-ta'am be-Rusyah,* 16–60.

2. Lederhender, *Road to Modern Jewish Politics,* 74ff.

3. For a description of the aristocracy, see Nathans, *Beyond the Pale,* 38–44.

4. From the early years of Russian rule, Jewish merchants had been allowed to enjoy many of the same rights as Christian members of the merchant guilds, and were exempted "from the rolls of the Jewish community proper, for crucial purposes such as taxation and military service." Stanislawski, "Russian Jewry, the Russian State, and the Dynamics of Jewish Emancipation," 267. See also Klier, *Russia Gathers Her Jews,* 67.

5. Nathans, *Beyond the Pale,* 40.

6. Gessen, *Istoriia,* II: 68 ("kuptsy ne platili podatei i potomu ne nesli material'noi otvetstvennosti za postuplenie podati s obshchestva"); Klier, *Russia Gathers Her Jews,* 67.

7. Gessen, *Istoriia,* II: 69–70.

8. Nathans, *Beyond the Pale,* 37.

9. Stanislawski, *Tsar Nicholas,* 40.

10. Levitats, *Jewish Community,* 7.

11. Dubnow, *History of the Jews in Russia and Poland,* I: 367; II: 60.

12. Gessen, *Istoriia,* II: 94.

13. *EE,* s.v. "Obshchina evreiskaia v Rossii."

14. Shohat, "Ha-hanhaga be-kehilot Rusyah": 163. Shohat surmises that the deputaty were the consultative body of the sborshchiki.

15. Levitats, *Jewish Community,* 11, 30, 58–59, 172.

16. Kappeler, *The Russian Empire: A Multi-Ethnic History,* 129.

17. G., "Pis'mo iz Kieva," *Vestnik evreiskoi obshchiny* no. 1 (Aug.) 1913: 37.

18. This kind of confusion was not unusual in the "undergoverned" provinces of the Russian empire before the Great Reforms; see Starr, *Decentralization and Self-Government in Russia, 1830–1870*, 3–50.

19. Shohat, "Ha-hanhagah be-kehilot Rusyah," 186; Gessen, *Istoriia*, II: 170.

20. Wirtschafter, *Social Identity*, 133.

21. Stanislawski, *Tsar Nicholas*, 127.

22. "Some municipal administrations, aiming to expand their own power, grant rights to the 'prosperous and settled,' on one hand, and to the 'ritual committee boards' [of prayer houses], which exist outside the law, on the other—rights that in reality belong to the entire community. *EE*, "Obshchina evreiskaia v Rossii."

23. Ibid.

24. Nathans, *Beyond the Pale*, 153–155.

25. Polishchuk, *Evrei Odessy i Novorossii*, 267; Shaw, "The Odessa Jewish Community 1855–1900," 175.

26. Shohat also comes to this conclusion, citing the prescient remark of Ludwig Phillippson, editor of the *Algemeine Zeitung des Judentums*, in that journal in 1845 (vol. 11, no. 47, 17 Nov. 1845: 696) that the abolition of the kahal was intended to make of Jewry (*Judenheit*) "eine todte Masse von Atomen." Shohat, "Ha-hanhagah be-kehilot Rusyah," 154.

27. This shift was symbolized by permission for *khoziaistvennye pravleniia* only, not *dukhovnye pravleniia*; a rough English-language parallel would be "synagogue management committees" versus "ritual committees." In a letter to the Kiev Chief of Police dated 18 Nov. 1869, Crown Rabbi Joshua Tsukkerman remarked that *dukhovnye pravleniia* were already banned within Kiev's Jewish prayer houses. DAmK f. 17 (Kievskaia gorodskaia duma), op. 4, spr. 2643 ("O provedenii vyborov ravvina"), ark. 31.

28. As we saw in Chapter 1, Russian bureaucrats were clearly influenced by Iakov Brafman's *Book of the Kahal*, an attack on the alleged power and global reach of the organized Jewish community that advocated the abolition of small prayer quorums, regulation of the selection of communal officials, and a reduction in the number of voluntary societies. Lederhendler, *Road to Modern Jewish Politics*, 143.

29. Ibid., 84–110, 157; Nathans, *Beyond the Pale*, 50–59.

30. Lederhendler, *Road to Modern Jewish Politics*, 111ff.

31. Raeff, "Patterns of Russian Imperial Policy toward the Nationalities," 35–37; Weeks, *Nation and State*; Geraci, *Window on the East*; Thaden and Thaden, *Russia's Western Borderlands*, conclusion; Starr, "The Tsarist Government: The Imperial Dimension," 3–38. For an analysis of the Ukrainian component in the imperial bureaucracy administering the Ukrainian lands, see Velychenko, "Identities, Loyalties and Service in Imperial Russia: Who Administered the Borderlands?" 188–208.

32. Crews, "Empire and the Confessional State: Islam and Religious Politics in Nineteenth-Century Russia," par. 16.

33. *Ha-magid* no. 22, 7 June 1871: 171.

34. *Zapiska o Kievskoi evreiskoi bol'nitse*, 3.

35. *Ha-magid* no. 22, 7 June (26 May o.s.) 1871: 171.

36. *Kol mevaser* no. 15, 20 April 1872: 115 ("Di yuden in Kiev"). This account is corroborated by a description of the dedication of the hospital's new building in 1885. *Ha-melits* no. 81, 1 Nov. 1885: 1311–17.

37. Vasil'chikova and Kupernik are identified by Tmol bar Yente only as "V." and "K.," but their identities are corroborated by other sources. The identity of "B." is unclear.

38. Konel'skii, "Kievskiia evreiskiia blagotvoritel'niia uchrezhdeniia," *Razsvet* no. 3, 17 Jan. 1880: col. 92.

39. *Zapiska o Kievskoi evreiskoi bol'nitse,* 3.

40. Ibid., 4. Six years later, however, the hospital still had only twenty beds. Zakrevskii, *Opisanie Kieva,* 129.

41. *Zapiska o Kievskoi evreiskoi bol'nitse,* 13.

42. *Kievlianin* no. 42, 7 April 1870: 3.

43. TsDIAU f. 707 (Upravlenie Kievskogo uchebnogo okruga), op. 87, spr. 5686, ark. 67–67zv.

44. *Kievlianin* no. 42, 9 April 1866: 161.

45. RGIA f. 733, op. 149, d. 39, ll. 1–2, cited in Nathans, *Beyond the Pale,* 226.

46. *Kievskii telegraf* no. 12, 29 Jan. 1865: 2.

47. Nathans, *Beyond the Pale,* 150.

48. DAKO f. 1 (Kievskoe gubernskoe pravlenie), op. 131, spr. 153 ("O Kievskom korobochnom sbore s 1890 po 1894 gg."), ark. 76zv.

49. There were at least seven Jewish city councilors before 1883, including Lazar' Brodsky, M. D. Vainshtein, G. M. Rozenberg, Avraham Kupernik, and Crown Rabbi Evsei Tsukkerman. *Kievlianin* no. 78, 3 July 1879; *Kievlianin* no. 60, 17 March 1883; *Voskhod* 17, 1904; *Zapiska o Kievskoi evreiskoi bol'nitse.* The Municipal Statute of 1870 created city councils (*dumy*) "elected on the basis of property qualifications," regardless of soslovie. Wirtschafter, *Social Identity,* 138; Nardova, "Municipal Self-Government After the 1870 Reform," 184.

50. "Iz Iugo-zapadnago Kraia," *Novoe vremia* no. 5270, 30 Oct. 1890, cited in TsDIAU f. 442 (Kantseliaria Kievskogo, Podol'skogo i Volynskogo general-gubernatora), op. 528, spr. 450 ("Ob osnovanii i deiatel'nosti evreiskikh molitvennykh domov i sinagog v g. Kieve"), ark. 1–4.

51. See Nathans, *Beyond the Pale,* 149–152.

52. DAKO f. 1, op. 131, spr. 153, ark. 76zv; RGIA f. 821 (Departament dukhovnykh del inostrannykh ispovedanii MVD), op. 8, d. 108 ("Ob ustanovlenii novogo poriadka deiatel'nosti evreiskikh blagotvoritel'nykh obshchestv i po voprosu o vozmozhnosti uprazdneniia evreiskhikh pogrebatel'nykh bratstv"), l. 182.

53. *Zapiska o Kievskoi evreiskoi bol'nitse,* 18.

54. In fact, when the hospital was granted a new charter in 1891 and the old hospital committee ceased functioning, Kiev's mayor asked Governor L. N. Tamara to whom the kosher tax funds for communal needs other than the hospital should now be given. Neishtube, *Istoricheskaia zapiska v pamiat' 50-ti letiia sushchestvovaniia Kievskoi Evreiskoi Bol'nitsy, 1862–1912 g.,* 48. Clearly, the hospital committee had allocated the funds for the entire community. See also Konel'skii, "Kievskiia evreiskiia blagotvoritel'niia uchrezhdeniia": "This committee [*popechitel'stvo*] is in actuality the only official representative [body] for Kiev Jews, not only in relation to the hospital, but in other affairs as well."

55. This is made clear by an 1890 memorandum from the provincial governor, referring to "the Jewish Committee, which was originally confirmed by the city council on 4 Aug. 1875 for Jewish Hospital affairs." DAKO f. 1, op. 131, spr. 153, ark. 76zv.

56. *Kol mevaser* no. 17, 4 May 1872: 125–126.

57. Dal', *Tolkovyi slovar' zhivago velikorusskago iazyka.* See also Pushkarev, *Dictionary of Russian Historical Terms from the Eleventh Century to 1917,* s.v. "Obshchestvo."

58. DAmK f. 17, op. 4, spr. 2643 ("O provedenii vyborov ravvina").

59. In Kiev, it was even used in the early nineteenth century, when a statute (*polozhenie*) of the Committee of Ministers from 1831 used the term: "At the request of the trustees of the Kiev Jewish Society/Corporation ("Kievskoe Evreiskoe Obshchestvo"), petitioning for the

extension of the delay granted to Kiev's Jews ("Kievskim Evreiam") for their expulsion . . ." Levanda, *Pol'nyi khronologicheskii sbornik,* 293.

60. For the 1876 figures, see *Ha-melits* no. 290, 30 Dec. 1892: 5–6. M. Konel'skii, "Kievskiia evreiskiia blagotvoritel'niia uchrezhdeniia," col. 92.

61. *Ha-melits* no. 73, 18 Sept. 1884: 1196; *Ha-melits* no. 85, 29 Oct. 1884: 1865–1866; *Jewish Chronicle* 25 June 1880: 12 and 2 July 1880: 10; *Ha-melits* no. 80, 28 Oct. 1885: 1302; *Ha-melits* no. 81, 1 Nov. 1885: 1311–1317. According to one account, the maternity clinic was founded independently by a group of wealthy Jewish benefactresses but was later appended to the hospital. Konel'skii, "Kievskiia evreiskiia blagotvoritel'niia uchrezhdeniia."

62. *Ha-melits* 26, 8 April 1885: 416–417; Khiterer, "The Social and Economic History of Jews in Kiev," 224.

63. *Ha-melits* no. 50, 29 June 1884: 835; no. 1, 4 Jan. 1885: 10–11; no. 26, 8 April 1885: 416–417; no. 85, 15 April 1891: 3; no. 24, 29 Jan. 1892: 2.

64. Klier, *Imperial Russia's Jewish Question,* 276.

65. *Kievlianin* no. 78, 3 July 1879.

66. M. Konel'skii, "Kievskiia evreiskiia blagotvoritel'niia uchrezhdeniia," col. 91.

67. TsDIAU f. 442, op. 528, spr. 450, ark. 1–4.

68. DAKO f. 1, op. 131, spr. 153, ark. 29–29zv.

69. See Nathans, *Beyond the Pale,* 141–142.

70. DAKO f. 1, op. 131, spr. 153, ark. 93.

71. DAKO f. 1, op. 131, spr. 153, ark. 100.

72. Kupernik, *Le-korot benei yisra'el be-kiyov,* 9.

73. Ibid., 9–11.

74. DAKO f. 1, op. 131, spr. 153, ark. 36.

75. The abolition of the committee may also have had something to do with the adoption of a new charter for the Jewish Hospital in 1891, which created a board subject to the authority of the governor of Kiev province. This development may have served to sever the last link between the governance of the hospital and general communal functions, including the distribution of the kosher tax revenues.

76. RGIA f. 821, op. 8, d. 108, l. 183ob.

77. *Kievskoe slovo* no. 2348, 28 July 1894: 2–3.

78. See, for example, Bradley, "Subjects into Citizens: Societies, Civil Society, and Autocracy in Tsarist Russia," par. 29 ("By the end of nineteenth century, the relationship between government and more and more associations became politicized and confrontational") and Lindenmeyr, *Poverty Is Not a Vice,* 176–178, 198–199.

79. RGIA f. 821, op. 8, d. 108, l. 185. The Russian term was *pogrebal'noe obshchestvo.*

80. See Klier, "Russkaia voina protiv 'Khevra kadisha,'" 109–114.

81. *EE,* s.v. "Blagotvoritel'niia uchrezhdeniia."

82. RGIA f. 821, op. 8, d. 108, l. 195.

83. Ibid., ll. 143–147.

84. Ibid., l. 176.

85. Cited in Rogger, *Jewish Policies and Right-Wing Politics,* 73.

86. RGIA f. 821, op. 8, d. 108, ll. 180–199.

87. Ibid., ll. 196–197ob. The governor-general did not specify to which "illegal goals" he was referring.

88. Rogger, *Jewish Policies,* 78–79.

89. Neishtube, *Istoricheskaia zapiska,* 40.

90. RGIA f. 821, op. 8, d. 108, l. 186.

91. *Kievskoe slovo* no. 2805, 2 Nov. 1895; *Nedel'naia khronika Voskhoda* no. 46, 12 Nov. 1895: 1265.

92. RGIA f. 821, op. 133, d. 782 ("Ob ustroistve khoziaistvennykh i dukhovnykh upravlenii pri evreiskikh molitvennykh uchrezhdeniiakh"), l. 4ob.

93. For example, the article in *Novoe vremia* discussed earlier in this chapter maintained that wealthy Jews preached "'an eye for an eye'—hate for all that is Russian." TsDIAU f. 442, op. 528, spr. 450, ark. 2zv.

94. See Klier, *Imperial Russia's Jewish Question,* 441.

95. TsDIAU f. 442, op. 528, spr. 450, ark. 71–71zv.

96. *Ha-melits* no. 63, 16 March 1895: 2.

97. *Ha-melits* no. 48, 26 Feb. 1896: 3.

98. *Ha-melits* no. 68, 22 March 1895: 2.

99. *Ha-melits* no. 63, 16 March 1895: 2; no. 48, 26 Feb. 1896: 3.

100. *Ha-melits* no. 88, 23 April 1895: 2.

101. *Ha-melits* no. 63, 16 March 1895: 2.

102. Rogger, *Jewish Policies,* 69.

103. *Nedel'naia khronika Voskhoda* no. 18, 1 May 1894: 488.

104. *Khronika Voskhoda* no. 30, 25 July 1899: 917–918.

105. *Khronika Voskhoda* no. 34, 15 Aug. 1899: 1036–1037.

106. Ibid., 1038–1039.

107. *Voskhod* no. 9, 3 Feb. 1900: 12.

108. Ibid.

109. Lindenmeyr, *Poverty Is Not a Vice,* 198–199.

110. *Khronika Voskhoda* no. 39, 19 Sept. 1899: 1194–1197.

111. Lindenmeyr, *Poverty Is Not a Vice,* 204. For a fuller discussion of Jewish philanthropy in Kiev, see Chapter 6.

112. *Voskhod* no. 95, 6 Dec. 1900: 18.

113. *Voskhod* no. 25, 12 April 1901: 15.

114. *Voskhod* no. 5, 21 Jan. 1901: 13.

115. *Voskhod* no. 25, 12 April 1901: 15.

116. Nathans, *Beyond the Pale,* 138–140.

117. *Voskhod* no. 9, 3 Feb. 1900: 12; no. 25, 12 April 1901: 14.

118. *Voskhod* no. 49, 5 Dec. 1903: 26–27.

119. TsDIAU f. 442, op. 628, spr. 190.

120. *EE,* s.v. "Ravvinat"; Levitats, *Jewish Community,* 85; *Voskhod* no. 25, 19 June 1903: 13. The system was indirect, with parishioners voting for electors, who then cast the deciding ballots.

121. DAmK f. 17 (Kievskaia gorodskaia duma), op. 4, spr. 659 ("O naznachenii v g. Kieve ravvina").

122. Freeze, *Jewish Marriage and Divorce,* 98–106.

123. Gessen, *Istoriia,* II: 175.

124. Shohat, *Mosad ha-rabanut,* 52, 56, 58; Freeze, *Jewish Marriage and Divorce,* 104–105.

125. At the dedication of the new building of the Jewish Hospital, for example: *Ha-melits* no. 81, 1 Nov. 1885: 1311–1317.

126. *Ha-melits* no. 108, 17 May 1896: 3–4.

127. TsDIAU f. 442, op. 525, spr. 172 ("Po prosheniiu Kievskogo ravvina Tsukkerman o prisvoenii emu zvanii potomstvennogo pochetnogo grazhdanina").

128. Communal dissident Shtammer's claim that Tsukkerman's annual income was very large—at least 6,000 rubles a year—is substantiated by Darewski's mention of the Crown rabbi's salary being 2,000 rubles after the two-thirds cut of all communal expenses by the governor-general in 1892. *Kto vinovat? K vyboram ravvina v Kieve*, 17. *Ha-melits* no. 290, 30 Dec. 1892: 5–6. To put this amount into perspective, one of the indigent spiritual rabbis of Kiev was given a monthly subsidy of 20 rubles to cover rent for what was probably a very modest apartment. *Ha-melits* no. 40, 16 Feb. 1896: 5.

129. Sholem Aleichem, *From the Fair*, 262–263.

130. *Kol mevaser* no. 40, 14 Oct. 1871: 298–300.

131. *Ha-melits* no. 11, 6 Feb. 1884: 169.

132. *Ha-melits* no. 34, 6 May 1885: 550–551.

133. *Ha-melits* no. 11, 6 Feb. 1884, p. 169; *Ha-melits* no. 34, 6 May 1885: 550–551.

134. *Ha-melits* no. 9, 11 Jan. 1894: 2–3.

135. *Ha-melits* no. 231, 21 Oct. 1894: 4–5; no. 49, 28 Feb. 1895: 1; no. 69, 23 March 1895: 1–2.

136. *Ha-melits* no. 290, 30 Dec. 1892: 5–6.

137. *Ha-melits* no. 112, 17 May 1894: 4–5.

138. *Ha-melits* no. 251, 13 Nov. 1892: 4–5.

139. Ianovskii, *Evreiskaia blagotvoritel'nost'*, 19.

140. *Ha-melits* no. 39, 19 Sept. 1899: 1194–97; Ianovskii, *Evreiskaia blagotvoritel'nost'*, 38.

141. Ianovskii, *Evreiskaia blagotvoritel'nost'*, 16, 39.

142. *Ha-melits* no. 251, 13 Nov. 1892: 4–5.

143. Shtammer, *Kto vinovat?* 17–18. I have not been able to find any information on Shtammer in other sources.

144. Shtammer, *Kto vinovat?* 5.

145. DAmK f. 163 (Kievskaia gorodskaia uprava), op. 7, spr. 2069 ("O naznachenii vyborov ravvina po gorodu Kieva na trekhletie s 1897 po 1899 god"), ark. 1–1zv.

146. DAmK f. 163 (Kievskaia gorodskaia uprava), op. 7, spr. 997 ("O vybore kievskogo ravvina"); *Kievlianin* no. 82, 13 April 1884: 1.

147. Shtammer, *Na Sud obshchestvennago mneniia*, 11–13. According to Shtammer, this occurred in 1886 (Shtammer, *Kto vinovat?* 5), but archival records seem to show that the Governor of Kiev guberniia told the municipal administration (*gorodskaia uprava*) *in 1881* that only permanent residents could vote. DAmK f. 163, op. 7, spr. 2069, ark. 1.

148. Shtammer, *Na Sud obshchestvennago mneniia*, 13–14; Shtammer, *Kto vinovat?* 14–15. There is evidence that may substantiate Shtammer's claim that the change was motivated by a request from within the Jewish community: an 1897 memorandum from the guberniia authorities to the municipal administration notes that several Kiev Jews had petitioned to preserve the previous manner of carrying out rabbinical elections in Kiev, and the governor-general had acceded to their request. DAmK f. 163, op. 7, spr. 2069, ark. 20–21. According to Polishchuk, however, these laws were for Odessa, too, so perhaps they were meant to cover the entire empire: first the law on all Jews having the right to vote, and then the law on electors. Polishchuk, *Evrei Odessy i Novorossii*, 287.

149. DAKO f. 1 (Kievskoe gubernskoe pravlenie), op. 141, spr. 497 ("O vybore chlenov khoziaistvennykh pravlenii v Kievskie evreiskie molel'ni"), ark. 4.

150. Shohat, *Mosad ha-rabanut*, 53; Levitats, *Jewish Community*, 56.

151. *Kol mevaser* no. 31, 31 July 1869: 317–319.

152. *Kol mevaser* no. 42, 22 Oct. 1870: 309–310.

153. DAKO f. 1, op. 336, d. 6197 ("Spisok sinagog i evreiskikh molitvennykh domov v g. Kieve i uezde"), ark. 1a–4zv.

154. *Kievlianin* no. 42, 9 April 1866: 161.

155. DAmK f. 17, op. 4, spr. 2643, ark. 31.

156. TsDIAU f. 442, op. 46, spr. 35 ("Delo o razreshenii ravvinu Tsukkermanu postroit' v g. Kieve molitvennyi dom").

157. *Kol mevaser* no. 31, 31 July 1869: 317–319.

158. [Kel'berin], *Desiatiletie Kievskago evreiskago khoral'nago molitvennago doma,* 5–6, 9.

159. Ibid., 7. The petition is also cited in RGIA f. 821, op. 8, d. 153, ll. 7–8ob.

160. Osip Rabinovich, "Novaia evreiskaia sinagoge v Odesse," in *Sochineniia* (Odessa, 1888), vol. 3, 373–374, cited in Stanislawski, *Tsar Nicholas,* 140.

161. TsDIAU f. 442, op. 528, spr. 450, ark. 17; *Ha-melits* no. 223, 8 Oct. 1891: 2. On Montefiore, see *Encyclopaedia Judaica,* s.v. "Moses Montefiore" (vol. XII: 271).

162. [Kel'berin], *Desiatiletie,* 8.

163. *Ha-melits* no. 198, 31 Aug. 1894: 2.

164. *Ha-melits* no. 108, 17 May 1896: 3–4.

165. *Ha-melits* no. 195, 31 Aug. 1898: 2.

166. *Ha-melits* no. 34, 6 May 1885: 550–551.

167. *Ha-melits* no. 6, 21 Feb. 1885: 88–93.

168. TsDIAU f. 442, op. 528, spr. 450, ark. 11zv; *Ha-melits* no. 223, 8 Oct. 1891: 2; *Ha-melits* no. 231, 21 Oct. 1894: 4–5; *Ha-melits* no. 108, 17 May 1896: 3–4.

169. Friedmann, *Sefer ha-zikhronot,* 195–196.

170. [Kel'berin], *Desiatiletie,* 14–15.

171. Ibid., 16–19.

172. TsDIAU f. 442, op. 528, spr. 450.

173. Kel'berin, *Desiatiletie,* 17.

174. *Nedel'naia khronika Voskhoda* no. 46, 12 Nov. 1895: 1265; TsDIAU f. 442, op. 528, spr. 450, ark. 46–51zv.

175. DAmK f. 163, op. 7, spr. 2069, ark. 1–1zv.

176. *Voskhod* no. 25, 19 June 1903: 13.

177. RGIA f. 821, op. 8, d. 153, ll. 26–33.

3. The Consolidation of Jewish Kiev, 1881–1914

1. Starozhil [Sergei Iaron], *Kiev,* 28.

2. The city's 1884 population is estimated at 154,000. *Istoriia Kieva,* I: 339.

3. *EE,* s.v. "Kiev."

4. Kievskoe Obshchestvo Gramotnosti, *Otchet za . . . god* (Kiev, 1896–1906).

5. *Khronika Voskhoda* no. 24, 13 June 1899; *Izvestiia Kievskoi gorodskoi dumy* no. 6 (June) 1906; Kievskaia gorodskaia uchilishchnaia komissiia, *Otchet . . . za 1909 g.* (Kiev, 1911).

6. *Sankt-Peterburgskie vedemosti* no. 175, 27 June 1884: 3.

7. Wynn, *Workers, Strikes, and Pogroms,* 111.

8. Cited in *Nedel'naia khronika Voskhoda* no. 35, 1 Sept. 1885: 948.

9. See, for example, *Nedel'naia khronika Voskhoda* no. 23, 5 June 1894. This was called *po etapu* in Russian.

10. *Voskhod* no. 60, 21 Oct. 1901: 14.

11. See, for example, *Die Judenpogrome in Russland,* II: 343.

12. Sholem Aleichem, *From the Fair,* 256.

13. Sholem Aleichem, *The Further Adventures of Menachem Mendl (New York-Warsaw-Vienna-Yehupetz)*, 163. For a description of a real-life oblava, see his letter to Simon Dubnow, 7 Aug. 1888, in Sholem Aleichem, *Mikhtevei Shalom-Aleikhem, 1881–1916*, 83.

14. *Nedel'naia khronika Voskhoda* no. 23, 5 June 1894: 634.

15. *Nedel'naia khronika Voskhoda* no. 19, 7 May 1895: 514.

16. Dubnow, *History of the Jews in Russia and Poland*, II: 346.

17. *Ha-melits* no. 85, 15 April 1891: 3 and no. 107, 15 May 1891: 2.

18. DAKO f. 1 (Kievskoe gubernskoe pravlenie), op. 131, spr. 185 ("O vyselenii iz Kieva evreia Simkhi Osadchego").

19. DAKO f. 1, op. 132, spr. 779 ("O vyselenii iz g. Kieva remeslennika-evreia Efshteina").

20. *Unzer leben* no. 279, 2 Dec. 1911: 4.

21. See Dubnow, *History of the Jews in Russia and Poland*, II: 399–406.

22. For "legislative pogrom," see Dubnow, *History of the Jews in Russia and Poland*, II: 309; for "cold pogrom," see Berk, *Year of Crisis, Year of Hope: Russian Jewry and the Pogroms of 1881–1882*, 180; for "silent pogrom," see Nathans, *Beyond the Pale*, 257.

23. *Voskhod* no. 35, 29 Aug. 1902.

24. Subbotin, *V cherte*, 157.

25. Lestschinsky, "Di idishe bafelkerung," 50.

26. Tsentral'nyi statisticheskii komitet, *Pervaia vseobshchaia perepis' naseleniia rossiiskoi imperii, 1897 g*, vol. 16: 2; Rubinow, *Economic Condition of the Jews in Russia*, 491.

27. Nathans, *Beyond the Pale*, 111; B. Gol'dberg, "O rodnom iazyke u evreev Rossii," 77.

28. *Pervaia vseobshchaia perepis'*, vol. 16: 2.

29. Ibid.; Freeze, *Jewish Marriage and Divorce*, 303.

30. *Pervaia vseobshchaia perepis'*, vol. 16: 2; Hamm, *Kiev*, 103.

31. Subbotin, *V cherte*, 181–182.

32. Lestschinsky, "Di idishe bafelkerung," 56.

33. Friedmann, *Sefer ha-zikhronot*, 215–216.

34. Rubinow, *Economic Condition*, 493.

35. Wirtschafter, *Social Identity*, 147.

36. See Soyer, *Jewish Immigrant Associations and American Identity in New York, 1880–1939*.

37. *Haynt* no. 144, 23 June 1910: 2.

38. Wirtschafter, *Social Identity*, 149.

39. Lestschinsky, "Di idishe bafelkerung," 50.

40. *Die Judenpogrome*, II: 339. Most of the population figures for cities covered in the volume are from the 1897 census, and indicated as such; not so with the figure for Kiev.

41. *Novyi voskhod* no. 37, 13 Sept. 1912.

42. Rozenblat, "Herzl u-mandelshtam," 583.

43. Gessen, *Istoriia*, II: 230

44. Sheinis, *Evreiskoe studenchestvo v tsifrakh (po dannym perepisi 1909 g. v Kievskom Universitete i Politekhnicheskom Institute)*, iii; Estraikh, "From Yehupets Jargonists to Kiev Modernists: The Rise of a Yiddish Literary Centre, 1880s–1914," 23.

45. DAKO f. 1, op. 142, spr. 407 ("O razreshenii evreiam, vospityvaiushchimsia v kievskikh uchebnykh zavedeniiakh, zhit' v Kieve"), l. 13 This *delo* has 472 folio pages of similar petitions.

46. DAKO f. 1, op. 140, spr. 350 ("O razreshenii Sone Zlobinskoi s sestrami zhit' v Kieve").

47. Haberer, *Jews and Revolution in Nineteenth-Century Russia*, 257.

48. Slutsky, *Ha-itonut ha-yehudit-rusit be-reshit ha-me'a ha-'esrim*, 133. See YIVO RG 80, folder 725, file 71, 4–5, for secret police memoranda from 1902 and 1903 that still refer to the group as "Frayhayt."

49. Nokhem Shtif, "Oytobiografye," *YIVO Bleter* 5 (1933): 195–225, cited in Dawidowicz, *The Golden Tradition: Jewish Life and Thought in Eastern Europe*, 258.

50. Subbotin, *V cherte*, 168.

51. Ibid., 170.

52. Ibid., 177–178.

53. Ibid., 173–174.

54. Jewish Colonization Association, *Récueil de Matériaux sur la situation économique des Israélites de Russie*, II: 196.

55. Subbotin, *V cherte*, 179.

56. Estraikh, "Yehupets Jargonists," 22.

57. *Pervaia vseobshchaia perepis'*, vol. 16: 2; Khodos, *Materialy po statistike naseleniia g. Kieva*, 140.

58. See, for example, *Ha-melits* no. 249, 12 Nov. 1896: 4, reporting on articles in *Kievlianin*.

59. Subbotin, *V cherte*, 170.

60. TsGIAU f. 1423 (Dokumenty, sobrannye Evreiskoi istoriko-arkheograficheskoi komissiei VUAN (Kollektsiia)), op. 1, spr. 28, cited in Khiterer, *Dokumenty sobrannye Evreiskoi*, 190–192. See also Kal'nyts'kyi, *Kyïv: turystychnyi putivnyk*, 575.

61. *Ha-melits* no. 33, 8 Feb. 1895: 2.

62. DAKO f. 1, op. 140, spr. 305 ("O razreshenii Tube Timen derzhat' razreshennykh v 1892 g. ee muzhu 5 prikazchikov v Kieve").

63. DAKO f. 1, op. 140, spr. 350.

64. DAKO f. 1, op. 140, spr. 686 ("Po khodataistvu Estry Gol'dshtein o razreshenii ei imet' v Kieve domashniuiu prislugu Khaiu Tsynman").

65. Jewish Colonization Association, *Récueil de Matériaux*, I: 349.

66. Subbotin, *V cherte*, 178–179.

67. *Pervaia vseobshchaia perepis'*, vol. 16: 2; Khodos, *Materialy po statistike naseleniia*, 140.

68. DAKO f. 1, op. 140, spr. 783 ("O razreshenii zhitel'stva v g. Kieve Rukhle Roitman kak beloshveike").

69. Freeze, "Making and Unmaking the Jewish Family," 270.

70. DAKO f. 1, op. 140, spr. 281 ("Po khodataistvu Fani Manilevoi o razreshenii ottsu ee zhit' pri nei v g. Kieve").

71. Jewish Colonization Association, *Récueil de Matériaux*, I: 368.

72. McReynolds and Popkin, "The Objective Eye and the Common Good," 111.

73. Jewish Colonization Association, *Récueil de Matériaux*, I: 369.

74. Otdel popecheniia ob evreiskikh devushkakh i zhenshchinakh g. Kieva pri Kievskom Otdelenii Rossiiskago Zashchity Zhenshchin, *Otchet za 1914 g. (god pervyi)* (Kiev, 1915).

75. On "the expansion of women's employment in positions requiring education," more generally, see Engel, *Between the Fields and the City: Women, Work, and Family in Russia, 1861–1914*, and idem, *Women in Russia, 1700–2000*, 111.

76. As a point of comparison, 42 percent of the mostly Russian and Polish women from outside Kiev residing at the shelter of the Kiev Branch of the Russian Society for the Defense of Women in 1912 were working in domestic service, while 6 percent were students at institutions of higher education. Kievskoe Otdelenie Rossiiskago Obshchestva Zashchity Zhenshchin, *Otchet za 1912 god* (Kiev, 1913).

77. Over one-quarter of all female students studying to be fel'dsher-midwives in the Russian Empire in 1910 were Jewish. Ramer, "The Transformation of the Russian Feldsher, 1864–1914," 152.

78. DAmK f. 163 (Kievskaia gorodskaia uprava), op. 5, spr. 23 ("O pravovom polozhenii torgovtsev evreiskoi natsional'nosti na gorodskikh bazarakh, 1890–1892"), ark. 5–8.

79. Obshchestvo letnikh sanatornykh kolonii dlia bol'nykh evreev neimushchago naseleniia g. Kieva, *Otchet po soderzhaniiu sanatornoi kolonii v Boiarke za 1910 god* (Kiev, 1911), 10.

80. Predstavitel'stvo po evreiskoi blagotvoritel'nosti pri Kievskoi Gorodskoi Uprave, *Otchet za 1913 god.*

81. Obshchestvo letnikh sanatornykh kolonii dlia bol'nykh evreev neimushchago naseleniia g. Kieva, *Otchet po soderzhaniiu sanatornoi kolonii v Boiarke za 1912 god*, 7–9.

82. TsDIAU f. 442 (Kantseliaria Kievskogo, Podol'skogo i Volynskogo general-gubernatora), op. 56, spr. 173, ark. 1–6. TsDIAU f. 442, op. 56, spr. 173 ("O vyselenii iz Kieva evreia Itska Kaganitsago pod firmoiu portnogo derzhit' dom terpimosti i zanimat'sia svodnichestvom"), ark. 1–6.

83. Kuprin, *Yama*, 54. For more on prostitution in the Russian Empire, see Bernstein, *Sonia's Daughters: Prostitutes and their Regulation in Imperial Russia.*

84. Kuprin, *Yama*, 104.

85. Starozhil [Sergei Iaron], *Kiev*, 6.

86. *Kievlianin* no. 203, 14 Sept. 1882: 2; no. 126, 9 June 1885: 2.

87. *Kievlianin* no. 163, 25 July 1881.

88. Sholem Aleichem, *The Letters of Menakhem-Mendl and Sheyne-Sheyndl and Motl, the Cantor's Son*, 19–37.

89. *Istoriia Kieva*, 479.

90. Kievskii komitet po okazaniiu pomoshchi postradavshchim ot pogromov 18–21 oktiabria 1905 g., *Otchet*, 154.

91. Gershon Badanes, "Kievskaia evreiskaia obshchina na Vserossiiskoi Vystavke 1913 g. v Kieve," *Vestnik evreiskoi obshchiny* (1913), 3 (Oct.): 19; *Haynt* no. 155, 6 July 1910: 2.

92. Obshchestvo letnikh sanatornykh kolonii dlia bol'nykh evreev neimushchago naseleniia g. Kieva, *Otchet . . . za 1910 god*, 10; *Haynt* no. 155, 6 July 1910: 2.

93. *Kievskoe slovo* no. 2538, 5 Feb. 1895; no. 2546, 13 Feb. 1895; no. 2559, 26 Feb. 1895.

94. Friedmann, *Sefer ha-zikhronot*, 209.

95. "Yakneho"z," in *Ale verk fun Sholem-Aleykhem* (each play paginated individually).

96. *Voskhod* no. 60, 21 Oct. 1901: 14.

97. *Izvestiia Kievskoi gorodskoi dumy* no. 5, May 1909: 22–31 (second pagination); *Kievskii Kalendar' na 1904 god* (Kiev, 1904).

98. Sementovskii, *Kiev, ego sviatyni, drevnosti, dostopamiatnosti i svedeniia neobkhodimye dlia ego pochitatelei i puteshestvennikov*, 216.

99. Sementovskii, *Kiev, ego sviatyni*, 247; *Voskhod* no. 9, 3 Feb. 1900: 12.

100. Obshchestvo letnikh sanatornykh kolonii dlia bol'nykh evreev neimushchago naseleniia g. Kieva, *Otchet . . . za 1910 god*, 11.

101. See, for example, *Kievlianin* no. 163, 25 July 1881.

102. TsDIAU f. 442, op. 528, spr. 450 ("Ob osnovanii i deiatel'nosti evreiskikh molitvennykh domov i sinagog v g. Kieve"), ark. 1–5.

103. DAKO f. 1, op. 336, d. 6197 ("Spisok sinagog i evreiskikh molitvennykh domov v g. Kieve i uezde"), ark. 1a–4zv.

104. See Lovell, *Summerfolk: A History of the Dacha, 1710–2000*, 58–117.

105. Sholem Aleichem, *Mikhtevei Shalom-Aleikhem,* 122.

106. See, for example, *Razsvet* no. 14–15, 5 April 1913: 50–51.

107. RGIA f. 1405 (Ministerstvo iustitsii), op. 530, d. 80 ("Nariad svedenii o rasprostranenii revoliutsionnykh izdanii, ob areste zapreshchennykh izdanii, zakrytii tipografii i privlechenii k otvetstvennosti izdatelei i redaktorov po Kievskoi sudebnoi palate"), l. 114.

108. Ibid., ll. 119–119ob. The proclamation was signed by the "Temporary Committee for Defense and Self-Protection."

109. Ibid., ll. 128–129.

110. *Voskhod* no. 18, 1 May 1903: 14.

111. See RGIA f. 1405, op. 530, d. 80, l. 120.

112. TsDIAU f. 275 (Kievskoe okhrannoe otdelenie), op. 2, spr. 49 ("Kopii pisem, nakhodiashchikhsia pod nabliudeniem lits, prinadlezhashchikh k evreiskim burzhuazno-natsionalisticheskim partiiam 'Poalei-Tsion' i dr. sionisticheskikh partii"), ark. 63–63zv.

113. Nokhem Shtif, "Oytobiografye," in Dawidowicz, *The Golden Tradition,* 258.

114. The pogrom is described and analyzed in detail and with perceptive insight in Hamm, *Kiev,* chap. 8. See also Hamm, "Kiev: Dubnov's Inferno of Russian Israel" and Khiterer, "The October 1905 Pogrom in Kiev." For an excellent survey and analysis of the pogrom "wave" of 1903–06, see Lambroza, "The Pogroms of 1903–1906," in *Pogroms,* ed. Klier and Lambroza, 192–247.

115. Hamm, *Kiev,* 178–188. The quotation is on p. 184.

116. Ibid., 185.

117. Turau and Kuzminskii, *Kievskii i Odesskii pogromy v otchetakh senatorov Turau i Kuzminskago,* 10.

118. For official descriptions of the "disorders" in the weeks leading up to the October pogrom, see CAHJP HM2, folder 8268 (original in TsDIAU f. 442, op. 855, spr. 391, ch. 1 and 2 ["Raporty, gazetnye vyrezki, perepiska i drugie materialy ob ulychnykh besporiadkakh, zabastovkakh, evreiskikh pogromakh . . . o merakh po predotvrashcheniiu ulichnykh besporiadkov i pogromov i ob organizatsii Komiteta po okazaniiu pomoshchi postradavshim ot pogromov v g. Kieve (Kantseliariia Kievskogo, Podolskogo i Volynskogo general-gubernatora")]).

119. See Ascher, *The Revolution of 1905,* II: 203–204.

120. Turau and Kuzminskii, *Kievskii i Odesskii pogromy,* 12, 16.

121. *Voskhod* no. 40, 8 Oct. 1905: 22–23.

122. See, for example, the report of Kiev Policemaster V. I. Tsikhotskii to Kiev governor P. S. Savvich about the demonstration of October 18, cited in *Vserossiiskaia politicheskaia stachka v oktiabre 1905 goda,* ed. Leonid Mikhailovich Ivanov, N. A. Mal'tseva, S. N. Valka, and A. M. Pankratova (Moscow and Leningrad: Izd-vo Akademii nauk SSSR, 1955), 124–127.

123. *Voskhod* no. 41, 13 Oct. 1905: 23.

124. Turau and Kuzminskii, *Kievskii i Odesskii pogromy,* 17–18.

125. *Voskhod* no. 40, 8 October 1905: 20.

126. Ratner was "a former populist and member of the SRs who had made Jewish causes his top priority as a result of the Kishinev pogrom." Hamm, *Kiev,* 183.

127. Turau and Kuzminskii, *Kievskii i Odesskii pogromy,* 21–22.

128. Hamm, *Kiev,* 188.

129. Turau and Kuzminskii, *Kievskii i Odesskii pogromy,* 30–32.

130. Hamm, *Kiev,* 189; Turau and Kuzminskii, *Kievskii i Odesskii pogromy,* 34–35.

131. This was the general pattern throughout the regions where pogroms took place in October 1905: "For the most part, they appear to have started when organized gangs

attacked demonstrators celebrating the opposition's victory over the autocracy." Ascher, *Revolution,* II: 254.

132. Khiterer, "October 1905 Pogrom," 25.

133. *Die Judenpogrome,* II: 359.

134. Turau and Kuzminskii, *Kievskii i Odesskii pogromy,* 64; Hamm, *Kiev,* 195; *Die Judenpogrome,* II: 363–365.

135. *Ha-zeman* no. 215, 26 Oct. 1905.

136. Ibid.

137. Sholem Aleichem, *Briv fun Sholem-Aleykhem, 1879–1916,* 48.

138. *Ha-zeman* no. 215, 26 Oct. 1905.

139. Ibid.

140. Mayzel, "Di ruslendishe revoliutsiye, di pogromen in 1905 un Sholem-Aleykhem," 63–64.

141. Letter to daughter Tissy, 22 October 1905, in Sholem Aleichem, *Mikhtevei Shalom-Aleikhem,* 27.

142. Khiterer, "October 1905 Pogrom," 26. For more on the school, see Chapter 6.

143. Cited in Khiterer, "October 1905 Pogrom," 25; Hamm, *Kiev,* 195.

144. Hamm, *Kiev,* 195; *EE,* s.v. "Kiev." Michael Hamm concludes that self-defense played a much smaller role in Kiev than in other large cities wracked by pogroms, both because of the apparent complacency of the local Jewish population and the relative weakness of the local Bundists. Hamm, *Kiev,* 192–193.

145. *Ha-zeman* no. 215, 26 Oct. 1905.

146. *Die Judenpogrome,* II: 373; *Ha-zeman* no. 215, 26 Oct. 1905; Khiterer, "October 1905 Pogrom," 32–33.

147. Khiterer, "October 1905 Pogrom," 27.

148. *Khronika evreiskoi zhizni* no. 32, 17 Aug. 1906: 24; Hamm, *Kiev,* 204–205.

149. Khiterer, "October 1905 Pogrom," 28.

150. Hamm, *Kiev,* 202; Hamm, "Kiev: Dubnov's Inferno of Russian Israel," 60.

151. TsDIAU f. 1423, op. 1, spr. 30, ark. 14–17, cited in Khiterer, *Dokumenty,* 202–204; Hamm, *Kiev,* 191.

152. Dubnow, *History of the Jews in Russia and Poland,* III: 154.

153. *Khronika evreiskoi zhizni* no. 11, 22 March 1906.

154. *Dos lebn* no. 77, 9 April 1906: 3.

155. *Khronika evreiskoi zhizni* no. 20, 25 May 1906.

156. *Khronika evreiskoi zhizni* no. 22, 8 June 1906.

157. *Der telegraf* no. 65, 20 March 1906: 3; no. 69, 24 March 1906: 4.

158. *Razsvet* no. 17, 3 May 1908.

159. *Razsvet* no. 25, 29 June 1908 and no. 30, 3 Aug. 1908. For a similar incident several years later, see TsDIAU f. 1010, op. 1, spr. 159 ("Vyreska iz gazety 'Rech'' ot 3 iiunia 1910 g. s zametkoi anonimnogo avtora 'Razgul soiuznikov'"), cited in Khiterer, *Dokumenty,* 180.

160. See, for example, *Razsvet* no. 20–21, 24 May 1909; *Evreiskii mir* no. 35, 23 Dec. 1910; *Novyi voskhod* No. 27, 5 July 1912. On the expulsion of 1910, see *Haynt* no. 149, 29 June 1910: 2.

161. *Haynt* no. 159, 11 July 1910: 3.

162. Lindemann, *The Jew Accused: Three Anti-Semitic Affairs: Dreyfus, Beilis, Frank, 1894–1915,* 176.

163. *Haynt* no. 76, 30 March 1911: 2. See also *Gut morgen* no. 434, 22 June 1911: 2.

164. Samuel, *Blood Accusation: The Strange History of the Beiliss Case,* 17.

165. *Haynt* no. 97, 28 April 1911: 2.

166. Liubchenko, "'Pogrom visit v vozdukhe': obshchestvennye nastroeniia v Kieve posle pokusheniia na P. A. Stolypina (po materiialam perliustratsii)," 272–286.

167. CZA, RG A3 (Mandelshtam, Max), folder 19 ("An Herrn H. Jork-Steiner in Wien").

168. The most incisive analysis of the case from the point of view of imperial politics is Rogger, "The Beilis Case: Anti-Semitism and Politics in the Reign of Nicholas II."

169. *Unzer leben* no. 274, 27 Nov. 1911: 3; *Novyi voskhod* no. 11, 15 March 1912: 11–12.

170. *Novyi voskhod* no. 12–13, 22 March 1912: 23–24; no. 14, 5 April 1912: 21.

171. *Ha-modia*, 30 March 1912: 389, cited in Levin, "Preventing Pogroms: Patterns in Jewish Politics in Early Twentieth Century Russia."

172. Samuel, *Blood Accusation*, 274 n. 62; *Haynt* no. 97, 28 April 1911: 2; *Haynt* no. 101, 3 May 1911: 3. On Margolin, see Khiterer, "Arnol'd Davidovich Margolin—zashchitnik Beilisa," 7, and idem, "Arnold Davidovich Margolin: Ukrainian-Jewish Jurist, Statesman and Diplomat," *Revolutionary Russia* 18, 2 (Dec. 2005): 145–167.

173. Sholem Aleichem, *Further Adventures*, 164.

174. Ibid., 168.

175. Lindemann, *The Jew Accused*, 185–186.

176. Samuel, *Blood Accusation*, 156.

177. Lindemann, *The Jew Accused*, 187.

178. Samuel, *Blood Accusation*, 166.

179. Kievskoe Russkoe sobranie, *Otchet o sostoianii s dekabria 1911 goda po 1 ianvaria 1914 goda*.

180. Shul'gin, *The Years: Memoirs of a Member of the Russian Duma, 1906–1917*, 104–105; Lindemann, *The Jew Accused*, 189.

181. Hamm, *Kiev*, 132.

182. *YIVO Encyclopedia of Jews in Eastern Europe*, s.v. "Beilis, Mendel."

183. *Novyi voskhod*, no. 37, 13 Sept. 1912.

184. Sholem Aleichem, *The Bloody Hoax*, 97.

185. *Haynt* no. 149, 29 June 1910: 2.

186. *Haynt* no. 155, 6 July 1910: 2. The other articles in the series appear in no. 144, 23 June 1910: 2 and no. 159, 11 July 1910: 3.

4. Modern Jewish Cultures and Practices

1. Frankel, "Assimilation and the Jews in Nineteenth-Century Europe: Towards a New Historiography?" 3.

2. Lederhendler, "Modernity without Emancipation or Assimilation? The Case of Russian Jewry," 324–343.

3. Nathans, *Beyond the Pale*, 45–79.

4. See, for example, Graetz, *The Jews in Nineteenth-Century France*.

5. Gordon, *Assimilation in American Life: The Role of Race, Religion, and National Origins*, 60ff.

6. Schnittker, "Acculturation in Context: The Self-Esteem of Chinese Immigrants," 56–76.

7. Slezkine, *The Jewish Century*, 127–144.

8. R. M. Kantor, ed., "'Ispoved' Grigoriia Gol'denberga," *Krasnyi arkhiv*, 30 (1928): 119–120, quoted in Haberer, *Jews and Revolution*, 159. Grigorii entered the revolutionary movement and eventually went to St. Petersburg where he helped to plan an attempt on the tsar's life.

9. Zipperstein, "Odessa and Jewish Urbanism." See also Zipperstein, *The Jews of Odessa*, 36–40.

10. See Stanislawski, *Zionism and the Fin-de-Siècle: Cosmopolitanism and Nationalism from Nordau to Jabotinsky*.

11. *Ha-melits* no. 231, 21 Oct. 1894: 4–5; Rozenblat, "Atsilei yisra'el be-kiyov," 269–270.

12. Friedmann, *Sefer ha-zikhronot*, 199, 205.

13. Hamm, *Kiev*, 152.

14. Friedmann, *Sefer ha-zikhronot*, 195.

15. Sholem Aleichem, *The Letters of Menakhem-Mendl*, 32. Sholem Aleichem began to write the Menakhem-Mendl/Sheyne-Sheyndl cycle in the early 1890s.

16. Kievskoe literaturno-artisticheskoe obshchestvo, *Otchet za 1903 god* (Kiev, 1904).

17. Sholem Aleichem *From the Fair*, 255.

18. *Leksikon fun der nayer yidisher literatur*, VIII: 678–679.

19. Mayzel, "Hakhamei Kiyov," 161.

20. Ibid., 152.

21. Nokhem Shtif, "Oytobiografye," *YIVO Bleter* 5 (1933): 195–225, cited in Dawidowicz, *The Golden Tradition*, 259.

22. Sholem Aleichem, *Dos Sholem-Aleykhem bukh*, 35. The letter was originally written in Hebrew.

23. *Leksikon fun der nayer yidisher literatur*, XIII: 680.

24. See Polishchuk, *Evrei Odessy i Novorossii*, 25.

25. Mayzel, "Hakhamei Kiyov," 157; *Encyclopaedia Judaica*, s.v. "Schulmann, Eleazar." See also Sholem Aleichem's account of coming to Kiev and finding him at Brodsky's mill in Sholem Aleichem, *From the Fair*, 257–259.

26. Friedmann, *Sefer ha-zikhronot*, 198.

27. YIVO, RG 80, folder 710, file 5b ("Briv fun Yehalel").

28. Yehalel's memoirs tell a different story, however: that he was banished from Kiev for disloyalty to the state (perhaps because of his Palestinophile activities?), and the rehabilitation that Brodsky kept promising him never materialized. Levin, *Yehudah Leib Levin: zikhronot ve-hegyonot*, 77.

29. *Ha-melits* no. 32, 29 April 1885: 513–514.

30. *Ha-melits* no. 49, 27 Feb. 1891: 3; no. 231, 20 Oct. 1891: 1–2; no. 230, 20 Oct. 1892: 2–3.

31. *Ha-melits* no. 213, 18 Sept. 1894: 2.

32. *Ha-melits* no. 187, 18 Aug. 1894: 2; no. 28, 2 Feb. 1896: 4.

33. *Ha-melits* no. 223, 9 Oct. 1894: 4–5.

34. *Ha-melits* no. 187, 18 Aug. 1894: 2; no. 241, 2 Nov. 1894: 3.

35. *Ha-melits* no. 28, 2 Feb. 1896: 4.

36. M. Rozenblat, "Mi-livtei ha-tenu'a ha-ivrit be-rusya," 855. Rozenblat relates that he rented apartments in the mouth of the beast, as it were—from members of the Black Hundreds who were Kiev city councilors and from the editor of *Kievlianin*. His explanations that the gatherings, which were actually meetings of Hebraists and Zionists, were about matters of pedagogy and biblical studies, were apparently accepted without question by his Judeophobic landlords.

37. *Ha-melits* no. 124, 5 June 1896: 3.

38. *Ha-melits* no. 195, 31 Aug. 1898: 2.

39. *Ha-melits* no. 223, 9 Oct. 1894: 4–5.

40. *Der yud* no. 17, 25 April 1901: 15–16.

41. *Ha-melits* no. 213, 18 Sept. 1894: 2.

42. The Hebrew is *yitpake'a,* corresponding to the Yiddish *platsn;* thus, in contemporary Jewish-English the sentence might read: "You could plotz looking for that book!"

43. Letter of 10–11 April 1902, Sholem Aleichem, *Mikhtevei,* 129. Sholem Aleichem was referring to two of Abramovitsh's most famous works.

44. *Ha-melits* no. 5, 7 Jan. 1898: 1–2, and no. 125, 9 July 1898: 2.

45. Friedmann, *Sefer ha-zikhronot,* 199.

46. Maor, *Ha-tenu'a ha-tsionit be-Rusya,* 53–54; Levin, *Zikhronot ve-hegyonot,* 73.

47. *Ha-melits* no. 85, 29 Oct. 1884: 1865 and no. 101, 24 Dec. 1884: 1657.

48. *Ha-melits* no. 21, 12 March 1884: 368.

49. TsDIAU f. 442 (Kantseliaria Kievskogo, Podol'skogo i Volynskogo general-gubernatora), op. 538, spr. 52 ("Delo o zakritii v g. Kieve obshchestva 'Bratstvo liubitelei siona,' sodeistvuiushchego pereseleniiu evreev v Palestinu"), ark. 13–15.

50. Mayzel, "Hakhamei Kiyov," 158.

51. CZA, RG A3 (Mandelshtam, Max), folder 19 ("An Dr. Kirstein in Berlin").

52. *Ha-melits* no. 213, 18 Sept. 1894: 2

53. Friedmann, *Sefer ha-zikhronot,* 215.

54. *Ha-melits* no. 231, 20 Oct. 1891: 1–2; no. 231, 21 Oct. 1894: 4–5.

55. Rozenblat, "Mi-livtei."

56. *Leksikon fun der nayer yidisher literatur,* XIII: 681.

57. *Ha-melits* no. 78, 7 April 1896: 1.

58. Friedmann, *Sefer ha-zikhronot,* 213; Evreiskii kolonial'nyi bank, *Spisok lits, podpisavshchikhsia na aktsii Evreiskago kolonial'nago banka do 20-go maia 1899 goda v g. Kieve* (Kiev: V universitetskoi tip., 1899).

59. *Ha-melits* no. 231, 21 Oct. 1894: 4–5.

60. TsDIAU f. 442, op. 538, spr. 52, ark. 16–16zv; this is corroborated by Yehalel's memoirs: Levin, *Zikhronot ve-hegyonot,* 75–76.

61. CZA RG A3, folder 18 ("Brief an Dr. M. T. Schnirer," Vienna, 22 Sept. 1897).

62. CZA, RG A3 (Mandelshtam, Max), folder 20 ("Rede über Zionismus geh. in Kiew nach dem 4ten Kongress in London 1900").

63. For records pertaining to Kiev as a Zionist center, see CZA, RG F7 (Russia, 1903–1914), esp. folder 79 ("Hozrim shel ha-murshe le-galil kiyov") and RG Z1 (Central Zionist Office, Vienna, 1897–1905), esp. folder 382, "Circulars of Kiev Region." On Zlatopol'skii, see Rozenblat, "Hillel Zlatopolski (bi-melo'ot lo shishim shana)," 55.

64. Nokhem Shtif, "Oytobiografye," cited in Dawidowicz, *The Golden Tradition,* 258.

65. Kaufman, "Cherta osedlosti v miniatiure," nos. 16, 17, 19, 649–650.

66. *Materialy dlia istorii antievreiskikh pogromov v Rossii,* ed. G. Ia. Krasnyi-Admoni, 395ff.

67. *Izvestiia Kievskoi gorodskoi dumy* no. 5, May 1909, 22–31; RGIA f. 821 (Departament dukhovnykh del inostrannykh ispovedanii MVD), op. 8, d. 153, ark. 139–139zv; TsDIAU f. 442, op. 628, spr. 388, ark. 30.

68. *Kievskie otkliki* no. 2, 2 Jan. 1906: 1.

69. B. Gol'dberg, "O rodnom iazyke u evreev Rossii," 77; Lestschinsky, "Di idishe bafelkerung," 54.

70. Kievskoe otdelenie Obshchestva rasprostraneniia prosveshcheniia mezhdu evreiami v Rossii, *Otchet za 1907 god,* 41–42.

71. Nathans, *Beyond the Pale,* 230 ff.; Estraikh, "Languages of 'Yehupets' Students," 65–70.

72. IR TsNB f. 321 (Kollektsiia evreiskikh rukopisei), op. 1, spr. OR 65, n. 40; Levitats, *Jewish Community,* 74. See also Bacon, "Ha-hevrot le-limud ve-gemilut hasadim be-mizrah Eiropa: hevrot magidei tehilim shel Kiev," 99–115.

73. *Ha-melits* no. 108, 17 May 1896: 3–4.

74. Sholem Aleichem, *The Bloody Hoax,* 97.

75. See Neishtube, *Istoricheskaia zapiska;* Bezplatnaia boiarskaia sanatoriia dlia bednikh chakhotochnykh evreev g. Kieva, *Otchet po soderzhaniiu sanitorii za 1904 god* (Kiev, 1905).

76. Bezplatnaia boiarskaia sanatoriia dlia bednikh chakhotochnykh evreev g. Kieva, *Otchet po soderzhaniiu sanitorii za 1908 god* (Kiev, 1909).

77. *Yudishe naye leben* no. 1–2, Jan.–Feb. 1914.

78. For an acute analysis of the influence of Russian and other languages on Yiddish, see Harshav, *The Meaning of Yiddish,* 27–73 and especially 67. For a similar case of Russian-inflected German in St. Petersburg, see Anders Henriksson, "Nationalism, Assimilation and Identity in Late Imperial Russia: The St. Petersburg Germans, 1906–1914," 343.

79. *Pervaia vseobshchaia perepis',* vol. 16.

80. Gol'dberg, "O rodnom iazyke," 77.

81. *Ha-melits* no. 49, 27 Feb. 1891: 3.

82. *Der yud* no. 17, 25 April 1901: 15–16.

83. Friedmann, *Sefer ha-zikhronot,* 197.

84. Sholem Aleichem, *The Bloody Hoax,* 104–105.

85. *Kiever vort* no. 1, 1 Jan. 1910.

86. Kirzhnits, *Di yidishe prese in der gevezener rusishe imperye, 1823–1916,* 30, 40; DAKO f. 2 (Kantseliariia Kievskogo gubernatora), op. 44, spr. 105 ("O dostavlenii svedenii o periodicheskikh izdaniiakh vykhodiashchikh v Kievskoi gubernii"), ark. 50zv-51.

87. TsDIAU f. 295 (Kievskii vremennyi komitet po delam pechati), op. 1, spr. 438 ("Otchety o rabote Kievskogo vremennogo komiteta po delam pechati za 1909–1913 gg. i prilozheniia k nim. Chernoviki"), ark. 96zv.

88. TsDIAU f. 295, op. 1, spr. 383 ("Uvedomlenie Kievskogo gubernatora o vydache Zil'bergergu I. E. svidetel'stvo na izdanie v g. Kieva gazety 'Iudishe nas leben' [Evreiskaia novaia zhizn'] na razgovornom evreiskom iazyke i o ee programme").

89. TsDIAU f. 295, op. 1, spr. 125 ("Uvedomlenie Kievskogo gubernatora o vydache Slonimu D. A. svidetel'stvo na izdanie v g. Kieva gazetu 'Folkshtime' na razgovornom evreiskom iazyke i o ee programme"); TsDIAU f. 295, op. 1, spr. 232 ("Uvedomlenie Kievskogo gubernatora o vydache doktoru Skomorovskomu D. A. svidetel'stvo na izdanie v g. Kieva gazetu 'Kiever-Tageblatt' . . . i o ee programme").

90. DAKO f. 2 (Kantseliariia Kievskogo gubernatora), op. 42, spr. 159 ("Po khodataistvu Leizera-Elii Fridmana o razreshenii emu izdavat' v g. Kieve na drevne-evreiskom iazyke gazetu, 'Gatsofe Umabit' t. e. 'Nabliudatl' i Zritel''"), ark. 1–8; TsDIAU f. 295, op. 1, spr. 34 ("Uvedomlenie Kievskogo gubernatora o vydache Fridmanu L. B. svidetel'stvo na izdanie v g. Kieva gazety 'Gatsofe umabit' na drevneevreiskom iazyke; programma gazety"); TsDIAU f. 295, op. 1, spr. 418 ("Uvedomlenie Kievskogo gubernatora o vydache Fridmanu L. B. svidetel'stvo na izdanie v g. Kieva gazety 'Gatsofe' . . . i o ee programme"); TsDIAU f. 295, op. 1, spr. 438, ark. 259zv-260.

91. Just how this might have occurred is suggested by the case of "L.," possibly an SS (Socialist Zionist) activist, who worked at a Russian newspaper in addition to editing a Yiddish newspaper that was soon to start publication in Kiev. This gives some sense of the multidimensional lives that intellectual, politically active Jews could lead in the context of the late imperial city. TsDIAU f. 705 (Iugo-Vostochnoe raionnoe okhrannoe otdelenie), op. 2, spr. 81, ark.

2–4zv. For more on *Nedel'naia khronika Voskhoda* and its "parent" journal *Voskhod,* see Slutsky, *Ha-itonut,* 142–309. For an overview and analysis of the challenges facing a Yiddish periodical press in the pre-1905 Russian Empire, see Fishman, "The Politics of Yiddish in Tsarist Russia," 159–163.

92. See Ury, "Red Banner, Blue Star: Radical Politics, Democratic Institutions and Collective Identity Among Jews in Warsaw, 1904–1907," 143–147, 166–177. On the press in the Russian Empire, see Brooks, *When Russia Learned to Read,* 109–165 and McReynolds, *The News under Russia's Old Regime: The Development of a Mass-Circulation Press.*

93. TsDIAU f. 705, op. 2, spr. 81 ("Perepiska s Departamentom Politsii i zhandarmskim upravleniem i perliustratsiia pisem so svedeniami o litsakh, prinadlezhavshikh k melkoburzhuazno i burzhuazno-natsionalisticheskoi [*sic*] partiiam 'Bund' i 'Poialei-Tsion'"), ark. 2–4zv.

94. Brooks, *When Russia Learned to Read,* 110.

95. Kievlianin no. 26, 1 March 1873, 1–2; this phrase was repeated in subsequent years.

96. Murav'ev, "Zapiska," 265.

97. *Ha-melits* no. 119, 2 June 1895: 4; no. 176, 5 Aug. 1894: 4–5.

98. For example, in 1880 the student body of the Third Gymnasium in the Podol district was 30 percent Jewish. *Kievlianin* no. 93, 25 April 1880: 1.

99. *Russkii evrei* no. 7, 11 Feb. 1881. It should be noted that, in addition to the official quotas established in official educational institutions with the introduction of the *numerus clausus* for Jewish males in universities and gymnasia in the mid-1880s, Jews began to be barred from other kinds of educational facilities on an ad hoc and individual basis.

100. Cited in Shohat, *Mosad ha-rabanut,* 184 n. 8.

101. [Kel'berin], *Desiatiletie Kievskago evreiskago khoral'nago molitvennago doma,* 5–6, 9.

102. *Ha-melits* no. 112, 17 May 1894: 4–5; no. 115, 20 May 1894: 3.

103. *Ha-melits* no. 4, 14 Jan. 1885.

104. Mayzel, "Hakhamei Kiyov," 158; *Leksikon fun der nayer yidisher literatur,* III: 403–405.

105. See Hyman, *Gender and Assimilation in Modern Jewish History: The Roles and Representation of Women,* 10–49.

106. Kotik, *Mayne zikhroynes,* II: 245–246. David Assaf, who has translated and annotated Friedmann's memoirs, has found corroboration of this astonishing account in the works of Yehudah Leib Levin (Yehalel). See Kotik, *Na va-nad: zikhronotav shel Yehezkel Kotik, helek sheni,* 183.

107. Kotik, *Mayne zikhroynes,* II: 244.

108. DAKO f. 1 (Kievskoe gubernskoe pravlenie), op. 332, d. 154 ("Svedenie o evreiskikh i karaimskikh religioznykh uchrezhdeniiakh gubernii 1889 g."), ark. 44.

109. Lederhendler, *Jewish Responses to Modernity,* 64.

110. Zipperstein, *The Jews of Odessa,* 131; Piotr Wrobel, "Jewish Warsaw before the First World War," 254.

111. Freeze, *Jewish Marriage and Divorce,* 241. In Warsaw there were reportedly "demoralised rabbis . . . who solemnised fictitious marriages and quick divorces for commercial gain." Wrobel, "Jewish Warsaw before the First World War," 254.

112. Friedmann, *Sefer ha-zikhronot,* 205. Zipperstein notes similarly erratic behavior in Odessa: "the same individual might fast on a minor holy day and then desecrate the Sabbath." Zipperstein, *The Jews of Odessa,* 131.

113. Friedmann, *Sefer ha-zikhronot,* 209.

114. Ibid., 215.

115. Bacon, "Ha-hevrot le-limud," 107.

116. See Zipperstein, *The Jews of Odessa*, 37.

117. An observer of 1905 Warsaw wrote: "It began with a compromise. The owner of a shop was standing there, and the Christian woman hired for Saturday was selling soda water and taking the money. After a few months, this mediation disappeared. . . ." H. Piasecki, "Żydowska Organizacja PPS 1893–1907" (Wrocław, 1978), 192, cited in Wrobel, "Jewish Warsaw before the First World War," 266.

118. Sholem Aleichem, *Menakhem-Mendl*, 42.

119. Ibid., 48. Peretz Smolenskin describes Odessa's freewheeling Jews in similar terms in his novel *Simhat ha-nef.* Zipperstein, *The Jews of Odessa*, 108–109.

120. *Ha-melits* no. 68, 22 March 1895.

121. CAHJP, Ru 81, Doc. 2 ("Tazkir ha-rav ha-Kiyovi A. Luria el mo'etset ha-ir be-Kiyov"), 20 Nov. 1903. That this was indeed the case is made clear by a 1906 petition submitted by members of that same elite, which noted that, with a few rare exceptions, prosperous Jews did not eat kosher meat. TsDIAU f. 442, op. 658, spr. 97, ark. 99.

122. *Ha-melits* no. 290, 30 Dec. 1892: 5–6.

123. *Ha-melits* no. 34, 9 Feb. 1895: 2.

124. *Ha-melits* no. 198, 31 Aug. 1894: 2.

125. *Ha-melits* no. 28, 2 Feb. 1896: 4; no. 40, 16 Feb. 1896; 5. These two items were written by different correspondents.

126. RGIA f. 821, op. 9, d. 46 ("O priznanii spravedlivoi zhaloby Ia. S. Gol'denveizera na ravvina, otkazavshegosia vnesti v metricheskuiu knigu akt o rozhdenii ego syna bez soversheniia nad nim obriada obrezaniia [1898–1908]").

127. RGIA f. 821, op. 81, d. 381 ("O predpisanii odesskomu ravvinu zanesti v metricheskie knigi novorozhdennogo syna vracha L. M. Shorshteina bez soversheniia nad nim obriada obrezaniia").

128. See Judd, "Circumcision and Modern Jewish Life: A German Case Study, 1843–1914," 142–155.

129. See Polishchuk, "Was There a Jewish Reform Movement in Russia?" 32.

130. *Ha-melits* no. 223, 8 Oct. 1891; Guterman, "The Origins of the Great Synagogue in Warsaw on Tlomackie Street," 185.

131. Polishchuk, "Jewish Reform Movement," 3.

132. Ibid., 16.

133. Friedmann, *Sefer ha-zikhronot*, 213.

134. Ibid., 225–229.

135. Polishchuk, "Jewish Reform Movement," 13.

136. *Ha-melits* no. 6, 21 Feb. 1885: 88–93.

137. *Ha-melits* no. 215, 3 Oct. 1896: 2.

138. *Ha-melits* no. 223, 8 Oct. 1891: 2.

139. *Ha-melits* no. 195, 31 Oct. 1898: 2.

140. Kel'berin, *K istorii evreiskago khoral'nago molitvennago doma v Kieve*, 18–19.

141. *Ha-melits* no. 108, 17 May 1896: 3–4.

142. *Ha-melits* no. 251, 13 Nov. 1892: 4–5.

143. Polishchuk, "Jewish Reform Movement," 23.

144. *Ha-melits* no. 109, 13 May 1894: 4–5.

145. *Ha-melits* no. 223, 23 Oct. 1898: 2.

146. Brodsky, *Smoke Signals*, 14.

147. Friedmann, *Sefer ha-zikhronot*, 337.

148. *Kiever vort* no. 5, 6 Jan. 1910. On Yiddish schools in the Russian Empire, see Fishman, "The Politics of Yiddish in Tsarist Russia," 167–170.

149. Friedmann, *Sefer ha-zikhronot,* 209.

150. Sholem Aleichem, *The Bloody Hoax,* 76–78.

151. The fictional character's wife wears a wig, which was apparently an unusual enough circumstance that the novelist found it worth noting. See Sholem Aleichem, *The Bloody Hoax,* 72.

152. RGIA f. 821, op. 8, d. 153, l. 85.

153. *Ha-melits* 262, 26 Nov. 1892. This may explain why many of his hasidim came to Kiev, as a more acculturated and educated rebbe might be more likely to allow his followers to come to the big city; or they themselves might have been more educated, and thus be more likely to migrate to the city.

154. *Ha-melits* no. 28, 2 Feb. 1896: 4.

155. *Ha-melits* no. 40, 16 Feb. 1896: 5.

156. *Ha-melits* no. 125, 9 July 1898: 2.

157. Mayzel, "Di ruslendishe revoliutsiye, di pogromen in 1905 un Sholem-Aleykhem," 70–71.

158. Friedmann, *Sefer ha-zikhronot,* 200, 205, 209.

159. Sholem Aleichem, *Menakhem-Mendl,* 22.

160. Friedmann, *Sefer ha-zikhronot,* 209–213.

161. Factories employing both Christian and Jewish workers, which by law had to be closed on Sunday, were usually open on Saturday. Thus, if a Jew insisted on keeping the Sabbath, he or she would have had to seek out a Jewish employer who hired only Jews. Many Jews in Kiev probably did not have this luxury. See Kahan, "The Impact of Industrialization," 41.

162. Kievskoe otdelenie Obshchestva rasprostraneniia prosveshcheniia mezhdu evreiami v Rossii, *Otchet za 1907 god.*

163. Predstavitel'stvo po evreiskoi blagotvoritel'nosti pri Kievskoi Gorodskoi Uprave, *Otchet za 1913 god,* vii.

164. *Kiever vort* no. 9, 11 Jan. 1910.

165. Alfasi, *Ha-hakham ha-mufla: Ha-rav Shlomo Ha-Cohen Aharonson, ha-rav ha-rashi ha-rishon shel Tel Aviv. Hayav u-fe'alo,* 18–19 passim; "Toldotav," *Ha-arets* 26 March 1935 and "R. Shlomo Aharonson—ha-rav," *Ha-arets* 15 March 1936, both in Central Zionist Archives RG F30, folder 230.

166. *Unzer leben* no. 276, 2 Dec. 1910: 4.

167. RGIA f. 821, op. 133, d. 705 ch. 1 ("Ob ustroistve evreiskikh molitvennykh domov"), ll. 253–253ob; RGIA f. 821, op. 8, d. 153, l. 103ob.

168. YoTse"R, *Mi-zeman le-zeman, mikhtav iti ha-yotse le-iti mi-bayit le-vayit be-format ka-zayit u-mi-hatser le-hatser MI-YoTs"eR LE-SHRETSER,* Letter XIII: "Va-yishakehu, o neshikah be-yom huladeto," 25.

169. *Voskhod* no. 43, 4 June 1900: 9.

170. See, for example, Zborowski and Herzog, *Life Is with People: The Culture of the Shtetl,* 51. Interestingly, the term used in the petitions was often *molitvennaia shkola* ("prayer school"), perhaps a kind of portmanteau embracing both the elements of worship and study found in the traditional "house of study."

171. *K kharakteristike evreiskago studenchestva (Po dannym ankety sredi evreiskago studenchestva g. Kieva v Noiabre 1910 g.),* 66.

172. Sheinis, *Evreiskoe studenchestvo v tsifrakh.*

173. See Weissler, "Women's Studies and Women's Prayers: Reconstructing the Religious History of Ashkenazic Women," 28–47.

174. Sheinis, *Evreiskoe studenchestvo.*

175. Nathans, *Beyond the Pale,* 302.

176. Sheinis, *Evreiskoe studenchestvo.*

177. Simon Dixon, "The Church's Social Role in St Petersburg, 1880–1914," 167–192.

178. Bartlett and Edmondson, "Collapse and Creation: Issues of Identity and the Russian *Fin de Siècle,*" 191. See also the articles in *Russian Orthodoxy under the Old Regime,* ed. Stavrou and Nichols.

179. Freeze, "'Going to the Intelligentsia': The Church and Its Urban Mission in Post-Reform Russia," 220.

180. Bartlett and Edmondson, "Collapse and Creation," 173–174.

181. Gassenschmidt, *Jewish Liberal Politics,* 72ff. The new political reaction had an impact on the national activities of other groups as well, such as the Ukrainians, many of whose organizations went underground after 1907. Kappeler, "The Ukrainians of the Russian Empire, 1860–1914," 113.

182. *Ha-melits* no. 103, 10 May 1895: 2; *Voskhod* no. 50, 12 Dec. 1902: 37.

183. *Khronika evreiskoi zhizni* no. 30, 3 Aug. 1906: 24.

184. *Razsvet* 1908, no. 15, 12 April 1908: 23–25.

185. Zipperstein, *Imagining Russian Jewry,* 46.

186. Rappaport, "Jewish Education and Jewish Culture in the Russian Empire, 1880–1914," 102.

187. TsDIAU f. 275 (Kievskoe okhrannoe otdelenie), op. 1, spr. 2828 ("Perepiska s sudebnym sledovatelem Chernigovskogo okruzhnogo suda, prokurorom Kievskogo okruzhnogo suda i drugimi litsami o sbore svedenii ob obshchestve dlia izucheniia drevne-evreiskogo iazyka 'EZRO' v gor. Kieve"), ark. 3–3zv.

188. *Razsvet* no. 50, 13 Dec. 1909: 16–18.

189. *Evreiskii mir* no. 28, 4 Nov. 1910: 33. On *Hovevei sefat ever* and the *Evreiskoe literaturnoe obshchestvo* more generally, see Veidlinger, *Jewish Public Culture in the Late Russian Empire.* For an overview of the significance of Hebrew literature in this period of Russian-Jewish history, see Averbach, "Hebrew Literature and Jewish Nationalism in the Tsarist Empire, 1881–1917," 132–150.

190. *Evreiskii mir* no. 10, 11 March 1910: 48; *Evreiskii mir* no. 12, 24 March 1911: 20.

191. *Evreiskii mir* no. 8, 25 Feb. 1911: 15.

192. *Razsvet* no. 50, 13 Dec. 1909: 16–18.

193. TsDIAU f. 1597, op. 1, spr. 279 ("Proekt ustava 'Evreiskogo natsional'nogo kruzhka studentov-evreev' Kievskogo politekhnicheskogo instituta i ustav evreiskogo studencheskogo kruzhka 'Kadima' pri KPI"), ark. 267–268.

194. *Ha-melits* no. 198, 31 Aug. 1894: 2; *Ha-melits* no. 34, 9 Feb. 1895: 2.

195. *Ha-melits* no. 187, 18 Aug. 1894: 2.

196. *Razsvet* no. 50, 13 Dec. 1909: 16–18.

197. Rozenblat, "Mi-livtei"; in another version, Rozenblat recalls a "Hebrew Week" held after the conference that included speeches by Hebrew poet Chaim Nahman Bialik and Zionist leaders Rabbi Jacob Mazeh, Menahem Ussishkin, and Nahum Sokolov. Rozenblat, "Ha-shavu'a ha-ivri be-kiyov," 423. On the founding of the Association for Hebrew Culture and Language, see Brenner, *The Renaissance of Jewish Culture in Weimar Germany,* 197–200.

198. *Gut morgen* no. 426, 14 June 1911: 3.

199. Kievskoe otdelenie Obshchestva rasprostraneniia prosveshcheniia mezhdu evreiami v Rossii, *Otchet za 1907 god*, 49.

200. *Razsvet* no. 40, 4 Oct. 1909: 20.

201. *Evreiskii mir* no. 18, 6 May 1910: 27.

202. *Razsvet* no. 41, 26 Oct. 1908: 26.

203. *Evreiskii mir* no. 7, 18 Feb. 1911: 18 and no. 12, 24 March 1911: 15.

204. Wolitz, "The Kiev-Grupe (1918–1920) Debate: The Function of Literature," 97.

205. Sherman, "David Bergelson (1884–1952): A Biography," 16.

206. I have drawn on Zipperstein, "Odessa and Jewish Urbanism," for inspiration in my conclusions on Jewish modernity in the city.

207. Cited in Mayzel, "Hakhamei Kiyov," 154.

208. A. S. Shmakov, *Pogrom evreev v Kieve*, 15–16, 19.

209. Estraikh, "Languages of 'Yehupets' Students," 68.

210. See for example, Gessen, *Istoriia*, II: 198: "Breaking off with religious ritual observance, Jewish *intelligenty* in Russia, not finding any other connection to their people, disengaged themselves from it completely, considering themselves to be, in a spiritual sense, nothing other than Russian citizens (*russkimi grazhdanami*)."

211. Darewski, *Le-korot ha-yehudim be-Kiyov*, 8.

5. Jew as Neighbor, Jew as Other

1. Endelman, *The Jews of Georgian England, 1714–1830: Tradition and Change in a Liberal Society*, 249.

2. On civil society in the Russian Empire, see Bradley, "Subjects into Citizens"; Engelstein, "The Dream of Civil Society in Tsarist Russia: Law, State, and Religion"; the helpful collection of articles in Clowes, Kassow, and West, *Between Tsar and People: Educated Society and the Quest for Public Identity in Late Imperial Russia*; and also McReynolds and Popkin, "The Objective Eye and the Common Good," 57–98. On voluntary and philanthropic associations, see especially Lindenmeyr, *Poverty Is Not a Vice* and Bradley, "Voluntary Associations, Civic Culture, and *Obshchestvennost'* in Moscow," 131–148.

3. Of course for some individuals this activity may have held the added potential of helping to combat antisemitism, as non-Jews witnessed the contributions of Jews to society and formed a more positive image of them. Paula Hyman speculates that this may have been the case with Jewish women's volunteer activity in Germany. Hyman, "Two Models of Modernization: Jewish Women in the German and the Russian Empires," 43.

4. Bradley, "Voluntary Associations, Civic Culture, and *Obshchestvennost'* in Moscow," 148. Charles Steinwedel writes that "in late imperial Russia, a type of enlightened civic inclusion and religion competed with ethnicity as bases for integration. . . ." Steinwedel, "To Make a Difference," 81.

5. Another city with a similarly diverse population and a vibrant, often ethnic group-specific associational life was Riga; see Henriksson, "Riga: Growth, Conflict, and the Limitations of Good Government, 194–197, 200.

6. Brower, "Urban Revolution in the Late Russian Empire," 329.

7. Hamm, *Kiev*, 169.

8. The most recent example of this is Slezkine's *Jewish Century*, where the author contrasts the traditional Jews of the Pale of Settlement, who inhabited a completely different life-world from that of their Christian neighbors, to the generation of young Jews striving toward

russification in the 1870s and 1880s whose "joyous return to Russian togetherness meant a permanent escape from the Jewish home" (137). See also Nathans, *Beyond the Pale,* 377.

9. See Klier, *Russia Gathers Her Jews,* 182–87; Katz, "Representations of 'the Jew' in the Writings of Nikolai Gogol, Fyodor Dostoevsky and Ivan Turgenev."

10. While ethnic identity is a highly problematic term in this period, if identified by native language these burghers were likely to be Poles, Ukrainians, Germans, or Armenians.

11. Ettinger, "Jewish Participation in the Settlement of Ukraine in the Sixteenth and Seventeenth Centuries," 28–29; Subtelny, *Ukraine: A History,* 277–278; Sysyn, "The Jewish Factor in the Khmelnytsky Uprising," 48; Rosman, *The Lords' Jews: Magnate-Jewish Relations in the Polish-Lithuanian Commonwealth During the Eighteenth Century,* passim. For an especially sensitive treatment of mutual perceptions, see Aster and Potichnyj, *Jewish Ukrainian Relations: Two Solitudes.*

12. Magocsi, "The Ukrainian National Revival: A New Analytical Framework," 1–2; Rudnytsky, "The Intellectual Origins of Modern Ukraine," 123–141.

13. For a summary of statements by seminal Ukrainian thinkers on the Jewish question, see Rudnytsky, "Ukrainian–Jewish Relations in Nineteenth-Century Ukrainian Political Thought," 69–83. For discussions of these issues in the Ukrainian press, see "Evreis'ka sprava i ukraïns'ki techii," *Slovo* no. 6, 1909 and Efremov, *Evreis'ka sprava na Ukraïni (Odbytok z "Rady").*

14. Klier, "*Kievlianin* and the Jews," 86–87.

15. See, for example, most issues of *Khronika evreiskoi zhizni,* 1906.

16. Boshyk, "Between Socialism and Nationalism: Jewish–Ukrainian Political Relations in Imperial Russia, 1900–1917," 177.

17. Hamm, *Kiev,* 251 n. 63, and 109; this is also attested to in a history of the Zionist movement written by two secret police officials in TsDIAU f. 274 (Kievskoe gubernskoe zhandarmskoe upravlenie), op. 1, spr. 2444 ("Spravka Departamenta politsii po istorii sionistskago dvizheniia"). It should be noted that the Spilka was a Marxist party that rejected nationalism as a meaningful political category of analysis. See Magocsi, *A History of Ukraine,* 279.

18. Harcave, "The Jews and the First Russian National Election," 38.

19. *Khronika evreiskoi zhizni* no. 18, 10 May 1906: 26–29; Emmons, *The Formation of Political Parties and the First National Elections in Russia,* 332.

20. McReynolds and Popkin, "The Objective Eye and the Common Good," 66.

21. This discussion is based on annual reports of the society, 1896 through 1906: Kievskoe Obshchestvo Gramotnosti, *Otchet za . . . god* (Kiev, 1896–1906). See also Hamm, *Kiev,* 165–166.

22. The library was the most popular in the city. By contrast, the most heavily visited of the municipal libraries received about 30,000 visits per year. Kievskoe Obshchestvo Gramotnosti, *Otchet za 1902 god* (Kiev, 1903), 87.

23. Kievskoe Obshchestvo Gramotnosti, *Otchet za 1902 god* (Kiev, 1903), 88–89.

24. Prosvita's Kiev branch was founded in 1906. For more on the Literacy Society, see Hamm, *Kiev,* 165–166.

25. Kievskoe Obshchestvo Gramotnosti, *Otchet za 1899 god* (Kiev, 1900). The society had to receive official permission for each Ukrainian play that it put on. Among those authorized were "Natalka Poltavka" and "Zaporozhskyy klad." Kievskoe Obshchestvo Gramotnosti, *Otchet za 1903 god* (Kiev, 1900), 65–66.

26. *Kievskie otkliki* no. 2, 2 Jan. 1906: 1; Kievskoe Obshchestvo Gramotnosti, *Otchet za 1903 god* (Kiev, 1904), 65.

27. Kievskoe Obshchestvo Gramotnosti, *Otchet za 1906 god* (Kiev, 1907), 2.

28. *Sistematicheskii ukazatel' zhurnala "Kievskaia starina" (1882–1906 g.)* (Poltava, 1911); "Evrei kozaki v nachale XVII veka," *Kievskaia starina* 5 (1890): 377–379; Galant, "K istorii uman'skoi rezni 1768 g.," 209–229. See also Galant, *K istorii Uman'skoi Rezni 1768 goda.*

29. See Kovalinskii, *Sem'ia Tereshchenko.*

30. While educational institutions are not usually considered an element of civil society because they are controlled by the government, there was an element of voluntary activity involved in the late imperial period because so many private schools and institutes were founded in those years by individuals or groups of one kind or another. These institutions were often under the official supervision of a government ministry but direct control was at a minimum.

31. See an 1891 memorandum from the economic department of the Ministry of Interior in RGIA f. 821, op. 8, d. 108, ll. 143–147 ("Delo ob ustanovlenii novago poriadka deiatel'nosti evreiskikh blagotvoritel'nykh obshchestv i po voprosu o vozmozhnosti uprazdneniia evreiskikh pogrebal'nykh bratstv").

32. *Khronika Voskhoda* no. 24, 13 June 1899: 732; *Izvestiia Kievskoi gorodskoi dumy* no. 6 (June), 1906.

33. Kievskaia gorodskaia uchilishchnaia komissiia, *Otchet . . . za 1909 g.* (Kiev, 1911).

34. *Evreiskii mir* no. 33, 9 Dec. 1910, 26.

35. Nathans provides a comprehensive analysis of the numerus clausus and its impact on the course of Jewish integration in *Beyond the Pale,* chap. 7 (257–307).

36. *Voskhod* no. 74, 24 Sept. 1900: 11.

37. *Khronika evreiskoi zhizni* no. 31, 10 Aug. 1906: 30.

38. *Khronika Voskhoda* no. 44, 24 Oct. 1899: 1386.

39. *Kievskie vesti* no. 55, 24 Feb. 1910.

40. Sholem Aleichem, *Further Adventures,* 164.

41. Ibid. Sholem Aleichem provides a similar vignette in his novel *In the Storm:* during the 1905 pogrom, several thugs attack a young Jew, "after which they got into an argument about whether he was a Jew or a Christian. If he was a Christian, how come he was a redhead? If he was a Jew, why was he clean-shaven?" Sholem Aleichem, *In the Storm,* 209.

42. *Ha-melits* no. 88, 23 April 1895: 2; no. 98, 4 May 1895: 1–2.

43. TsDIAU f. 442 (Kantseliaria Kievskogo, Podol'skogo i Volynskogo general-gubernatora), op. 661, spr. 273, ark. 29–30zv. ("Ob uregulirovanii blagotvoritel'nykh uchrezhdeniiakh v Kievskoi gubernii").

44. The Jewish initiators were members of the Literacy Society, but it is unclear whether the Jewish activists working together with the Society of Day Shelters were members of that society.

45. Kievskoe Obshchestvo Gramotnosti, *Otchet voskresnykh shkol za 1899–1900-i god* (Kiev, 1901). A Jewish presence was nonexistent or negligible in the society's four other Sunday literacy schools.

46. *Voskhod* no. 15, 13 April 1897, 426; Obshchestvo dnevnykh priiutov dlia detei rabochego klassa, *Otchet za 1900 god* (Kiev, 1900); *Voskhod* no. 51–52, 25 Dec. 1897: 1435; Kievskoe Obshchestvo Gramotnosti, *Otchet za 1898 god* (Kiev, 1899).

47. Kievskoe Obshchestvo Gramotnosti, *Otchet za 1901 god* (Kiev, 1902).

48. Kievskoe popechitel'stvo o narodnoi trezvosti, *Otchet o sostoianii vechernikh klassov dlia vzroslykh s 1 ianvaria 1904 po 1 ianvaria 1906 g.* (Kiev, 1906).

49. The Jewish community paid for kosher meals to be provided for Jews admitted to these institutions. See Konel'skii, "Kievskiia evreiskiia blagotvoritel'nyia uchrezhdeniia."

50. *Ha-melits* no. 58, 2 Aug. 1885: 937; *Die Judenpogrome in Russland,* II: 348.

51. *Voskhod* no. 9, 4 Feb. 1901: 20; Obshchestvo Popecheniia o bednykh remeslennykh i rabochikh evreiakh g. Kieva, *Otchet za 1907 god* (Kiev, 1908), vi–viii.

52. *Voskhod* no. 50, 12 Dec. 1902: 37.

53. For more on the society see Hamm, *Kiev,* 160.

54. Kievskoe Otdelenie Rossiiskago Obshchestva Zashchity Zhenshchin, *Otchet za 1912 god* (Kiev, 1913), 37. It is unclear which organizations are being referred to, as the Kiev Literacy Society and *Prosvita* had been closed several years earlier, in 1908 and 1910, respectively (for the latter, see *Rada* no. 81, 9 April 1910: 1). The Kiev branch of the Jewish Enlightenment Society had not been shut down.

55. Kievskoe Otdelenie Rossiiskago Obshchestva Zashchity Zhenshchin, *Otchet za 1912 g.,* 7, 19.

56. Otdel popecheniia ob evreiskikh devushkakh i zhenshchinakh g. Kieva pri Kievskom Otdelenii Rossiiskago Zashchity Zhenshchin, *Otchet za 1914 g. (god pervyi)* (Kiev, 1915)

57. *EE,* s.v. "Sankt-Peterburg."

58. The society may have been perceived as antisemitic due to the fact that when in 1906 it "urged the Ministry of Justice to strengthen the laws against procuring, it noted that 'a majority' of white-slave traders were 'Russian and Galician Jews.'" Engelstein, *The Keys to Happiness: Sex and the Search for Modernity in Fin-de-siècle Russia,* 308.

59. Aster and Potichnyj write that "although the jury of Ukrainian peasants found Beilis innocent, the trial itself legitimized and perpetuated the perception of the Jew as a threatening figure in the minds of the people." Aster and Potichnyj, *Jewish Ukrainian Relations: Two Solitudes,* 56.

60. Hamm, *Kiev,* 138.

61. See *Evreiskii narod* no. 6, 22 Nov. 1906: 23, for a report of the Governor-General closing a shoemakers' society because it was majority Jewish.

62. TsDIAU f. 442, op. 636, spr. 647, ch. 1, ark. 252–260, 554–566 ("Ob obshchestvakh i soiuzakh, utverzhdennykh na osnovanii zakona 4-go Marta 1906 g.").

63. Hamm, *Kiev,* 212; TsDIAU f. 442, op. 636, spr. 647 ch. 8, ark. 689, 893.

64. *Kiever vort* no. 2, 3 Jan. 1910; no. 9, 11 Jan. 1910.

65. TsDIAU f. 442, op. 636, spr. 647 ch. 3, ark. 704–712; DAKO f. 10 (Kievskoe gubernskoe po delam ob obshchestvakh prisutstvie), op. 1, spr. 129, ark. 19zv, 32 ("O registratsii Kievskago Podol'skago obshchestvennago kluba"); *Kiever vort* no. 6, 5 Jan. 1910.

66. A similar club existed in Odessa in the 1860s. See Zipperstein, *The Jews of Odessa,* 110.

67. Kievskoe obshchestvennoe sobranie, *Otchet za 1910–1911 g.* (Kiev, 1911).

68. Kievskoe obshchestvennoe sobranie, *Otchet za 1915 g.* (Kiev, 1916).

69. Friedmann, *Sefer ha-zikhronot,* 363–364.

70. TsDIAU f. 442, op. 636, spr. 647 ch. 8, ark. 224–229, 374–384, 906. The organization's charter does not explain the use of the descriptor "Russian" (in the ethnic and not the all-imperial sense) in the name.

71. *Kievskii telegraf* no. 12, 29 Jan. 1865: 2.

72. *Kiever vort* 1 Jan. 1910.

73. See, for example, no. 76, 3 April 1910: 1 and no. 77, 4 April 1910: 1.

74. *Kievskoe slovo* No. 3595, 13 Jan. 1898.

75. *Balaguly* was used in the 1874 Kiev census. Iugo-Zapadnoe otdelenie Imperatorskago Russkago Geograficheskago Obshchestva, *Kiev i ego predmestiia.* A reference to *marvikher* can be found in *Kievskoe slovo* no. 3585, 3 Jan. 1898.

76. *Hamelits* no. 108, 17 May 1896: 3–4; Kievskoe Obshchestvo Gramotnosti, *Otchet za 1906 god* (Kiev, 1907).

77. Owen, "Impediments to a Bourgeois Consciousness in Russia, 1880–1905," 84–85.

78. *Ha-melits* no. 223, 23 Oct. 1898: 2.

79. For an analysis of Russian government policy in the Ukrainian provinces and nationalist responses, see Weeks, *Nation and State*. For the Russian right, see Rogger, "The Formation of the Russian Right: 1900–06," 188–211.

80. Rogger, "Conclusion and Overview," 342; Avrutin, "Racial Categories and the Politics of (Jewish) Difference in Late Imperial Russia," 36.

81. Edelman, "The Russian Nationalist Party and the Political Crisis of 1909," 33–34.

82. For more on the national Russian Assembly, see Rogger, "The Formation of the Russian Right: 1900–06," 191–193.

83. Kievskoe Russkoe sobranie, *Otchet o sostoianii s dekabria 1911 goda po 1 ianvaria 1914 goda* (Kiev, 1914).

84. TsDIAU f. 442, op. 636, spr. 647 ch. 8, ark. 224–229, 374–384, 906.

85. Rawson, *Russian Rightists and the Revolution of 1905*, 102–103.

86. Ibid., 184, 194.

87. Ibid., 220.

88. *Khronika evreiskoi zhizni* no. 32, 17 Aug. 1906: 24; Hamm, *Kiev*, 204–205.

89. *Novyi voskhod* no. 11, 15 March 1912: 11–12.

90. *Novyi voskhod* no. 14, 5 April 1912: 21.

91. Lindemann, *The Jew Accused*, 187. Vitalii Shul'gin claims that Archbishop Anthony of Volhyn gave a speech from the pulpit after the Kishinev pogrom of 1903 condemning the *pogromshchiki*, who, he averred, "dare not call themselves Christians." Shul'gin, *The Years*, 74.

92. See, for example, *Nedel'naia khronika Voskhoda* no. 23, 5 June 1894 and no. 60, 21 Oct. 1901.

93. Kievskoe Obschchestvo Gramotnosti, *Otchet za 1905 god* (Kiev, 1906).

94. Rogger, "Conclusion and Overview," 342.

95. Hamm, *Kiev*, 194–196.

96. *Kievskoe slovo*, 9 Nov. 1905 quoted in Gusev, "Bund i ievreis'ki pohromy v 1905 roku," 36.

97. *Khronika evreiskoi zhizni* no. 20, 25 May 1906.

98. *Evreiskii mir* no. 12, 25 March 1910: 24; *Khronika evreiskoi zhizni* no. 7, 21 Feb. 1906: 25.

99. *Evreiskii narod* no. 8, 8 Dec. 1906.

100. *Evreiskii mir* no. 3, 21 Jan. 1910: 30; *Kiever vort* no. 6, 5 Jan. 1910.

101. See, for example, Mosse, "The Revolution of 1848: Jewish Emancipation in Germany and its Limits," 389–401. Eli Lederhendler also rejects "a theory of Eastern European exceptionalism" in his "Modernity Without Emancipation or Assimilation?" 324–343.

102. Frankel, "Assimilation and the Jews in Nineteenth-Century Europe: Towards a New Historiography?" 22.

103. Chew Sock Foon, "On the Incompatibility of Ethnic and National Loyalties: Reframing the Issue," *Canadian Review of Studies in Nationalism* 13, No. 1 (1986), 1–11, cited in Magocsi, "The Ukrainian National Revival," 51. On situational identity, see Aneta Pavlenko and Adrian Blackledge, "Introduction: New Theoretical Approaches to the Study of Negotiation of Identities in Multilingual Contexts," 1–33.

104. I am grateful to Benjamin Nathans for his insightful comments on this theme.

105. Murav, *Identity Theft: The Jew in Imperial Russia and the Case of Avraam Uri Kovner*, 190 and passim. Murav and Safran both explore the ways in which Jewish acculturation destabi-

lized and subverted "the idea of the innateness of identity, whether religious, national, or personal. Safran, *Rewriting the Jew,* 193.

106. David Sorkin calls this "parallel sociability." Sorkin, "Religious Reforms and Secular Trends in German-Jewish Life: An Agenda for Research," 182. See also Sorkin, *The Transformation of German Jewry, 1780–1840,* 113–114; Katz, *Out of the Ghetto: The Social Background of Jewish Emancipation, 1770–1870,* 177; Liedtke, *Jewish Welfare in Hamburg and Manchester, c. 1850–1914,* 10–12; Schüler-Springorum, "Assimilation and Community Reconsidered: The Jewish Community in Konigsburg, 1871–1914," 110; Zipperstein, *The Jews of Odessa,* 110; Rozenblit, *The Jews of Vienna.*

107. See, for example, Liedtke, *Jewish Welfare in Hamburg and Manchester,* 10ff.

108. On associational life among German Jews, see Sorkin, "The Impact of Emancipation on German Jewry: A Reconsideration," 177–198. Women played a particularly important role in the new Jewish associations, especially those in the realm of welfare. "Although German-Jewish women were prominent in the work of the non-sectarian German women's movement and in the advancement of social work, the majority of organized Jewish women remained within Jewish local or national organizations." Kaplan, "Gender and Jewish History in Imperial Germany," 218. See also Kaplan, *The Making of the Jewish Middle Class: Women, Family, and Identity in Imperial Germany,* 192, and Meir, "Mnogostoronnost' evreiskoi blagotvoritel'nosti sredi evreev Kieva, 1859–1914 gg.," 185–216.

109. See, for example, Endelman, *The Jews of Britain, 1656 to 2000,* 99–101.

110. *Novyi voskhod,* no. 37, 13 Sept. 1912. On the Jewish policy in the last years of the empire, see Rogger, "The Jewish Policy of Late Tsarism: A Reappraisal" in idem, *Jewish Policies,* 25–39.

111. In the realm of politics, too, many Jews found it more and more difficult to remain active in all-imperial liberal parties and groupings, or at least to do so without also contributing their energies to specifically Jewish liberal groups as well (such as the Union for the Full Rights of the Jewish People in Russia). See Gassenschmidt, *Jewish Liberal Politics,* esp. 19–44.

112. Bradley, "Subjects into Citizens," par. 13.

6. Varieties of Jewish Philanthropy

1. Penslar, *Shylock's Children: Economics and Jewish Identity in Modern Europe,* 92.

2. Löwe, "From Charity to Social Policy: The Emergence of Jewish 'Self-Help' Organizations in Imperial Russia, 1800–1914," 53–54.

3. Penslar, *Shylock's Children,* 96.

4. Lindenmeyr, *Poverty Is Not a Vice,* 99.

5. TsDIAU f. 442 (Kantseliaria Kievskogo, Podol'skogo i Volynskogo general-gubernatora), op. 661, spr. 273 ("Ob uregulirovanii blagotvoritel'nykh uchrezhdeniiakh v Kievskoi gubernii"), ark. 87–98.

6. For an analysis of the communities of Hamburg and Manchester see Liedtke, *Jewish Welfare in Hamburg and Manchester.*

7. Penslar, *Shylock's Children,* 182.

8. The term originates in the Hebrew word meaning "support" or "assistance."

9. Obshchestvo Popecheniia o bednykh remeslennykh i rabochikh evreiakh g. Kieva, *Otchet za 1910 god* (Kiev 1911); Obshchestvo Posobiia bednym evreiam g. Kieva "Gmilus-Khesed," *Otchet za 1910–11 god* (Kiev, 1911).

10. Liedtke reaches a similar conclusion regarding Hamburg and Manchester; see *Jewish Welfare,* 10–12.

11. Nathans, *Beyond the Pale,* 146.

12. See Kaplan, *The Making of the Jewish Middle Class,* 8ff.

13. Gershon-Badanes [G. E. Gurevich], *Evreiskiia obshchestvennyia dela v Kieve,* 10, 28.

14. See, for example, the photograph on Obshchestvo lechebnits dlia khronicheski-bol'nykh detei v g. Kieve, *Obzor X-ti letnei deiatel'nosti* (Kiev, 1910), 15. Perhaps the grandest form of recognition for philanthropic efforts were government awards such as those granted to Lazar' Brodsky: the French Order of the Legion of Honor and the Russian medals of Stanislav, Anna and St. Vladimir. Khiterer, "The Social and Economic History of Jews in Kiev," 228.

15. *Zapiska o Kievskoi evreiskoi bol'nitse,* 18.

16. Ibid., 5; Neishtube, *Istoricheskaia zapiska,* 27.

17. *Zapiska o Kievskoi evreiskoi bol'nitse,* 6–7, 16–23; Neishtube, *Istoricheskaia zapiska,* 164. It is unclear whether the plot proposed for purchase on Starozhitomirskaia (later L'vovskaia) was the same as that which housed the hospital between 1876 and 1885.

18. *Ha-melits* no. 81, 1 Nov. 1885: 1311–17.

19. V. S. Perlis, *Meditsinskii otchet po rodil'nomy otdeleniiu pri Kievskoi evreiskoi bol'nitsy za 1891, 1892 i 1893 god* (Kiev, 1895), 4, cited in Epstein, "Caring for the Soul's House," 175.

20. Dedication ceremonies accompanying the opening of other modern Jewish hospitals in the Russian Empire, such as those in Simferopol and Berdichev, were similar to the one described here in their attempt to present a modern and civilized face of Russian Jewry to the surrounding society. Epstein, "Caring for the Soul's House," 181.

21. *Ha-melits* no. 81, 1 Nov. 1885: 1311–17.

22. Ibid.

23. *Ha-melits* no. 80, 28 Oct. 1885: 1302.

24. *Ha-melits* no. 81, 1 Nov. 1885: 1311–17.

25. Epstein, "Caring for the Soul's House," 6.

26. *Ha-melits* no. 6, 21 Feb. 1885: 88–93.

27. *Kievskiia gubernskiia vedemosti* no. 79, 9 July 1874: 362.

28. *Ha-melits* no. 81, 1 Nov. 1885: 1311–17.

29. *Ha-melits* no. 73, 18 Sept. 1884: 1196.

30. *Ha-melits* no. 26, 8 April 1885: 416–17.

31. Liedtke, *Jewish Welfare,* 10–12.

32. *Zaria* no. 58, 2 Aug. 1885: 937.

33. Neishtube, *Istoricheskaia zapiska,* 40.

34. TsDIAU f. 442, op. 544, spr. 90 ("Ob uchrezhdenii Obshchestva podaniia pomoshchi bol'nym detiam"), ark. 62, pp. 2–4.

35. *Ha-melits* no. 80, 9 April 1896: 3–4.

36. *Kievskii kalendar' Iugo-Zapadnago kraia na 1899 g.* (Kiev, 1899), 65ff. In 1905, Jews made up about 15 percent of students at the Polytechnical Institute, and at least 40 percent in 1909. DAmK f. 18, op. 1, spr. 535 ("Statisticheskie svedeniia o kolichestve, sotsial'nom i natsional'nom sostave studentov za 1904–1905 gg.; spiski studentov institute"); DAmK f. 18 (Kievskii Politekhnicheskii institut), op. 1, spr. 206 ("O provedenii mitingov i zabastovok evreiskimi studentami v institute"). The full story of the establishment of the institute, which was actually a kind of bargain involving the regulation of sugar prices that was struck between Chairman of the Council of Ministers S. I. Witte and the sugar magnates of the Russian southwest, is told in Kovalinskii, *Metsenaty Kieva,* 170–173.

37. *Ha-melits* no. 73, 18 Sept. 1884: 1196.

38. TsDIAU f. 442, op. 544, spr. 90, ark. 62, p. 3.

39. *Nedel'naia khronika Voskhoda* no. 49, 4 Dec. 1894: 1297; *Ha-melits* no. 48, 26 Feb. 1895: 5.

40. *Nedel'naia khronika Voskhoda* no. 48, 27 Nov. 1894: 1274. For example, 30 percent of students at Kiev's Fifth Girls' Gymnasium and 15 percent at the Duchinskaia Private Girls' Gymnasium were Jewish, as were a substantial number of students at the Beitel' Girls' Gymnasium. Kel'berin, *Kievskoe evreiskoe uchilishche imeni S. I. Brodskago*, 3; TsDIAU f. 707 (Upravlenie Kievskogo uchebnogo okruga), op. 149, spr. 45 ("Ob ustanovlenii v zhenskikh gimnaziiakh i progimnaziiakh protsentnoi normy dlia uchashchikhsia-evreev"), ark. 27–29.

41. *Ha-melits* no. 80, 9 April 1896: 3–4.

42. *Ha-melits* no. 237, 29 Oct. 1896: 5–6.

43. Neishtube, *Istoricheskaia zapiska*, 167. See also Epstein, "Caring for the Soul's House," 173.

44. Neishtube, *Istoricheskaia zapiska*, 163.

45. Ibid., 163.

46. *Ha-melits* no. 111, 20 May 1891: 1–2.

47. *Nedel'naia khronika Voskhoda* no. 45, 6 Nov. 1894: 1194.

48. *Ha-melits* no. 243, 8 Nov. 1895. This may have been due in part to the closure of the Kirillov Hospital, leaving the Jewish Hospital as the only medical facility serving the Ploskaia and Lukianovskaia districts (Neishtube, *Istoricheskaia zapiska*, 54). But Epstein shows that "Jewish medical personnel and the Jewish community displayed a disproportionately active response" to crises such as cholera epidemics. Epstein, "Caring for the Soul's House," 200.

49. Neishtube, *Istoricheskaia zapiska*, 55, 166.

50. *Nedel'naia khronika Voskhoda* no. 45, 5 Nov. 1895: 1236.

51. *Nedel'naia khronika Voskhoda* no. 32, 10 Aug. 1897: 889.

52. *Novoe vremia* no. 5270, 30 Oct. 1890.

53. Neishtube, *Istoricheskaia zapiska*, 43.

54. *Ha-melits* no. 26, 8 April 1885: 416–17.

55. *Nedel'naia khronika Voskhoda* no. 48, 27 Nov. 1894: 1274; *Ha-melits* no. 281, 19 Dec. 1896: 3.

56. Vasil' Halaiba, "Likarnia, instytut, uchilishche, rynok . . . : Z istorii̇̈ evreis'koho blahodiintstva v Kyevi," *Khronyka 2000: ukraïns'kyi kul'turolohichnyi al'manakh* (1998): 109–110.

57. On productivization in Jewish philanthropic efforts in Western and Central Europe, see Penslar, *Shylock's Children*, 205–216.

58. *Jewish Chronicle* 25 June 1880 and 2 July 1880.

59. Subbotin, *V cherte evreiskoi osedlosti*, 179–180.

60. Rubinow, *Economic Condition*, 492.

61. *Ha-melits* no. 11, 6 Feb. 1884: 169.

62. *Ha-melits* no. 34, 6 May 1885: 550–551.

63. *Ha-melits* no. 129, 14 June 1895: 2.

64. It is also unclear if the Talmud Torah was still in existence at this point.

65. TsDIAU f. 707, op. 217–A, spr. 42 ("Po voprosu o khodataistve kuptsa B. Kats-nel'sona o razreshenii prepodovat' v sushchestvuiushchem v g. Demievke khedere russkii iazyk"). According to an 1893 law, Kiev's Jews were permitted to maintain 31 heders but no more. DAKO f. 2 (Kantseliariia Kievskogo gubernatora), op. 227, spr. 245 ("Po khodataistvu komiteta Kievskogo otdeleniia OPE o razreshenii otkryt' v g. Kieve pedagogicheskii muzei nagliadnykh posobii dlia . . . evreiskikh khederov i obshchestvennykh shkol"), ark. 1.

66. *Ha-melits* no. 34, 6 May 1885: 550–551.

67. Gershon Badanes, "Kievskaia evreiskaia obshchina na Vserossiiskoi Vystavke 1913 g. v Kieve," 19.

68. Kel'berin, *Kievskoe evreiskoe uchilishche,* 12–13, 15–16.

69. Ibid., 12.

70. Ibid., 18.

71. *Der yud* no. 17, 25 April 1901: 15–16.

72. *Voskhod* no. 35, 29 Aug. 1902: 30–31.

73. Obshchestvo letnikh sanatornykh kolonii dlia bol'nykh evreev neimushchago naseleniia g. Kieva, *Otchet po soderzhaniiu sanatornoi kolonii v Boiarke za 1910 god* (Kiev, 1911), 5–6.

74. *Kievskii kalendar' Iugo-Zapadnago kraia,* 65–101; Rieber, *Merchants and Entrepreneurs in Imperial Russia,* 107. Kovalinskii maintains that the great captains of industry in Kiev donated large sums for the Polytechnical Institute in exchange for a promise from Minister of Trade Witte that the government would regulate sugar prices, which were then falling. Kovalinskii, *Metsenaty Kieva,* 170–173.

75. Brodsky, *Smoke Signals,* 13, cited in Estraikh, "From Yehupets Jargonists to Kiev Modernists," 23.

76. DAmK f. 18, op. 1, spr. 535.

77. Ibid., spr. 206, ark. 69–139.

78. Kovalinskii, *Metsenaty Kieva,* 172; Michail Kalnizkij, "Juden in Kiew—Ein Gang Durch die Jahrhunderte," 21.

79. TsDIAU f. 1423 (Dokumenty, sobrannye Evreiskoi istoriko-arkheograficheskoi komissiei VUAN (Kollektsiia)), op. 1, spr. 12 ("Anonimnyi donos Kievskomu, Podol'skomu i Volynskomu general-gubernatoru"), cited in Khiterer, *Dokumenty,* 180.

80. Kievskoe blagotvoritel'noe obshchestvo, *Godovoi otchet za 1899 god* (Kiev, 1900), 172; *Khronika Voskhoda* no. 24, 13 June 1899: 731. The Tereshchenko family also had a connection to Kiev's two Free Night Shelters, both of which were named after N. A. Tereshchenko. *Ves' Kiev* (Kiev, 1900), 307.

81. *Ha-melits* no. 111, 20 May 1891: 1–2.

82. *Ha-melits* no. 235, 29 Oct. 1895: 2 and no. 243, 8 Nov. 1895.

83. *Ha-melits* no. 267, 8 Dec. 1896: 4.

84. Neishtube, *Istoricheskaia zapiska,* 166–167.

85. Ger. Bad—s, "Kievskaia evreiskaia obshchina v 1913 g.," *Vestnik evreiskoi obshchiny* no. 3 (March 1914): 34; Gershon Badanes, "Kievskaia evreiskaia obshchina na Vserossiiskoi Vystavke 1913 g. v Kieve," 31.

86. Neishtube, *Istoricheskaia zapiska,* 3.

87. Citing 1858 as the date for the first admittance of Jews into Kiev by Alexander II was a common error in the literature about the city.

88. Neishtube, *Istoricheskaia zapiska,* 36.

89. *Zapiska o Kievskoi evreiskoi bol'nitse,* 12–14.

90. Neishtube, *Istoricheskaia zapiska,* 38.

91. Ibid., 40.

92. Ibid., 43–44.

93. *Ha-melits* no. 215, 12 Oct. 1898: 3–4.

94. *Ha-melits* no. 206, 9 Sept. 1894: 5–6.

95. Neishtube, *Istoricheskaia zapiska,* appendix.

96. *Kiever vort* no. 6, 7 Jan. 1910.

97. Gershon Badanes, "Kievskaia evreiskaia obshchina," 20–21.

98. Ger.Bad—s, "Kievskaia evreiskaia obshchina v 1913 g.," *Vestnik evreiskoi obshchiny* no. 2 (Feb. 1914): 53.

99. *Voskhod* no. 9, 4 Feb. 1901: 20; no. 20, 15 May 1903.

100. [Predstavitel'stvo po evreiskoi blagotvoritel'nosti pri Kievskoi Gorodskoi Uprave,] *Otchet po okazaniiu pomoshchi bednym bol'nym evreiam g. Kieva na domu* (Kiev, 1898); *Ha-melits* no. 26, 8 April 1885: 416–417; Obshchestvo Popecheniia o bednykh remeslennykh i rabochikh evreiakh g. Kieva, *Otchet za 1907 god* (Kiev, 1908), vi. The genesis of the society is uncertain: an item in the press in 1896 reporting that Ionna Zaitsev had proposed a Bikur Holim society that would furnish free doctor's visits and food for the poor seems to indicate that it was founded not long after that date. However, we have mentions of Bikur Holim in Kiev in the 1880s, which may refer to an earlier, more primitive organization for visiting the sick; in that case, Zaitsev's call may have been to create a modern home visiting society—in other words, to transform the *hevra* into an *obshchestvo.*

101. Lindenmeyr, *Poverty Is Not a Vice,* 116.

102. McReynolds and Popkin, "The Objective Eye and the Common Good," 60.

103. Levitats, *Jewish Community,* 79–82, 125.

104. IR TsNB f. 321 (Kollektsiia evreiskikh rukopisei), op. 1, spr. OR 71, n. 39 ("Pinkas de-havura mishnayot Kiev de-Beit ha-Midrash Makariv be-po Kiev"), ark. 20.

105. Bacon, "Ha-hevrot le-limud," 107.

106. McReynolds and Popkin, "The Objective Eye and the Common Good," 65. Martha Bohachevsky-Chomiak notes that throughout the Russian empire "women were more likely to join community than overtly political organizations," such as the "Ukrainian Women's Community (*Zhinocha hromada*)," a broadly educational but also semipolitical group. Bohachevsky-Chomiak, 161, 169.

107. Epstein confirms these findings for Russian Jewry as a whole; see Epstein, "Caring for the Soul's House," 186–188.

108. Neishtube, *Istoricheskaia zapiska,* 15; TsDIAU f. 707, op. 87, spr. 5686, ark. 66 ("S perepiskoiu po raznym predmetam," 1873); *Ha-melits* no. 81, 1 Nov. 1885: 1311–17.

109. TsDIAU f. 442, op. 539, spr. 11 ("Delo ob uchrezhdenii Kievskogo obshchestva priiutov dlia devochek evreiskogo veroispovedaniia"). The founders were El'ka Rozenberg, Sofiia Mandel'shtam, Beila Merpert, Berta Brodskaia, Gitel'-Beila Tul'chinskaia, Elisaveta Ettinger, Eva Brodskaia, and Mariia Rozenberg. On the growing need for such shelters as more and more women entered the workforce, see Rose L. Glickman, "The Russian Factory Woman, 1880–1914," 75–76.

110. Kievskoe evreiskoe obshchestvo dlia vspomoshchestvovaniia postradavshim ot bezporiadkov na iuge Rossii 1881 g., *Otchet . . . po 1-e oktiabria 1881 goda* (Kiev: Ern. Perlis, 1882), 6.

111. *Ha-melits* no. 34, 9 Feb. 1895: 2.

112. Bezplatnaia boiarskaia sanatoriia dlia bednikh chakhotochnykh evreev g. Kieva, *Otchet po soderzhaniiu sanitorii za 1902 god* (Kiev, 1903); *Kievlianin* no. 78, 5 July 1866: 34.

113. *Voskhod* no. 74, 24 Sept. 1900: 12.

114. Kievskii piatyi dnevnoi priiut dlia detei rabochego klassa Iudeiskago veroispovedaniia, *Otchet za 1900–1913 gg.* (Kiev, 1914).

115. *Voskhod* no. 9, 4 Feb. 1901: 20 and no. 20, 15 May 1903: 29–30.

116. *Ha-melits* no. 98, 4 May 1895: 1–2.

117. *Nedel'naia khronika Voskhoda* no. 24, 11 June 1895: 662.

118. *Nedel'naia khronika Voskhoda* no. 35, 28 Aug. 1894: 934.

119. *Ha-melits* no. 124, 5 June 1896; Mikhail Kal'nitskii, *Sinagoga Kievskoi iudeiskoi obshchiny, 5656–5756: Istoricheskii ocherk,* 13.

120. Kotik, *Mayne zikhroynes,* II: 239.

121. *Nedel'naia khronika Voskhoda* no. 7, 16 Feb. 1897.

122. *Ha-melits* no. 48, 24 Feb. 1892: 2.

123. Kievskii komitet po okazaniiu pomoshchi postradavshim ot pogromov 18–21 oktiabria 1905 goda, *Otchet* 4; TsDIAU f. 1423, op. 1, spr. 30, ark. 24, cited in Khiterer, *Dokumenty,* 206–207.

124. *Ves' Kiev* (1907), cols. 708–709.

125. *Voskhod* no. 41, 13 Oct. 1905: 7–9. See also Adele Lindenmeyr, "Maternalism and Child Welfare in Late Imperial Russia," *Journal of Women's History* 5, 2 (Fall 1993): 114–125.

126. Predstavitel'stvo po evreiskoi blagotvoritel'nosti pri Kievskoi Gorodskoi Uprave, *Otchet za 1913 god,* appendix.

127. Kievskoe otdelenie Obshchestva rasprostraneniia prosveshcheniia mezhdu evreiami v Rossii, *Otchet za 1907 god* (Kiev, 1908).

128. Obshchestvo Posobiia bednym evreiam g. Kieva "Gmilus-Khesed," *Otchet . . . ot 1 Sentiabria 1912 g. po 31 Avgusta 1913 g.* (Kiev, 1913).

129. See Lindenmeyr, *Poverty Is Not a Vice,* 126.

130. Gershon Badanes, "Kievskaia evreiskaia obshchina," 38–40.

131. Obshchestvo letnikh sanatornykh kolonii dlia bol'nykh evreev neimushchago naseleniia g. Kieva, *Otchet po soderzhaniiu sanatornoi kolonii v Boiarke za 1908 god* (Kiev, 1909).

132. Obshchestvo letnikh sanatornykh kolonii dlia bol'nykh evreev neimushchago naseleniia g. Kieva, *Otchet . . . za 1902 god* (Kiev, 1903).

133. Kaplan, *The Making of the Jewish Middle Class,* 192.

134. *Khronika Evreiskoi zhizni* no. 11, 22 March 1906: 34–35.

135. *Evreiskii mir* no. 14–15, 15 April 1911: 21–26.

136. Documentation on the Kiev OZE can be found in RGIA f. 1546 (Evreiskii komitet pomoshchi zhertvam voiny v Petrograde), op. 1, spr. 61 ("Donesenie upolnomochennogo Komiteta Ioffe o deiatel'nosti komitetov v gg. Kieve, Ekaterinoslave i Khar'kove," 1915–17).

137. Hamm, *Kiev,* 131.

138. *Kiever vort* no. 5, 6 Jan. 1910; Gershon-Badanes, *Evreiskiia obshchestvennyia dela,* 11.

139. *Kievskoe utro* no. 132, 31 Dec. 1910.

140. *Razsvet* no. 19, 17 May 1908: 34.

141. Kievskoe Otdelenie Rossiiskago Obshchestva Zashchity Zhenshchin, *Otchet za 1912 god* (Kiev, 1913), 37.

142. *Dos folk* no. 13, 15 Dec. 1906.

143. TsDIAU f. 442, op. 661, spr. 273 ("Ob uregulirovanii blagotvoritel'nykh uchrezhdeniiakh v Kievskoi gubernii," 1908–09).

144. Liedtke, *Jewish Welfare,* 99, 228.

145. Kievskoe evreiskoe obshchestvo dlia vspomoshchestvovaniia postradavshim ot bezporiadkov na iuge Rossii 1881 g., *Otchet,* 6–8.

146. *Materialy dlia istorii antievreiskikh pogromov v Rossii,* ed. G. Ia. Krasnyi-Admoni, 532–533.

147. Ibid.

148. *Ha-melits* no. 56, 26 July 1885: 901–904. See also Frankel, *Prophecy and Politics,* 62. Frankel notes that the Kiev delegation was a "highly unusual step . . . [seen as a] direct challenge in St. Petersburg."

149. Frankel, *Prophecy and Politics,* 61.

150. TsDIAU f. 1423, op. 1, spr. 30, ark. 14–17, cited in Khiterer, *Dokumenty*, 202–204. The Committee's work was so complex that it had to organize separate Financial, Legal, and Schools Commissions.

151. Kievskii komitet po okazaniiu pomoshchi postradavshchim ot pogromov 18–21 oktiabria 1905 g., *Otchet*, 89, 104, 127, 133, 154.

152. Ibid., 112, 115, 139.

153. Ibid., 133, 139, 161.

154. TsDIAU f. 1423, op. 1, spr. 30, ark. 20–21, cited in Khiterer, *Dokumenty*, 206.

155. *Voskhod* no. 47–48, 1 Dec. 1905: 53.

156. TsDIAU f. 1423, op. 1, spr. 30, ark. 20–21, cited in Khiterer, *Dokumenty*, 206.

157. *Evreiskii mir* no. 32, 2 Dec. 1910: 43.

7. Revolutions in Communal Life

1. Aronson, "V bor'be za grazhdanskie i national'nye prava (Obshchestvennye techeniia v russkom evreistve)," 224–238.

2. See Frankel, *Prophecy and Politics*, 167–169.

3. Wirtschafter, *Social Identity*, 157.

4. Kappeler, "The Ukrainians of the Russian Empire," 113.

5. Frankel, *Prophecy and Politics*, 155–156.

6. For example, the Kiev board of the Nonparty Jewish Organization (discussed below) recommended to Jews in the provinces that, rather than isolating themselves and choosing only Jewish candidates, they join forces with progressive Christian forces. *Evreiskii narod* no. 6, 22 Nov. 1906. On Jewish involvement and attitudes toward the elections, see Levin, "Russian Jewry and the Duma Elections, 1906–1907," 233–264.

7. Slutsky, "Dr Max Mandelshtam bi-tekufat ha-tsionut ha-medinit," 64.

8. Zimmerman, *Poles, Jews, and the Politics of Nationality: The Bund and the Polish Socialist Party in Late Tsarist Russia, 1892–1914*, 234.

9. See, for example, Lederhender, *Road to Modern Jewish Politics*, 154–157.

10. One parallel to the Kiev case—of many throughout Eastern Europe—including an attempt to democratize a communal structure that had always been dominated by the plutocracy, a struggle between different nationalist factions over the direction of the community and especially education and welfare, and an attempt to craft a Jewish politics of pride and self-respect, can be found in Kassow, "Jewish Communal Politics in Transition: The Vilna *Kehile*, 1919–1920," 61–92.

11. See Nathans, "The Other Modern Jewish Politics: Integration and Modernity in Fin de Siècle Russia," 20–34.

12. Tobias, *The Jewish Bund in Russia: From Its Origins to 1905*, 8.

13. Wirtschafter, *Social Identity*, 146.

14. Tobias, *The Jewish Bund*, 117.

15. TsDIAU f. 1423 (Dokumenty, sobrannye Evreiskoi istoriko-arkheograficheskoi komissiei VUAN (Kollektsiia)), op. 1, spr. 10, ark. 13, cited in Khiterer, *Dokumenty*, 218–221.

16. Nathans, *Beyond the Pale*, 283; TsDIAU f. 275 (Kievskoe okhrannoe otdelenie), op. 1, spr. 547 ("Delo o razrabotke pisem, poluchennykh agenturnym putem, soderzhashchikh svedeniia o deiatel'nosti Kievskogo raionnogo 'Evreiskogo tovarishcheskogo s"ezda'"), ark. 2.

17. TsDIAU f. 838 (Kollektsiia listovok), op. 2, spr. 941 ("Listovka Kievskoi gruppy Bunda 'Pogrom v Smele'"); YIVO, RG 1400, MG 7, folder 67 ("Der pogrom in Smela"). Ad-

ditional leaflets distributed by the Kiev group in 1904, preserved in the same YIVO record group, are "Der yidisher proletariat in zayn klasen-kampf" (The Jewish Proletariat in Its Class Struggle) and "Ko vsem uchashchimsia v sredne-uchebnykh zavedeniiakh" (To All Students of Secondary Schools).

18. CAHJP, HMF 211 ("O besporiadkakh po sluchaiu ob"iavleniia prizyva zapasnykh i sluchaiakh nasiliia poslednikh po otnosheniiu k evreiam"); TsDIAU f. 838, op. 2, spr. 942 ("'Pobedy revoliutsii, evreiskie pogromy' [Listovka Bunda]"); Hamm, *Kiev,* 178.

19. Hamm, *Kiev,* 182. Hamm adds that "it was reported that only 20 to 40 supporters attended the Bund's agitational meetings, compared with estimates of 500 in Kishinev, 2,000 in Minsk, 3,500 in Dvinsk, and up to 5,000 in Warsaw!"

20. TsDIAU f. 274 (Kievskoe gubernskoe zhandarmskoe upravlenie), op. 1, spr. 2444 ("Spravka Departamenta politsii po istorii sionistskogo dvizheniia"), ark. 18.

21. Seimists were "autonomists [who] maintained that the Palestinian versus territorialist questions should be postponed until a Jewish national parliament in Russia deliberated over such issues. In the meantime, SERP called for recognition of the Jews in Russia as a national body with rights to national autonomy and claimed some thirteen thousand members by the end of 1906." The other parties were the SS/Zionist Socialist Workers Party, founded in Odessa in 1905, and the Jewish Social-Democratic Workers' Party—Poale Zion, founded 1906 in Poltava. Zimmerman, *Poles, Jews, and the Politics of Nationality,* 230.

22. *Evreiskii narod* no. 3, 3 Nov. 1906: 39.

23. *Khronika evreiskoi zhizni* no. 7, 21 Feb. 1906: 29; Slutsky, "Dr. Maks Mandelshtam," 62; CZA, RG A3 (Mandelshtam, Max), folder 24, 52–70.

24. Slutsky, "Dr Max Mandelshtam," 63–66. See also Leshchinskii, *Gal'vestonskaia emigratsiia i emigratsionnaia politika*; Alroey, "'Erets le-am ve-lo am le-erets': ha-histradrut ha-teritorialistit ha-yehudit (ITO), ha-tenu'a he-tsionit ve-ha-hagira ha-yehudit be-reishit ha-me'a ha-20," 537–564 and idem, "Galveston and Palestine: Immigration and Ideology in the Early Twentieth Century," 129–150. The Territorialist movement awaits its historian.

25. On Brodsky's involvement with the Galveston Project, see Khiterer, "The Social and Economic History of Jews in Kiev," 238–244.

26. Otto Müller, *Intelligencija: Untersuchungen zur Geschichte eines politischen Schlagwortes* (Frankfurt, 1971); Daniel R. Brower, "The Problem of the Russian Intelligentsia," *Slavic Review* 26 (1967): 638–9, 646, both cited in Wirtschafter, *Social Identity,* 89–90.

27. On polu-intelligenty, see Nathans, *Beyond the Pale,* 233; on activist professionals, see Wirtschafter, *Social Identity,* 91.

28. Haimson, "The Problem of Social Identities in Early Twentieth Century Russia," 3–4.

29. On the establishment of the Union, see Gassenschmidt, *Jewish Liberal Politics,* 20–23, and Vovshin, "Tahalikh ha-hitgabshut shel yahadut rusyah leor pe'ilut 'ha-berit le-hasagat melo ha-zekhuyot avur ha-am ha-yehudi be-rusya' bi-tekufat ha-mahapekha ha-rusit ha-rishona, 1905–1907." For related documents, see TsDIAU f. 275, op. 1, t. 1, spr. 869 ("Delo o deiatel'nosti 'Kievskogo soiuza dlia dostizheniia polnopraviia evreiskogo naroda v Rossii'"); TsDIAU f. 275, op. 1, spr. 1122 ("Perepiska s Departamentom politsii, Kievskim GZhU i drugimi uchrezhdeniiami o sbore svedenii o mestnoi organizatsii 'Soiuz soiuzov'"), ark. 13–16; and TsDIAU f. 1423, op. 1, spr. 9, ark. 6–7, quoted in Khiterer, *Dokumenty,* 250.

30. Harcave, "The Jews and the First Russian National Election," 35, 38.

31. RGIA f. 1565 (Soiuz dlia dostizheniia polnopraviia evreiskogo naroda v Rossii), op. 1, d. 24, l. 8.

32. *Voskhod* no. 28, 14 July 1905: 21; Hamm, *Kiev,* 183.

33. RGIA f. 1565, op. 1, d. 24 ("O vyborakh v Gosudarstvennuiu Dumu i na s"sezd 'Obshchestva polnopraviia' v g. Kieve"), l. 23ob.

34. Ibid., ll. 31, 32, 35.

35. Ibid., ll. 36–37.

36. See Emmons, *The Formation of Political Parties*, 149.

37. RGIA f. 1565, op. 1, d. 24, ll. 71–74, 76–79ob. At a province-wide conference in March 1906, a delegate from Cherkassy fulminated that "almost all those advanced as candidates for Duma members belong to the Jewish haute bourgeoisie (*krupnaia evreiskaia burzhuaziia*), and they weren't even required to state their political credos or even to promise to support the political program of the Union for Equality." It is also noteworthy that the membership of the local branch of the Union for Equality overlapped substantially with that of the Pogrom Aid Committee (discussed in chapter 6), which was "notable"-heavy and accused of favoritism.

38. Ibid., ll. 89–90ob, 92–94.

39. Ibid., ll. 123–124ob.

40. Ibid., l. 138ob.

41. Harcave, "The Jews and the First Russian National Election," 39.

42. Emmons, *The Formation of Political Parties*, 278, 291.

43. Gassenschmidt, *Jewish Liberal Politics*, 33.

44. *Evreiskii narod* no. 6, 22 Nov. 1906: 11–12.

45. Shtammer, *Kto vinovat? K vyboram ravvina v Kieve*, 7.

46. Ibid., 13.

47. Crown rabbis had always been elected, but never by a universal franchise, and had thus never been seen as "popular" leaders or accountable to their constituents heretofore.

48. Shtammer, *Kto vinovat?* 9.

49. *Khronika Voskhoda* no. 17, 25 April 1899: 509; Shohat, *Mosad ha-rabanut*, 121.

50. Iampol'skii, *Vstupitel'naia dukhovnaia beseda: chitano v molitvennom dome L. Brodskago v subbotu 3 ianvaria 1900 g. Kievskim gorodskim ravvinom doktorom F. A. Iampol'skim.*

51. CZA, RG A24 (Ussishkin, Menahem), folder 8, file 130, emphasis in original.

52. *Khronika Voskhoda* no. 34, 15 Aug. 1899: 1036–7.

53. Shtammer, *Na Sud obshchestvennago mneniia* (Kiev, 1908), 15.

54. *Voskhod* no. 9, 3 Feb. 1900: 12.

55. A decision of the State Council (*Gosudarstvennyi sovet*) of 8 June 1901 had interpreted the existing law (PSZ 1896, vol. XI, pt. 1) to mean that those eligible to vote for electors in rabbinical elections were "members of prayer societies, Russian subjects of male sex, not younger than 25 years old and having been members of a prayer society no less than two years prior to the election." Mysh, *Rukovodstvo k russkim zakonam*, 87–88.

56. When he was elected Crown rabbi in Kiev, he was called a "well-known litterateur" by a correspondent from Kiev. *Voskhod* no. 3, 16 Jan. 1903: 18. See also *EE*, s.v. "Lur'e, Solomon."

57. [S. A. Lur'e], *Curriculum Vitae* (Kiev, 1898), 3.

58. *Voskhod* no. 25, 12 April 1901: 14.

59. *Kievskii kalendar' Iugo-Zapadnago kraia na 1899 g.* (Kiev, 1899), App. I, 36.

60. DAmK f. 163 (Kievskaia gorodskaia uprava), op. 7, spr. 2069 ("O naznachenii vyborov ravvina po gorodu Kieva na trekhletie s 1897 po 1899 god"), ark. 36–37.

61. *Kievskaia gazeta* no. 264, 24 Sept. 1903.

62. *Kievskaia gazeta* no. 283, 14 Oct. 1903. The exchange is recapped in *Voskhod* no. 40, 5 Oct. 1903: 12–13 and no. 44, 10 Oct. 1903: 16.

63. *Kievskaia gazeta* no. 288, 18 Oct. 1903.

64. *Kievskaia gazeta* no. 292, 23 Oct. 1903.

65. CAHJP, Ru 81, Doc. 2 ("Tazkir ha-rav ha-Kiyovi A. Luria el mo'etset ha-ir be-Kiyov), 20 Nov. 1903; emphasis in original.

66. That this was indeed the case is made clear by a 1906 petition submitted by members of that same elite, which noted that, with a few rare exceptions, prosperous Jews did not eat kosher meat. TsDIAU f. 442 (Kantseliaria Kievskogo, Podol'skogo i Volynskogo general-gubernatora), op. 658, spr. 97 ("Ob otdache s torgov korobochnykh sborov po KIEVSKOI gubernii na chetyrekhletie s 1906 goda"), ark. 99.

67. *Voskhod* no. 3, 23 Jan. 1904: 18.

68. *Voskhod* no. 21, 26 May 1905: 37–38.

69. *Voskhod* no. 49–50, 16 Dec. 1905: 59.

70. *Khronika evreiskoi zhizni* no. 3, 24 Jan. 1906: 23.

71. *Der telegraf* no. 65, 20 March 1906: 3.

72. *Voskhod* no. 24, 16 June 1905: 34.

73. TsDIAU f. 294 (Kantseliariia Kievskogo otdel'nogo tsenzora), op. 1, spr. 422 ("Ob izdanii zhurnala 'Kievskii Evreiskii Vestnik'").

74. *Khronika evreiskoi zhizni* no. 32, 17 Aug. 1906: 26.

75. *Evreiskii narod* no. 6, 22 Nov. 1906: 21.

76. *Evreiskii narod* no. 1, 18 Oct. 1906: 36.

77. *Voskhod* no. 15, 15 April 1904: 21; *Khronika evreiskoi zhizni* no. 8, 28 Feb. 1906: 36.

78. See Frankel, *Prophecy and Politics*, 62.

79. *Khronika evreiskoi zhizni* no. 17, 26 April 1906: 22.

80. TsDIAU f. 442, op. 635, spr. 165 ("Po zhalobe evreev g. Kieva na ravvina za trebovanie s bednykh platy za sovershenie religioznykh obriadov").

81. DAKO f. 1 (Kievskoe gubernskoe pravlenie), op. 141, spr. 248 ("O vybore Kievskogo Kazennogo Ravvina 1-go uchastka"), ark. 1.

82. Ibid., ark. 4.

83. Ibid., ark. 13.

84. TsDIAU f. 442, op. 636, spr. 485 ("Delo o predanii sudu kievskogo kazennogo ravvina Lur'e za vedenie metricheskikh knig na russkom iazyke bez perevoda na evreiskii").

85. *Khronika evreiskoi zhizni* no. 5, 8 Feb. 1906: 33.

86. YIVO, RG 80, folder 703, item 20 ("Oyfruf fun Kiever rabiner Lurye tsu di bazukhers fun di sinagoges, 8 X 1906").

87. RGIA f. 821 (Departament dukhovnykh del inostrannykh ispovedanii MVD), op. 8, d. 153 ("Evrei v g. Kieve"), ll. 113–114.

88. DAKO f. 1, op. 141, spr. 248, ark. 18, emphasis added.

89. Shtammer, *Na sud obshchestvennago mneniia*, 20–21. Azriel Shohat also believed that the division of the city was engineered in order to eliminate Lur'e. Shohat, *Mosad ha-rabanut*, 121.

90. RGIA f. 821, op. 8, d. 153, ll. 110–112ob.

91. TsDIAU f. 442, op. 658, spr. 97, ark. 93–94zv.

92. Ibid., ark. 239–241zv.

93. DAKO f. 2 (Kantseliariia Kievskogo gubernatora), op. 44, spr. 292 ("Po khodataistvu Kievskomu otdeleniiu OPE o razreshenii emu otkryt' v g. Kieve biblioteku"), ark. 1.

94. *Razsvet* no. 27, 13 July 1908: 26; no. 28, 20 July 1898: 12–14; no. 29, 27 July 1908: 18–20.

95. DAKO f. 1, op. 141, spr. 287 ("O vybore Kievskogo kazennogo ravvina 2-go uchastka"), ark. 184.

96. RGIA f. 821, op. 8, d. 448 ("O rassmotrenii zhalob razlichnykh uchrezhdenii i otdel'nykh lits na vymogatel'stvo, pritesneniia, zloupotrebleniia vlast'iu, raskhishchenie obshchestvennykh deneg i drugie sluzhebnye i ugolovnye prestupleniia ravvinov (1875–1909)"), for example, contains many denunciations of Crown rabbis for corruption or other offenses.

97. DAKO f. 1, op. 141, spr. 287, ark. 185.

98. *Dos folk* no. 19, 22 Dec. 1906.

99. For a broader account of the changes within the OPE across Russia in 1905, see Horowitz, "Victory from Defeat: 1905 and the Society for the Promotion of Enlightenment among the Jews of Russia," 79–95.

100. I. Sergeeva and O. Gorshikhina, "Deiatel'nost' Kievskogo otdeleniia Obshchestvo dlia rasprostraneniia prosveshcheniia mezhdu evreiami v Rossii v kontse XIX–nachale XX vv.," in *Istoriia evreev v Rossii,* ed. Eliashevich, 124–125.

101. Friedmann, *Sefer ha-zikhronot,* 317. R. M. Kulisher was one of those who was also active in the OPE even before the Kiev branch was established (see Sergeeva and Gorshikhina, "Deiatel'nost' Kievskogo otdeleniia," 124).

102. *Voskhod* no. 17, 28 April 1905: 24–25.

103. Rappaport, "Jewish Education and Jewish Culture," 73.

104. Ibid., 100–101.

105. Ibid., 113; Frankel, *Prophecy and Politics,* 160–161.

106. Rappaport, "Jewish Education and Jewish Culture," 114.

107. Fishman, *The Rise of Modern Yiddish Culture,* 33–47.

108. *Voskhod* no. 17, 28 April 1905: 24–25.

109. *Voskhod* no. 2, 19 Jan. 1905: 26–27. Tsitron's proposal was passed.

110. *Voskhod* no. 28, 14 July 1905: 21; Hamm, *Kiev,* 183.

111. *Voskhod* no. 25, 23 June 1905: 10–13.

112. *Voskhod* no. 29, 21 July 1905: 19–20.

113. DAKO f. 348 (Kievskoe otdelenie Obshchestva dlia rasprostraneniia prosveshcheniia mezhdu evreiami v Rossii), op. 1, spr. 1 ("Protokoly zasedanii komiteta otdeleniia ob-va za 1903–1907 gg."), str. 71 (Board meeting, 25 Sept. 1905). It is unclear how far we can trust internal Territorialist documents claiming that the coup was a party action ("recently territorialists in Kiev have put in a lot of work and managed to take over the branch of the Jewish Enlightenment Society"). At the very least, a good number of the democratic activists were probably Territorialists. CZA, RG A3 (Mandelshtam, Max), folder 24 ("Rabota v g. Kieve," approx. 27 Sept. 1905), 25–26. A similar "coup" took place within the St. Petersburg OPE; see Fishman, *The Rise of Modern Yiddish Culture,* 39.

114. *Voskhod* no. 39, 29 Sept. 1905: 12–16.

115. Fishman, *The Rise of Modern Yiddish Culture,* 38.

116. V. K. Plehve, Minister of the Interior from 1902 to 1904, was widely hated for his role in the government's reactionary policies in the years leading up to the Revolution of 1905.

117. *Voskhod* no. 41, 13 Oct. 1905: 7–9.

118. *Voskhod* no. 39, 29 Sept. 1905: 12–16; no. 41, 13 Oct. 1905: 7–9.

119. Ibid., 2–16.

120. *Khronika Evreiskoi zhizni* no. 15, 19 April 1906: 28–30.

121. *Voskhod* no. 25, 23 June 1905: 10–13.

122. *Khronika Evreiskoi zhizni* no. 15, 19 April 1906: 28–30.

123. Gershon-Badanes [G. E. Gurevich], *Evreiskiia obshchestvennyia dela v Kieve,* 8.

124. *Evreiskii mir* no. 28, 4 Nov. 1910: 30.

125. Gershon-Badanes, *Evreiskiia obshchestvennyia dela,* 4.

126. Ibid., 8.

127. Ibid., 3.

128. *"Ves' Kiev" na 1907 g.,* ed. M. Boguslavskii (Kiev, 1907), cols. 391–414, 593.

129. *Nedel'naia khronika Voskhoda* no. 3, 15 Jan. 1895: 56–57.

130. Gershon-Badanes, *Evreiskiia obshchestvennyia dela,* 17.

131. Ibid., 4.

132. Ibid., 6.

133. Ibid., 6–8.

134. *Raszvet* no. 46, 15 Nov. 1909: 17–18 and Gershon-Badanes, *Evreiskiia obshchestvennyia dela,* 7.

135. Gershon-Badanes, *Evreiskiia obshchestvennyia dela,* 4.

136. *Razsvet* no. 17, 3 May 1908: 24–25.

137. *Razsvet* no. 45, 9 Nov. 1908: 28–30.

138. Gershon-Badanes, *Evreiskiia obshchestvennyia dela,* 11.

139. Ibid., 15, 19; *Razsvet* no. 46, 15 Nov. 1909, 17–18.

140. *Razsvet* no. 48, 14 Dec. 1908: 35–36.

141. Gershon-Badanes, *Evreiskiia obshchestvennyia dela,* 12–13.

142. *Razsvet* no. 45, 9 Nov. 1908: 28–30. Others argued that the supervisors' salaries should be paid by the holder of the meat tax lease, as was done in Odessa and other cities, and not allocated out of the proceeds themselves. *Razsvet* no. 48, 14 Dec. 1908: 35–36.

143. *Razsvet* no. 48, 14 Dec. 1908: 35–36.

144. *Razsvet* no. 45, 9 Nov. 1908: 28–30.

145. *Razsvet* no. 48, 14 Dec. 1908: 35–36.

146. Gershon-Badanes, *Evreiskiia obshchestvennyia dela,* 10.

147. Ibid., 19–20.

148. Ibid., 10–11.

149. Gershon-Badanes [G. E. Gurevich], *S odnogo vola tri shkury: (K voprosu o polozhenii evreev v Kieve)* (Kiev, 1907), 22–23; *Khronika Voskhoda* no. 34, 15 Aug. 1899: 1038–39.

150. Gershon-Badanes, *Evreiskiia obshchestvennyia dela,* 9; Kommissiia po pogrebeniiu evreev v Kieve, *Otchet . . . v 1907 g.* (Kiev, 1908), 9.

151. DAKO f. 1, op. 141, spr. 497 ("O vybore chlenov khoziaistvennykh pravlenii v Kievskie evreiskie molel'ni"), ark. 4

152. DAKO f. 1, op. 141, spr. 287, ark. 3–11zv.

153. Ibid., ark. 3zv.

154. Ibid., ark. 5.

155. Petitioners from Prayer House No. 11 wrote that not being able to vote in rabbinical and governing board elections caused them to suffer injury and hindrance religiously as well as materially. It is unclear what they meant by this but clearly the elections played a very important role in Jewish life within and possibly also outside the synagogue.

156. *Der telegraf* no. 60, 14 March 1906: 4–5.

157. Kievskoe otdelenie Obshchestva rasprostraneniia prosveshcheniia mezhdu evreiami v Rossii, *Otchet za 1907 god* (Kiev, 1908), 13–14.

158. Ibid., 13–14, 26–27.

159. *Razsvet* no. 42, 2 Nov. 1908: 20–22.

160. Kievskoe otdelenie Obshchestva rasprostraneniia prosveshcheniia mezhdu evreiami v Rossii, *Otchet za 1908 god* (Kiev, 1909), 41.

161. Ibid., 16–17.

162. Ibid., 42.

163. Ibid., 38; *Razsvet* no. 42, 2 Nov. 1908: 20–22.

164. Kievskoe otdelenie Obshchestva rasprostraneniia prosveshcheniia mezhdu evreiami v Rossii, *Otchet za 1908 god,* 45–50. See also *Vestnik OPE,* no. 5, March 1911: 54–55 ("Soveshchanie Komiteta Obshchestva Prosveshcheniia s predstaviteliami otdelenii, 25–28 marta 1910 g.").

165. While the OPE did not go to the authorities for relief in Kiev, it did submit petitions on behalf of small-town schools hoping to receive a portion of the so-called "remainders" of the kosher tax.

166. The following account is based on reports of the meeting in *Kievskaia mysl'* no. 320, 18 Nov. 1908: 3 and *Razsvet* no. 48, 14 Dec. 1908: 35–36.

167. Kievskoe otdelenie Obshchestva rasprostraneniia prosveshcheniia mezhdu evreiami v Rossii, *Otchet za 1907 god,* 18.

168. *Voskhod* no. 39, 29 Sept. 1905: 12–16.

169. *Khronika evreiskoi zhizni* no. 15, 19 April 1906: 28–30.

170. Kievskoe otdelenie Obshchestva rasprostraneniia prosveshcheniia mezhdu evreiami v Rossii, *Otchet za 1907 god,* 22.

171. *Kievskaia zhizn'* no. 25, 2 March 1906: 5.

172. *Khronika Evreiskoi zhizni* no. 15, 19 April 1906: 28–30.

173. Ibid.

174. *Razsvet* no. 13–14, 5 April 1909: 28–29.

175. Kievskoe otdelenie Obshchestva rasprostraneniia prosveshcheniia mezhdu evreiami v Rossii, *Otchet za 1907 god,* 34; Otchet za 1908 god, 25.

176. *Razsvet* no. 49, 6 Dec. 1909: 33–34.

177. Hamm, *Kiev,* 177.

178. Kievskoe otdelenie Obshchestva rasprostraneniia prosveshcheniia mezhdu evreiami v Rossii, *Otchet za 1909 god* (Kiev, 1910), 5–6.

179. Idem, *Otchet za 1908 god,* 69.

180. Idem, *Otchet za 1909 god,* 12; *Otchet za 1908 god,* 11.

181. Wladeldo, "Kiev (Iz kul'turnoi zhizni mestnago evreistva)," *Evreiskii mir* no. 7, 25 Feb. 1911: 19.

182. Kievskoe otdelenie Obshchestva rasprostraneniia prosveshcheniia mezhdu evreiami v Rossii, *Otchet za 1910 god* (Kiev, 1911), 19; idem, *Otchet za 1911 god* (Kiev, 1912), 18; idem, *Otchet za 1912 god* (Kiev, 1913), 27.

183. Idem, *Otchet za 1909 god,* 12–13.

184. Ibid., 44.

185. Idem, *Otchet za 1910 god,* 50.

186. Predstavitel'stvo po evreiskoi blagotvoritel'i pri Kievskoi Gorodskoi Uprave, *Otchet za 1913 god,* xiii–xiv.

187. Kievskoe otdelenie Obshchestva rasprostraneniia prosveshcheniia mezhdu evreiami v Rossii, *Otchet za 1909 god,* 7.

188. Ibid., 15.

189. Rozenblat, "Mi-livtei," 29.

190. Kievskoe otdelenie Obshchestva rasprostraneniia prosveshcheniia mezhdu evreiami v Rossii, *Otchet za 1909 god,* 10.

191. Obshchestvo Popecheniia o bednykh remeslennykh i rabochikh evreiakh g. Kieva, *Otchet za 1906 god* (Kiev, 1907), i-iii.

192. TsDIAU f. 442, op. 636, spr. 647, ch. 1 ("Ob obshchestvakh i soiuzakh, utverzhdennykh na osnovanii zakona 4-go Marta 1906 g."), ark. 346–356, str. 1–3.

193. Obshchestvo Popecheniia o bednykh remeslennykh i rabochikh evreiakh g. Kieva, *Otchet za 1907 god* (Kiev, 1908), v.

194. TsDIAU f. 442, op. 636, spr. 647, ch. 1, ark. 346–356, str. 3–5.

195. Obshchestvo Popecheniia o bednykh remeslennykh i rabochikh evreiakh g. Kieva, *Otchet za 1906 god* (Kiev, 1907).

196. Obshchestvo Popecheniia o bednykh remeslennykh i rabochikh evreiakh g. Kieva, *Otchet za 1907 god* (Kiev, 1908).

197. *Razsvet* no. 19, 17 May 1908: 34.

198. Obshchestvo Popecheniia o bednykh remeslennykh i rabochikh evreiakh g. Kieva, *Otchet za 1907 god*, ix.

199. Ibid., viii.

200. Bacon, "Ha-hevrot le-limud," 103. The pinkas is in the collection of the Vernadsky National Library of Ukraine: IR TsNB f. 321 (Kollektsiia evreiskikh rukopisei), op. 1, spr. OR 65, n. 40. See also Yohanan Petrovsky-Shtern, "Hasidism, Havurot, and the Jewish Street," 20–54.

201. Bacon, "Ha-hevrot le-limud," 105.

202. Ibid., 106–107.

203. Heinz-Dietrich Löwe reached a similar conclusion in Löwe, "From Charity to Social Policy," 69.

204. See, for example, *Unzer leben* no. 276, 29 Nov. 1911: 2.

Conclusion

1. Rawson, *Russian Rightists,* 98.

2. Ibid., 91.

3. See Rawson, *Russian Rightists,* 171.

4. Avrutin, "Racial Categories," 16.

5. Ibid., 25. For the earlier Russian "Judeophobia," see Klier, *Imperial Russia's Jewish Question,* 370–383 and Klier, "German Anti-Semitism and Russian Judeophobia in the 1880s," 524–540.

6. Avrutin, "Racial Categories," 33.

7. Ibid., 33, and Avrutin, "A Legible People."

8. On Jewish converts to Christianity who returned to Judaism after the 1905 law on religious freedom because conversion had done little to remove the stigma of Jewishness, see Avrutin, "Returning to Judaism after the 1905 Law on Religious Freedom in Tsarist Russia," 1.

9. My discussion of a "Jewish public sphere" in Kiev is informed by Ury, "Red Banner, Blue Star."

10. *Haynt* no. 144, 23 June 1910: 2; *Novyi voskhod* no. 26, 28 June 1912: 12.

11. See Ury, "Red Banner, Blue Star," 210–211.

BIBLIOGRAPHY

Archival Documents

Central Archives for the History of the Jewish People, Jerusalem

Record groups HMF and Ru 81

Central Zionist Archives, Jerusalem

Record groups A24 (Ussishkin, Menahem) and A3 (Mandelshtam, Max)

Russian State Historical Archive, St. Petersburg

f. 821 (Departament dukhovnykh del inostrannykh ispovedanii MVD)
f. 1405 (Ministerstvo iustitsii)
f. 1546 (Evreiskii komitet pomoshchi zhertvam voiny v Petrograde)
f. 1565 (Soiuz dlia dostizheniia polnopraviia evreiskogo naroda v Rossii)

Central State Historical Archive of Ukraine, Kiev

f. 274 (Kievskoe gubernskoe zhandarmskoe upravlenie)
f. 275 (Kievskoe okhrannoe otdelenie)
f. 294 (Kantseliariia Kievskogo otdel'nogo tsenzora)
f. 295 (Kievskii vremennyi komitet po delam pechati)
f. 442 (Kantseliaria Kievskogo, Podol'skogo i Volynskogo general-gubernatora)
f. 705 (Iugo-Vostochnoe raionnoe okhrannoe otdelenie)
f. 707 (Upravlenie Kievskogo uchebnogo okruga)
f. 838 (Kollektsiia listovok)
f. 1423 (Dokumenty, sobrannye Evreiskoi istoriko-arkheograficheskoi komissiei VUAN (Kollektsiia))
f. 1597 (Ekaterinoslavskoe okhrannoe otdelenie)

State Archives of the City of Kiev

f. 17 (Kievskaia gorodskaia duma)
f. 18 (Kievskii Politekhnicheskii institut)
f. 163 (Kievskaia gorodskaia uprava)
f. 237 (Kievskaia gorodskaia politsiia)

State Archive of Kiev Oblast'

f. 1 (Kievskoe gubernskoe pravlenie)
f. 2 (Kantseliariia Kievskogo gubernatora)
f. 10 (Kievskoe gubernskoe po delam ob obshchestvakh prisutstvie)
f. 348 (Kievskoe otdelenie Obshchestva dlia rasprostraneniia prosveshcheniia mezhdu evreiami v Rossii)

Manuscript Division of the Vernadsky National Library of Ukraine, Kiev

f. 321 (Kollektsiia evreiskikh rukopisei)

YIVO Institute for Jewish Research, New York

RG 80 (Mizrakh yidisher historisher arkhiv, Berlin)
RG 1400 (Bund Archives)

Newspapers

Kiev

Dos folk
Izvestiia Kievskoi gorodskoi dumy
Kiever vort
Kievlianin
Kievskaia gazeta
Kievskaia mysl'
Kievskaia zhizn'
Kievskie otkliki
Kievskie vesti
Kievskii telegraf
Kievskiia gubernskiia vedemosti
Kievskoe slovo
Kievskoe utro
Rada
Slovo
Yudishe naye leben
Zaria

St. Petersburg, Odessa, Warsaw, Moscow, Lyck, London

Der fraynd
Der telegraf
Der yud
Evreiskii mir
Evreiskii narod
Gut morgen
Ha-melits
Ha-magid
Haynt
Jewish Chronicle
Khronika evreiskoi zhizni
Kol mevaser
Nedel'naia khronika Voskhoda; Khronika Voskhoda; Voskhod
Novoe vremia
Novyi voskhod
Razsvet
Russkii evrei
Russkii kur'er
Sankt-Peterburgskie vedemosti
Unzer leben
Yudishes folks-blat

Prerevolutionary Works

Bezplatnaia boiarskaia sanatoriia dlia bednikh chakhotochnykh evreev g. Kieva. *Otchet po soderzhaniiu sanitorii za 1902 god.* Kiev, 1903.

Bezplatnaia boiarskaia sanatoriia dlia bednikh chakhotochnykh evreev g. Kieva. *Otchet po soderzhaniiu sanitorii za 1904 god.* Kiev, 1905.

——. *Otchet po soderzhaniiu sanitorii za 1908 god.* Kiev, 1909.

Bliokh, I. S. *Sravnenie material'nogo byta i nravstvennago sostoianiia naseleniia v cherte osedlosti evreev i vne ee. Tsifrovye dannye i issledovaniia po otnosheniiu k evreiskomu voprosu.* St. Petersburg, 1891.

Boguslavskii, M., ed. *"Ves' Kiev" na 1907 g.* Kiev, 1907.

Dal', Vladimir Ivanovich. *Tolkovyi slovar' zhivago velikorusskago iazyka.* S.-Peterburg: Izd. T-va M.O. Bol', 1904.

Darewski, Israel. *Le-korot ha-yehudim be-Kiyov.* Berditshov: Hayim Ya'akov Sheftel, 1902.

Efremov, S. O. *Evreis'ka sprava na Ukraini (Odbytok z "Rady").* Kiev, 1909.

Evreiskaia entsiklopediia: svod znanii o evreistve i ego kulture v proshlom i nastoiashchem. Sankt Peterburg: Obshchestva dlia nauchnykh evreiskikh izdanii i izd-vo Brokgauz-Efron, 1906–13. 16 vols.

Evreiskii kolonial'nyi bank. *Spisok lits, podpisavshchikhsia na aktsii Evreiskago kolonial'nago banka do 20-go maia 1899 goda v g. Kieve.* Kiev: V universitetskoi tip., 1899.

Galant, I. *K istorii Uman'skoi Rezni 1768 goda.* Kiev, 1908.

Galant, I. V. "K istorii uman'skoi rezni 1768 g." *Kievskaia starina* 11 (1895): 209–229.

Ger. Bad—s. "Kievskaia evreiskaia obshchina v 1913 g." *Vestnik evreiskoi obshchiny* (1914), 2 (Feb.): 49–54.

Gershon-Badanes [G. E. Gurevich]. *Evreiskiia obshchestvennyia dela v Kieve.* Kiev: tip. S.G. Sliusarevskago, 1910.

——. "Kievskaia evreiskaia obshchina na Vserossiiskoi Vystavke 1913 g. v Kieve." *Vestnik evreiskoi obshchiny* (1913), 2 (Sept.): 29–42 and 3 (Oct.): 17–25.

——. *S odnogo vola tri shkury: (K voprosu o polozhenii evreev v Kieve).* Kiev, 1907.

Gessen, Iulii. "Getto v Rossii." *Evreiskii mir* no. 13 (1 April 1910): 57–62.

——. "Mnogostradal'naia obshchina." *Evreiskii mir* 22 (25 Sept. 1910).

Gol'dberg, B. "O rodnom iazyke u evreev Rossii." *Evreiskaia zhizn'* (1905), 4 (April): 70–86.

Gol'denveizer, Aleksei. "Mandel'shtamm i studenchestvo." In *Pamiati Maksa Emel'ianovicha Mandel'shtamma: rechi, stat'i i nekrologi,* 34–50. Kiev, 1912.

Iampol'skii, P. A. *Vstupitel'naia dukhovnaia beseda: chitano v molitvennom dome L. Brodskago v subbotu 3 ianvaria 1900 g. Kievskim gorodskim ravvinom doktorom F.A. Iampolskim.* Kiev: Izd. "Akhiasafa," 1900.

Ianovskii, S. Ia. *Evreiskaia blagotvoritel'nost'.* Saint Petersburg: Gos. tip., 1903.

Iugo-Zapadnoe otdelenie Imperatorskago Russkago Geograficheskago Obshchestva. *Kiev i ego predmestiia.* Kiev, 1875.

Jewish Colonization Association. *Récueil de Matériaux sur la situation économique des Israélites de Russie.* Paris, 1906.

Kaufman, A. E. "Cherta osedlosti v miniatiure." *Russkii evrei* (1880), 16, 17, 19: 611–616.

[Kel'berin, I. P.] *Desiatiletie Kievskago evreiskago khoral'nago molitvennago doma.* Kiev, 1909.

Kel'berin, I. *Kievskoe evreiskoe uchilishche imeni S. I. Brodskago.* Kiev: Lur'e i K°, 1905.

——. *K istorii evreiskago khoral'nago molitvennago doma v Kieve.* Kiev, 1909.

Kiev i ego sviatynia. Moscow, 1867.

Kievskii kalendar' Iugo-Zapadnago kraia na 1899 g. Kiev, 1899.

Kievskii komitet po okazaniiu pomoshchi postradavshchim ot pogromov 18–21 oktiabria 1905 g. *Otchet.* Kiev, 1906.

Kievskii piatyi dnevnoi priiut dlia detei rabochago klassa Iudeiskago veroispovedaniia. *Otchet za 1900–1913 gg.* Kiev, 1914.

Kievskoe evreiskoe obshchestvo dlia vspomoshchestvovaniia postradavshim ot bezporiadkov na iuge Rossii 1881 g. *Otchet . . . po 1-e oktiabria 1881 goda.* Kiev: Ern. Perlis, 1882.

Kievskoe literaturno-artisticheskoe obshchestvo. *Otchet za 1903 god.* Kiev, 1904.

Kievskoe obshchestvennoe sobranie. *Otchet za 1910–1911 g.* Kiev, 1911.

——. *Otchet za 1915 g.* Kiev, 1916.

Kievskoe Obshchestvo Gramotnosti. *Otchet voskresnykh shkol za 1899–1900-i god.* Kiev, 1901.

Kievskoe otdelenie Obshchestva rasprostraneniia prosveshcheniia mezhdu evreiami v Rossii. *Otchet za 1907 god.* Kiev, 1908.

——. *Otchet za 1908 god.* Kiev, 1909.

——. *Otchet za 1909 god.* Kiev, 1910.

——. *Otchet za 1910 god.* Kiev, 1911.

Kievskoe Otdelenie Rossiiskago Obshchestva Zashchity Zhenshchin. *Otchet za 1912 god.* Kiev, 1913.

Kievskoe popechitel'stvo o narodnoi trezvosti. *Otchet o sostoianii vechernikh klassov dlia vzroslykh s 1 ianvaria 1904 po 1 ianvaria 1906 g.* Kiev, 1906.

Kievskoe Russkoe sobranie. *Otchet o sostoianii s dekabria 1911 goda po 1 ianvaria 1914 goda.* Kiev, 1914.

K kharakteristike evreiskago studenchestva (Po dannym ankety sredi evreiskago studenchestva g. Kieva v Noiabre 1910 g.). Kiev: Tip. Rabotnik, 1913.

Kommissiia po pogrebeniiu evreev v Kieve. *Otchet . . . v 1907 g.* Kiev, 1908.

Konel'skii, M. "Kievskiia evreiskiia blagotvoritel nyia uchrezhdeniia." *Razsvet* no. 3, 17 Jan. 1880: col. 92.

Kotik, Yekhezkel. *Mayne zikhroynes (tsveyter teyl).* Warsaw: 1914.

——. *Na va-nad: zikhronotav shel Yehezkel Kotik, helek sheni.* David Assaf, ed. and trans. Tel Aviv: Beit Shalom Aleichem and Tel Aviv University, 2005.

Kulisher, M. I. "Evrei v Kieve: Istoricheskii ocherk." *Evreiskaia starina* 5 (1913), 351–366, 417–438.

Kupernik, Avraham. *Le-korot benei yisrael be-kiyov.* [Berdichev]: Ya'akov Sheftel, 1891.

Kutaisov, P. I. "Pogromy v Kieve i Kievskoi gubernii." In *Materialy dlia istorii antievreiskikh pogromov v Rossii,* ed. G. Ia. Krasnyi-Admoni, II: 425–429. Petrograd-Moscow: Gosudarstvennoe izdatel'stvo, 1923.

Leshchinskii, Iakov. *Gal'vestonskaia emigratsiia i emigratsionnaia politika.* Kiev, 1912.

Levanda, V. O. *Pol'nyi khronologicheskii sbornik zakonov i polozhenii, kasaiushchikhsia evreev.* Sankt Peterburg, 1874.

Levin, Yehudah Leib. *Yehuda Leib Levin: Zikhronot ve-hegyonot.* Jerusalem: Mosad Bialik (Sifriyat "Dorot"), 1968.

[Lur'e, S. A.] *Curriculum Vitae.* Kiev, 1898.

Merder, A. "Melochi iz arkhivov iugo-zapadnago kraia." *Kievskaia starina* 71 (1900), 10 (October): 21–24 (section II).

Murav'ev, Andrei Nikolaevich. "Zapiska o sokhranenii samobytnosti Kieva (Nachalo 1870-kh gg.)." *Iehupets* 5 (1999), 259–267.

Mysh, M. I. *Rukovodstvo k russkim zakonam o evreiakh.* St. Petersburg: 1914.

Neishtube, P. T. *Istoricheskaia zapiska v pamiat' 50-ti letiia sushchestvovaniia Kievskoi Evreiskoi Bol'nitsy, 1862–1912 g.* Kiev, 1913.

Obshchestvo lechebnits dlia khronicheski-bol'nykh detei v g. Kieve. *Obzor X-ti letnei deiatel'nosti.* Kiev, 1910.

Obshchestvo letnikh sanatornykh kolonii dlia bol'nykh evreev neimushchago naseleniia g. Kieva. *Otchet po soderzhaniiu sanatornoi kolonii v Boiarke za 1910 god.* Kiev, 1911.

——. *Otchet po soderzhaniiu sanatornoi kolonii v Boiarke za 1912 god.* Kiev, 1913.

Obshchestvo Popecheniia o bednykh remeslennykh i rabochikh evreiakh g. Kieva. *Otchet za 1906 god.* Kiev, 1907.

——. *Otchet za 1907 god.* Kiev, 1908.

Otdel popecheniia ob evreiskikh devushkakh i zhenshchinakh g. Kieva pri Kievskom Otdelenii Rossiiskago Zashchity Zhenshchin. *Otchet za 1914 g. (god pervyi).* Kiev, 1915.

Pamiati Maksa Emel'ianovicha Mandel'shtamma: rechi, stat'i i nekrologi. Kiev, 1912.

Pantiukhov, I. *Opyt sanitarnoi topografii i statistiki Kieva.* Kievskii gubernskii statisticheskii komitet, 1877.

Predstavitel'stvo po evreiskoi blagotvoritel'nosti pri Kievskoi Gorodskoi Uprave. *Otchet za 1913 god.* Vasil'kov: V. M. Reingol'd, 1915.

Sementovskii, Nikolai Maksimovich. *Kiev, ego sviatyni, drevnosti, dostopamiatnosti i svedeniiam neobkhodimye dlia ego pochitatelei i puteshestvennikov.* Kiev: N. Ia. Ogloblin, 1900.

Sheinis, D. I. *Evreiskoe studenchestvo v tsifrakh (po dannym perepisi 1909 g. v Kievskom Universitete i Politekhnicheskom Institute).* Kiev, 1911.

Shmakov, A. S. *Pogrom evreev v Kieve.* Moscow: Tipografiia Imperatorskago Moskovskago Universiteta, 1908.

Sholem Aleichem. *The Bloody Hoax.* Trans. Aliza Shevrin. Bloomington: Indiana University Press, 1992.

——. *Briv fun Sholem-Aleykhem, 1879–1916.* Tel Aviv: Beit Shalom-Alekhem; Y. L. Perets Farlag, 1995.

——. *Dos Sholem-Aleykhem bukh.* New York: Sholem-Aleykhem Bukh Komitet, 1926.

——. *From the Fair.* Trans. Curt Leviant. New York: Viking, 1985.

——. *The Further Adventures of Menachem Mendl (New York-Warsaw-Vienna-Yehupetz).* Trans. Aliza Shevrin. Syracuse, N.Y.: Syracuse University Press, 2001.

——. *In the Storm.* Trans. Aliza Shevrin. New York: G.P. Putnam's Sons, 1984.

——. *The Letters of Menakhem-Mendl and Sheyne-Sheyndl and Motl, the Cantor's Son.* Trans. Hillel Halkin. New Haven, Conn.: Yale University Press, 2002.

——. *Mikhtevei Shalom-Aleikhem, 1881–1916.* Tel Aviv: Am oved be-shituf im Beit Shalom-Aleikhem, 1998.

——. "Yakneho"z." In *Ale verk fun Sholem-Aleykhem,* vol. 4. New York: Forverts, 1944.

Shtammer, L. *Kto vinovat? K vyboram ravvina v Kieve.* Kiev: I. I. Gorbunov, 1897.

——. *Na Sud obshchestvennago mneniia.* Kiev, 1908.

Starozhil [Sergei Iaron]. *Kiev v vosmidesiatykh godakh: vospominaniia starozhila.* Kiev: Petr Barskii v Kieve, 1910.

Subbotin, A. P. *V cherte evreiskoi osedlosti. Otryvki iz ekonomicheskago izsledovaniia v zapadnoi i iugo-zapadnoi Rossii za leto 1887 g.* St. Petersburg, 1888.

Turau, E. F., and A. M. Kuzminskii. *Kievskii i Odesskii pogromy v otchetakh senatorov Turau i Kuzminskago.* Sankt-Peterburg, 1907.

Tsentral'nyi statisticheskii komitet. *Pervaia vseobshchaia perepis' naseleniia rossiiskoi imperii, 1897 g.* St. Petersburg, 1899.

YoTse"R. *Mi-zeman le-zeman, mikhtav iti ha-yotse mi-bayit le-vayit be-format ka-zayit u-mi-hatser le-hatser MI-YoTs"eR LE-SHRETSER.* Kiev, 1911.

Zakrevskii, Nikolai. *Opisanie Kieva.* Moscow: V. Grachev, 1868.

Zapiska o Kievskoi evreiskoi bol'nitse. Kiev: A. N. Ivanov, 1889.

Zionist Organisation. *Die Judenpogrome in Russland.* Köln und Leipzig: Jüdischer Verlag, 1910.

Post-1917 Works

Alfasi, Yitshak. *Ha-hakham ha-mufla: Ha-rav Shlomo Ha-Cohen Aharonson, ha-rav ha-rashi ha-rishon shel Tel Aviv. Hayav u-fe'alo.* Tel Aviv: 1985.

Allworth, Edward, ed. *Soviet Nationality Problems.* New York: Columbia University Press, 1971.

Almog, S., ed. *Transition and Change in Modern Jewish History: Essays Presented in Honor of Shmuel Ettinger.* Jerusalem: Zalman Shazar Center for Jewish History, 1987.

Alroey, Gur. "'Erets le-am ve-lo am le-erets': ha-histradrut ha-teritorialistit ha-yehudit (ITO), ha-tenu'a he-tsionist ve-ha-hagira ha-yehudit be-reishit ha-me'a ha-20." *Iyunim bi-tekumat Yisra'el* 14: 537–564.

——. "Galveston and Palestine: Immigration and Ideology in the Early Twentieth Century." *American Jewish Archives* 56, nos. 1–2 (2004): 129–150.

Aronson, G. Ia. "V bor'be za grazhdanskie i national'nye prava (Obshchestvennye techeniia v russkom evreistve)." In *Kniga o russkom evreistve,* ed. Gregor Aronson, Ia. G. Frumkin, and A. A. Gol'denveizer, 224–238. New York: Union of Russian Jews, 1960.

Aronson, Gregor, Ia. G. Frumkin, and A. A. Gol'denveizer, eds. *Kniga o russkom evreistve.* New York: Union of Russian Jews, 1960.

Aronson, I. M. "Geographical and Socioeconomic Factors in the 1881 Anti-Jewish Pogroms in Russia." *Russian Review* 39 (1980), 1 (January): 18–31.

Aronson, I. Michael. "The Anti-Jewish Pogroms in Russia in 1881." In *Pogroms: Anti-Jewish Violence in Modern Russian History,* ed. John D. Klier and Shlomo Lambroza, 44–61. Cambridge: Cambridge University Press, 1992.

Aronson, Irwin Michael. *Troubled Waters: The Origins of the 1881 Anti-Jewish Pogroms in Russia.* Pittsburgh: University of Pittsburgh Press, 1990.

Ascher, Abraham. *The Revolution of 1905.* Stanford, Calif.: Stanford University Press, 2001.

Assaf, David. *Ne'ehaz ba-sevakh: pirkei mashber u-mevucha be-toldot ha-hasidut.* Jerusalem: Merkaz Zalman Shazar, 2006.

Aster, Howard, and Peter J. Potichnyj. *Jewish Ukrainian Relations: Two Solitudes.* Oakville, Ont.: Mosaic Press, 1983.

Atkinson, Dorothy, Alexander Dallin, and Gail Warshofsky Lapidus, eds. *Women in Russia.* Stanford, Calif.: Stanford University Press, 1977.

Averbach, David. "Hebrew Literature and Jewish Nationalism in the Tsarist Empire, 1881–1917." In *The Emergence of Modern Jewish Politics: Bundism and Zionism in Eastern Europe,* ed. Zvi Y. Gitelman, 132–150. Pittsbugh: University of Pittsburgh Press, 2003.

Avrutin, Eugene M. "A Legible People: Identification Politics and Jewish Accommodation in Tsarist Russia." Ph.D. diss., University of Michigan, 2004.

——. "Racial Categories and the Politics of (Jewish) Difference in Late Imperial Russia." *Kritika* 8, no. 1 (Winter 2007): 13–40.

——. "Returning to Judaism after the 1905 Law on Religious Freedom in Tsarist Russia." *Slavic Review* 65 (2006): 90–110.

Bacon, Gershon. "Ha-hevrot le-limud ve-gemilut hasadim be-mizrah Eiropa: Hevrot magidei tehilim shel Kiev." *Bar-Ilan* 24–25 (1989): 99–115.

Baron, Salo W. *The Russian Jew under Tsars and Soviets.* New York: Macmillan, 1964.

Bartal, Israel et al., eds. *Anti-Jewish Violence: Rethinking the Pogrom in East European History.* Bloomington: Indiana University Press, forthcoming.

Bartlett, Rosamund, and Linda Edmondson. "Collapse and Creation: Issues of Identity and the Russian *Fin de Siècle.*" In *Constructing Russian Culture in the Age of Revolution: 1881–1940,* ed. Catriona Kelly and David Shepherd, 165–216. Oxford: Oxford University Press, 1998.

Bartoszewski, Wladyslaw T., and Antony Polonsky, eds. *The Jews in Warsaw: A History.* Oxford: Basil Blackwell in association with the Institute for Polish-Jewish Studies, Oxford, 1991.

Berk, S. M. *Year of Crisis, Year of Hope: Russian Jewry and the Pogroms of 1881–1882.* Westport, Conn. and London: Greenwood Press, 1985.

Bernstein, Laurie. *Sonia's Daughters: Prostitutes and their Regulation in Imperial Russia.* Berkeley: University of California Press, 1995.

Birnbaum, Pierre, and Ira Katzenelson, eds. *Paths of Emancipation: Jews, States, and Citizenship.* Princeton, N.J.: Princeton University Press, 1995.

Bohachevsky-Chomiak, Martha. "Women in Kiev and Kharkiv: Community Organizations in the Russian Empire." In *Imperial Russia, 1700–1917: State, Society, Opposition,* ed. Ezra Mendelsohn and Marshall S. Shatz, 161–174. DeKalb: Northern Illinois University Press, 1988.

Boshyk, Yury. "Between Socialism and Nationalism: Jewish–Ukrainian Political Relations in Imperial Russia, 1900–1917." In *Ukrainian–Jewish Relations in Historical Perspective,* ed. Peter Potichnyj and Howard Aster, 173–202. Edmonton: Canadian Institute of Ukrainian Studies, 1988.

Bradley, Joseph. "Subjects into Citizens: Societies, Civil Society, and Autocracy in Tsarist Russia." *American Historical Review* 107, no. 4 (2006): 1094–1123.

———. "Voluntary Associations, Civic Culture, and *Obshchestvennost'* in Moscow." In *Between Tsar and People: Educated Society and the Quest for Public Identity in Late Imperial Russia,* ed. Edith W. Clowes, Samuel D. Kassow, and James L. West, 131–148. Princeton, N.J.: Princeton University Press, 1991.

Brenner, Michael. *The Renaissance of Jewish Culture in Weimar Germany.* New Haven, Conn.: Yale University Press, 1998.

Brodsky, Alexandra Fanny. *Smoke Signals: From Eminence to Exile.* London and New York: Radcliffe Press, 1997.

Brooks, Jeffrey. *When Russia Learned to Read: Literacy and Popular Literature, 1861–1917.* Evanston, Ill.: Northwestern University Press, 2003.

Brower, Daniel R. "Urban Revolution in the Late Russian Empire." In *The City in Late Imperial Russia,* ed. Michael F. Hamm, 319–353. Bloomington: Indiana University Press, 1986.

Burbank, Jane. "Revisioning Imperial Russia." *Slavic Review* 52, no. 3 (Fall 1993): 555–567.

Clowes, Edith W., Samuel D. Kassow, and James L. West, eds. *Between Tsar and People: Educated Society and the Quest for Public Identity in Late Imperial Russia.* Princeton, N.J.: Princeton University Press, 1991.

Crews, Robert. "Empire and the Confessional State: Islam and Religious Politics in Nineteenth-Century Russia." *American Historical Review* 108, no. 1 (2003): 50–83.

Dawidowicz, Lucy S. *The Golden Tradition: Jewish Life and Thought in Eastern Europe.* Syracuse, N.Y.: Syracuse University Press, 1996.

Deich, Genrikh M. *Arkhivnye dokumenty po istorii evreev v Rossii v XIX-nachale XX vv.: putevoditel'.* Pittsburgh: Izd-vo "Blagovest"; Russian Publications Project, Center for Russian and East European Studies, University of Pittsburgh, 1994.

Dement'eva, V. E., ed. *Istoriia Kieva.* Kiev: Akademiia nauk URSR, Kiev: Institut istorii; Izdatel'stvo Akademii Nauk Ukrainskoi SSR, 1963.

Dixon, Simon. "The Church's Social Role in St Petersburg, 1880–1914." In *Church, Nation and State in Russia and Ukraine,* ed. Geoffrey A. Hosking, 167–192. London: Macmillan and the School of Slavonic and East European Studies of the University of London, 1991.

Dubnow, Simon. *History of the Jews in Russia and Poland, From the Earliest Times Until the Present Day.* Philadelphia: Jewish Publication Society of America, 1916.

Edelman, Robert. "The Russian Nationalist Party and the Political Crisis of 1909." *Russian Review* 34, no. 1 (1975): 22–54.

Eklof, Ben, John Bushnell, and L. G. Zakharova, eds. *Russia's Great Reforms, 1855–1881.* Bloomington: Indiana University Press, 1994.

Eliashevich, D. A., ed. *Istoriia evreev v Rossii: problemy istochnikovedeniia i istoriografii: sbornik nauchnykh trudov.* St. Petersburg: St. Petersburg Jewish University, Institute of Jewish Diaspora, 1993.

Emmons, Terence. *The Formation of Political Parties and the First National Elections in Russia.* Cambridge, Mass.: Harvard University Press, 1983.

Encyclopaedia Judaica, 1st ed. Jerusalem; [New York]: Macmillan, 1971–1972.

Endelman, Todd M. *The Jews of Britain, 1656 to 2000.* Berkeley: University of California Press, 2002.

———. *The Jews of Georgian England, 1714–1830: Tradition and Change in a Liberal Society.* Philadelphia: Jewish Publication Society of America, 1979.

Engel, Barbara Alpern. *Between the Fields and the City: Women, Work, and Family in Russia, 1861–1914.* New York: Cambridge University Press, 1996.

———. *Women in Russia, 1700–2000.* Cambridge: Cambridge University Press, 2003.

Engelstein, Laura. "The Dream of Civil Society in Tsarist Russia: Law, State, and Religion." In *Civil Society before Democracy: Lessons from Nineteenth-Century Europe,* ed. Nancy Bermeo and Philip Nord, 23–42. Lanham, Md.: Rowman and Littlefield, 2000.

———. *The Keys to Happiness: Sex and the Search for Modernity in Fin-de-siècle Russia.* Ithaca, N.Y.: Cornell University Press, 1992.

Epstein, Lisa Rae. "Caring for the Soul's House: the Jews of Russia and Health Care 1860–1914." Ph.D. diss., Yale University, 1995.

Estraikh, Gennady. "From Yehupets Jargonists to Kiev Modernists: The Rise of a Yiddish Literary Centre, 1880s–1914." *East European Jewish Affairs* 30, no. 1 (2000), 17–38.

———. "Languages of 'Yehupets' Students." *East European Jewish Affairs* 22, no. 1 (Summer 1992): 63–72.

Ettinger, Shmuel. "Jewish Participation in the Settlement of Ukraine in the Sixteenth and Seventeenth Centuries." In *Ukrainian-Jewish Relations in Historical Perspective,* ed. Peter Potichnyj and Howard Aster, 23–30. Edmonton: Canadian Institute of Ukrainian Studies, 1988.

Fishman, David E. "The Politics of Yiddish in Tsarist Russia." In *From Ancient Israel to Modern Judaism: Intellect in Quest for Understanding,* ed. Jacob Neusner, Ernest S. Frerichs, and Nahum M. Sarna, IV: 155–171. Atlanta: Scholars Press, 1989.

———. *The Rise of Modern Yiddish Culture.* Pittsburgh: University of Pittsburgh Press, 2005.

Frankel, Jonathan. "Assimilation and the Jews in Nineteenth-Century Europe: Towards a New Historiography?" In *Assimilation and Community: The Jews in Nineteenth-Century Europe,* ed. Jonathan Frankel and Steven Zipperstein, 1–31. Cambridge: Cambridge University Press, 1992.

———. *Prophecy and Politics: Socialism, Nationalism, and the Russian Jews, 1862–1917.* Cambridge: Cambridge University Press, 1981.

———, and Steven J. Zipperstein, eds. *Assimilation and Community: The Jews in Nineteenth-Century Europe.* Cambridge: Cambridge University Press, 1992.

Freeze, Chae-Ran Y. *Jewish Marriage and Divorce in Imperial Russia.* Hanover, N.H.: Brandeis University Press and University Press of New England, 2002.

———. "Making and Unmaking the Jewish Family: Marriage and Divorce in Imperial Russia, 1850–1914." Ph.D. diss., Brandeis University, 1997.

Freeze, Gregory L. "'Going to the Intelligentsia': The Church and Its Urban Mission in Post-Reform Russia." In *Between Tsar and People: Educated Society and the Quest for Public Identity in Late Imperial Russia,* ed. Edith W. Clowes, Samuel D. Kassow, and James L. West, 215–247. Princeton, N.J.: Princeton University Press, 1991.

Friedmann, E. E. *Sefer ha-zikhronot,* vol. 2. Tel Aviv, 1926.

Gassenschmidt, Christoph. *Jewish Liberal Politics in Tsarist Russia, 1900–1914: The Modernization of Russian Jewry.* Basingstoke: Macmillan in association with St Antony's College, Oxford, 1995.

Geraci, Robert P. *Window on the East: National and Imperial Identities in Late Tsarist Russia.* Ithaca, N.Y.: Cornell University Press, 2001.

Gessen, Iulii I. *Istoriia evreiskogo naroda v Rossii.* Leningrad: 1925.

Ginzburg, Shaul. "Ghetos in amoliken rusland." In idem, *Historishe verk,* III: 335–340. New York: Shoyl Ginzburg 70-yohriger yubiley komitet, 1937.

———. *Historishe verk.* New York: Shoyl Ginzburg 70-yohriger yubiley komitet, 1937.

Gitelman, Zvi Y., ed. *The Emergence of Modern Jewish Politics: Bundism and Zionism in Eastern Europe.* Pittsburgh: University of Pittsburgh Press, 2003.

Glickman, Rose L. "The Russian Factory Woman, 1880–1914." In *Women in Russia,* ed. Dorothy Atkinson, Alexander Dallin, and Gail Warshofsky Lapidus, 63–83. Stanford, Calif.: Stanford University Press, 1977.

Gordon, Milton Myron. *Assimilation in American Life: The Role of Race, Religion, and National Origins.* New York: Oxford University Press, 1964.

Groberg, Kristi, and Avraham Greenbaum, eds. *A Missionary for History: Essays in Honor of S. M. Dubnow.* Minneapolis: University of Minnesota Press, 1998.

Gusev, Viktor. "Bund i ievreis'ki pohromy v 1905 roku." In *Ievreis'ka istoriia ta kul'tura v Ukraïni: materialy konferentsiï, Kyïv, 2–5 veresnia 1996,* 35–37. Kyiv: 1997.

Guterman, Alexander. "The Origins of the Great Synagogue in Warsaw on Tlomackie Street." In *The Jews in Warsaw: A History,* ed. Wladyslaw T. Bartoszewski and Antony Polonsky, pp. 181–211. Oxford: Basil Blackwell in association with the Institute for Polish-Jewish Studies, Oxford, 1991.

Gutman, Israel, ed. *The Jews of Poland between Two World Wars.* Hanover, N.H.: Published for Brandeis University Press by University Press of New England, 1989.

Haberer, Erich E. *Jews and Revolution in Nineteenth-Century Russia.* New York: Cambridge University Press, 1995.

Haimson, Leopold. "The Problem of Social Identities in Early Twentieth Century Russia." *Slavic Review* 47, no. 1 (1998): 1–21.

Halaiba, Vasil'. "Likarnia, instytut, uchilishche, rynok . . . : Z istoriï evreis'koho blahodiintstva v Kyevi." *Khronyka 2000: ukraïns'kyi kul'turolohichnyi al'manakh* (1998): 102–118.

Hamm, Michael F. *The City in Late Imperial Russia.* Bloomington: Indiana University Press, 1986.

———. *Kiev: A Portrait, 1800–1917.* Princeton, N.J.: Princeton University Press, 1993.

———. "Kiev: Dubnov's Inferno of Russian Israel." *A Missionary for History: Essays in Honor of S. M. Dubnow.,* ed. K. Groberg and A. Greenbaum, 55–63. Minneapolis: University of Minnesota, 1998.

Harcave, Sidney. "The Jews and the First Russian National Election." *American Slavic and East European Review* 9, no. 1 (1950): 33–41.

Harshav, Benjamin. *The Meaning of Yiddish*. Berkeley: University of California Press, 1990.

Henriksson, Anders. "Nationalism, Assimilation and Identity in Late Imperial Russia: The St. Petersburg Germans, 1906–1914." *Russian Review* 52 (July 1993): 341–353.

——. "Riga: Growth, Conflict, and the Limitations of Good Government, 1850–1914." In *The City in Late Imperial Russia*, ed. Michael F. Hamm, 178–208. Bloomington: Indiana University Press, 1976.

Hoffman, Stefani and Ezra Mendelsohn, eds. *The Revolution of 1905 and Russia's Jews*. Philadelphia: University of Pennsylvania Press, 2008.

Horowitz, Brian. "Victory from Defeat: 1905 and the Society for the Promotion of Enlightenment among the Jews of Russia." In *The Revolution of 1905 and Russia's Jews*, ed. Stefani Hoffman and Ezra Mendelsohn, 79–95. Philadelphia: University of Pennsylvania Press, 2008.

Hrushevskyi, M., ed. *Kyïv ta ioho okolytsia v istorii i pamiatkakh*. Kiev: Derzhavne vyd-vo Ukraïny, 1926.

Hyman, Paula. *Gender and Assimilation in Modern Jewish History: The Roles and Representation of Women*. Seattle: University of Washington Press, 1995.

Hyman, Paula E. "Two Models of Modernization: Jewish Women in the German and the Russian Empires." *Studies in Contemporary Jewry* 16 (2001): 39–53.

Ievreis'ka istoriia ta kul'tura v Ukraïni: materialy konferentsiï, Kyïv, 2–5 veresnia 1996. Kyïv: Instytut iudaïki, 1997.

Iubileynyy zbirnyk na poshanu akademika D. I. Bahaliia z nahody 70-oï richnytsi zhyttia ta 50-kh rokovyn naukovoï diial'nosti. Kyïv, 1927.

Ivanov, Leonid Mikhailovich, N. A. Mal'tseva, S. N. Valka, and A. M. Pankratova, eds. *Vserossiiskaia politicheskaia stachka v oktiabre 1905 goda*. Moscow: Izd-vo Akademii nauk SSSR, 1955.

Johanson, Christine. *Women's Struggle for Higher Education in Russia, 1855–1900*. Kingston: McGill-Queen's University Press, 1987.

Judd, Robin. "Circumcision and Modern Jewish Life: A German Case Study, 1843–1914." In *The Covenant of Circumcision: New Perspectives on an Ancient Jewish Rite*, ed. Elizabeth Wyner Mark, 142–155. Hanover and London: Brandeis University Press, 2003.

Judge, Edward H. *Easter in Kishinev: Anatomy of a Pogrom*. New York: New York University Press, 1992.

Kahan, Arcadius. *Essays in Jewish Social and Economic History*. Chicago: University of Chicago Press, 1986.

——. "The Impact of Industrialization in Tsarist Russia on the Socioeconomic Conditions of the Jewish Population." In Kahan, *Essays in Jewish Social and Economic History*, 1–81. Chicago: University of Chicago Press, 1986.

Kal'nitskii, Mikhail. *Sinagoga Kievskoi iudeiskoi obshchiny, 5656–5756: Istoricheskii ocherk*. Kiev: Institut iudaiki, 1996.

Kalnizkij, Michail. "Juden in Kiew—Ein Gang Durch die Jahrhunderte." In *Thora und Krone: Kulturgeräte der jüdischen Diaspora in der Ukraine. Austellungskatalog des Kunsthistorischen*

Museum, Wien, ed. Wilfried Seipel, 15–24. Vienna: Kunsthistorisches Museum Wien, 1993.

Kal'nyts'kyi, Mykhailo. *Kyïv: turystychnyi putivnyk.* Kyïv: Vydanystvo "Tsentr Ievropy," 2001.

——, comp. "Ievreis'ki adresy Kyieva." Kyïv: Instytut Iudaïky, 2001.

Kaplan, Marion. "Gender and Jewish History in Imperial Germany." In *Assimilation and Community: The Jews in Nineteenth-Century Europe*, ed. Jonathan Frankel and Steven Zipperstein, 199–224. Cambridge: Cambridge University Press, 1992.

——. *The Making of the Jewish Middle Class: Women, Family, and Identity in Imperial Germany.* New York: Oxford University Press, 1991.

Kappeler, Andreas. *The Russian Empire: A Multi-Ethnic History.* New York and London: Longman, 2001.

——. "The Ukrainians of the Russian Empire, 1860–1914." In *The Formation of National Elites*, ed. Andreas Kappeler, Fikret Adanir, and Alan O'Day, 105–132. Dartmouth, Eng.: European Science Foundation and New York University Press, 1992.

——, Alan O'Day, and Fikret Adanir, eds. *The Formation of National Elites.* Dartmouth, Eng.: European Science Foundation and New York University Press, 1992.

Kassow, Samuel. "Jewish Communal Politics in Transition: The Vilna *Kehile*, 1919–1920." *YIVO Annual* 20 (1991): 61–92.

Katz, Elena M. "Representations of 'the Jew' in the Writings of Nikolai Gogol, Fyodor Dostoevsky and Ivan Turgenev." Ph.D. diss., University of Southampton, 2003.

Katz, Jacob. *Out of the Ghetto: The Social Background of Jewish Emancipation, 1770–1870.* New York: Schocken Books, 1978.

Kelly, Catriona, and David Shepherd, eds. *Constructing Russian Culture in the Age of Revolution: 1881–1940.* Oxford: Oxford University Press, 1998.

Kel'ner, V. E., ed. *Evrei v Rossii. XIX vek.* Moscow: Novoe literaturnoe obozrenie, 2000.

Khiterer, Victoria. "The Social and Economic History of Jews in Kiev before February 1917." Ph.D. diss., Brandeis University, 2008.

Khiterer, Viktoriia. *Dokumenty sobrannye Evreiskoi istoriko-arkheograficheskoi komissiei Vseukrainskoi akademii nauk.* Kiev: Institut iudaiki, 1999.

Khiterer, Viktoriya. "The October 1905 Pogrom in Kiev." *East European Jewish Affairs* 22, no. 2 (Winter 1992): 21–38.

——. "Arnol'd Davidovich Margolin—zashchitnik Beilisa." *Vestnik Evreiskogo universiteta v Moskve* 3 (1994), 7: 156–162.

Khodos, M. R. *Materialy po statistike naseleniia g. Kieva.* Kiev, 1926.

Kirzhnits, A. *Di Yidishe prese in der gevezener rusishe imperye, 1823–1916.* Moscow: Tsentraler felker-farlag fun F.S.S.R., 1930.

Klapholz, Israel Jacob. *Admorei Tshernobil.* S.l., [1971].

Klier, John D. "German Anti-Semitism and Russian Judeophobia in the 1880s." *Jahrbücher für Geschichte Osteuropas* 37 (1989), 4: 524–540.

Klier, John Doyle. *Imperial Russia's Jewish Question, 1855–1881.* Cambridge: Cambridge University Press, 1995.

———. "*Kievlianin* and the Jews: A Decade of Disillusionment, 1864–1873." *Harvard Ukrainian Studies* V (1982), 1: 83–101.

———. *Russia Gathers Her Jews: The Origins of the "Jewish Question" in Russia, 1772–1825.* DeKalb: Northern Illinois University Press, 1986.

———. "Russkaia voina protiv 'Khevra kadisha.'" In *Istoriia evreev v Rossii: problemy istochnikovedeniia i istoriografii: sbornik nauchnykh trudov*, ed. D. A. Eliashevich, 109–114. St. Petersburg: St. Petersburg Jewish University, Institute of Jewish Diaspora, 1993.

———. "S. M. Dubnov and the Kiev Pogrom of 1882." In *A Missionary for History: Essays in Honor of S. M. Dubnow*, ed. Kristi Groberg and Avraham Greenbaum, 65–72. Minneapolis: University of Minnesota, 1998.

Klier, John D., and Shlomo Lambroza, eds. *Pogroms: Anti-Jewish Violence in Modern Russian History.* Cambridge: Cambridge University Press, 1992.

Kovalinskii, Vitalii. *Metsenaty Kieva.* Kiev: Severin-press, 1995.

———. *Sem'ia Tereshchenko.* Kyïv: Presa Ukraïny, 2003.

Krasnyi-Admoni, G. Ia., ed. *Materialy dlia istorii antievreiskikh pogromov v Rossii.* Petrograd-Moscow: Gosudarstvennoe izdatel'stvo, 1923.

Kubijovyĉ, Volodymyr, ed. *Ukraine: A Concise Encyclopedia.* [Toronto:] Published for the Ukrainian National Association, University of Toronto Press, 1971.

Kuprin, Aleksandr. *Yama.* Trans. Bernard Guilbert Guerney. Westport, Conn.: Hyperion Press, 1977.

Lambroza, Shlomo. "The Pogroms of 1903–1906." In *Pogroms: Anti-Jewish Violence in Modern Russian History*, ed. John D. Klier and Shlomo Lambroza, 192–247. Cambridge: Cambridge University Press, 1992.

Landau, H. "Der ontayl fun yidn in der rusish-ukraynisher tsuker-industriye." *Shriftn far ekonomik un statistik* 1 (1929): 98–103.

Lederhendler, Eli. *Jewish Responses to Modernity: New Voices in America and Eastern Europe.* New York: New York University Press, 1994.

———. "Modernity Without Emancipation or Assimilation? The Case of Russian Jewry." In *Assimilation and Community, The Jews in Nineteenth-Century Europe*, ed. Jonathan Frankel and Steven Zipperstein, 324–343. Cambridge: Cambridge University Press, 1992.

———. *The Road to Modern Jewish Politics: Political Tradition and Political Reconstruction in the Jewish Community of Tsarist Russia.* New York: Oxford University Press, 1989.

Lestschinsky, Yakov. "Di idishe bafelkerung in Kiev fun 1897 biz 1923." *Bleter far idishe demografye, statistik un ekonomik* 5 (1925): 49–67.

———. *Dos idishe folk in tsifern.* Berlin: Klal Verlag, 1922.

Levin, Vladimir. "Preventing Pogroms: Patterns in Jewish Politics in Early Twentieth-Century Russia." In *Anti-Jewish Violence: Rethinking the Pogrom in East European History*, ed. Jonathan Dekel-Chen et al. Bloomington: Indiana University Press, forthcoming.

———. "Russian Jewry and the Duma Elections, 1906–1907." *Jews and Slavs* 7 (2000): 233–264.

Levitats, Isaac. *The Jewish Community in Russia, 1844–1917.* Jerusalem: Posner and Sons, 1981.

Liedtke, Rainer. *Jewish Welfare in Hamburg and Manchester, c. 1850–1914.* Oxford: Clarendon Press, 1998.

Lindemann, Albert S. *The Jew Accused: Three Anti-Semitic Affairs: Dreyfus, Beilis, Frank, 1894–1915.* Cambridge: Cambridge University Press, 1991.

Lindenmeyr, Adele. *Poverty Is Not a Vice: Charity, Society, and the State in Imperial Russia.* Princeton, N.J.: Princeton University Press, 1996.

Litvak, Olga. *Conscription and the Search for Modern Russian Jewry.* Bloomington: Indiana University Press, 2006.

Liubchenko, Volodymyr. "'Pogrom visit v vozdukhe': obshchestvennye nastroeniia v Kieve posle pokusheniia na P. A. Stolypina (po materiialam perliustratsii)." *Vestnik Evreiskogo universiteta v Moskve* 1, no. 19 (1999): 272–286.

Lovell, Stephen. *Summerfolk: A History of the Dacha, 1710–2000.* Ithaca, N.Y.: Cornell University Press, 2003.

Löwe, Heinz-Dietrich. "From Charity to Social Policy: The Emergence of Jewish 'Self-Help' Organizations in Imperial Russia, 1800–1914." *East European Jewish Affairs* 27, no. 2 (1997): 53–75.

——. "Pogroms in Russia: Explanations, Comparisons, Suggestions." *Jewish Social Studies (n.s.)* 11, no. 1 (2004): 16–24.

Maor, Yitshak. *Ha-tenu'a ha-tsionit be-Rusya.* Jerusalem: Ha-sifriya ha-tsionit, 1973.

Mayzel, Nahman. "Di ruslendishe revoliutsiye, di pogromen in 1905 un Sholem-Aleykhem." In idem, *Undzer Sholom-Aleykhem,* 62–82. Warsaw: Yidish Bukh, 1959.

——. "Hakhamei Kiyov—benei doro shel Shalom Aleikhem." *He-'avar* 13 (1946), Iyar 5626: 150–162.

Magocsi, Paul R. *A History of Ukraine.* Toronto: University of Toronto Press, 1996.

Magocsi, Paul Robert. "The Ukrainian National Revival: A New Analytical Framework." *Canadian Review of Studies in Nationalism* XVI, nos. 1–2 (1989): 45–62.

McReynolds, Louise. *The News under Russia's Old Regime: The Development of a Mass-Circulation Press.* Princeton, N.J.: Princeton University Press, 1991.

——, and Cathy Popkin. "The Objective Eye and the Common Good." In *Constructing Russian Culture in the Age of Revolution: 1881–1940,* ed. Catriona Kelly and David Shepherd, 57–98. Oxford: Oxford University Press, 1998.

Meir, Natan M. "Mnogostoronnost' evreiskoi blagotvoritel'nosti sredi evreev Kieva, 1859–1914 gg." *Ab Imperio* 4 (2004) 1: 185–216.

Mendelsohn, Ezra. *Class Struggle in the Pale.* Cambridge: Cambridge University Press, 1970.

Mendelsohn, Ezra, and Marshall S. Shatz, eds. *Imperial Russia, 1700–1917: State, Society, Opposition.* Dekalb: Northern Illinois University Press, 1988.

Mosse, Werner E. "The Revolution of 1848: Jewish Emancipation in Germany and its Limits." In *Revolution and Evolution: 1848 in German-Jewish History,* ed. Werner E. Mosse, Arnold Paucker, and Reinhard Rürup, 389–401. Tübingen: Mohr, 1981.

——, Arnold Paucker, and Reinhard Rürup, eds. *Revolution and Evolution: 1848 in German-Jewish History.* Tübingen: Mohr, 1981.

Murav, Harriet. *Identity Theft: The Jew in Imperial Russia and the Case of Avraam Uri Kovner.* Stanford, Calif.: Stanford University Press, 2003.

Nardova, Valeriia A. "Municipal Self-Government after the 1870 Reform." In *Russia's Great Reforms, 1855–1881,* ed. Ben Eklof, John Bushnell, and L. G. Zakharova, 181–196. Bloomington: Indiana University Press, 1994.

Nathans, Benjamin. *Beyond the Pale: the Jewish Encounter with Late Imperial Russia.* Berkeley and Los Angeles: University of California Press, 2002.

——. "On Russian-Jewish Historiography." In *Historiography of Imperial Russia: The Profession and Writing of History in a Multinational State,* ed. Thomas Sanders, 410–417. Armonk, N.Y.: M. E. Sharpe, 1999.

——. "The Other Modern Jewish Politics: Integration and Modernity in Fin de Siècle Russia." in *The Emergence of Modern Jewish Politics: Bundism and Zionism in Eastern Europe,* ed. Zvi Y. Gitelman, 20–34. Pittsburgh: University of Pittsburgh Press, 2003.

Neusner, Jacob, Ernest S. Frerichs, and Nahum M. Sarna, eds. *From Ancient Israel to Modern Judaism: Intellect in Quest for Understanding.* Atlanta: Scholars Press, 1989.

Niger, Shmuel, and Yakov Shatski, eds. *Leksikon fun der nayer yidisher literatur.* New York: Congress for Jewish Culture, 1956.

Owen, Thomas C. "Impediments to a Bourgeois Consciousness in Russia, 1880–1905: The Estate Structure, Ethnic Diversity, and Economic Regionalism." In *Between Tsar and People: Educated Society and the Quest for Public Identity in Late Imperial Russia,* ed. Edith W. Clowes, Samuel D. Kassow, and James L. West, 75–89. Princeton, N.J.: Princeton University Press, 1991.

Parush, Iris. *Reading Jewish Women: Marginality and Modernization in Nineteenth-Century Eastern European Jewish Society.* Waltham, Mass.: Brandeis University Press, 2004.

Pavlenko, Aneta and Adrian Blackledge. "Introduction: New Theoretical Approaches to the Study of Negotiation of Identities in Multilingual Contexts." In *Negotiation of Identities in Multilingual Contexts,* ed. Aneta Pavlenko and Adrian Blackledge, 1–33. Clevedon, Eng.: Multilingual Matters, 2004.

——, eds. *Negotiation of Identities in Multilingual Contexts.* Clevedon, Eng.: Multilingual Matters, 2004.

Penslar, Derek Jonathan. *Shylock's Children: Economics and Jewish Identity in Modern Europe.* Berkeley: University of California Press, 2001.

Perlmann, Joel. "Literacy among the Jews of Russia in 1897: A Reanalysis of Census Data." The Levy Economics Institute of Bard College Working Paper No. 182, December 1996.

Petrovskii-Shtern, Iokhanan. *Evrei v russkoi armii, 1827–1914.* Moscow: Novoe literaturnoe obozrenie, 2003.

Petrovsky-Shtern, Yohanan. "Hasidism, Havurot, and the Jewish Street." *Jewish Social Studies* (n.s.) 10, no. 2 (Winter 2004): 20–54.

Polishchuk, M. *Evrei Odessy i Novorossii: Sotsial'no-politicheskaia istoriia evreev Odessy i drugikh gorodov Novorossii, 1881–1904.* Jerusalem and Moscow: Gesharim and Mosty kul'tury, 2002.

Polishchuk, Mikhail. "Was There a Jewish Reform Movement in Russia?" *Shvut* 8, no. 24 (1999): 1–35.

Polonska-Vasylenko, N. "The Ukrainian Church in the Lithuanian-Polish Realm and the Kozak Hetman State." In *Ukraine: A Concise Encyclopedia*, ed. Volodymyr Kubijovyĉ, 154–155. [Toronto:] Published for the Ukrainian National Association, University of Toronto Press, 1971.

Potichnyj, Peter, and Howard Aster, eds. *Ukrainian–Jewish Relations in Historical Perspective.* Edmonton: 1988.

Pritsak, Omeljan. "The Pogroms of 1881." *Harvard Ukrainian Studies* 11, no. 1–2 (June 1987): 8–43.

Pushkarev, Sergei G., comp. *Dictionary of Russian Historical Terms from the Eleventh Century to 1917.* George Vernadsky and Ralph T. Fisher, Jr., eds. New Haven and London: Yale University Press, 1970.

Raeff, Marc. "Patterns of Russian Imperial Policy toward the Nationalities." In Edward Allworth, ed., *Soviet Nationality Problems*, 22–42. New York: Columbia University Press, 1971.

Ramer, Samuel C. "The Transformation of the Russian Feldsher, 1864–1914." In *Imperial Russia, 1700–1917: State, Society, Opposition*, ed. Ezra Mendelsohn and Marshall S. Shatz, 136–160. DeKalb: Northern Illinois University Press, 1988.

Rappaport, Steven. "Jewish Education and Jewish Culture in the Russian Empire, 1880–1914." Ph.D. diss., Stanford University, 2000.

Rawson, Don C. *Russian Rightists and the Revolution of 1905.* New York: Cambridge University Press, 1995.

Rieber, Alfred J. *Merchants and Entrepreneurs in Imperial Russia.* Chapel Hill: University of North Carolina Press, 1982.

Rogger, Hans. "The Beilis Case: Anti-Semitism and Politics in the Reign of Nicholas II." In idem, *Jewish Policies and Right-Wing Politics in Imperial Russia*, 40–55. Berkeley and Los Angeles: University of California Press, 1986.

———. "Conclusion and Overview." In *Pogroms: Anti-Jewish Violence in Modern Russian History*, ed. John D. Klier and Shlomo Lambroza, 314–372. Cambridge: Cambridge University Press, 1992.

———. "The Formation of the Russian Right: 1900–06." In idem, *Jewish Policies and Right-Wing Politics in Imperial Russia*, 188–211. Berkeley and Los Angeles: University of California Press, 1986.

———. *Jewish Policies and Right-Wing Politics in Imperial Russia.* Berkeley and Los Angeles: University of California Press, 1986.

Ro'i, Yaacov, ed. *Jews and Jewish Life in Russia and the Soviet Union.* Tel Aviv: The Cummings Center for Russian and East European Studies, Tel Aviv University, 1995.

Rosman, Murray Jay. *The Lords' Jews: Magnate–Jewish Relations in the Polish–Lithuanian Commonwealth during the Eighteenth Century.* Cambridge, Mass.: Harvard University Press for the Center for Jewish Studies, Harvard University and the Harvard Ukrainian Research Institute, 1990.

Rozenblat, Moshe. "Atsilei yisra'el be-kiyov." *Ha-do'ar* 8, no. 16 (1929): 269–270.

——. "Ha-shavua ha-ivri be-kiyov." *Ha-do'ar* 5, no. 23 (1926): 423.

——. "Herzl u-mandelshtam." *Ha-do'ar* 8, no. 34 (1929): 583–584.

——. "Hillel Zlatopolski (bi-m'lot lo shishim shana)." *Ha-do'ar* 8, no. 4 (1928): 55–56.

——. "Mi-livtei ha-tenu'a ha-ivrit be-rusya." *Ha-do'ar* 26, no. 29 (1947): 855.

Rozenblit, Marsha L. *The Jews of Vienna, 1867–1914: Assimilation and Identity.* Albany: State University of New York Press, 1983.

Rubinow, Isaac M. *Economic Condition of the Jews in Russia.* Washington: U.S. Government Print Office, 1907.

Rudnytsky, Ivan. "The Intellectual Origins of Modern Ukraine." In *Essays in Modern Ukrainian History,* ed. Ivan Rudnytsky, 123–141. Edmonton: Canadian Institute of Ukrainian Studies Press, 1987.

——. "Ukrainian–Jewish Relations in Nineteenth-Century Ukrainian Political Thought." In *Ukrainian-Jewish Relations in Historical Perspective,* ed. Peter Potichnyj and Howard Aster, 69–84. Edmonton: Canadian Institute of Ukrainian Studies, 1988.

——, ed. *Essays in Modern Ukrainian History.* Edmonton: Canadian Institute of Ukrainian Studies Press, 1987.

Ruppin, Arthur. *Jewish Fate and Future.* London: Macmillan, 1940; repr. Westport, Conn.: Greenwood Press, 1972.

Rybyn's'kyy, V. P. "Z istorii getta v Kyïvi." In *Iubileynyy zbirnyk na poshanu akademika D. I. Bahaliia z nahody 70-oï richnytsi zhyttia ta 50-kh rokovyn naukovoï diial'nosti,* 938–955. Kyïv, 1927.

Safran, Gabriella. *Rewriting the Jew: Assimilation Narratives in the Russian Empire.* Stanford, Calif.: Stanford University Press, 2000.

Samuel, Maurice. *Blood Accusation: The Strange History of the Beiliss Case.* London: Weidenfeld & Nicolson, 1967.

Sanders, Thomas, ed. *Historiography of Imperial Russia: The Profession and Writing of History in a Multinational State.* Armonk, N.Y.: M. E. Sharpe, 1999.

Schnittker, Jason. "Acculturation in Context: The Self-Esteem of Chinese Immigrants." *Social Psychology Quarterly* 65, no. 1 (2002): 56–76.

Schüler-Springorum, Stefanie. "Assimilation and Community Reconsidered: The Jewish Community in Königsburg, 1871–1914." *Jewish Social Studies* (n.s.) 5, no. 3 (Spring/Summer 1999): 104–131.

Seipel, Wilfried, ed. *Thora und Krone: Kulturgeräte der jüdischen Diaspora in der Ukraine. Austellungskatalog des Kunsthistorischen Museum, Wien.* Vienna: Kunsthistorisches Museum Wien, 1993.

Sergeeva, I., and O. Gorshikhina. "Deiatel'nost' Kievskogo otdeleniia Obshchestvo dlia rasprostraneniia prosveshcheniia mezhdu evreiami v Rossii v kontse XIX–nachale XX vv." In *Istoriia evreev v Rossii: problemy istochnikovedeniia i istoriografii: sbornik nauchnykh trudov,* ed. D. A. Eliashevich, 122–133. Sankt-Peterburg: St. Petersburg Jewish University, Institute of Jewish Diaspora, 1993.

Shamrai, Serhii. "Kyïvs'kyi odnodennyi perepys 2-go berezolia 1874 roku (Storinka z istorii marksyzmu na Ukraïni)." In *Kyïv ta ioho okolytsia v istorii i pamiatkakh,* ed. M. Hrushevsky, 351–392. Kiev: Derzhavne vyd-vo Ukraïny, 1926.

Shaw, Peter. "The Odessa Jewish Community, 1855–1900: An Institutional History." Ph.D. diss., Hebrew University of Jerusalem, 1988.

Shcherbyna, Volodymyr Ivanovych. "Do istoriï zhinochoï osvity u Kyïvi." In V. I. Shcherbyna, *Novi studiï z istoriï Kyïva*, 159–164. Kiev: Vidala Ukraïns'ka Akademiia Nauk, 1926.

Sherman, Joseph. "David Bergelson (1884–1952): A Biography." In *David Bergelson: From Modernism to Socialist Realism*, ed. Joseph Sherman and Gennady Estraikh, 7–78. Leeds: Legenda, 2007.

——, and Gennady Estraikh, eds. *David Bergelson: From Modernism to Socialist Realism*. Leeds: Legenda, 2007.

Shmeruk, Chone. "Yiddish Literature and Collective Memory: The Case of the Chmielnicki Massacres," *Polin* 5 (1990): 173–183.

Shohat, Azriel. "Ha-hanhaga be-kehilot Rusya im bitul ha-kahal." *Tsiyon* 42, nos. 3–4 (1977): 143–233.

——. *Mosad ha-rabanut mi-ta'am be-Rusya*. Haifa: University of Haifa, 1975.

Shul'gin, V. V. *The Years: Memoirs of a Member of the Russian Duma, 1906–1917*. Tanya Davis, trans. New York: Hippocrene Books, 1984.

Slezkine, Yuri. *The Jewish Century*. Princeton, N.J.: Princeton University Press, 2004.

Sliozberg, G. B. *Dela minuvshikh dnei*. Paris, 1933.

Slutsky, Y. "Dr Maks Mandelshtam." *He-avar* 4 (July 1956): 56–76.

Slutsky, Yehudah. "Dr Max Mandelshtam bi-tekufat ha-tsionut ha-medinit." *He-avar* 5 (1957): 44–68.

——. *Ha-itonut ha-yehudit-rusit ba-me'a ha-tesha-esre*. Jerusalem: Mosad Bialik, 1970.

——. *Ha-itonut ha-yehudit-rusit be-reshit ha-me'a ha-esrim*. Tel Aviv: Tel Aviv University, 1978.

Sorkin, David. "The Impact of Emancipation on German Jewry: A Reconsideration." In *Assimilation and Community: The Jews in Nineteenth-Century Europe*, ed. Jonathan Frankel and Steven Zipperstein, 177–198. Cambridge: Cambridge University Press, 1992.

——. "Religious Reforms and Secular Trends in German-Jewish Life: An Agenda for Research." *Leo Baeck Institute Year Book* 40 (1995): 170–184.

Sorkin, David Jan. *The Transformation of German Jewry, 1780–1840*. New York: Oxford University Press, 1987.

Soyer, Daniel. *Jewish Immigrant Associations and American Identity in New York, 1880–1939*. Detroit: Wayne State University Press, 2001.

Stampfer, Shaul. "Gender Differentiation and Education of the Jewish Woman in Nineteenth Century Eastern Europe." *Polin* 7 (1992): 187–211.

——. "Patterns of Internal Jewish Migration in the Russian Empire." In *Jews and Jewish Life in Russia and the Soviet Union*, ed. Yaacov Ro'i, 28–47. Tel Aviv: Cummings Center for Russian and East European Studies, Tel Aviv University, 1995.

——. "Yedi'at kero u-khetov etsel yehudei mizrah eiropa ba-tekufa ha-hadasha: heksher, mekorot va-hashlakhot." In *Transition and Change in Modern Jewish History*, ed. S. Almog, 63–87. Jerusalem: Zalman Shazar Center for Jewish History, 1987.

Stanislawski, Michael. "Russian Jewry, the Russian State, and the Dynamics of Jewish Emancipation." In *Paths of Emancipation: Jews, States, and Citizenship*, ed. Pierre Birnbaum and Ira Katzenelson, 262–283. Princeton, N.J.: Princeton University Press, 1995.

——. *Tsar Nicholas I and the Jews: the Transformation of Jewish Society in Russia, 1825–1855*. Philadelphia: Jewish Publication Society of America, 1983.

Starr, S. Frederick. *Decentralization and Self-Government in Russia, 1830–1870*. Princeton, N.J.: Princeton University Press, 1972.

——. "The Tsarist Government: The Imperial Dimension." In *Soviet Nationality Policies and Practices*, ed. Jeremy R. Azrael, 3–38. New York: Praeger, 1978.

Stavrou, Theofanis George, and Robert L. Nichols, eds. *Russian Orthodoxy under the Old Regime*. Minneapolis: University of Minnesota Press, 1978.

Steinwedel, Charles. "To Make a Difference: The Category of Ethnicity in Late Imperial Russian Politics, 1861–1917. In *Russian Modernity: Politics, Knowledge, Practices*, ed. David L. Hoffman and Yanni Kotsonis, 67–86. New York: St. Martin's, 2000.

Subtelny, Orest. *Ukraine: A History*. 2nd ed. Toronto: University of Toronto Press, 1988.

Sylvester, Roshanna P. *Tales of Old Odessa: Crime and Civility in a City of Thieves*. DeKalb: Northern Illinois University Press, 2005.

Sysyn, Frank. "The Jewish Factor in the Khmelnytsky Uprising." In *Ukrainian–Jewish Relations in Historical Perspective*, ed. Peter Potichnyj and Howard Aster, 43–54. Edmonton: Canadian Institute of Ukrainian Studies, 1988.

Thaden, Edward C., and Marianna Forster Thaden. *Russia's Western Borderlands, 1710–1870*. Princeton, N.J.: Princeton University Press, 1984.

Tobias, Henry. *The Jewish Bund in Russia: From Its Origins to 1905*. Stanford, Calif.: Stanford University Press, 1972.

Ury, Scott. "Red Banner, Blue Star: Radical Politics, Democratic Institutions and Collective Identity among Jews in Warsaw, 1904–1907." Ph.D. diss., Hebrew University of Jerusalem, 2006.

Velychenko, Stephen. "Identities, Loyalties and Service in Imperial Russia: Who Administered the Borderlands?" *Russian Review* 54 (April 1995): 188–208.

von Hagen, Mark. "Does Ukraine Have a History?" *Slavic Review* 54, no. 3 (1995): 658–673.

Vovshin, Ilya. "Tahalikh ha-hitgabshut shel yahadut rusyah le-or pe'ilut 'ha-berit le-hasagat melo ha-zekhuyot avur ha-am ha-yehudi be-rusya' bi-tekufat ha-mahapekha ha-rusit ha-rishona, 1905–1907." M.A. thesis, University of Haifa, 2008.

Weeks, Theodore R. *Nation and State in Late Imperial Russia: Nationalism and Russification on the Western Frontier, 1863–1914*. DeKalb: Northern Illinois University Press, 1996.

Weinryb, Bernard D. *Neueste Wirtschaftsgeschichte der Juden in Russland und Polen*. Breslau, 1934.

Weissler, Chava. "Women's Studies and Women's Prayers: Reconstructing the Religious History of Ashkenazic Women." *Jewish Social Studies* 1, no. 2 (1995): 28–47.

Wirtschafter, Elise Kimerling. *Social Identity in Imperial Russia*. DeKalb: Northern Illinois University Press, 1998.

Wolitz, Seth. "The Kiev-Grupe (1918–1920) Debate: The Function of Literature." *Yiddish* 3, no. 3 (1978): 97–106.

Wrobel, Piotr. "Jewish Warsaw before the First World War." In *The Jews in Warsaw: A History*, ed. Wladyslaw T. Bartoszewski and Antony Polonsky, 246–277. Oxford: Basil Blackwell in association with the Institute for Polish-Jewish Studies, Oxford, 1991.

Wynn, Charters. *Workers, Strikes, and Pogroms: The Donbass-Dnepr Bend in Late Imperial Russia, 1870–1905*. Princeton, N.J.: Princeton University Press, 1992.

The YIVO Encyclopedia of Jews in Eastern Europe. New Haven, Conn.: Yale University Press, 2008.

Zborowski, Mark, and Elizabeth Herzog. *Life Is with People: The Culture of the Shtetl*. New York: Schocken, 1952.

Zimmerman, Joshua D. *Poles, Jews, and the Politics of Nationality: The Bund and the Polish Socialist Party in Late Tsarist Russia, 1892–1914*. Madison: University of Wisconsin Press, 2004.

Zipperstein, Steven J. *Imagining Russian Jewry: Memory, History, Identity*. Seattle: University of Washington Press, 1999.

——. *The Jews of Odessa: A Cultural History, 1794–1881*. Stanford, Calif.: Stanford University Press, 1985.

——. "Odessa and Jewish Urbanism." Public lecture at the University of Maryland, 6 Nov. 2002.

INDEX

Italicized page numbers indicate figures.

Natan M. Meir is the Lorry I. Lokey Professor of Judaic Studies at Portland State University in Portland, Oregon. Raised in Jerusalem, Montreal, and Teaneck, New Jersey, he received his undergraduate and graduate degrees from Columbia University, and previously taught at the University of Southampton in the United Kingdom. His teaching and research interests concern the social and cultural history of East European Jews, especially the Jews of Imperial Russia; modern Jewish identity; and subaltern groups within Jewish society.

Lightning Source UK Ltd.
Milton Keynes UK
UKHW021941220622
404815UK00008B/483